Also by Stacy M. DeBroff

The Mom Book: 4,278 of Mom Central's Tips . . . for Moms, from *Moms*

Mom Central: The Ultimate Family Organizer (with Marsha Feinberg)

SIGN ME UP!

The Parents' Complete Guide to Sports,
Activities, Music Lessons, Dance Classes,
and Other Extracurriculars

Stacy M. DeBroff

THE FREE PRESS   *New York London Toronto Sydney Singapore*

FREE PRESS

A Division of Simon & Schuster, Inc.

1230 Avenue of the Americas

New York, NY 10020

FREE PRESS and colophon are trademarks

of Simon & Schuster, Inc.

For information regarding special discounts for bulk purchases,

please contact Simon & Schuster Special Sales

at 1-800-456-6798 or business@simonandschuster.com

Designed by Bonni Leon-Berman

Manufactured in the United States of America

1 3 5 7 9 10 8 6 4 2

Library of Congress Cataloging-in-Publication Data is available.

ISBN 0-7432-3541-X

ACKNOWLEDGMENTS

For the Herculean task of writing *Sign Me Up!,* the expression "many hands make light work" has never been more true. The research for this book involved gathering in-depth information from over 560 coaches, parents, and instructors, not to mention long, long hours of writing and editing the text and culling the best of everyone's thoughts, advice, and experience.

I write from a small lovely office tucked into the back corner of my house, overlooking my steep, rock-laden garden and deep woods behind it. With its three computers nestled snugly together, we have affectionately named the office "the Treehouse," as we seem to be up in the trees. I have declared the amazing interns who work with me "Treehouse Goddesses," without whom this book would never have been possible. These research and editorial wizards who have put in countless hours over the past year are as follows: Kate Coppola, Jennifer Smith, Mirella Misiaszek, Erin Walsh, Emily Hyman, Caroline Brancatella, and Beth Withers. They are, simply put, amazing, and it has been an honor to be graced by their reflective intelligence, dedication, organizational mastery, and editorial prowess.

I owe a deep debt of gratitude to Michelle Zeitler for her editorial insights, putting in nights and weekends reviewing the manuscript and offering her wise insights, grammatical precision, and wry sense of humor. This book was also launched with invaluable help from Jill Martyn, who worked with me on *The Mom Book* before becoming the senior writer for the president of Harvard University. I also owe huge thanks to Violeta Stoyneva, who served as my Sherlock Holmes of the Internet, helping me to track down thousands of instructors to contact, as well as Gulcan Nakipoglu, who helped us put in many of the edits.

I also would not have kept my sanity without my amazing women friends. Mimi Doe, a close friend and fellow parenting author, lent me her brilliant creativity as I worked to frame the book and its publicity. Moreover, she helped to keep everything in a humorous perspective when I was buried in all the work. Sara Hunter Hoagland, a children's book author herself, sent gorgeous flowers to energize me as I strove to meet my deadline. The phone rang off the hook with friends checking up on me and cheering me on, and I want to thank just a few of them for being there so steadfastly for me during this process: Alexa Shabecoff, Janine Idelson, Sylvia Maxfield, C. A. Webb, Amy Boesky, Cindee Lacasse, Bryann Bromley, Priscilla Cohen, Lisa Butler, Betsy Drucker, Deb Drake, Allison Rimm, Karla Todd, and Karen McGoldrick DeBroff.

A former editorial intern, Stephanie James, created all the wondrous and fun artwork inside the book. She was doodling one day when I realized what an amazingly talented artist she was, until then having focused on her 4.0 GPA and exceptional research and writing skills. Her illustrations capture the spirit of *Sign Me Up!* and breathe life into all its text.

I am lucky to have one of the best editors in the business, Andrea Au. Authors often complain about being treated like neglected stepchildren, chastised for needing attention and sent to a remote corner to write a book. When forced to give up their creation to the editors like a heart-wrenching adoption, authors are told to be content with semiannual updates on its progression. In contrast, Andrea is a fabulous, hands-on editor, who has been a delightful colleague. She has been a miracle worker when it has come to shepherding this book through the myriad details, from its conceptualization to detailed design process and publicity. She's thoughtful, insightful, and warm, and has put in untold overtime hours to get this book out on a tight publication timetable. She receives a long standing ovation from me.

I have been repeatedly touched by the e-mails and conversations I have had with coaches and teachers across the country, and as far flung as South Africa, Australia, England, and Canada, about their sports and activities. It's remarkable how much passion they bring to their work, and I have been moved by their generosity to take the time from the midst of football practices, chess club meetings, concert tours, and even Olympic training to share all their thoughts. In many ways, *Sign Me Up!* is a tapestry of hundreds of voices, capturing coaches' and teachers' amazing knowledge to help make the process of choosing among activities and pursuing them less stressful for both you and your child. I have also spent hundreds upon hundreds of hours interviewing parents to gather their experiences, advice, and insights about the activity-mania phenomenon that seems to have all of us in its grip. It has been thought provoking to realize how deeply most parents wrestle with this issue and vastly reassuring that everyone agrees something must change to lessen the pressure around sports and activities for our children.

Lastly, being a mom comes first and foremost to me, and I have two wondrous children, Kyle, 10, and Brooks, 9, who continually delight me with their amazing thoughts about the world, their passionate pursuits, and their love of adventure and fun. Both have felt deeply invested in the process of writing this book. As I typed away, they would continually pop into my office to check on my progress and share their thoughts on everything, from why they think kids like sports, to how I spend too much time staring at my computer screen, to new activities I should sign them up for!

I also could never have even attempted to write this book without the immense support of my husband, Ron Remy, who took over as "the mom" while I frantically worked to make the book's deadline. He also served as my most important reader, offering insightful edits and comments, and even laughing out loud by my side in agreement with many of the quotes (which gave me hope at 1 a.m. as I stared at 1,200 pages of a draft manuscript). He has always been my number one adviser and cheerleader over the course of the past 19 years we have been together. I adore him and rely on him always to give me the strength and courage to persevere, and he's always the one clapping loudest on the sidelines.

Now, how lucky can one girl get?

—*Stacy DeBroff*

CONTENTS

Part II: SPORTS

8 Guide to Specific Sports 179

9 Other Physical Activities 423

10 Sports Resources 435

Part III: ART AND PERFORMING ARTS

11 General Music Considerations 459

Part IV: INTELLECTUAL AND COMMUNITY ACTIVITIES

PART I
ACTIVITY MANIA

The Big Picture

It is not enough to be busy . . . the question is: What are we busy about?
—*Henry David Thoreau,* Walden

Tell me, what is it you plan to do with your one wild and precious life?
—*Mary Oliver,* The Summer Day

As a parent of two children, a girl and boy ages 10 and 9, I experience every day the ultra-scheduled, time-pressured reality known as activity mania. In my family, Saturdays resemble a militarized zone, with my husband and me tag-teaming and mapping out complex strategies to manage our hectic schedules. Cell phones become critical to confer en route between events. Activities cascade on top of each other during the day, from soccer games to basketball practices to flute lessons to birthday parties. Name any day of the week, and I can roll off at least three commitments between my two kids, not to mention those of my husband or myself. One e-mail between us pretty much sums up our typical weekend insanity:

Stace: Tomorrow is going to be busy and I need some help. Here is the best schedule I can come up with:

10:00–11:15: I take Kyle to her one and only indoor soccer team practice.

11:00–noon: You take Brooks to his basketball practice at the Newton Community Center.

Noon-12:45: We all meet for lunch at Blue Ribbon BBQ.

1:00–2:00: We all go to Kyle's basketball game at Day Middle School. You take Kyle home after the game.

1:30–3:30: I take Brooks to his indoor soccer game and then we come home. OK?

Like my husband and me, many of today's parents devote their lives to pickup duties and weekend afternoons on the sidelines. Imagine the suburban mom in the minivan or SUV, coffee in the cup holder, dashing a daughter to gymnastics, a son to T-ball, stopping by the store to replace a lost mouth guard, and taking a spare moment to flip through brochures for summer camp. On one occasion, as I was interviewing a mom on the sidelines of our daughters' soccer game, she suddenly jumped up startled, asked me the time, and said, "Oh my! I want to make sure I don't miss my son's end-of-the-year gymnastics show on the other side of town— I've got to dash! Can you drop my daughter off at home for me?"

Free play in backyards and wooded neighborhood lots has been replaced with organized sports, after-school programs, religious education classes, private music lessons, organized play dates, and carpooling between them all. Not only are we, as parents, the busiest generation to come along in eons, but we have created schedules for our kids that resemble the calendar of a CEO. The culture of excess, in which more is better, has worked its way down and entwined itself around the hours of our children's lives.

In the midst of this frenzy, I, like many parents, have felt the tremendous burden of having to help my children make thoughtful, strategic choices in picking activities that are both fun and personally enriching, and that hopefully will also sustain them when they are older. But short of saying all kids should be drifting carefree in tire swings in the afternoons, it's hard to manage which activities to choose and how to approach issues of pressure, competition, practice, and quitting. I've heard many parents ruminating about helping their sons or daughters "find their thing," wanting to cultivate their children's gifts for the world to recognize and applaud. And to further complicate the issue, we feel we have only a limited period of time to get it right before it's too late. So now you see parents fretting about how to schedule even their toddler's time in order to get a leg up on the competition for college, scholarships, jobs, and life in general fifteen years into the future.

And so our children's busy schedules keep growing and growing. Now we have infant and toddler pre-curricular activities, from classes in tumbling, art, music, and swimming to Spanish. By the time a child reaches kindergarten, she may play a

The pushy parents of one girl were commenting on their daughter's soccer experience in the prior season, criticizing the coach based upon the team's performance in matches. The mother said, "Look, I didn't go to Harvard to be a loser! We didn't move to this town to have our daughter be a loser! I expect better quality coaching and better results from our daughter's team!"

—*Anonymous*

My daughter has been doing gymnastics since she was 18 months old in a Mommy and Me class. She now practices four hours a day, four times a week with her gymnastics team. There are days when I have to push her to go, but once she gets there, she's happy and doesn't want to leave. In addition to practice, we have away meets every other weekend, often causing us to travel up to four hours just to get there. I don't think all this is about her making the Olympics, but I do think that it's about making her competitive in high school gymnastics. Then again, there's an intensity to her training that almost precludes everything else. On top of gymnastics, she plays competitive travel soccer. But if she comes or goes with any soccer paraphernalia near her, the gymnastics coach goes berserk! I really hope that my girls will be able to get athletic scholarships to college. I'm still trying to find a Title IX sport that will help my oldest daughter get into college, as a lot of the top schools are now looking for strong female athletes. Maybe ice hockey or wrestling?

—*Cathy, mom of Samantha, 13, and Kimberly, 10*

My oldest son wanted to try the learn-to-skate ice hockey program this winter. He can rollerblade but not ice-skate. A lot of his friends started ice hockey in kindergarten, and while my son was a beginner, he really wanted to be with his fourth-grade friends. First, he flipped out because he didn't have the full hockey regalia for the first day of practice, which includes a helmet, skates, shoulder pads, and hockey stick (at least $300 for the whole deal). We registered him to be on the Squirts team and out we went to get the gear. When we arrived on the first day of practice, my son was upset because he still didn't have the official shirt, and he wasn't wearing the "right" sweatpants. A half-hour later he came off the ice crying. He, of course, couldn't skate as well as his friends and was profoundly frustrated and sad. It was definitely a life lesson for him, but at the same time, should I be kicking myself for not having signed him up a few years ago so that he would have been more on par with his friends? It was very painful. I found myself wondering if my son should have private lessons or go to a special camp or clinic to catch up. You want your child to feel like he could do anything, and not feel discouraged because he didn't start a particular activity at age 5. But I couldn't add more to Philip's plate without him (or me!) burning out.

—*Deborah, mom of Philip, 10, Patrick, 8, and William, 3*

My kids like to do everything, so when I tell them they have to give something up, they complain. Then I usually cave in, because the main reason I'm saying no is because I don't want to drive around in the car all the time. It has gotten to the point where they're so booked up that there's no time to do anything.

—*Anonymous*

sport, dabble in the arts, speak a little French or Spanish, and feel pressured to add a second dance lesson each week if she wants to stay competitive. Free time must practically be penciled into the family calendar, and when a break in the action finally comes, most kids dive in front of the TV, computer, or video game to console them in a desperate retreat from activity overload. It's no surprise that our kids burn out! Childhood has become like training for the Olympics of "Adulthood." With activities gearing up each fall with the back-to-school season, by the time your jack-o'-lantern begins collapsing on your porch at Halloween, your child may find herself feeling similarly caved in.

THE DEMOGRAPHICS SAY IT ALL

The general increase in population, coupled with a more intense lifestyle for children, has sent the participation levels of various sports and activity organizations through the roof. Staggering statistics attest to the tremendous size of this market. According to American Sports Data, of the 48.5 million 6- to 17-year-olds in America, 26.2 million play on at least one organized sports team. Another 10 million children play team sports, but only in casual pickup situations. Some 11.4 million girls ages 6–17 (48% of all girls) are members of an organized sports team, compared to 14.8 million boys (59% of all boys).

In a 1998 study, researchers at the University of Michigan's Institute for Social

Research compiled time diaries of 3,586 children nationwide, ages 12 and under from virtually every ethnic, social, and financial background. They found children's leisure time has dropped from 40% of the day in 1981 to 25% two decades later. In particular, involvement in sports rose almost 50% from 1981 to 1997: boys now spend an average of four hours a week playing sports, while girls log half that time.

Other statistics of note: The American Youth Soccer League alone has 630,000 players and 250,000 volunteers. There are now more than 7,400 Little League programs in more than 100 countries around the globe, with more than 2.8 million registered participants. The Boys and Girls Club of America has 2,851 clubs nationwide serving 3.3 million boys and girls each year. The number of youths involved in 4-H in 2000 was 6.8 million.

The pressure to perform has begun to manifest itself on and off the field. After signing up for activities in record numbers, children quit in record numbers as well. The Institute for the Study of Youth Sports of Michigan State University found that 70% of children drop out of organized sports by age 13.

FEAR UNDERLYING THE FRENZY

A huge parental fear lurking in the background is that if we don't push, our children will somehow fail, and we will be at fault. In our more anxious moments, we worry about our children's untapped and stunted potential, limited educational choices, and meager job opportunities. We worry that these mistakes or flaws will build upon themselves in a tidal wave of mediocrity sweeping into adulthood. If our children are not learning an instrument, a sport, or a language by age 6, they have already fallen behind their peers.

The fundamental structure of childhood has shifted, and now resembles a sort of elaborate Stanley Kaplan cram course for life. It's not just playing with toys, but with supercharged toys marketed to expand your child's mind and deepen his intelligence. We play classical music to boost the intelligence of our fetuses, enroll toddlers who have just learned to walk in tumbling classes, and pop foreign language tapes in the car as we career around to the next hopefully optimizing event. Like a strategic stock pick or investment, parents try to determine which activities or lessons or equipment will pay off in the long run. Hanging out no longer counts as a constructive activity, but rather a waste of time that quickly descends into the horror of having a complaining, whiny, bored child on your hands. You hear from all fronts that you have to infuse your child with self-esteem boosters and help her acquire new skills to frame her sense of self. You want her to feel not only competent but proud of herself.

Our children's prowess at activities and sports reassures us that we are raising successful children. And if a young prodigy loses interest, it is easy to feel betrayed or worried that she is squandering her talent. Your child may be interested in music, dance, gymnastics, or another sport, but she doesn't need to do all of them at the same time. Moreover, if you overexpose your child to an activity early, you run the risk that she will tire of something she would otherwise have enjoyed for years. Pursue the few things that your child wants to do the most, and you can always add or substitute another activity down the line.

You can also look for a family activity that you can all do together. Lots of programs involve children and adults. If you have a pet, take a dog-training class together. If your child plays soccer, see what it takes to be a coach. If she is interested in painting or learning an instrument, take lessons together. For the past four years, I have taken karate classes once a week with my kids. I started off sitting in the hallway and reading for an hour, but found myself mesmerized by the lessons and asked both the instructors and my kids if I could join the class. I watched cautiously to see how my kids responded to my being there, and to my surprise, they adored it. They found it amusing in the beginning as I struggled to learn punches, kicks, and forms they had long since mastered. I overheard another child telling my son

I'm big on activities that are team-oriented and provide a good amount of physical exercise. Since teams are a big source of friends for my girls, we focus on them. We also set the limit of one sport at a time, as our daughters have Hebrew school two days a week in addition to Sunday school and piano lessons one day a week. And that pretty much covers the week, except Wednesday, when my oldest daughter is free, with no activities and with time for friends. Plus, it all adds up when you factor in homework for school, piano practice, and a half-hour of required reading for each day. There's just not enough time for all the things our oldest daughter wants to do and the things that she has to do.

—*Cliff, soccer coach for 5 years and dad of Rachel, 10, Amanda, 8, and Jenny, 1*

It all starts out so easy: a game a week when the kids are young. Then they start adding on mid-week practices. Then they introduce travel teams, which means away games and travel on Saturdays or Sundays. Everything escalates as you go along, and then that new schedule becomes the baseline on which even more things are added. It's hard not to be caught up in the madness, as you want your child to be the best and on the number one team if she can.

—*Andy, dad of Samantha, 13, and Kimberly, 10*

he had the coolest mom in the universe, to which my son (thankfully) agreed. My kids rushed up to embrace me and told me how proud they were when I earned my first belt. Now, even though I've surpassed them in rank, they still love the fact that I come to class to share in the fun. This fall, three other moms have joined their kids in our class, and I feel I have forged a unique path for parents to bond with their children by embracing their interests and passions. We all learned something new, got to spend time together, and I became more than the chauffeur waiting for a lesson to end.

HARD TO STEP OUT OF THE CRAZE

In our world of whirling motion, sitting, talking, having a leisurely family dinner, or just hanging out no longer counts as valuable or productive. Backyard play and neighborhood roaming with rules set by children and boundaries set by mealtimes has shifted to carefully structured lessons and events with omnipresent adults. You may find yourself in the deeply consuming role of ultimate arranger and regulator of your child's activities.

When I started writing this book, I felt so good that four of my son's five days after school were *not* scheduled. Then the phone started to ring. First it was the mom of his friend Cary, who reminded me how much our seven-year-old boys loved playing chess together. "There's a one-hour class after school on Mondays. Does Brooks want to go with Cary?" she asked. "We could carpool and it would be such fun for the boys. They could play afterward." "Well, yes, I think so," I said as Brooks enthusiastically nodded to me. The phone rang again. His friend Danny's mom, Claire, told me that while at her house for a playdate, the boys had decided it would be fun to take a Skins and Scales course after school on Fridays to study snakes, lizards, and other reptiles with a zoologist. "Could Brooks do that? Would you call the registrar first thing in the morning to make sure he gets in while there's still room available?" Brooks was ecstatic at the idea. Suddenly the afternoon commitments were piling up . . . but when I thought of the long, dark afternoons of winter, when the TV beckoned to my son like an irresistible lure, the thought of all these new activities sounded appealing. Before I knew it, he was completely overbooked and balking at leaving the house, while I carpooled from one side of town to the other, waiting for snakes to be prodded and chess pieces tucked away.

As a parent in today's culture, you will inevitably find yourself part of the activity craze. Short of moving your family to remote reaches of the rural countryside, disconnecting the TV set, and tending to your homestead, there's no way to escape it. You need instead to modulate the activities in which you immerse your child, or allow her to immerse herself.

Every parent feels anxiety about this topic. We all want the best for our kids, and

I was so over the top about activities when my girls were younger that I actually would take them out of school one day a week fifteen minutes early so that we could get to ballet class on time. I'd send them to school with pink tights under their clothes, have them change into ballet clothes in the car, and shove food down their throats en route.

—*Amy, mom of Sacha, 11, and Libby, 8*

It's hard for this activity craze not to hook you a little bit. You naturally want the best for your kids, but our generation is insane. We have some kind of anxiety driving us to push our children in ways that we weren't pushed. I do think we're doing them a disservice, and that they would be fine if we just left them alone. I don't get why we're doing it to them, as it seems neither healthy nor productive.

—*Claire, mom of Ben, 14, Alison, 11, and Danny, 8*

I think of activities as falling into lots of different categories. For sports, there are team sports, club sports, vacation and family sports, and even private vs. public school sports. Then there's art: performance, dramatic, creative arts, going to theater and appreciating it and liking it (opera, theater, musical theater). I have friends who, if their kids can't sit through a performance of *The Magic Flute*, are freaking out! Then there's dancing for girls, which often starts with ballet; then they add on different types of dance. Plus, there's cultural activities: ethnic, religious, learning a language related to a parent background, gospel groups, Jewish education, going to each other's cultural nights. Some parents are so politically correct that they drag their kids to every cultural and ethnic event going on in our town. All these activities can be blown out to be your whole life, which is wildly unrealistic. It's a lot we're expecting of our kids.

—*Karla, mom of Karl, 9, Max, 6, and Leo, 3*

many of us see early involvement as the way to give our kids a head start in a competitive world. When you find yourself drowning in carpools and a crowded calendar, you're far from alone. It's so easy to overload your kids on activities because it all sounds so good. But a little goes a long way. Your child will likely rebel if every minute of her week is scheduled, even if she enjoys the activities. Kids need downtime. They need unstructured playtime. Not only does this unstructured time give your child the chance to recuperate physically and emotionally, but it forces her to engage in creative play. You've got to try a whole lot of things and see what sticks. Easing up and scaling back may be the best thing you can do to benefit your child. If you fear she will "lose out" by not starting golf at age 3, step back and re-evaluate your definition of success for your kids—which is more likely about the kind of people they are rather than the length of their extracurricular résumés. If all else fails, remember that you turned out just fine, even though you might not have done seven activities a week.

TRICKLE-DOWN THEORY: CHILDREN'S HECTIC LIVES REFLECT OUR OWN

As a parent, you have tremendous influence on your child. Not only do you influence the way she spends her time, but you also mold her values and shape her opinions of what she considers important. Your power to inspire your child, as well as to dampen her enthusiasm, means you have to be particularly careful in the messages you give her about activities. Behind every overextended child, there is usually an overextended parent. A crowded schedule of activities is how we live our lives, and it's filtering into our children's world as well.

We live in an excessively competitive society, in which there's no rung on the achievement ladder high enough. As parents, most of us feel a constant pressure to compete in our careers, and this pressure has infused our children's days to become a normal way of life for them. Competitiveness and winning has become a highly desirable attribute not only in ourselves, but also in our children. So it should come as no surprise to us that many parents scream their lungs out at sports games. The same goes for harassing the umpires, the outright attacks on other parents (in one instance, a Boston hockey-rink dad killed another dad in a fight after a practice), and the searing criticism of a child leveled by parents right in front of everyone else. The team-sports atmosphere fosters rivalry at early ages: between competing teams, between players on the same team competing for positions and playing time, and between siblings seeking parental attention and praise.

I had a nuclear "soccer mom" moment recently that made me realize just how pernicious this competitiveness can be. It started with a two-and-a-half-hour trek across the entire state of Massachusetts so my carsick nine-year-old daughter, Kyle, could play in an away soccer match for her travel club team. Kyle and I left the house at 10:30 a.m. in order to make the 2:30 p.m. game. By the time the ref's whistle had blown, I was taking Advil, and my daughter was alternating between

> Children mirror their parents and if the parents are overscheduled, so are their kids.
>
> —Janine, mom of Ben, 10, and Andrew, 7
>
> As parents we're so used to fast-paced and pressured environments that we bring our children into that same mode because we can't relax. We force them into the same amount of activity, and thus they can't relax. Every Sunday morning in our house begins with Dad saying, "What should we do today?"
>
> —Ellen, mom of Rachel, 10, Ben, 7, and Josh, 3

staring at the clouds and kicking the grass. As I slumped in my collapsible chair in a remote field in Northampton, I watched her stand around, zoning out, hands on hips and barely breaking into a run. Her usual soccer passion was nowhere to be found, or perhaps we had left it a couple of hours back on the highway. Her team lost 5–0, and she came off the field disappointed. "You look upset, Mom," she said. At which point my frustration came to a head. "Well, Kyle, you didn't even try! You put no effort into the game. We drove all the way out here—couldn't you make a run for the ball at least once?" As our weekends (and often, our weeknights too) become consumed by our children's extracurricular activities, we sometimes forget that these games are supposed to be fun.

Even before kindergarten, we introduce our children into the ultra-busy, competitive world of adults without a moment to spare. Almost every waking hour of our children's lives gets programmed in the hopes that they do not miss anything. Given the activity mania we're swept up in, take a step back the next time your child wants to add another activity into the mix, or doesn't make the travel team. Make sure that you both remember that there's much more to life.

WHAT A CONTRAST TO OUR CHILDHOOD

It used to be that kids got together, organized their own games, created their own rules, and worked through disputes without any adults in sight. Most of us were sent outside to play until the dinner bell rang. Oftentimes our moms didn't even know where we were. We could ride our bikes several miles to a friend's house. We hung out with our siblings, friends, or the neighborhood gang. We watched TV and made forts in the backyard, had water fights, climbed trees, rounded up kids for kick the can, and put on imaginary plays.

Now, if we stuck a group of nine-year-olds out on a field with a soccer ball, many

I've become one of those people mournful and nostalgic for the days when you just opened the back door and sent your kids outside to play. When my friends' kids who are maxed-out on activities have unstructured time, they don't know how to play outside or build a fort, because they haven't taken a class on it. Now, instead of pickup games, we have soccer with rules and over-the-top parents running the practices and games. There's no longer a chance to be free, reveling in unstructured time. At the same time, adults want to be children, taking up activities such as snowboarding, and searching for carefree moments.

—*Amy, mom of Sacha, 11, and Libby, 8*

Growing up, all you had to do was step outside to be barraged by a pack of kids. There were things constantly going on after school, from stickball and capture the flag, to kick the can. Plus, these activities would bring together kids of widely disparate ages. Usually there'd be a mom inside watching out for us, and cars would slow down as they expected to have kids dashing about the streets all the time in the midst of these games. When we bought our house, we looked for a really quiet street where our kids could play outside and have similar experiences to this childhood. The cul-de-sac where we now live is fairly isolated, and has about 40 kids living in its houses.

—*Jonathon, dad of Alia, 8, and Asher, 5*

As a girl, I could be a Girl Scout or go to dancing school. The boys had Scouts, Pop Warner football, and Little League. That was it, and I grew up in a city of 100,000. Now, in our town of 12,000, we have year-round soccer and hockey, seasonal basketball and baseball, football in a neighboring town, martial arts, dance schools, Scouts, Spanish classes, and two schools offer after-school care and activities. And I'm sure there are more that I haven't heard about yet!

—*Anne, mom of Rob, 10, and Tim, 8*

wouldn't take the initiative or know how to organize themselves into teams; instead, they would wait around for an adult to show up to get things started. The by-products of adult influence can be seen everywhere: from travel teams, to regional and national tournaments, to fancy team uniforms and trophies. Free play and unstructured games have given way to organized sports, with many children starting to train in preschool.

Things have changed dramatically from when most of us were growing up. Just imagine what would happen if adults took over the game of hide-and-seek. We would most likely have volunteer parent coaches, intense training sessions, and weekend tournaments culminating in a national championship. Tryouts for elite teams would start at age 7, aimed at recruiting strategic hiders and aggressive seekers. But of course, we would also have to consider team camouflage uniforms and special quiet shoes so essential for team play. All of a sudden, it's hard to imagine where the fun has gone.

WHY THE ACTIVITY MANIA?

Impact of the Evolving Workforce and Working Moms

Given the number of homes where both parents work, many families depend on organized activities to fill the after-school void. With more mothers working outside of the home, a heavily structured schedule ensures that children are safe, engaged, and not getting into trouble. About 70% of mothers with children age 12 and younger work full- or part-time, which has created an intense demand for structured programs and activities between the time school lets out and work ends. And corporate culture demands that people put in longer and longer hours at the office. According to the International Labor Organization, fathers now work an average of 50.9 hours a week, while mothers work 41.4 hours.

Few of us feel that we have an abundance of time to spend doing fun things with our children. Having your child partake in what you hope will be engaging activities helps alleviate the guilt of not being with her, and makes up for your absence during the week. It's more comforting to immerse your child in enriching activities than to imagine her sitting around at home with nothing to do. Plus, if you are a working parent, the structured sequencing of your child's activities can become critical to your family's day running smoothly.

And if you're a stay-at-home parent, you often feel your worthiness is judged according to your child's behavior and accomplishments. You are probably familiar with caricatures of the Power Mom tooling around the suburbs in her sport utility

> Nowadays, there are so many families with two parents who work outside the home that parents feel guilty thinking about their children sitting around bored with a babysitter. It's much more appealing to fill up their time with what we think of as fun, constructive activities.
>
> —*Cathy, mom of Samantha, 13, and Kimberly, 10*

> Signing kids up for activities is a natural attempt to make our lives more predictable. Honestly, as a working parent, it's nice to have a set routine.
>
> —*Mark, dad of Ben, 9, and Jacqueline, 6*

vehicle sipping Starbucks, while zealously contemplating which local gymnastics programs will give her agile four-year-old the best edge in future competitions.

No One Home to Play With

With so many kids are enrolled in organized activities, it's increasingly difficult to find neighborhood kids for spontaneous play. Moreover, other moms aren't around to lend a supervising hand from the back porch or kitchen window anymore. Many kids have their free time booked solid. Just coordinating a play date often involves an elaborate search for overlapping free time of the two children involved. Often, you may call another parent to schedule a play date with your child and you are told the friend is only free on Thursday at 3:30 because every other afternoon is booked with activities.

When we were growing up, parents didn't stand outside with clipboards checking off teams or listing skill-enhancing activities. They said, "Go outside and play. Find someone to play with. Find something to do!" And off we went, with dozens of other kids varying widely in age to romp around the neighborhood.

Now the streets can be eerily quiet. Swing sets in backyards go dormant. Instead of kids climbing trees, romping through backyards, or racing along in bikes, they're off to organized activities or after-school programs while parents work. The streets themselves are busier with traffic as SUVs screech around corners carrying kids who are late for softball practice or flute lessons. There are fewer vacant neighborhood lots to hang out in, and the local parks or woods don't feel safe enough to let your child meander there unsupervised. The action has moved from the swing sets to the softball fields and gymnasiums.

Our son is not in organized sports, and there's no one around to play with him, not even to toss around a Frisbee.

—Jonathon, dad of Alia, 8, and Asher, 5

My husband and I would always be saying to our daughter, "Go play with the kids next door!" She kept telling us it just didn't work that way. So one day my husband walked her over to the next-door neighbor's house. When they opened the door, they looked at him with guilty shock and said, "Oh my! Did we have a playdate scheduled that we forgot about?" Nine times out of ten the kids are already booked with a playdate or dashing off to a soccer game or class. It's a far cry from when we were kids and played outside until we heard the call of "Dinner's ready!"

—Jill, mom of Stella, 5

It's easy to pooh-pooh all of these classes and teams for kids, but it's hard to create opportunities for informal activities. Not everyone has a backyard where they can let kids go out and play, or a pond out back on which to skate.

—Deborah, mom of Philip, 10, Patrick, 8, and William, 3

It's Not Safe Out There

Many of us grew up with our bikes as our ticket to freedom, flying along streets, vacant lots, and playgrounds, free to go as far as our legs and bikes could carry us. A roving gang of neighborhood kids, ranging from young kids to adolescents, formed a critical mass and could look out for each other's safety. Today, neighborhoods where parents feel they can send their children out to romp around unsupervised are scarce. We feel like we live in a more dangerous and unpredictable world. We fear that even the most innocuous park near our homes may be teeming with sexual predators, drug dealers, or potential kidnappers. We know that on today's busy roads, there are reckless drivers who won't slow down for kids crossing the street, riding a bike, or chasing down a ball.

Many of us have a sense that the world's a more dangerous place than when we grew up. When I was my kids' age, I would come and go as I pleased, riding a three-mile radius to friends' houses on my bike. Now my wife and I don't feel like we can let our kids wander the neighborhood by themselves. We have a field right behind our house, but I wouldn't let them go play there without an adult watching in case a stranger came along. So if our kids can't program for themselves, we have to program for them.

—*Arnie, dad of Tessa, 11, and Jake, 8*

When I was growing up, we ran outside and played pickup sports. It was more fun, but today I wouldn't let my kids just run around the neighborhood. At age 10, my parents let me hop on my bike and ride a mile to my friend's house. And they wouldn't know where I was until dinner. Unfortunately, in this day and age, I am afraid to do that. Whether real or imagined, I'm just afraid of strangers, and while I know my kids are intelligent, to be ignorant of the dangers would be crazy. Ergo, we have organized everything when it comes to sports and activities.

—*Andy, dad of Rachel, 10, Ben, 7, and Josh, 3*

I worry about my kids when they're out of my sight, because I just know that there are people who will take advantage of your child's comfort zone and whisk them off. It can happen anywhere, and it doesn't matter where you live.

—*Dean, dad of Evan, 10, and Olivia, Justin, and Shelby, 8*

We worry about injuries during unsupervised play. We've even heard horror stories of guns in the house on playdates, or nannies, baby-sitters, or other parents who don't pay the least bit of attention to the kids, who stuff themselves with junk food and computer games.

We no longer feel comfortable giving our children the ability to be independent, even letting them ride a mile on their bikes to a buddy's house, and we go with the "rather be safe than sorry" approach. So parental and adult involvement is required to get kids to activities and organize them once they're there. In structured activities, we know our kids are both safe and engaged in educational and skill-building recreation. Organized activities hold intense appeal, since they are theoretically safe and overseen by responsible adults who monitor what's going on in our absence.

Cutbacks in Programs at Public Schools

Many kids need after-school sports and activities to make up for what's no longer being offered at public schools. From gym classes lacking sophisticated equipment, to art, to music, to theater, these programs are usually the first to go, since many see them as superfluous to the core educational needs of students. Parents rely on after-school activities to make up for the lack of all these. Even some of the sports are becoming privatized as many kids forgo middle school and high school teams in order to play on elite club or travel teams.

Thinking Ahead to the Teenage Years

As we are bombarded with media images of troubled youth, we feel the need to do everything possible to protect our children. Negative peer groups, drugs, sex at an early age, depression, dropping out of school, or resorting to violence make up but a few of our concerns. Research supports our worst fears, as kids who are nonparticipants in sports have been found to be 57% more likely to drop out of school, 49% more likely to use drugs, and 35% more likely to smoke cigarettes. One advan-

There's a lot to be said for keeping your kids busy and off the streets and out of trouble with their peers by having them do organized sports and activities.

—Jane, mom of Carolyn, 17, and Peter, 11

With all the hang-ups teenagers have and their struggle to figure out where they fit in, it really helped me growing up to have an activity as an outlet. During my teen years, I found that being on a tennis court was the one way I felt confident, and it provided a place to which I could escape. Based on my experience, I want my kids to learn one thing that they'll take with them through their teen years and into their adult life. Anything else on top of that would be great, but not completely necessary.

—Sarah, mom of Taylor, 8, and Cameron, 6

tage of having your child immersed in sports and activities is the idea of immunizing her against these dangers, of which we are reminded daily as we peruse the newspaper headlines. As kids enter their teenage years, parents cling to activities as a wholesome alternative to their child hanging out with undesirable peers and getting into trouble.

IN A CULTURE OF OVERACHIEVEMENT, IT'S HARD TO KEEP UP WITH THE JONESES

Parental Peer Pressure

It's hard to pare down your own child's activities when the kids next door and at school are going full tilt. You have to be adamant about your decision, and recognize what's going on around you. The activity frenzy spreads like a virus: It's contagious when you're in close proximity with other anxious parents or their overachieving kids. You want to give your child an edge. Talking with a bunch of intense parents can cause your conviction about downtime to crumble in a matter of minutes.

Just as adults will ask one another, "What do you do for work?" as an identity validator, parents will inquire of you, "What activities do your children do?" The subtext here is really, "What does your child do to stand out from the crowd? What has she already accomplished, and how does she stack up against my child? Should my child be doing or achieving more?" We often find ourselves surrounded by driven parents who can strike an anxious chord in even the most laid-back of us. If you say, "I don't think my child's going to do any activities this year," you will get concerned looks from other parents, who think you may be bordering on child abuse.

My husband saw on our daughter's travel soccer league Web site that they were offering an eight-week Special Academy for four girls from each town who played on their town's number one or two teams. He thought that it would be a great opportunity for our daughter, and mailed in the registration. I jokingly suggested that he should FedEx it, since some parents, anxious to get their daughters in, would do that. He laughingly dismissed the intensity I perceived. He e-mailed other families about the academy, who thanked him for passing on the information. Later that weekend, he ran into one of the other dads at a soccer game, who told him that he had personally driven over to the coordinator with the application on his way to work the very next morning. Suddenly my husband was concerned about the pos-

I feel guilty when I listen to so many people talking about all the things they've signed their kids up for. My kids like staying home and playing with their friends. I have to keep reminding myself that when I was growing up, we played out in the yard and turned out okay. Most other parents I know feel the same way but keep enrolling their kids in more and more activities because they're afraid not to.

    —Deb, mom of Evan, 10, and Olivia, Justin, and Shelby, 8

When I talk to a mom who has her kids involved in lots of different activities, I wonder whether my child will miss the boat. It's hard not to feel the pressure of "everyone else is doing it."

    —Ellen, mom of Alison, 6, and Hilary, 2

I sometimes feel the competition between parents to be overwhelming. My three-year-old already knows how to swim, dance, and tumble, and yet her friends are doing more. It makes you second-guess yourself, and you have to remind yourself that all these early sign-ups for activities are totally unnecessary.

    —Leslie, mom of Katie, 3, and Lily, 2

sibility that our daughter wouldn't get a spot and their daughter would—and the intensity of the competitive atmosphere never seemed more apparent.

Fear of Being an Inadequate Parent

The effort you make to immerse your child in the best growing and developing activities or sports often becomes intertwined with your concept of yourself as a good, dedicated parent. We don't just want to turn out a perfect child, we want to be recognized as perfect parents by both other parents as well as our own children. Describing your child in any way as "average" or "ordinary" has become a pejorative. We now hold the image of a child waiting to be perfected, buffed by experience and exposure, until she shimmers as an emerging adult.

As a collective, we have become overly invested in our children, who have taken

Even though I believe it's necessary not to overload my kids with activities, I also feel subtle pressure from other parents. One friend told me that her daughter was joining the T-ball league. I thought, maybe Grace should join too. Maybe softball will be the sport that she excels at, and I should get her involved now. How am I to know what her sport will be? But I reminded myself that I didn't want Grace or my family spread too thin, so we did not sign her up for T-ball.

—*Lisa, mom of Grace, 6, Ben, 4, and Maddie, 1*

People define success by where they are in life: The most driven parents seem the most successful. And unfortunately, we communicate to our children that to be successful they have to meet or surpass what we've achieved as their parents. It creates a lot of pressure on our kids, and they feel terrible if they don't live up to these expectations.

—*Janine, mom of Ben, 10, and Andrew, 7*

I think that in today's fairly materialistic society, having the busiest kids is like a currency or a flashy car. I hear people comparing how busy they and their kids are, and it's almost like a contest to see who wins. It's become unacceptable for a kid to simply play for an afternoon, or have idle time. Much like a wallet, if a child's day isn't full, something must be wrong.

—*Paul Hobart, PGA teaching professional, Tartan Fields Golf Club*

over the center of our adult universe. Much of what would be our free time has become devoted to giving our children a leg up and plunging them into one enrichment activity after another. It gets to the point where we can barely catch our breath, and collapsing on the couch after a round of soccer games, music lessons, and other scheduled events becomes the highlight of our weekend. The superenriched, activity-drenched lifestyle may be like taking a vitamin overdose—ultimately, it's not good for you. We have become unwilling to vest control in children to chart their own course of talents and skills or to explore their own passions. We feel that our child will otherwise be vulnerable, and won't have the skills to thrive in a highly educated, success-oriented culture.

My daughter's friend Katie came over one day for a playdate. Kyle had just taken up the flute, and I loved listening to all the squeaks and efforts at perfection. But Katie, at age 8, pulled out her violin, promptly played a concerto, and told us how excited she was to have been picked for our city's youth orchestra. As I said, "That's so great for you, Katie!" I was cringing with worry, just thinking about how behind Kyle must be after having just started to play and hoping that she didn't blame me for not starting her lessons sooner! I knew how ridiculous my thoughts were, but these types of comparisons are sometimes tough to avoid.

The Push to Excel Starting in the Womb

We start trying to craft superkids practically from birth. We have our babies listening to Mozart in utero. Once they're born, we feel guilty if they're not staring at complex mobiles and listening to stories we read them to stimulate their brains. We want our child to be among the first to start talking, walking, running, and reading.

We inwardly wince in baby playgroups when one parent announces a new milestone her child achieved. The push for excellence is beginning younger and younger. At age 5, many children are already precluded from advanced gymnastics teams. One friend who saw the first inkling of strength in her seven-year-old child's swimming ability promptly found her a coach, a team to compete on, and a place to practice twice a week. Is this craziness or just parental savvy? What is going on here? When my child lounges around after school on a Tuesday early release day, why do I feel uneasy about the slightest complaint of boredom or move toward the TV remote control, my anxiety provoking thoughts of possible extracurricular activities? Perhaps it has something to do with those fearful visions of my child growing up with a dearth of outside hobbies or interests, shaped by an early slump into laziness and lack of motivation. But it's easy to forget the fact that elementary school can run from 8:20 a.m. to 3 p.m., and kids are often beat at the end of an intense day.

There is a distinct pressure on you to produce a successful child, which easily and often translates to pressure on your child to be a winner. Life should not be lived in a state of perpetual rush. All these nonstop activities and frantic running around are not in the best interest of your child. You may find it's like resisting an addiction. Remind yourself that slowing down doesn't mean ruining your child's life. Remember that you're trying to raise a great person, not create a great résumé.

Holding Your Child Back from Kindergarten

Many parents anxious to have their kids be the best both academically and athletically keep their five-year-olds, especially boys, in preschool for an extra year. The thinking behind this decision is that the child will be older, more mature, bigger, and more skilled when entering kindergarten. This trend has become an epidemic

So many of my daughter's friends are doing an extra preschool year, it's unbelievable! Parents want to give their kids an extra edge, so that their child will be the best, brightest, and most athletic in the class.

—Jill, mom of Stella, 5

Our town is so obsessed with sports that tons of kids are being held back each year before they start kindergarten in the hopes they will have a better chance of emerging as an athletic star. In fact, my friend Amy's daughter was born in October and every single person she talked with told her to hold her smart, engaged daughter back. I found that incredible, and I think it reflects the lengths to which parents will go to give their child a leg up.

—Janine, mom of Ben, 10, and Andrew, 7

in many suburbs. Thirty years ago only 5.8% of all kindergartners were 6 or older, while today this statistic has risen to more than 13.2%, according to the U.S. Department of Education.

Moreover, the trend continues into the early elementary school years, with more principals getting flooded with requests for children to repeat a grade. It's not that the kids are failing academically, but rather that parents want their children to be the oldest in the class, to excel both in school and in sports, and to thereby have a competitive edge over their peers. Yet, you run the risk of your child being bored and unchallenged academically, towering over her classmates, and feeling she is letting you down if she does not live up to your expectations to excel. You should enroll your five-year-old child who meets age-entrance requirements in kindergarten rather than hold her back.

LOOKING AHEAD: THINKING ABOUT COLLEGE

Sports and activity sign-ups have become more about "packaging" your child in a way that will appeal to college admissions officers than about helping your child develop and mature. We start worrying about what will distinguish our children when they're only four-year-olds. At what will they excel? What will get them into

I work at an Ivy League school, where I'm surrounded by kids who speak five languages, are musicians, or sing beautifully, or are champion Irish step-dancers, or master chess players, or all of the above, in addition to being brilliant. When I look at these wonderful, accomplished people, a part of me wants my kids to be like them. It's hard not to want your child to be remarkable.

—*Alexa, mom of Adam, 11, and Sophie, 8*

I'll hear parents talking on the sidelines about what sports will help get their children into college, saying things like, "I think she can get into Dartmouth with this sport."

—*Jane, mom of Carolyn, 17, and Peter, 11*

We have already thought about college applications, and my wife and I have had serious discussions about relocating down the road to a more rural setting where there is not as much competition so that our daughter could stand out a bit more. There are a lot of smart, well-rounded, oversubscribed kids in our neighborhood.

—*David, dad of Alexandra, 10*

It seems impossible to get into a good college these days, as the bar has risen so high. I basically got a letter along those lines from my alma mater that implied I should keep those alumni checks coming, as they listed the unbelievable number of class valedictorians and total applicants this year. We're hoping that our children will excel in an activity to help get them into college. However, it may be that the surefire route to college is doing a more obscure activity.

—*Leslie, mom of Alexandra, 10, and Jack, 9*

Actually, college applications are ten years from now! Nothing could be further from my mind.

—*Arnie, dad of Tessa, 11, and Jake, 8*

I worry all the time about how competitive it has become to get into college and think anxiously that I'd better start making bigger contributions to my alma mater or there will be no way my kids will get in! I've taught Harvard undergraduates for four years, and I think that if you don't come from a geographically diverse place or have a unique racial background like American Samoa, it's so hard to get in. I worry about my white, upper-middle-class, East Coast son not even having a chance. My best friend from high school moved her family out to Montana, which she did for a lot of reasons, not the least of which was being very strategic about getting her children into an elite college. I think my kids will have a lot harder time getting into a good school than my husband and I did, and I want the best for them.

—*Sylvia, mom of Max, 13, and Kate and Zoe, 10*

Activities can help with college admission, but if parents are so worried about this at an elementary age, I really think they need to get a life of their own. There is a difference between wanting the best for your child and living through them. Children need to have the autonomy to make their own choices. Some kids will function okay being "pushed" into a specific activity. However, if you start a kid on a serious basketball or tennis training program when they are 7, what if they're stressed out and burned out by the time they hit high school? They won't be using that to get into college!

—*Jessica Carleton, elite competitive archer, coaching for 10 years*

a good school, be that a private elementary school or college? In today's competitive society we feel pressured to max out our kids' schedule to achieve these goals. Therefore, instead of focusing on what our kids love, helping them discover passions and hobbies that will carry them into their adult years, and getting them out for exercise and fresh air, we have an eye on what's most impressive to the outside world and future admissions officers.

We now have a sense that unless our child is a topnotch tennis player, chess wizard, artist with gallery shows by age 12, or has otherwise distinguished herself by high school, along with getting great grades, she cannot get admitted to top colleges. An increasing number of parents believe that if their children do not go to a certain level of elite college, their chances of succeeding in life will be significantly diminished. The accumulation of credentials intensifies as well: The "right" graduate school looms after college, and the "right" sequence of jobs is next.

Many believe that extracurricular activities ultimately end up helping good students stand out from the crowd. A 3.8 grade point average is no longer enough. Instead, your child has to have a two-page résumé sparkling with all her amazing additional achievements. And it seems we have good reason to be concerned. Take statistics from Harvard College's class of 2005. Only 10.7% of the 19,009 applicants for Harvard's class of 2005 were accepted, marking an all-time low. The applicant pool included 2,900 valedictorians, not to mention all those with perfect SAT scores. Of the incoming freshmen, more than 60% listed a sport, 26% said that music was their most serious extracurricular pursuit, and 22% listed drama, dance, or some form of the arts.

From writing outstanding essays to creating the perfect list of extracurriculars, admissions standards have been raised to new levels each year. One of the main anxieties is your child will need to "sell" herself to a college admissions board. It's easy to worry about what will distinguish your child from the rest of the applicants, and one of the main questions that parents have concerns what a child should be doing after school to boost her "brag sheet." Should your child be the master of one or two activities, or should she become involved in as many activities as can be crammed into an afternoon? Are college counselors looking for specialization in one activity or after-school activity overload?

College admissions boards are not looking for well-rounded students but for well-rounded student bodies. In other words, your child should not get involved in ten extracurricular activities just to appear to be the Renaissance student. When it comes to a student's extracurriculars, colleges like to see dedication, consistency, and commitment. It is better for your child to be wholeheartedly involved in a couple of activities for several hours a week over her high school career than to pursue nine or ten activities that change from year to year, lest she appear fickle or noncommittal. She should immerse herself in a few activities that she is truly interested in and that require a commitment of two or more hours a week. You don't want your child so busy shaping a résumé that might appeal to an elite college that she loses genuine enthusiasm for the underlying activities.

YOUTH SPORTS AND ACTIVITIES HAVE BECOME BIG BUSINESS

A billion-dollar industry has emerged from this activity mania, which further fuels the drive to get and keep kids enrolled in activities and sports. The growth of youth sports reflects the intense popularity of professional sports in our society. The U.S. sports apparel and equipment industry rakes in over $40 billion a year. Married couples with children spend over $1.8 billion every year for recreational lessons.

Stop for a minute and consider how much money you have or will be contributing to sustaining them.

From commercials promoting kids' sports gear to schmaltzy ones capturing the joyously tear-stained cheeks of parents watching their child's first dance recital, the message is strong: Spend more in order to raise an awesome child. Corporate marketing plays on our parental insecurities and encourages us to constantly spend more to give our child every advantage.

HOW THIS BOOK CAN HELP YOU HANDLE ACTIVITY MANIA

Sign Me Up! has been designed to offer you in-depth information and guidance for selecting from the plethora of children's organized activities, lessons, sports, and social groups available from toddlerhood through high school. Selecting your child's activities until now has been an elaborate guessing game. Do you choose the same activity as all the neighbors' kids, one at which you suspect your child might excel, one in which your child has expressed interest, or something that will make your child stand out from the crowd?

Often you lack personal experience with the activities your child wants to do, or those in which you are interested in enrolling her. Ask most parents the differences between the major types of karate taught in the United States—from self-defense to full-scale assault training—and they don't have a clue about the philosophy of the studio down the block in which they have just enrolled their child. It helps enormously to consider all of your child's options, understand what each activity involves, and learn what types of activities suit the needs and temperament of your unique child.

This book has two sections. The first offers advice about how to structure your child's life after day care or school: How to choose activities that your child will enjoy, how much is too much, what to do when your child wants to quit, and how to deal with a bad sport. The second section offers a detailed look at specific childhood activities, from sports to dance to musical instruments, including information about the best age to start, the advantages and disadvantages of each activity, and what types of kids tend to excel in each. The chapters provide quick and easily accessible answers as you and your child try to decide among or wade through new activities. Children and parents lack the information to make informed decisions when selecting activities, and often end up feeling frustrated, overwhelmed, or disappointed. *Sign Me Up!* takes much of the guesswork and angst out of choosing activities and sports. Use the insights in Parts II, III, and IV to help you sort through the morass of choices for your child and to solve the problems that sometimes arise. The idea behind the book is choosing wisely. Take the time to find out as much concrete information as you can, particularly about the commitment involved, and think about and discuss activities your child wants to sign up for rather than quickly making decisions on the fly.

The wealth of opportunities available to your child is amazing and mind-boggling. We have done extensive research to bring you the most helpful and informative tips on the most popular athletic and artistic pursuits for kids. The book does not include extreme sports that experts consider dangerous for children, such as freestyle boxing and scuba diving, or everyday activities such as biking, skateboarding, canoeing, fishing, or inline skating, which usually don't involve lessons or classes.

Due to space limitations, we've also chosen not to include more obscure pursuits for children or ones that start very late into high school or college, such as paddle tennis, speed skating, water polo, and riflery. We also do not address the innumerable types of worthwhile intellectually or academically driven school-based clubs and pursuits. Keep the intellectual alternatives in mind as your child gets older, as these mainly begin in high school. Just a few options include speech and debate clubs, the Model United Nations program, the Academic Decathlon, science fairs, poetry and writing magazines and competitions, math tournaments, spelling bees, and so on. Your child can also engage in many different volunteer and religious institution-based activities.

In each section, we've listed organizations and resources to help you track these options down. Also, first and foremost, ask parents with older children in your community for advice on local options. Tap into the network of local parents to find out more about your child's activity, choices. The Web sites in the Resources chapters have been designed to help you find options in your local community. Call your local parks and recreation department as well for information about local leagues and classes.

To write this book, we interviewed over 560 coaches, teachers, musicians, dancers, artists, specialists, and parents around America and the world to gather their best insights and advice. Interspersed throughout are their stories, tips, and advice. Parents also share their own experiences, from how to survive early morning ice hockey practices to dealing with adult screamers in the bleachers. I have used first names only for parents in order to encourage them to candidly share their experiences. Teachers, coaches, and parents shared their opinions about what type of children excel at or enjoy a given activity, how you should structure your involvement, and what to expect down the road if your child embarks on a particular activity or sport. *Sign Me Up!* is a reference guide designed to be useful for years, available every season for evaluating activities, selecting them, and helping your child thrive. Come to my Web site at **www.momcentral.com** for more resources and updates.

How to Choose

Making thoughtful, informed, and strategic choices about what and how many activities to expose your child to when she is young—as well as teaching her how to do this for herself as she gets older—is the heart of *Sign Me Up!* Added into this mix is the trend toward activity mania, and the need to sort out the complexities of your own ambitions and fears for your child, as well as gain insight into which activities will likely be best suited to your child's personality, temperament, and skills.

CLARIFY WHAT YOU BRING TO THE TABLE

Trying to Divine Your Child's Unique Potential

🐾 You want to help your child grow up to realize her full potential in areas where she is particularly gifted. The examples of child prodigies such as Mozart come to mind: What if his parents had not introduced him to the piano at age 3?

🐾 Each slight interest becomes an untapped potential to be explored: What if your child could be the next great piano, soccer, or chess player? If your child starts piano and does really well, does that mean switching to the best teacher in the area?

🐾 The plethora of activity choices puts you in a position of constantly screening your child's potential talent or passion. For some kids, this becomes readily apparent, but for the vast majority, it's tough to do with a kindergartner. Then suddenly

This obsession of having to figure early what activities your child will excel in is ridiculous: How can you know at age 4 or 5? I was at a coffee meeting at the beginning of school and one mom lamented with worry, "Kevin tried baseball, soccer . . . but doesn't like anything at all." But Kevin is in kindergarten!

—Karen, mom of Max, 9, Sophie, 7, Celia, 5, and Jake, 2

I often feel tense and anxious, like I'm getting behind or missing out on critical opportunities for my kids if, for example, they haven't learned to play a musical instrument by age 7. Should I be sending my son to French class every week because they say that kids learn best when they're little? Oh my goodness! Plus, it puts our kids under a lot of pressure. Even my friends back in England say that it's just as bad there, with pressure to have their children participate in so many activities at such young ages.

—Sarah, mom of Taylor, 8, and Cameron, 6

There's nothing like finding your child's sweet spot and nurturing that, helping them to develop and bring it forward. I approach each activity as the one that might unlock the true essence of my child.

—Dean, dad of Evan, 10, and Olivia, Justin, and Shelby, 8

My husband was a national champion dancer, and he has the strong opinion that you excel at what you do well. He thinks it's our mission as parents to help our kids find their natural gifts, realizing that they will be mediocre at some things but great in others.

—Naomi, mom of Talia, 11, Arielle, 10, Aaron, 8, and Daniella, 5

by age 9, it's too late to start many, unexplored competitive activities, and your child is, for competitive purposes, prevented from participating.

Wanting the Best for Your Child

As a conscientious parent, you naturally want the best for your child. Yet it's often easy to confuse wanting the best with being the best.

✤ Parental love has become entwined with a perceived responsibility to indoctrinate your child into the land of opportunity. If you love your child, you will provide her with the best lessons, classes, activities, and sports exposure to help her grow into an exemplary adult.

✤ Don't fall into the trap of considering early achievement to be all-important. You only have to read the newspaper to see examples of young children's quests gone awry, such as seven-year-old Jessica Dubroff crashing her plane on a quest to set a new solo flying record.

✤ We are raising our children in what some have come to think of as "the Age of Anxiety." You need to step back and carefully consider what is the ultimate goal of all this activity mania and what will ultimately make your child successful.

✤ Jam-packed schedules and activities are simply not the cornerstone of shaping your child's adult self-actualization or a guarantee of her future happiness.

✤ Shift the emphasis in your words and actions to encouraging and supporting your child to do her best, rather than try to be the best.

It starts off innocently, as parents want the best of everything for their children. But then suddenly, kids' sports become so competitive that people go off the deep end. Many parents who have participated in a particular sport have fond memories of doing it and they want their children to share those same experiences and memories. Give kids a broad spectrum of exposure and be open to them liking different things than you did.

—*George Campbell, swimming program director for 20 years, middle school physical education director for 32 years, and dad of three grown kids*

Consider if it is *really* your child that you are thinking about. Why does your child have to be the "best," the "smartest," or the "most talented"? Too often, parents can get competitive with each other or with idealized pictures of overachieving families seen in the media. Consider the distressing rise in the phenomenon of "sports rage" where parents get so out of control at their children's games that it often turns physical, sometimes with fatal results. This is hardly about the child anymore.

—*Tanah Haney, professional performer and private harp, piano, and recorder teacher for 12 years*

Don't Relive Your Own Childhood

❧ Try not to impose your own passions on your child, as many parents do despite their best intentions. It's hard not to relive your youth through your child, bringing your own hopes and aspirations to the table. It's difficult to accept that while you were a tennis ace, your child has absolutely no interest in picking up a racket.

❧ Conversely, activities that you failed in as a child can be as emotionally laden as activities in which you excelled. You want to make sure that your own childhood experience doesn't lead you to push your child in the opposite direction. It's tempting to experience vicariously something that may have been lacking from your own childhood. Take a moment to be clear about whose needs are being served. Selecting a sport only because you felt unfairly teased for not making the team as a kid is not the way to go.

❧ What motivates you about your child participating in a particular sport or activity and what motivates your child are often fundamentally different. Your child may not love the sports you did as a child or you have picked for her to do, and you have to respect that, as well as recognize how hard it may be for your child to tell you this outright.

❧ Resist selecting only those sports that you personally enjoy or excelled at or want to coach, particularly if your child shows no interest in them.

Another part of my desire for a remarkable kid is because I feel that I wasn't very well rounded myself. I took music lessons for years, but dropped piano like a hot potato as soon as my parents let me. I took Spanish lessons for years but never became fluent. As an adult, I have lots of friends who are well rounded, and I feel rueful and wish I was more accomplished. It spills over to my expectations for my children.

—*Alexa, mom of a Adam, 11, and Sophie, 7*

My parents didn't sign me up for many activities growing up, and I felt kind of deprived. I felt programmed to do only what my parents did, which was sail and play tennis, and I think that I missed the whole social aspect of childhood without doing Girl Scouts. My mom worked the whole time I was growing up, and the logistics, such as getting us kids places, were too hard.

—*Leslie, mom of Katie, 3, and Lily, 2*

Your Child's Success as Reflected Glory on You

✦ Reflected glory can be sweet and intoxicating. When someone says to you, "You're the parent of ———?!" who just scored the winning goal or played a concert solo, you beam with pride and accomplishment.

✦ Remember that your child is not an extension of yourself, but rather a person with her own likes and dislikes, setting out to realize her own goals. Respect your child's uniqueness and the fact that she might have different dreams and ways of doing things than you'd expect.

As a child progresses, expectations from parents add to the already inherent pressure that comes with playing a sport. It is important for parents to monitor themselves and not let their own needs for success and achievements get connected to their child's experience.

—*Timothy Smith, director of junior tennis at Longwood Cricket Club and codirector of New England Academy of Tennis, teaching for 18 years*

We feel a compulsion to do more for our kids than we had done for us. A lot of us came from simple, hardworking parents and the level of organized sports was a bunch of kids hanging out at the playground and around the neighborhood. Just like we buy better homes, we all want to step up to elevate our kids to an even better life.

—*Dean, dad of Evan, 10, and Olivia, Justin, and Shelby, 8*

Valuing Your Child as a Human Being vs. a Human Doing

✦ There is an underlying pernicious message our children absorb: They must not be good enough just being, it's only through doing that they validate themselves in your eyes and in those of their peers, coaches, and teachers.

✦ Your child will thrive most when she has a close relationship with you, a happy, relaxed family life, and a deep understanding that she is loved just for being herself, and not because of the activities at which she excels.

One of the things I teach each of my children every single day is that they're precious just because they're here. I believe that our job as parents is to build children up so that they can go out and face the world every day. If they go out of the house without a full cup, it's like leaving home without breakfast. So instead of sending them out to all these activities, spend time filling that child up, giving them something to carry them through the day and through their lives.

—*Diana, mom of six children*

Back to the Basics: All About Having Fun

🐾 First and foremost, activities can and should be fun for your child. The more fun it is, the more likely your child will continue to stay active later in life.

🐾 Look for an activity that your child can continue to play and appreciate into her adult years.

I believe that everything that's not school-related is supposed to be fun. I actually feel lucky that neither of my kids is gifted athletically. What I strive for them to be is capable, nothing more.

—*Arnie, dad of Tessa, 11, and Jake, 8*

My bottom line is the pleasure principle. If you love taking your toddler to swim, and it's relaxing for you and your baby, and it gets you away from changing diapers for an hour, great.

—*Amy, mom of Sacha, 11, and Libby, 8*

I tell my kids that regardless of what the coach and people scream at you in games, this is for fun. Yes, you have to work hard to win, but it's just a game. It's not the be-all and end-all. When the sport wasn't fun anymore for my oldest, she quit and moved on to band.

—*Kim, mom of Brandi, 19, Courtney, 13, and Colleen, 10*

✦ Excelling and winning in the forms of all-star games, trophies, Little League World Series Championships and Youth Super Bowl titles have taken precedence over having fun. This is true for music, dance, and other competitions too.

✦ Stay in touch with your child's feelings about the program. If he does not enjoy himself, find another activity for the time being.

DECIDING AMONG ALL THE TANTALIZING POSSIBILITIES

✦ Between sports teams, gymnastics, karate, dance classes, art lessons, and exposure to a second language, the enticing smorgasbord of possibilities seems endless. Should your child take swimming lessons, join a soccer team, learn to play the piano or flute, sign up for T-ball, or join a Spanish-language or chess club?

✦ There are just so many choices, all with differing strengths. In fact, it's entirely too easy to overload our kids' after-school hours with multiple activities, accompanied by a never-ending number of car trips and inevitable fast-food dinners. Cou-

In the earlier stages, with four young kids, there was no way I could have each kid do more than one activity during the week. So by necessity, I didn't get caught up in the activity overload. Now all the activities and sports seem okay: not so stressful, inappropriate, or so out of control. My kids get ready for the activities themselves, and now that I can leave my kids for a few minutes at home to do homework while I pick someone up from an activity, it's not affecting everyone else as much.

—*Bridgitt, mom of Taylor, 10, Connor and Chloe, 8, Brian, 6*

On top of four gymnastics practices a week, our youngest daughter plays competitive travel soccer, so in the spring and fall she alternates between gymnastics and soccer practices on Wednesdays. The other two afternoons a week and on Sundays she has religious school, and soccer games on Saturday mornings. Of course, our family (that is, everyone but me!) can't stand downtime. Even when we go on a family vacation, we do a thousand activities a day!

—*Cathy, mom of Samantha, 13, and Kimberly, 10*

All these activities are a substitute for a natural neighborhood. We now create activity-based neighborhoods instead of proximity-based neighborhoods.

—Ron, nationally licensed youth soccer coach and dad of two, ages 10 and 8

Frenzied activity is the term I'd use to describe our only daughter's life. She's typically over-subscribed (she takes after her mother)! Monday it's Girl Scouts and basketball practice at night, Tuesday is dance, Wednesday is swimming, Thursday is piano, and Saturday is soccer and basketball. On top of it all, she's in aftercare, which we consider to be like hanging out in the neighborhood.

—David, father of Alexandra, 10

pled with growing homework loads, free time for children is becoming as scarce as it is for their parents, if not more so.

🦋 Rather than seeing activities and sports as fun ways to engage our children, our generation has shifted to viewing the immersion of children as essential to their future successes as adults.

Think of Ages 4–10 as the Trial Years

🦋 Your community likely offers a staggering number of children's activities. Determining which are best for your child can be an overwhelming endeavor.

🦋 Treat the years between ages 4 and 10 as the "trial years," a time for your child to explore interests without pressure, discover passions while having fun, and see what she wants to stick with and pursue further. Aim for a wide exposure to lots of different activities and sports, watching to see what sparks your child's interest and passion. These are the years to introduce your child to a rich array of possibilities and opportunities.

🦋 Think of how many hobbies, sports, and other pursuits you have happily taken up and dropped across the course of your lifetime. There is an important value in being able to dabble around in a lot of other things that hold your interest for only a short stretch of time.

🦋 Allow your child to experiment casually with many different sports and activities and then encourage the ones she seems to enjoy the most.

🐟 Developing interests generally come from an exposure to a wide variety of activities. Aim to allow your toddler and elementary school child many experiences across a diverse spectrum of activities. This way she can figure out what she likes, and begin to define herself.

🐟 Remember not to make sweeping judgments about your child's abilities or skills when she's young. Innumerable athletes were told as young children that they lacked the physical abilities to succeed. Ask your child which activities she has an interest in or thinks she might enjoy.

My philosophy is that you should let your kids try a lot of stuff, not expect much, and focus on helping them figure out what they like. You use the trial years to try all sorts of different activities to narrow down and discover what interests and engages your child. Otherwise, you may find in a few years that while other kids have found their thing, your kid is still trying to perform a whole bunch of stuff he hates and is fighting with you about doing them. As a parent, you have to accept that you're not necessarily going to find that each child in your family loves sports, art, music, and excels academically. It's important that the trial years are viewed as exactly that: finding what your child responds to and likes best.

—*Karla, mom of Karl, 9, Max 6, and Leo, 3*

I put my kids in all types of activities prior to starting kindergarten. By starting early, we've weeded out things that were nice to do, but they don't care to continue. For instance, my five-year-old daughter has taken several sessions of ice-skating lessons, has been in gymnastics since she was 16 months old, has played hockey and soccer, and is taking dance lessons. She decided that hockey and soccer aren't for her and will continue with dance and gymnastics. My son has done most of the same actvities and likes hockey and soccer and may discontinue gymnastics. Do I get tired of hauling my kids all over? Of course! But I look at it as opportunities for them to experience various sports. If they don't like them, that is perfectly okay. They never have to do it again. I just want to give them choices.

—*Kim, mom of five-year-old twins*

My oldest was one of those kids who had a real interest in certain things. He wanted to play soccer and baseball, and at various times to take chess, magic, karate, and reptile classes. His interests drove what he did, and he definitely cycled through different activities. Now he's into guitar lessons, skiing, and tennis once a week. Basically, whatever my kids are into at the time, I go along with to see what sticks. But this is what I got for not having signed up my third child for any activities for seven years: Now it's "Quidditch for Muggles" on Monday, karate for beginners on Tuesday, Wednesday is rock wall climbing, Thursday is cartooning, and Friday is classes with the reptile man. This is the most overscheduled child I've ever had. And it's all come from him. I'm defenseless. How do you say no when your child says, "I have to take this reptile class—it's got live animals!"

—*Claire, mom of Ben, 14, Alison, 11, and Danny, 8*

As kids get older, they're not as willing to try new things. They get into a comfort zone and don't want to take an unknown step. Exposing kids to lots of things while they're young helps diminish that resistance if they want to try the activity again at a later date.

—*Dean, dad of Evan, 10, and Olivia, Justin, and Shelby, 8*

Helping Your Child Find the Right Fit

🐾 Look for clues about what your child might enjoy by how she spends her free time at home, whether it is jumping and climbing, staging plays, or doing art projects.

🐾 Encourage your child to pursue her natural interests. As soon as your child starts expressing her opinions, let her weigh in on choosing her own activities.

🐾 Explain when financial or transportation considerations limit her choices.

🐾 Agree to a trial period for each activity to see how well it fits with your child's interests and needs, as well as your schedule.

🐾 Other factors to consider when choosing an activity for your child:

   ☻ Does your child know any of the other children participating?

   ☻ What do other parents have to say about the class, the organization, and the specific teacher or coach?

   ☻ Will your child have time to get her homework done?

- How does your child handle: risk taking? losing? winning? playing with others on a team?

- How aggressive is she?

- How self-disciplined is your child when it comes to practice?

- Is your child willing to put in the commitment that the activity requires?

✦ If your child has no particular sport in mind, then you might try enrolling her in an all-sports program at a recreation department or similar facility. This type of program will give your child a taste of several different sports in a relatively non-competitive and stress-free environment.

Matching Activities to Your Child's Physique

✦ Evaluate your child's body type and physical strengths. Some sports, activities, and musical instruments, as seen in the specific activity sections that follow, require a very specific body type. Some types require being as tall as a basketball or volleyball player, while others require being petite like a gymnast or figure skater.

✦ This doesn't mean that your child has to fit the stereotype in order to have fun or succeed. Many children come up with ways to maximize their abilities or overcome their physical limitations through determination and skill development. Still other children simply love a sport and do not mind that they may not be the best at it.

✦ Moreover, your child's body can change dramatically during adolescence and puberty, with some children not becoming fully grown until the end of high school.

✦ If your child is small, find a program that groups kids by size as well as by age. Or if your child is up for it, have her join a team with kids a year younger.

✦ In many activities, being small is an asset. This ranges from endurance sports like running and swimming to sports like gymnastics and dance that require agility and balance over strength or bulk.

✦ Each individual sport and activity section of Part II addresses the typical physique or physical attributes required to either get started or excel competitively.

The Role and Influence of Your Child's Friends

✤ Find out which activities your child's friends are doing. If your child is reluctant to join activities, she may be more likely to participate in an activity that she can do with them.

✤ Establishing friendships and forming peer groups are of vital importance to your child.

✤ Many kids pick up a sport because it's social and allows them time with their friends.

✤ If your child ends up not quite fitting in with her friends' activities, you'll need to balance her social needs with trying less popular activities that may be better suited to her interests and strengths.

✤ One great benefit of activities is that they enable your child to meet other kids from different schools in your town. By the time she reaches middle school, your child will already know many of her new incoming classmates.

✤ For those children in private school, activities serve as the link to neighborhood-based friendships.

Now at age eleven, what my daughter likes most is the social side of the activities, as she gets to do fun things with a group of friends.

    —Amy, mom of Sacha, 11, and Libby, 8

I'm very focused on structured activities for my son with his neighborhood buddies so that he doesn't feel excluded from his community because he's in private school.

    —Janine, mom of Ben, 10, and Andrew, 7

Lily likes the team aspect of soccer, especially as she goes to a private school. Through community sports, she has met lots of kids in our town, and now seems to know someone everywhere she goes.

    —Debbie, mom of Zachary, 12, and Lily, 10

Pressure to Follow the "In-Crowd"

🍂 Every community has its passions, and at some point along the way, you or your child will undoubtedly encounter enormous peer pressure to join in your community's most popular structured activities.

🍂 Depending on the activities in your community, you'll find the parenting

The pressure in our neighborhood to enroll toddlers in activities is quite intense. Attending preschool is routine for kids as young as 2 1/2. My three-year-old is the only child of his age in our social circle who isn't, and I still feel at times I have to explain myself when friends wonder why Ben isn't in preschool. I am often asked why my daughter isn't currently in soccer, T-ball, ballet, or gymnastics like the rest of her friends even though she has already done preschool, soccer, ballet, Gymboree, swimming classes, Sunday school, and Spanish classes at various times over the last five years.

   —Lisa, mom of Grace, 6, Ben, 4, and Maddie, 1

Our town is like a soccer factory. If your child doesn't start early, they get so far behind their peers that it's impossible to catch up and make the highly competitive top tiers.

   —Jill, mom of Stella, 5

There's tons of social pressure to sign your children up for the programs that all the other kids in your town are doing. If you don't, other parents start viewing you as an outsider and act as if there's something wrong with you.

   —Dean, dad of Evan, 10, and Olivia, Justin, and Shelby, 8

I definitely limit my boys' activities, which is hard in the community in which I live. I see what everyone else is doing, such as all my son's friends playing basketball in the winter, and then I think, Should we? But I love the fact that he's having a break.

   —Dee, mom of Carey, 8, and Danny, 6

in-crowd heading in a certain direction. Remind yourself to help your child pick activities based on her interests, instead of being swept up in the herd mentality. Sometimes your child wants to pursue an activity or sport not in vogue at the moment in your community or among her peers.

✺ Those sports will be highly organized, with extensive parent volunteering, lots of attendance at events, and sign-ups that begin at very young ages. Moreover, these popular activities will have better facilities and equipment, more crowds watching, be intensely competitive—which makes both the successes and the failures more public—and garner more peer recognition for your child.

✺ The real issue is whether the activity is a good match for your child. Even if your child does not excel, she may greatly enjoy being part of her peer group.

✺ Be willing to think outside the box when it comes to choices. Do not limit your choice to the most popular sports; consider alternative activities, such as fencing or Odyssey of the Mind. So what if soccer is the most popular sport in your area? If your child dislikes it, look off the beaten path for an alternative, whether it be archery, karate, or volleyball.

✺ If you haven't heard it a dozen times yet, you will soon hear your child announce, "But everyone else is doing it!"

✺ When every child in your neighborhood starts signing up for the most popular activity, such as soccer, at age 4, your child will be hopelessly behind and struggling to catch up if she decides to embark on the activity a few years later.

✺ Counterbalancing this should be the unique preferences, talents, and interests of your child. Your kid may be the one to hate softball in a community that lives and breathes it on the weekends.

Fear Your Child Will Be Left Behind by Her Peers

✺ You may find yourself in the midst of a struggle between what age is too early versus when you will have waited too long.

✺ If your eight-year-old decides he wants to try a sport, such as ice hockey or soccer, he may find himself way behind peers who started four years ago. It will be hard, if not impossible, to catch up, as well as frustrating and disheartening.

It's hard not to make comparisons. My friend Sally's son does everything: a musical instrument, sports, the elementary school newspaper—what every parent wants their child to be like. My son's the polar opposite of hers. I try to kick back and say it's okay that my son only does karate, but it's hard not to be neurotic.

—*Alexa, mom of Adam, 11, and Sophie, 7*

It really depends on the type of person you are and your parenting personality. When some of my friends hear another child playing the piano, they respond by saying, "Oh my gosh, I better get my kids to take piano lessons right away!" But the kids could care less.

—*Karen, mom of Max, 9, Sophie, 7, Celia, 5, and Jake, 2*

I sometimes get caught up in comparing my son to his peers, such as this little boy Josh who's already a stellar athlete at age 10. His parents have him taking golf, tennis, gymnastics, basketball, soccer, and he now wants to play peewee football next year. Another good friend has put her son, who's also the same age as my oldest, into tennis, soccer, basketball, and skiing. She's driven to have him excel at these sports and be on the travel team. It makes me feel that if Ben doesn't do those things too, then he can't hang out with his friends. I have to catch myself and put it all in perspective.

—*Janine, mom of Ben, 10, and Andrew, 7*

I never learned to ski as a child, and now that I'm just a beginner with my kids, I'm finding it very difficult. So many activities are easier to learn as kids and so much harder to pick up later, like swimming, skiing, or horseback riding. If you introduce these activities to a child in an appropriate setting, they learn to love them and will continue them as hobbies into adulthood.

—*Amy, mom of Sacha, 11, and Libby, 8*

How Young Is Too Young?

❦ We enroll our two-year-olds in preschool programs and myriad activities intended to enrich and provide social opportunities for them. From swimming or tumbling to ballet or music appreciation, these activities offer parents the chance to meet, talk, and share the experience with others who have children of the same age. Furthermore, it gives you a chance to get out of the house and do something engaging with your child.

❦ Most children are open to trying lots of different things from toddlerhood up through early elementary school years. Toddlers with Mom, Dad, or baby-sitter in tow can start classes at age 1. Many three-year-olds are already activity veterans.

❦ Starting as early as your child's second birthday, you will likely feel pressure to start signing your child up for classes and activities, whether it be Gymboree, a Mommy and Me class, beginning dance, rhythm and music, or tumbling.

Nowadays, if your kid is not playing tennis by age 9, he can't be competitive. I was a state swimmer, but did not even start until I was 11. The bar has been raised incredibly high for our kids.

    —Lisa, mom of CJ, 10, and Maddie, 8

I feel very conflicted. While I think it's not a good idea to start so early with all these activities, at the same time, because of the way my kids' lives are structured given that I work full-time, it's sort of a fact of life.

    —Deborah, mom of Philip, 10, Patrick, 8, and William, 3

The younger kids train, the better they will become at a sport. Ask Tiger Woods if he started too early. But it should be based on your child's wanting to pick up the sport. My kids all tried various sports and made their own decision about what they wanted to play. My youngest decided at 9 that she wanted only to play soccer. It was her decision and now she's a regional team player. But it happened because it was what *she* wanted.

    —Jeffrey Sanderson, soccer coach for 12 years, and dad of a 14-year-old daughter

✦ Part of the belief underlying this frenzy stems from the myth "the earlier the better." You fear that if your child hasn't mastered a particular skill early, the window of opportunity for that sport or activity will rapidly close. So as early as second grade, your child may be precluded from excelling at this sport or activity, or even participating at all due to a late start.

✦ Before you plunge in and try to keep up with the parenting crowd, ask yourself why you are signing your child up for particular activities, and whether she's stimulated or overwhelmed.

WHO DOES THE CHOOSING?

✦ Who should take the initiative in deciding what activities to pursue, lessons to sign up for, or teams to join? It's best if the desire comes from your child.

✦ You have a tremendous influence over your child's activities, even when just suggesting a particular hobby or sport to your child.

✦ Sort out your child's skills and talents from her passions and interests.

✦ Consult your child before making commitments to classes or activities. Gauge her level of interest, and clarify what appeals to her the most. Is it that her best friend's taking the class along with her, or that she inherently enjoys the activity itself?

✦ Evaluate how many of your child's activities are initiated by her, and how many have been chosen or insisted upon by you. You also have to factor in the age and temperament of your child in order to figure out where it's best to draw this ever-shifting line.

✦ It's easy to end up micromanaging your child's choices because you feel responsible for her success.

✦ Staying deeply involved in every detail of your child's life prevents her from learning to structure her own schedule and find a personal balance between activities and downtime.

✦ Motivation to engage in an activity will likely change as your child gets older. In preschool and early elementary school years, most children sign up because their parents want them to.

✦ For your child under the age of 5, you may need to guide her choices much more than you will for her at age 9. If you want an activity that helps broaden your child's interests, think about those that push her 10% against the grain. If your child is not naturally inclined to do anything athletic, find an activity that gets her active without forcing her into competitive, strenuous activities she views as torturous.

❧ The motivation then shifts at age 8 to activities they intrinsically enjoy, ones they are good at, and ones where they can be with friends.

I guess my feeling is that if you ask your kids how many desserts they would like after dinner, they would prefer five, not one. If you asked what time they'd like to go to bed, it would probably be midnight. We don't let them choose in those situations, so why when it comes to activities should they suddenly become the choosers? But no matter what side you come down on this debate, kids eventually sort it out themselves and gravitate to the things they enjoy most. As parents, we overemphasize our personal opinions about this stuff.

—Amy, mom of Sacha, 11, and Libby, 8

By forcing your child to do activities, you run the risk of screwing up your relationship with him. Kids have natural inclinations of their own that you need to follow. The idea that your kids have to like everything: Give me a break! If your kid can't handle a lot, you have to accept him and love him for who he is. You really can only force your child to do one or two things in terms of trying new activities or sports.

—Karla, mom of Karl, 9, Max, 6, and Leo, 3

My kids have the final say, but I definitely direct them to certain sports and activities I think they'll like. I want them to try a lot of different things now while they are young, because as they get older, they'll have to decide between sports, such as whether to stick with baseball rather than soccer.

—Sarah, mom of Taylor, 8, and Cameron, 6

My daughter's a very social being and loves all the activities for that aspect. I make sure sports and music are covered, while her mom's in charge of the other arts. We kind of break it up. It's about 50/50 about who chooses between her and us.

—David, dad of Alexandra, 10

Following Your Child's Lead

❦ In order for something to ultimately become a passion for your child, it has to be of her own choosing. Even as a preschooler, she will likely have ideas and instinctive reactions about whether she finds something engaging and interesting.

❦ When your child makes her own decisions, it forges stronger character development than when you are the one running the show. Children acquire self-reliance and resilience through making mistakes and getting beyond them. In order for your child to develop a strong sense of herself, she has to feel not only free to fail, but to experience failure and move beyond it. The message you send your child when you choose is that she lacks the ability or maturity to make responsible or thoughtful decisions on her own.

❦ Your child will start having very strong opinions and want to make her own choices between ages 9 and 12.

❦ Plus, as your child reaches puberty, any prior acquiescence to your activity suggestions or preference often comes to an abrupt halt, and she may promptly decide to drop the activity altogether. To get past this phase, the drive and perseverance has to come from your child, not you. If she selects the activities in which she wants to participate, she'll be more likely to stick them out.

Danny discovered that he likes to draw, and started taking a cartooning class. For me, that's such a compelling reason to schlep across town to take him there. Kids should be able to try many different things and discover what they want to do. It's about helping them find their passions. It's so important to nurture your kids, encourage their interests, and lay off trying to impose a master plan.

—*Claire, mom of Ben, 14, Alison, 11, and Danny, 8*

I grew tired of always saying, "Come on, it's time to practice" or "Hurry up, get your hockey stuff on, we're running late." Now the attitude I've arrived at with our kids is that they have to want to do an activity and initiate things on their own in order for me to sign them up.

—*Lisa, mom of CJ, 10, and Maddie, 8*

My daughter has already informed me that this fall she wants to take ballet, tap, skating, singing, and piano! That would be an activity every day of the week proposition. I'm going to do it because I want her to find herself, and learn what she's good at and what she enjoys doing. Maybe it will be one of these things, or maybe it will be something else altogether.

—Jill, mom of Stella, 5

My kids pick their own activities. Sydney chose jazz and tap dancing lessons. Michael chose a rock-climbing course at a local gym. I can't keep up with what everyone else in our town is doing, so I just let my kids pick a couple things that interest them.

—Susan, mom of Sydney, 8, and Michael, 7

Not allowing your child to make decisions about what fits well for him deprives him of the opportunity to grow in ways he really needs to grow. Especially when they hit middle school, some kids, like my oldest, spend a lot of time trying to figure out who they are and who they want to become. They need the room, the space, and the downtime to sort it out. They may even need a year or two, as my son did, to not do many activities at all, before they emerge ready to take on ones that are good fits. My son came out of this period immersed in fencing, drama, musicals, and the Model United Nations. As a parent, you need to relax and trust in your child's coming out of a retreat period.

—Elizabeth, mom of Robert, 15, and David, 10

Prioritizing and Goal-Setting with Your Child

❦ Ask any child under age 8 about the score in a game, and even those tracking it will get it wrong most of the time. There will be games your child's team loses handily only to have your child declare it an all-out victory, as she really has no idea of the score unless debriefed by an adult. For this age group, it's all about the fun, the excitement, getting to participate, being with friends, and building new skills.

❦ What motivates you to have your child participate and what motivates your child may be vastly different without your even fully realizing the disparity. What do you want your child to get out of the activity in general? Try this exercise of categorizing and prioritizing activities with your child: Each of you rank activities your child wants to do on a rating scale from 5 to 1, with 5 = indispensable to you, and 1 = indispensable to your child.

❧ It is also important to set meaningful and attainable goals with your child. Concrete goals help because they allow your child to work toward something and enable her to monitor her progress along the way. Goals should depend on age, experience, and skill. Goals could be, for instance, getting in at least three-quarters of first serves in a tennis match. Clarify what your child hopes to gain from participating and support her in her own goals.

❧ Realize that your child's goals may change throughout the years. It is also important that these goals are not set in stone and that there is some wiggle room. In the long run, it's not natural ability that will keep your child playing and improving, but a sense of accomplishment and joy.

We tend to visualize activities in bundles. By doing "block scheduling," we trade apples for apples, not impacting the other bundles. When my daughter reached high school, she traded in the sports bundle year-round competitive soccer for spring tennis and a regularly used health club membership. The music bundle works this way too. Elise has studied instrumental music since age 5, when she began taking piano lessons. By fifth grade, she was choosing music over other activities and adding instruments with a current focus on piano, tuba, and organ. Music lessons, individual practice time, ensemble rehearsals, and performances are scheduled by the week, making necessary tradeoffs within the music block. My daughter is very energetic and has learned over the years to balance three or four simultaneous bundles. Some kids would go for two or three; I doubt a healthy child could handle more than four. This is very important, since a critical part of stress management for a child is to protect the social and sleep bundles!

—*Kathy, mom of Elise, 15*

If there is a new activity in which our kids want to participate, we look at the cost, time commitment, and what our child will get out of the experience before adding it to our schedule.

—*Dana, mom of three, ages 9, 7, and 5*

Insisting on Certain Non-Negotiable Activities

✦ Parents clearly fall into two camps on this issue of forcing your child to pursue a particular activity or sport. Some are totally opposed, while others either care passionately about an activity, such as music being an integral part of their family culture, or consider an activity fundamental, such as learning to swim.

✦ There may be some things you consider either fundamental "life skills" such as knowing how to swim, or something very important to your family that you feel essential for your child to know, such as learning to ski for family ski trips or learning to play a musical instrument.

✦ Forcing your child to continue an activity she doesn't enjoy turns it into a control issue, and you risk having a deeply resentful, willful, and rebellious child on your hands. When you make your child do something she does not want to, you will endure endless glares, sullen pouts, and occasional tantrums.

✦ On the other hand, there are countless stories of athletes and musicians who feel grateful that their parents forced them to take or stick with an activity, and stories from fellow adults who regret either never having tried an activity at all or having dropped out.

Recently when I took my kids skating at a local ice rink, I saw a kid howling as her mom pushed her onto the ice. It just broke my heart. That's a sure way to lose your child's trust and make your child feel like her opinions don't count.

—Amy, mom of Sacha, 11, and Libby, 8

While I mostly let my kids pick their own activities, I insist on Red Cross swimming lessons each Saturday because I want my boys to achieve a certain level of proficiency in swimming as a life skill. I then try to accommodate other requests from my children, such as other activities they want to try or the instrument they want to learn at school.

—Deborah, mom of Philip, 10, Patrick, 8, and William, 3

I think that you should never insist on an activity that your child constantly complains about—except, of course, religious school and piano lessons. Hmmm . . . I take that all back!

—*Ellen, mom of Rachel, 10, Ben, 7, and Josh, 3*

You cannot force your child to do something and not expect a fight (I know as a parent of two children). Rather, talk with your child to see what things they are interested in or would like to try. Suggest or cajole, but do not press. A joint child-parent decision is best.

—*John Mueller, assistant professor of trombone and euphonium, University of Memphis, and professional musician, teaching for 21 years*

Requiring activity is not harmful; dictating what those activities must be is.

—*Stephen Gregg, USSRA director of junior development and squash coach*

LIMITING THE NUMBER OF SIMULTANEOUS ACTIVITIES

✦ Ice skating, hockey, children's theater, soccer, ballet, modern dance, chess club, French lessons, piano lessons, swimming . . . "Gotta catch 'em all!" as the Pokémon mantra admonishes our kids.

✦ It would be great if there was a simple, uniform answer to the question of how many activities to allow—such as one sport, one musical instrument, one language— and call it a day. Instead, it's a constant dilemma that reappears each time seasons change, a class comes to an end, and you have to decide whether to reenroll, and so on.

✦ There are some, albeit few, parents who pull their kids from all organized activities, but they are clearly the exception. For the rest of us, we do not want to approach activities in such an all-or-nothing fashion. Activities in moderation can offer tremendous benefits, from physical exercise to helping your child develop hobbies and passions.

✦ Yet you do need to set limits. Just as you don't allow your child to gorge herself on ice cream after dinner, you cannot say the sky's the limit for activities after

We started out with soccer, as everyone in our community does, and sports have progressed from there. My son does all the following at various times during the year: travel team soccer, Little League baseball, Pop Warner, tennis, ice hockey, and local basketball league. We have a ski house in the winter, so there's ski school every weekend and he's become an exceptional skier. He does summer tennis camp and a couple of weeks of baseball, and an intensive week of football camp. Plus, my husband takes him out during the summers to a nearby golf driving range.

—Leslie, mom of Alexandra, 10, and Jack, 9

I have limited my sons' activities to those that promote lifelong enjoyment (tennis, swimming, chess, etc.), specific interests (music, science, art), and family involvement (church activities, Japanese lessons).

—Lisa, mom of Connor, 10, Garrison, 6, and Mitchell, 1

In our town, there is peer pressure to keep kids enrolled in many activities, so we are constantly fighting to keep our family time our own and not have our days and nights be a series of car pools and rushing from place to place. My three kids have already participated in a lot of activities (tumbling, Spanish, preschool, soccer, ballet, art classes, Sunday School, etc.), and I really try to keep the number of activities within reason. When I hear friends talk about having sports practice or games for their kids six nights out of seven, my head spins.

—Lisa, mom of Grace, 6, Ben, 4, and Maddie, 1

We are on the underside of programming our kids. I'm a big believer that collectively we overprogram our kids. There's so much they can do now that they're too easily bored. Picking even three activities doesn't feel like enough for them. But when I was growing up, after school I would watch TV, read, play pickup games outside with my friends, and have extremely limited organized activities. Perhaps because I loved hanging out, I'm fairly oblivious to pressure. I'm not trying to keep up with anyone. In my case, I may actually project my lack of ambitions onto my kids!

—Arnie, dad of Tessa, 11, and Jake, 8

school. While each sport or activity can be worthwhile in and of itself, they become overly stressful and time-consuming in the aggregate.

Your Child's Temperament and Energy Level

🦐 There is no ideal number of simultaneous extracurricular activities. You need to take into account the personality of your child, her tolerance levels, and your needs as a family.

🦐 Kids have such widely ranging temperaments that you have to think carefully about what works best for your child. What overloads one child will seem just perfect to another. Some kids thrive on jam-packed schedules, always look for the next thing to do, and still have energy to burn after the myriad activities of a day. For this whirling dervish, a packed schedule seems fabulous. Other children complain about how two commitments a week seems oppressive and gives them no downtime with their friends or to hang out at home. Keep close tabs on how your child thrives or burns out on a given schedule.

I have had my oldest son signed up for activities since he was four years old. I've found that he needs one-hour-long activities to keep him entertained otherwise he's always looking for me to play with him. He's just not the sort of kid who goes to his room or the basement to play, which my youngest son will do for hours on end. So I take him to sports activities a few times a week to enable him to get rid of some of his excess energy. Plus, he really enjoys them. But he also likes downtime too, so I have to find the right balance.

—*Sarah, mom of Taylor, 8, and Cameron, 6*

Our son loves all the sports he does. Outside of sports, he likes TV, his dog, and his best friend, but he has no artistic ability or musical interest whatsoever. We're willing to go with his sports passion. Also, he's always been one of those kids that don't need that much sleep, and has no problem with homework. If he ever exhibited disinterest, seemed tired, or said, "It's too much," we'd ratchet it down. But he hasn't, and so we just take every year as it comes.

—*Leslie, mom of Alexandra, 10, and Jack, 9*

I have two kids at opposite extremes when it comes to activities. My daughter is interested in everything, immersed in soccer, pottery, ballet, and musical theater, and loves them all. On the other hand, my son's only activity is karate once a week. When it comes to picking activities for your kids, it's very individually based on each child's personality. My daughter can absorb a lot, and my son can't.

—*Alexa, mom of Adam, 11, and Sophie, 7*

My oldest son is somewhat athletically challenged and has a laid-back personality, which he managed to accommodate in his sports choices. He loved playing soccer, and found that being a defensive player best suited his temperament and skills.

—*Elizabeth, mom of Robert, 15, and David, 10*

🐾 Many parents limit their children, especially younger ones, to one activity at a time. Some children cannot handle more than this, because they don't have the endurance and attention span needed for more.

🐾 Other parents take their cues from their children. While it's true that some kids need more downtime, it's also true that some children simply do not do well without structure. When they don't have planned activities, they "don't have anything to do!" or are "bored." If your child complains of this, then it may be time to get her involved in something. If she is already involved in an activity, maybe she is ready to take on something else.

🐾 Children who do well with downtime are children who are great at entertaining themselves. A drawback to having lots of scheduled activities, however, is that there will inevitably come a time when there is not as much to do. If a child has little experience with unstructured time, she is going to be miserable.

How Much Is Too Much?

🐾 Often, your child is as conflicted as you are concerning how much is too much. Despite sighing about having to trudge off to a class or activity, being tired, or evidencing signs of the pressure, your child may at the same time tell you how much she likes the various activities she does and how she doesn't want to drop any of them.

🐾 Our culture sends you powerful messages that to be a successful modern par-

Follow your kids' lead. I guess I feel fortunate that I have stamina. We can afford to do lots of activities, and my husband has the interest and willingness to do a lot of the driving to night practices and weekend games.

—Leslie, mom of Alexandra, 10, and Jack, 9

With four kids, I set limits on how many activities each can do. To be fair to everyone, I will only allow them one sport a season. A lot of kids at their school and in our neighborhood do more, but with four I can barely handle one sport each. For games, I split them up with my husband, and we tag team, but we still have at least one of the younger kids with us being bored on the sidelines. We worry already about the future as our two youngest get old enough to start sports because of all the conflicting practices and games even with each child doing only one sport.

—Karen, mom of Max, 9, Sophie, 7, Celia, 5, and Jake, 2

I don't want to overbook my kids, but I do want them to learn tennis and swimming. I would also like them to be able to ice-skate and appreciate music. It's overwhelming, as there are tons of things you want your kids to try, and you're never sure about which activity to sign them up for when they're too young to really choose on their own. I want my girls to explore lots of things to discover what they enjoy.

—Leslie, mom of Katie, 3, and Lily, 2

ent, you should keep your child constantly stimulated. Yet you can't let the constant drumbeat of this message drown out the cues from your child about what works best for her.

🐦 While an activity or sport can offer your child a different skill or aspect of personal development, in the present they can be overwhelming, stripping your child's day of free time and putting her under enormous pressure.

🐦 If your child wants to add an activity and you think she's overloaded, ask her to consider giving up one current activity in exchange for the new one.

🐾 Urge your child to slow down, and talk over what should come off her schedule.

🐾 Try to limit your child to one competitive sport a season, given the time commitment practices and games usually entail, so you do not find your entire weekend absorbed with carpooling and spending too much time in the bleachers.

Your Active Child Wants Even More Activities

In addition to his other sports, my son wanted to play on an ice hockey team, but it involved four practices a week and games on the weekends. I feel it's too much of a commitment in addition to the football that he already did. So I said no, and he actually was okay with that.

—Lisa, mom of CJ, 10, and Maddie, 8

🐾 Many kids would book themselves up every spare moment if they could. Just because your child wants to spend her every waking minute filled with activities doesn't mean you should facilitate this or allow it. With this child, your challenge is to ensure a balanced schedule, preserving some downtime each day.

🐾 What if your child does twelve things a week, seems to be thriving in them, and handle the commotion just fine? It's like living on a diet of Oreo cookies: Your child may still be growing, but it's ultimately not nutritious. For this child, the challenge will be teaching her how to become self-reliant and self-entertaining in free time.

🐾 Monitor your energetic child to make sure she does not overextend herself.

Getting Your Resistant Child to Try Something New

🐾 Fear of the unknown or of failure often keeps children from trying new things.

🐾 Drawing the line between activities your child initiates and those you push is key.

🐾 You may find yourself with a reluctant participant when it comes to activities. Your child may balk at activities that require physical exertion or risk-taking, or shy away from team-event or competitive situations.

🐾 You may need to help your resident couch potato develop a healthy and fit lifestyle. Your challenge is to find ways your child enjoys being active.

Each year for my birthday, I ask my kids to try something new they haven't ever done before. This year they took a few guitar lessons, which they found fun. It's a great way to expose them to something new.

—*Karla, mom of Karl, 9, Max, 6, and Leo, 3*

Too many activities have never been a problem for our children. Finding something that *they* wanted to do has been the key. My daughter never wanted to do anything until high school, when she suddenly sat up off the couch and said she'd decided to join the swim team. My husband and I were floored because until then she'd been the world's loveliest couch potato. We said weakly, "But sweetie, you don't even put your face in the water." "Oh, details, details!" said Dinah, and joined. Well, she got a varsity letter, never complained about the 5:30 a.m. practices in that cold, cold water—just loved it and made excellent friends. So let your child choose!

—*Karen, mom of Dinah, 16, and Toby, 12*

One thing I encourage in my kids is to at least try something. One of my twins kept saying that he wanted to sign up for soccer, but when it came time to do so, he didn't want to because he thought he wasn't very good. I told my son, "While you can stand there and think you'll not be good at it, you should give it a try. You keep telling me you want to play, and the season is only ten games long. Don't just stand at the sidelines, jump in and try it." He did, turned out to be good at the sport, and enjoyed himself. At the end of the season he decided that he preferred basketball and wanted to make that his focus. I was very impressed with him being able at age 9 to say, "You know, Mom, I like this, but I'd just rather play basketball." And I respected his choice. He did what I asked, which was try it. He made a life decision to just do basketball, and it's his life to live.

—*Diana, mom of 6 children*

CONSIDER THE LOGISTICS

✦ Before enrolling your child, take into consideration total time commitment, expectations for practicing outside of class, and fees. What commitment are you willing to make in terms of time, money, and energy?

✦ It can begin to feel like you are mobilizing an army when it comes to covering all the bases with sports and activities, with all their accompanying transportation logistics and time demands on the family schedule. One mom complained that trying to get everyone where they needed to be on time in her family was a task that would make a hardened air-traffic controller weep. Keeping it all straight can seem like an exercise in calendar optimization.

I was recently offered a consulting project. I asked my husband, who was encouraging me to take it on, if he was willing to come home from work to take the kids to all their activities. I ultimately turned the offer down, as keeping up with the logistics of three kids has become a full-time job in and of itself.

—Claire, mom of Ben, 14, Alison, 11, and Danny, 8

Because I work almost full-time, my daughter's activities are almost all packed in on Saturdays. One day a week she takes pottery that is offered right at her school, and after class, she just goes over to aftercare in the same building. Once a week my mom, who lives nearby, takes her to musical theater. Two afternoons a week I'm home early from work, and I love just puttering around the house with my kids without any activities to which I have to get them to, and sitting down together for family dinners.

—Alexa, mom of Adam, 11, and Sophie, 7

While our kids are very scheduled, I like to think of it as organized mayhem. Although it sounds like a lot, my wife has it down to a science. She drops one kid off, runs errands during karate, and then she's off to Rachel's dance class. I'm so impressed by how she coordinates it so there's no lost time.

—Andy, dad of Rachel, 10, Ben, 7, and Josh, 3

Using Your Family Calendar Strategically

🦋 Put a large master family calendar up on your refrigerator, as it's a central location where everyone will look. Find one with large squares that gives you plenty of space for notes.

🦋 Post events on the family calendar to remind everyone of upcoming games and practices. You can assign each family member a different-colored pencil for recording activities and commitments in order to tell at a glance who needs to be where and when.

🦋 Mark off sacrosanct family time in ink on your calendar.

🦋 Block out a week on your family calendar with a colored marker to show the hours of each day taken up with organized activities for a typical week. Highlight family dinners missed and invitations declined because of activity conflicts. Putting it all down on paper can be a shock to show the amount of the time your family loses without realizing it.

🦋 Mapping out a weekly seasonal schedule in advance can help your child get a concrete, visual sense of how much she intends to do.

I purchased a black thin notebook for each child and inserted dividers where we needed to keep paperwork, such as coaches' names, sign-up days, after-game snack list, etc. It has really helped find key information at critical times.

—*Chris, mom of Hayden, 8, and Emma, 4*

Near my family calendar area, I have a file folder for each of my children's school activities, sports activities, and church-related activities. This way I don't have all those papers pinned to my bulletin board and loose flyers around driving me crazy.

—*Karon, mom of Thomas, 11, Jeffrey, 9, and Bryce, 6*

Scheduling Strategies

✦ You can't talk about kids and activities without having to contend with transportation. No longer can you just open the back door and send your child outside to play. Instead, getting your child to games, activities, and practices often involves lots of driving around or elaborate carpool arrangements, or use of local children's transportation services.

✦ When it comes to carpooling, find others who have like-minded ideas about

For swimming, I book my two-year-old for a parent-tot swim and my five-year-old for a swimming lesson of his level at the same time. I have to register at a center further away, but the time it saves waiting with a child who is bored is worth it. For my son's soccer game, I have registered for the league that plays in a park with a play area for the two-year-old. I can watch my son play and keep my daughter entertained.

   —*Jana, mom of two, ages 5 and 2*

With two kids, I pick the same two days a week for all their activities. That way three days a week they have afternoons free for playdates.

   —*Susan, mom of Sydney, 8, and Michael, 7*

Last Saturday, my husband had done eleven different sporting things with our kids by the end of the day. One big break for us is our older kids are finally old enough to be left at home alone, so we can run five minutes away to pick someone up without having to drag everyone around with us. Having four kids, I rely a lot on neighborhood carpools.

   —*Bridgitt, mom of Taylor, 10, Connor and Chloe, 8, and Brian, 6*

With four children ranging in age from 10 years to 2 years, I have been saved by a sense of humor and lots of solicited help from my husband, family, and friends. Building a community of friends whom I can call on for things such as carpools has been critical.

   —*Deborah, mom of Aminadav, 10, Eliav, 8, Avidan, 5, and Temima, 2*

snacks in the car, promptness, and how to handle sick days or days when your child just doesn't want to go.

✦ Look for simultaneous classes at the same location if you have two or more children of different ages and abilities.

Activity Bags and Equipment

✦ To save time, prepack a bag for each sport or activity your child participates in regularly. Have these stocked by the door and ready to go. Prepack your child's game bag with tissues, sun block, lip balm, a sweatshirt, and nonperishable snacks. Toss a towel into your child's equipment bag to wipe off items that get wet during use.

✦ Designate a bag or make a spot on a shelf for items that your child wears to the game. Set a rule that certain items go into the wash immediately after each game. Help your child make a checklist of each item she needs, and give her a sturdy equipment bag to store it in. If the gear isn't in use, tell her it should be in the bag.

✦ Buy an extra mouth guard, and for your son an extra jockstrap, and keep them in the glove compartment of your car, especially for sports where your child cannot play without them.

To help keep things more organized, I have given each of our kids his own soccer bag. The first thing they do when they come home is to take stuff off, put it in their soccer bag, and replenish the water. We also keep a whole shelf of pop-up water bottles right by these bags so kids can take their soccer bag off the shelf, grab a water bottle, and go.

—*Elise, mom of Zeke, 16, Jeremy, 14, and Adam, 12*

Food, Drinks, and Snacks

✦ Make sure your child drinks plenty of fluids before, during, and after exercise. Store full water bottles in your refrigerator to take before practices and games.

✦ Keep containers of finger food in the refrigerator, such as sliced fruit, sliced-up cold cuts, or string cheese, so your child can grab a snack on the way to a game.

✦ Stock up on low-fat granola or protein bars, serving-size packages of applesauce and dried fruit, fresh fruit, juice and chocolate milk boxes, and carrot and celery sticks for snacks on the go.

🍂 Get a soft-sided insulated lunch box with a cold pack to keep drinks cool and provide emergency relief for any bumps.

There turned out to be an unexpected downside with one of my carpools. The mother would feed the kids pure junk food and fake juice in the car. The healthiest stuff she gave them appeared to be licorice. On the days she drove, I found my son was not eating dinner, so it ended up being a big problem that we had to discuss.

—*Bridgitt, mom of Taylor, 10, Connor and Chloe, 8, and Brian, 6*

ASSESSING AN AFTER-SCHOOL PROGRAM

🍂 When the bell rings to signal the end of the school day, working parents face the dilemma of what to do with their school-aged children until early evening when at least one parent gets home from work. For those parents who cannot afford or do not want a nanny, quality after-school programs provide a crucial alternative to the increasing number of latchkey children. Elementary school children are too young to responsibly care for themselves, and older children often lack the maturity to stay home.

🍂 An after-school program can offer a structured, safe, and supervised environment. Also, instead of having to patch together numerous activities, you can instead send your child to a single program offering a diverse array of activities, with both downtime and homework time built in.

🍂 The National Center for Education Statistics reports that more than 2.5 million children between kindergarten and eighth grade participate in after-school programs.

🍂 There tend to be two primary types of after-school programs:

    ◉ Many school districts run on-site after-school programs. One distinct advantage is that your child does not need transportation to get to the program, which is a logistical challenge for community-based programs.

- Well-established community organizations, like Boys and Girls Clubs, YMCAs, YWCAs, religious institutions, local colleges, and town recreational departments, also run programs.

✦ A program has to meet your child's needs and interests, be that quiet, arts-related activities or a social or sports free-for-all.

✦ Ask the following questions when assessing the quality of an after-school program:

- What activities and sports are offered? Look for physical activities that will serve as an outlet for your child's pent-up energy after having sat at a desk or table most of the day.

- What choices will my child have in terms of the schedule and participation?

- Does the program provide quiet time for getting homework done or tutoring help if your child needs it?

- Do the children spend any time watching movies or playing computer games?

- How much flexibility exists if I run late at work? Are there late fees?

- How are the children grouped, how large are the groups, and what is the staff/child ratio?

- Is the staff trained in first aid and CPR?

- How does the program handle discipline issues?

- What happens if my child gets sick while there?

- Are snacks provided?

- Can my child attend only a few times a week instead of every day?

- Does the program run on any days that are school holidays?

- Do the children go on field trips and if so, where? Are any extra fees involved for these?

✦ Talk to the directors of prospective programs and make a visit while kids are there.

✦ Pay particular attention to the interactions between the children and caregivers, and whether the children seem to be having fun. You should hear lots of laughter and lively conversations.

✦ Make sure that the environment is clean, cheerful, bright, and well equipped.

✦ Ask if the program is licensed or accredited, either by a state agency or the National School-Age Care Alliance (NSACA). With a mission to ensure higher quality programming in after-school care, NSACA evaluates programs based on a set of standards that include programming, staffing, and supervision, as well as health and safety issues. Ask if the program you are considering has been accredited.

The Need for Downtime

THE VALUE OF DOING NOTHING

❧ Wanting to provide your child with the most opportunities to further her growth and development does not have to mean intensive daily exposure to as much as possible. Being on the run all the time isn't great for anyone, especially a child, so it's important to remember to choose carefully and slow down a bit.

❧ Many parents become concerned about the dreaded possibilities of boredom, lack of motivation, or laziness if a child is not challenged round the clock and in a constant state of motion or in an engaged, structured activity. This attitude leads to intense schedules and rushing around with no time to just kick back and relax.

❧ It used to be that the work of childhood was play, exploration, and experimentation, not in the context of structured classes or lessons with adults, but in free time roaming outside when not in school. Those were the days of skipping, hopscotch, jungle gyms, tag, and "let's pretend."

❧ While your child might have a number of opportunities to pursue after-school activities, she also needs time to relax at home. School takes a lot of energy, and your child needs some downtime to play with friends and siblings and to partici-

Kids need personal time factored into the daily routine—time that's not structured and when they have no commitments to other people. Between school, homework, and sports, kids need time to daydream, fantasize, just drift a little bit, and do all the things we have no time for as adults. Some of the most precious moments of childhood come from downtime. Our kids' day starts at 7 a.m., and when you factor in school, homework, practice or a game, dinner, reading, and bedtime, it's a full 13-hour day. That's a long time to be constantly mentally and physically challenged. We don't expect a lot of adults to maintain that kind of schedule.

—*Dean, dad of Evan, 10, and Olivia, Justin, and Shelby, 8*

I schedule activities so that my kids all have Monday, Thursday, and Friday free to relax at home and have friends over to play. I'm amazed at the schedules of my best friends' kids, who do something every day. For me, it's really important that my kids have downtime.

—*Susan, mom of Sydney, 8, and Michael, 7*

When it comes to sports and activities, less is more. Kids have about ten years to try different things and it does not need to be ten in one year. Okay, maybe I'm preaching, but I see so many worn-out kids in school, grocery stores, and around town. My kids have had to remind me too, "Mom, we just need a stay-at-home day today to play!"

—*Suzanne*

pate in family activities. She may be interested in music, dance, gymnastics, or another sport, but she doesn't need to do all of them at the same time.

✦ When kids have downtime every day, they learn to thrive on spontaneity and creativity.

MAKING TIME FOR UNSTRUCTURED PLAY

❦ Advocate a little boredom for your child. When we were growing up and complained about being bored, our moms promptly showed us the back door and told us, "Go outside and find something to do!" And remarkably, we did. We found neighborhood buddies to climb trees with, chase around the block, and start a pickup game. We examined bugs in the yard, made angels in the snow, and built secret forts. We curled up with a paperback book on the porch or in a comfy chair somewhere at home. We used our imaginations and came up with hours of entertainment that didn't involve our parents or any electronic device.

❦ Downtime is not wasted time. Our culture sends parents a message that unstructured leisure hours waste valuable time. Play appears frivolous, taking away from the future success of your child, in a society that places a premium not only on being "successful," but also on being a star.

❦ Free time provides your child with the opportunities to be self-motivated and follow whatever captures her interest in the moment. Play is not a matter of doing something for positive adult feedback or measurable achievement, but done for the sheer joy of being immersed in a fun activity and exploring things on her own.

In free play, kids develop creativity so much more than in structured activities. You would not believe the creative worlds my son comes up with, whether with Robotics, Legos, or boxes and tape. Free time has also indirectly taught my boys time-management skills, such as only having a half-hour before supper to finish up their game, which has carried over to being able to pace and manage their homework themselves. They don't look for constant outside direction from a parent. It takes *days* for my kids to get bored. It makes me sad to think about those poor kids who have no downtime, but instead a frenetic overlay on their days. They will have so many years as adults of working hard. Letting your children be carefree and having time to play is a real gift you can give them.

—*Elizabeth, mom of Robert, 15, and David, 10*

Kids need more downtime at home where they can relax. So do I! My life is very structured with work, and my idea of a fun time is decorating cookies with my kids at home. I love being playful with my children during downtime, whether this be going for a long bike ride, rollerblading, or hiking. Plus, there are some things like building a great snow fort that no class can ever teach. One afternoon when my oldest had nothing to do, she curled up on the floor with markers and pens and created her own comic book. When both girls are together, they'll make up plays, draw, play outside, read, or even knit. It's amazing how they find stuff to do. My youngest needs enormous amounts of downtime, during which she immerses herself in a dreamy, imaginary world, where she gets dressed up and talks to herself. She really needs that time; it's very important to her.

—*Amy, mom of Sacha, 11, and Libby, 8*

Parents who sign their kids up for many activities are doing a real disservice to their children. It's too much pressure. Kids need time to stare off into space, to know how to dream, and use their imaginations. And if you're carving up time for all these activities, your children don't have that as a resource. Kids get used to constant activity and start taking a sound-bite approach to life. They want to be fed, entertained, and the household loses its rhythm. It's important to me that we sit down for dinner together every night.

—*Dee, mom of Carey, 8, and Danny, 6*

Dealing with Declarations of Boredom

✦ You need to ease your child into finding creative ways to entertain herself when you hear the dreaded words "I'm bored," and to stop depending on you as a constant source of entertainment.

✦ As she learns to entertain herself, your child will inevitably struggle and feel frustrated, complaining of having nothing to do. Try to be supportive without being directive, and resist the temptation to jump into the fray with an organized activity of your own, or a quick solution that involves your participation. Tolerating the complaints without intervening enables your child to come up with her own forms of entertainment.

✦ You'll be amazed at how quickly your child learns to alleviate her boredom and create unexpected ways to solve problems. She will learn to entertain herself without the structure of organized activities or the pressure of competition or performance. Give her opportunities to play with other kids without adult intervention or

Downtime encourages kids to use their imagination. When one of my kids tells me, "I'm bored," I think how much I would love to be bored and curl up on the sofa and read my book for an hour! Kids expect entertainment from an early age, and I find that you have to teach them how to amuse themselves. Quiet play is essential because it allows kids to work out some of the stresses they encounter on a daily basis, even if they're not aware of it. When my kids come home from school, they explode through the door. They need chill time after a packed day at school. This could mean drawing, playing with blocks, reading, or playing with siblings. It helps diffuse all the stimulation they get. I've even started limiting playdates. With three or four a week, it was getting too much for me, and I realized it was too much for them. Now the rule is that they can have a friend over one day a week at our house, and they can go to someone else's house on a different day.

—Karen, mom of Max, 9, Sophie, 7, Celia, 5, and Jake, 2

Rachel was home only 15 minutes for Christmas vacation when she started complaining she was bored. I pointed out to her that for the holidays she just got thirty toys that she could play with, and she looked at me like I was crazy. And I realized it's because I've made my kids that way. I'm an enabler. Instead of saying, "I'm doing something or I'm cleaning up, go find something to do on your own" I'll say, "all right, honey, give me five minutes and let's do something together," "Let's go somewhere," or "Let's get on the phone and arrange a playdate." I can't do that now with a toddler at home; he's sleeping, or it's six at night and I'm not going to bundle him up to go. So I've had to slowly teach my children how to entertain themselves.

—Ellen, mom of Rachel, 10, Ben, 7, and Josh, 3

When time starts feeling overscheduled, my kids will frequently say, "I really want to stay home." I've learned at those times to go with my gut about what they need. My daughter is a preteen who realizes she's growing up fast. She recently said to me, "Mom, I just want to play." She chose to cut back and not do any karate right now whereas before, she was doing it three times a week.

—Joy, mom of Chris, 15, and Victoria, 11

organization. Plus, a little solitary downtime can go a long way in helping her recharge her battery.

✦ Part of the purpose of downtime is to get your child to exercise her imagination, whether it's investigating the backyard or inventing a new game with friends.

✦ These hours of unstructured play form a critical backbone in your child's development, as they allow her to explore, discover, use her imagination, and problem-solve on her own.

✦ Consider the time you spend easing your child into learning to self-entertain as an investment in her autonomy that will carry her through the rest of her life. Your initial investment of time will help your child develop independence and rely on herself for amusement sometimes.

How to Approach Downtime During Summer Months

✦ That long stretch of unscheduled time we call summer "vacation" often poses quite a dilemma, especially when deciding how to fill in free time for elementary-age children.

✦ Just considering the plethora of summer options can make your head swim. There's the intensive sports camp, the all-around day camp, the sleep-away camp, or music camp—many of which you have to start looking into in September.

✦ If you choose to give your child some big chunks of unscheduled time in the summer, you will likely feel as if you're swimming against a strong riptide. Hanging out doesn't lend itself to measurable skill development or a success check-off. Moreover, many sports are quickly evolving to year-round affairs, with training sessions, practices, and games running continually through summer and vacations alike.

Every day, several people ask me what I'm doing about summer camp for my boys. People are fanatical about camp. I think they're scared to spend a summer of unstructured time with their kids. If your child doesn't go to summer camp, there's no one home to play with. I finally signed my son up because I was scared about his being sad and bored hanging out all by himself during the day.

—*Sarah, mom of Taylor, 8, and Cameron, 6*

My summer rule is to have only two planned weeks per month. For instance, in July we took our annual family vacation and my son had his art camp. That's it. The rest of the time is for smaller projects, unstructured days, spontaneous trips, and play dates.

—*Tammy, mom of Nathaniel, 6, and Madeline, 3*

At the end of the school year the question is always, "So, what camp(s) are your kids doing this summer?" My answer has been "Mommy Camp" and downtime in our own backyard.

—*Dana, mom of three children, ages 9, 7, and 5*

🐟 Yet summer need not and should not be totally consumed by highly structured programs. It is perfectly okay for your child to have time to just goof off. If you can work out the logistics in terms of childcare if you work, allow your child a couple of weeks each summer with nothing scheduled.

NOT ENOUGH DOWNTIME: WARNING SIGNS OF STRESS AND BURNOUT

🐟 Activities can suddenly pile up until your child feels smothered under their collective weight. All the things that your child wanted to do can very quickly become "have-to-dos."

🐟 Just like when your computer gets overloaded and a message flashes across your screen, "Disk full," warning signs of stress let you know when your child has overloaded.

🐟 Your child will usually let you know either verbally or by acting out if she's had enough. Be vigilant about noticing behavioral changes that indicate something may not be right in her life.

🐟 Symptoms such as irritability, restlessness, and combativeness to feelings of dejection, apathy, fatigue, or inability to concentrate or sleep often emanate from

I overheard my daughter telling one of her friends, who had exclaimed that she couldn't wait for the weekend to come, that her weekend is more stressful than her weekdays because of all the games and practices involved with her sports. It definitely does take a toll in terms of downtime, and if she didn't enjoy it as much as she does, I would look to cut back.

—*Cathy, mom of Samantha, 13, and Kimberly, 10*

I usually take my cue from the children whether they want to continue a sport or not. I can tell if they are excited to go to an activity or if it is a hassle to get them out the door. If their interest naturally declines, then I don't sign them up again.

—*Lisa, mom of Grace, 6, Ben, 4, and Maddie, 1*

We want to give our children so much that we bombard them with activities to either compensate for lack of quality time, to expand their horizons, or keep them occupied. We wonder what happened to the age of innocence. As we push our children to be "super" children, we kill their ability to be children. I see some children stressed out from too many activities and the demands on their time and performance. Children need balance too.

—*Karen, mom of Kyle, 1*

Last year, my girls were totally "activitied-up" taking piano, karate, soccer, a choral group, and Girl Scouts. They burned out and we had to cut back, which created time for playdates and more socializing. Unfortunately, the end result was that they got immersed in petty girl politics, which left them each at different times feeling miserable and left out. So this year we're going back to organized activities. We've sat down and gone over the list of things they want to do, so that we're clearer about how much they'll take on.

—*Sylvia, mom of Max, 13, and Kate and Zoe, 10*

I have learned to take cues from my kids. Two years ago, when my son, David, was in second grade, he tearfully told me that he had no time just to play with his friends. Quitting religious school was not an option, so we let David decide which of his other two afternoon activities to quit. We were all much happier once that decision was made.

—*Rebecca, mom of David, 10, and Talia, 6*

overscheduling and relentlessly intense weekly schedules, pressure to excel, or a combination of both.

✦ If your child dreads going to an activity or practice, this should raise an immediate red flag. Other signs of stress include: uncharacteristic tantrums, headaches and stomachaches, loss of appetite, stress or depression, being lethargic or unmotivated, falling behind in schoolwork, being exhausted or withdrawn all the time, refusing to go to practice, intense anxiety before competitions or performances, irritability, misbehavior, moodiness, and aggressiveness.

✦ Talk with your child about how she's doing. Does she wish she had more time hanging out around the house? More spontaneous play dates like bringing a friend home from school? Time to be alone? Sleeping in? Playing with kids next door? Curling up with a book and reading during the day for pleasure? Also, ask open-ended questions to allow her to vent.

✦ Make sure your child is getting enough sleep. From elementary school through high school, your child needs 9–11 hours of sleep every night, and most kids do not get this.

✦ When you sense that your child is overwhelmed, step in to make some concrete schedule changes and implement them right away. Give your child the freedom to scale back. While you don't want her to develop a pattern of dropping out of an activity as soon as she tires of it, when the activity turns stressful, it can be detrimental to your child's physical well-being. If it's not just a quickly passing phase, encourage your child to redirect her energies elsewhere and take a break.

✦ Seek professional help for your child if she shows severe signs of stress.

LIMITING TV AND ELECTRONICS: PASSIVITY CENTRAL

✦ Our children live in the age of the digital playground, with electronic devices luring them into hours of solitary, sedentary entertainment. Kids often bury themselves in electronic games for solitude and freedom from adult micromanaging.

✦ Never has the comforting, passive distraction of the computer, television, or electronic entertainment been so readily available for our children. The average American household now has three televisions, two VCRs, three radios, two tape players, two CD players, a video game player, and a computer!

✦ With all this technology in our homes, children have the entertainment they need without venturing outside to play. Even playdates become consumed by the latest video game, handheld electronics adventure, or TV shows.

✦ Left to her own devices, your child may opt to amuse herself electronically for hours on end. She may simply shut out the outside world in favor of such entertaining escapes as television or Game Boy. Children now watch an average of three to five hours of television each day, which ends up totaling billions of hours each year that all our children spend sacked out on the couch.

✦ The time your child spends plugged-in is time she does not spend exercising her body, expanding her mind, or exploring her environment. Moreover, time glued to the television makes your child the passive absorber of often violent and commercial television programming. Excessive television has recently been linked to long-term behavioral problems in children, such as violent behavior, obesity, shorter attention spans, decreased sociality, poor performance in school, sexual precociousness, and drug use. Quite the litany, and enough to strike fear in any parent's heart.

Establishing Family Rules

✦ Set limits on TV, computer, and electronic games to get your child to engage in more active, rather than passive, play. While in limited doses, television enables your child to both relax and keep up with cultural references by peers, even educational television and games limit your child's imagination. When the TV goes off, your child can rediscover imaginary play with Legos, blocks, toys, and board games.

✦ Pick one week to mark down exactly how much TV your child watches. You will likely find yourself amazed at how quickly it adds up when you factor in morning shows or cartoons, movies, videos, and a week's worth of time on the couch.

One day, I got completely frustrated with the time my oldest son was spending in front of the TV. So I declared it arts and crafts day and we cut out and colored TV tickets worth 30 minutes apiece. I gathered them all up and put them in a "TV ticket envelope." I gave him three tickets every morning. And when he was out of tickets, he was out of TV time. It worked so well that my son intrinsically knows when his time is up. Now I see him engaging in more imaginative play and finding much more creative things to do with his time.

    —Phyllis, mom of Nicholas, 5, Ian, 3, and Reagan, 1

When the TV's on, my kids wouldn't hear me even if I spoke with a bullhorn. Plus, in the mornings I couldn't get the boys dressed or get them to breakfast, as they were watching cartoons. My solution that's worked wonders: I just eliminated TV altogether from Monday to Friday.

    —Dee, mom of Carey, 8, and Danny, 6

We always discouraged TV, and it eventually got to a point where we set a limit on the hours per day it was on. It was hard because I am not a TV watcher but my husband is, so he would tell them one thing and I would tell them another. But, thanks to limited TV, my daughter is now very motivated, resourceful, and reads a lot of books.

    —Shawn, mom of Taylor, 17, and Mikaela, 15

We started a policy in our family beginning in elementary school that there's no TV from Sunday night to Friday, except for occasional news, an educational show or sports event. Then, during the summer, anything goes. Lately, my kids have been consumed by instant messaging, and will walk into our house and go straight to the computer. We have been somewhat successful in limiting them on the computer to an assigned thirty minutes a day.

    —Elise, mom of Zeke, 16, Jeremy, 14, and Adam, 12

I teach my kids how to limit TV, but if you turn it into a forbidden object, it becomes more desired.

    —Cynthia, mom of Zachary, 10, Stephanie, 8, and Nicholas, 3

It's so easy for kids to turn on the TV and veg out. To cut down on the amount of TV my son watched when he was younger, we got an entertainment unit where the doors that close around the TV can be locked. That way when the allotted time for TV is up, it's over without hassling.

—*Sibylle, mom of Lane, 16*

✤ Monitor the shows your child watches regularly. Catch the show once to make sure that the content and messages are what you consider to be age- and values-appropriate. Talk with your child about the show afterward, and ask questions to get a more in-depth understanding of her thinking about what you saw together.

✤ Discuss the reasons why there are commercials on TV and how advertising tries to get you to buy toys and other things. Teach your child how to be both critical and skeptical of the advertising messages, and to distinguish commercials from other types of television programming. Point out what exaggerations the advertisers use. Even toddlers can begin to acquire a skeptical, savvy approach to commercial messaging by manufacturers.

✤ Be clear about what stations your child is allowed to watch and what stations are forbidden.

✤ Rather than having your child channel-surf in search of an appealing show, map out in advance what programs she wants to watch. Agree to turn the TV off when the agreed-upon show ends.

✤ For one hour a day, your child chooses when and what she wants to watch.

✤ No TV before completing household tasks.

✤ Allot your child a particular number of TV-viewing hours per week, and let her choose how she uses them with your supervision. Unused hours could be cashed in for a small treat.

✤ Use a kitchen timer to set a time limit on your child's computer or electronic game time. When the buzzer goes off, time's up. Make sure your child understands that the computer or game must be turned off and that it can be saved for another day.

✤ Do not put a television set in your child's room.

✤ Do not allow any TV in the morning if you find yourself scrambling to get your child off in time to day care, activities, or school.

✤ Offer trade-offs: For every hour of TV time, your child has to spend an hour running around in the backyard or doing some other form of physical activity.

✦ Limit TV time for your entire family and model the habits you want your child to adopt. Set a good example yourself with your own viewing habits and by not leaving the TV on as background noise.

✦ Keep TV time as healthy as possible. Make up physical games to play during the commercials, like a jumping jack contest, and do not put out too many snacks for your child to munch on while she watches TV.

✦ Pick one day a week or one week a year when nobody in the family can watch the TV. National TV Turn-off Week is scheduled for every April. Make this a celebratory time, with family game nights and outings. Your child might just learn how easy it is to live without it.

✦ Pretend for one night that you're living in the 1800s and have no electricity.

Computer and Electronic Games

✦ It's hard to talk about downtime for your child these days without addressing the issue of video games or computers as their downtime of choice.

✦ To limit video games, make the rule that your child can only play after dark for a set amount of time, which curtails when she can play and stops her from asking during the day.

✦ Once your child reaches the age that she can surf the Internet by herself, invest in software or choose an Internet service provider that allows you to limit her access to inappropriate sites.

✦ Have two chairs side by side at your computer so you can surf with your child.

✦ Keep your family computer in a public place so you can better supervise its use and monitor how much time your child spends on it.

We don't have a PlayStation and it's becoming a real problem with our six-year-old. Ben will go on playdates to other people's houses to play it. I can't limit it there, as it just depends on who's watching them. We never say no to the computer we have at home, as we feel 99% of the programs our kids play have educational value, whereas PlayStation doesn't. But our computer only allows one kid to play at a time (though they do learn to take turns).

—*Andy, dad of Rachel, 10, Ben, 7, and Josh, 3*

I would rather have my son spend three hours of creative play with a discarded appliance box than playing educational computer games. We need to keep in mind that simpler is often better. I am not slamming educational computer games—they can entertain and educate children in many positive ways, but moderation is needed.

—*Karen, mom of Kyle, 1*

CARVING OUT TIME TOGETHER AS A FAMILY

🔱 To make a statement about how over the top things have become, the town of Ridgewood, New Jersey, organized one collective night off, and it took nine months of planning, an 18-member committee, meetings, discussions, and negotiations with school, athletic, and religious leaders just to pull it off. The fields stood empty with lights turned off, no practices or games were held, lessons were canceled, teachers assigned no homework, and families just spent the night together. Families wanted to make the point about how rushed and fragmented their lives had become with the nonstop whirlwind of activities culminating in strenuous homework, a brief kiss, lights out, and another day waiting in which to run themselves ragged. So they took a night off to have a leisurely family dinner, to play games, relax, and hang out. And this was considered radical enough to get coverage in almost every major media outlet.

🔱 The small town of Wayzata, Minnesota, also garnered national media attention when they organized Family Life 1st (www.familylife1st.org), a grassroots group solely focused on reclaiming family time. They do so by urging parents to think carefully before signing children up for new activities and not to sign them up for one activity after another. They also work to get coaches and other activity leaders to recognize the importance of family togetherness by not scheduling practices for the family dinner hour or penalizing kids for missing games for family-related events, holidays, or religious commitments. Lastly, they created a seal of approval so parents would be able to know beforehand if a particular organization respects the needs of families in its scheduling policies.

🔱 Once your child hits elementary school, your typical family weekend can easily devolve into an endless array of sporting events, practices, sleepovers, and play-dates. When you have more than one child who becomes heavily involved in sports, you may find yourself spending more hours in your car and on sports fields than you imagined possible. Evenings quickly become consumed by lessons, practices, and games.

🔱 Suddenly your schedule needs to accommodate these activities, which spill over into evenings and weekends, taking away from what used to be sacrosanct family time. Family dinners, weekend outings, and just hanging out together often go by the wayside. Even school holidays, such as Thanksgiving, winter break, and spring vacation can often become long treks to tournaments rather than time spent relaxing together as a family.

🔱 When your family has too much going on, it leaves everyone cranky and on edge. If your family life becomes so fragmented that you barely have time together, it's time to call a family meeting and to make some hard choices about what needs to change. Sit down to talk about how you're doing as a family and how your child's time is structured. How many hours each week do you want to preserve for family time, as opposed to how many you actually spend together now? Use this as an opportunity to make a carefully thought-out decision about whether you have enough downtime to hang together as a family or if you feel out of balance.

🐟 Establish family traditions that take precedence over outside activities, no matter how busy each family member becomes. Make spending time with each other a

My whole life has become "Where do we have to be?" Sometimes it does seem like too much and gets tiring, especially when I feel that I've simply become the girls' taxi driver. If only I could set my car to autopilot!

    —*Cathy, mom of Samantha, 13, and Kimberly, 10*

We were so relieved to have the fall soccer season end. For a while it was fun to see everyone at the games, but it was even nicer to have a free chunk of time every Saturday afternoon.

    —*Ken, dad of Carey, 8, and Danny, 6*

By having my boys participate in sports clinics rather than league play, we have our weekends free for family time instead having the pressures of so many practices and games.

    —*Lisa, mom of Connor, 10, Garrison, 6, and Mitchell, 1*

I have three children and have watched my friends and acquaintances wear themselves down over getting their kids to various sports or other activities. I decided very early on that I was not going to be spending my whole life in the car, and went on a quest to find alternatives to the "taxi mom" syndrome. We finally found a weekly activity club at our church to which all of us could go that has been great.

    —*Kristen, mom of three*

priority and strengthening family bonds a concentrated focus. It's often on week-end mornings spent lounging around the house in pajamas that everyone in your family gets to unwind and talk to each other.

🐾 Set aside and embrace downtime for yourself and your family, including time to connect and go on adventures. Downtime should be fun, and does not necessarily have to enhance your child's development or put pressure on either of you.

The Erosion of the Family Dinner

🐾 Dinner offers your family the chance to regroup. The family dinner hour often devolves into the family half-hour and finally into the fast-food circuit, where you do drive-through and eat on the go between your child's flute lesson and basketball practice. Amid all the scurrying about, it's easy to forget how gathering around a table to eat and talk centers your family.

🐾 According to research by the University of Minnesota, in the past 20 years, there has been a 33% decline in the number of families who eat dinner together regularly. It's gone so far that we even have an American National Eat Dinner Together Week, from October 1 to 7, to remind us to gather around the dinner table!

🐾 To make family dinners a priority, resolve to eat dinner together at least four times a week even if it's just takeout pizza. It doesn't have to be gourmet, it just has to be relaxed and not rushed. Keep it simple on chaotic evenings.

Frequently I have days when I leave the house when the kids get home from school and don't return until past dinnertime. You get home, and it's stressful. Dinner has become catch as catch can. I go get half-done prepared foods and salad bar items from the grocery store, and lots of takeout food.

—Leslie, mom of Alexandra, 10, and Jack, 9

🐾 Have your child grab a snack to tide her over on tough nights when you can't sit down to eat dinner until everyone finishes activities or comes home from work. Even if one parent can't make it home from work in time, it is still valuable to have a family dinner.

🐾 The dinner hour should be a time for talking, catching up, and sharing tidbits from your day, laughing together, and building intimacy as a family—things you can't do from the sidelines of a game, or rushing about in the car.

🐾 Keep the conversation light and upbeat, as the whole point is to enjoy each other, and not to use mealtime to air major grievances or discuss serious issues.

> My general and flexible guidelines to preserve family time and downtime that have worked well are: No activities between 5:30 and 7 p.m. for family dinner. Keep weekends as clear as possible. Have a half-hour every day after school free, with at least one afternoon free. Lastly, as the whole family supports the person involved in the activity, it must work for all of us.
>
> —*Lisa, mom of Connor, 10, Garrison, 6, and Mitchell, 1*
>
> I always feel the pressure to add more activities, but I set strong boundaries. Where we live there's so much stuff to choose from, and kids do so much. I'll look through activity offerings and everything sounds good. But then I realize that tap dancing at 5 p.m. on Thursdays is going to ruin our family dinnertime and make everyone cranky that night.
>
> —*Melissa, mom of Alia, 8, and Asher, 5*

✦ Turn off the TV and the radio. Let an answering machine pick up any phone calls.

✦ Even your baby or toddler should be invited. Even though they don't participate in the actual conversation, they listen, watch, and feel a part of things.

Set Aside Family Time

✦ It doesn't matter what your family does, but that you do it together. If nights are tough for you, pick a morning or afternoon once a week. The key is setting the time aside once a week, every week. Have family pizza nights playing board games, laughing, and hanging out together.

✦ Decide on something that everyone considers fun and can do together. Go out to a movie, play miniature golf, go to a museum, walk on the beach, play Laser Tag, or splurge on ice-cream sundaes.

> This past weekend was the most luxurious family time we've had in a while. My husband and I didn't go out either night. We watched a football game together. We played games. We watched a movie with the kids. I've found that it's so important to schedule in that kind of downtime.
>
> —*Bridgitt, mom of Taylor, 10, Connor and Chloe, 8, and Brian, 6*

✦ Some families decide that Saturday lunch or Sunday breakfast works best as a

We have tried to keep activities away from the weekends, which has meant ruling some things out, such as art, swimming, or dance, and allowing each of our girls to do only one sport that they like during the fall and spring sessions.

—Amy, mom of Sacha, 11, and Libby, 8

standing family meal and time you can always count on to sit down together. But realize that a single Sunday brunch won't counterbalance a week of no shared meals.

Take Up Sports and Hobbies as a Family

🍀 Join a community center or gym where the whole family can swim, exercise, or take different classes, whether it's a local recreation center, the YMCA, or a Jewish community center, where options are abundant.

🍀 Try to make exercising together a regular part of your family life. Come up with physical activities your family loves to do together, be that hiking, skiing, bike riding, rollerblading, canoeing, kayaking, rock climbing, swimming, skating, playing golf or tennis, ice skating, or even walking the hallways of a nearby science, children's, or art museum.

🍀 Involve your child in making plans, and ask if she has any creative suggestions.

🍀 Little changes work as well: Take the stairs instead of elevators, shovel snow or rake leaves outdoors, or walk instead of circling around for the closest parking spot.

I've been thinking lately that it would be great to have a family sport, so that we can play tennis or golf with our kids, or go skiing or hiking together. Especially with kids specializing in different sports, you don't want all your family time to be just about shuffling them around.

—Deborah, mom of Philip, 10, Patrick 8, and William, 3

Instead of sitting on the couch, watching TV, and eating, it's important to have a family sport or hobby. For many, this could be skiing, biking, golf, hiking, or sailing. It's really cool to have something about which your whole family's passionate. I have seen this be the glue for many families as their children get older and for when they leave home.

—Karla, mom of Karl, 9, Max 6, and Leo, 3

We rely on tennis and biking as our family sports—it's so nice when you can go out with the kids.

—*Jane, mom of Carolyn, 17, and Peter, 11*

In the winter, we go skiing on weekends as a family, which means our kids can't sign up for any sports that involve weekend games. On our ski weekends, we spend lots of time together on the slopes, have big family dinners, and soak in the hot tub after a long day. We let our kids go hard core on sports in the fall and spring, and are willing to run them around to many activities because we have our winters to relax and counterbalance this.

—*Sheri, mom of Allison, 11, and Eric, 9*

🦋 Take a weekly lesson with your child, such as karate or yoga class.

🦋 Once a week have a family sports night or weekend outing.

🦋 Many programs involve children and adults. If you have a pet, take a dog training class together. If your child plays soccer, coach her team. If she is interested in painting or learning an instrument, take lessons together.

Missing Games or Practices for Family Travel or Social Events

🦋 Stories abound from parents about coaches benching kids because they missed practice for a family wedding, or missed scheduled tournaments over school vacation or holiday weekends like Thanksgiving or Easter.

🦋 If your child misses a practice or a game for a doctor's appointment, family event, or religious reason, you may easily find yourself or your child worrying that it will affect her standing on her team. You may also be concerned, with good reason, that the coach will think your child lacks commitment or her teammates will think she is letting them down.

🦋 Tolerance for missed practices and games diminishes as children get older. While an occasional unexpected conflict will be unavoidable, discuss in advance any foreseeable conflicts with your child's coach and what repercussions your child should anticipate (such as not being allowed to play in a game after a missed practice).

We have a rule on our team regarding missed practices: Faith, family, and school are all acceptable reasons for absence.

—*Robert Wade, head softball coach for 5 years*

Parents should never lie to coaches or make excuses for their children about missing practices or games. First of all, the coach generally finds out through the grapevine where the kid really went and then loses trust for the family. More important, when parents make or allow excuses, it sends a message to the child that excuses and dishonesty are acceptable ways to resolve conflict.

—*Rich Janor, Wheatland Travel Baseball Club coach for 5 years*

We have all had to deal with this at one time or another. My rule is the coach should let the parents and players know what is expected of them at the very beginning of the season and not as the season progresses. Parents need to let the coach and their daughter know what trips or special events have been previously planned. That way, surprises are kept to a minimum. Parents and athletes need to fully realize that when they sign up for a team sport, regardless of which league, they are making a commitment to be there. Team sports require 100% participation by all. If the parent or athlete cannot agree with that, they should look at an individual sport that may afford them more flexibility.

—*Gale Bundrick, softball coach, Canyon Del Oro High School, teaching for 25 years*

Sometimes it is unavoidable, but leisure commitments are extremely disruptive to the team, sending a message that it is okay to skip practice and games and that the team is not that important. Especially in a small high school, there are enough conflicts with academics and other extracurricular events to drive a coach nuts. Parents need to make arrangements and realize that just because the school calendar has a vacation, it doesn't mean that the sports teams have a vacation. Year in and year out I fight this out at spring break. This is the best time of the season to get the most work done and it is the most disrupted by personal types of activities.

—*Randy Watt, youth softball coach for 14 years*

Family comes first. However, social events are another story. If a student misses because of a choice rather than an obligation, he is not encouraged to participate in any special events or competitions.

> —Rick Foley, Elmwood Center director and chief instructor in tae kwon do and hapkido, teaching for 26 years

No Time for Religion

✦ Giving your child a spiritual and religious background becomes another piece that you have to fit into the activity puzzle.

✦ Moreover, a growing number of clergy bemoan the fact that they're losing children from services and religious school to weekend sports games that now take place on both Saturday and Sunday. Despite pleas and protests from religious leaders, many youth leagues say they have no choice, due to limited playing fields.

Preventing Family Burnout

✦ If you or your family is stretched to the max to accommodate your child's schedule, then you need to cut back on or say no to activities. The quality of family life and pace you set for your children are a core part of their well-being.

✦ Your child's activities often take vast amounts of time and commitment on your part from the driving, the waiting, the cheering at games, the shopping for sports equipment, to the sign-ups and the scheduling. When children get involved with youth sports, it often reaches the point where you can't even go away for the weekend as a family without having to cancel four events.

✦ As activities pile up, you may discover that the process of shuttling your child from one activity to

We are a religious family, and quickly found that many of the athletic events our children wanted to pursue, such as soccer, conflicted with time we would otherwise be in synagogue services. After many years of dealing with the misery and growing hostility of our kids, who resented not being able to play on sports teams or be with their friends, we finally realized that we had to evolve our ideology and become more flexible. We decided that Friday nights would be time spent at services together just as a family, with no exceptions, but we gave up going to weekend services. It's actually been a huge issue and concern for many different religious leaders in our town, as no one goes to services anymore.

> —Naomi, mom of Talia, 11, Arielle, 10, Aaron, 8, and Daniella, 5

the next is not only a hassle, but dragging you and the rest of your family down, leaving everyone irritable (not to mention tired of being in the car all the time). Many moms feel that instead of being stay-at-home moms, they're actually "stay in the car" moms.

🌿 It is not healthy to focus your family life around your child's sports and activities schedule, or to give up vacations, family meals, weekend downtime, and holidays. Plus, by having all your plans center on accommodating your child's activities, she takes away the impression that the world centers on her, while you might end up finding yourself resentful of her self-centeredness.

🌿 It's your ongoing challenge to keep your child, yourself, and your family centered and in balance. Set limits that fit your family's needs.

We drive ourselves insane taking our son to all his practices and games. If my husband were not such a sports fanatic, willing to drive him everywhere, it just wouldn't happen. Our son has two hours of practice every day of the week in the fall: 6 p.m.–8 p.m. for football, and 3 p.m.–5 p.m. two times a week for soccer. Then games take over the weekends. It's been a strain on me with all the driving and waiting around—thank goodness for cell phones and the fact that I love to read.

    —Leslie, mom of Alexandra, 10, and Jack, 9

When all my boys' activities start up, Saturdays get very busy with swimming lessons, soccer games, baseball, and a learn-to-skate program. Sundays are religious school in the mornings. We've deliberately avoided lessons or sports that involve Sunday afternoon, keeping it free as our one time during the week to do something around the house together or go on a family outing. For us as working parents, two weekend days full of stuff becomes too much like the week.

    —Deborah, mom of Philip, 10, Patrick, 8, and William 3

I usually only let my kids pick one activity each, but this summer I didn't do that. Eric had sports camp during the day and karate at night. Tina had dance at night and they both had swimming lessons three times a week. We had really overscheduled and were always in the car. The kids didn't mind, but I vowed, "Never again will I do this!"

    —Stephanie, mom of Eric, 5, and Tina, 3

BALANCING ACTIVITIES WITH TIME FOR HOMEWORK

✻ Schools give homework more than ever before and children 6 to 8 years old have three times as much homework as they did in 1980.

✻ In organized sports, a large number of volunteer coaches are working parents who hold weekday practices late in the afternoon or early evening hours. Suddenly homework has to get done right after school when your child wants to shut down her brain after seven long hours in class. Otherwise, homework takes place after an evening practice when your child is starting to become cranky, easily discouraged, and frustrated when trying to memorize spelling words, write sentences, or solve math problems.

✻ For your elementary school child, make sure you leave enough time for homework. The minute homework starts feeling rushed, your child's frustration level will likely go through the roof. You do not want the time demands placed on your child by extracurricular activities to cause her academic performance to suffer.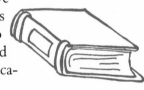

 ✻ Any activity that routinely keeps your child up late at night doing homework needs to be restructured. Your child will be hard-pressed to explain uncompleted homework when the cause is a baseball game or soccer tournament.

✻ Given how early in elementary school kids find themselves piled up with homework and reading time each night, it often has to be factored in as a significant component of your child's weekdays.

✻ If you hear from your child's teacher that she is sluggish, tired, or unfocused in school, she may be doing too much in terms of after-school activities and not getting enough downtime or sleep.

⊙∼⊙∼⊙∼⊙∼⊙∼⊙∼⊙

My 16-year-old son got involved in too many things and his grades started to reflect this. We told him he had to cut back on his activities, but gave him the option of deciding which ones he would give up.

—*Diana, mom of six children*

4

Ongoing Management

SIBLING STRATEGIES

Avoiding Comparisons Between Children

❧ It's natural for your children to compete for your attention. Sibling rivalry becomes even more intense when the children are the same gender and within three years of age.

❧ Don't compare siblings, hoping to challenge or motivate your straggler to perform as well as your higher achiever. Comparisons among siblings only serve to make one child feel bad or less loved, and to intensify an already inherently competitive relationship. Trying to win your approval or outshine a sibling can soon eclipse the activity itself.

❧ Avoid comparing your children to each other or assigning roles such as "David is our star athlete, but Brad is our super-smart chess player."

❧ Your child will quickly pick up any comparisons you make and despair at any shortcomings of her own. As a result, she may start making judgments about herself in relation to her siblings and peers that mirror your opinions.

I have found that activities are extremely hard on siblings, especially if that sibling is a lot younger than her older brother and sister. They get dragged around to all the different fields, classes, and arenas. Sometimes the younger sibling can't do an activity because it conflicts with an older sibling's well-established involvement in another activity.

—Lisa, mom of Grace, 6, Ben, 4, and Maddie, 1

It took me a long time to find my middle son a gymnastics program that works with our family schedule. Timewise, I couldn't be in two places at once. It's the same issue with swimming lessons; because of the two-year age difference between my oldest boys, they can't get lessons at the same time. So I sit during two different sessions every Saturday morning, and one boy waits with me while the other swims. With three kids, I'm really concerned when my two-year-old becomes old enough to want activities of his own. I have no idea how my youngest will do anything!

—Deborah, mom of Philip, 10, Patrick, 8, and William, 3

When Your Children Compete Head-to-Head

🍂 Sometimes siblings work out and thrive on competition, such as the tennis stars and sisters Venus and Serena Williams. The two often directly compete with each other in major tournaments and have had a running competitive rivalry for years, but still manage to remain best friends. Others find directly competing against one another creates a tense rivalry. In this case, help diffuse the situation by encouraging your children to pursue different activities, enter different leagues, or separate them so that they do not compete against each other.

🍂 It's natural for kids to compare themselves to their siblings and peers, and your challenge is to minimize sibling conflict, not aggravate it further.

🍂 Never confide in one child that she is better or more talented than her sibling.

🍂 Praise your children for supporting, teaching, or cheering each other on.

Although it's counterintuitive, do different activities for your kids to prevent sibling rivalry. Don't double up, even though it's so easy to drop them off at the same place. I saw this with my girls both taking lessons from the piano teacher who came to our home. While it was convenient, it had them making comparisons and stepping on each other's toes.

—Amy, mom of Sacha, 11, and Libby, 8

Since your oldest one starts activities first, the younger ones, by default, get tied into the rigid schedule of the older one. But our middle son lacked the focus to follow the karate instructions, and it wasn't the right activity for him. It was also better for Philip not to have his younger brother in karate class with him.

—Deborah, mom of Philip, 10, Patrick, 8, and William 3

Twins or Multiples: Same Team?

🐟 Sets of multiples differ dramatically in their preferences based on personality and gender. Some have very different preferences from one another or don't get along well, while others prefer to do everything together.

🐟 The needs of your children have to inform your decision about whether to enroll them in the same classes or on the same team. While it's much more convenient from a scheduling perspective to do so and to only have to get to one soccer practice instead of two or three, it may be detrimental to their growing sense of independence and personal development.

Up to this point, my twin sons have always asked to be on the same team. They're extremely close and draw strength from each other. They compete well together, and are even good against one another.

—Diana, mom of six children

🐟 If your multiples need a lot of space from one another, sign them up for different activities to give them the chance to shine individually and have the opportunity to make separate friends.

Following in the Footsteps of a Sibling Star

✦ Feelings tend to get hurt when one sibling outshines the other.

✦ If one child feels overly pressured because of a sibling superstar reputation, encourage her to consider different activities or sports, and to develop special interests and skills of her own.

✦ If you have a child whose interests demand large investments of parental time, make sure your other children do not feel left out or jealous. If your family goes out to dinner to celebrate a successful game or performance, toast siblings for being supportive and thus contributing to the success.

✦ Let your child decide for herself if she wants to pursue the same activity or sport as a sibling.

✦ Teach your child who is the star to be sensitive to her sibling's feelings by not gloating about her triumphs around the house, not making diminishing comments about her sibling, and lending encouragement.

LARGER FAMILIES

✦ Parents with four or more kids tend to fall into two camps when it comes to philosophies about activities. They either sign kids up as a group or get help with transportation in order for each child to be able to pursue individual interests.

Honestly, I draw up maps every morning figuring out how our day is going to unfold and making deals with other parents about carpooling! With four kids, finding others to carpool with has a huge influence on what activities my kids do. Arielle takes four hours of dance (jazz, tap, and ballet) a week at a local dance studio. She's a really gifted dancer for her age, and the dance studio is not my favorite, but we've kept her there, as she's in a fantastic carpool with her friends. If I thought she was going to become a professional dancer, then maybe I'd reconsider, but the logistics of getting her there and back home for each of these classes makes carpooling the determining factor. Often, when I can't drive legs of the carpool as much as the other parents because I'm a working mom, I make it up in creative ways other than driving such as by having all the kids over to our house for lunch on the weekends after the games.

—Naomi, mom of Talia, 11, Arielle, 10, Aaron, 8, and Daniella, 5

I have highly involved kids, and I want each to be able to pursue individual interests. With four kids so close together in age, I used to rely on the luxury of forty hours a week of baby-sitting help and a lot of carpools in order to make all their activities possible. The baby-sitter could run out and pick up one kid here or another one there while I was home fixing dinner or helping with homework. It made it so much easier to keep things calm. If I hadn't been able to afford the help, my kids would have just been incredibly limited in the activities they could do. I still have to be sophisticated about getting to classes on different days; otherwise, I end up having the other three kids sitting in the car for an hour, as none of these classes have good waiting spaces.

—*Bridgitt, mom of Taylor, 10, Connor and Chloe, 8, and Brian, 6*

Having four kids is a huge challenge, because you can't be in more than one place at a time. We rely on a network of parents to help by trading off carpooling. Two of our triplets are on the same soccer team, which works out great. They talk about their accomplishments but don't use them against each other. It's a great way for them to be together without fighting over something.

—*Dean, dad of Evan, 10, and Olivia, Justin, and Shelby, 8*

DEALING WITH YOUR CHILD'S COACH

Letting the Coaches Coach

🦋 If the coach or instructor doesn't call for an initial meeting with parents, ask for one at the beginning of the season so that you can understand the expectations and goals.

🦋 Be clear about the coach's expectations for your child, such as the time commitment as well as the consequences of missing team events. Same goes for rehearsals for music or dance recitals, or any other group activities.

🦋 Punctuality makes a huge difference to your child's teacher. Make sure that your child arrives on time with the proper equipment. If she will miss a practice, game, or lesson, or be late, call or e-mail one of the coaches to let him know with as much advance notice as possible.

✦ Ask the coach if there is any specific way you can help out. Offer to serve as a team volunteer or apply yourself to one of the many jobs crucial to the success of a team, such as tournament coordinator, team registrar, field setup, or snacks, or for performance-based activities, usher or costumes.

✦ Once you feel satisfied that your child is in good hands, give the coach the space and freedom he needs to coach well.

✦ Periodically, thank the instructor for the time and energy he gives to your child.

Dealing with a Problematic Situation

✦ If your child is having a problem, encourage her, if she's mature enough, to directly approach her teacher, rather than having you jump in as the first recourse to fix things.

As a volunteer coach, I find I generally have the most problems with the parents, not the kids. I have parents who want to coach from the sidelines, during the game, and during practice; parents who don't listen to league instructions, such as not addressing the referees; and parents who don't pay attention to their phone messages, read their mail, or return their calls. These are things I find most frustrating.

—*Cliff, soccer coach for 5 years and dad of Rachel, 10, Amanda, 8, and Jenny, 1*

Most of the youth and high school coaches I have interacted with agree on one thing: Parents can be much more difficult to deal with than children, especially those notorious for getting their two cents' worth with regard to strategy and coaching. Once you find a talented coach to work with your child, be supportive at games, but leave the coaching to the coaches. Shouting instructions from the stands during a game drives coaches crazy, regardless of whether or not the advice is sound. Be supportive of the coach and do not criticize him in front of your child. Any issues should be discussed one-on-one between parent and coach in a professional manner without players present. Nothing can erode the intricate fabric of teamwork faster than players doubting the capabilities of their coaches.

—*Rich Janor, Wheatland Travel Baseball Club coach for 5 years*

✦ If your child dreads going to practices or games, has been coming home from lessons unhappy, or has talked about dropping out, consider the following strategies:

- ⌐ Talk to your child and try to determine what the actual problem seems to be from her perspective. Realize that she may be reluctant to open up. She may fear your reaction or what might happen if you decide to talk to the instructor based on what she has said.
- ⌐ Attend some practices to observe what's going on firsthand.
- ⌐ If you feel a need to talk things over with your child's coach, ask for an appointment at a convenient time. Never have a serious conversation right before or after a game, when there are too many emotions, distractions, and children needing the coach's attention.
- ⌐ Approach your child's coach or teacher with a focus on problem solving and cooperation rather than confrontation. Before telling the coach what you think, ask the coach for his view of the issue or situation. You may be surprised to find yourselves in agreement.
- ⌐ If the issue involves a decision the instructor made, start by saying that you respect his decision but want to understand more clearly the rationale behind it. Avoid coming across as accusatory. Give the instructor a chance to correct a misunderstanding.
- ⌐ If, despite these collaborative efforts, the problem still cannot be resolved, you may need to go to the program's director or administrator. You also may need to move your child to a different team, school, or league.

IMPROVING YOUR SKILLS AS SPECTATOR

✦ At almost any game, you are bound to hear some parents yelling loudly from the sidelines, their voices carrying over the others. You'll see parents screaming at the ref, shouting out instructions to their children (such as "Run faster" or "Down the left side"), hollering, gesturing, and jumping out of their seats. You'll also, no doubt, experience parents berating their children from the sidelines ("Focus, Sam!") or being ecstatic depending on the play of the moment, and in general, modeling inappropriate and immature behavior. Also, in the anonymity of a crowd, you'll often hear parents screaming things that they might otherwise never say. Many team coaches have resorted to insisting that parents sit sequestered on the opposite side of the playing field from the kids.

✦ Given the tremendous amount of anxiety and ambition parents bring to the table when it comes to their child's activities, it's not surprising that parents are los-

Lily had one basketball coach with a short temper, but he taught her a valuable lesson. Despite his lack of patience, he was great at teaching the girls skills. Lily learned that not every coach had to be sweet, lovely, huggy, and kissy in order to be good.

—*Debbie, mom of Zachary, 12, and Lily, 10*

As a parent you have to ensure that the coach is not acting in ways detrimental to your child. I sat through one practice in 95-degree weather where the coach had the team running up and down a hill. I had to step in and let him know that I didn't think it was right for my kid, who was exhausted but trying to keep up. At times, volunteer parent coaches will unknowingly push kids into injuries, not maliciously or deliberately, but because they don't have professional experience in training kids.

—*Elizabeth, mom of Robert, 15, and David, 10*

We had one terrible coach. He yelled at the kids, cussed, and told them things like, "I'm going to be picking the number one team in your division next year, and if you don't play your heart out today, keep in mind I'm watching you." Many parents complained, and he wasn't allowed to coach anymore. The lesson I took away from this experience was that you've got to speak up.

—*Bridgitt, mom of Taylor, 10, Connor and Chloe, 8, and Brian, 6*

Our soccer coaches realized that they were getting too emotional during games, so they bought themselves two folding chairs. When things get too intense, they sit down, take a breather, and calm themselves! However, we had one coach who didn't seem to realize he was going over the top. He would start each game with a history lesson. One day, the topic at hand was Napoleon at Waterloo, with advice on how his team of young girls could use the example of the French emperor's experience to beat the other team, which, by the way, they couldn't follow at all! I thought to myself, This is so out of control!

—*Cathy, mom of Samantha, 13, and Kimberly, 10*

ing their cool on the sidelines at youth sporting events. In many areas of America, this behavior has gotten out of hand. Take, for instance, an argument between two fathers after a youth hockey practice in Massachusetts that cost one of them his life. In Florida, a furious parent shot a referee at a child's soccer match. In California, a baseball coach for eight-year-olds went into the stands wielding an aluminum bat to silence a hostile crowd during a game.

I can remember sitting in the bleachers telling my son to watch the ball, or yelling, "You gotta swing the bat," but after hearing a father yelling at his kid, "Catch the D—— ball!" I was so mad. Only to have my wife remind me, "You just yelled at your son the same way." Wow! That was the last time.

—*Larry Cook, softball coach for 30 years*

✦ Theoretically, it all sounds perfectly easy to stay calm and positive, until one kid on the opposing team elbows your six-year-old in the ribs for the third time during a soccer game. It's hard not to lose yourself in the tension of your child's competition.

✦ The word *fan* is short for "fanatic," and at times, you will inevitably find yourself struggling to keep from acting angry, frustrated, or emotionally out of control at your child's games or meets.

✦ For some coaches and leagues, their toughest job has become training parents to act appropriately. Many youth leagues have adopted zero-tolerance policies in which a referee can stop a game at any time to demand that a verbally abusive parent leave the premises. Over 14 states have passed laws imposing stiffer penalties for assaulting an amateur sports official. In addition to issuing codes of conduct for parents, many leagues have volunteer parents serving as "culture keepers" to keep the peace at competitive games.

✦ Just like an athlete who needs improvement, you can refine your performance on the sidelines.

✦ Let the coach be the only one giving instructions to the team or individual players. Leave it up to your coach to talk with your child on the sidelines when she takes a break in the action. When your child hears you calling out instructions to her on the field, she may easily think you are yelling at her instead of trying to help her. Games typically get competitive enough without having numerous adults screaming out conflicting instructions.

✦ Figure out what really gets to you as a spectator at your child's games, whether it's seeing your child get pushed, a bad or missed call by the referee, your child not playing well, your child constantly sitting out, or feeling impatient with your child's lack of skill development.

✦ Anticipate these inevitably frustrating moments so that you can modulate your response. Empathize with the referee, who's most likely trying his best, and ac-

One girl's mom would scream relentlessly at her daughter during soccer games. When asked to quiet down by other parents, she replied, "I'm going to yell at my kid and cheer her on. My kid wants to hear my voice!" No wonder our team did not win the trophy given out by the soccer league for the best-behaved parents as voted by the referees!

—*Cathy, mom of Samantha, 13, and Kimberly, 10*

One father this year was so upset on the sidelines he kept yelling, "Jeez, Emily, hit the ball," He kept making a fool of himself. Granted, she wasn't the most coordinated kid, but she was having fun. She's not the worst one on the team. I felt so sorry for her, as she was trying her best. It made me think to myself, What's the goal here?

—*Karen, mom of Max, 9, Sophie, 7, Celia, 5, and Jake, 2*

Sometimes, when we drove my son to a game, we would stay in the minivan when we felt like we might be pressuring him, telling him to go over here or there, or giving him too much direction. Some parents get way too into it, live vicariously through their kids, and try to control the whole thing. We learned to just let it be his sport and his thing.

—*Rochelle, mom of Chris, 21, Erika, 16, and Amy, 13*

Kids are simply not capable of consistency. Youth sports is just this incredibly endless arena for mistakes. A child can't always control the ball or make the shot. Even pros strike out, miss foul shots, and have intercepted passes. Yet parents shout at their kids from the sidelines about making mistakes. Children are very intuitive, always watching and looking. After hundreds of games of looking at adult responses, they must be thinking, Why is everyone so nervous, worried, and taking all this so seriously?

—*Dean Conway, state head coach and director of coaching for Mass. Youth Soccer Association and former teacher*

knowledge that your child's team may simply be outmatched in a particular game, your child may just be having a bad day, or the opposing players have resorted to rough play because they're losing.

✦ Your child learns self-control by watching you display it on the sidelines. Actions speak louder than words. Your child will be constantly observing and learning how to react during competitions from you. If you're a poor sport, your child will surely follow suit. Being calm and positive will set the standards for your child, who will often rely more on how you act than how you tell her to behave. If you tell your child to display self-control and be respectful and gracious to opponents, but then she sees you losing your cool or yelling at a game, your efforts will be completely undermined.

Sideline Dos and Dont's

DO
✦ Be your child's biggest fan by attending as many games as you can, offering support and encouragement.

✦ Make your job on the sidelines that of your child's unconditional, positive supporter, especially when she's having a tough game. Let the coach be the one to offer up any criticism, skill pointers, or game strategy.

✦ Be supportive and help your child keep the competition in perspective. Becoming angry or letting your disappointment show when your child doesn't perform well will leave her questioning whether this means you love her less.

✦ Cheer and call out encouragement instead of directions. Cheer enthusiastically for great skills, not just for scoring.

✦ Always cheer positively. Root for all the kids on the team, not just your own, and not against their opponents. "Sam, get the ball!" from the sidelines becomes, "Go, Vipers" or "Go, defense."

✦ Limit yourself to a few generic words of praise, such as "Great goal," "Nice pass," or "Go, Panthers!" Doing so will not only take pressure off your child but also inspire other parents to tone it down as well.

✦ Smile and show confidence and faith in your child. Your child will watch you closely during a performance and will feel dejected by your cries of frustration, or shouts to try harder.

✦ Thank the coaches, referees, or umpire at the end of the competition for their hard work.

Yelling instructions such as "Kick it," "Pass it," or "Run" will likely cause your player to pause instead of play. As an example, my daughter's team played the toughest opponent in our division. With five minutes to play and our team down a goal, our left wing stole the ball at midfield, beat one defender and was dribbling toward the goal with only a single defender in front of her. She was about 25 yards out when her parent yelled, "Shoot! Shoot!" loud enough to be heard all the way to the other side of the field. Instead of seeing our right forward wide open 10 yards in front of the goal, she fired off a weak 25-yard shot that bounced twice before the opposing goalkeeper easily scooped it up. If you feel the need to shout, by all means let out a "Go [name of your child's team]" or "Great play," but if you are about to yell out a command, please hold it in.

—*Ron, nationally licensed youth soccer coach, and dad of two, ages 10 and 8*

When my twelve-year-old was refereeing for younger kids' games, the parents would completely ignore her and run it the way they saw fit. They would declare when they were done with half time, insist on subbing in players when they felt like it, and change even the basic rules of how many kids play on each side. They ran roughshod over the teen referees, often yelling at them. It got to the point where I would go with her to sit and watch the games she refereed. It was so hard for her just to be heard to say, "Can we please get started!"

—*Cathy, mom of Samantha, 13, and Kimberly, 10*

DON'T

🐾 Don't yell at your child from the sidelines, as it only serves to confuse and potentially embarrass her. Doing so destroys your child's concentration. Moreover, you put her in a no-win situation if you end up yelling out advice that contradicts that of her coach.

🐾 Do not lose your temper no matter how bad a call from a referee is or what your child's opponent or their parents do or say. Walk off the stress or leave. Getting angry accomplishes nothing. Just as you don't want your child to embarrass you, don't embarrass her.

🐾 If you get more worked up and excited than your child, something's wrong. Take a break from attending a game to regroup and gain perspective.

🐾 Watch nonverbal disapproving signals you give your child, particularly looks of disappointment or disgust. In addition, realize that being silent or not giving your child any feedback after a game will likely be taken as implicit criticism.

🐾 Put away your video camera, as it takes competitive performance pressure off your child and can make her feel self-conscious in the midst of a game.

🐾 Don't shower your child with extravagant praise. Your child will quickly pick up on it, when you're cheering madly and all she did was pass the ball once to a teammate.

🐾 Don't offer your own negative critique about your child's performance after a game. Your child most likely already feels bad about any mistakes she made.

5

Dealing with Difficult Issues

Once your child becomes immersed in activities, problematic situations often emerge from dealing with a sense of failure to relating well to a particular instructor. This section focuses on the most common of these recurrent issues, offering strategies to help your child build life strategies, such as how to learn to win and lose gracefully, how to persevere, and when quitting or taking a hiatus from a depleting or frustrating activity makes the most sense.

SUPPORTING YOUR CHILD AFTER A GAME OR PERFORMANCE

✦ After a game or recital, focus your comments on how your child performed. Provide support for your child by listening to her and try to understand her feelings. Ask your child open-ended questions such as, "Did you enjoy yourself?" "What did you think of the game today?" or "How did you think it went?"

✦ For sports, shift the emphasis from the win or lose outcome. How you react to wins and losses of your child's team can set up a dynamic in which your child wants mostly to win to please you and make you proud.

✦ Instead of just having fun and enjoying the activity, parental approval or coach approval becomes your child's driving motivation. After a practice, ask about what your child learned, what skill she thinks she's best at or most needs to improve, and if she enjoyed it.

🍀 Praise your child for her effort and the new skills she acquires. "What a *great* effort against a tough team!" becomes the slogan for a lost game.

🍀 The car ride home might seem like the perfect place and time to discuss your child's performance. However, your child is often exhausted, working through her own reaction to the situation, and vulnerable to criticism. Ask questions focused on what your child thought of the experience, rather than offering your own impressions and observations.

🍀 Don't offer much in the way of unsolicited advice, unless your child asks for your help or input. Leave it up to her coaches and teachers to offer constructive feedback and tips for how to improve.

🍀 Develop a fun postgame or performance ritual, such as taking everyone out to a cheap-eats dinner after the game. Make it part of your ritual on game days to stop for ice cream or pizza, win or lose.

🍀 Ask what she enjoyed the most about performing. You might be surprised that the answer is not scoring the winning goal, but some other moment that was fun.

You can tell at games which parents try to live vicariously through their child for failed sports dreams from their past; it's the mom or dad who is so hard on the child after a bad performance.

—*Ian Coffey, assistant swimming coach at Syracuse University, coaching for 8 years*

What to Say After a Tough Loss

🍀 Make sure that your child knows that win or lose, you love her, appreciate her efforts, and do not feel disappointed in her. This will prevent her from fearing your disapproval if she fails. This applies also to bad music recitals or drama performances.

🍀 Don't be a fair-weather fan, liking your child most when she performs well, or becoming frustrated or angry when she does poorly.

🍀 Be the one person your child can always look to for encouragement and positive reinforcement.

🍀 While you want to reassure your child, you also want to acknowledge a hard loss and be open to hearing about any frustration, discouragement, anger, or self-criticism your child feels in response.

🍀 Don't give false praise, which your child will instantly detect and resent. Your child tends to know when she didn't play her best or made critical mistakes.

As adults and coaches, we can help every kid find something positive in their performance even if it is just one shot they made. How they finish with the other competitors is but a small part of the total experience.

—*Tom Barker, Texas Junior Olympics archery development coordinator, coaching for 9 years*

As hard as it may be, always make your child feel like he is not any less of a person just because he didn't score the winning run. When the other kids are saying mean things and even the coach is disappointed, your child has to know that you still think he is the best. If your child wants to talk about it, be honest. Point out his contributions even if the team didn't win and talk about things that didn't go his way, but be gentle. Your child does not want to hear that nobody will ever be as good as him or the other kids are idiots. Kids see right through that and tune you out even though you may really mean it. I have learned not to talk about the game in the car ride home unless my son brings it up.

—*Nancy, mom of a son age 13*

Keeping Winning in Perspective

🍂 Emotions often run high at games because the stakes feel high, given all the practices, time, energy, and family investment that goes into your child's participating. It's natural to want your child, and by extension your child's team, to do well. It can also feel at times like your child's failures are your own.

🍂 Instill in your child a deep-seated belief that you love her no matter what, regardless of how well she performs, the milestones she achieves, or the wins she accumulates. You don't want your child to be the one that fears that you will be mad if she blows it at a critical performance or game.

🍂 It is a constant struggle to keep reminding your child that winning is not the most important thing. Make sure you share with her all the other values that are important in participating in sports, activities, or being part of a team. These include skill building, the opportunity to test those skills against a worthy opponent, the value of being a part of a team, and the satisfaction of having given your best effort. Other values to emphasize include fun, fitness and being physically active, improvement, fair play, persistence, and tenacity. Encourage your child to always think broadly about what accomplishment means. There are important benefits less quantifiable than trophies or awards. Emphasize in actions and words to your child that winning isn't always the ultimate goal and that there are many equally important ways to be successful.

✦ Winning can't be discounted, as it's important in a competitive situation, but it should be secondary when your child is striving to build skills and achieve personal goals. If you emphasize skill building, you motivate your child to improve. This places the emphasis on things your child has control over, unlike the outcome of a team game. Lending your child contextual perspective on winning or losing helps your child set achievable goals for herself.

I tell all my students that a "winner" is a person who accepts responsibility for his or her actions, sees mistakes as lessons to be learned, understands that periods of slow progress will pass with persistence, and comes to appreciate losses as actually offering the greatest opportunity for personal improvement.

—*Omar Pancoast III, chess director, C&O Family Chess Center, teaching for 30 years*

My experience as a parent, music teacher, and Little League baseball coach has led me to appreciate the many little successes that shape a child. Pay enough attention to your child to appreciate the good single and not just the home run or winning the game. Know what it took for your child to hold on to third chair in band and don't worry if he does not end up in Carnegie Hall. The praise and appreciation you give in these endeavors at a young age greatly affect your child for rest of his life.

—*John Mueller, assistant professor of trombone and euphonium, University of Memphis, and professional musician, teaching for 21 years*

When it comes to organized sports, minimize the competitive aspects for as long as you can get away with it, without denying that the competition exists. To accomplish this, I will tell my sons things like, "Yeah, it feels great to win, but I'm glad you're having fun."

—*Alma, mom of three sons, ages 12, 6, and 4*

Stress Effort, Not Performance

✦ Praise your child for trying hard, regardless of the outcome of a game or performance.

✦ If your child sees winning as the only acceptable outcome, then she'll spend most of her energy during a game or competition trying to avoid making mistakes, and blaming others when those mistakes inevitably happen.

✦ Accept that there will be plenty of times when you bear the brunt of your child's anger and frustration.

✦ Tell your child that while winning isn't everything, trying to win is, and that you will consider your child successful if she puts forth her best effort every time she plays.

✦ Measure your child's performance by the effort she puts forth, the skills she acquires, and her achievement of personal goals. Get your child competing against herself with realistic goals, and concentrating on doing her personal best. If your child conceptualizes success in terms of "Am I getting better?" she will focus on mastering new skills and likely stick with the sport longer. If your child's primary focus is on winning, she will be more likely to want to quit in the face of failure.

✦ Stress as well the importance of teamwork, self-discipline, and perseverance.

✦ Don't expect your child to be or become one of the best players on the team, and recognize that every child has inevitable lulls in skill development.

✦ There will be times you watch your child play poorly, and you have to downplay your own frustration or disappointment.

✦ It's so important that your child know that you value her efforts above all else. That's not to say that you won't praise her accomplishments and cheer her victories, but it does mean that you won't disparage her failures, setbacks, or lack of raw talent at a particular endeavor.

Don't Push Too Hard

✦ Children do their best and benefit from activities that they feel comfortable doing. If you try to rush your child, you can make her feel intimidated and

I get wary as soon as I hear parents using the word "we" when referring to their child's activities. That's when you know that they're getting carried away. They get swept up in the intense competition and the frenzy of it all, and lose sight of what activities are really all about: It has to be fun for the kids.

—*George Campbell, swimming program director for 20 years and middle school physical education director for 32 years*

turn her off the activity. Kids need to progress at their own pace. The less you push her, the more likely she will take it upon herself to succeed.

🍂 Viewing your child as an extension of yourself puts unhealthy pressure on her. You can tell when this is happening when you start referring to sports and activities in which your child participates in plural terms, such as, *"We* do karate, soccer in the fall, and T-ball in the spring."

Avoid Comparing Your Child to Her Peers

🍂 Comparing your child to her peers or teammates is unhealthy and demoralizing for you both. It can make you and her feel anxious and inadequate. Instead of trying to figure out who is outpacing your child, ask yourself, "Is my child having fun? Has she been learning and gaining new skills?" As long as this is the case, push your worries aside.

🍂 Your child will take a different path, learn different activities at different speeds, and achieve different levels of success than you or her peers have experienced.

It's impossible not to compare your child to others. I find myself doing it all the time, almost to a fault. It's not fair to her, and I know she'll be fine, but it's hard when one friend is doing something really well and she hasn't even tried it yet. It's hard work to step back from that kind of thinking.

—*Jill, mom of Stella, 5*

I try not to compare my kids to others. I tell them, "I don't care what everyone does, I just care what you do." There are going to be kids who are better than mine, and some worse than they are. I just don't want kids who are so competitive that they're the one making fun of the kid who can't kick the soccer ball.

—*Karen, mom of Max, 9, Sophie, 7, Celia, 5, and Jake, 2*

DEALING WITH A BAD SPORT

✦ Your child practices good sportsmanship when she treats everyone around her with respect, from fellow teammates and opponents, to coaches and referees. It is as simple as shaking hands with opponents before a game, cheering good plays made by others, and accepting bad calls from referees with grace. It also means learning how to win without gloating and lose without complaining.

✦ It's tough to congratulate opponents after losing a competition of any form. Set a good example for your child by congratulating the parents of kids on the other team.

✦ Point out examples of sportsmanship in professional athletes, and point out why incidents of bad sportsmanship upset you. When a player makes a critical mistake or gets angry, point out what it takes to collect yourself and get mentally back into the game. When a player hoots and hollers after scoring, talk about how badly that makes the opponent feel. If a player gets penalized for fighting or arguing with a referee, talk with your child about how that penalty hurts the entire team. Note examples of opponents acknowledging one another's good plays.

✦ By emphasizing effort, hard work, practice, and learning from mistakes over the final product, you will enable your child to be more resilient when confronting challenges.

✦ Even the best kids have moments of appallingly bad sportsmanship, which can often be profoundly embarrassing for you as all parents look your way. Even though you feel frustrated, stay calm when talking to her about her behavior. Listen thoughtfully to your child's recounting of what happened, whether it was that she got pushed, thought the referee made a bad call, or wanted so badly to win. Let your child know that while it is okay to feel angry or disappointed, there are more appropriate ways to vent these emotions.

✦ Make sure your child knows precisely what sportsmanship entails, including:
   ➤ Abiding by the rules of a game and never cheating or playing unfairly
   ➤ Avoiding arguments with teammates, opponents, coaches, and referees or officials
   ➤ Encouraging teammates, even when they make mistakes
   ➤ Accepting the decisions of game officials

✦ Remind your child that all athletes and teams make mistakes and don't have great games every time. Explain that the true test of a champion is being a good sport after losing a big game.

✦ Talk with your child about how you deal with your own mistakes, frustration, and disappointment. Model the behavior you want to see in your child. Dedication, sportsmanship, focus, and confidence are qualities she absorbs by watching you. Make sure that your child does not see you or other adults at your house screaming at the TV because of referee calls, or acting out when losing a game you're playing. Play board games with your child to work on appropriate reactions to winning and losing.

When bad sportsmanship occurs at a game or practice, discuss other ways the situation could have been handled.

Sportsmanship, like a forehand or a backhand, can be taught, and it should be one of the highest priorities for the coaches and the parents.

—*Stephen Gregg, USSRA director of junior development and squash coach*

Your child has watchful eyes and will mimic your every move.

—*Douglas Veronesi, kempo and jujitsu studio owner and instructor for 4 years*

My son had a bad baseball experience where he was playing with a group one year behind him agewise. He had stayed out of baseball for a couple of years, and we wanted him to be able to play in a less competitive league. Still, kids had started pitching instead of adults, and they were also keeping track of strike-outs at bat. It was hard for my son to sustain that level of frustration. During one game he stamped off the field, and I told him he had to go back into the game and support his team. He refused. The coach spoke with him, and still he refused. I talked further with him, and told him if he didn't go back out, we wouldn't let him play the rest of the season because he was being such a bad sport. He still refused, and that was that.

—*Alexa, mom of Adam, 11, and Sophie, 7*

Sportsmanship should be a requirement, not an afterthought.

—*Mike Gaffney, assistant head softball coach, Hesser College, coaching for 15 years*

WHEN YOUR CHILD WANTS TO QUIT

When is it okay for your child to stop participating in an activity or sport? How do you respond when your child announces, "I quit!" two practices into a sport? What do you do when your child declares, "I hate flute and I'm never going back!" Of course, this is often the same activity she begged you to sign her up for in the first place.

Your child's desire to quit can become emotional for you as well, given all the time, money, and emotional investment you make in her activities. After spending thousands of dollars on lessons, elite teams, travel, specialty camps, and tournaments, it is natural to want to see a return on your investment. This could either take the form of your child achieving a certain level of success or happiness from the pursuit. Blowing off flute or ballet after years of lessons no longer becomes a casual decision.

When your five- to eight-year-old says "I want to quit!" the first recourse is to try to ignore them and see if they forget all about it the next day.

—*Roger Boskus, waterskiing instructor for 3 years*

Many kids act irrationally when they are upset, and especially when they announce something so dramatic as "I quit." Parents shouldn't initially give in to quitting, because children will get the idea that they can quit anything when it becomes too difficult or not enjoyable. If a child is truly miserable, then they should obviously quit, but sometimes it is just a bad day, and kids don't necessarily want to quit. Parents should encourage them to stay with it, but when it becomes the dreaded topic of every day, then they should pull their child out.

—*Matthew Barrowclough, youth sailing instructor for 2 years*

When frustration strikes and a child is not enjoying the game, the words "I quit!" may only signal the need for a break or a shift in the level of seriousness.

—*Omar Pancoast III, chess director, C&O Family Chess Center, teaching for 30 years*

✤ Sometimes you can address your child's frustration and quickly resolve it, while at other points moving on to something else makes the most sense. At other times, you may want your child to stick out the activity either because she made a commitment or you consider it to be essential.

✤ Never use bribes, rewards, or the threat of punishment in order to get your child to continue an activity. The minute you find yourself tempted to do so, it's likely that you are bringing your own strong feelings about the activity into the mix. The point of activities should be fun, learning, and skill building. Using rewards to keep her going undermines the character building and internal motivation that activities can ignite.

✤ Your difficult job is to help your child ascertain when quitting makes sense, as it raises important issues, including burnout, overload, commitment, perseverance, and getting enough physical exercise.

Uncover the Heart of the Matter

✤ If your child wants to quit a sport, find out what the problem is before you do anything rash. Deciding how much to push your child in a particular activity involves a thoughtful assessment of why she wants to quit in the first place.

✤ More than 70% of children below age 13 drop out of youth sports because of an overemphasis on winning, abusive coaches, or because they don't get enough chances to play in games.

✤ Compare notes with other parents. When waiting on the sidelines of a game or dropping off and picking up from a practice or lesson, take the time to talk with other parents about their children's experience. Determining if their children express similar concerns as your child will help you assess the validity of her complaints.

✤ Go to a practice, but don't watch. Instead, close your eyes and listen for a while. What you hear will give you a great indication of what's really going on. You should hear laughter and not silence from the kids or shouting from the coach. The tenor of the interactions among the kids as well as with the coach can give you a great deal of insight to the emotional underpinnings of a situation. Observe how your child responds to the coach or teacher and to her peers. Evaluate what in the dynamic leaves her feeling frustrated and discouraged.

✤ Whatever reasons your child offers for wanting to quit, there is more than likely an underlying cause of her unhappiness. Your goal is to get beyond your child's superficial complaint, which may be as evasive as "I don't have fun" or "I just don't want to do it anymore." Her desire to quit may even be the symptom of another problem of which she's not even fully aware. Did she say she wanted to quit in a moment of intense frustration, or did she really mean it?

✦ If your child comes home sullen, downcast, or sulky after practice, find out what's troubling her. Try to get to the heart of the matter by carefully listening to her feelings. Ask your child specific questions about her experience to see if you can remedy the situation, or if she's better off moving on to the next activity.

✦ Ask your child why she wants to quit and what prompted her decision. Just give her time to vent and then go from there. Look for a practical solution.

✦ Help your child understand her reasons for wanting to quit. When she says, "I'm bored," this may mask underlying feelings of incompetence or tension with other teammates. Try to get to the specifics when it comes to your child's frustrations and dislikes, and assess whether these can be changed.

It is important to find out why. Are they quitting because they are not good at it? Is it because of the coach? Is it not fun anymore? Are they injured? The answer will determine the appropriate course. Sometimes you may agree that it is time to quit. Other times it may be time for a change of venue to put a different perspective on it. Sometimes it is burnout, and they just need to put it away for a while. "I quit" from a kid may be "I need a break" but not "forever." Unfortunately, sometimes they may want to quit because it is a parent's dream and not theirs.

—Tom Barker, Texas Junior Olympics archery development coordinator, coaching for 9 years

The main reason kids struggle and eventually quit is the lack of fun. If children are not enjoying a sport, then they will struggle and not have a positive experience. Sometimes the child just grows out of the sport and doesn't want to play, and then it's time to move on to a different challenge. Another common reason for wanting to drop out is being overcommitted. I've seen some families that go to youth hockey after a soccer game, then head to a lacrosse match after hockey. The kids need rest!

—Matthew Mincone, Martha's Vineyard High School boys' varsity coach for 4 years

When Your Talented Child Wants to Quit

✦ You may feel particularly angry, disappointed, and frustrated if your child has exceptional talents in a particular activity and still wants to walk away. Clearly she has the skills, but perhaps feels too much pressure or that expectations are set too high for her performance.

✦ As a parent you walk a fine line between encouraging your child through tough times and allowing her to quit. You will likely find yourself wondering whether your child will end up being grateful to you for making her stick it out when she is older, or if your pushing will just leave her feeling unhappy or resentful. This becomes even more crucial if you, as an adult, lament the fact that your parents let you quit an activity, and think wistfully of what you might have achieved if you had continued. Your personal regrets may dramatically color how you view your child's complaints or pleas to quit.

✦ You want your child to be successful, and part of that success has to include your child's decision to redirect her energies into something better suited to her temperament and skills. This philosophy extends from the earliest activities to college years and beyond, when your child will be making decisions on her own about what to do with her life.

One of the worst things a parent can hear is that his or her child hates the game the parent so desperately wants them to love. Being made to go, forced to practice, or pressured to improve and make a team are all things kids rebel against. Let them walk away, and they will find their way back in good time. As with a lot of things, we all like things better when we think they are our idea.

—*Paul Hobart, PGA teaching professional, Tartan Fields Golf Club*

✦ While wrestling with decisions over quitting, listen carefully to what your child says and how she feels, and teach her to make well-thought-out decisions. This process will give her the invaluable gift of life skills.

Dealing with Your Own Frustration

✦ The decision to drop out of sports can be very emotional for both you and your child.

✦ Especially if you have invested a lot of time, money, and emotion in your child's pursuit of a sport, it can feel like a personal betrayal when your child suddenly decides she's had enough.

✦ You may find yourself worrying that your child may become a habitual quitter, lazy, or waste her potential. Just because your child quits ballet or karate at age 8 does not mean she will be a quitter as an adult.

🌀 If you are friends with other parents through an activity, your child's quitting may mean you do not get to hang out with them anymore, such as on the sidelines.

In eighth grade, our son announced that he did not want to play ice hockey again. I know I was disappointed. We had built our winters and our friendships around youth hockey. Now that Ben is 18 years old, I asked him why he decided to quit when he did. He said it was because the sport had become more important to us as parents than to him. To this day, I don't know how I misread his feelings so badly. And we blame ourselves for ruining this experience for him.

—Linda, mom of Ben, 18

ADDRESSING REASONS YOUR CHILD MAY GIVE FOR QUITTING

🌀 Sometimes your child joins an activity because everyone else is doing it, only to discover that she doesn't really like it, or she wants to quit because all of her friends are doing something else and she wants to be with them. Or maybe her friends tease her because they consider the activity to be "uncool."

🌀 Below are some of the more common reasons children have for calling it quits, and ways to address each.

Just Not Having Fun

🌀 Often an activity just isn't as much fun as your child imagined it would be.

🌀 According to the National Alliance for Youth Sports, of the over 20 million kids who sign up for youth soccer, baseball, football, hockey, and other competitive sports each year, some 70% quit organized sports by age 13 and never return. The number one reason cited for this is that it has stopped being fun.

🌀 Your child's interest and dedication will wane as soon as a sport stops being fun for her. Fun doesn't have to mean "entertaining," but often comes from skill development and feeling challenged in a "doable" way.

🌀 Watch for the warning signs that a particular sport or activity has stopped being fun. If your child continually feels unhappy, disappointed, or is struggling with her self-esteem, discuss it with the coach or instructor, and watch a lesson or two.

🦐 Kids start dropping out in big numbers as they enter middle school, when "fun" takes a back seat to winning. During this vulnerable stage your challenge is to keep your child engaged in sports and activities she enjoys.

🦐 Set up a time to speak privately with your child's coach or teacher to gather his input. Explain that your child does not seem to be enjoying herself, and ask for the instructor's insight as to what might be happening. Don't confront the instructor and blame him for the problem. Rather, frame it in terms of seeking advice that will help you understand the reasons for your child's frustration. A team approach to evaluating and solving the problem will likely get you a more satisfying resolution.

My philosophy has become that as long as an activity interests my kids, they keep up with it, and are not complaining, it's fine. But I tell them if I hear a complaint, such as about having to drive a half hour to practice, then we have to reevaluate their participation in that activity. The bottom line is, it should be fun.

—Elise, mom of Zeke, 16, Jeremy, 14, and Adam, 12

After having gotten her black belt, my daughter decided to take a break from karate, even though she had just been asked to be on the demo team of kids that go around to schools and show off their skills. She said, "Okay, I've achieved what I wanted to," and then she said, "I want to play!" I made her go a couple more times, just to make sure she felt okay with the decision and it wasn't just spur of the moment or because she was feeling lazy. I asked her several times if she wanted to go back, but every time I asked, she informed me, "No, Mom. I just want to play!"

—Joy, mom of Chris, 15, and Victoria, 11

Children usually quit at adolescence because they think that they're missing out on being with friends and cruising the mall.

—Linda Kola, master-rated figure-skating coach, teaching for 26 years

Feels Incompetent or Untalented

🦋 Make sure your child is in the right class for her skill level. Her lackluster performance can affect her self-esteem, making her feel negatively about herself in comparison to her friends.

🦋 Your child may feel too much pressure from you, her coach, or her teacher in areas such as skill acquisition, performance, and competition.

🦋 Give your child extra attention to see if it makes a difference. Set up a place in your home or backyard that's conducive to casual practice and take the time to play with her just for the sheer fun of it.

🦋 Your child may find a new activity more difficult than she thought and feel frustrated because she lacks the skills to do it well at first. Your child may also find a particular skill or learning situation, whether a new soccer move or a specific musical piece, frustrating and difficult to master. Her desire to quit may reflect her feeling that this stumbling block is insurmountable. Help her shift her attitude toward practicing, and encourage her to be patient for the time it takes to acquire proficiency with each new skill.

🦋 Another reason that kids get discouraged is when they are not progressing as quickly as they want or getting the constant stream of praise they became accustomed to as a beginner. As your child's skill advances, more will be expected of her, and she will get praised less often.

🦋 Around ages 12–13, specialization becomes more of an issue, and those children who aren't the

The simple truth is that not being good at something is not fun. And that's why recreational leagues tend to dwindle by middle school. Kids who are really good go onto elite teams and everyone else drops by the wayside.

—*George Campbell, swimming program director for 20 years and middle school physical education director for 32 years*

best at something feel discouraged and stop having fun. Children feel that it's no longer worth the effort it takes for practices, lessons, and games, therefore missing out on social time with friends. Many kids drop out because other players have matured faster, and as a result, they are unable to keep up.

🦋 Determine if more encouragement or individual attention from you or the instructor can resolve the issue at hand. Discuss the possibility of a different teaching approach or perhaps work on a particular skill to overcome a hurdle. This could be anything from difficulty reading music and coordinating finger movements to how to make solid contact with the ball.

🦋 If your child balks at competition, find ways that she can continue the activity without this element, whether it means playing in the backyard or with another league or group.

Feels Underchallenged or Bored

✸ It can also be a problem if your child's skills have surpassed her peers, and she feels bored, underchallenged, and finds the activity tedious.

✸ In this case, your child may need to switch teams or classes to participate in a more appropriate skill level.

Struggling in the Opening Forays

✸ Being in a new situation terrifies some children. Opening forays for any child in team competition can also be intimidating. The timing may be wrong, as your child may lack the maturity, discipline, or physical skills that the activity requires.

✸ Your child may need some extra help adjusting, or need you to stay through the first few classes, lessons, or practices.

Bad Fit with the Coach, Teacher, or Other Kids

✸ Your child may threaten to quit in a tantrum or when angry with a coach, teammate, or referee. A cooling-down period followed by a clearheaded discussion about the situation may resolve the issue.

✸ Assess whether there is a personality or learning-style conflict between your child and the coach or teacher. If so, change instructors to find someone more in sync with your child. This can make a world of difference and transform your child's attitude about the activity.

Both times my older son has wanted to quit, he was on a team with a coach who wasn't really enthusiastic or knowledgeable, and it occurred fairly late in a losing season. We feel it is important for kids to be responsible about commitments they make, and explained to our son that in a team situation, there are a number of people depending on him to follow through and "stick it out" for the season. He did finish the season, and even had some fun.

—Anne, mom of Rob, 10, and Tim, 8

✤ Perhaps your child does not get along with one or more of the other children in her group. Talk with the coach and bring up any peer issues that seem to be playing a part in your child's unhappiness in the activity.

Burnout

✤ Your child may simply be overcommitted and want to quit some or all of her activities in order to have more free time.

✤ Evaluate whether there are intermediate steps to quitting. Could your child miss one of the two practices a week and still play on the team? Could she switch from an elite team to a recreational one that places fewer time demands or pressure on her?

ENCOURAGING YOUR CHILD TO STICK WITH IT A WHILE LONGER

✤ Many kids go through periods when they question their commitment to an activity. Your job is to help your child ascertain if it is a phase that will pass or an irresolvable issue.

✤ Agree with your child that she must do her best for a specific amount of time. Talk with your child about giving new activities a fair chance. Set a "wait and see" time period for the rest of the season or the remaining prepaid lessons. After that point, she can decide whether she still wants to quit or wants to stick with it. This extra time may enable her to enjoy the activity, or at the very least be able to make a more informed decision about quitting.

✤ Quitting teaches your child instant gratification as opposed to working hard at something that has a deeper, lasting satisfaction and sense of accomplishment. It also promotes a philosophy of simply jumping from one thing to the next the minute something doesn't make her feel good. You don't want your child to make giving up a repeated pattern that carries over to other areas or into her adult life.

✤ While you should take her feelings seriously, make it a basic family rule that your child should "stick it out" unless her physical or emotional well-being is at stake. Your child must then put thought into the sign-up process, understanding that she must honor her commitments, especially to a team who is depending on her.

✤ Take your child to events that build up or sustain a passion for the activity, where she gets to see the activity performed on a professional level.

My oldest daughter periodically announces that she wants to quit piano. We say fine, although we do encourage her to play a musical instrument. She actually did quit once, only to decide that she wanted to do it again. I think she changed her mind and chose to restart because of peer pressure, as a lot of her friends play piano.

    —Cliff, soccer coach for 5 years and dad of Rachel, 10, Amanda, 8, and Jenny, 1

When my kids announce they want to quit something at the beginning of the season, we'll tell them, "You just started and you should stick it out." Most of the time, they're just having a bad day, which they're entitled to, and it turns out to be a great thing that they didn't quit.

    —Jane, mom of Carolyn, 17, and Peter, 11

Sometimes it's hard if your child doesn't want to continue a particular activity. My oldest son announced he has had it with karate, but I felt conflicted because he had already gotten his green belt, invested hundreds of hours in classes, and was over the hump of being a beginner.

    —Deborah, mom of Philip, 10, Patrick, 8, and William 3

My eight-year-old son quit karate because he didn't like testing for a new belt. Even though I told him that they only test you when you're ready to pass, he didn't want to have anything to do with it. My instinct was that he should have stuck it out, but I didn't feel like turning it into a battle. Of course, I think to myself that he might feel better about himself if he had earned that orange belt.

    —Dee, mom of Carey, 8, and Danny, 6

The parent should say, "You need to honor your commitment to your team and give it a try for the rest of the season. If you don't like it after that, I'll bet we can find another activity that interests you." Sometimes kids will decide to reenter the program when they are ready and on their own terms.

    —Ted Tye, president of Newton Girls' Soccer, coach for 13 years, and dad of an 18-year-old and 12-year-old twins

✦ Reasons to discuss with your child why you want her to keep going:
- ❧ You've invested a lot of money and time in lessons or equipment, or have prepaid for a season.
- ❧ You feel that your child hasn't really given it a fair chance.
- ❧ You feel that this particular activity benefits your child, giving her something she wouldn't otherwise have, such as exercise, a team experience, a base of musical knowledge, or simply something to do on Tuesday afternoons other than hang out with you or a baby-sitter.
- ❧ She complains about going, you have a hard time motivating her to get out the door, but once she's there, she has a great time. It may be that your child has a difficult time transitioning from home or straight from school to an activity.
- ❧ She has not been engaged in the activity very long. Teaching perseverance and commitment has its merits, but you must weigh these principles against the misery your child feels.
- ❧ Your child has waffled in the past, but with your encouragement has come to love activities she has stuck out.
- ❧ Teammates are depending on her, and if she quits mid-season, they will be left in the lurch.

Making It a Family Policy Not to Quit

✦ In order to teach your child about commitment and responsibility, make it a general family policy that your child commits to finishing what she starts. This helps shift the angst of the process to carefully thinking through sign-ups, instead of on dropping out of a particular activity. Encourage lots of discussion and investigate options before signing up. That having been said, clearly you don't want to force your child to continue an activity that's creating a great deal of stress, anxiety, unhappiness, or making her feel bad about herself.

✦ Some parents feel it's simply unacceptable to quit a team except in extreme circumstances. If this is how you feel, tread cautiously and take into consideration your child's age. If your elementary school child is trying out team sports for the first time, the experience will be new to her. However, as your child gets older, you should be more adamant about her seeing a commitment through, except under extreme circumstances or if your child is profoundly unhappy.

✦ Carefully consider whether you think a particular activity is good for her (such as exercise she wouldn't otherwise get) or something you consider essential (like learning to swim).

I don't let my kids quit activities at the first sign of frustration or the first complaint. My father imbued in me the philosophy that once you start something, you should see it through. I try to impress this ethos on my kids, but I don't overdo it and will, with reluctance, let them quit something they're truly unhappy doing. It's often a confusing and difficult decision to make.

—*Arnie, dad of Tessa, 11, and Jake, 8*

Quitting is not even an option for our kids. Our family philosophy is that once you join something, you owe it to your team to go to practices and games. Our kids have bought into this, but it's not always easy. It becomes especially hard when conflicts like birthday parties come up and the kids want to skip a practice or game or when they want to quit altogether. But we believe that part of growing up involves understanding that once you've made a commitment, you see it through for that season.

—*Sheri, mom of Allison, 11, and Eric, 9*

I tell my kids that if they ask to do something, and I pay for it, they pretty much have to stick it out. Of course, I haven't held true to that when my kids are truly miserable doing something.

—*Karla, mom of Karl, 9, Max, 6, and Leo, 3*

We tell our kids that by quitting they will be letting the whole team down. So an activity is a responsibility that they need to commit to and stick with through to the end of the season, and then they can choose not to sign up to do it again.

—*Dean, dad of Evan, 10, and Olivia, Justin, and Shelby, 8*

TIMES WHEN CALLING IT QUITS MAKES SENSE

✦ Ultimately, your job is to teach your child to make independent and thoughtful decisions about what's in her best interest. Quitting piano may end her chances to

While my oldest daughter has a beautiful voice, she decided that she was doing too many things and wanted to quit the chorus she was in. We discussed it, and we let her quit, as every single day after school she had something going on and it had become too much for her.

—*Naomi, mom of Talia, 11, Arielle, 10, Aaron, 8, and Daniella, 5*

My daughter started gymnastics in kindergarten and loved it, but when she was in second grade, we moved across town and she had to change gyms. She found it a whole different atmosphere: very competitive and very strict. She hated it, and my daughter has always been right in tune with what she wants. So she happily dropped gymnastics and switched to taking karate with her brother.

—*Joy, mom of Chris, 15, and Victoria, 11*

I've always been lax about letting my kids quit when they don't want to do an activity or take a class anymore. Of course, none of them have ever shown so much potential in one thing that I thought it would be a waste for mankind and for them. What's interesting is that things naturally drop off along the way and your child goes on to pick up something else.

—*Claire, mom of Ben, 14, Alison, 11, and Danny, 8*

Don't force your child to continue if she does not want to. My 7-year-old nephew told his parents he did not want to play T-ball anymore because it was "so-o-o boring," so they asked him if he was sure, and he said, "Yes." T-ball season came around and all of his friends were playing and he was so mad he was not. But now he wants to play more than ever! It will work itself out.

—*Christie Lynn McCoy, assistant softball coach, Syracuse University, for 5 years*

be a concert pianist or win a college music scholarship, but that may very well not matter a bit to her, as her passions lie elsewhere. Moreover, pushing your child against her will may only serve to make her hate the activity and feel resentful toward you.

❧ Although it is important to encourage your child's interests, don't keep pushing a passion. In letting your child make her own decisions, you are acknowledging that passions sometimes wane. Give your child the right to quit when she has taken it as far as she wants.

❧ If your child is miserable, frustrated, and has taken an ego beating, she may well be justified in washing her hands of a particular endeavor. In fact, she may be following a strong intuition that the situation is wrong for her. Your child's health and emotional well-being should come first and foremost, and she may be the best judge of this.

❧ If you've tried everything and your child still moans and groans before every lesson or practice, then it's time to back off. Let her stop the activity so her frustration doesn't become generalized to hating all music, sports, or lessons.

THE PROCESS OF QUITTING ITSELF

❧ Once the final decision has been made, support your child's choice. Tell your child, "Okay, we support you," and have your actions mirror that sentiment as well. At this point, wholeheartedly supporting your child's decisions is important for her feelings of self-worth. Don't be afraid that you may be raising a perennial quitter when your elementary-age child decides she has had enough.

❧ Talk about quitting in terms of taking a hiatus. Tell your child, "It sounds like you need a break." Emphasize that this is not a permanent decision. Leave your child the option to take the activity up again later if it becomes more appealing. Sometimes a child just needs a sabbatical from the activity to regroup.

❧ Ask your child to go with you to tell her coach/teacher that she has decided to leave the activity and why. Even if this is the most basic of explanations and exchanges, it will provide your child with much-needed closure.

❧ Offer your child the option of switching to a different activity, so that if she quits soccer, she agrees to try a different sport that will continue to build her physical skills and fitness.

PART II
SPORTS

6

General Sports Considerations

READY FOR ORGANIZED SPORTS?

✦ With visions of Olympic medals, lucrative professional contracts, or college scholarship money, many parents feel tempted to start their children as early as possible in order to get as much experience as possible. Unfortunately, this early-start approach can also lead to early burnout long before a child gets anywhere close to her parents' lofty goals.

✦ Because every child and every sport is different, there are no absolute answers about the best time to start. You may be able to measure your child's readiness for organized, competitive sports in terms of motor skills, social maturity, and the ability to understand and follow rules and regulations. But the best indication of readiness comes from your child. She should be eager to try the sport and enjoy it once she starts.

✦ You should never push your child into team sports, but by the time she is six years old, you may want to see if she is ready. The American Academy of Pediatrics recommends that your child not start team sports prior to this age, but you know your child best. Just because she meets the suggested or minimum age for a particular program doesn't mean she's ready for the activity. If the demands exceed your child's developmental level, she may feel frustrated. In addition to age, you also need to consider your child's physical coordination, size, and emotional maturity.

To better understand the mania of overscheduling kids, it helps to consider the evolution of youth sports over the past 60 years. In my view, this evolution occurred over five distinct eras: the sandlot era (circa 1930–1940s), the Little League era (circa 1950s), the TV era (circa 1960s), the Title IX era (circa 1970s) and the Mega-sports era (circa 1980s). Youth sports changed dramatically after World War II with the startup and growth of Little League baseball. Little League got parents involved as coaches, team moms, and league administrators, and children starting play at age 6 or 7. The TV boom of the 1960s and 1970s aided this change, as it brought sports into the home. No longer did kids have to imagine how their favorite athlete performed—they could see him or her in slow motion and instant replay and imitate what they saw on TV. With organized Little League and the exposure of television came fancy uniforms, sophisticated equipment, trophies, mini-stadiums, All Stars, most valuable players, playoffs, championships, the Little League World Series, and an intense pressure and focus on winning. Title IX brought female athletics into the game, and the Mega-sports era made the lucrative lure of college scholarship and extremely high professional sports earnings compelling for many parents and their athletic kids.

—*Jerry Norton, director of Ponte Vedra Development Football League and youth coach for 36 years*

Your child should be able to take direction, cooperate, express an interest in joining a team, and focus on a task for more than ten minutes.

🔱 Until then, enroll her in a program that emphasizes fun and physical exercise, not one whose primary concerns are rules and competition.

🔱 Many parents begin trying to find sports and activities that pique their children's interest as early as 3 years old. Yet many preschoolers get stressed if a parent does not stay right by their side. Others have trouble listening, following directions, or getting along with others.

🔱 Sports teams for children under 5 have cropped up everywhere, leading many children to be proficient at a sport by age 7, while their peers who have not started yet feel hopelessly behind. Many children aren't ready for team play until well into elementary school when they can understand the rules, cooperate with teammates, and practice good sportsmanship.

🔱 Make sure your child is in a class or program with other children of similar age and ability. Consider the age range of children playing. If your child is on the

It's been my observation that if your child doesn't start certain sports like soccer early, it's very tough to catch up. With so many kids starting early, it puts others who begin an activity later at a real disadvantage. They might feel like klutzes, or their self-esteem plummets because they think they're the worst ones on the team. It's hard to learn when everyone else is whizzing by you, and you're just a beginner without enough experience to keep up. So as a parent, you are faced with a difficult decision, not wanting to have your kids start too early, but also hoping they won't miss out on opportunities to do certain activities because they will be less advanced than their peers. It's a double-edged sword.

—*Karen, mom of Max, 9, Sophie, 7, Celia, 5, and Jake, 2*

Having coached my daughters' soccer and basketball teams, I think that either kindergarten or first grade is a good time to start organized sports. The kids don't get a ton out of it from a skill perspective, but they get friendships and have fun, which is what it is all about.

—*Cliff, soccer coach for 5 years and dad of Rachel, 10, Amanda, 8, and Jenny, 1*

My biggest mistake with my children's activities was starting them too young, especially with my first. First, I tried to take her to Gymboree as an eight-month-old, and she was not into it at all. She cried, she hated the parachute game, and would sit on my lap on the side and hang on to me. So I thought, Well, I just haven't found her activity yet. I was on a crusade. I signed her up for baby swim, on Saturday mornings. It took an hour just to get out the door, between the bathing suit and diaper bag and being pregnant with my second. She would just cry and cry in class. I really felt like I was a failure, she was a failure, and all these dads were giving me a look like, "What's wrong with your child?" Next up was ballet class at age 3. The dance studio had a steel door with no window between the class and the hallway where the parents waited. All the little ballerinas would go in, but no parents were allowed. My daughter cried and cried, and we sat outside ballet class for eight weeks. They wouldn't let me in, and I wouldn't leave her crying. She was too young, and they were too rigid. Once she was old enough, she loved the activities to which she went, and even turned out to love dance. Finally, I learned that activities were supposed to be for her and not some form of boot camp.

—*Amy, mom of Sacha, 11, and Libby, 8*

> ⓔ
>
> My son is a star football player, but he never did it when he was young. You can take your child out to the backyard to toss around the football. At a young age, competition is not necessarily healthy. Your child's natural abilities will probably rise to the surface on their own. My son is a star player because of himself, not because we did something when he was little. Take the time to get to know your kid and who they are. When you do, the rest of it falls into place.
>
> —*Diana, mom of six children*

younger side, will the older kids overwhelm her? It is important that players of similar size, maturity, and skills are matched as opponents and the rules or play area should be adjusted for the age, ability, and size of the participants. For example, the basketball net should be lowered and the size of the soccer field reduced for younger players.

🐟 Physical and emotional maturity can vary greatly among children of the same age. If your child is physically much smaller than her peers, you may want to wait an extra year before beginning organized sports.

SPECIALIZING EARLY

🐟 In an age of such prodigies as Tiger Woods and Venus Williams, a common parental temptation is to find your child's strength early and focus on helping her to realize that potential to its fullest. However, having your child specialize early in a sport or activity has tremendous repercussions. Even if your child says she enjoys the concentrated focus, early specialization precludes trying other activities or sports, and can result in a complete lack of downtime.

🐟 The three-sport athlete is disappearing, to be replaced by the year-round specialist. Most elite teams go year-round, including summer training camps or programs. Summer sports specialty camps have proliferated for kids age 5 and older. To participate in even two competitive sports often involves incredible time-management skills and tough sacrifices for your child and family.

🐟 You may find yourself torn between allowing your child to specialize when she is younger and engaging her in numerous activities that build different skills. Most Olympic sports now try to identify future stars for specialized training before the end of fifth grade. Media coverage of sports, such as gymnastics, ice skating, and tennis, highlight very talented young athletes, and hold them up as models for others to follow.

✦ Let your child explore a myriad of options before settling on only one sport in which to specialize. By sampling and participating in a variety of diverse sports and activities, your child develops a wide range of skills, experience, interests, and passions. A key advantage to encouraging your child to diversify her interests is that

Trying to pigeonhole a child too early can be a mistake. Focusing intensely on a single activity deprives children of other meaningful experiences that can help shape their physical and emotional development.

> —Jerry Norton, director of Ponte Vedra Development Football League and youth coach for 36 years

I am a firm believer that kids should not even think about specializing until, perhaps, high school. Interests change quickly. Kids, for instance, become better soccer players by playing basketball, hockey or taking a gymnastics class, and taking a break over the winter helps avoid long-term burnout.

> —Ted Tye, president of Newton Girls' Soccer, coach for 13 years, and dad of an 18-year-old and 12-year-old twins.

I see kids pick up new sports all the time in middle school. So you can expose children to certain sports early, but realize those won't necessarily be the ones they choose to pursue later on. Some kids grow a foot in one year, and suddenly they're great basketball players. Many high-profile professional athletes, like Michael Jordan, got cut from their junior high and high school teams. Then there are kids like my son who took up cycling at age 14. He started out not being very good, but he kept getting a little bit better, and by his senior year he was the East Coast champion and just missed getting picked for the U.S. Cycling Team after training with them.

> —George Campbell, swimming program director for 20 years, middle school physical education director for 32 years, and dad of three grown kids

less success in one activity can be offset by more successes in others. Delaying an exclusive single-sport focus also helps ensure the opportunity for your child to pursue a sport that really interests her rather than fulfilling your or a coach's aspirations.

🔖 Children who participate in a variety of sports and specialize only after puberty tend to become more consistent and less injury-ridden athletes. Also, research indicates that the greater the number of sports a pre-adolescent child plays, the more she will succeed in a specific sport in later years.

🔖 Specializing early should not only be a matter of talent, but also really be about your child's passion for the activity. Through increased exposure, your child can pick and choose among what she likes best and what makes use of her talents and natural gifts. She'll have a comparative base, and her self-esteem and identity won't be wrapped up in one activity.

🔖 Keep in mind that for every young Olympic star, there are thousands of children who specialized in a sport at an early age, devoted vast amounts of leisure time to pursuing it during countless afternoons and weekends, and did not make the cut as they got older for elite and high school teams. Of the many kids who seem to be incredibly gifted at a sport or activity at age 6, very few will still stand out at age 11. Most early athletic prowess stems from how fast children physically develop, rather than core differences in inherent talent. When it seems that you have a talented child on your hands, the pressure mounts for you to encourage her to specialize in the activity. Yet when other kids start catching up around puberty, your child can feel that all the time and energy that she put into the sport hasn't paid off, or that she has failed to live up to the coach's or your expectations for greatness.

Aiming for a College Scholarship to Defray Tuition

🔖 The fact is that very few athletes end up going to college on a full or partial athletic scholarship, especially at the Division I level. Only 1 in 4 top elementary school athletes are standouts in high school. Of the 35 million kids participating in youth sports, only a small fraction will even make a college team. Fewer than 1% of the kids playing sports today will qualify for any kind of college athletic scholarship, according to the National Center for Educational Statistics.

🔖 Many children and parents feel crushed or angry if all the devoted years of athletic training doesn't result in a college scholarship. Many kids feel disappointed in themselves for not living up to their early potential. For others, the single-minded pursuit of one activity precluded them from developing other interests or exploring other areas of talent and passion.

My son, Jack, loves baseball and football, but he's going to have to choose between them. We're always being told by coaches how our son is highly "coachable" and has tremendous natural talent. Our son's unique, and I'm sure we have friends talking about us behind our back saying that we're angling for a professional athletic career, but I don't care. School ends at 2 p.m. and my son goes to bed at 9 p.m., so what's he going to do with all that time? He has playdates too, and we keep the focus on having fun. We think we'll start hearing from football coaches at private schools around eighth or ninth grade, and we're hoping that our son will have an advantage when it comes to applying to college and being scouted for scholarships. After all the time, effort, and money we've already invested, if my son doesn't get into a college on a sports scholarship or get drafted, I don't know what I'll do. But of course, it's impossible to know if he'll be as terrific at 19 as he is at 9 and still be the big fish in the small pond.

  —*Leslie, mom of Alexandra, 10, and Jack, 9*

If a parent is worried about college, they should take all the money that they would spend on travel sports in the hopes that their child gets a college scholarship, invest it, and by the time their child gets to college, they will have more than enough.

  —*Jeffrey Sanderson, youth soccer coach for 12 years*

I have a friend whose son's entire focus in life has been basketball. It's all he's ever done sportswise, and he just found out that he didn't make the high school varsity team. He's depressed and feels that all those years of effort and sacrifice to solely focus on basketball weren't worth it. His parents are devastated. The scary thing is that this could happen to any of our kids who have thrown themselves entirely into one pursuit.

  —*Anonymous*

The Possibility of a Professional Sports Career

✤ Keep your secret hopes for your child's professional or Olympic career in perspective. Early participation in organized youth sports is not necessarily a launching pad for pro athletes. The Center for the Study of Sports in Society at Northeastern University has calculated that only 1 in 12,000 high school athletes will become a

Salaries for professional athletes have skyrocketed in the past 20 years, and a sports career now represents a potential Golden Egg, even though the probability of an individual's ultimate success is minimal. The lure of lucrative college scholarships also drives parents and their athletic children to participate, excel, win, and be recognized in a sport or multiple sports. In search of the elusive championship, today's youth sports teams practice four or five times a week, several hours a day. In the case of a potentially elite athlete, the time spent practicing can be far greater than rewards and the costs astronomical for specialty coaches and facilities.

—*Jerry Norton, director of Ponte Vedra Development Football League and youth coach for 36 years*

My kids have never shown prodigy tendencies, and even if they had, I'm not sure I would have been interested in pursuing that. I've always wanted normal kids. I never thought I'd have Olympians or kids performing at Carnegie Hall. So it's not on my radar screen. For me, activities are about being active, well rounded, balanced, and having friends with whom my children can connect.

—*Claire, mom of Ben, 14, Alison, 11, and Danny, 8*

If your child has talent and enjoys the activity, then go for it. My oldest is the best squash player in the world, and in order to do this, he gave up competing in all other sports by age 12 and stopped school at 16. But he speaks two languages fluently, has traveled many times to all corners of the world, and is very financially secure.

—*John Power, head coach of men's and women's squash at Dartmouth, coaching for 25 years*

Parents worry too much about their kids being superstars. The odds are so remote, perhaps one in a million, that your kids will become professional. You just can't run your life around this outside possibility.

—*Sheri, mom of Allison, 11, and Eric, 9*

professional in any sport. It's statistically more difficult to become an Olympic athlete than a brain surgeon.

Starting Early Often Means Burning Out Early

🦅 If you push your child into organized sports too soon, you run the risk of injury, burnout, or turning your child off altogether to something she may otherwise have loved when she was older.

🦅 Having started soccer or baseball at 4, many kids have had it by age 12 and walk off the field in protest.

CHOOSING SUBJECTIVELY VS. OBJECTIVELY JUDGED SPORTS

🦅 Another factor to consider with competitive sports is how they are judged. Some, such as gymnastics, diving, or figure skating, involve subjective evaluation and rating by judges.

🦅 Others offer more concrete ways of measuring success, such as your time in swimming or the number of goals scored in soccer, with subjective calls coming up only in officials' or referees' decisions, such as a false start or a penalty.

🦅 Your child's tolerance level for subjective decisions over which she does not have control should factor into your activity considerations as well.

Ben loved karate, doing it with this great little group of friends who all progressed quickly through their belts together. They came up in a fairly short time for their junior black belt test. The teacher said that in order to get ready, they had to go to the karate studio five times a week for a month prior to the test. Each session of training lasted two hours. Ben made himself sick doing it, coming one night nauseated and stressed that he wouldn't make it, and having to stay up late at night to get his homework done. One of his best friends cried in the middle of the test because it was so intense. Once Ben made junior black belt, in order to continue, the instructor required him to take two karate classes plus one private lesson a week. I complained to the teacher that these kids were only 8 years old and that Ben would have to give up all the other things he was doing to keep that schedule. The teacher said, "That's right." I think it's inappropriate for a child that age to specialize so early. Ben doesn't do karate anymore and neither does a single one of his friends. It became too intense and stopped being fun. The lesson I took away from all this was that the teacher pushed them too hard. Otherwise, Ben would still be doing karate and enjoying it.

—Janine, mom of Ben, 10, and Andrew, 7

The great thing about competitive swimming is that you can measure how you're doing objectively, as it's based simply on your times swum during meets or competitions. This is quite a contrast to sports like soccer where you can't necessarily tell who is doing the best. In subjectively judged sports, the person who's always hogging the ball gets recognized as the star, while they might not really be the best person on the team or the one contributing most to the goals scored.

—Margy Halloran, swim team coach for 4 years and competitive collegiate swimmer

TEAM VS. INDIVIDUAL SPORTS

How do you decide whether a team or individual sport is right for your child? While some kids adore team sports and thrive on camaraderie, others gravitate to and prefer individually driven activities. Ideally, your child will have a chance to participate in both.

Children should do both team and individual sports at some time in childhood. Team sports are great because they teach kids how to get along with others and work for a common goal. Individual sports are wonderful because they teach kids that they can achieve success on their own.

—Stephanie Doyle, varsity women's sailing coach, University of South Florida, and youth coach for 10 years

Team Sports

Team sports offer your child the social opportunity of being with friends and meeting new ones. They also enable kids to work on interpersonal relationship building, cooperation with others, and developing conflict-resolution skills. In team sports, everyone is working together toward a common goal.

In a team environment, there is less pressure on individual performance, as success or failure does not ride on your child's shoulders alone. Many kids thrive on the support and encouragement that team sports can provide.

Learning to be a member of a team is often hard for children, as it involves placing team goals ahead of personal ones. Suddenly things such as "hogging the ball" instead of passing become detrimental to the team's success. In a team sport, a child is part of a group of athletes striving for a common goal, and the interests of the team are set above those of the individual player. Team sports teach kids how to think "we" instead of "me."

✦ The majority of children will not have an opportunity beyond high school to play major team sports, so you may want to encourage your child to play at least one organized team sport in elementary school.

Individual Sports

✦ Individual sports, such as gymnastics, singles tennis, martial arts, and horseback riding attract children who would rather rely on themselves than others and are very self-motivated. Your child can measure her progress by skill acquisition, striving for a personal best, and through head-to-head competition with others.

✦ In contrast to team sports, the spotlight is on individual performance, and there is no one else to blame for losing. Because your child's own performance determines successes and failures, the pressure accompanying individual performances overwhelms some kids.

✦ While some kids don't like the loner part of individual sports and prefer the camaraderie with other kids on a team, there are many instances where individual sports are

Team and individual sports are different animals. All sports teach determination, perseverance, courage, critical thinking, emotional self-control, accepting defeat, and being a gracious winner. However, team sports also teach cooperation, trust in your teammates, responsibility and dependability, loyalty, and teamwork.

—Ray Lokar, head basketball coach at Bishop Amat High School, coaching for over 25 years

I want my girls to learn to be team players, as I think it's an important skill in life, family, business, and social situations. Part of this means teaching your child to realize that individual accomplishment in that setting is secondary to that of team. I tell the girls on the soccer and basketball teams I coach never to do anything better for yourself if it's not better for your team. We have incidents where one girl might get mad at another girl on the team, and we spend a lot of time working on how to get along socially.

—Cliff, soccer coach for 5 years and dad of Rachel, 10, Amanda, 8, and Jenny, 1

My husband and I both feel strongly that team sports instill values and training for life that you don't get in individual sports. They teach good sportsmanship. For instance, our son plays defense on his soccer team, which is not a great position because he doesn't get to score many goals, but he understands his importance to the team.

—Leslie, mom of Alexandra, 10, and Jack, 9

Individual sports give you a more limited set of excuses for failure. No coach calls the plays; nobody else can fumble. You win and lose by your own efforts.

> —*Rick Foley, Elmwood Center director and chief instructor in tae kwon do and hapkido, teaching for 26 years*

These days very few sports are true individual sports. For example, many high schools have varsity golf, tennis, and swimming. Even though the athlete may be on her own in the pool, she is still part of a team.

> —*Neil Becker, high school spring, softball coach, coaching for 7 years*

Both my kids shy away from competition with other kids, and my son isn't a particularly big risk taker, so they both are much better suited to individual sports. Competition against other kids tends to undermine my son's confidence, since he is not especially athletic.

> —*Brenda, mom of Madeline, 11, and Bernard, 8*

practiced in a team environment. For example, individual sports, such as swimming, ice skating, gymnastics, archery, and golf, use team scoring at the youth competition level to create a team environment.

🍂 Another benefit of individual sports, such as golf, tennis, skiing, running, cycling, and swimming, is that they more easily extend into adult years.

RECREATIONAL VS. ELITE TEAMS

🍂 Relatively early in your child's sport career, you may find yourself dealing with the issue of playing on a recreational versus a competitive or "elite" team, as well as with the intensity that often accompanies the tryout and selection process for the elite teams.

🍂 Recreational teams or leagues tend to be low-key, with children of varying skill levels playing side by side. There are also usually team policies making sure that every child plays a significant portion of the games so that bench warming rarely becomes an issue.

❧ Starting around age 8 or 9, many towns or programs form "elite" teams for the best athletes in an age group. This is done in order to raise the level of competition and group children with similar skills for more advanced training.

❧ Keep in mind that skill levels can change dramatically as kids approach and go through puberty. Especially during the developmental ages from 8 to 14, one season can make a huge difference. A child may have a bad experience in the season, such as not having fun or playing on a team where she's not challenged or developing new skills. In addition, kids' bodies change so rapidly that the best players can become mediocre and the mediocre ones excel. The intense competition in many youth sports begins at the age when many children are still struggling to master a sport's fundamentals.

Recreational Teams

❧ A recreational team competes primarily within its own community, and the emphasis remains squarely on your child's having a good time, getting to participate in games, improving her sportsmanship, learning skills and game fundamentals, and fostering a love for the sport.

❧ Recreational teams do not hold tryouts. In most recreational leagues, policies mandate that all players play at least one half of each game and there is very little travel, just local games and usually practice once a week at most.

❧ Volunteer coaches are almost always the parents of children on the team.

My son is still playing recreational soccer in sixth grade, and loves it. He has no interest in anything more competitive. He arranges all the rides himself and loves hanging with his friends.

—*Sylvia, mom of Max, 13, and Kate and Zoe, 10*

My daughter has always been much more of an art kid than a sports kid. She wasn't too interested in organized sports until fourth and fifth grade, when other girls started doing intramural sports and she got drawn into their team spirit. None of the girls were jocks. They just like playing soccer, basketball, and softball with their friends. Now Alie plays soccer pretty well, but faces the last year of intramural soccer in our town and has the choice to join a travel team or stop. The system is set up for a much more competitive environment that doesn't interest my kids. For kids who just want to play recreationally, it's a much more difficult road to navigate.

—*Claire, mom of Ben, 14, Alison, 11, and Danny, 8*

Our daughter began playing soccer in second grade with all the other little girls in town. She had amazing natural talent and loved the game. There was some pressure to put her on a more competitive team, but we felt that sports for little kids should be about fun and friends first, sportswomanship second, with skill and proficiency way down on the list. By sixth grade she was getting frustrated when some of the kids in the town team were losing interest and not giving the game their best effort, so we let her join another, more serious and more advanced "club" team. But she still plays on her original team, for friendship's sake.

—*Nancy, mom of Hallie, 14, and Tessa, 10*

Playing Up with an Older Age Group

🌼 If your child is big for her age or shows a strong talent in a particular sport, you may want or the coach may suggest that she play in a level higher than her grade or age group. (Conversely, in rare circumstances, a coach or you may want your child to play with younger children because she is a beginner and needs to work more on fundamentals.)

🌼 This issue of "playing up" starts to present itself in the early elementary grade years, and while flattering to your child's ego as well as your own, the decision merits careful consideration.

🌼 Your child may lose the confidence and leadership skills that come with being one of the strongest players on an age-appropriate team.

Travel, Select, or Elite Competitive Teams

🌼 If your child gets serious about a sport, she will likely join a club or traveling team. These private leagues or "elite" teams offer higher levels of coaching and competition, but often entail a substantial commitment level in terms of playing a sport for more than one season or even year-round, as well as higher costs for coaching and traveling. An offer for your child to join one of these select teams or programs is difficult to resist, as both your child and you will be flattered and it gives your child a chance to stand out from her peers.

🌼 A travel team organization provides competition among teams from neighboring communities, other states, and sometimes even other countries. Players at this level already possess above-average skill, so time is now spent honing skills and learning tactical play in a very competitive atmosphere.

🦋 Your child may be a candidate for a competitive travel team if she has excellent athletic ability and speed, wants to improve her game with more practices and games, and possesses a desire to play in higher levels of competition.

🦋 Keep in mind that travel teams usually do not guarantee playing time for your child.

🦋 The commitment required for most select teams includes practice two or three times per week before and during the season for approximately 90 minutes per session. Be sure to ask about practice schedules before committing to a team. Some teams even reduce playing time for a player who misses practices or is consistently late.

🦋 Travel leagues are generally grouped by age (under age 10, under 12 or 13, and so on) with a set cutoff date for all age groups. These leagues are usually locally based, organized by town or city, and some teams stay together for an entire year.

🦋 Teams are divided into levels within the travel teams, and different-level teams play in different competitive divisions (Division I being the highest, then Division II, and so on). Teams are assigned to divisions based on the track record of the team or prior year's team from that town or league.

🦋 Teams bring in outside expert players or coaches to enhance training by volunteer coaches (who have mostly played competitive sports up to the college level, and often continue to play in adult leagues).

🦋 Variants between recreational and competitive travel teams exist in different parts of the country, some with less travel, some with more open enrollment and mixture of skill levels.

🦋 For travel teams, ask:
- What will the costs be, and what do those fees cover (tournaments, uniforms, coaching fees, travel expenses for coaches)?
- How much travel will there be to out-of-town games or tournaments, and how far away will they be?
- What criteria will be used to select players, and how are tryouts run?

With the travel teams, the sports suddenly shift from years of being a democracy, where all kids get equal playing time and rotate positions, to a meritocracy, where the better kids get more coaching time and more play time.

—*Ron, nationally licensed youth soccer coach and dad of two, ages 10 and 8*

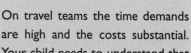

On travel teams the time demands are high and the costs substantial. Your child needs to understand that as the levels increase, so do the expectations.

—*Nat Gonzalez, men's head soccer coach, University of California Riverside, for 13 years*

We have struggled with competitive sports, as my experience over the years has been that you're picked for the elite teams either because you're extremely talented or you have extremely pushy parents. But if a kid's just above average, he can easily get lost in the sauce because his parents weren't pushing anything. For instance, with soccer travel teams, kids get tracked way before they need to, and who gets selected for what team becomes a political hotbed among the parents. I'm amazed by the mean-spiritedness and hypocrisy of it. What's it all about? I felt so disgusted with the scene with Ben that I didn't go there with Alison. It's just not worth getting hyper about all these activities.

—*Claire, mom of Ben, 14, Alison, 11, and Danny, 8*

> ∼ Will there be a second round of tryouts?
> ∼ How soon will people be notified about team placements after the tryouts?
> ∼ How many seasons will the team stay together?
> ∼ How often, when, and where will the team practice?
> ∼ Are there any team obligations during the "off season"?

Elite Team Tryouts

🦋 Competitive tryouts involve coaches selecting team members after watching them go through a variety of drills or competitive play in games. For towns with a lot of kids trying out, this process often involves multiple tryout sessions. A process of elimination takes place in the first session in order to make it into the second round. It also involves some hard, subjective decisions by coaches.

🦋 Once a child makes one team, it's easier for her to make the next cut, so the first team your child tries out for is critical.

🦋 If a child gets cut or doesn't make a team, she is often discouraged and drops the sport. Remind your child that stories abound of middle-of-the-road young athletes who went on to excel in their high school years and beyond. Their enjoyment of the game kept them interested and improving during critical years of the game, while their more skilled peers may have lost interest.

🦋 Keep in mind that it's often incredibly difficult for even the more experienced coaches to differentiate among all the children who show up for the tryouts. Coaches can often easily spot the best and the least advanced 10%, but attempting to discriminate among the middle 80% is almost impossible.

✦ Ask in advance about what coaches will be looking for in a player and the commitment you and your child need to make if she makes the team.

✦ For programs that make "cuts," it is important for your child to know in ad-

Elite team tryouts are just that. They are for the elite players and they are team tryouts. That means that the coach already has a team in place and is usually looking to fill a few positional slots. Try to find out what positions they need before the tryouts. You could save yourself a lot of time and aggravation. Also, once players have made the roster of an elite team, they must continually improve or they may be cut at subsequent tryouts. These teams are designed for the players that want to compete at a very high level.

—Owen Boyd, youth soccer coach for 15 years

My daughter didn't make our town's travel soccer team in their first round of tryouts, which was really disappointing and hard for her. But I pointed out to her that she hadn't really practiced to make the team. My daughter's not a natural soccer player, and I've found as a coach that very, very few kids are naturally gifted. I had told her that most kids who made a team spend their time practicing in the backyard or on the weekend. So she set herself the goal of trying to make it onto a travel soccer team at the next set of tryouts six months later, and spent time with me practicing in the field near our house. Just this week she found out that she made a team. I thought that the whole experience had been a great life lesson for her. It was something not that important in life, but terribly important to her, and she was able to put hard work into it and achieve her goals.

—Cliff, soccer coach for 5 years and dad of Rachel, 10, Amanda, 8, and Jenny, 1

The elite team tryouts in our town left me feeling angry, as there was tremendous unfairness in team selections. My daughter was consistently better in her ball-handling skill than many who made the travel teams, but it all came down to parent politics. Playing in the recreational league this year, she has clearly lost skills, not being challenged. It has been a horrible year for her from a skill perspective and very disappointing, as it felt like a waste of play. I finally took her out of the league and got her a private coach. It's very hard not to get worked up about it.

—Anonymous

vance that she may not make a team. This can be tough for your child to handle, and for this reason consider carefully how she will handle this before sending her to try out.

BENCH WARMING

My son isn't going to make the elite soccer teams in our town. I feel sad for him in that he knows he won't make the cut. It bums him out when he gets sidelined during the games, though he handles it as well as he can and feels happy when his team wins. There are times when I see him sitting there with his head between his legs, never getting put in during the games' more competitive moments, and I feel so bad for him. For his intramural soccer team (which should not have been competitive), Ben's coach played him only about a quarter of the time. He justified his decisions by telling Ben, "Sorry, but it's really important that we win. I'll put you in the next game." In the second half of the championship game, they needed a replacement goalie, and when the coach asked for volunteers, Ben immediately raised his hand. This was an incredible high-stakes risk, as he had never played goalie before. My heart was pounding out of my chest because I was so concerned he would go from feeling bad to worse. He gave it his all, performed well, and we were so proud of him for taking the chance.

—Janine, mom of Ben, 10, and Andrew, 7

✦ Every child likes to play, and resents time sitting on the sidelines. Sitting on the bench watching the stronger players can cause frustration and dwindling self-confidence in your child. Plus, when your child feels unwanted, it's easy for you to feel protective, frustrated, or angry.

✦ Clarify the participation philosophy of each youth sports program you are considering. The reality is that in some sports programs, a child who isn't among the best players will find herself watching from the sidelines more than she and you would like. Other coaches may bench your child for missing a scheduled practice or making a mistake.

✦ While a youth coach will usually allow each child under age 12 equal playing time, starting with kids as young as age 8, many youth sports coaches adopt the philosophy of "play the best and bench the rest." Coaches have their own biases.

✦ Ideally, your child's coach keeps track of how much each child is playing and in what positions during games. But if you or your child feel she isn't getting a fair amount of playing time, it's worth talking to the coach. You can open the discussion with the coach by asking, "How can my child improve her game so that she can get more time on the field?"

✦ If your town or club team has different levels of competition for the same age group, encourage your child to play in a program that

> The single biggest topic of discussion between upset parents and coaches is playing time. If you have an issue with your child's playing time, take a step back and give it some time before addressing it. As a coach, I always try hard to balance individual development with the success of the team. Many parents who voice playing-time concerns see their child's talent level through rose-colored glasses. In short, while you should look out for the best interests of your child, try to be patient and level-headed about playing time.
>
> —*Rich Janor, Wheatland Travel Baseball Club coach for 5 years*

matches her skill level and passion about the sport. Getting your child to play on a team with more skilled or older players could relegate her to the bench during highly competitive games.

WHAT TO DO WHEN YOUR CHILD HATES SPORTS

✦ Organized youth sports have become so embedded in our culture that a child who doesn't participate seems to be missing out on a crucial part of life.

✦ Yet some children simply aren't interested in sports. Fortunately, many alternative ways to keep fit and active are available. As long as your child does not become sedentary and gets some exercise, there's no reason to worry if she resists joining organized sports activities.

✦ Before giving up on sports, make sure first that you understand the motivations behind your child's resistance to organized teams. If she's simply not interested, that's one thing, but if she's resistant because she fears competition or is worried about being made fun of or has low self-esteem in that area, you need to encourage her to tackle those fears. See pages 113–117 on reasons why kids want to quit.

✦ Encourage your child instead to take up lifelong activities like cycling, rollerblading, dance, horseback riding, running, swimming, strength training, martial arts, yoga, tennis, or hiking. These are all activities that can promote fitness on an individual, noncompetitive level.

✦ Even if your child never belongs to a sports team, there are many other activities, such as after-school clubs, school and volunteer activities, band or singing

My son Danny's not much of an athlete. But he found his way into rock climbing and karate. For him, these activities let him feel good about himself, get a little exercise, and to do them, he doesn't need to be supercoordinated.

—*Claire, mom of Ben, 14, Alison, 11, and Danny, 8*

My middle child doesn't like athletics, so I'm not forcing him. He's my brainiac—he taught himself to read, loves math, but he has two left feet. He would be out on the soccer field looking at all the bugs, and it made no sense at all to him why he should be chasing a little ball on the field.

—*Karen, mom of Josh, 7, Dalton, 5, and Alexa, 3*

I have a nephew who lives in South Africa who, as an adolescent, was obsessed with cricket but had no skill at all when it came to playing. Instead, he got trained as a referee, which he thought was fabulous. At age 13, he became the youngest referee of adult cricket games in South African history, and it goes to show that supporting your kids' desires is huge.

—*Amy, mom of Sacha, 11, and Libby, 8*

groups, acting or debating groups, and community service that can teach your child teamwork and cooperation.

NEED FOR PHYSICAL EXERCISE: THE CULTURE OF OBESITY

Obesity in Children: Why You Should Be Concerned

🐟 We are raising a generation of couch potatoes. Obesity has emerged as a serious and growing childhood disease. The statistics are both astonishing and alarming: About 25% of all U.S. children are seriously overweight, and 15% are obese. The Harvard School of Public Health found there are 11 million obese children between the ages of 6 and 11 alone, an increase of 54% over the last 40 years.

❧ Severely overweight children face a 70% likelihood of becoming obese as adults, which raises the risk of diabetes, high blood pressure, heart disease, stroke, and certain forms of cancer. Obesity may also negatively impact children's relationships with their peers. Research shows that overweight kids ages 6 and older tend to get excluded from social groups, have fewer friends, are less involved with extracurricular activities, are more depressed, and have lower self-esteem than their peers.

❧ According to the Academy of Pediatrics, only 2% of the 18 million schoolchildren taking the President's Physical Fitness Test were physically fit enough to receive the award. Fitness tests given recently in California found only 1 in 5 students (grades 5, 7, and 9) met their fitness standards for cardiorespiratory endurance, muscular strength, muscular endurance, flexibility, and body composition.

❧ A recent study by the Harvard School of Public Health showed that 70% of kids are out of shape, while 90% of parents are convinced that their child is fit.

❧ The statistics get worse, since children's physical activity levels decline sharply as they approach adolescence: 30% of high school students do not get regular cardiovascular exercise; 44% do not even take a physical education class, thanks to reduced physical education programs in schools.

❧ According to the National Association for Sport and Physical Education, children between the ages of 5 and 12 should be physically active on most days of the week, with a recommendation of at least 30 minutes of daily physical activity, including 10- to 15-minute bursts of moderate to vigorous activity.

What's Causing the Increased Obesity?

❧ Lack of physical activity is the number one reason kids become overweight. Many children simply don't get enough physical activity to burn off the calories they consume. When your child spends her time sitting at a desk in school, sitting in front of the television or a computer, and at a table doing homework at night, it's not time spent doing exercise. Plus, most kids now take a bus or are driven to school instead of walking or riding their bikes. Even getting to activities involves being chauffeured around.

❧ Your child will burn an average of 60 calories in an hour of watching TV, while playing and running around outside will burn over 200 calories.

❧ Poor eating habits also contribute to the obesity epidemic. We are eating more fast-food meals and takeout food, which are high in fat, sugar, and overall calories. The U.S. Department of Agriculture estimates that restaurant meals are 20% higher in total fat content and 15% higher in saturated fat than those prepared at home. Today more than one-third of the calories consumed every day come from food purchased outside the home, almost double the amount 30 years ago. Restaurant portions and packaged foods also come in much larger portions now, and most people still eat the entire plate served, according to an American Institute for Cancer Research restaurant survey.

🍀 TV commercials encourage your child to snack on junk food. Research has found that children who view four or more hours of television each day have greater body fat and mass than those who viewed less than two hours a day.

Ways to Curtail Obesity in Your Child

🍀 Even when you're in a rush, avoid the temptation to whisk your child into a fast-food restaurant for food on the go or to pick up fast food for dinner at home. Instead, pick up a quick-fix cookbook for recipes that are fast and easy to make, like sandwiches or stir-fries.

🍀 Provide low-fat, low-sugar, and low-calorie nutritious snacks and meals. Encourage your child to eat slowly. Rather than telling your child not to eat something, don't buy it for your home. Instead, keep healthy snacks accessible, such as fresh or dried fruit, graham crackers, cereal, or yogurt.

🍀 Don't resort to nagging, criticizing, or humiliating your child in an effort to inspire her to lose weight.

🍀 Encourage your child to be physically active in some way every day. Select fun activities that allow your child to support her body weight and keep her moving.

🍀 Consult with a physician or registered dietitian for a guided weight-loss program that also helps modify your child's eating habits.

Role Modeling: Be Physically Active Yourself

🍀 Your attitude toward exercise will largely influence how your child feels about exercising.

🍀 Get your own act into gear. The best way to inspire your child to be physically active is to make exercise a priority in your own life. If your child sees that you enjoy exercise, she'll be motivated to follow in your footsteps.

🍀 Leave the dishes in the sink, the laundry in the dryer, and go for a walk as a family after dinner.

🍀 Find family activities that involve exercising together, such as a bike ride or swimming outings in the summer.

✦ Go outside in the fall and rake leaves together—give your little one a child-size rake to help along.

✦ Plan vacations and outings that include some exercise, and focus on taking up a family hobby, be that skiing, tennis, or hiking, that gets everyone outside doing something fun together.

✦ Starting in elementary school, pick one exercise- or fitness-related gift for your child's birthdays: from a starting tennis racket to a mini-trampoline to a new baseball or softball mitt you can try out together.

CONSIDERATIONS FOR YOUR ATHLETIC DAUGHTER

Title IX and Girls in Sports Today

✦ Since the passage of Title IX in 1972, which requires institutions receiving federal funding to provide equal athletic opportunity for both sexes, the number of girls playing sports has gone from 1 in 25 to 1 in 3, while boys' participation level of 1 out of every 2 has remained the same.

✦ Girls now account for 44% of all members of school-age sports teams. Some 11.4 million girls ages 6–17 (48% of all girls) are members of an organized team, compared to 14.8 million boys (59% of all boys).

✦ Girls now engage in athletics in record numbers and women athletes enjoy more attention than ever before. Today, record numbers of women are competing in the Olympics and much attention is focused on the U.S. Women's Soccer team or the new Women's National Basketball Association.

✦ The President's Council on Physical Fitness and Sport Positives found that sport participation enhances girls' body image, self-esteem, and confidence. It also concluded from its research that sports participation enables girls to achieve more academic success, score higher on tests, have better mental health, experience less depression, and have a greater lifetime earning potential. Girls who play sports are more likely to turn away from risky behavior, being 92% less likely to get involved with drugs and 80% less likely to have an unwanted pregnancy.

Tips to Avoid Gender Stereotyping

❦ Don't let gender interfere with your child's desire to participate in the sport of her choice. Girls can be as tough as boys in football or hockey, while boys can excel in gymnastics, dance, and figure skating.

❦ Society's conceptions of gender strongly influence the way girls feel about physical activity. Whether your daughter wants to take part in an activity is largely determined by whether it is considered to be "gender appropriate." Society not only teaches that girls and boys are different, but also that they are opposite. This "gender opposition" teaches that if boys are one thing—more aggressive or more athletic—then girls must be the other.

❦ Don't characterize activities as either "girls' sports" or "boys' sports." That being said, acknowledge that a select few sports still remain predominately separated by sex. Baseball is mostly played by boys; softball by girls. Football is still a male sport, whereas a few sports, like synchronized swimming, rhythmic gymnastics, and field hockey, are only for female athletes.

Same-Sex vs. Coed Sports Teams

❦ Before puberty, boys and girls tend to be equivalent in size, weight, strength, endurance, and speed. For this reason they are usually equally matched when playing sports together. Skill, agility, and coordination serve as the primary differentiators between children at this age, but local teams still often separate children by sex starting in their earliest years.

❦ After puberty, boys gain an advantage in terms of both strength and size, and this can also create safety concerns. For this reason, the American Academy of Pediatrics recommends that boys and girls over 12 years of age should no longer compete against each other, particularly in contact and collision sports.

❦ After age 13, boys overall become taller, heavier, faster, stronger, bigger, and more powerful than girls due to testosterone. When these physical differences manifest themselves in boys, think carefully about coed contact and collision sports before enrolling your daughter.

❦ Ultimately, your child is best off in a league playing with kids of comparable abilities. If your daughter's skill level parallels that of players on a coed team, then it's probably the better choice for her, assuming that the coed option appeals to her. Some girls find it easier in same-sex situations to take the initiative as a leader, and feel more comfortable learning new skills.

When Your Daughter Wants to Play on the Boys' Team

🐾 The two main reasons that girls want to play organized sports with boys are that there is no organized girls' league for a particular sport, or the existing girls' league has inferior resources and facilities. This often occurs under age 12 in team sports such as soccer, baseball, and basketball.

🐾 Gauge your child's comfort level, and let that be your guide. She may not want to take on the challenge of overcoming a gender barrier. She may also feel intimidated, particularly if teased, bullied, or ignored by boys whose masculinity is threatened by having a girl on their team. A lot of boys cannot accept the fact that girls may be able to outperform them, and will laugh at mistakes or sit in stony silence if outplayed by a girl.

🐾 For these reasons, if your daughter decides that this is what she wants to do, she will need your support and positive encouragement. You and your child will also need to sit down for a discussion with the coach to solicit his input and to ensure his support and help. If a coach is opposed to your daughter joining the team, she will likely find herself discouraged and humiliated during the season.

🐾 Also, make sure that your daughter's skills are such that she can maintain an equal footing with the boys and that she will thrive on the competitive atmosphere. For some girls, playing on a boys' team instills confidence in that they can keep up with the boys both physically and psychologically.

🐾 Once your child reaches puberty, most girls choose to switch over completely and compete only against girls.

This spring my eight-year-old daughter will be playing boys' soccer because she's too young to try out for the girls' travel soccer team, and she is not getting enough competition on the girls' intramural teams. She wanted to try it for one spring season, as a couple of her friends are doing it, and one little girl who did it last fall found herself thriving in the middle of the pack on the boys' team.

—Bridgitt, mom of Taylor, 10, Connor and Chloe, 8, and Brian, 6

My daughter insisted on signing up for Little League baseball instead of softball, which a couple of older girls in our neighborhood have done. I explained to her that she'd be the only girl on the team, but she declared, "That's okay. That's what I want to do!" I was struck by what a big change this was for her to be pursuing what she wants to do instead of just what's social and allows her be with her friends.

—Lisa, mom of CJ, 10, and Maddie, 8

Girls Dropping Out of Sports Entirely Around Puberty

✦ Encourage your daughter to stick with sports during puberty, between ages 11 and 14, as these are the ages when most girls walk around them.

✦ It is typical for girls starting in early adolescence to drop out of sports and become more sedentary. By age 14, girls drop out of sports at a rate six times higher than boys. The primary reason this takes place is that girls become preoccupied with sorting out who they are during puberty, and many start to consider sports unfeminine or fear that it is viewed as such by their peers whom they are trying to impress. For those girls who have developed athletic passions, the connection to the sports will endure through this transitional period.

SPORTS FOR YOUR SPECIAL NEEDS CHILD

✦ Many children with special needs are faced with a sense of frustration and failure at school, so it's important to pick physical activities in which they can feel successful and good about themselves. It's also critical because, statistically, as children with disabilities get older, they tend to decrease their physical activity levels, reaching a peak between ages 10 and 12 and then declining through adolescence and adulthood.

✦ Discuss with a program's teacher or coach whether there's a good match, and enable the teachers to be more effective by knowing about your child's issues. Ask how much of an issue your child's special needs will be, both in terms of your child feeling frustrated or disrupting the program or class. If your child has a chronic illness, find ways for her to participate so she does not always feel overprotected, sheltered, and lacking in independence.

✦ Many sports have modified forms and adaptations, along with special leagues. The term "adapted sport" refers to a sport that is modified or created to meet the unique needs of individuals with disabilities, either with able-bodied participants or in sepa-

One of my twins lost most of his hearing at four months old with meningitis. He wears hearing aids, knows sign language, and it turns out that he's incredibly athletic and better than most of the kids on his soccer team. We taught the coaches some basic sign language to help them communicate with him when he's on the field. Of course, there was one time that an opposing coach thought these were unfair signals for secret moves!

—*Diana, mom of six children*

rate environments. Numerous organizations now enable disabled athletes to participate, with the largest ones highlighted in the resource section in Chapter 10.

My son has ADHD, and he gets overwrought and exhausted if he has too many things going on. He also has very limited interests. We haven't found much in terms of activities that really interest him, and to be honest, this has been very disconcerting to my husband and me, as we can't help but have anxiety about how he's going to get into a good college if he has no interests.

—*Anonymous*

David has a congenital bone deformity that prevents him from holding his hand out, so things like baseball, because it involves a glove, or doing piano, aren't physically possible. So soccer has been great.

—*Elizabeth, mom of Robert, 15, and David, 10*

I have learned as a parent of a child with special needs to focus on what your child can do. Take your child everywhere, and get her involved in regular activities. As time goes on, you see the disability less and less. Amy is just Amy.

—*Rochelle, mom of Chris, 21, Erika, 16, and Amy, 13*

Choosing the Right Sport for Your Child

KIDS WHO EXCEL

✦ All sports and activities require passion, interest, and commitment to be successful. Many kids who are highly motivated, determined, dedicated, and hardworking eventually surpass their peers with more "raw talent." Many kids who are primarily doing an activity due to parents' pressure eventually burn out and drop out.

✦ Again and again, coaches talk about the determination to succeed, perseverance, supportive parents, and positive reinforcement and feedback. They also agree that the kids who excel are the ones who are willing to listen and follow directions, are open to feedback, and who do not get frustrated easily. These kids have what they call "great coachability."

Those who excel are resilient, desire to be better, set goals for themselves, and want to play at the next level.

—*Randy Watt, youth softball coach for 26 years*

Kids who excel have a love and passion for the game. I see children drop out because they have unrealistic expectations, thinking that with a little practice they will be hitting the ball like the pros they see on TV and not recognizing that becoming an accomplished tennis player takes years of diligent practice. It is important for coaches and parents to emphasize the long-term learning process more than immediate results and to create a learning environment where a child can experience and celebrate small successes along the way toward more lofty goals.

    —Timothy Smith, director of junior tennis at Longwood Cricket Club and codirector of New England Academy of Tennis, teaching for 18 years

Successful athletes have an inordinate desire to excel, are competitive by nature, demonstrate a willingness to work harder than their opponents, and take risks in order to be successful. Most important, they enjoy the process and don't focus solely on the end result.

    —Heather Lewis, head field hockey coach at Bucknell University, coaching for 17 years

Kids who excel at individual sports are internally motivated and enjoy competing against themselves as well as others.

    —Jan Brogan, head coach women's tennis, University of California, Berkeley, teaching for 25 years

GENERAL SPORTS BENEFITS

Physical Benefits of Exercise

Regular physical activity in children can:

- counter factors contributing to heart disease and strokes in adulthood, like obesity, high blood pressure, and poor cholesterol levels
- lower the risk of chronic diseases such as hypertension, Type II diabetes, cardiovascular disease, osteoporosis, and certain cancers
- boost your child's immune system

- increase bone density
- increase cardiovascular fitness, endurance, and muscular strength
- improve flexibility, coordination, and balance
- hone large and small motor skills including hand-eye coordination
- boost energy levels and improve sleep patterns
- inspire physical confidence and instill future exercise habits

Psychological and Emotional Benefits

Playing sports also includes many psychological payoffs. It can:

- build self-esteem, self-image, and confidence
- alleviate feelings of depression and anxiety and create an emotional outlet for stress, tension, aggression, or other pent-up emotions
- instill the value of self-discipline, commitment, sportsmanship, teamwork, loyalty, resilience, perseverance, hard work, goal-setting, practice, determination, and personal responsibility
- demonstrate how to handle failure and overcome adversity

Athletics are person builders. Every positive value needed for success in later life can be developed through a young person's involvement in sports. Hard work, discipline, striving for attainable and far-reaching goals, enduring setbacks, dealing with sudden success, dealing with unexpected failure, and many other core values are taught and reinforced daily.

—*Daryl Hayes, high school head wrestling coach for 9 years*

Last season was one my son will never forget, the sort that a parent always hopes their child will experience sometime. He was on a baseball team that won the state championship, and played a tournament in another state while living in the college dorms. He learned about teamwork, sacrifices, friendships, and bonded with the team, since they played together every day for almost 6 months.

—*Nancy, mom of a son age 13*

Social Benefits

To be a successful athlete, your child will develop:

- self-esteem, independence, assertiveness, pride, and confidence, traits that will enable your child to be better prepared in any walk of life

- the ability to work in a team and get along with peers and coaches, learning teamwork and leadership skills

- a sense of belonging with teammates and a wide circle of acquaintances through sports participation

Mental Benefits and Educational Success

Various studies have found that kids who participate in sports and other activities are more likely to:

- be able to focus in class

- achieve good grades, higher standardized test scores, and a higher level of education

- attend school on a regular basis with fewer unexcused absences

- exhibit fewer behavior problems in and out of the classroom, including misbehaving in class, using drugs, committing delinquent acts, or dropping out of school

FINDING THE RIGHT COACH FOR YOUR CHILD

Volunteer Coaches

Each year, 3 million American adults volunteer to coach more than 25 million young athletes between the ages of 6 and 18 in non-school-run sports. They comprise one of the largest volunteer corps in the country, and they all possess different expectations, skills, and knowledge. Only 20% have any formal training in coaching. The turnover rate for coaches averages 40% a year, with the average youth sports coach leading teams for only three to five years.

These coaches can have a great deal of influence on your child. The National Youth Sports Coaches Association (NYSCA) found that the average youth sports coach spends 80 hours a season with his or her players. Often, it is your child's coach who determines whether she will enjoy the experience, and can profoundly influence your child both physically and emotionally.

✦ Among the most common reasons kids give for dropping out are abusive coaches, not enough chances to play, and overemphasis on winning.

✦ Ask the league officials what training, if any, is required for volunteer coaches and how coaches are selected. Ask if police background checks are run on the coaches. In an attempt to curb the number of out-of-control coaches or those with criminal records, many organizations now perform background checks before allowing coaches to take the field.

✦ Ask about how the coach will handle discipline issues.

Youth programs in any sport usually have coaches who are volunteers. More often than not they are the parent of one of the players. Like anything else, there will be good and bad coaches. There will be coaches who are knowledgeable about the game but too intense for the early years, and there will be coaches who know nothing about the game who are just great role models for your child. When getting started, a "good-hearted" mom or dad with limited experience can be a better coach than a former All-American who doesn't have realistic expectations.

—*Jeff Hoyle, high school girls' basketball coach, teaching for 19 years*

Most, if not all, programs are run on a volunteer basis. Quality control can be difficult. Not all coaches are good and may not connect well with every child. This is one of the reasons that we encourage switching coaches and teammates from season to season.

—*Ted Tye, president of Newton Girls' Soccer, coach for 13 years, and dad of an 18-year-old and 12-year-old twins*

When You Have the Ability to Pick

❧ If you have a choice among several coaches in a league sport, look for a coach who has an even temper, encourages all the players, and will serve as a positive role model for your child. Ask around the community about the best coaches, and go to games the year before you sign your child up to see how they interact with the kids.

❧ With professional instructors in sports and activities such as tennis, golf, skiing, or music, you can choose your child's coach, unlike many team leagues.

❧ Often a coach's ability to teach has no relation to how well he or she plays the game, so while a competitive background is helpful, it's not always an indicator of coaching capability.

My kids have very different learning styles and what they want and need from a coach is fundamentally different. My oldest son is a nonaggressive type of kid who likes sports and being part of a team, but does not like coaches so focused on learning and winning that they forget to also stress fun. Some coaches become more vested in the team winning than they should, and it's come to the point that I've had to have discussions with our town's soccer league about some of the worst offenders.

—Elizabeth, mom of Robert, 15, and
David, 10

Get to know the coach and his or her values. Choose someone who's mature, trustworthy, and someone you would want your child to look up to, since this person will have an impact on your child's life.

—Siobhan Bahan, former Sunnyside High
School varsity coach

❧ Observe the coach in action at practice and games. Coaches vary dramatically in style. Seek out a coach particularly suited to your child in order to avoid difficulties stemming from a personality or teaching style conflict. When evaluating a coach, his attitude is the key. How will he motivate or correct your child?

❧ Many overzealous coaches use intense training methods, and are demanding and emotionally insensitive in an effort to create a star team or star athlete. Some kids thrive under this approach, while many others wither.

❧ Other issues to consider:
  ➤ What is the coaching and league policy regarding playing time in games?
  ➤ How much value does the coach place on winning or on having the stronger athletes play?
  ➤ What counts as excused absences and how does the coach feel about missed practices?
  ➤ What is the coach's prior experience? Has he ever coached this level before?
  ➤ Does the team have an assistant coach, and what is that person's role?

I've seen lots of moments when coaches and parents (since they're usually one and the same!) can be too focused on winning or having the kids make fewer mistakes. But the way we truly learn things in life is from our mistakes, rather than from being told what to do. While it's great to teach children rules and mechanics of games and for them to experience winning, it's a far larger thing for children to learn from team moments together and rallying around the weakest player. That's life stuff.

Signs of Great Coaching

In general, a great coach:

- builds enthusiasm among the players and is enthusiastic both about the sport and coaching it

- has a solid technical knowledge of the sport and the ability to teach technique and tactics to children of your child's age

- has gone through a coaching training or certification program

- communicates easily with the kids and is patient with them

- builds kids up when they make mistakes instead of criticizing them

- recognizes that all kids go through plateaus in their skill development and have growth spurts that can adversely affect their coordination

- serves as a role model for your child and his teammates

- requires a warm-up and mandates that kids wear protective equipment at both practices and games

- has been certified in first aid/CPR and has first-aid supplies on the field

At practices, a great coach:

- has highly organized practices, with kids actively participating instead of just standing around waiting for their turn

- is fair, patient, and listens well

- works with everyone, not just the best players

A coach's primary goal should be that everyone will play again next year.

    —Andrew Crane, Henrico County sports supervisor, coaching youth basketball for 26 years

Look for a coach with intelligence, kindness, patience, and a good sense of humor.

    —Madeleine Austin, owner and head trainer, Imajica Equestrian Center, teaching for 30 years

A coach must have a passion for what he teaches, and coming to practice should be the highlight of his day. Many parents make the mistake of assuming that just because someone has played a sport professionally, he must be a good instructor. Completely false! I have seen so many former professionals who know the fundamentals but lack the ability to communicate them to children in an effective manner. A good program is one that has good coaches!

    —Rich Janor, Wheatland Travel Baseball Club coach for 5 years

Excellent teaching involves accommodating your child's learning style and providing the necessary motivation to help your child make it through the "plateau periods" when his or her game does not seem to be progressing. When a child feels that his teacher genuinely cares about him and his progress, he will work very hard and persevere through difficult times because of this strong relationship.

    —Roger Mitten, Mid-Town Tennis Club head tennis professional, and founder of tennis opportunity program for economically disadvantaged children, teaching for 15 years

Look for coaches who are very well organized and very self-aware. We're constantly telling our coaches and parents: Don't worry about winning big. It's ultimately the quality of teaching that matters most in turning out the best players as time goes by.

    —Dean Conway, state head coach and director of coaching for Mass. Youth Soccer Association

One distressing observation I've made as a youth soccer coach is how much constant praise and positive reinforcement kids today are used to getting on a daily basis, to the point where it's become trivialized. Even with the smallest achievement, the expectation is for heaps of praise. Instead, as coaches, we point out errors and offer constructive ways of doing things better, rather than just letting the errors slide. And, if you're consistent, the kids really, really appreciate when they've done something well and have much greater personal pride in the accomplishment.

—*Ron, nationally licensed youth soccer coach and dad of two, ages 10 and 8*

Look for an enthusiastic coach who understands how to communicate and knows how to correct without making it seem like a punishment.

—*Kelly Boyd, volleyball coach at Southern Indiana University, coaching for 7 years*

- spends some of the practice time talking to kids individually or in small groups
- uses positive reinforcement, focusing on your child's progress and efforts instead of mistakes or shortcomings
- patiently and effectively teaches fundamental technical and tactical skills, especially since the key developmental ages are from 8 to 14

During games, the coach:

- emphasizes sportsmanship and fair play at all times, especially during tough games
- has an "everyone plays" mentality, giving each member of the team the opportunity to play at least half of every game, and giving younger players the opportunity to play different positions
- values playing one's best and mastering the sport ahead of winning
- keeps winning and losing in perspective, graciously accepting defeat or victory
- does not fly off the handle and never screams at players
- treats players as individuals
- pays attention to safety issues, including warm-up, equipment, and field conditions

We've been lucky because our son has had fabulous coaching. The best coach he ever had walked into the locker room before a big game and said, "I really don't care if we win or lose. I want to see you play your best." It was such an important message for those kids.

—*Jane, mom of Carolyn, 17, and Peter, 11*

One fabulous soccer coach my son had told the kids that he would not instruct from the sidelines during a game. He told them that instead they had to learn to think like a team, anticipate where the ball was going to be, and talk to each other positively. By the end of the season, the kids felt like they owned the game. His low-key style taught them independence and gave them a love of the sport.

—*Elizabeth, mom of Robert, 15, and David, 10*

A coach should be a great example when it comes to sportmanship. I know lots of the kids that I coach watch me bowl and interact with others, and listen to me talk. I want to win as bad as anyone around in competition so I am always trying my best. But always, win or lose, I try to be the best sportsman possible.

—*Doug Barker, Louisville youth bowling coach for 16 years*

Telltale Signs of Poor Coaching

- doesn't want to hear from the parents
- argues with or openly criticizes a referee, umpire, or official
- makes winning the driving force of team play
- harshly, publicly, or personally criticizes players for failures, rather than giving constructive advice based on performance (e.g., "You stink," as opposed to "You played like you were tired")
- makes kids feel bad when they lose and worthy only when they win
- uses leadership built on intimidation
- flies off the handle frequently, especially during games or matches

Many coaches are well intentioned, but lack perspective. This results in behaviors like being overly focused on winning in the second grade or coaches not giving kids equal playing time in recreational programs.

—*Ted Tye, president of Newton Girls' Soccer, coach for 13 years, and dad of an 18-year-old and 12-year-old twins*

Less skilled, less talented, or less athletic kids can get intimidated or otherwise turned off by insensitive, abusive coaches. Highly competitive coaches, imitating their college or professional counterparts, often get carried away, such as with excessive calisthenics, push-ups or running laps, which drives kids away quickly.

—*Jerry Norton, director of Ponte Vedra Development Football League and youth coach for 36 years*

I simply don't like those coaches who push and scream. Sometimes it has meant going across town to find the right nurturing coach for our kids rather than joining a team right in our neighborhood.

—*Sarah, mom of Lauren, 12, and Parker, 7*

- yells, screams, or uses profane language
- plays his own child more than others
- consistently gives better players more playing time
- fails to break up fights or allows children to tease each other
- condones breaking the rules or cheating, saying "Everyone does it"
- pushes players beyond their limits

EVALUATING A TEACHER

❧ Every instructor presents his or her knowledge in a different way. Ultimately, you want a person who "connects" with your child, someone who is friendly and understanding, yet stimulating and inspiring. It is essential that the teacher can form a bond of trust with your child. A great teacher should demand respect but also allow room for creative ideas and student responses.

❧ Professional training, degrees, and experience working with children are crucial areas to investigate when choosing a teacher for your child. Realize that some teachers are really good at an activity but don't know how to teach it, while others who are not as talented are excellent teachers whom kids love.

❧ Organization is also important. Does the teacher prepare a curriculum? Does she keep a log of her work with your student? Is class or lesson time used effectively?

❧ The teacher should reflect professionalism in her appearance and interactions with both you and your child. She should have patience and sensitivity when dealing with your child's strengths and limitations, and find a balance between constructive criticism and encouragement.

❧ Observe any class before getting your kids involved. The teacher should be enthusiastic, aware of all of the students' needs, reasonable in the goals she sets, well trained and qualified, and prepared. In a class, the kids should be grouped in ways that seem age- or skill-appropriate, and should be enjoying themselves.

The teacher should have a clear idea of the skills, the craft, and how to help the students enjoy their study. A teacher who is too skill-obsessed or too fun-obsessed will not provide the student with the balance of hard work and enjoyment that ultimately lead to success.

—Bob Thomas, dance director, Dean College, teaching for 26 years

Look for an instructor who clearly enjoys working with children, makes the whole experience *fun*, and strives for each child to be successful in his or her own way. Beginners need lots of encouragement, and a good instructor will always try to find the strengths of each student.

—Janet Darvill, U.S. Professional Tennis Registry–certified tennis professional, teaching for 4 years

COACHING YOUR OWN CHILD

Making the Decision

✦ Approximately 1 in 5 parents will become volunteer coaches for their child's team. Before doing so, you will need to clarify both how your child feels about this decision and how you feel about taking on the hard work involved in being a coach. Many parents mean well when they volunteer to coach, but don't fully realize how much time and effort it takes to do this successfully.

✦ Some parents have found that coaching helps get and keep their children involved in an organized sport. Others find coaching their own children a recipe for disaster because the child resents the switch from nurturing parent to neutral or demanding coach who can't play favorites.

✦ Discuss the decision with your child:
  ➤ How does she feel about you coaching? Ask your child if it's okay with her. Talk with her about how you will need to pay equal attention to all the kids involved. Explain how you will treat her just like the other members of her team during practices and games, but take off your coaching hat when you leave the field.
  ➤ Is she concerned that your coaching will impact her friendships with other kids on the team?
  ➤ Make sure that your child feels both comfortable and enthusiastic about having you as a coach, is willing to share your attention and praise with her teammates, and is able to accept your directions and criticism.

✦ Even though coaching can be immensely fulfilling, it can also be a challenge, especially if you are dealing with your own child. Before rushing into coaching your child's team, take a moment to clarify your motives. Ask yourself the following questions when considering if you will make the commitment:
  ➤ Why do I want to coach? What are my goals for my child and her team? Make sure that you're not signing on as a coach to help make your child a star or ensure your child gets extra playing time.
  ➤ Do I have the skills and qualifications it takes to be a coach? How well do I understand the sport and its rules? What will it take for me to get up to speed? Will I need to get certified or licensed? Keep in mind that with more advanced players, you'll need a more sophisticated awareness of the game.
  ➤ Can I treat my own child the same as the other members of her team and have the same expectations for her? Can I be objective in team assignments, and not favor my child? Not only does this mean avoiding favoritism, but it also requires not being tougher on your child than on the other players. You have to be willing to accept your child no matter where she is in terms

For a dad, being able to coach your daughter is a bonding experience second to none. It gives me time to spend with my daughter that isn't forced or manufactured, and it's time we both really enjoy. With me as her coach, my daughter is a more active participant and enjoys sports more. It also gives her a level of comfort, particularly at the beginning of the season when the environment is new. That may change as she gets older and would like more independence from me. From my personal standpoint, all coaches need to be evenhanded when coaching their children. I am probably so much so that I actually give her a slight disadvantage over her peers.

—*Ron, nationally licensed youth soccer coach and dad of two, ages 10 and 8*

Being a T-ball coach has been a great life experience for me. The pressures of your job and home can definitely take you out of your child's life. Being a coach forces you to stop everything else and puts you back in touch with your children. It gives you a real sense of what's going on with them, and allows you to see their weaknesses along with their strengths. You can then work with them outside of practice to address the emotional challenges they have, sportsmanship, or physical skills they need to work on.

—*Dean, dad of Evan, 10, and Olivia, Justin, and Shelby, 8*

Because my husband has become our daughter's soccer coach, he's taken so much responsibility off my shoulders. He's thrown himself completely into it. He really connects with the kids. And since Dad's involved, they share this as a special bond. Of course, the downside of Dad as coach is that he ultimately does care if the team wins or not. Fortunately, the team has had big successes, winning a recent Columbus Day tournament. It was so exciting, and very good for her.

—*Bridgitt, mom of Taylor, 10, Connor and Chloe, 8, Brian, 6*

of both skill ability level and motivation, and not push her at all times to be the best one on the team.

➣ Can I make the required commitment given my schedule?

➣ Can I modulate my emotions, especially during highly competitive situations?

- Can I be patient when a child does not perform as I hoped or expected?
- Can I avoid comparing my child's athletic achievement to my own?
- Will I be able to pay equal attention to the stars and the more average players?
- Do I have the energy and enthusiasm that it takes?
- Will my other children feel excluded or jealous?

If you're thinking about coaching your child's team, try assisting for a season first—to learn, observe, take on fewer responsibilities, and see how it works for both of you.

Coaching your child allows you to get to know her peers and gives you something to share and talk about with her, but it can also become a source of tension. Keep a watchful eye on how your child is handling your new role, as she may become overly concerned about gaining your approval, or feel even more devastated by your disapproval.

You will have to continually work to keep your roles as parent and coach separate:
- When your child experiences frustration after a game, she will want you to console her as her parent, not offer advice as her coach.
- Resist the temptation to talk with your child about other team members' performances, or to solicit her advice on strategy or what positions other children should play. Once you leave the field, leave the game behind as well.
- Don't let your child's sport become the central focus of your conversations or of the quality time you spend together.

Part of successfully coaching your child means recognizing when it's time to have someone else take over the role, either because your child has progressed beyond your own skill level or because coaching has caused both of you frustration.

Dealing with Other Parents

Start off with an initial parents' meeting to clarify expectations, rules about sideline behavior, and practice and game schedules. Discuss the league's and your own philosophy regarding playing time and position assignments.

Encourage parents to immediately seek you out with questions, concerns, or constructive feedback.

A coach should communicate well with both kids and parents. I always consider "parent train-ing" as important as "kid training."

　—Ted Tye, president of Newton Girls' Soccer, coach for 13 years, and dad of an 18-year-old and 12-year-old twins

As a coach, the only negative behavior I've had to deal with from other parents is when they forget that we're volunteering and not paid teachers or coaches. They forget we do this for the love of the game or because we are coaching our kids and that we're not experts in child psychology or caregivers. I've been blessed, as it's been pretty rare for me, but other coaches have nightmare stories.

　—Ron, nationally licensed youth soccer coach and dad of two, ages 10 and 8

As a coach, I try to be a voice of reason with the other parents. These are kids' sports, yet some of the parents act like this is the seventh game of the World Series. They forget that kids should just go out and have fun.

　—Andy, dad of Rachel, 10, Ben, 7, and Josh, 3

WHAT TO LOOK FOR IN A SPORTS PROGRAM

🐟 Step back and carefully reflect on the cost, both in terms of time and financial commitment, before your child jumps into the fray. Before you say yes, make sure you and your child really understand how much time the activity will require, in-cluding the amount of practice between lessons or games, the length of practices, the length of the season, and travel time.

🐟 Look at the other kids who are involved, the teaching style of the coach, what the goals of the program are, and what the expected level of commitment will be when choosing a program for your child.

🐟 Ask the following questions:
　➤ How many practices will occur each week and for how long?

- Where will the practice sessions be held?
- Are practices held during the holidays and on days following tournaments?
- In how many tournaments will the team compete? When and where will the tournaments take place?
- Who is the coach, and is he trained or certified? Is there more than one coach?
- How are teams formed to ensure balanced competition? Are the kids currently on the team at a comparable skill level or physical size as your child?
- What are the fees, and what is supplied with registration?
- What parental involvement is required?

In the right type of youth sports program, kids learn that the essence of sports competition is not winning but rather striving to win.

    —Jerry Norton, director of Ponte Vedra Development Football League and youth coach for 36 years

Find a program that makes kids first priority. Good organization is very important, as well as time management and preparation. A program should make it clear to kids and parents what the time commitments are, and what is to be expected of both so that everyone is on the same page. You also want to look at the coaches themselves and make sure they are good people who you feel you can trust. It is important that a program is not overly competitive, especially with younger children. A good indicator of the quality of a program is the number of children they currently have and the number that come back year after year.

    —Larry Shaw, head wrestling coach, Oak Glen High School, and 2002 National Wrestling Coaches Association State Coach of the Year, coaching for 24 years

The issue with kids being grouped by age in sports is that boys mature at such different rates that there are huge physical disparities. Recently, I watched my son at 80 pounds going up against a 130-pound kid who towered over him. It can definitely leave you feeling uneasy!

    —Jane, mom of Carolyn, 17, and Peter, 11

~ Does a larger organization or agency sponsor the league, such as the YMCA?

~ What kind of equipment is used, and who is responsible for providing it?

✦ When observing a practice or game, look for kids having fun, all team members participating, the other children's skill level paralleling your child's, an emphasis on good sportsmanship, organized and responsive coaches treating the players with respect, and well-maintained equipment or fields.

OVERALL SAFETY AND INJURY CONSIDERATIONS

✦ According to the National Youth Sports Safety Foundation, of the 40 million children and adolescents participating in organized sports each year, approximately 5 million seek medical treatment for injuries.

✦ Surprisingly, over 60% of organized sports injuries occur during practice rather than during games.

✦ The seriousness of injuries increases with age and the level of competition. Especially for contact sports, children should be matched against children of similar weight, size, and skill development, as this helps reduce injuries. As children grow bigger, risk of injury increases because of the increasing bulk of force at impact.

✦ Especially around puberty, ages 11–13 for girls and 12–16 for boys, safety should be critically considered, as children are more vulnerable to injury during rapid growth spurts.

✦ Lack of proper coaching education has been identified as a key reason why many sports injuries occur. Ninety percent of youth sport coaches in the U.S. have never taken training classes in the sport they coach. Make sure your child's coach makes warm-ups and cool-downs routine before and after your child's sports practices or games. Team coaches should also have training in first aid and CPR.

Proper Equipment

✦ Always have your child wear a mouth guard in contact sports, such as basketball, soccer, hockey, baseball and karate. Not only does a mouth guard prevent teeth injuries, it also acts as a shock absorber that protects against jaw and neck injuries. If your child has difficulty finding one that fits properly and comfortably, her dentist can make a custom mouthpiece.

✦ Helmets significantly reduce head injuries among skiers, bicyclists, skaters, baseball and football players, as well as horseback riders.

✦ A face mask or goggles should be worn for all impact sports in which your child participates. Baseball and basketball are accountable for most eye injuries. Make sure your child wears protective eyewear with lenses made of polycarbonate material. Polycarbonate is lightweight, scratch-resistant and amenable to prescription lenses. If your child uses prescription lenses, they should be set into a sports frame that can hold the lenses firmly in place.

✦ Improper footwear is a major cause of injuries to feet, knees, and ankles. Avoid hand-me-down shoes, as they often fit poorly and have worn-down treads. And don't send your child out to play in shoes that have not first been broken in.

✦ Equipment and safety gear that fits your child is essential for injury prevention. Insist that your child wear the appropriate protective gear both during practice and games, as it greatly reduces the likelihood and severity of injuries.

✦ Be sure that the coach insists that safety gear be purchased and used at all times.

Preventing Heatstroke, Dehydration, and Frostbite

✦ When the temperature reaches over 85 degrees or humidity exceeds 70%, heat exhaustion and heatstroke become issues. On such days, your child should drink at least two glasses of water before playing sports, and replenish fluids every 15 to 20 minutes during the practice or game.

✦ In cold weather, make sure your child is properly dressed in warm, insulating layers, and teach her to recognize the warning signs of frostbite, such as tingling in fingers, toes, and face.

Overuse Injuries

✦ Overuse injuries result from repetitive motions, especially those that affect the vulnerable cartilage at the end of your child's bones where tendons attach. These include stress fractures, muscle tears, or even bone deformities. Children who alternate between different sports are less likely to overuse the same set of muscles and joints. These injuries may be the result of inadequate warm-up, too much physical exertion, or improper technique. Children are particularly vulnerable to overuse injuries because of the softness of their growing bones and the tightness of their ligaments, tendons, and muscles during growth spurts.

✦ As a result of overuse injuries, an entire specialty of pediatric sports medicine has arisen. Because of the rising number of overuse injuries in children, the American Academy of Pediatrics felt compelled to issue a new policy statement warning of the serious health risks that can come with concentrating too intensively or too early on a single sport.

✦ Chronic injuries, such as tennis elbow, swimmer's shoulder, and shin splints are on the rise as more children play organized sports at younger ages, specialize and play a single sport year-round, and attend intensive summer sports specialty camps or training programs. Encouraging your child to play a variety of sports and cross-train will help prevent these overuse injuries from occurring.

✦ If your child begins complaining of pain, take her immediately to see her pediatrician, who may recommend seeing a sports medicine or pediatric orthopedic specialist. The first indication will usually be sore muscles after practice or a game, which gradually starts persisting into the next day. Left untreated, the pain often begins during the training itself, and will finally show up in simple daily movements like lifting an arm or walking. Often, treatment involves modifying or temporarily eliminating the physical motion or activity that caused the injury.

✦ If your child plays in pain, she may end up needing surgery or do irreversible damage.

Getting Ready for the Start of a New Season

✦ Encourage your child to do preseason physical exercise and conditioning, building up to several times a week, in order to get in shape. At the beginning of a new season, injuries often occur because children do too much too soon, particularly if they've been relatively inactive prior to the season opener. As a result, many kids end up with strains, tendonitis, and stress fractures.

✦ Take your child to see her physician for a preseason sports physical examination. Have her physician check conditions that might affect her ability to play sports and to discuss protective measures for any previous injuries.

EATING DISORDERS

✦ Eating disorders have become a rising epidemic among young athletes. Athletes are at significantly greater risk when participating in sports where a lean body is critical, such as gymnastics, ballet, figure skating, long-distance running, diving, and synchronized swimming. The incidence of eating disorders in young female athletes has been estimated at 62%, compared to 3% in the general population of girls. It can also be found in boys, especially in weight-driven sports such as wrestling.

✦ Watch out for sports where coaches instruct the team on what to eat and how to count calories, demand weight loss, or make team decisions based on weight. If a coach suggests your child lose weight in order to increase her performance, as is likely at higher levels of competition, your child may become obsessed with weight loss and pursue it with the same intensity and perseverance that makes her so successful in the sport.

✦ For some sports, such as gymnastics, girls may also fear the onset of puberty because it means developing hips and breasts that might hinder their performance. These girls may use excessive measures to maintain a thin and girlish figure to stay competitive.

✦ Eating disorders also stem from psychological issues. A child who feels a lack of control and low self-worth will turn to something she can control—her eating habits and weight. Even though she may be within a healthy body weight, she will obsess about being or getting fat, and decide to eat less and lose a certain number of pounds.

✦ The most common eating disorders, which usually appear around age 16, are:
  - Anorexia nervosa, which involves self-starvation. The anorexic views herself as overweight, even though she is extremely thin. If your child avoids eating, loses a significant amount of weight without being sick, exercises compulsively, goes three months without her period, or expresses an intense fear of gaining weight, this eating disorder may be affecting her.
  - Bulimia, which involves repeated incidents of binge eating, followed by purging through laxatives, diuretics, or vomiting after meals. Your child may develop swollen neck glands due to the vomiting. Because a sufferer of bulimia continues to both binge and purge, weight loss is not necessarily one of its many harmful side effects. Also be on the lookout for "exercise bulimia," where instead of purging, a child intensely exercises to work off what she eats, often for several hours a day.

✦ Athletes who have a close relative diagnosed with an eating disorder are 50% more likely to develop one than are athletes with no family history of the disease.

Effects of Eating Disorders

Depending on how severe the eating disorder is and how long it has been going on, the most common effects include:

- weight loss
- loss in endurance, coordination, muscular strength, and speed
- muscle cramps, dizziness, or fatigue
- hair loss and yellow or damaged teeth
- amenorrhea, the absence of normal menstruation, which can lead to premature osteoporosis, low bone density, stress fractures, along with fertility issues later in life
- loss of concentration and focus
- feelings of inadequacy, worthlessness, and low self-esteem
- being angry, sullen, socially withdrawn, or defiant
- sleeplessness, lack of motivation, agitation, irritability, and unusual mood swings
- anxiety, fear, panic over weight gain, or depression

What to Watch Out For

Both anorexia nervosa and bulimia often go undiagnosed for some time, as a person suffering from these eating disorders finds ways to hide her bingeing, purging, or self-starvation. Take note if your child:

- begins to diet and makes comments about food being too fattening to eat
- obsesses about food or weighs herself frequently
- gives excuses during meals for not being hungry
- disappears after meals into the bathroom
- makes disparaging comments about her body

What to Do

Keep a vigilant lookout for any of the signs noted above. If you notice these symptoms in your child:

◉ Take her immediately to a pediatrician or a trained specialist in the eating disorders field. Eating disorders progress in severity, and can prove life-threatening if left untreated. Recognize that this is a complicated illness and that, from an emotional perspective, your child will have to work very hard to overcome it.

◉ Consult your child's pediatrician if she has amenorrhea. The pediatrician should measure her body fat, hormone levels, vitamin and mineral levels, and assess overall nutrition and stress levels.

◉ Make sure you model healthy eating behavior.

◉ Do not make disparaging comments about your child's body or your own, about eating fat or about being on a diet.

OVERALL COST CONSIDERATIONS

✦ Sports are becoming increasingly expensive, especially when protective equipment for intensive sports becomes necessary or additional private lessons, coaching, and club fees are essential for your child to excel.

✦ "You've got to pay to play," the saying goes. With three sports seasons in a year and multiple enrollments within a family, the price of participation can escalate shockingly fast. Whether it means signing your child up for private lessons, or paying registration fees for team sports, it will likely cost you hundreds, if not thousands, of dollars annually to fund your child's activities. The added costs of expensive athletic equipment can strain your family's finances well beyond what you originally anticipated. It has been estimated that parents spend an average of $2,100 a year on their children's sports, with some spending as much as $12,000 for traveling teams and their accompanying hotel costs.

✦ Find out how much the sport will cost, and decide if that number falls within your family budget at the level at which your child will be pursuing it. Some sports, such as ice hockey or skiing, may involve high costs for equipment, while others, such as soccer, may merely involve purchasing only cleats, shin guards, and a ball. Ask about additional costs outside the basic enrollment fee that might arise later. The hidden costs of children's activities run the gamut from a team uniform to a $150 pair of hockey gloves or high travel costs for away tournaments. While many sports dramatically escalate in cost for those children who get serious about pursuing them, don't let this influence your decision about exploring sports on a recreational level.

Budgeting Know-How

Before signing your child up for an activity, sport, or lesson, clarify the following:
- What are the basic costs or registration fees?
- What will your expenses be over the long run if your child sticks with the activity?
- Are there any tournaments or performances that will involve additional expenses?
- What equipment will your child need to buy or rent?
- What kind of travel will be involved, and does any of it mean staying overnight and incurring the expenses of lodging and meals?
- What mandatory fund-raising activities will your child or you have to participate in?
- How much of your time will you be expected to volunteer?
- Will your child be encouraged to attend any specialty workshops or camps, and if so, how much do they cost?

✦ Talk to parents who have children already participating in the activity about hidden costs as well as common expenses to anticipate.

✦ Find out what lessons, classes, or leagues your city or town offers, as they usually involve substantially lower costs.

✦ Write down a list of your child's activities, their anticipated costs for the season, and when you will likely incur those expenses. This will help you anticipate spikes in costs, such as in September, January, or June, when new activities, sports, and lessons are just gearing up.

✦ You can reduce what you pay in lesson fees by pairing your child up for semi-private lessons with a friend who has a comparable skill level and interest. The two can compete with each other and work together.

Buying Equipment

✦ Start a relationship with a good sports shop so you can get expert advice about what your child really needs to perform well and stay safe. Ask other parents for recommendations when you're at games or practices.

✦ Spend your funds first on equipment that will protect your child from injuries. Then consider glow-in-the-dark batting gloves with matching sunglasses.

I was recently at my boys' swimming lesson talking with the mom of a boy in my son's class, and her philosophy was this: For big time-commitment and equipment sports such as ice hockey and lacrosse, her kids can pick one sport each. They then have to commit to it for two to three years because of the cost involved for equipment, lessons, or extras like ice time. Her son picked lacrosse this year, but this meant no baseball for him this spring and he was really, really disappointed about that. Should you, as a parent, set those rules? What if your child changes his mind?

—*Deborah, mom of Philip, 10, Patrick, 8, and William, 3*

We are not wealthy people, and have raised our kids on very little. If it is something the child wants, do what you have to do to get him into the sport. Seek out award scholarships for basketball or eat hot dogs a couple of extra nights to save money.

—*Diana, mom of 6 children*

Even having signed my kids up for just a couple of activities, it gets really expensive really fast! When I sign my three-year-old up for a class, we will first try it a couple of weeks in a row, because if she doesn't like it, I don't want to waste money by signing her up for a whole season and then have her refuse to go.

—*Leslie, mom of Katie, 3, and Lily, 2*

🐟 Buying used equipment can save you hundreds of dollars a season, as well as enable your growing athlete to get better equipment than you would otherwise be willing to splurge for. But make sure the equipment isn't all used up. Check it carefully. Be sure to look for name-brand gear that's in good condition, and start searching well before the season begins. Besides shared equipment from older siblings, cousins, or friends with older kids, look for neighborhood swaps and scout out garage sales.

Sometimes we parents forget what it's like to have other kids' opinions matter. No child wants to look like a geek on the field. That's not to say you have to spend millions on looking good, but maybe buying that fancy bat will make your child feel like he is a pro even if he's not. Give such items as birthday gifts if they tend to be expensive.

—*Nancy, mom of a son age 13*

Ways to Save Money on Your Child's Sports Expenses

✦ Make presents out of needed sports equipment, such as a new tennis racket or lacrosse stick.

✦ If your child has an avid interest in a particular activity, it pays to buy new, high-quality equipment that will last if it's an item that your child won't outgrow.

✦ Sometimes renting equipment off-site from a sports store saves money compared to renting it on the premises, such as ice skates, skis, or snowboards.

8

Guide to Specific Sports

ARCHERY

Overview

As the legend of Robin Hood attests, archery competitions date back at least to medieval times. Today's archers still honor the famous outlaw with the term "Robin Hood," referring to splitting the shaft of an arrow already in the target with another arrow. While archery equipment has had dramatic technological improvements since then, the sport remains essentially the same. Fiberglass recurve bows and graphite arrows have replaced wooden ones, but archery still depends on steady hands, a strong upper body, accurate aim, and unflinching nerves. Archery was featured in the Olympic Games several times from 1900 to 1920, and then became a permanent part of the Games in 1972.

Although archery has traditionally been associated with summer camp, participation is on the rise, as children are practicing archery long after camp has ended. In addition, many Boy Scout troops offer archery as a means to earn a badge and introduce kids to the sport. Moreover, your child may decide that archery has great allure after watching Robin Hood and his merry men in such action movies as *Robin Hood: Prince of Thieves* with Kevin Costner.

Often compared to martial arts, archery requires a great amount of concentration and patience in order to aim the arrow, let it fly, and hit the target accurately as each shot is carefully choreographed. In archery, your child will be taught about the complex variables that go into pulling back the bow and launching a feathered arrow into that large traditional target with its bright, concentric red, yellow, and blue rings. Everything from the tightness with which your child holds the bow to the solitary standing at the target line makes the ultimate challenge of archery a personal one.

General Benefits

◎ Improves hand-eye coordination

◎ Teaches mental concentration, focus, and composure

◎ Instills patience and self-discipline

◎ Gives a child body awareness, tones the back and arm muscles, and builds upper-body strength

◎ Promotes physical strength and stamina. A typical archery tournament round consists of 60 arrows for the beginning divisions and 120 arrows for older divisions. Given the typical draw weight of the bows, this can add up to over 3,600 pounds pulled in a few hours

Kids Who Tend to Excel

◎ There are no "natural born archers," meaning that just about any child can take

Archery is an intensely personal experience. When stripped down to its essence, it's only the archer, the bow, and the target—whether it's local practice or going for the gold in the Olympic Games. Archery is also a lifetime sport. At the national championships, there are youth under 10 and masters over 70 shooting on the same line.

—*Ruth Rowe, Olympic recurve archer, coaching for 15 years*

◎

There is an almost euphoric and magical enthusiasm of watching an arrow fly and actually going where you were looking and where your mind told it to go. Plus, in archery, there is a lot of social interaction—I tell people that archery practice is a big party that is occasionally interrupted by the shooting of arrows.

—*Tom Barker, Texas Junior Olympics archery development coordinator, coaching for 9 years*

up the sport and have some level of success at it, depending on her level of commitment. Adjustable targets enable kids of all ages, sizes, and abilities to join in.

Ultimately, success in archery is more mental than physical, requiring intense focus. While some muscle strength is needed, the ability to be absolutely consistent from shot to shot is most important. An archer needs steady hands, great focus, and the patience to work on precision aiming.

Many children drawn to archery are introspective and prefer individual to group activities.

Archery is a sport of consistency, control, and finesse, and those who excel typically are perseverant perfectionists. Archery ultimately involves more mental ability than physical ability, once the basics are learned and ingrained in an athlete's repertoire. It is a sport where everything must be performed correctly, every time, in order to be accurate. So there is always room for improvement, in one's form, with one's equipment, with one's mental game.

> —Kathy Miller, president, Chicagoland JOAD club, NAA Level II coach, and mom of Stephanie, 17, and Jonathon, 15

The laid-back atmosphere of archery appeals to many kids. They can go at their own pace, and even if they are not as good as the other kids, they don't stick out like a sore thumb. With practice, it is possible for anyone to excel at archery. Plus, there are always ways to create new challenges, such as moving the target farther away or challenging yourself to get a higher score. No one can shoot five perfect bull's-eyes in a row.

> —Jill Locasio, summer camp archery instructor for 5 years

The great thing about archery is that just about anyone can do it. It's a great sport for children who "think" they're not good at sports. We have people with different personalities who excel at the sport, from quiet, focused individuals to extroverted athletes—anyone who has a desire can excel.

> —Jessica Carleton, elite competitive archer, coaching for 10 years

Archery is a sport that even disabled kids can participate in with success, and archery tournaments accommodate three different levels of impairments. My daughter Lindsey was born with a rare disorder where one's bones are not strong and reliable, and she can only walk with the use of crutches. A middle school teacher suggested she might be able to "do" archery, and we found the nearest program to investigate. In short, three years later she won a national title in her age group among all able-bodied archers. I was notified today by the coach for the U.S. Paralympic Archery Team that based on Lindsey's performance at Outdoor Target Nationals, they have ranked her as a national training team member.

—*A. Ron Carmichael, archery coach for 4 years*

Best Age to Start

◎ Your child can begin taking formal archery lessons as young as 5 years old if she has:

- ⁓ the strength to hold the bow in front of her with an outstretched arm;
- ⁓ the coordination to notch an arrow and shoot it;
- ⁓ the strength to draw back a bow at least 18 inches (which is enough to allow a light aluminum arrow to reach an indoor target and stick consistently);
- ⁓ the ability to concentrate;
- ⁓ the maturity to follow safety rules.

◎ While children as young as 6 or 7 have taken well to archery using beginners' bows, they often find it tedious after about 15 minutes. For this reason, many instructors prefer children to begin around 10 years old.

What to Look For When Getting Started

❧ Children should start learning archery on a recurve bow. A beginning archer will use a recurve bow of around 20 pounds, while women use around 38 pounds and men go up as high as 48 pounds.

❧ Beginners' lessons should focus on proper technique and shooting procedure, as well as helping your child achieve consistency when shooting. Even though officially there are different types of archery, the basic technique is pretty much the same. Only the angles and the bows differ.

❧ Look for an instructor who enables your child to have success in increments, first learning how to shoot an arrow, then in hitting the target, in hitting the bull's-eye, and finally in shooting consistently.

🏹 Make sure your child's teacher is certified by the National Field Archery Association (NFAA), or by the National Archery Association (NAA), which has four levels of instructors, the first level being a summer camp counselor and the fourth level being an Olympic coach. Ask if the teacher is a competitive archer herself.

🏹 Look for an instructional program that also enables your child to practice shooting outside of class time.

Competitive Archery

🏹 There are three primary types of shooting. Most archers start with target archery, where your child shoots arrows at circular targets with varying sizes based on their distance from the target; this is the type featured in the Olympics. Field (or "bush walkabout") archery is more advanced, and involves small, circular targets. These targets are laid out over a varied woodland setting, at different distances in order to simulate a hunting environment. In 3-D archery, foam replicas of game animals are used as targets.

🏹 The Junior Olympic Archery Development, or JOAD, program is a national youth archery program organized for the purpose of introducing, instructing, and

A key benefit of youth archery is the sportmanship fostered. I cannot tell you how many times I have seen someone forget a piece of their archery equipment or have something malfunction and their competitor offers their spare to the other kid to get them back in the game. It is like, "I want to beat you, but I want to do it against your best game." While winning is a part of the game, improvement and personal best are emphasized more.

—*Tom Barker, Texas Junior Olympics archery development coordinator, coaching for 9 years*

At the most recent Olympics, out of the top 10 scores registered by all athletes, shooting the same type arrows using the same type bows, shooting the same distance (70 meters) at the same-size targets, 6 out of the top 10 scores were performed by women. In the modern Olympics, women *can* outperform men.

—*A. Ron Carmichael, archery coach for 4 years*

> I took a team of 32 kids ages 13–18 to the Czech Republic this summer for the junior world championships, and the top 16 went for free. This event takes place every other year and is a major goal for our top junior shooters. There are also several national championships each year. The top kids earn positions on the junior U.S. archery team and train for a week at the Olympic Training Center in San Diego. There are also many local youth tournaments throughout the country.
>
> —Lloyd Brown, 2000 and 1996 Olympic team coach and resident athlete coach, Olympic Training Center, teaching for 23 years

developing future archers. JOAD clubs are all over the U.S. and host local tournaments. The National Archery Association and National Field Archery Association also run events for youth at local, state, national, and international levels.

❦ Most competitive archers follow a physical fitness program that involves strength training and cardiovascular exercises.

Types of Bows Used

❦ Most archery schools or facilities will provide equipment for your child as part of their lesson fee and also have equipment that can be rented or used for practice.

❦ For beginners, instructors use lighter bows to minimize how quickly your child fatigues.

❦ There are four primary types of bows used in archery:
- *Recurve Bow:* This bow is used mainly for target archery. Similar to a longbow, this bow offers more power, speed, and accuracy.
- *Compound Bow:* This more technical but most popular bow has mechanical pulleys to make drawing the bow back easier, while dramatically increasing its power and straight arrow flight.
- *Longbow:* This is the traditional "Robin Hood" bow of English archery.
- *Target Bow:* This bow has sights to allow more accurate aiming, and a stabilizer to stop the bow from moving around when drawn back and to dampen vibrations when the arrow is fired.

Safety and Injury Concerns

🪶 Archery has a great safety record, based on very strict rules of shooting. An instructor should be in strict control when children are shooting by using a whistle or another type of clear signal to indicate when shooting can begin and when it is safe to retrieve arrows. Even though an arrow is a potential weapon, for any serious injury to occur during an archery lesson or practice session, someone would have to do something really reckless.

🪶 Many shooters develop calluses and blisters on their fingers from shooting a great deal. Changing one's grip and wearing a finger tab will help protect the fingers.

🪶 Other injuries may occur that are related to overshooting, poor form, or being "over-bowed" (shooting a bow with poundage that is too heavy for the child to handle safely), such as "tennis elbow," "golfer's elbow," and rotator cuff injuries. Many archers also complain about sore shoulders and back muscles.

🪶 Your child should always wear an arm guard, also called a bracer, which is used to prevent the string, when released, from striking the forearm holding the bow. If this occurs, it can leave a bruise or cut on an unprotected area. A bracer also helps prevent clothing from being caught in the string as it is released. It needs to be of sufficient thickness to shield your child's arm. The arm guard comes in a forearm-

Occasionally archers get rotator cuff injuries, but these are likely to occur from many years of shooting, not at the onset. Some kids get shoulder problems from shooting too many pounds; a good coach will only incrementally increase the weight being pulled back.

—*Jessica Carleton, elite competitive archer, coaching for 10 years*

The biggest concern with youth archery is over-bowing, which is when a youth archer uses a bow with too much mass weight or draw weight. As far as mass weight is concerned, the child needs to be able to comfortably hold the bow up at arm's length but not drawn for about 30 seconds. As far as duration is concerned, I try to limit the kids to 60 arrows per day. After that, form begins to break down and bad habits creep in. It is more about quality than quantity of practice.

—*Tom Barker, Texas Junior Olympics archery development coordinator, coaching for 9 years*

only or a full-arm style, depending on the type of bow your child uses and how she holds it.

❧ Pulling back the bow's string and holding it in a drawn position puts a lot of pressure on the fingertips, which can create calluses. To protect the release hand, a shooting glove or finger tab (a flat piece of leather) is commonly used to protect the three fingers that actually draw the string.

Cost Considerations

❧ While you will have to pay for lessons, range fees, and perhaps a membership fee for an archery club, the key expense comes with the decision to buy your child her own equipment. To join a club or archery organization usually costs between $20 and $50 per year.

❧ Typically, group classes cost under $10 at a local archery center, while private lessons vary dramatically in price regionally, costing from $20 to $50 an hour. The cost for a child to use the range for practice is generally $1–$8 an hour. Individual and family memberships in clubs, associations, and private ranges can range anywhere from $35 to $140 per year.

❧ Investing in personal equipment can be expensive. But if your child gets extremely involved in archery, it might be a worthwhile investment due to the increased accuracy of custom-fitted equipment. You can anticipate that if your child starts around age 7, she will likely go through approximately three bows by the time she is 12 years old.

❧ While you can find beginners' (lightweight, low poundage) bows for less than $100 for your under-ten-year-old child, a decent set of equipment, including a bow, arrows, accessories, and safety gear, will typically cost between $250 and $350. The initial accessories, such as arrows, a quiver, rest, sight, chest protector, and a finger tab, as well as a case to transport it all in, adds up to another $100 to $150.

❧ The bow needs to be fitted to the contours of your child's body. Things to look for:
- You want a bow that can accommodate your growing child, with an adjustable draw length system. Most youth starter bows' draw length range from 19 to 22 inches.
- Draw weight (this determines how hard the bow is to be pulled back) is very low for entry-level models and is usually between 15 to 20 pounds for a child under age 10. If your child develops a serious interest in archery, she may want a bow in the range of 25 to 45 pounds to start.

- Beginners' bows should weigh two pounds or less. However, starting around age 7, as your child's arm muscles grow stronger, an instructor may introduce heavier bows.
- The axle-to-axle length should be less than 35 inches, with the best starter bows around 30 inches in length.

★ Arm guards cost around $10, finger tabs $3, and 6 arrows cost approximately $20.

If an archer is to be successful, he or she must have their own equipment, after learning on very lightweight equipment to achieve proper technique. The limbs (which determine the draw weight and partly determine the length of the bow) and the arrows will change as the child grows. One caution: The cheaper bows will quickly be a limiting factor on performance, usually within months after purchase.

—*Ruth Rowe, Olympic recurve archer, coaching for 15 years*

The great thing about recurve bows is that, at the very early beginning ages, they are fairly inexpensive. As children continue to participate, if they get a "take down" recurve bow, then instead of having to buy a whole new bow, they can simply buy new limbs in a higher poundage.

—*Jessica Carleton, elite competitive archer, coaching for 10 years*

Every archer is different, and equipment must be chosen to suit that person. The length and weight of the riser and limbs, the poundage of the limbs, the draw length, the size and type of the arrows and how they are tuned to the bow, are all considerations that differ for every person. In the last 10 years, my children have each had about 5 different bows, and have changed limbs and arrows countless times over the years. Even as teenagers, they are constantly changing limbs and arrows, but at this level, it is due to finding the state-of-the-art equipment that will produce optimum results.

—*Kathy Miller, president, Chicagoland JOAD club, NAA Level II coach, and mom of Stephanie, 17, and Jonathon, 15*

BADMINTON

Overview

Competitive badminton differs dramatically from the game you play with your child in the backyard. Many Americans still stereotype badminton as a nonserious sport, but it is actually the fastest of all racket sports. The shuttlecock, which players hit with their rackets, can reach speeds of over 180 m.p.h.

Badminton was invented at least 2,000 years ago, and initially played in ancient Greece, India, Japan, and China. The sport takes its name from the estate of Badminton in Gloucestershire, England, where the current version of the game emerged in the 1850s. British players introduced badminton to the United States in 1878. Still played widely in Asia and Europe, badminton became an Olympic sport in 1992, with athletes competing in singles, doubles, and mixed doubles.

After soccer, badminton is the world's most popular sport, played by an estimated one billion people. It's particularly popular in the crowded areas of Southeast Asia and Europe, as badminton facilities don't take up a great deal of space. According to USA Badminton, the sport's governing body, there are over one million active badminton players in the United States, 140,000 of them between the ages of 6 and 11, and 275,000 between ages 12 and 17. Badminton has yet to be played in America at the college level. USA Badminton has embarked on an ambitious grassroots program to get American youth involved, including teaching programs for young children using a lowered net and a smaller racket.

Unlike other racket sports, badminton uses a shuttlecock ("birdie") instead of a ball, made of a rounded cork base with goose feathers attached in competitive play, and plastic for casual play. Players use the racket, which is smaller and lighter than a tennis racket, to strike the shuttlecock, which can never touch the ground. Similar to tennis, badminton is a racket sport for singles or doubles play.

General Benefits

◉ Improves muscular strength, speed, agility, reflexes, quickness, hand-eye coordination, and flexibility.

◉ Builds endurance, stamina, and cardiovascular conditioning from all the running and sprinting that takes place during a game. A badminton game can last up to two hours, and in a typical match, players will cover just about every inch of the court and run more than one mile.

Best Age to Start

◉ While kids can start learning badminton between ages 8 and 12, many do not pick up the sport until their teenage years.

Kids Who Tend to Excel

◉ This lightning-fast sport demands constant motion, and players need both explosive speed and aerobic endurance. Quickness and accuracy are valued more highly than power and strength.

◉ Those who excel in badminton are those with finesse, agility, stamina, and the strategic thinking to play to an opponent's weaknesses. Players also need strong hand-eye coordination.

Safety and Injury Concerns

✦ Badminton injuries are the same as tennis, and the most common include muscle strains, tennis elbow, sprained ankle, Achilles' tear, or bruised heel.

Cost Considerations

✦ Badminton racket, between $50 and $170. Your child will need an extra racket if she becomes a serious player in order to have a spare available at tournaments. Tournament fees average $50.

✦ Shuttlecocks, which cost around $12 a set. Your child will need a new set every few weeks.

BASEBALL, SOFTBALL, AND T-BALL

Overview

Nearly 6 million children ages 5–14 participate in organized baseball and softball leagues in the United States, and baseball is the most popular sport for boys in the country. Over 4 million girls play softball in America, making it the second most popular sport for girls after soccer. The thousands of Little League programs across the country have made America's national pastime one of the most community-oriented activities in which a child can participate. Originally started as an indoor version of baseball, softball was first played in the late 1800s and continues to be played recreationally by millions. Many children start by playing T-ball, a modified version of the game in which balls are hit off a torso-high tee rather than being pitched to the batter.

Although baseball, softball, and T-ball are technically team sports, a great deal of individual attention is focused on specific athletes. For instance, a pitcher is alone in executing a pitch. Similarly, a baseman must singularly field a ball that could determine the outcome of a game played by nine teammates. The player at bat has all eyes focused on him. Many children love this moment in the spotlight, combined with the intense team camaraderie.

T-ball: The Start for Both Baseball and Softball

🐾 An estimated 2.2 million children participate in T-ball, about 65% of them boys and 35% girls.

🐾 There are no pitchers in T-ball. Instead, players use a soft safety ball and hit it off a torso-high tee. All players have the opportunity to bat and play the field. No strikes and balls are called on the batter. A coach or umpire will assist if the child has not hit the ball after many swings. Runners must remain on base until the ball is hit and are not allowed to steal bases. An inning is over when all children have batted once. T-ball games usually have a time limit rather than an inning limit. Otherwise, a nine-inning T-ball game could last for over three hours.

🐾 Most children start out by playing T-ball between ages 4 and 8.

🐾 By age 8, children move on to baseball or softball.

Little League Baseball

🐾 Approximately 3 million children around the globe play Little League. Ten years ago, Little League baseball began "Second Season," with 350 leagues participating in nontraditional fall and winter play. Last year there were 2,342 of these leagues.

My eight-year-old son *loves* baseball. He will try out this year for Little League, which is great because it's intramural and age-appropriate. When he found out about the tryouts, it became clear that he so desperately wanted to be good at baseball. I was feeling guilty about not getting out in the backyard as much as I should. So our solution was that my husband takes him to a batting cage on Saturday mornings at 8:00. They first stop for doughnuts, and then they practice hitting balls. It's their special time together. So he bonds with his dad and has a chance to live out his little-boy dreams of practicing to become a great baseball player when he grows up.

—*Bridgitt, mom of Taylor, 10, Connor and Chloe, 8, and Brian, 6*

✦ Rules require that every child play in every game, and teams are organized by grouping kids with others of similar age and by sex.

Softball

✦ Softball is a form of baseball in which players use a larger, softer ball and an underhand-style pitch. It became an organized sport in the United States in 1933, and an Olympic sport in 1996. Both boys and girls can play softball in elementary school, but only girls pursue it competitively in high school and beyond.

✦ A softball is 12 to 16 inches in circumference, while a baseball is only 9 inches around. There are ten players on the field during a softball game, rather than the nine players in a baseball game, with the extra player covering a portion of the outfield. Also, a softball field is smaller than a baseball field. Finally, in softball, the pitcher throws the ball underhand, unlike in baseball, where the pitcher throws the ball overhand.

✦ Softball consists of several disciplines: fast pitch, slow pitch, and modified fast pitch. Fast pitch allows two main underhand pitching deliveries, one that involves an entire revolution and the other where the pitcher's arm comes back and then forward. Slow pitch requires the pitcher to lob the ball underhanded in an arc. A modified fast pitch allows underhand deliveries, but the arm must not make a complete revolution around the shoulder socket. Internationally, fast pitch is the dominant game. In the United States, slow pitch is played by millions of people in recreational leagues.

Softball is a sport for life. It can be enjoyed at all ages, at all competitive levels, and in all environments. It is a social sport, bringing together people in school, work, and churches, etc. It is also a coed sport where men and women can compete and play together on the same field.

—*Charlie Dobbins, head softball coach, Peace College, teaching for 30 years*

Softball is a great sport for kids because it is fairly inexpensive to get started, it offers all different levels of play with a variety of skill positions needed both offensively and defensively, it's fun, and builds relationships and friendships for both the kids and parents.

—*Larry Cook, softball coach for 30 years*

My daughter's baseball passion has been an outgrowth of us both being Red Sox fans. Baseball has been a great way for us to be kindred spirits and spend time together.

—*David, dad of Alexandra, 10*

Baseball is a great game for kids to pursue because of the life lessons learned playing it. Striking out with the bases loaded and allowing the winning run to score on an error taught me how to handle embarrassment in life. Being retired on a well-hit ball and watching as a teammate committed an error taught me how to handle frustration. Being hit in the back with a fastball and going back into the box for another at-bat taught me how to deal with fear and to fight through it. Watching an umpire make a bad call and winning a championship game taught me to control my emotions. Playing the outfield and having no balls hit to me all day taught me how to deal with loneliness. Baseball is great for a kid's self-confidence. It has been said that hitting a moving baseball is the single most difficult skill in all of sports. It requires the utmost concentration and mental toughness. Since this is so difficult, when a kid feels the crack of the bat on a solid hit, a great sense of accomplishment ensues.

—*Rich Janor, Wheatland Travel Baseball Club coach for 5 years*

General Benefits

- Builds overall muscle strength and conditioning, with upper body strength development from batting, and lower body strength from running

- Increases agility and balance

- Improves hand-eye coordination

- Teaches teamwork

Kids Who Tend to Excel

- Your child will excel in baseball or softball if he enjoys the team aspect of the game. While there is room for individual accomplishment, baseball is essentially a team sport involving coaches, teammates, and fans. The most successful teams are those that draw from the strengths of all involved and don't count on the star quality of a few players to achieve success.

- Any body type can participate in softball if they can hit, pitch, and field well. It is helpful if a player has strength, speed, agility, and size, but he can still excel at this game with one or more of these qualities missing.

- An important requirement is hand-eye coordination. This skill is integral to hitting or fielding a ball in motion.

Best Age to Start

- The first step is usually T-ball, which is recreational and noncompetitive, at about ages 5–6.

- The next step is recreational baseball and softball, where the coaches pitch, generally between the ages of 7 and 8.

◉ Little League baseball and softball start at age 9, with kids pitching around age 10, which is the age at which most acquire the skills needed to throw consistently.

◉ Girls have opportunities to play baseball at a recreational or youth level and veer off to softball around the fifth grade. Peer pressure is probably the greatest motivator for girls to go with softball.

◉ In elite programs, the top-level players start standing out by the time they are 10 and 11.

◉ While some naturally talented kids can pick up baseball or softball in middle school and still excel, most good players tend to start by second grade.

Baseball can be enjoyed by just about any kid. A player need not be tall, like in basketball; he need not be big, like in football; and he need not be fast, like in soccer. As long as a child has a desire to work hard, a willingness to practice and improve, and a love for the game, he or she can have fun on the field. The first quality I look for when assessing a young ball player is "coachability"—an openness to coaching and instruction. Other important qualities include a relentless work ethic, discipline, determination, and a positive attitude. Physical qualities include hand-eye coordination, quickness and agility, and upper and lower body strength.

　　—Rich Janor, Wheatland Travel Baseball Club coach for 5 years

The game of softball is a game of motion—the pitcher is moving, the ball is moving, and the hitter is moving. As a result, it requires a high degree of coordination.

　　—Gale Bundrick, softball coach, Canyon Del Oro High School, teaching for 25 years

Qualities such as speed, agility, and arm strength are those traits that the kids who excel usually possess. It helps to remind your child that in baseball, even if you fail 70% of the time, you will be a great player!

　　—Chris Huesman, Dublin, Ohio, high school baseball coach for 13 years

Start early, and the earlier the better. Trying to teach your son baseball at age 10, while the rest of the kids on the team have played since they were 4, will be very hard on him. Besides feeling like he'll never measure up to the rest of the kids, it puts a lot of pressure on him to perform well at something new.

    —Nancy, mom of a son age 13

Girls who play Little League baseball make great softball players. Many areas of the country do not offer softball programs for youngsters, so T-ball and baseball develop the necessary skills.

    —Neil Becker, high school softball coach, coaching for 7 years

If your child doesn't start softball until 12, it's not a big deal! However, I would have her playing by age 12 if she plans to participate in high school.

    —Gale Bundrick, softball coach, Canyon Del Oro High School, teaching for 25 years

What to Look For When Getting Started

🐟 Most baseball, softball, and T-ball teams are community-based organizations. A town or district usually has its own rules and regulations. In official Little League baseball, leagues can only accept players who live within their zoned area, so forming teams doesn't become a competition to acquire the best player.

🐟 Before signing your child up for a baseball, softball, or T-ball team, consider the following issues to team composition:
- Do you want your child to be on a coed or single-sex team?
- What will be your reaction if your child is the only girl or boy on the team?
- What type of practice and game schedules should you expect throughout the season?
- Will playoffs extend the season?

🐟 Leagues with players under the age of 10 should use adult pitchers or batting tees.

✦ Most leagues are organized by age groups that overlap a bit, so some children can move ahead, while others stay with a comparable skill and age level group.

✦ Look for a coach who insists that all players rotate through the lineup and have a chance to play different positions, offers only constructive criticism, and whose first priority is having fun and learning rather than winning.

✦ Look for a team with no more than 14 players to ensure that your child gets enough time on the field and at bat.

✦ For most eight-year-olds, two one-hour practices a week and one game a week should be expected. As your child's age, skill, fitness, and interest increase, so too will the length and frequency of practices and games.

✦ As players get better, many take lessons from a private pitching, hitting, or throwing coach to work one-on-one on skill development. Look for a quality private instructor who can help your child gain in-depth working knowledge of various techniques.

Safety and Injury Concerns

✦ With safety precautions in place, the majority of injuries in baseball and softball are minor, consisting mainly of scrapes, muscle sprains and strains, jammed fingers, bruises, and fractures to the ankle and knee. Coaches should teach the proper techniques for throwing a ball, running the bases, and sliding into a base.

✦ Breakaway bases, which dislodge if slid into by a runner, prevent most softball and baseball sliding injuries to the hands, ankle, foot, and knee. A field can be equipped with this type of base for about $400.

✦ Make sure your child starts to practice throwing the ball before the start of a season so as to help reduce soreness or tendonitis during the first few weeks.

✦ Getting hit by the ball poses the greatest danger. Baseball has the highest number of sports-related eye injuries in children. For this reason, batting helmets with face guards should be worn during both practice and games by all batters, batters waiting on deck, and base runners. Face guards, made of clear plastic that attach to the sides of a batting helmet, also help prevent mouth, dental, and eye injuries if your child gets hit by a ball. As players mature, the pitching and hit balls become faster.

✦ Many children who pitch suffer overuse injuries to the shoulder, rotator cuff, and elbow from too much pitching or from improperly releasing the ball. Approximately 45% of pitchers under age 12 have chronic elbow pain, rising to around 58% for high school pitchers. Make sure pitching time is limited to protect your

Arm injuries are the most common injuries I have seen in youth baseball. If a coach allows a player to pitch too much, he runs the risk of ruining that player's career. I know high school pitchers who needed arm surgery because their youth coaches overpitched them or taught them to throw breaking pitches too early. A pitcher should not learn to throw a curveball until at least age 12. It drives me nuts when I see a coach overpitching a kid at any level. The coach becomes so consumed with winning a particular game (in several years, no one will even remember the score or the outcome) that he compromises the health and safety of his young athlete. Most leagues have rules about appropriate amounts of rest between pitching appearances. A good coach observes these rules and is even more conservative if possible.

—*Rich Janor, Wheatland Travel Baseball Club coach for 5 years*

Sliding injuries are fairly common. The headfirst slide into home plate is a source of many broken or dislocated fingers and wrists caused by colliding with a catcher blocking the plate. Feet-first slides also have their dangers. A lot of players get scared about sliding and slide late, risking jammed or broken ankles.

—*Randy Watt, youth softball coach for 26 years*

child. To decrease shoulder and elbow problems from excessive pitching, Little League baseball has set a limit of six innings of pitching per week and requires pitchers to rest between appearances.

✦ In T-ball or on a team with young players, safety balls are much softer and don't hurt a player who gets hit by the ball. This also helps keep children from developing a fear of the ball. Softer baseballs or softballs, which have a foam core instead of cork or rubber, also lessen the severity of ball-impact injuries. Little League baseball allows the use of these balls in games.

✦ Make sure the coach inspects the playing field for holes, glass, and other debris before a game or practice.

✦ While catastrophic injuries are rare, about three or four children die each year from getting struck in the head or chest with a ball or bat.

Cost Considerations

✦ Your child should have his own glove for practices and games. You will need to take the time to find a well-fitting glove your child feels comfortable wearing. To break in a leather glove, use softening oil or saddle soap, and tie a ball into the glove using rubber bands or string to form a well-defined pocket.

✦ Most league fees include a team T-shirt or uniform and cap. The teams generally provide bats, balls, helmets, and catcher's gear.

✦ Standard player equipment that your child will likely need to purchase includes a glove ($30–$150), bat ($50–$150, but can cost as much as $400 for a high-end model), baseball shoes with rubber cleats ($20–$80), and sliding pants ($25–$40).

For baseball, you will need at least a baseball glove and, depending on your child, maybe batting gloves, a bat bag, additional pants and socks, their own bat and even a specialty glove for a specific position, all of which can get quite expensive. Granted these are not required, but your child may want these because they really do help his game or "all the other kids on the team have them." Looking the part is just as important as playing the part in a child's eye!

—*Nancy, mom of a son age 13*

The big expense in youth baseball for parents who choose to have their kids work with an instructor one-on-one is private lessons, perhaps the best way to put a child on the fast track toward a successful baseball career. Private lessons with a professional instructor cost between $30 to $80 per hour! Anyone who charges less probably isn't any good, and anyone who charges more is probably taking you to the cleaners.

—*Rich Janor, Wheatland Travel Baseball Club coach for 5 years*

When an athlete gets involved with a travel team, the cost really takes off. These programs generally cost thousands of dollars per player. On top of these fees, you must also include travel expenses such as motels, meals, gas, and plane tickets or wear and tear on the family car. Some teams travel great distances to find the right competition or get the exposure to college coaches.

—*Randy Watt, youth softball coach for 26 years*

More serious players might have their own helmet ($25–$50) and batting gloves ($25–$50).

🔸 The catchers need additional protective equipment, such as a catcher's mitt, face guard, shin guards, throat guard, long chest protector, and protective cup for boys. The total cost ranges between $100 and $300. An advanced player may want to own equipment of a higher quality.

🔸 Registration fees for a typical youth baseball program range from $50 to $250 per year, depending if the cost of uniforms, referees, or paid coaches is included. Private coaching sessions typically cost $35 for a half-hour lesson.

🔸 Travel baseball programs, which are more competitive and intense, range from $250 to over $1,000 per season, depending on the number of games and ability to find sponsors. Many children also attend special training camps, which adds to the expense. You might also have to factor in travel costs, particularly if the team will be participating in out-of-state tournaments.

BASKETBALL

Overview

Basketball is a fast-moving team sport that can be played on both outdoor and indoor courts, as well as on school playgrounds and in driveways. Although an organized game of basketball requires 10 players, it can easily be altered to suit fewer players, because the skills needed to play the sport can be worked on and practiced individually.

Dr. James Naismith is recognized for inventing the game of basketball. In December 1891 he put a pair of peach baskets up at a YMCA gymnasium in Springfield, Massachusetts, and shot a soccer ball into them. A few weeks later, women at Smith College picked up the game. A basketball replaced the soccer ball and the metal hoops were introduced in 1893, followed by backboards in 1895. That same game, with rule refinements and open nets, today is played by more than 300 million people worldwide and has been prominently featured at the Olympic Games since 1936. With superstars like Michael Jordan, Magic Johnson, and Larry Bird, the sport inspires millions of kids to play each year.

There is something special for those of us who love the game: the squeak of the sneakers, the bounce of the ball, the swish of the net. It is something that keeps many of us playing in over-40 pickup leagues or taking backyard jump shots well beyond our prime.

—*Jeff Hoyle, high school girls' basketball coach, teaching for 19 years*

General Benefits

- Improves overall strength, endurance, and conditioning, as it involves continual sprinting, jumping, shooting, and rebounding

- Improves hand-eye coordination.

- Teaches interdependence and teamwork.

Kids Who Tend to Excel

- Basketball is often considered a game dominated by tall players who use their height to their advantage over smaller players. If your child is tall for his age, he will likely have an edge over his peers when he starts to play. Also, many times in basketball, the size of your child will determine what position he plays.

- However, height is not the determining factor of who will be a good basketball player. If your child is short, he can learn how to play smart by getting into proper position on the court and improving his ball-handling skills. Many short players can outplay taller players by relying on their speed and agility.

- Basketball players need to be quick and strong. They need to have good hand-eye coordination to dribble, pass, and shoot the ball. Athleticism and concentration are both important, to keep up with the aerobic intensity of the game and the quick turnarounds in play.

Basketball teaches passion, discipline, selflessness, respect, perspective, courage, leadership, responsibility, resilience, and imagination. As you work on improving your game, your practice builds confidence, and confidence builds success. What a valuable lesson!

—*Jeff Hoyle, high school girls' basketball coach, teaching for 19 years*

I look around at some of the parents who push their kids so hard at basketball but don't realize that their kids will probably never be in the NBA. There are so few slots. What are the chances? My kids are too short, but playing basketball is a skill I want them to learn and one that will allow them to play pickup games in the driveway with their friends.

—*Deb, mom of Evan, 10, and Olivia, Justin, and Shelby 8*

Once you pick up the fundamentals of basketball, you have to practice hard to master them, even if you're athletically gifted. Introverted kids do well, as they often rise to the challenge. Plus, all kids learn that they have to work together as one cohesive team.

—*Eric Edward, youth basketball coach for 6 years*

The best players I have coached are not only good athletes but also have the drive to go out and work at the many different physical and mental skills basketball requires, and then apply them in a team setting. Ball handling, shooting, passing, rebounding, defensive slides, being able to play with your back to the basket, make shots or free throws in pressure situations, as well as teamwork are key skills. You also don't see many overweight basketball players running up and down the court because basketball requires strength and good cardiovascular conditioning.

—*Jeff Hoyle, high school girls' basketball coach, teaching for 19 years*

Kids who excel are extremely coordinated, aggressive, and quick. As they get older, size, an understanding of the game, and a willingness to practice their skills become important.

—*Andrew Crane, Henrico County sports supervisor, coaching youth basketball for 26 years*

In basketball, all players should learn perimeter fundamentals and guard skills because you never know when a kid will stop growing, and a 13-year-old center may have to be his high school's point guard by the time he is a senior.

—*Ray Lokar, head basketball coach at Bishop Amat High School, coaching for over 25 years*

Best Age to Start

 Most youth basketball leagues accept boys and girls beginning at age 5.

 Children ages 5–7 concentrate on skill development, while children ages 8 and older compete on teams. The younger children usually do not have the strength yet to shoot or handle a ball. If your young child wants to play in games, find a youth league that uses smaller balls and lowers baskets to only seven or eight feet.

 When your child reaches 8 years of age, he can begin more regulated team competitive play. Yet many children do not become competitive in basketball until middle school.

Kids can really begin to learn the basics such as dribbling, shooting, and the rules of the game as early as age 6. But it's not until age 7 or 8 that they become coordinated enough to handle the ball and move with it.

> —*Eric Edward, youth basketball coach for 6 years*

Most collegiate athletes begin at a young age. At the early stages in development, parents should look for coaches who are knowledgeable and who are willing and able to take the time to make a child feel important and successful.

> —*Bobbi Morse, assistant women's basketball coach, St. Louis University, coaching for 18 years*

My daughter started playing basketball at 5 years old, and it was so hilarious. The kids would pass the ball two inches away from each other and shoot at the wrong basket. She loved wearing the team uniform, but I'm not sure it justified the expense, as it wasn't quite what we were hoping she'd get out of it!

> —*Lisa, mom of Lars, 8, Elsa, 6, and Peter 4*

What to Look For When Getting Started

🦃 Most youth leagues start out playing on a half-size court, with lowered baskets, and a smaller, lighter-weight ball that the kids can more easily manipulate with their hands. It helps lower the frustration level when learning the game and trying to shoot baskets.

🦃 You must also decide if your child wants to start in a coed or single-sex program, as many leagues do not divide according to gender until middle school.

🦃 Make sure the coach gives equal playing time to all the players regardless of skill level.

🦃 A typical league basketball team holds one hour of practice and one game per week. However, traveling or more competitive leagues require a much heavier time commitment with longer daily practices and games at least once or twice a week.

A common oversight among basketball coaches is spending too much time teaching plays and not enough time teaching how to play. Teams need to have organized offenses and plays, but it is far more important to be able to execute the fundamentals of movement, ball handling, dribbling, passing, and shooting than it is to know how to run through a particular offense. Along with all of the individual fundamentals, players need to understand the concept of "relative motion." That can best be described as realizing how one player fits into the space on the floor, given the relative positioning of the other players, both offense and defense. A player with this understanding will know how to move to get open, create proper spacing, pass angles, and play well on ball defense.

—*Ray Lokar, head basketball coach at Bishop Amat High School, coaching for over 25 years*

In basketball, stature, quickness, and skills determine the position played. Usually height will be the basis for a coach to play the child in a particular position, with the specific skills for that position then being taught.

—*Ronald Crawford, past national chairman, AUU Sports, coaching junior high and high school basketball for 27 years*

Safety and Injury Concerns

🦶 The most common injuries are jammed fingers, sprained ankles, knee injuries, and muscle strains. Preseason conditioning, stretching before practice or a game, and high-top basketball shoes are the best preventive measures.

🦶 Eye injuries are frequent and basketball is one of the leading causes of sports-related eye injuries in children. Along with baseball, basketball accounts for half of all sports-related mouth injuries. The most common causes of injuries are scrambling for loose balls, falls, and collisions between players.

🦶 Most injuries turn out to be minor, causing a player to miss the remainder of the practice or game, but be able to play again within the week. Of those injuries requiring surgery, knee injuries account for the most. Basketball as a sport has the highest rate among girls of knee injuries requiring surgery.

🦶 If your child wears glasses, switch to safety glasses or use glass guards for eye protection.

🐾 Do not let your child wear jewelry or chew gum during practice or games.

🐾 Have your child use a mouth guard to protect his teeth.

Cost Considerations

🐾 One great thing about basketball is that you don't need a lot of equipment to play, just a court with basketball hoops, a good pair of shoes, and a basketball.

🐾 Most youth basketball leagues charge fees that cover team uniforms, which can cost anywhere between $15 and $100. If your child joins a travel team, such as those sponsored by AAU, the fees can run up to the thousands of dollars to cover coaching and travel costs.

🐾 Since basketball requires a great deal of running, jumping, and pivoting, your child's basketball shoes are his most essential piece of equipment. A good pair of basketball shoes will cost between $70 and $100, but often stores have closeouts on prior models that can be picked up at a significant discount. Basketball shoes come in low- and high-top styles, with the latter offering extra ankle support. Given the quick running, jumping, sudden stopping, and turning, high-top styles might be the better choice, as they will help prevent ankle injuries. Your child should wear thick white athletic socks with the shoes, and should wear them when trying on shoes at the store.

There really aren't that many risks involved in basketball, as most injuries will be minor. The worst thing I've seen happen is a kid smack his head on the floor and require a few stitches. Occasionally we have some bloody noses, bumps, and bruises, things like that, but nothing too serious.

　　—*Rich Bradley, Basketball City youth coach for 2 years*

The common injuries range from sprained ankles to torn knee ligaments and can be avoided by proper weight training, conditioning, and diet.

　　—*Coral Sage, women's basketball assistant coach, University of California, Riverside, for 2 years*

🐾 Basketballs come in varying sizes, and children generally start with a size 5 ball. Check what size basketball your child will be using in the league before purchasing one. A ball costs between $10 and $40.

🐾 Basketball hoops can range from $150 to thousands of dollars. A quality basketball hoop for your home will cost around $350. You may also incur an installation charge if the hoop is not freestanding.

BOWLING

Overview

Historians trace bowling back to the Stone Age, when people used a round stone and stick, though the earliest archeological record of bowling dates back 7,000 years to ancient Egypt, where a round object and marble bars, resembling a bowling ball and pins, were found in a pyramid. Tenpin bowling, as found in today's bowling, was developed in the United States in the 1800s, based on a nine-pin European game. Today millions of people around the world play individually or on league teams. Bowling can be played both socially or at a competitive level. More than 80 countries belong to an international governing body for ten-pin bowling, and bowling is also one of the Special Olympics summer sports.

Your child may be very interested in getting involved in sports but lack the athletic ability to compete with his peers. Bowling is a good option to explore. It offers a great alternative to outdoor sports, especially during bad weather. Plus, it's a sport that can be played for a lifetime.

Taking up bowling is very inexpensive, and there is bound to be a bowling alley in or near your community. If your child loves bowling, you can sign him up for a youth bowling league. As in swimming, individual athletes compete in separate lanes against each other. Like archery, scores are determined by the accuracy of hitting the target. The scoring in bowling is objective and depends purely on your ability to knock down the pins.

There are about 18,000 leagues in over 4,500 bowling centers across the United States. Competition starts at the very beginner level and moves up to an elite national and international level. Currently, 10 states offer high school varsity level competition for male and female athletes, and the number grows each year. The National Collegiate Athletic Association

---

On a youth level, during the course of a typical three-game series, a young bowler will use 134 muscles and walk over 2 miles while carrying 864 pounds. Plus, there are no "bench sitters" in bowling. With the handicap or equalization system used in most beginner and intermediate programs, the differences in abilities are equalized, allowing all competitors an opportunity at winning.

—*James Zebehazy, executive director, Young American Bowling Alliance, coaching for 20 years*

Bowlers perform an approach that requires coordination of every limb of their body, and to perform it well requires years of practice, coaching, and desire. Math skills are learned in scorekeeping and as the bowler advances, in adjusting on the lanes, as well as some basic physics of the bowling ball construction and reaction. Plus, bowling can be a team or individual sport.

—*Doug Barker, Louisville youth bowling coach for 16 years*

(NCAA) just recognized girls' bowling as a championship sport with over 40 colleges offering NCAA-recognized competition.

General Benefits

- ◉ Builds strength, endurance, flexibility, and balance
- ◉ Develops good hand-eye coordination
- ◉ Builds control and accuracy
- ◉ Provides anaerobic exercise

Kids Who Tend to Excel

◉ Bowling is not dependent upon strength or size. The key is being able to execute the same bowling stroke again and again with precision. Like a baseball pitcher, a bowler needs consistency to deliver the ball toward the target.

Bowling is great for kids because any child can do it regardless of size or quickness. Kids who excel have a desire to physically improve and are open to trying new techniques. It attracts kids who thought they were not capable of competing in a sport. I've coached really overweight kids and very insecure kids, kids with muscular dystrophy, multiple sclerosis, and a number of other disabilities. To see their self-confidence grow is one of the things bowling is all about.

—Doug Barker, Louisville youth bowling coach for 16 years

To excel at the top levels of bowling, an athlete needs a high degree of hand-eye coordination and timing as opposed to size, speed, and strength. The bowler has to be able to deliver a ball with a very consistent speed within about a 4-inch area on a lane that is 42 inches wide, and hit at least one other "target" between 15 and 30 feet down the lane. The elite athlete does not have a particular body type, which is one of the attractive aspects of our sport. Anyone can participate.

—James Zebehazy, executive director, Young American Bowling Alliance, coaching for 20 years

◉ Kids who take up bowling tend to be self-disciplined and are often introverted, highly analytical, and able to focus and visualize the path they need the ball to take.

◉ From a tactical perspective, bowling is an easy sport to learn but difficult to master, as it requires a great deal of thought, concentration, and strategy.

Best Age to Start

◉ Your child can begin recreational bowling as soon as he can safely pick up and roll a six-pound ball with two hands. Peewees start bowling with bumpers at age 3. By the time they are 6, they generally have learned enough to start bowling without bumpers.

◉ Children should begin to take serious bowling lessons around age 8 or 9. Before this age, your child's body will struggle to properly glide the bowling ball around his hip.

What to Look For When Getting Started

🦋 For young children who are just starting out, the lighter pins and smaller balls of candlepin or duckpin bowling make it easier for them to learn to bowl. Candlepins, about the same height as a tenpin, and duckpins, which are shorter, are considered "small ball" games. The bowling ball is about the size of a softball and weighs about 3 pounds. These regional games are found only in New England and parts of

Look for a program when your child is 6 years or older, as there are safety factors to consider such as the fact that bowling balls weigh between 6 and 16 pounds.

—Don Boggs, USA Bowling silver-level coach and Junior Olympics master instructor for 18 years

We actually have members as young as 2 years old. As you can imagine, they do not use a traditional delivery, but Mom and Dad have them out on the lanes. Typically, our members start at age 6. Many of our programs provide coaching at this level, but it is between ages 8 and 10 when children develop the maturity and ability to understand the coaching theory and recommendations, and where the best chance of success takes place.

—James Zebehazy, executive director, Young American Bowling Alliance, coaching for 20 years

For a youth bowling league, seek out a program with a good coach/child ratio (no more than ten kids per coach during regular league competition) and ensure that the program for kids 11 and under stresses fun, sportsmanship, and team play over individual achievements. The occasional child under 12 who shows unusual talent and promise can further develop skills with private coaching or by moving to the "junior" league (ages 12–14) at an earlier age. Kids bowling in a recreational league usually spend between two and three hours at the bowling center every Saturday. As they become more involved with the sport, they might go to the center one or two afternoons a week for individual practice or lessons. Once the "competitive" bug gets them, they will probably bowl more than one league each week, practice three or four times each week, and enter tournaments a couple of times a month.

—*Maryfran Milbank, U.S. Olympics silver-level certified bowling coach for 10 years*

Bowling presents a number of options for competing. You can be a casual bowler, who does not feel pressure to score well but enjoys the socialization and activity. You can be a serious bowler, who is there more for the score and to reach a higher level of ability and skill. When looking at a program for your child, look for coaches that are on the lanes talking, laughing, and advising. Watch the kids. Are they having fun, or are they all frustrated if they aren't bowling well?

—*Doug Barker, Louisville youth bowling coach for 16 years*

There are organized youth leagues in just about every bowling center across the country on Saturday mornings. Many centers also offer after-school programs. High school bowling is rapidly expanding across the country leading into more collegiate programs. The NCAA is scheduled to formally recognize women's bowling as a varsity sport within the next month. There are traveling youth leagues that visit different bowling centers on a weekly basis and an extensive offering of tournaments on a local, state, and national level.

—*Christine Zahn, NCAA's National Director of High School Bowling, teaching for 32 years*

Maryland and Virginia. Scoring is the same as in regulation tenpin bowling, except that you are allowed three balls per frame.

❧ Many children get frustrated continually watching their balls roll into the gutter. Children should start with fold-down bumpers to keep the balls in play and out of the gutter, and give them the thrill of knocking down pins.

Most injuries occur when a child is not adhering to the rules, rather than resulting from the physical performance of the game. The first concern is a child getting hit by someone swinging a bowling ball. Many kids don't remain in the bowler's area, but play around on the approach. If they are playing with the bowling balls at the ball return there is the probability of pinched fingers. Inquisitive types put their faces in the ball return to see if they can see the ball coming, which results in injury.

—*Christine Zahn, NCAA's National Director of High School Bowling, teaching for 32 years*

The most common injuries you see in bowling are mashed fingers between balls and a ball hitting a child's ankle. As kids get older, you see injuries to the rotator cuff, wrist, and elbow of the bowling arm, and the hip, knee, or ankle of the sliding (non-bowling-side) leg.

—*Doug Barker, Louisville youth bowling coach for 16 years*

Bowling centers have a reputation as "smoke filled" and frequented by beer-guzzling adults, but nothing could be further from the truth. Today's bowling facilities are clean and bright, and more and more are 100% smoke-free even beyond their youth programs.

—*James Zebehazy, executive director, Young American Bowling Alliance, coaching for 20 years*

⚜ Look for a junior league that has an instructor who specializes in teaching children and who is knowledgeable about the fundamentals and intricacies of bowling.

⚜ Ask about the ratio of coaches to children, whether the coaches have been certified through the national programs such as the Young American Bowling Alliance, and how long the bowling program has been in existence.

⚜ Lessons should teach the fundamentals: rules, proper approach, hand position, follow-through, ball dynamics, footwork, different bowling techniques, and scoring. Your child's muscle memory progresses until bowling becomes a mental game and the physical portion takes place automatically.

⚜ You want an instructor who will focus on helping your child develop a fundamentally sound game before moving on to power moves.

Safety and Injury Concerns

⚜ Muscle strains on the upper body joints, arm, hand, and shoulder can occur if your child uses a ball that is too heavy for him or improperly fitted, or if he tries to pick up the ball with just one hand. Muscle soreness or ankle bruises can also result when a beginner tries to throw a ball instead of using a proper swinging technique. Sore hamstring muscles result from bending from the waist instead of at the knee.

❧ In order to prevent these types of injuries, your child should work with a qualified coach on his bowling technique, and have the fit of his bowling ball checked and adjusted every six months.

Cost Considerations

❧ When your child is first starting out, shoes cost only a few dollars to rent from a bowling center, and the house bowling balls are free. Bowling shoes cost between $15 and $40 a pair, and your child may want a pair if he gets serious about bowling, though children tend to outgrow them as fast as sneakers.

❧ If you buy your child his own ball, he will have the advantage of being able to

Do not go to a discount chain store to purchase a bowling ball, as the clerks who work at these stores are not properly trained to fit a ball to a bowler's hand, and serious ligament and tendon injuries could occur. As a child's skills develop, equipment becomes more important. Like in golf, where different types of clubs are used for different types of shots, there are different types of bowling balls for different types of shots. After a child has learned the fundamentals with his or her own "first" ball, the next step would be to purchase a second ball. In many cases, the bowler's first ball is plastic, which is more suited to use for spares, so the second ball (urethane or reactive urethane) will enable the bowler to learn a "hook" shot, which is more reliable for scoring strikes.

—*Maryfran Milbank, U.S. Olympics silver-level certified bowling coach for 10 years*

A polyester bowling ball, great for beginning bowlers, will run in the neighborhood of $60 including drilling by a professional. Make sure your child has the proper grip (hole sizes and span) and proper weight ball. You will need to replace the ball with a heavier ball as your child gets older and stronger. The grip (hole sizes and distance between the thumb and finger holes) will also change as your child's hand grows. A ball can be plugged and redrilled for a fraction of the cost of a new ball. Have the ball checked every 6 months by a pro shop to ensure a proper fit, as it's hard to improve skills with a ball that is too light or no longer fits the hand comfortably.

—*Cary Pon, manager of coach development and certification for USA Bowling and instructor for 25 years*

build up more consistently by not bowling with a different fit and weight each time he plays. He will need a light ball that weighs under 8 pounds, a ball bag, and a hand towel to wipe the ball off as well as dry his hands while bowling.

✦ When you decide to purchase your child a bowling ball, get one professionally fitted from a reputable pro shop. A beginning ball generally costs between $30 and $75, and many pro shops give discounts to youth league bowlers.

✦ Your child's ball will need to be refitted approximately every 6 months to accommodate his growing finger size. Some pro shops offer a used-equipment exchange program that, for a fee, enables your child to exchange balls for increased weight as he grows. Bowling balls run from 6 pounds for youths to 16 pounds, which is the heaviest weight allowed by rules governing the sport. Generally a ball is good for about 9 months.

✦ As your child's expertise grows, he will likely need several different types of bowling balls. For elite athletes, bowling balls can cost up to $200 each, and an athlete may need 6 or 8 bowling balls for use on the differing lane conditions.

✦ When a child first joins a youth bowling league, he must pay an annual registration fee of around $12 to the Young American Bowling Alliance (YABA), a national membership organization for youth bowlers. Tournament fees average about $10 each event, and young athletes usually bowl three events.

✦ Ongoing expenses for a child in a league include weekly fees for lane usage, which are usually under $10, as well as possibly being asked to contribute to a prize fund to provide end-of-season trophies or scholarship funds.

✦ Private lessons vary considerably in cost, but usually run between $15 and $50 an hour.

✦ Bowling centers generally give youth league bowlers discounted prices for bowling practice outside of league play.

CHEERLEADING

Overview

Cheerleading was launched in 1898 when Johnny Campbell led the first cheers at a Minnesota University American football game. This phenomenon later developed into a type of organized support group that cheered teams on and built school spirit at sporting events. There are now more than 3.3 million boys and girls involved in cheerleading throughout the United States. Despite the fact that cheerleading was started by a boy, most cheerleaders are girls, with typically only one or two boys found on high school squads.

Cheerleading has evolved over the past few decades from a pastime for popular kids to a highly choreographed and complex athletic activity requiring strength, agility, grace, and stamina. Cheerleading shares many attributes with gymnastics and dance, plus it has a unique teamwork element. In addition to cheers, jumps, rolls, tumbles, pyramids, and athletic stunts are used to dazzle the audience.

With this new athleticism, competitive cheerleading has increased. While many cheerleading squads simply entertain spectators of the home team and build team spirit, approximately 30% of school teams will also participate in cheerleading competitions. At these competitions, held regionally and at the national level, squads perform complex maneuvers and difficult skills in nonstop routines lasting up to three minutes. Many coaches and participants want cheerleading to be considered a serious sport so that schools will pay for qualified coaches and uniforms, and the community will recognize the athleticism required for modern cheerleading. Until the majority of squads make competitions their primary mission, though, cheerleading will not likely be recognized as an official sport.

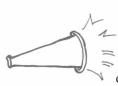

General Benefits

◉ Provides strenuous aerobic exercise through stunts, dancing, tumbling, jumping, and conditioning

◉ Builds upper and lower body strength

Cheerleading is performed in front of large crowds. Kids learn how to excel under pressure, because in games and competitions there is no such thing as a second chance. Cheerleading is also a sport based solely on teamwork. When stunting, cheerleaders learn the importance of every part of the stunt—not just the flyers, but the backs and bases as well. Before stunting, a squad usually engages in "trust" exercises so that flyers and bases feel comfortable with one another.

—*Anna Wong, head coach, Tufts University Football/Basketball Cheerleading Squad, for 2 years*

- Develops balance, flexibility, agility, and coordination

- Teaches teamwork and a high level of trust for teammates, especially as the stunts increase in difficulty

Kids Who Tend to Excel

- Cheerleading takes physical strength, agility, poise, stamina, and flexibility.

- Children who excel usually come from playing other athletic sports like softball, soccer, swimming, and gymnastics.

- Those who are outgoing and are driven by the adrenaline rush of competing usually enjoy cheerleading the most.

Best Age to Start

- Cheerleading coaches differ widely in terms of what they consider the best age to start, with some advocating it for five-year-olds, while others suggesting kids get involved at much older ages after first becoming trained in gymnastics, tumbling, or dance.

What to Look For When Getting Started

- Ask about the philosophy of the cheerleading program, how children are selected, and the type of skills or athletics that will be incorporated into routines.

- The athleticism required of modern cheerleading necessitates the need for a coach, as well as spotters for any stunts. Look for a coach who has some type of coach training or certification in proper skill development and safety procedures.

The kids who excel the most in cheerleading are those who pay the most attention and work their hardest to fix mistakes. Motions have to be tight and locked. Stunting has to be done to specific counts. The level of accuracy and attention to detail is very high. I think the "cheerleader" stereotype has died down in the last decade largely due to its emphasis and portrayal in the media and mainstream culture as a competitive sport. Male cheerleaders are rare, but when I do meet one, they are among the nicest, sweetest, most athletic and strongest people I've ever met. Male cheerleaders transcend the "obnoxious jock" stereotypes to define the epitome of a competitive athlete.

—Anna Wong, head coach, Tufts University Football/Basketball Cheerleading Squad, for 2 years

A child will excel in cheerleading if she has persistence, willingness to try anything new, and the ability to master fear.

—Maggie Hendricks, cheerleading coach, Chicagoland Pop Warner, for 6 years

Children can begin cheerleading as young as 4 or 5 years old. At that age, they can learn the basics and get in front of a crowd. As they get older, programs start incorporating stunts and jumps, and at around age 8–10, they can start performing some of the advanced skills.

—*Jim Lord, executive director of American Association of Cheerleading Coaches and Advisors, coaching for 18 years*

For cheerleading, starting a child in gymnastics as young as 2 years old helps ensure better success at cheerleading, as it teaches not only basic tumbling but also all-around skills from hand-eye coordination to balance.

—*Regina Fraticelli, Junior Elite Allstar cheerleading coach for 7 years*

Attend a sporting event, and watch the chemistry of the squad and how the coach treats them.

🌿 Make sure that there is supervision at all practices and games, as well as a mat provided for practice. Also ask if the squad works on the conditioning and flexibility needed for any of the moves.

🌿 The Pop Warner football program has cheerleading squads, starting in elementary school around age 8, and offers cheer competitions at the local, regional, and national level.

Many communities have for-profit cheer gyms, with squads coached by paid professionals instead of volunteer moms, as is the case in a nonprofit organization such as Pop Warner. Cheer gyms usually have tryouts and place kids on teams that suit their level. In my Pop Warner squad, we take all kids who want to sign up, and have some kids who have never cheered before as well as those who are very good. We are geared more toward having fun than winning at competition.

—*Kari Dodge, Pop Warner junior cheer head coach for 2 years*

Children in a youth organizations such as peewee football are going to spend much less but get minimal training because staff are usually volunteer high school cheerleaders and limited in their experience. If you want your child to get a good feel for cheerleading, competitive cheerleading programs offer a great experience. The extra costs can be high, but what you get out of it in one year you can't get in four to five years of youth cheerleading.

—*Regina Fraticelli, Junior Elite Allstar cheerleading coach for 7 years*

Many kids don't realize the level of commitment required in cheerleading. Every child needs to be present at every practice, as many times a routine cannot be practiced or put together because a single person is missing.

—*Anna Wong, head coach, Tufts University Football/Basketball Cheerleading Squad, for 2 years*

Safety Issues and Concerns

🔰 Cheerleading can be a dangerous sport because of the way it combines other sports such as gymnastics, acrobatics, and dance. The most common injuries are usually minor and involve rolled ankles, sore wrists, pulled muscles, shin splints, or bruises from tumbling or cartwheels.

🔰 Falls are common if a squad does stunts and can result in broken hands or wrists, black eyes, as well as back or knee injuries. For this reason, it's essential that your child's coach teach proper falling techniques that will protect against injury. Adequate protective matting is also essential, along with spotters during practices.

🔰 Your child should do stretching and warm-up exercises before any practices, games, pep rallies, and competitions.

🔰 The American Association of Cheerleading Coaches and Advisors (AACCA) has developed a Cheerleading Safety Manual for cheerleading gymnastics, which includes very specific safety rules for stunts, pyramids, and tumbling. These range from prohibitions on certain moves, such as diving rolls or vaults, as well as general safety prescriptions, such as all pyramids and partner stunts are limited to two persons high. The AACCA also runs safety courses for coaches nationwide.

Most injuries occur during stunting. Usually the flyer falls and hurts herself as well as the cheerleader who is trying to catch her. Minor cuts and bruises are also common. The best way to avoid any cheerleading-related injuries is to keep fingernails short, take off all jewelry, never chew gum or eat candy while cheering, don't wear any hair clips and keep hair out of your face, wear proper practice attire, and most important, pay attention!

—*Anna Wong, head coach, Tufts University Football/Basketball Cheerleading Squad, for 2 years*

Cost Considerations

🌿 Cheerleading costs vary from squad to squad, but in addition to a registration fee, your child will usually need to purchase a uniform (skirt, shell, and liner, if used), socks, shoes, pompoms, rain jacket, warm-ups, and hair ribbons for girls. The uniform itself typically costs around $100, but the cost often ends up between $200 and $300 for all the extras. Cheerleading shoes cost between $25 and $50, and pompoms cost $10–$15.

🌿 Some squads attend cheerleading camps or clinics, for which they have to pay an additional registration fee, and many take gymnastic classes on the side.

🌿 Potential hidden costs include competition fees (generally between $20 and $50) and travel fees.

🌿 Cheerleading groups usually rely on fund-raisers and sponsors to help defray costs.

In terms of travel costs, the cost to go to our regional competitions is about $200 per cheerleader and travel to nationals averages $1,200 to $1,500 per cheerleader.

—*Kari Dodge, Pop Warner junior cheer head coach for 2 years*

Basic uniform apparel and a home camp can be as little as $300 per child, but can run as much as $1,000 or more if they are a competitive team that requires gymnastics lessons, camp and competition fees, and more elaborate uniforms.

—*Jim Lord, executive director of American Association of Cheerleading Coaches and Advisors, coaching for 18 years*

CLIMBING

Overview

Over the years, rock climbing has gained a reputation as an extreme sport, but modern techniques and equipment have greatly increased the safety level. Until recently, rock climbing involved scaling daunting cliffs or mountain peaks. With the advent of rock gyms and indoor climbing on artificial walls, along with shorter outdoor climbs that can be found within a few hours of almost anywhere in America, climbing has soared in popularity.

Rock-climbing competitions began in Europe in the 1970s with speed-climbing challenges on real rock outdoors. Indoor climbing started with rock climbers seeking to train year-round or in bad weather. Within a few years, the first indoor rock-climbing walls were created and indoor competitions became more popular. Indoor walls had the advantage of not having any weather issues, and one can place holds to create different types of routes. Today indoor climbing has evolved into its own sport, complete with climbing competitions done on indoor rock walls. Climbing on indoor rock walls is both convenient and less costly than having to buy equipment for outdoor climbs. Basic climbing skills mastered in an indoor rock gym can be easily transferred to outdoor climbing, which is a more exciting but more dangerous sport. Today there over 3,000 indoor climbing gyms holding about 500 climbing competitions each year worldwide. Over 6 million Americans climb an artificial rock wall at least once annually, and climbing as a whole has been growing exponentially both as a recreational and competitive sport.

Rock climbing, described as being "ballet on a vertical surface," has emerged as a popular sport for active children wishing to experience a workout that is challenging, exhilarating, and fun. Climbing vertical walls indoors or scaling mountain faces provides a unique combination of mental and physical prowess, as well as an all-around conditioning workout.

General Benefits

◉ Teaches intense concentration, problem solving on the go, patience to make a calculated next move, and perseverance to reach the top

◉ Strengthens mental acuity, self-reliance, and fear-coping skills

◉ Offers an aerobic workout that exercises almost every muscle group for full-body conditioning

◉ Improves strength, endurance, balance, flexibility, and coordination

- Offers the satisfaction of mastering a challenge

- Outdoor climbs offer spectacular scenery

Kids Who Tend to Excel

- If your child loves to climb and is fascinated by heights, then rock climbing may be just the thrill he is looking for.

- Your child does not need to have a super-strong upper body to be a good climber because flexibility is actually more important. Strength is eventually needed to work with ropes, as well as to excel at the elite youth climbing levels. Climbers who concentrate on their footwork instead of just trying to hoist themselves up with their arms tire less quickly. Your child's legs are much stronger than his arms, and will take him much farther.

- Climbers need to have creative problem-solving ability so that when a hold is out of reach, they can improvise in order to complete a route.

- The mental challenge of rock climbing requires intense concentration, determination, resilience, and the ability to overcome any fear of heights.

Best Age to Start

- Indoor climbing lessons generally start for kids between 5 and 10 years old.

- For a more aggressive pursuit of the sport, perhaps leading to outdoor climbing, kids are usually at least age 12. Children usually need to be around 13 years old before they learn to belay.

What to Look For When Getting Started

- Your child should start with indoor climbing, as it offers a more controlled learning environment

Climbing teaches kids tenacity, perseverance, focus, pattern perception, and problem solving. It uses all muscles in the body pretty equally, from the toes to the fingertips, and puts all joints through their full range of motion. It is low impact, builds and tones muscle, and increases flexibility. With increased proficiency, balance, core torso strength, and footwork become more important than upper-body strength. Climbers come in all shapes and sizes.

—Lisa Coyne, mom of a 12-year-old daughter who climbs, and regional coordinator in the Pacific Northwest for USCCA

Kids who have a wiry build take to the sport quickly because climbing depends more on good tendon strength/weight ratio than large muscles. Typically, these kids are the ones who don't do that well at team sports like football and soccer because they are physically too small or lack the muscular development those sports require.

—Matt Stark, New Jersey rock head route setter and climbing coach for 8 years

Climbing can be a great avenue for personal discovery and growth, but it needs to be at your child's individual pace. Everyone with a sense of adventure can enjoy climbing.

—Paul Diefenderfer, Phoenix rock gym owner, teaching for 25 years

Climbing is a very intuitive sport, similar in many ways to climbing trees. A sense of balance and willingness to try moves that don't seem immediately logical helps. The only thing I see some kids struggle with is a fear of heights, but almost every kid can get past that with encouragement.

—Clay Tyson, Rockville Climbing Center manager and teacher for 2 years

Top youth climbers are very self-motivated and disciplined. Most prefer individual-type sports to team sports. More often than not, they seem to be children thought of as quiet or shy. They are motivated by the personal challenge of figuring out the sequence of moves and then accomplishing them in order to progress to the top of a route.

—Karen Lage, former board member of the Junior Competition Climbing Association and mom of a competitive climber, Lisa, 18

Kids who always act like monkeys, climbing everything and anything that comes their way, invariably enjoy rock climbing. Kids who excel quickly often come from a gymnastics background. Since climbing involves planning a sequence of movements to push upward on differently shaped and positioned holds, kids who like puzzles and problem solving thrive.

—Lisa Coyne, mom of a 12-year-old daughter who climbs, and regional coordinator in the Pacific Northwest for USCCA

and tends to be less intimidating for kids who need to conquer their fears. The ropes and walls are regularly inspected and belayers tested.

❧ The rock gym should provide climbing walls of varying levels of difficulty equipped with movable holds, ropes, and pulleys. Reputable rock gyms will provide expert instruction and rent climbing shoes, harnesses, and other equipment your child will need to climb safely.

Kids should definitely start indoors. The objective dangers such as rock fall are nearly eliminated. In the controlled environment of a climbing gym with qualified instructors and good equipment, kids can enjoy the sport and keep risks to a minimum. When your child makes the transition to outdoor climbing, it should only be done with a qualified guide, preferably one who is certified by the American Mountain Guide Association.

—*Clay Tyson, Rockville Climbing Center manager and teacher for 2 years*

Great climbers don't always make great coaches, but a coach with prior climbing competition experience can understand and relate to the psychological demands associated with rock climbing. If a child is looking to be competitive in the sport, an instructor should know specific training tactics that will help prevent injuries and allow the child to excel at a quicker rate.

—*Matt Stark, New Jersey Rock Gym head route setter and climbing coach for 8 years*

Competition climbing is evolving and becoming more popular throughout the world. One comment I often hear from parents and observers is that climbing tends not to be a cutthroat type of competition. Most climbers understand that the real competition is between the climber and the route set on the wall, not between climbers.

—*Karen Lage, former board member of the Junior Competition Climbing Association and mom of a competitive climber, Lisa, 18*

We have found that kids' competition climbing attracts a really diverse group of kids who display good sportsmanship and a great sense of fun.

—*Lisa Coyne, mom of a 12-year-old daughter who climbs, and regional coordinator in the Pacific Northwest for USCCA*

🌿 In a beginner's class, your child should learn climbing and belaying fundamentals and proper technique. Like other sports, climbing is best learned through practice.

🌿 Once your child masters rock climbing indoors, he can turn to conquering outdoor climbing. Before making the transition from indoor to outdoor climbing, your child needs to learn resting positions, how to place protection devices in rocks, and many other skills. Almost all basic climbing skills mastered in a rock gym can be transferred to outdoor climbing.

✦ Your child should never attempt to rock climb without expert instruction. Your child should tackle outdoor climbs with a reputable climbing school, rock gym, or guide company. Before moving outside, he should know how to tie himself into his harness and belay, which is the act of taking up slack in the rope as the climber ahead ascends, so the climber will fall just a couple of inches in case he loses a grip. He should also be taught various holds, climbing maneuvers, and how to tie basic knots, such as the figure-eight knot. Your child should practice all he has learned under the watchful eyes of a qualified instructor. The number of beginner lessons he will need depends on his aptitude for knot tying, his fitness level, and many other factors.

✦ The U.S. Competition Climbing Association (USCCA) sanctions over 120 regional climbing competitions all over the country. Youth compete in age categories: 11 and under, 12–13, 14–15, 16–17, and 18–19. The season runs approximately from February to July, depending on how far a climber advances. Each region has a championship from which six kids in each of several age and gender categories are chosen to advance to a divisional competition. The top climbers from these competitions go on to the nationals. Winners progress to divisional championships and finally a youth national championship.

Checking Out an Indoor Climbing Gym

✦ Many reputable gyms seek certification for both their instructors and their facilities from the Climbing Gym Association (CGA), a subgroup of the Outdoor Recreation Coalition of America (ORCA). Their certification also ensures that the facility meets the proper safety standards.

✦ When signing your child up for a class, look for small class sizes, ideally four to six people.

✦ When observing the facility, look to see if the climbing wall is in good repair. Check for broken handholds or footholds, worn paint, and exposed or splintered wood. Ask the staff about the air-circulation system, as with a lot of climbers in a small space, the air can quickly fill with chalk. If your child plans to climb during the summer, be sure the gym has air conditioning.

✦ Make sure the gym offers routes for all levels, including novices, intermediates, and experts, as well as different kinds of climbing, such as face climbing, crack climbing, and different overhang angles. Look to see if the equipment is set up to practice lead climbing or just top roping.

🦂 When you sign your child up, be sure he will have plenty of opportunities to practice. Ask how crowded the gym can become and what the peak climbing hours are.

🦂 Ask the staff and a few climbers whether they make regular changes to the routes.

🦂 Look for a relaxed, friendly gym environment that encourages questions, conversation, and camaraderie for your child. If the atmosphere seems intense and competitive, your child should probably seek another gym that is more suited for beginners.

Types of Climbing

CLIMBING COMPETITIONS

🦂 In speed climbing, climbers compete against time, not against each other.

🦂 Red point competitions provide many climbing routes and assign points based on the level of difficulty of each route. Climbers earn points only for completed routes.

🦂 During On Sight competitions, climbers get only one preview of a route and have just one attempt to climb it. Points are awarded based on the height the climber achieves. Climbers are kept in an isolated area so that they cannot see the other climbers' attempts and learn from the routes tried. This is the preferred format for sanctioned events. Flash competitions are a variant of this, in which climbers get to watch the other competitors.

🦂 A bouldering competition is characterized by short routes and high-strength moves without the use of ropes. In a gym, bouldering routes usually do not exceed 12 feet in height.

OUTDOOR CLIMBS

🦂 Sport climbing shares the same rope technique as free climbing except that it uses bolts for protection that have already been preset into the rock face. This means that climbers don't need to set their own anchors into the rock, making sport climbing the most popular form of outdoor climbing. It also involves short, intense climbs with athletic moves up steep vertical rock faces. A belayer hangs on to the rope to ensure that if the climber falls, the rope doesn't move, which makes this the safest of the outdoor climbs.

✦ Traditional ("trad") climbing on big rock faces emphasizes the use of holds and various protection devices inserted into cracks as a climber ascends. These devices take skill and effort to place correctly.

✦ Free climbing uses natural rock features to climb with ropes to protect against falls. A lead climber puts protection into small irregular cracks in the rock, often a chock (a wedge-shaped chunk of steel with a wire attached), placed so that a downward pull drives it tighter into the rock. The rope runs through a metal loop, attached to the chock, and attaches to a climber via a sit harness. A partner feeds out the rope as needed through a belay device. If you fall, your partner "locks off" the rope and stops your fall.

✦ Bouldering involves climbing boulders low to the ground. These are very short climbs with explosive, experimental moves, where a climber's feet never get more than a few feet off the ground. Climbers do "boulder problems," which often involve moves too risky to try when high up. Climbers use no ropes or gear to protect from falling except sometimes a mat to lessen the impact of a fall.

Safety and Injury Concerns

Young climbers remain injury-free relative to most sports. They do, however, get really stinky feet from wearing those little climbing shoes without socks. Roll down the windows when carpooling these kids back from the climbing meet!

—Lisa Coyne, mom of a 12-year-old daughter who climbs, and regional coordinator in the Pacific Northwest for USCCA

✦ Risks of injury or accidents in rock climbing are very low as long as safety precautions are followed.

✦ Most rock-climbing injuries are caused by excessive strain, and affect the fingers, hands, wrists, forearms, elbows, and shoulders. These injuries include tendon pulls, carpal tunnel syndrome, and strains, which often result from overtraining. Bigger kids doing difficult climbs on small holds or pockets may strain or tear ligaments in their fingers. The key is to gradually increase the difficulty of the climbs to allow the muscles and ligaments time to strengthen to meet the demands of difficult moves.

✦ While the incidence of falling is very low, outdoor rock climbing can be dangerous, and even the most experienced climbers go out in pairs. Your child should go outdoors to climb only with an experienced climber, to ensure the use of good techniques as well as to point out any potential hazards in the climb.

Cost Considerations

🦋 Start by having your child rent gear at a gym. Most indoor rock gyms include equipment within the cost of the class or program. Other indoor gyms rent beginner's equipment at an inexpensive rate. Most of the kids who are looking to compete and move on will start to buy their own gear.

🦋 The only thing a beginning climber really needs is a pair of climbing shoes, which cost between $70 and $150. Rock shoes protect your child's feet as well as grab and hold the rock surface. Unless your child is climbing a lot, it is probably cheaper to rent if his feet are still growing.

🦋 Buying your own climbing equipment can be costly. Equipment for an indoor climber generally costs between $150 to $200, half of which usually goes for climbing shoes. A basic set of outdoor climbing gear can cost up to $500. The basic equipment consists of:
- a climbing harness that accommodates your child's body shape and climbing style ($30–$120);
- a belay device ($15–$80);
- lightweight, metal snapping links called carabiners ($8–$15);
- shoes ($60–$140);
- a chalk bag ($20).

🦋 Classes for children generally cost between $10 and $15, with private lessons costing around $30 hourly. Yearly gym memberships vary dramatically in cost, starting around $50 and going up as high as $450 a year. Many gyms issue day passes to use their climbing walls, which generally cost around $12 a day.

🦋 Entering into a competition usually costs between $25 and $35.

CREW/ROWING

Overview

Rowing is one of the oldest and most physically demanding sports in the world, requiring tremendous stamina and muscular strength. It started as a form of transportation and has evolved into one of the most popular international sports in the world. It's been part of the Olympic Games since 1896, with women's events added in 1976.

The long crew boat is often referred to as a shell because its hull is only about a quarter-inch thick to make the boat as light as possible. Formerly made of wood,

Nobody is *the* star in a crew team. Rowing is the most collaborative sport because every crew member must share the work and is forced to be a team player if they want to win.

—John Riley, former Olympian and national team rower, teaching for 10 years

Rowing utilizes all physical aspects of the human body: cardiovascular (both aerobic and anaerobic system), strength (full-body sport), and skill (balance). Mentally, children learn the aspects of team, devotion, dedication, and hard work.

—Fred Honebein, assistant rowing coach, University of Washington, coaching for 6 years

Rowing is a great sport that builds focus and concentration—as you have to stay in time with the other rowers in your boat—along with stamina, strength, and overall conditioning.

—Cathy Coffman, head coach, Rivanna Rowing Club, teaching for 17 years

most shells today are made of composite materials such as carbon fiber or fiberglass, and constructed as narrowly as possible. A U-shaped oarlock mounted to the shell's body holds each rower's oar in place.

There are two types of rowing: In sweep rowing, each rower handles a single oar. Sweep boats can have two, four, or eight rowers. In sculling, a rower uses two oars, called sculls. Sculling races have one, two-, and four-person boats. The eight-person boats have a coxswain, who sits at the bow or stern of the boat directing the crew, urging them on, and using a rudder to steer. Steering in smaller boats is done using a foot pedal to control a small rudder, or by applying more power to the oars on one side of the shell.

Each rower has her back facing the direction the shell is moving and sits on a sliding seat with wheels set on a track called the slide. Speed is generated using a set sequence involving the legs, back, and arms. The rower closest to the stern, known as the stroke, must be a strong rower with excellent technique, as she sets the rhythm for her teammates. Four major factors determine how fast a shell moves through the water: timing, form, power, and conditioning. If any of these factors is off, a boat won't run fast.

General Benefits

● A highly aerobic activity that improves cardiovascular fitness and exercises all major muscle groups

● Particularly strengthens the back, legs, abdominals, and buttocks

● Builds teamwork and camaraderie, given the intense collaborative effort and precise team timing needed to be successful

- ℗ Relatively injury-free

- ℗ Bench warming is not an issue, since everyone rows

Kids Who Tend to Excel

℗ Rowing races take incredible endurance, balance, and strength. While it looks like only upper-body strength is important, the strength of the rowing stroke comes from the legs.

℗ The rowing personality enjoys team sports and loves the outdoors, tolerating them even the bad weather. Cold, rain, and light winds are all conditions for practice.

Rowing does not come naturally, so the kids who do the best have lots of willpower and de-termination. Kids who excel in rowing are strongly achievement-based, goal-oriented, and be-lieve hard work will produce results. They have to be go-getters who will get up early and practice, then go to school, then possibly work out again after school.

—*John Riley, former Olympian and national team rower, teaching for 10 years*

Typically, good rowers have aerobic fitness, the ability to train with or without others effec-tively, willingness to be a part of something that is hard to master, and personal drive. Kids who drop out either feel that rowing takes too much time or they feel like they cannot handle the physical work load.

—*Fred Honebein, assistant rowing coach, University of Washington, coaching for 6 years*

Children who excel at rowing are usually smart academically, responsible, self-motivated, competitive, tall, as well as good all-around athletes. Many kids who are not good enough to compete in basketball, volleyball, or swimming do well in our sport. It does not take the hand-eye coordination of many sports.

—*Kris Sanford, rowing coach, Syracuse University, teaching for 15 years*

The great thing about rowing is that since it is not a "traditional American sport," everyone starts off on an even level with no prior knowledge of the sport and has an opportunity to excel. Physical ability can be created through smart training. Honestly, though, rowers are generally taller and lankier individuals. Rowing is about leverage, and taller is better. However, all sizes can participate, and many smaller people outperform their larger counterparts. Many programs even offer a weight-specific category (commonly called "lightweights"). For the smallest children the job of coxswain is an option. The coxswain is the "quarterback" of the boat, and this job requires mental, other than physical prowess. A coxswain must be smart, mentally quick, dynamic, and motivating. Rowing is a physically demanding sport, and not all children enjoy such a level of activity. Some students don't care to sit in a boat on the river, in 50-degree weather when it is raining. The sport also demands a lot of time.

—*George Kirschbaum, Jr., Washington and Lee varsity women's coach, teaching for 14 years*

Rowers usually hit the water to practice as the sun is rising, so your child has to be up for the very early morning routine.

Perfecting the rowing stroke requires tremendous practice and dedication, and simultaneous blade work as a team is critical to success.

Kids don't need to be muscular giants, as the strength skills can be learned.

The average starting age is 13 or 14 years old, which I think is best. We get some eighth graders participating and many do well, depending on the child's mental and physical maturity.

—*George Kirschbaum, Jr., Washington and Lee varsity women's coach, teaching for 14 years*

Best Age to Start

At the age of 9, kids can start sculling (two oars for each rower), but not sweep rowing (one oar for each rower). Sweep rowing—while many programs start it around eighth grade—should not be practiced until college. Since only one oar is used, kids who start sweep rowing too early tend to develop asymmetrically.

What to Look For When Getting Started

Look for a coach who has been certified by U.S. Rowing. A coach's technical knowledge is very important. Observe how much emphasis he places on injury prevention and how he relates to his athletes. Speak to the athletes on the team and their parents to find out if they are happy with the coach.

❧ Inquire about the time commitment, how much racing your child will do, and where meets will take place. Ask about the coach-to-boat ratio to help ascertain how much individualized attention your child will get from the coaching staff. Organized squads can range in size anywhere from 2 to 100 kids.

❧ Racing competitions take place for kids under age 17 through schools or inter-club competitions. All boats race in heats, with the winners advancing to the next level. The races are divided into sculling and sweep oar, with heavyweight and lightweight divisions. Rowers' speed is measured in terms of strokes per minute (SPM).

❧ Expect bad weather during some meets, as crew races are rowed unless there is thunder and lightning. During the school year there are races all over the country, with concentrations in Philadelphia, Northern Virginia/D.C., New England, Florida, California, and Washington State. During the summer, club racing takes place throughout the country. During the fall, head races (3 miles) abound all over the country. The biggest and most well known is the Head of the Charles in Boston, with over 7,000 competitors, including youth races.

The best way for kids to start lessons is to join a team, and parents can expect lots of time at practice. Training usually includes running, strength training, and rowing on the erg (rowing machine). Rowing meets are like swim meets—long, a little boring, but really exciting in a tight race.

—*Cathy Coffman, head coach, Rivanna Rowing Club, teaching for 17 years*

Spring, the primary racing season, divides the country into high school rowing and junior club rowing. For the most part, the two do not compete against each other, because clubs can pick top athletes from a larger pool, creating a perceived advantage over high school teams. During the other seasons of the year, most students row for a club program. Summer and fall races are usually open to all ages and skill levels, although they compete in separate events for fairness.

—*George Kirschbaum, Jr., Washington and Lee varsity women's coach, teaching for 14 years*

Safety and Injury Concerns

✦ Your child needs to know how to swim well, with clothes on and in cold water, especially since sea conditions, weather, currents, and winds can change suddenly.

✦ Boats should have a whistle, a bailer, a line to secure a damaged oarlock, and a towline on board in case of an emergency situation on the water.

✦ The coach should track local weather patterns, water hazards, and traffic patterns.

✦ Lower-back injuries or wrist tendonitis can occur if a rower uses improper stroke technique, or if the shell is not mechanically set up correctly. Your child should also be doing some form of training off the water to develop sufficient strength in the lower back, abdominals, and hip flexors.

✦ Blistered and callused hands are par for the course.

✦ Two other risks are hypothermia and overexposure to the sun. To guard against hypothermia, your child should have spare clothes stored in the boathouse to change into after coming off the water. A hat or cap to keep warm or for sun protection and a water bottle for practice on really hot days are also recommended.

Cost Considerations

✦ Taking up rowing is usually a simple matter of joining a local club and paying a small membership fee for instruction and use of the club's shells and equipment.

✦ Club team programs typically cost $300–$500, while school-funded programs are much less. Fund-raising is usually an integral part of being part of most programs to pay for equipment. New boats with eight rowers and one coxswain, the most commonly rowed boat class, cost anywhere from $16,000 to almost $30,000 new.

✦ If your child decides to join a rowing club, club dues range from $10 to $50 per year, and usually include instruction and use of scull and safety equipment. Traveling to regattas can be expensive depending on how many regattas a team plans to attend. Team uniforms can be another cost.

CURLING

Overview

Resembling shuffleboard or boccie, curling is a team sport played on ice. Often described as "chess on ice," curling involves intense strategy. Curling originated in the 1500s on the ponds of Scotland and northern Europe and eventually found its way to Canada and America in the 1800s, finally becoming an Olympic Games medal sport in 1998.

Today over 1.5 million people around the world curl. The U.S. Curling Association has over 135 affiliated curling clubs and over 15,000 curlers in 28 states, mostly across the north. Curling has traditionally thrived in northern states—the Great Lakes, New England, and the mid-Atlantic states—with Wisconsin and Minnesota having the greatest concentration of curlers. But after gaining TV exposure at the Olympics, new curling clubs are starting all over the country, such as in Florida, Tennessee, and Oregon. Curling is a sport that your child can enjoy his entire life, as well as a sport in which boys and girls can compete on an equal basis.

A curling match has all the excitement and tenseness of a close golf game going into the final holes. The most fun in curling is the bonspiel (competition or tournament), where competitors range from 5 years old to 100.

—*Ed Lukowich, athlete development director with USA Curling, founder of the World Curling Tour, curling for 40 years*

The biggest thing about curling is that not too many people know about it. Curling is still a low-participation sport in the U.S., so just finding a place to play, period, can be a challenge. It is one of the few sports that a family can play together. We had three generations represented on a team at one of our recent events. No expensive equipment to purchase, just great fun!

—*Doug Deleff, president of the Denver Curling Club, coaching for 10 years*

The Basics

🎏 Curling is played on special indoor ice in a rectangular shape. Unlike hockey ice, the curling surface is groomed by frequent shaving to keep it perfectly level.

🎏 In each match, there are two teams of four players. The object of the game is to slide ("deliver") 42-pound polished granite rocks down the sheet of ice to the center of a 12-foot diameter target painted on the ice. Junior curling stones weigh 25 pounds. Each player "delivers" two stones, with each team trying to get their stones closest to the target or knock the opposing team's stone out of the way.

🎏 Rocks traveling down the ice sometimes curve or "curl." High-level strategy comes into play in planning shots and then controlling their speed and direction. Ever-changing ice conditions add to the challenge.

🎏 The four players each take on one role: the lead, second, third, and skip. During the delivery of each stone, the skip calls the shot, two players sweep the stone to help control its speed and accuracy, and one player throws the stone. The skip is responsible for determining whether sweeping is necessary. When players sweep, or brush, the ice in front of the rock, the friction caused by the sweeping polishes the ice by briefly heating the surface, making the rocks travel farther and straighter.

🎏 Just millimeters in the final destination can mean the difference between a loss and a win.

General Benefits

◉ Improves balance, flexibility, and concentration

◉ Teaches finesse; the slide requires gracefulness and care

◉ Builds strength; sweeping the stone depends on strength and endurance

◉ Teaches quick responses and adaptability, as ice conditions change dramatically during a game

◉ Hones strategic thinking, as each player must think many moves ahead

---

Curling gives kids a sense of camaraderie and participating on a team, and teaches them to make snap decisions when the called shot isn't working and stay calm under pressure. Plus, as my son says, "People don't realize how fun it is until they try it!"

—*Clare Bergquist, director of the junior curling program at the Milwaukee Curling Club and mom of three curlers, ages 11, 9, and 7*

Curling is a great family sport. My wife and I have curled for about 17 years. Our 15-year-old son plays in a junior league and plays with us in weekend tournaments (called bonspiels).

—*Doug Potter, president of the Granite Curling Club of Seattle*

◉ Teaches players how to work closely and communicate as a team

Kids Who Tend to Excel

◉ Kids who excel in curling are generally flexible and have good coordination. There is no ideal body size or shape for curling.

◉ Throwing a rock requires flexibility and balance.

◉ Sweeping requires strength and stamina. Moving up and done on the ice can cover a few miles each game.

◉ Strategy and analytic skills are needed to anticipate what the other team is doing.

◉ Teamwork is critical, as the whole team is part and parcel of each shot.

◉ Curling is often compared to reading a putting green, and kids who love challenges and are able to stay very focused do well.

Kids who excel at curling know how to think strategically, remain calm under pressure when making a key shot, recognize their teammates' and opponents' strengths and weaknesses and capitalize on them, have the ability to motivate teammates, and like to be around people and socialize.

—*Clare Bergquist, director of the junior curling program at the Milwaukee Curling Club and mom of three curlers, ages 11, 9, and 7*

◉

The ability to work with your teammates and focus on your particular role is critical. Different people on the team have different skills. For instance, the lead (first shooter) has to be a strong sweeper and have great feel for draw weight (the ability to get the stone to stop where they want it). The skip (last shooter) has to perform under pressure and be able to make a wide range of shots.

—*Doug Deleff, president of the Denver Curling Club, coaching for 10 years*

Although curling is an easy sport to learn, it is a most difficult sport to master (a lot like golf). Some people excel at leadership and become skips (they relate more to the mental side of the game) while other players enjoy front-end positions (offers more physical exertion in the game).

> —Ed Lukowich, athlete development director with USA Curling, founder of the World Curling Tour, curling for 40 years

If a child is an excellent shot maker, strategist, and team morale builder, he can specialize in being the skip on a curling team, but he should however always be able to sweep in the event he is asked to play another position. Children who are more social tend to like to play lead or second on a curling team, since they are not as absorbed in the pressure shots or strategy making on the team.

> —Clare Bergquist, director of the junior curling program at the Milwaukee Curling Club and mom of three curlers, ages 11, 9, and 7

Best Age to Start

While kids can start as young as age 5, most junior programs start training kids between the ages of 10 and 14.

What to Look For When Getting Started

If there is a curling club near you, ask about whether it has a junior program.

Instructors should focus on skill development.

These are great opportunities for competition on the youth level. Junior tournaments take place at the larger curling clubs. In addition, there are state or regional competitions, with the winners proceeding to the national competition and then the USA Nationals and World Juniors. Young athletes fall into two divisions grouped by age: youth curlers are 13 years old and under, and the Junior Curler division is for kids ages 14–21.

Kids can start earlier, but when they weigh about twice what a rock weighs, around 60 pounds, roughly ages 10–12, is when they can start to make real progress.

　　—*Doug Potter, president of the Granite Curling Club of Seattle*

With little rocks (smaller stones) kids can start early and learn to do their slide delivery right away.

　　—*Ed Lukowich, athlete development director with USA Curling, founder of the World Curling Tour, curling for 40 years*

Safety and Injury Concerns

🌱 Curling is a relatively injury-free sport. Aside from some muscle strains and knee injuries, the only source of injury comes from slipping and falling on the ice, which happens rarely. A key part of curling instruction should focus on how to move across the ice safely. Some beginners wear helmets to protect the back of the head when hitting the ice if an accidental slip occurs.

Cost Considerations

🌱 Curling is relatively cheap, especially compared with other winter sports such as hockey or skiing.

🌱 Your child will have to pay a club membership, with dues ranging from club to club but often costing as low as $50 for a season. Equipment costs are relatively low to start, as most clubs have loaner sliders, grippers, and brooms. Your child just wears stretchy slacks and a warm sweater or jacket.

🌱 A slip-on slider only costs $15–$20 and is a piece of Teflon, plastic, or steel that is slipped onto one foot in order to easily slide down the sheet of ice. A rubber-soled shoe is worn on the other foot, to grip the ice. One foot pushes while the other slides. Right-handed curlers push with their right foot and slide on their left.

🌱 Clubs will most often supply the brooms or brushes used to sweep the ice.

🌱 Eventually, buying an outfit and equipment becomes more expensive, with

A curling instructor should be enthusiastic and knowledgeable. Young people often get bored and the instructor has to have the skills and flexibility to adapt the sport to a child's needs. An instructor has to teach the basic fundamentals but then has to let the kids play! It is not that important that they get it exactly right the first time they try. It is more important that they have fun and that it is not competitive at the younger age level.

—Beverly Schroeder, national team leader for U.S. Curling Association, teaching for 17 years

Once children master the basic shooting skills, curling becomes a physical skill and mental strategy competition. Kids need to develop patience to wait for the opportunity for certain shots. They need to develop finesse and touch: Curling is not a "power" game. Curling is a very inclusive sport because a good strategy will win over good skills on most days.

—Iain Hueton, president of Ogden, Utah, Curling Club, coaching for 4 years

curling shoes ranging from $75 to $100, brooms costing between $20 and $80, and pants and a jacket costing between $100 to $200.

DIVING

Overview

One of the most popular sports to watch at the Summer Olympics, diving combines grace, power, and courage, while mesmerizing spectators. Diving is more strongly linked with gymnastics than with swimming, having originated in 17th-century Germany and Sweden when gymnasts spent summers on the beaches and acrobatics over the water became a new activity.

In competitive diving, there are two types of diving surfaces: springboard and platform. Springboards, usually only a few feet above the water, have bounce that enables high jumps and more time for diving moves above the springboard. In platform diving, a solid platform is high above the water and offers no bounce. All the diving moves take place between the platform and the water.

Judges score dives based on elements that include each dive's approach, takeoff, distance from the diving board or platform, height, speed of rotation, execution, position when entering the water, and entry into the water. Each dive is worth up to ten points. Points are further adjusted based on the dive's degree of difficulty and types of maneuvers the diver attempts, such as flips, twists, pikes, or tucks.

General Benefits

◎ Instills bravery and courage, since the diver must overcome the fear of flipping, twisting, and backward diving

◎ Teaches intense self-discipline, concentration, and body awareness

◎ Improves motor skills, along with upper- and lower-body strength

Best Age to Start

◎ Your child can start diving as young as age 5, as long as she is a strong enough swimmer to have passed a pool's deep end test, and can come back to the surface after a dive and over to the side of the pool safely and independently. She also has to be able to push far enough off to clear her head and feet from the diving board. Otherwise, she does not have to have mastered swimming strokes first.

◎ Most children start diving between the ages of 8 to 12, although some elite divers do not start until high school or college.

A diver's entire body becomes equally strong, as the legs are used for jumping; the abdominals, and back for lifting legs and keeping tight through the water; and the neck, arms, and shoulders for entry into the water, particularly off the platform. The best divers are not only powerful, but learn to be graceful as well.

—*Anneliese Tuymer, U.S. Diving Florida Gold Coast Administration, involved with diving for 19 years*

Diving imparts balance, grace, timing, rhythm, kinesthetic awareness, conditioning, and general athleticism.

—*Cynthia Potter, head diving coach at The Westminster Schools in Atlanta, coaching for 21 years*

Kids Who Tend to Excel

◎ Diving involves flying through the air, twisting, flipping, and somersaulting. Thus, being athletic, flexible, and courageous is key, as well as overcoming any fear of heights.

◎ It requires persistence. Your child will need to be dedicated, motivated, and willing to practice frequently. Children often become frustrated, as it can take six months or longer to master a complicated new dive.

Kids who excel most in diving are coordinated, fearless or able to control their fears, enjoy vertigo-type activities, and have lots of patience, for it takes a great deal of practice to succeed in diving.

—*Rick Schavone, director of men's and women's diving, Stanford University, teaching for 30 years*

Most kids who dive are pretty fearless. Yet each time children try a new type of dive, such as the first backward dive or flip, they usually feel scared out of their minds. But the first time they smack their backs on the water, they realize it's not that bad. The next biggest step after backward dives are "reverses," where you jump off the board forward but dive backward. A coach has to talk your child through each new dive, and encourage the persistence and practice needed to master it. About 75% of good divers start out in gymnastics. Diving is a very driven, individualistic sport that attracts perfectionists. Plus, kids have to be willing to tolerate the subjectivity of the scoring.

—*Debbie Sperling, diving team coach, Brae Burn Country Club, teaching for 3 years*

Kids who excel at diving have flexibility, strength, kinesthetic awareness, spatial awareness, and are visually adept. They also need to be strong psychologically, as even talented kids feel scared that they will become lost in a dive.

—*Julian Krug, diving coach, University of Pittsburgh, teaching for 30 years*

What to Look For When Getting Started

🐟 Diving is a very technical sport, and should be taught by a highly specialized coach. Look for an organized diving program under the instruction of coaches who have been certified by U.S. Diving.

🐟 Your child will have to face and conquer considerable fears associated with learning new moves and dives. You want a diving coach who understands your child, and has knowledge of what motivates her and what helps her overcome the challenge or fear of a new dive. Your child may reach a point when she would rather quit than face a difficult new dive. This often occurs after taking some time off from practice. Look toward a coach to help assess your child's progress.

In terms of learning to dive, kids start on the pool deck, then gradually work their way to a low one-meter board, followed by the three-meter board, and eventually move to platform diving.

—*George Campbell, swimming program director for 20 years, middle school physical education director for 32 years, and dad of three grown kids*

Make sure the swimming club your child joins continually raises the bar for kids to improve, instead of allowing kids to settle into a comfort zone of dives that limit their potential. Clubs with divers at different talent levels are the best because this allows younger divers with less experience to learn from other athletes as well as the coach.

—*Caesar Garcia, competitive diver on board of directors for U.S. Diving*

Look for a coach with experience who has been around a long time, and has maturity and professionalism. Top-level national coaches can usually be found at major universities. Diving is an easy sport to say you can coach and just start coaching, but it is a dangerous sport, so good coaching is critical to safety and improvement.

—*Rick Schavone, director of men's and women's diving, Stanford University, teaching for 30 years*

Diving is an individual sport where it's often your child against his or her own mind, especially when your child is afraid of a particular dive, doing a new dive for the first time, or moving to a higher diving board or platform. This also makes the sense of personal accomplishment enormous.

—*Anneliese Tuymer, U.S. Diving Florida Gold Coast Administration, involved with diving for 19 years*

❧ Many programs have rigorous out-of-the-pool dry-land exercises, which are just as important as practicing the dives in the pool.

❧ Diving is highly specialized, and your child will have to join a special club to pursue it seriously. Once your child joins a diving club team, you can anticipate practice being 4 to 5 times per week year-round.

✦ There are local competitions year-round, many under the auspices of U.S. Diving, in addition to summer leagues offered at pools all over the country. Each area association of U.S. Diving typically holds about 10 meets annually. Junior divers compete in progressive age groups through age 19. Additionally, USD hosts a Junior National Championship at different sites each summer for which regional and zone championships serve as qualifiers.

Safety and Injury Concerns

✦ Diving has the reputation of being one of the most dangerous activities around, with stories of paralysis and spine injury. Yet according to U.S. Diving, in the past 100 years, no competitive divers in the United States have suffered catastrophic injuries.

✦ A Consumer Product Safety Commission study found fewer accidents related to diving than to golf, bowling, or sitting in bleachers. A second study by the National Spinal Cord Injury Data Research Center found that half of all diving injuries occur in rivers, lakes, and oceans and most result from a combination of horseplay and bad judgment.

Cost Considerations

✦ Your child needs only a team swimsuit, a facility in which to train and practice, and lessons from a seasoned diving coach. Costs for lessons depend on their frequency and the quality of the coach.

✦ Team costs range from $100 to $400 a month at the club level. In addition, your child may have to join a pool. Private lessons average between $60 and $100 per hour.

✦ If your child enters into the more elite levels, traveling expenses to competitions become an additional cost.

EQUESTRIAN SPORTS

Overview

Riding horses can be anything from pleasure trail riding to intense competitions and shows. Horseback riding is a recreational activity in which any child can participate, regardless of ability, handicap, size, or weight.

Tracing back many centuries, equestrian competitions have been considered the ultimate in team sports, as horse and rider must work together for years to hone feats of grace, daring, agility, and speed. The only sport where man and animal are teammates, siding builds a relationship of respect and confidence between rider and horse. Equestrian events have been part of the Olympics since 1900, and men and women have been competing against each other in these events since 1952. Equestrian sports are one of the few in which men and women compete on equal terms.

General Benefits

⊙ Learning to tend and care for a horse helps children develop a sense of responsibility, commitment, and teamwork with the horse.

⊙ Riding improves posture, as learning to sit properly in the saddle teaches alignment.

⊙ Stamina, coordination, balance, and muscular endurance are improved.

⊙ Riding enhances muscle tone in the lower body, especially the inner thighs, buttocks, abdominal area, and lower back, all of which are used to support posture in the saddle. Having feet in the stirrups stretches out heels and calves.

⊙ When trotting or galloping at some speed, riding provides an aerobic workout.

⊙ Riding is great for relaxation and offers an activity in which your whole family can participate.

Riding helps children to develop a sense of responsibility, independence, and compassion from caring for a horse, along with balance, good posture, and muscle control.

—Jessica Rattner, Region Six U.S. Dressage Federation Junior/Young Rider executive board member and competitive dressage rider

Kids Who Tend to Excel

⊙ Your child should love animals, not be afraid of getting close to a horse, or mind getting dirty.

⊙ Muscular strength, coordination, and balance are needed to hold the proper position in the saddle.

⊙ Children have to have the ability to focus, understand the horse's movements, and flow with its actions. They also need courage to overcome the fear factor involved.

There's no question that the kids who do the best are athletic types. They just have more muscle and body control, which they need for this physically demanding sport. In terms of personality, I have plenty of outgoing kids, but there are also quiet ones. The quiet ones tend to enjoy the one-on-one time with the horses, such as the grooming and brushing.

　　—Cheryl, instructor, Milestone Equestrian Center, teaching for 15 years

Kids who excel are analytical, coordinated, and have an enthusiasm for life. Riding requires co-ordination and body awareness, similar to gymnastics. Your child needs to know where she is in a moving space and be able to calmly interact with her environment while in that rapidly moving space. Horses are energy, and your child must learn how to influence that energy toward a mutually beneficial purpose. She must have a passion for perfection, an awe of the beauty and intelligence of the horse, and a desire to help the horse find peace and happiness. To ride well, you need serenity, feeling, and participation with the horse in the use of its energy.

　　—Kathleen Harjess, director of Equilibrium Horse Center, teaching for 20 years

Kids who excel in dressage are typically Type A personalities who enjoy striving for perfection and are the fearless ones. Fear transfers to your horse and puts both horse and rider in a dangerous situation. Most of the best riders are tall, although I myself (as well as some of the top dressage riders) am 5'2".

　　—Jessica Rattner, Region Six U.S. Dressage Federation Junior/Young Rider executive board member and competitive dressage rider

Best Age to Start

 Because riding comes with a great deal of responsibility, your child shouldn't start until she is ready to learn how to groom and care for the horse.

 The appropriate age to begin riding depends on your child's physical and emotional maturity and the type of horses at the stable where your child chooses to ride. Sign up for an introductory lesson to determine your child's level of commitment to riding and caring for horses.

◉ Small children won't be able to ride until they are older, as their legs don't reach the stirrups.

◉ Families who grow up around horses often have their children riding as young as age 2, but only for short stretches with parental assistance.

◉ Instructors usually accept children ages 6 and older, but many instructors feel age 8 is the best age to start, as children at that age have enough physical strength and mental focus to get the most out of their lessons.

What to Look For When Getting Started
FINDING A STABLE AND TRAINER

✦ Visit several stables before setting up any lessons. Riding stables vary considerably both in how they are run and how they treat their horses. When evaluating a riding facility, look for a clean stable, well ventilated, neat and organized, and with easygoing horses used for beginner lessons. The horses should have shiny coats and look well maintained. While there, watch a lesson in progress and observe the instructor's interaction with the children.

✦ Inquire about the instructors' teaching experience, the quality of their safety record, and whether they have insurance. Ask about the program costs, training, showing time, and the level of commitment that will be required.

Look for an instructor who listens to both the student and the horse, and has good eye contact when speaking to you. The teacher must show a rapport and very personal, kind interaction with the horse; the horses should appear to like the teacher and easily come to the teacher when beckoned. Also look for a training program where no restraining equipment is used, such as tie-downs or draw reins. The horses must be free to do their work willing, and not forced.

—*Kathleen Harjess, director of Equilibrium Horse Center, teaching for 20 years*

An instructor should have clear and established rules and protocol for riding and handling horses. Horses that are safe and experienced for beginners are critical. The riding ring must be safe, enclosed, and not too large for beginners.

—*Janine Malone, Rosinburg Farm owner and riding instructor for 40 years, and committee member with USA Equestrian and the U.S. Dressage Federation*

Look for a beginning program that balances safety, fun, and education, and places the emphasis on your child connecting with the horse. Pony Club is an excellent program when there is an active chapter in your area, as it balances horsemanship with educational and competitive opportunities in a variety of areas such as eventing, dressage, or jumping, and also often provides means for to reduce the expenses.

—*Linda Allen, course designer, judge, and clinician, teaching riding for 45 years*

A child should begin with private riding lessons and then move to a small group when she has the ability to control her own horse. The one-on-one instruction makes a real difference in the beginning.

—*Madeleine Austin, owner and head trainer, Imajica Equestrian Center, teaching for 30 years*

🍃 If your child doesn't want to compete and only wants to ride recreationally, find a stable that caters to beginners. If your child wants to pursue riding more seriously, look for a stable that grooms competitive riders.

🍃 Some stables concentrate on either English or Western riding lessons, while some have instructors who teach both. The discipline your child chooses to pursue will depend on the type of lessons available in your area and the extent of your child's aspirations.

🍃 Local pony clubs run jumping and dressage programs for children, along with giving them a solid base in horsemanship.

🍃 Initially, almost all programs will give your child a horse to ride, but if your child becomes serious about riding, you will eventually face the decision about buying your own horse.

PRIVATE VS. GROUP LESSONS

🍃 While group lessons can be more affordable, trainers recommend private lessons for beginning riders. Your child's first lesson should include the correct way to approach, lead, work, mount, and dismount the horse. Lessons start with learning mounting techniques, and how to ride while staying in balance. The instructor often uses a leading rein in order to control the horse.

🍃 Once your child has mastered the basics of how to walk, trot, gallop, and control the horse, group lessons can add a spirit of friendly competition to her riding experience.

ENGLISH VS. WESTERN RIDING

🍃 English riding descends from fox-hunting traditions in England and is often referred to as the classic form of horseback riding. English riders wear jodhpurs, which are a pair of long, tightfitting riding pants, along with a hard riding helmet to protect the head in the case of a fall.

✦ Western riding evolved in the American West on cattle ranches, influenced by the style of riding used by Spanish conquistadors who had migrated north.

✦ The main difference between English- and Western-style riding involves the saddle. The Western saddle is slightly wider, designed to be more comfortable for a rider during long days out on the range, which makes it more restrictive on a horse's movements. The English saddle, which is smaller, flatter, and weighs significantly less, is designed to give the rider closer contact with the horse. The English saddle is used during shows, races, and competitions.

✦ Western riders sit farther back in the saddle and use one hand to control the horse. English-style riding requires the rider to grip the reins with two hands, while Western riders take both reins in one hand, allowing their other hand to fall naturally at their side or thigh.

I only offer private lessons so that kids can't compare themselves to each other. Say two kids start out in the same class and in three months one is jumping, while the other one is still learning the basics. If they're apart, they don't know that, or at least they don't see that. It helps each kid feel comfortable learning at his own pace.

—Cheryl, instructor, Milestone Equestrian Center, teaching for 15 years

The first year of riding is a crucial stage in which to a child develops a "proper seat." A child must have individual attention to do this, so I recommend private lessons to start.

—Jessica Rattner, Region Six U.S. Dressage Federation Junior/Young Rider executive board member and competitive dressage rider

✦ In English riding, the rider uses the reins, saddle, leaning of weight, and legs to control the horse's speed and direction. English riders train their horses to move in the opposite direction from their signals, whereas Western riders teach their horses to move in the same direction as their signals.

Most Popular Types of Riding Competitions
SHOW JUMPING

✦ Modern jumping events emerged out of Ireland's fox-hunting tradition, with British and American hunting enthusiasts seeking ways to test horses' talents more systematically. Jumping involves negotiating a course of about 15 to 20 obstacles, including triple bars, parallel rails, water jumps, and simulated stone walls. A rider is penalized for jumps taken out of order, if a horse refuses a jump or knocks down a jump rail, or for exceeding the time limit for the course. The riders wear dark-colored hunt coats, helmets, tan pants, gloves, and field boots. Riders may also wear spurs and carry a crop. Each horse's mane and tail are braided.

While Western is easier to learn and sometimes safer, dressage and English riding is for those really wanting to ride correctly and seriously.

    —*Lendon Gray, chairman U.S. Dressage Federation Junior/Young Rider Council and president of Gleneden Dressage, teaching for 38 years*

The style of horse riding that a child starts out doing depends on where you live, the availability of different styles, and your child's desire. On the East Coast, it is more common to find stables that offer English instruction. If the child wants to learn to jump, English style is the best. Conversely, if your child sees herself as a future rodeo queen, she should start in a Western program. Most children who start in a specific program will stay with that type of riding.

    —*Madeleine Austin, owner and head trainer, Imajica Equestrian Center, teaching for 30 years*

DRESSAGE

❦ A second form of English riding competition, dressage, is often described as horses performing ballet. In dressage, a horse and rider perform a set of intricate stepping maneuvers in response to a rider's subtle signals. Dressage developed as a method of training horses for war, teaching them precise movements.

❦ When dressage made its introduction at the 1912 Olympics, it was for military riders exclusively and remained so for another 40 years. Eventually competition became open to and dominated by civilian riders. Riders wear a white shirt, a black coat with tails, white pants, and riding boots. Horses' manes and tails are braided. One to five judges evaluate the performance based on the execution of the moves, pace, rider's position, and ability to control the horse.

WESTERN RIDING COMPETITIONS

❦ Reining events judge the ability of a ranch-style horse and rider to execute approved patterns of movement and stops in a show arena. The moves originated from the need to work with cows on a ranch. Riders and horses are judged on controlled speed and finesse when performing the various maneuvers. Some Western horse shows often offer competition classes for juniors in which the reins can be held with two hands.

✦ In Western trail competitions, a horse and rider navigate a course consisting of small jumps, poles, gates, and bridges.

✦ In all Western classes, the riders wear Western attire: a tuxedo shirt with a vest or jacket, riding pants, hat, and gloves. The clothes can be almost any color. The horses wear bridles and saddles with silver decorations.

Safety and Injury Concerns

✦ Your child should be taught how to safely dismount the horse in an emergency, so that she knows how to fall off in a way that will sustain the least amount of injury.

✦ A safety-approved helmet is a must to prevent head injury.

✦ While equestrian activities are inherently dangerous in terms of getting thrown off a horse, severe injuries are rare. A recent study of 121,274 horse-related injuries treated at hospital emergency rooms showed that only 1% occurred at a riding school facility.

✦ The most common injuries involve strains to neck and low back, and bumps and bruises from falls.

Cost Considerations

✦ For your child's first riding lessons, ask the instructors if they have riding helmets to borrow. Riders under the age of 18 are required by law to wear approved safety helmets. The most important item that you will need to purchase is a good helmet

Children must be supervised when working around a horse. Horses are animals of flight, and if frightened and "cornered," they will kick or bite. Just an accidental stepping on a horse's foot can result in broken bones or a horse tossing its head in the child's face.

—*Lendon Gray, chairman U.S. Dressage Federation Junior/Young Rider Council and president of Gleneden Dressage, teaching for 38 years*

Riding involves many risks, in that all sorts of things can happen—from getting your foot stepped on to falling and breaking your neck. It all depends on the teacher, how in control they are of the situation, and how well they read the horses. If you have a hyperactive child, chances are that you don't want to let him near a horse. It's dangerous and it's grueling on the trainer.

—*Cheryl, instructor, Milestone Equestrian Center, teaching for 15 years*

Injuries can be severe and are most often caused by unsafe riding or handling habits, an unsafe or inappropriate horse for the level of the rider, poor instruction, improper tack and equipment, or attempting to ride at a level at which the rider or horse is not proficient.

—*Janine Malone, Rosinburg Farm owner and riding instructor for 40 years, and committee member with USA Equestrian and the U.S. Dressage Federation*

with an adjustable chin strap. A basic safety helmet can be purchased for around $50, while a traditional black velvet helmet costs about $80. Look for a helmet with an adjustable chin strap.

🌱 Your child will need to wear hard leather shoes or boots with a heel. Ask the riding instructor what type she prefers. With a half- to one-inch-heeled shoe, your child's foot will not slip through or become caught in the stirrup. Though unnecessary unless required by the riding instructor, specialized jodhpur boots can be used for riding, as well as full-length riding boots made of leather or rubber.

🌱 Ask the riding instructor if your child can wear jeans or if she needs to buy a pair of riding pants.

🌱 In wet weather, a pair of gloves stops the reins from slipping from your child's hands.

🌱 Lessons typically cost around $35 for a half-hour.

🌱 If your child wants to compete in shows, be aware there are additional costs depending on where the show is held, how many classes your child enters, and the appropriate riding gear required to compete. Other costs include show fees, extra equipment, specific riding clothes, and travel costs to get to the competitions.

🌱 If your child is serious about riding, there will come a point when she will want to own a horse, which can cost tens of thousands of dollars. After the initial purchase price, it will cost between $7,000 and $10,000 a year, at a minimum, to board the horse at a stable. Owning a horse also involves a huge time commitment in terms of caring for the horse and riding it. Leasing a horse for your child is an initial option you might want to consider. Larger stables often lease horses for those not yet ready to make the commitment of a purchase.

FENCING

Overview

All it takes is for your child to see a film with choreographed Zorro-type moves and repeated cries of *"En garde!"* for fencing to capture his imagination. Fencing is on the rise in clubs and classes, and the number of children registered with the U.S. Fencing Association (USFA) has tripled since 1996. Now half the membership of the USFA is under age 20. Plus, over 30% participating are girls. The popularity of fencing stems from its combination of fun competitive sparring and the discipline of individual training in swordplay. Once your child understands the basics, fencing becomes an art that can take a lifetime to master and one that draws deeply on individual creativity and strategy.

Fencing is one of only four sports that has been featured at every modern Olympic Games since 1896, where it combines the swashbuckling moves of Errol Flynn with an electronic scoring system.

As a sport, fencing has greatly evolved since its bloody origins in the duel of swordsmen's blades. Instead of leaping between balconies or swinging from the drapery, fencers spar on a rectangular strip, 6 feet by 40 feet. A fencer in competition must "hit" his opponent by touching him with the blade in a specified target zone as many as fifteen times, a far cry from the single decisive thrust of yore. However, much of the social decorum lingers in fencing conventions, from saluting an opponent in a bout to retrieving a lost blade if it falls from your opponent's hand.

Modern fencing is fluid, fast, and athletic. It has been compared to the martial arts, and described as "a conversation of blades." Participants call fencing "chess at 100 miles an hour."

Fencing is often described as "one-third ballet, one-third physical chess, and one-third legal homicide." It is not for the faint of heart.

—*Rita Finkel, mom of three fencers and manager of The Fencers Club*

Fencing is actually considered a martial art mainly because of the discipline and concentration that it involves.

—*Meghan Gardner, director of Guard Up, teaching for 3 years*

My son picked fencing after watching *The Parent Trap*. I went on the Internet and found the U.S. Fencing Association as well as the one place offering fencing in Jacksonville, Florida, where we live. My son started fencing at age 7, and he loves it. We tried soccer, but I came to the conclusion that my son was not a team player, as he wanted to do everything or blame other people when they didn't win. His temperament is much better suited to an individual sport like fencing.

—*Karen, mom of Josh, 7, Dalton, 5, and Alexa, 3*

In fact, the movements in competition are so fast that electronic scoring is used in matches to detect the blade in designated target areas. Those new to fencing are always awed by the lightning speed of the fencer's movements.

Upon being attacked, a fencer defends himself with a parry (an action that deflects the opponent's blade), after which the fencer counterattacks with a riposte (an answering attack). In accordance with the historical objective of trying to wound your opponent without sustaining any blows or injuries to yourself, training teaches a fencer how to touch an opponent with the blade without being touched.

As an individual sport, children learn to stand on their own two feet and make decisions for themselves in competition. It is similar to tennis in that there is very little coaching from the sidelines.

—*Sherry Posthumus, assistant athletic director, Stanford University, coaching fencing for 14 years*

Fencing combines constant motion punctuated by explosive movements from the legs with small, precise hand movements. Fencing most closely resembles tennis and racquetball in the type of explosive leg movement that it requires, but the upper body uses more minor muscles to work the weapon than those sports.

—*R. Cole Harkness, fencing master, Halberstadt Fencers Club in San Francisco, teaching for 17 years*

General Benefits

Fencing is one of the few sports where girls and boys, as well as children of various ages, can compete against each other on equal terms. Moreover, it's one of the few sports where a small child has a fighting chance of beating a larger child.

Fencing builds endurance, self-discipline, and concentration. Fast-paced footwork offers a great aerobic workout and increased stamina. Quick, explosive movements sharpen reflexes and increase poise. Lunging and sparring strengthen and tone leg muscles. Sparring teaches a fencer to be focused and emotionally levelheaded.

Fencers benefit from improved balance, flexibility, coordination, agility, dexterity, and speed.

The intense strategic component rewards mental acuity, critical thinking, responsiveness, and decisiveness on one's feet. In addition, facing an opponent presents a tactical and intellectual challenge. The strategy of fencing encompasses skills from driving attacks to crafty elusion and defense, all adapted to the movements of varying opponents.

A sense of camaraderie, fair play, and integrity prevails even in the most heated of bouts. The gallantry of the sport encourages gracious manners and courtesy toward the opponent.

Kids Who Tend to Excel

◎ A wide range of kids excel at fencing. Those who are able to concentrate and stay levelheaded when squaring off with an opponent tend to have an advantage.

◎ Fencing is more athletic and complex than many people expect, and physically, it helps to have speed, endurance, strength, precision, flexibility, agility, coordination, and quick reaction time. Sheer force or speed is not enough in fencing.

◎ Left-handers usually enjoy a slight advantage in competitions. While 15% of all beginning fencers are lefties, 50% of world champions are lefties.

◎ Kids who excel at fencing exhibit strategic thinking, self-drive, patience, tenacity, hand-eye coordination, balance, and individuality (fencers train as part of a team, but the competition is one-on-one).

◎ Fencing involves patience, as it typically takes a long time to develop correctly, and is not a sport of instant gratification.

My son Robert discovered fencing at age 11 at summer camp and fell in love with it. He loves fantasy books, and I think that many of the kids drawn to fencing are very imaginative, and maybe see themselves secretly as knights in shining armor when they fence. My son joined a local fencing club and takes weekly lessons. When he started, no one seemed to have heard of fencing, but then, lo and behold, it became the rage and started being offered at his middle school as well.

—*Elizabeth, mom of Robert, 15, and David, 10*

The kids who excel in fencing tend to be very introverted, and it's actually the bookworms who do the best. You'll get a kid who's kind of quiet, who doesn't really play a lot of sports, and he'll come in and discover that this is what he always wanted to do. Especially with things like *Harry Potter* and *Lord of the Rings,* fencing attracts a certain type of kid, the one who loves the game Dungeons and Dragons. No level of athleticism is really required. We had one mom who came in with her four boys. She said that fencing was the only activity they'd do, otherwise they were couch potatoes. They really weren't athletically inclined kids, but loved fencing because it really engaged their imaginations.

—*Meghan Gardner, director of Guard Up, teaching for 3 years*

Most of our fencers are quite intelligent and in the top 10% of their class. Many high school kids try to use fencing as a means of gaining scholarships into Ivy League schools that have fencing teams. It is very hard for a kid to compete in, say, football or ice hockey on a national level before college. In fencing it is very possible.

    —Kenneth Strattan, fencing instructor for 5 years, and Valentin Nikolov, Olympic fencer and head coach for the Bulgarian National Team for 30 years

Successful fencers need brains (this is a smart sport) and fearlessness. Having someone coming at you with a weapon is a daunting thing for many.

    —Rita Finkel, mom of three fencers and manager of The Fencers Club

Best Age to Start

Most coaches recommend that kids start fencing between the ages of 9 and 12, although some programs will take children as young as age 5 and the USFA offers competitive divisions for children 10 and under. Younger kids often lack the hand-eye coordination, patience, and concentration needed for fencing, and lack the arm strength to hold up the weapon for any length of time.

What to Look For When Getting Started

When selecting a program, ask if the club provides all the needed equipment for practice as well as for competitions so you have a clear understanding of the costs involved.

Ask whether bouting is self-regulated or if the instructors monitor all bouts.

Beginning lessons focus on footwork, balance, rules of the game, and required courtesy. Your child will also learn drills that teach him the various techniques of positions such as guard, attack, parry, and riposte, deception and counter-deception. As an individual combat sport, fencing classes usually involve a lot of footwork, sparring, drills, and cross-training for endurance.

Not only will your child work to develop sensitivity to his opponent's actions and reactions, weaknesses, and habits, but he will also learn how to use these per-

The very young usually do not posses the upper-body strength to wield the weapons without acquiring bad habits. For this reason, kids should start between the ages of 10 and 12, and first do a general large-muscle sport to build their athletic base, such as soccer or judo.

—*R. Cole Harkness, fencing master, Halberstadt Fencers Club in San Francisco, teaching for 17 years*

Younger kids have too short an attention span and usually not enough arm strength. Doing footwork until they are strong enough to do handwork is usually too boring for them.

—*Roberta Harding, Circle d'Escrime School of Fencing and USFCA foil instructor for 14 years*

The very young require a special program and equipment. We don't let them play with steel weapons; instead they get "Smurf" sabers.

—*Jim Kelly, instructor, Cape Cod Fencing Club, teaching for 10 years*

ceptions and exploit them to his advantage. Since there is a wide variety of styles and techniques, learning the ability to analyze opponents and adapt to their strategies is key.

🌿 As a beginner, your child will use shorter blades that are light and quick. Blades used in fencing vary considerably based on their stiffness, flex point, weight, length, and balance.

🌿 Regional and national competitions are available for children, and are broken down into the age categories of under 10, under 12, under 14, and under 17.

🌿 Fencing in the United States is gradually developing an accreditation program for coaches. The U.S. Fencing Coaches Association (USFCA) issues three levels of certification: moniteur, prevost, and master. The first is qualified to teach beginners; the second, to coach teams and train intermediate-level fencers; and the third, to work at the highest level of national and international competitive fencing. Similarly, the U.S. Fencing Association (USFA), the recognized national governing body under the International Olympic Committee, has a five-level coaching development program.

If someone says they don't do competitive fencing (or "USFA fencing") or says that they teach "classical" or "historical," that usually means that what you will get is a stylized version of the modern Olympic sport of fencing that is more historical reenactment than sport. Useful for theater, however.

—*R. Cole Harkness, fencing master, Halberstadt Fencers Club in San Francisco, teaching for 17 years*

Most instructors teach beginners with the foil, because it's the "classic" weapon and because skills from foil transfer to the other weapons more easily than the other way around (although about 75% of the technique is the same in all three weapons). Some prefer épée for its simplicity (the whole body is a valid target and the rule is simply that the first to hit an opponent scores a point). Starting a child with saber demands caution, because the use of the sharp edge of the weapon (foil and épée are point-only) can lead to wild, swinging actions that are both incorrect and dangerous. Some coaches teach all three concurrently and allow the students to choose whichever suits them best (or to continue with more than one).

—*Scott Tundermann, Northampton Fencing Center owner and instructor for 6 years*

We start kids on foil because it is the lightest weapon and a great teaching tool. The fencer who starts on foil learns distance, weapon control, timing, and right of way, to name a few. Plus, by having everyone on foil, that means that on a really slow club night when only 5 people show up, everyone can still fence together with foil.

—*Kenneth Strattan, fencing instructor for 5 years, and Valentin Nikolov, Olympic fencer and head coach for the Bulgarian National Team for 30 years*

🐟 Ask about a coach's fencing background and if he is or was a rated competitor (ratings are A through E, with A being the highest), as well as if his students are rated.

Basic Types of Fencing

Fencing as a sport involves sword fighting with one of three different weapons: the foil, épée, or saber.

FOIL

✦ The most popular blade used in beginner training and competitions is the foil. Of all the weapons, the foil teaches the basics the best, and also takes the most finesse to master.

✦ Originally a training weapon in the 18th century, the foil—a small sword—has a thin, light, flexible blade just under three feet long and a small bell guard. Children's blades are short and light. In bouts, the point of the blade anywhere on the front or back of an opponent's torso scores touches. Training emphasizes strong defensive moves with the blade and quick, penetrating attacks with the tip.

✦ Until recently, women could only compete internationally in foil. Now national competitions for women include épée and saber. Internationally, women's épée was added to the Olympic Games for the first time in 1996.

ÉPÉE

✦ Descended from the dueling swords of the mid-19th century, the épée is heavier than the foil, with a stiff blade and a large bell guard to protect the hand from being hit.

✦ Épée training emphasizes timing, control, and strong counterattacks. In bouts, touches are scored only with the point of the blade, and anywhere on an opponent's body is considered a valid target. Moreover, very few rules govern sparring.

✦ Most épée fencers think of themselves as practical, no-nonsense sword fighters.

SABER

✦ Fencers turn to the saber to experience the adrenaline rush of a typically fast, aggressive sword fight. Descended from the slashing cavalry swords of the late 19th century, a saber, while similar in length and weight to a foil, has a light, flat blade and a knuckle guard.

✦ In bouts, touches can be scored with either the point or the edge of the blade touching an opponent's body anywhere above the waist (simulating the area of a rider on a horse). The mask has added protection with a metal covering, as the head is a valid target area.

✦ Saber technique emphasizes speed and strong offense.

Safety and Injury Concerns

❦ Fencing has an excellent safety record, as the bendable swords for beginners are capped at the tip with a rubber button or metal tip, and players wear gear that protects them during the beginner's drills and practice-fighting bouts. The foil's blade should be flexible enough to make it difficult to hurt an opponent, even accidentally. All blades should be free of rust or sharp bends.

❦ A clean fencing attack does not hurt, but feels more like a tap on the shoulder, with the flexible blade absorbing most of the blow. The worst your child might experience are bruises, pulled muscles, twisted ankles, sprains, or strains. Minor welts sometimes occur in sparring with inexperienced fencers who have not yet acquired a feel for the sport. Your child should also be taught proper footwork so that stress that can injure the ligaments is not put on his knees.

❦ Your child should wear full protective gear. This includes long-legged pants and a long-sleeved shirt. Covering this will be a padded chest and underarm protector,

The first lesson that new fencers get pounded into their heads is safety. We never let up. We treat the swords as if they were guns! The most potential danger comes from a broken blade—it was the cause of the only fatal fencing accident in modern times in the old Soviet Union.

—Jim Kelly, instructor, Cape Cod Fencing Club, teaching for 10 years

Fencing is an extremely safe sport due to the safety equipment worn, the absence of direct physical contact, and the low-impact nature of the movements.

—Michael Elder, head coach, Miami Fencing Club, teaching for 38 years

If done correctly, fencing should cause no injuries, although there are some inevitable hard hits that may leave a bruise. Serious injuries from the weapons are almost unheard-of, as the protective jacket and mask are made to stop even a broken-off blade from doing real damage. In general, fencing is one of the safest sports around.

—Scott Tundermann, Northampton Fencing Center owner and instructor for 6 years

called a plastron, that cushions any blows. A girl usually also wears a hard plastic chest plate ("dinger") to protect her chest. Boys wear athletic cups. A standard metal mesh helmet protects the head. A more experienced fencer wears a suit made of puncture-resistant white cloth. A leather glove with a long cuff covering the sleeve opening and padding is used to protect the sword hand.

🗡 Many saber fencers get fencer's elbow, similar to tennis elbow. Also, shoulder rotator cuff injuries can be caused by poor technique.

🗡 Your child should always warm up and stretch before practice or a competition.

🗡 When they do occur, injuries are mostly the "pulled muscle" type due to overexertion.

Cost Considerations

🗡 Fencing is a relatively inexpensive sport, until your child enters competitions or buys his own fencing equipment and gear. Many introductory programs will provide all the equipment, while others require everyone to purchase their own gear.

🗡 A beginner's set of fencing equipment, including a sword, jacket, mask, and glove, will cost approximately $120–$150. Competitive gear costs more, usually between $200 and $300, with high-end gear costing upward of $1,000–$1,200 for uniform, mask, and weapons.

🗡 Instead of expensive fencing shoes, light, flexible, thin-soled, indoor tennis shoes offer an excellent low-cost alternative. In addition, more experienced fencers use hard heel cups or softer rubber inserts to absorb the impact of lunges.

🗡 Class fees range from $30 to $80 per month, depending on how many classes your child takes.

🗡 If your child fences in a club, costs run about $10 per session, or sometimes around $20 a month.

When the fencer is ready to enter competitions, he will have to add a lame, body cord, and an electric weapon. This adds another $125 to the fencer's equipment cost. Also, the hidden expenses are always there. As a fencer moves up, the competitions move farther and farther away. I have traveled thousands of miles so that my 10-year-old son could compete in a North American Cup competition.

—Kenneth Strattan, fencing instructor for 5 years

Competitive fencing involves dramatically escalated costs. If competing in épée, your child will need two electrified weapons, two body cords, and a fencing knicker costing around $200. Foil requires, in addition to this, a metallic vest costing around $75. Competing in saber is the most expensive given electric scoring, and additional equipment costs around $300. Moreover, this equipment often requires repair and replacement.

—Jim Kelly, instructor, Cape Cod Fencing Club, teaching for 10 years

🦯 Your child must belong to the U.S. Fencing Association to fence in a competition, which costs $40 for a junior membership.

🦯 Local competitions usually cost between $5 and $10 for each event being fenced, while competition at a national championship costs around $50 per event.

🦯 Additional equipment for competition will often cost another $250, so it's helpful if your child's fencing club has competition equipment to rent or borrow.

🦯 There is also the cost of traveling to competitions, particularly those taking place at the regional or national level.

FIELD HOCKEY

Overview

Field hockey is one of the world's oldest competitive team sports. Variants on today's game were played in the Nile Valley as well as among the Greeks, Romans, Ethiopians, and Aztecs, and evolved in England in the 19th century. This energetic sport demands teamwork, speed, strategic thinking, determination, and a certain amount of fearlessness. Body-checking and blocking are allowed.

In field hockey, eleven players on each team use a short, curved wooden stick to move a very hard small ball down a field to shoot goals. There are two halves, 30 minutes each. The hardwood field hockey stick has a curved head, rounded on one side and flat on the other. The ball must be passed or dribbled down the field using only the flat side of the stick. A goal is scored when an attacker strikes the ball into the goal from within the striking circle, which is a semicircle 16 yards away from the goal. Players may not shield the ball using their body or stick.

Although there are NCAA Division I field hockey programs, field hockey is not a nationally recognized sport. Field hockey is mainly played on the East Coast—from Maine down to North Carolina—along with Colorado, Texas, and California. Schools have been the primary place where kids learn field hockey, though club teams are just now beginning to develop. While some Midwestern states have field hockey, many haven't fully embraced it as a sport for their children, so it may be challenging to find teams in those areas.

General Benefits

◎ Cardiovascular workout from the running involved, as well as stamina

- Quickness, adaptability, balance, and agility

- Overall strengthening

- Improved hand-eye coordination

- Teamwork

Kids Who Tend to Excel

- Fitness is a key factor, as field hockey is a physically demanding and highly aerobic sport. Players are constantly running from one end of the field to the other. Speed is necessary when dribbling the ball or getting into a strategic position to pass or block the ball. Children with endurance can keep up best with the fast-paced running.

- Good hand-eye coordination and upper-body strength are required to strike the ball with the hockey stick. Strong stick skills, which require a great deal of practice, make a huge difference in field hockey performance.

- One rule in field hockey is that a player may not raise the end of her stick above her shoulder; thus a taller player has a definite advantage.

- Children who are agile, competitive, assertive, and thrive in a team situation do well.

Field hockey involves constant motion and change that requires the continual involvement of all players—it is truly a sport that encompasses every participant on the field.

—*Heather Lewis, head field hockey coach at Bucknell University, coaching for 17 years*

Mental benefits of field hockey include self-esteem, communication skills, membership in a group effort, and endorphins released from activity. Physical benefits include cardiovascular endurance, great muscle tone, and skill development. Children with any body type can be successful. Kids who excel are well-conditioned athletes with the ability to be intense and have cognitive ability to see one move ahead and the skill level to execute. In other words, kids who excel are "tactically aware."

—*Marge Redmond, head field hockey coach at Ohio Wesleyan, coaching for 17 years*

All small kids excel at field hockey. The basic skills involve dribbling, passing, receiving, and shooting. As kids get older, the best players are coordinated, fit, hardworking, and creative.

—*Shellie Onstead, head field hockey coach at UC Berkeley, coaching for 20 years*

In Europe, Asia, South America, and Africa, children start playing field hockey as early as age 3. Some have a stick in their hand from the time they are born. In America, I would hope they could start just as early. However, most school systems do not offer the sport until eight or ninth grade, and even then, it's only offered to girls.

—*Sammie Merrill, assistant field hockey coach at Rutgers University, coaching for 5 years*

Field hockey for the most part isn't played until high school, and we expect 14-year-olds, who are going through so many physical and emotional changes already, to pick up a stick and be good at something that is very demanding and skill-oriented. So I recommend starting your child earlier, ideally around age 7 or 8.

—*Shannon Hlebichuk, University of Massachusetts, Lowell, head field hockey coach for 1 year*

Best Age to Start

Field hockey players generally start playing through school programs and begin around age 12 in middle school or during the first year of high school. One advantage of a start in the junior high years is that all the children begin on an equal footing, as they're all new to the sport.

There's a movement afoot trying to expose girls to field hockey at a younger age; some club teams now start children as young as age 8 in their programs.

What to Look For When Getting Started

Ask how many children have stayed with the program or club team for a long time. You want a program that creates a love for the sport and an active interest in playing.

Ask as well about the type of surface on which the club team plays field hockey. A child should be exposed to artificial turf early on, so she can work on skills needed for higher-level competitions.

Safety and Injury Concerns

✦ Most injuries involve broken or jammed fingers, turf burn on the knees and knuckles, and anterior cruciate ligament (ACL) injuries to the knee.

✦ If a player is in poor physical shape, a lot of stress gets put on her back, because instead of bending with the knees to play, she bends at her waist, which can cause lower-back strain.

✦ The hard ball used in field hockey frequently goes flying at very high speeds and players can get hit with it anywhere on their bodies. Except for the goalie, most players wear only shin guards, mouth guards, and sometimes goggles as protective gear.

✦ Your child must not only be alert to the swinging wooden sticks, but also be aware that players move fast and sometimes collide.

✦ Your child should wear a mouth guard to protect against injury to her teeth, especially as she gets to higher levels of play.

✦ Some states, such as Massachusetts, now require that players wear goggles to protect against eye injuries from contact with the ball or a stick.

✦ Cleats are important, especially if your child will be playing on wet grass.

Cost Considerations

✦ Field hockey equipment costs depend on the position of the player. A field hockey player needs the following basics: field hockey stick, field hockey ball, cleats, and shin guards.

✦ A good field hockey stick can cost anywhere from $25 to $150, with a beginner stick usually costing between $35 and $45. The stick usually needs to be replaced every one to two years. When choosing a stick for your child, you need to make sure it's the proper length by placing the stick perpendicular to the ground. The top of the stick should come up to her hip joint. Where sticks used to be made exclusively of wood, some are now made of a composite material. Sticks have different shock absorption based on their composition, so ask about this when making your purchasing decision.

✦ Shin guards cost around $15, cleats cost around $20, and a standard mouth guard typically costs $5. Eye goggles cost around $10 to $20.

✦ Programs or schools usually provide goalie equipment, as it costs around $700, and let the players buy their own sticks.

> I consider myself a traditionalist of the sport and recommend a wood stick. However, some players are now playing with a composite stick that allows for better "hits" during the game, thus giving the players a sense of accomplishment because the ball moves harder and faster.
>
> —Shannon Hlebichuk, University of Massachusetts, Lowell, head field hockey coach for 1 year

❦ Most field hockey events are U.S. Field Hockey Association sanctioned and every participant must be a member, costing about $35. Tournament fees run between $50 and $200.

❦ Club teams cost about the same as any softball or soccer club, generally between $200 and $800. Summer camps for field hockey run anywhere from $300 to $500 a week.

FIGURE SKATING

Overview

Skating, like many other winter sports, originated as an efficient way for hunters and warriors to travel across frozen water, using wood or bone runners attached to the feet. Skating became a recreational pastime with the development of an iron blade in the mid-1500s. Although skating developed in Europe, modern figure skating was invented by an American, Jackson Haines, who in the mid 1800s broke with convention by introducing dance moves into what had been highly stiff and formal skating. Figure skating has often been described as "ballet on ice," with routines blending athleticism and grace. Figure skating was first added to the Olympic program in 1908 and became an official Winter Olympic Games sport in 1924.

Like gymnastics, figure skating is a very popular sport among young girls. Similarly, it gains most of its popularity from the Olympics. Young girls idealize the strength and grace of young stars. However, as a parent, you should know that between rink time and lessons, ice skating can be quite expensive and an intense time commitment.

General Benefits

◉ Provides all-around muscle strengthening

◉ Increases cardiovascular fitness

◉ Improves coordination, balance, posture, muscle control, and body awareness

◉ Exposes a child to dance and music

◉ A great family activity

◉ Can be enjoyed for a lifetime, and can be done in so many different places, from indoor rinks to frozen ponds

Figure skating is a wonderful sport because it provides the athleticism of gymnastics with the grace of ballet. Skating provides a means for self-expression and creativity that can't be found in many other sports. Between recreational and competitive skating, everyone has a place to excel. Skating is mostly a short anaerobic sport but can be trained aerobically as well. Skaters gain muscular endurance, coordination, strength, and mental toughness.

—*Louise LoBosco, figure-skating coach, The Classical Academy, teaching for 25 years*

Skating creates physical strength in harmony with stamina and agility. Skaters learn how to think about moves before they do it, how to mentally prepare for competitions and performances, and how to push their limits.

—*Larisa Gendernalik, director of skating, Breckenridge Ice Rink, coaching for 30 years*

Skating teaches how to concentrate on the elements you are doing while at the same time putting in an artistic expression and making it look effortless. You have to focus while appearing to not be focusing, and learn how to pay attention to the 50-plus different things that your body has to do at the exact same time.

—*Alyna Douglass, ice-skating instructor for 3 years*

Kids Who Tend to Excel

◎ Skating is a physical sport that requires muscle strength, flexibility, endurance and grace.

◎ Children who excel are typically extroverted, like moving at fast speeds, and are somewhat fearless, as you need a bit of reckless abandonment to learn the jumps.

◎ Those who are willing to work and concentrate do best. For competitive skaters this often means skating 5–6 days a week, for at least 2–3 hours a day

◎ Coordination and body awareness are similar to those required for dance and gymnastics. Children who succeed in competitions usually do some sort of rhythmic activity such as ballet, modern dance, or gymnastics on the side.

◎ They also have to able to deal with the subjectivity involved in judging competitions, as well as the considerable tension and pressure put on them as individual performers.

I've had children as young as age 8 start competing—it just depends on their body build and daringness.

—*Linda Kola, master-rated figure-skating coach, teaching for 26 years*

Best Age to Start

◎ While you will occasionally see children under 3 in skates, most kids that age lack the required ankle strength. As a result, many rinks will not accept children for group classes who are under 4 years old.

◎ Ages 5–7 is a good time to sign your child up for lessons to see if she enjoys skating.

◎ Most children are coordinated enough to make significant progress in skill development by the time they are 8.

What to Look For When Getting Started

✦ Skaters normally begin to skate and learn basic skills in a group-lesson environment. Many children will join a skating club or begin working with a private instructor to further develop skills. Many rinks have figure-skating clubs and junior clubs.

✦ You should look for coaches who are members of the Professional Skaters Association (PSA), which organizes, trains, and rates coaches and certifies them, with the highest levels of certification being senior and master. The U.S. Figure Skating Association (USFSA) also rates coaches. Most coaches are former competitive skaters, and you should ask about their own skating experience and teaching background. Also, ask about the level of students with whom the coach currently works.

❀ Watch a lesson with a coach to see if you like the way that coach runs the session. Your child needs someone who matches her personality and uses a teaching style to which she responds best, especially since many skaters go their entire skating career with the same coach.

❀ Discuss your child's goals with the coach, whether she wants to test to advance in levels, and what degree of competition and travel makes sense. Ask the coach what will be required of your child in terms of time, commitment, and competitions. Private lessons are necessary for competitive skating, and club skaters can practice as many as 12 to 15 hours per week, depending on their level of interest and competitiveness.

Types of Competitive Skating
SINGLES FREESTYLE

❀ A competitive skater performs a program set to music and composed of elements such as jumps and spins. In a singles competition, the skater has to perform both a technical program of eight required moves, as well as a longer, free-skating program. Judging is based upon the quality of elements performed, difficulty of the program, technical performance, presentation, creativity, expression, and choreography.

In addition to group lessons, we found that doing one private lesson at the start of the season gives your child an infusion of individual focus that's worth its weight in gold.

—*Amy, mom of Sacha, 11, and Libby, 8*

When you're looking for a private coach, watch her working with students for a couple of weeks to see if she can demonstrate the exercises that she's teaching. Before your child starts jumping and spinning, she or he should master basic skills to prevent technical mistakes.

—*Natalya Khazova, former international competitor, coaching for 15 years*

❀ Skaters compete within groups of other skaters with similar ability levels. Levels are determined based on official USFSA tests, taken in front of judges at designated "test sessions." In singles freestyle, there are eight different test levels, each with specific required elements. In the very first test, skaters have to perform jumps and spins as separate elements. The singles freestyle test levels are: pre-preliminary, preliminary, pre-juvenile, juvenile, intermediate, novice, junior, and senior.

PAIRS FREESTYLE

❀ Pairs skating is free skating performed in unison by partners. Routines feature overhead lifts, throw jumps, pair spins, and synchronized spins and jumps, and

Kids should switch from recreational to competitive skating when they feel ready. If they wish, there are levels of competition that are achievable in less than a year. Others become serious and dedicated skaters without competing much. Testing and show opportunities can provide satisfying goals if your child doesn't like to compete.

—*Eric Neubauer, skating coach, Lehigh Valley Ice Arena, teaching for 25 years*

If a child is skating in a club or program and shows natural talent, one of the coaches will identify this and approach the parent to suggest private coaching. In most cases, the child usually requests private lessons when she feels she wants to compete. Some children, however, feel more comfortable in a group environment and don't want to take the step into competitive skating.

—*Carol Brown, South African international figure-skating judge for 18 years, coaching for 4 years*

Watch for burnout with the younger ones. Children can only handle so much intensity at a young age. The highly competitive world of figure skating causes athletes to think that if they can't be among the top four in the nation that they can't continue.

—*Louise LoBosco, figure-skating coach, The Classical Academy, teaching for 25 years*

are done with exact timing and in tandem. Judging is based both on the difficulty and creativity of the moves, along with how well the pair stays synchronized in body lines, gestures, and footwork. Competitions consist of both a long and short program.

❦ The skaters have usually skated for two or three years before beginning pairs skating. All basic skating skills, single jumps, and spins need to be mastered first. Pairs skating and ice dancing have risen in popularity in recent years, and children now start entering pairs-skating competitions sponsored by the International Skating Union as early as age 9.

ICE DANCING

❦ Ice dancing is the newest Olympic figure-skating event, debuting in the 1976 Olympic Games, and emphasizing rhythm, musical interpretation, and precision. Ice dancing is performed by a couple and emphasizes the beauty and artistry of the sport, rather than the athleticism.

❦ Ice-dancing competitors perform four routines: two compulsory dances, one original dance to a specific rhythm, and one free dance. All this involves edgework, flow, and fluid combined motions coordinated to music. Most children do not start ice-dancing competitions until their preteens.

SYNCHRONIZED TEAM SKATING (PRECISION SKATING)

❦ This new style, introduced in 1990, involves a team of anywhere from eight to over twenty skaters performing skating patterns and routines to music. Teamwork and timing are critical.

Safety and Injury Concerns

🍂 Overall, figure skaters have surprisingly few injuries given the speed and jumps on the ice and the lack of protective gear. The most common skating injuries are twisted ankles, bruised knees, minor cuts, and sprains.

🍂 A typical injury for lower-level skaters is falling forward and splitting open the chin. Your child should be taught to retract her fingers when falling to prevent cuts. Helmets and kneepads also help protect beginner skaters.

🍂 More serious skaters have to watch out for tendonitis, overuse injuries to the ankle and back, and stress fractures. Competitive skaters often wear "crash pads" while practicing jumps, which lessen the impact of a fall.

Injuries are more common today due to the triples and quads expected at a young age. I expect my athletes to follow an order of jump progression to help keep training in check and ensure appropriate strength. My skaters have to perform clean, fully rotated double jumps before beginning double axels. Many athletes start difficult jumps too soon.

—*Louise LoBosco, figure-skating coach, The Classical Academy, teaching for 25 years*

Cost Considerations

🍂 Rent skates for your child until she shows sustained interest in, for instance, a 6- or 8-week class. Make sure the skates fit correctly. If they're too loose, your child won't be able to control her skates. Your child should be able to wiggle her toes up and down, but not side-to-side or be able to lift her heel. Check that the blade edges feel sharp.

🍂 Your child may lobby for hockey skates, but figure skates offer more stability for beginners because both their longer blades and toe pick, located near the front end of each blade, help with stopping. The toe pick also helps your child to better grip the ice.

🍂 A new pair of ice skates is essential if your child decides to seriously pursue skating lessons. Beginner skates run about $50–$90, while skates for an advanced skater can run up to $1,000 a pair. Your child's blades need to be sharpened regularly, and blade protectors should be used when walking on the skates off the ice.

🍂 Other costs include group or private lessons, with prices varying regionally but often running about $15–45 for a half-hour, along with $2–$10 for ice time.

🍂 If your child gets into competitive figure skating, costs will include coaching fees, ice time, and costumes. Competitions all charge an entry fee ranging from $25 to $65.

FOOTBALL

Overview

American football has been played for well over a century. Developed in the late 1800s, its roots stem from two popular sports at the time, soccer and rugby. At first this sport consisted mostly of running and kicking field goals as the primary means of scoring. The forward pass came about only when President Roosevelt threatened to abolish football in 1905 because too many players were being killed due to the rough nature of the game. The creator of this forward pass was coach Pop Warner, and today youth football leagues endorsed with his name can be found across America. With the forward pass came a new scoring system, including touchdowns counting for 6 points and field goal for 3 points.

Millions of children now play football in the United States, with over 3 million playing Pop Warner, an organization for children ages 7–16 similar to Little League baseball. Despite the creation of a National Women's Football League in 1974, and the advent of flag football (which does not involve tackling and attracts both girls and boys) football remains primarily for boys and men. Although football often gets a bad rap for being an injury-ridden and male-dominated sport, it remains a character-building American tradition.

General Benefits

◉ Improved conditioning, muscle strength, stamina, and cardiovascular fitness

◉ Teaches agility, dexterity, and coordination

◉ Considered one of the ultimate team sports, it teaches cooperation and teamwork

In football, kids learn about individual responsibility in a very structured team environment. Each player has a well-defined role that is critical to the success of the entire group. Players learn how their assignments relate to team objectives, and they learn special techniques needed to perform their assignment in each play.

—Jerry Norton, director of Ponte Vedra Development Football League and youth coach for 36 years

Kids Who Tend to Excel

◉ Your child doesn't need to have a big, stocky build to play football, as different positions require different body types. For example, receivers need to be lean, tall, and fast.

◉ Football allows your physically aggressive child a socially acceptable and controlled outlet for his energy.

Girls in Football

✦ While a professional women's football league has been launched, girls in football are still a rarity.

✦ You'll find girls participating in youth football, but stopping around high school. If your daughter decides to pursue football in middle school or high school, she will still likely be the only girl on the team.

Best Age to Start

◉ Flag football programs can start as young as age 5, but the average starting age in most youth programs is 7 or 8.

◉ Tackle football starts around age 9.

◉ Make sure your child is playing on a team with kids who are at his level in terms of skill, strength, age, and size.

◉ Youth football permits kids ages 11, 12, and 13 who are particularly small to play in an "older/lighter"

Most of us, male or female, can't take the physical stamina and threshold for pain necessary to compete, and most girls can't handle the physical toll that football puts on one's body. Now, not to sound completely sexist, in most cases boys and even men can't take the physical punishment the body takes during a tackle football game. Girls and women have more choices than 50 years ago for participation in athletics, so the need to go coed in sports like football isn't as much of a necessity as it once was.

—*Gary May, youth football coach for 18 years, and youth baseball coach for 5 years*

Three girls, ages 9, 10, and 11, played in our youth program within the past five years, a very small percentage considering our total annual enrollment is about 200 kids. They each said they signed up because they wanted to have the experience of playing what is traditionally a male sport and enjoyed playing but quit after a year. Girls turn out in slightly larger numbers for our flag football program, a non-contact type of football. Over the past five years we've had about a dozen girls play, mostly in the younger divisions on coed teams.

—*Jerry Norton, director of Ponte Vedra Development Football League and youth coach for 36 years*

In the region where I coach, there aren't many girls out for football. Coaches might see one every now and again on a little league or middle school team, but rarely do they see one on a high school team. It is not that they can't play, it is just not the "in" thing to do.

—*Mark Calvin, football coach, Hubert Middle School, for 3 years*

It's the smaller guys who run the show. The captains of the team are the quarterbacks, running backs, and defensive backs. And they're not the big guys. What we look for is a player's desire to play the game with a big heart. Unfortunately, society puts a lot of pressure on the larger kids. The pressure generally starts at home and then continues at school with peers. The kid who will eventually back out of football is the one who can't escape the stereotype of the physical giant.

—*Gary May, youth football coach for 18 years, and youth baseball coach for 5 years*

The kids who perform the best in football have speed and a large, sturdy frame. However, these attributes don't really matter in youth football because boys have not fully developed. Competitiveness and a little mean streak help a kid most while playing in a game.

—*Lee Perry, Scorpion youth football president and head coach for 8 years*

The truth is that many kids today start playing football too young. Anything before the age of 12 can cause injury. Therefore, I advise parents to wait to put kids into football until they're a little older.

—*Gary May, youth football coach for 18 years, and youth baseball coach for 5 years*

My son Eric plays youth football for five- and six-year-olds and gets pretty excited about it. Players have to reach 55 pounds before they can move on to the next level. He'll be there for a while because he is now only 40 pounds. It's really funny to watch the kids play. There isn't really any tackling.

—*Stephanie, mom of Eric, 5, and Tina, 3*

category. Because they are likely to have more skill and experience than many of their teammates, league rules permit a maximum of eight "older/lighter" players per team.

Weight regulations requiring children to play with others their own size make youth football an ideal sport for a smaller child. Due to this type of grouping, there is a decreased chance of collision injuries common in later years when high school players are grouped only by age, resulting in size disparities.

What to Look For When Getting Started

When evaluating leagues, look into the past history of the program and the quality of the coaches.

Your child should be participating on a football team that:
- provides players with properly maintained and fitted equipment;
- emphasizes a physical conditioning program appropriate to your child's group;
- provides the team with a trainer or support staff knowledgeable in first aid.

Your child should be participating in a league that:
- uses only nationally certified officials;
- Provides safe and well-maintained playing fields.

Pop Warner Football

Currently Pop Warner is the only national youth football and cheerleading organization in the U.S. with

Finding the right program and the right coach is the single most important thing parents must do before allowing their child to play football, or for that matter, any youth sport. Overzealous coaches are far too common in youth football. In our program, we expose all players to each major position and provide instruction in how to play each one. By using this "try it to see if you like it" approach, we are able to fit kids into positions in which they can excel. Football coaches need to keep in mind that while practice and games are important, this is not the Super Bowl or the World Series. There is a life other than football for a child, although there are far too many coaches who don't endorse this radical idea.

—*Jerry Norton, director of Ponte Vedra Development Football League and youth coach for 36 years*

Always look at the head coach first. This will tell you how good the rest of the staff is.

—*David Hess, football coach, Abilene Christian University, for 3 years*

This is what the football coach said at my nine-year-old son's most recent practice, "Unlike coaches in soccer and baseball who lecture you about teamwork and sportsmanship, this is football and this is about winning! So let's start with some push-ups!" That about seems to sum football all up.

—*Anonymous*

leagues in 38 states. The Pop Warner league has flag football for its youngest players, and tackle football for older children, as well as over 35,000 volunteer coaches. In Pop Warner, there are around 140 leagues and conferences, and over 1,200 local associations. Teams compete all the way to regional and national championships, and an annual Super Bowl is held at Disney's Wide World of Sports.

The Pop Warner league has very strict safety requirements along with academic achievement conditions for its youth players. It also offers low-priced insurance coverage.

Its goal is to familiarize children with the fundamentals of football, and all teams are formed on a first-come basis. Tryouts are prohibited. Pop Warner also has a "Mandatory Play Rule," so every child plays in every game.

Safety and Injury Concerns

As long as the children have proper, well-fitting safety equipment, learn proper tackling techniques, and compete against kids who are relatively the same age, weight, and skill level, football has been shown to be a fairly safe sport. The U.S. Consumer Product Safety Commission found that organized football among children ages 5–15 had 12% fewer injuries per person than organized soccer. The most common are neck injuries and pulled muscles.

I have only had one season-ending injury, a dislocated elbow, on an indirect hit. That's it! It's been very surprising to me that boys this age could play as hard as they do and not suffer any more injuries.

—*Donny Goodall, Austin youth football head coach and high school coach for 5 years*

Improved equipment, proper coaching of safe blocking and tackling techniques plus proper conditioning have reduced injury rates in football dramatically over the past several years. In all my years of coaching youth football, the most significant injuries I've seen were a broken wrist and a broken finger. Mostly, I see bumps and bruises.

—*Jerry Norton, director of Ponte Vedra Development Football League and youth coach for*

🏈 Yet football can be dangerous as a contact sport. Just recently, a ten-year-old girl in Chicago died of head injuries she sustained during a tackle on her otherwise all-boys team during a full-contact practice.

🏈 Players should do stretching and warm-up exercises to help prevent the pulling of hamstring muscles.

🏈 Standard safety equipment includes a helmet, which your child should wear with the chin strap tightly fastened, as well as pads (shoulder, knee, thigh, hips, tailbone), cleats, and mouth guard. In addition, Pop Warner requires all their players to wear vests that protect ribs and long girdles over all the padding to keep the pads from slipping.

🏈 In order to find a helmet that correctly fits when trying helmets on, dampen your child's hair as it will be when he's playing. Make sure there is a one-inch gap between the front bottom of the helmet and his eyebrows. The helmet should fit snugly enough that when you tug on it, your child's forehead skin should crinkle and the helmet should not move. For your child who is under age 14, look for a helmet with a polyethylene shell, which weighs less but holds up to the lower impact levels.

🏈 If your child plays in intense heat, make sure that the coaches watch out for dehydration.

Cost Considerations

🏈 Except for personal items such as jock straps, undergarments, and footwear, most organized football teams will supply equipment to their players.

Football has tons of additional costs such as mouthpieces, travel expenses, meals, neck brace for youth football helmets, cooler for drinks, mister to use during halftime to cool down, shoes, socks, jerseys, practice pants, practice jerseys, girdle, halftime refreshments whenever it is your turn, end-of-season party expenses, and coaching gifts!

—Donny Goodall, Austin Youth Football head coach and high school coach for 5 years

Costs for being on a football team vary depending upon what equipment the program provides. Our program charges each player $125 for a complete set of certified equipment, including helmet, shoulder pads, game pants with pads, two game jerseys and one mouthpiece. Players are covered by extra medical insurance. All equipment except one of the jerseys is returned at the end of the season. Players provide their own athletic shoes, supporters, and cups. Our fee also includes costs for referees, field use, and other operating expenses. I would expect that the cost for most programs throughout the country would be in the range of $100 to $250 per player.

—Jerry Norton, director of Ponte Vedra Development Football League and youth coach for 36 years

🦙 Season costs vary tremendously, with an average of $100 to $150 per season, partially depending on how much equipment the program loans out.

🦙 Some teams charge a "towel," or laundry, fee, often about $2 a week.

🦙 If you wish to purchase your child his own equipment, buy equipment that fits at the time you buy it as opposed to things that he will grow into.

GOLF

Overview

The history of golf goes back more than 550 years, and the most accepted theory is that golf as we know it today started in Scotland in the early 1400s. The first written reference to golf came in 1457, when the king of Scotland demanded a formal Act of Parliament to make playing golf illegal as soldiers were spending more time playing golf than practicing archery. It was not until the mid-1700s that the first written rules of the game appeared. While it has become more sophisticated as a sport, the object of the game remains the same: to advance a ball into each hole's cup using as few strokes as possible.

Golf is an individual game and kids learn quickly that the results they get are based on their efforts alone. The sense of accomplishment and satisfaction that kids receive when they perform well, or just better than they have before, is evident in their smiles and the way that they carry themselves. The ability to see improvement and success based on one's own efforts provides a great life lesson in our instant society.

—*Paul Hobart, PGA teaching professional, Tartan Fields Golf Club*

With the advent of Tiger Woods and high-profile television coverage of the sport, golf has finally come into its own as one of the nation's most popular pastimes. There are over 18,000 golf courses in America, and nearly 27 million golfers with approximately 2.1 million junior members. Junior golf programs are proliferating all over the country. According to the National Golf Foundation, 6 out of every 10 children exposed to golf through a structured junior program will become active adult golfers. Moreover, adults who participated in a junior golf program play 50% more rounds than those exposed to golf in an unstructured way. However, many kids leave golf almost as fast as they enter, because it's a hard game to learn and takes vast amounts of time and practice to do well.

Golf can be a sport that your whole family plays together. Because of its handicap system as well as junior tee boxes, everyone can have fun and still enjoy some competition.

Golf is a game for life, unlike other popular sports such as gymnastics, soccer, or hockey, which few kids will play on the college level or continue on with as adults. Golf also has more integrity than what you find in most sports, in terms of its strong code of etiquette, and players calling penalties on themselves. Unlike other youth sports where everything's set up by parents, who often scream, yell, and can't let go, golf involves four hours on your own, uninterrupted by adults.

> —Mike Bailey, Brae Burn Country Club head golf professional and Class-A PGA teaching pro for 27 years

When you realize that golf is a lifetime sport, it makes the net time your children spend learning it worthwhile, as they can play it over such an extended time frame. Golf will be something that your child can use for socializing and business networking later in life.

> —Kelli Kostick, head teaching professional and LPGA/PGA certified pro for 12 years

General Benefits

◉ Playing golf strengthens your child's muscles, especially in the upper body, and increases flexibility, balance, and range of motion. If your child carries her own clubs when playing an 18-hole course, it will build her stamina.

◉ Golf improves your child's level of concentration and focus. When approaching each shot, your child has to exercise independent thinking and strategic decision making. Children also learn to give all their attention to one shot at a time.

◉ Learning to strike the ball enhances hand-eye coordination.

◉ Your child will learn golf etiquette as she develops into a golfer, as well as the specific rules of a course being played. Golf teaches respect, honesty in keeping track of your own score, consideration for other players, and good sportsmanship.

◉ Learning golf requires lots of patience and perseverance. Your child may whiff five times before she hits a great drive, but this will show her that practice goes a long way toward improving her game.

The best age to start your child in an organized program is around age 7. Before that, most children don't have the needed attention span or enough dexterity to handle a club. Anything sooner than that should last no more than a half-hour, one-on-one.

—*Kelli Kostick, head teaching professional and LPGA/PGA certified pro for 12 years*

We have kids as young as 4 in our clinics. The biggest deal in teaching kids golf is transferring knowledge of the golf swing. It's much harder to learn during adolescence.

—*Mike Bailey, Brae Burn Country Club head golf professional and Class-A PGA teaching pro for 27 years*

⊙ Walking an 18-hole course means your child will have the opportunity to spend four hours outside in a beautiful setting getting exercise that improves her fitness level, and talking to and making friends with other kids her own age and ability.

Best Age to Start

⊙ Depending on your child's size, attention span, and interest, lessons generally start anywhere from age 5 to 10. Most children are not ready for formal golf instruction until age 8, when they have enough self-discipline.

⊙ Tiger Woods may have started at age 2, but for most children it's best to start when they are both interested and able to follow the teacher's instructions, which for some children may not be until around age 12.

⊙ Since golf is a game of patience and perseverance, kids tend to burn out faster on golf than in other sports. It's often better to wait until your child's really interested in learning the sport and physically and emotionally mature enough to start tackling the sport's intricacies.

Kids Who Tend to Excel

⊙ Unlike many other competitive sports, your child's size and speed does  not determine how well she will play golf. Golf takes intense focus, concentration, and the discipline to spend hundreds of hours practicing the basics. It is a game of patience and perseverance, with such a slow learning curve that the average age of tour players is 32.

⊙ Even though golfers do not need to be in stellar shape, the sport does require that your child have strength, stamina, flexibility, coordination, balance, concentration, great hand-eye coordination, and skill.

Kids who do the best are disciplined, tenacious, and realize that golf is a game you have to constantly practice.

—*Kelli Kostick, head teaching professional and LPGA/PGA certified pro for 12 years*

There seems to be a polarity in the qualities associated with good junior players. The good athletes and the bigger, stronger kids do well. The interesting segment, and one that produces a lot of great players, is the smaller, less gifted kids. They learn very early that in golf you do not have teammates, and as such, it's all about you. If you're smaller and not as strong, you have to find creative ways to compete. The smaller children learn very early that good course management, a good short game, and a "never give up" attitude can place them on equal or better footing than the "athletes." Once they grow up and do get bigger and stronger, they can become tremendous all-around players.

—*Paul Hobart, PGA teaching professional, Tartan Fields Golf Club*

Kids learn golf by watching. I've noticed that it's the quieter kids who concentrate best on learning the sport. Kids whose energy level tends to run high have a tough time with it.

—*Fred Rosa, class-A PGA golf professional, teaching children for 6 years*

What to Look For When Getting Started

🦋 Look for a respected instructor who not only knows how to teach the basics, but also has patience, stays positive, and has himself played competitive golf.

🦋 Yearly clinics for junior golfers offer group lessons and generally are designed to introduce children to the basic fundamentals of golf. The group setting helps children feel less intimidated.

🦋 Look for a program that moves your child from one activity to the next; otherwise, kids get bored and lessons become tedious.

🦋 Golf is a game of fundamentals that can be hard to unlearn and then relearn the right way. Your child will learn everything from the proper grip, set-up, posture, alignment, ball position, and swing.

Look for a fun golf-learning environment that will motivate, challenge, and educate your child. You also want a teacher who's personable, friendly, has extensive knowledge of the club swing, and creates a nurturing environment. Your child will have to master many basics, such as how to hold the club, position to the ball, aim, and have a correct posture. Otherwise, she will not be able to hit the ball and will get frustrated. Plus, there's putting, chipping, pitching, a full swing, and sand play to learn. In the introductory stages of learning golf, you need a teacher who builds ways for your child to be successful in what is a difficult sport. Many of the activities I do in my beginning junior classes have nothing to do with playing on a golf course, but instead are all about building the skills needed to control a golf club and master hand-eye coordination. Lastly, try to find a program that allows your child access to facilities to practice, from a driving range, putting green, sand trap practice area, to a course that does not involve showing up before 5 a.m.

—*Kelli Kostick, head teaching professional and LPGA/PGA certified pro for 12 years*

Ask about the student/teacher ratio in a program. Anything over 6:1 has the potential to be unsafe, out of control, and probably not provide much individual attention. As kids progress, the group scenario provides less and less learning material, and children looking to really accelerate their learning are best served by taking lessons one-on-one.

—*Paul Hobart, PGA teaching professional, Tartan Fields Golf Club*

WHAT TO EXPECT IN LESSONS

✤ Most professionals feel that introducing your child to golf through golf lessons is essential to learning the basics of the game the right way.

✤ A group setting may help your child feel less intimidated, and if she likes it, she can go into private lessons after that.

✤ At first, your child should focus exclusively on the basics. Most junior golf programs work on grip, set-up, posture, and alignment as the key foundations to a great golf swing. In addition to working on striking the ball correctly, your child will work on putting, chipping, and pitching. But the key thing is that your child is having fun, and focusing on the golf ball and the target of where she wants to try to hit it. Bogging your child down in the mechanics of a golf swing can leave her frustrated and hating to golf.

Learning to play golf is like learning to walk—you learn by imitation, not instruction. It's amazing how many kids will swing a golf club just like their father. If you try to instruct a child between the ages of 4 and 8 in the details, you're going to lose him and it becomes not a lot of fun. Group situations make learning golf feel less threatening. There are more people who the instructors can focus on so that your child doesn't feel as if he's being scrutinized, and it gives kids comfort to see others hitting poorly and struggling to learn golf just like them. It's not usually until around age 10 that your child will be ready for individual lessons with a pro. Most pros will also discount their hourly rates by 25%–50% off the normal adult price for a child's lesson.

   —*Mike Bailey, Brae Burn Country Club head golf professional and class-A PGA teaching pro for 27 years*

A semi-private lesson works better for kids who have high energy and trouble paying attention. Try to sign your child up with a buddy, as golf is inherently a social game meant to be played with others. You want your child to develop a sense of camaraderie around golf, and have other people with whom he can go out and play. Forty-five minutes is the perfect lesson time, as it will enable the teacher to move around to a couple of different activities.

   —*Kelli Kostick, head teaching professional and LPGA/PGA certified pro for 12 years*

In getting started, the first thing that you want to teach kids about golf is behavior and respect. Obviously, if the kid is much younger, you just give him a club and let him try swinging. But we teach kids about what kind of game golf is before we ever give them a club. It's about manners and treating your opponents well. Then you start teaching kids the basics: grip and swing, nothing too technical at first and then you work from there. We teach in group clinics and individual lessons.

   —*Eric, City Golf instructor, teaching for 8 years*

✦ You don't have to belong to a private golf club to get your child started on golf. Lots of other places such as public golf courses and driving ranges offer junior group clinics and individual golf lessons for children.

Safety and Injury Concerns

✦ Most kids don't get hurt playing golf, but there are risks to keep in mind, such as getting hit by a golf ball, lower-back pain caused by the rotational pressure the golf swing can place on the spine and muscles, and golfer's elbow (the same as tennis elbow).

✦ Kids will swing a golf club at a moment's notice, so an instructor needs to make sure that everyone is positioned far enough apart.

Cost Considerations

Before starting your child in golf, realize that it can be a very expensive sport. Costs include:

✦ greens fees, which can range from $10 on a local public course up to $100 on a high-end private course;

✦ club fees, which can be a few hundred dollars for joining a local semi-public club to thousands of dollars for a private club and paying for your child to have junior golf privileges;

✦ lessons, with junior private lessons costing between $25 and $80 hourly, and junior clinics generally costing around $10–$25 each time;

✦ golf shoes, with plastic spikes, which cost between $25 and $50;

✦ golf balls and tees, about $15 for a dozen balls;

✦ golf gloves, around $15 a pair, which need to be replaced every couple of months—your child will need to keep a spare pair in case the first pair gets wet on the course;

✦ entry-level fees for tournaments, generally between $25 and $200.

Availability of golf courses and practice facilities is probably at an all-time high right now. Course and driving range construction is way up, and most areas have public facilities that will welcome kids. So if you do not belong to a golf club, a quick call to a local municipal course will probably lead to a bunch of info regarding lessons, junior camps and leagues, and reduced-fee opportunities.

—*Paul Hobart, PGA teaching professional, Tartan Fields Golf Club*

BUYING YOUR CHILD HER OWN SET OF CLUBS

✦ Once your child has decided to make a commitment to golf, purchasing clubs and other equipment can become expensive. A set of junior clubs usually starts around $70, but figure that it will cost you between $130 and $180 for a junior set and bag. Manufacturers have realized that there's a great market out there in junior golfers, so there's lots to choose from.

✦ Many pros recommend your child start with the minimum amount of equipment and build from this set as she gets older. Your child will need to start out with one wood, a putter, and three irons.

✦ Although cut-down clubs may be less expensive, the adult shafts are too heavy and stiff for your child. It's detrimental to your child to start off with these as a beginner and can really impact the fundamentals of her swing.

✦ Special-ordering a customized set should be reserved for older and more advanced youth golfers.

✦ The first step is to consult a professional, who can custom-fit your junior for a set of clubs. Without a properly fitted set, your child can easily fall into bad swing habits and end up with years of frustration in lessons.

✦ Important factors in selecting a set of clubs for your child include the following:
- ❤ The club's shaft flexibility should match your child's swing speed. Junior clubs generally come with ultra-flexible shafts.
- ❤ An overly heavy club will cause your child to overswing at the top, lose her balance, and hit inconsistent shots.
- ❤ The clubs should have a junior-size grip.

Junior club sets should be half sets, even- or odd-numbered irons and one wood (a 5 or 7 wood). The most important thing is to find a set of clubs that are not too heavy or too stiff in the shaft, as this could prevent your child from making a proper swing in balance. The old days of cutting down an old set of Mom's or Dad's clubs are a thing of the past. Manufacturers do a terrific job making clubs that fit juniors.

—Brendan Walsh, head golf professional, The Country Club, teaching for 17 years

➤ The club's shaft length should be matched to your child's height to enable her to make solid contact with the ball.

GYMNASTICS

Overview

Gymnastics has been around for over 2,000 years, spreading from Egypt to Greece and Rome. Ancient Persia, China, and India used gymnastics to prepare young men for battle, but as a competitive sport, it is just over 100 years old. The first large-scale modern men's gymnastics competition was at the 1896 Olympics in Athens, with women's gymnastics finally being added in the 1928 Olympics. In 1962 rhythmic gymnastics became officially recognized as a sport. Current fashion in judging women's gymnastics favors flexible, acrobatic movements, and as a result, the age of competitors, particularly among women, has dramatically lowered to the teens.

A fusion of strength and agility, athletics, and aesthetics, gymnastics has emerged as one of the defining sports of the Olympic Games. Gymnastics hits the spotlight every four years during the Summer Olympic Games as young gymnasts like Shannon Miller and Kerri Strug perform feats of strength, coordination, and risk-taking that leave audiences breathless. Miller's poise on the balance beam and Strug's confidence on the vault have enthralled and inspired even the shyest and most unathletic of children. Gymnastics builds confidence and self-reliance because it is an individual sport, and allows your child to work toward a goal of performing something that she has never done before.

General Benefits

◉ With classes offered at various levels, your child can pursue gymnastics for fun or to compete.

◉ Gymnastics increases your child's flexibility, total body strength, balance, and concentration. Other benefits of gymnastics include physical courage, determination, perseverance, expressiveness, self-confidence, self-discipline, and body awareness.

◉ Gymnastics requires a unique combination of strength and grace.

◉ It teaches coordination, hand-eye and foot-hand coordination, and large- as well as small-muscle coordination.

◉ Gymnasts must overcome real fears, such as the fear of heights, and therefore learn bravery and strength.

Kids who excel have dedication, determination, perseverance, patience, attention to detail, and time-management skills. Because high-level gymnastics requires an incredible amount of training time, our kids learn at a young age how to manage their time. Gymnastics, especially at the higher levels, is mainly a mental sport. It requires a high degree of determination and mental toughness.

—*Eduardo Ovalle, head coach women's gymnastics at MIT, coaching for 14 years*

The typical qualities of kids who excel in gymnastics include a small to medium body type, good coordination, balance, and strength. However, I have also seen taller girls do well in gymnastics.

—*Chrystal Chollet-Norton, head coach women's gymnastics, Rutgers University, coaching for 26 years*

There are many qualities that seem to rise to the surface after training has begun. The main thing is their love of the sport. I have seen many gymnasts that were not predisposed to doing well in the sport, i.e., not very flexible, strong, or athletic, but who excelled to the top levels. Determination to succeed and receiving positive feedback along the way is key to increasing the love of the sport.

—*K. Jay Hogue, Orlando Metro Gymnastics women's coach and owner*

In gymnastics, the mind is more important to doing well than the body. Sure, kids need flexibility and strength, but all these factors can be overcome with the mind. On the other hand, some kids have natural ability but cannot take a correction. I tell them, "If you can't do it, we can do it together, and eventually you can do it on your own."

—*Neysa Packard, instructor, Gymnastics & More, teaching for 30 years*

Usually, it is not the boys who have any gender misconceptions about gymnastics, but rather the parents. Many parents have misconceptions about what gymnastics involves for boys. After the first class, they say, "Wow! This is a great sport!" because they realize how much it will teach their sons about their bodies and how it will challenge them to find their limits and go beyond them.

—Neysa Packard, instructor, Gymnastic & More, teaching for 30 years

Danny takes an all-boys gymnastics class with a male instructor from Russia and loves it. For him, gymnastics has been like unstructured occupational therapy. For kids who have under-skilled motor coordination or have issues around sensory integration, gymnastics works great. On the other hand, our oldest son had taken a class at another gym where he was just one of two boys in an all-girls class and that bombed.

—Dee, mom of Carey, 8, and Danny, 5

My son is small but incredibly coordinated. My husband volunteered in his gym class at school and figured out that he was really good at tumbling. We then signed him up for gymnastics, and two months later he was doing back flips. It suits his physique, as he can't really do big-muscle sports well.

—Naomi, mom of Talia, 11, Arielle, 10, Aaron, 8, and Daniella, 5

Kids Who Tend to Excel

Kids who excel have:

- power, muscle endurance, dexterity, and flexibility;

- ability to get past the fear associated with difficult moves;

- mental stamina to compete under pressure;

- dedication, as gymnasts must devote many hours to practice and improvement.

Boys in Gymnastics

- Gymnastics for boys demands physical strength and usually starts around age 6.

- It offers a great way to vent energy and build courage, balance, strength, agility, and coordination.

- Many boys who have upper-body strength love moves such as doing flips on the rings, balancing on the parallel bars, or working on tumbling skills.

- Many boys who are physically small find that gymnastics proves a great competitive sport for them, as strength rather than height helps determine how well boys do in the sport. For these smaller boys, it can be a strong self-esteem builder.

Best Age to Start

◎ Many gymnastics schools offer basic tumbling classes for children around age 2.

◎ Talented children are often identified as young as 5 or 6 years old. Having a muscular, petite physique is so important that some of the most intense coaches will reject children from entering into serious training if even one of their parents is tall.

◎ The youngest age to start competitive gymnastics is usually age 6.

MOMMY AND ME TUMBLING CLASSES

✦ As soon as babies begin to crawl, many parents sign them up for beginning tumbling classes.

✦ Usually, activities will include a plethora of familiar equipment, such as ladders, slides, stepping stones, tunnels, beams, and perhaps a mini-trampoline.

Motor skills can be taught as early as 18 months, but I see no need to do anything other than recreational classes until they are 5 or 6.

—K. Jay Hogue, Orlando Metro Gymnastics women's coach and owner

Gymnastics is such a great sport to start as a little kid. Most of them start at 18 months, but if the child is a sibling of an older child, we let them start as young as 16 months! A lot of really little kids are sometimes even scared to go up to the second rung on the ladder. A good teacher will take the focus off the fear by holding them, encouraging them to try, and then telling them to give Mom a kiss. Once the focus is Mom and not the fear, it is not scary anymore.

—Neysa Packard, instructor, Gymnastic & More, teaching for 30 years

I signed all of my kids up for tumbling classes because in addition to the physical exercise, gymnastics builds the coordination and dexterity needed for other sports.

—Lisa, mom of Grace, 6, Ben, 4, and Maddie, 1

❧ Beginning gymnastics movements may also be taught, such as forward rolls, swinging under ladders, skipping, and jumping.

❧ As children grow older, classes should not remain stagnant but should become more physically challenging.

What to Look For When Getting Started

❧ Look for a well-organized program that puts a strong emphasis on safety.

❧ You should look for such things as floor-level trampolines, spotting harnesses,

Look for structure and fun. Gymnastics should be exciting each day. At a younger age you do not want your child to think of it as a job.

—*Chrystal Chollet-Norton, head coach women's gymnastics, Rutgers University, coaching for 26 years*

You need a very hands-on gymnastics instructor with young children in order to keep them safe, such as on the balance beam. Trust becomes a huge issue, and you want a teacher who really cares about your child. Some children learn by listening, some are more hands-on, and others have to see the instructor do it correctly in order to do it. A good instructor will be sensitive to the learning style of each child.

—*Neysa Packard, instructor, Gymnastics & More, teaching for 30 years*

Kim has been doing gymnastics since she was 18 months old in a Mommy and Me class. Now she practices four hours a day, four times a week with her gymnastics team. There was one day where Kim had practice from 4 to 8 on Friday, and then had a makeup practice from 7–11 on Saturday morning. There are days when I have to push her to go to practice, but once she gets there, she's happy and doesn't want to leave at the end of practice time. Then we have away meets every other weekend, often having to travel up to four hours just to get to the meet, so it becomes an all-day affair.

—*Cathy, mom of Samantha, 13, and Kimberly, 10*

and safety pits filled with foam blocks where gymnasts can land after doing more difficult maneuvers. The floor mats should be padded or have springs underneath to reduce the impact of landings.

🦋 Ask whether the program has been designed to produce competitive gymnasts and about the ratio of coaches to children in a class.

🦋 Make sure that the coach has passed his safety or coaching certification from U.S.A. Gymnastics, the sport's governing body. Look for a "take it slow" type of coach who will teach your child the basics of gymnastics. You don't want your child attempting the more difficult maneuvers until she has mastered the easier ones.

🦋 Recreational gymnastics is done strictly for fun typically one or two hours a week, with the focus on teaching children basic skills.

🦋 Competitive gymnastics is ranked on a level system from 1 to 10, 10 being the elite and Olympic level. The competitive gymnast has to practice and compete throughout the year in order to both progress in her skill level and excel. Moreover, the intensity level grows proportionately to the competition level.

Types of Competition
ARTISTIC GYMNASTICS

Female gymnasts perform routines on four different types of apparatus:

🦋 *Vault.* The gymnast runs across a platform and launches off a springboard, with the goal of pushing herself off an elevated padded platform called a horse, and landing on a mat without taking a step or falling. The gymnast can perform flips and turns when doing this to increase the difficulty. Gymnasts perform two vaults each.

🦋 *Balance beam.* The balance beam is an event in which the gymnast performs her routine atop an elevated beam, emphasizing strength and grace. Gymnasts perform a routine no longer than 1½ minutes that must include a variety of skills without any extra steps or wobbles. This event takes tremendous concentration and balance.

🦋 *Uneven bars.* This involves a routine flipping and spinning between uneven bars and ends with a dismount. Each gymnast's performance must use both bars, have changes of direction and 10–12 continuous moves, such as swings, handstands, and release and catch moves. A gymnast needs a tremendous amount of strength to avoid stops or extra swings.

🦋 *Floor exercise.* A tumbling routine is performed to music and combines artistic choreography with gymnastic skills. The gymnast has to integrate a choreographed dance with a creative series of acrobatic moves and tumbling. Like the balance beam, the routine lasts no longer than 1½ minutes.

Male gymnasts performing routines on six different types of apparatus, including:

✦ *Floor exercise.* This tumbling routine without music requires movements demonstrating strength, flexibility, and balance.

✦ *Pommel horse.* Routines consist of smooth, continuous circular and pendulum-type swings, double leg circles, scissors movements, and undercuts using all parts of the horse.

✦ *Long vault.* Vaults combine height, length, rotations, and a controlled landing.

✦ *Parallel bars.* Gymnasts perform a combination of swinging moves with strength holds.

✦ *Rings.* Routines combine a series of swings, holds, and an acrobatic dismount.

✦ *High bar.* Clean swinging movements involve changes of grip and direction, along with an acrobatic dismount.

RHYTHMIC GYMNASTICS FOR GIRLS

✦ In addition to artistic gymnastics for men and women, which are the traditional forms seen in the Olympic Games, rhythmic gymnastics is strictly a women's competition. The gymnasts, accompanied by music, perform on a square floor area doing routines using a rope, hoop, ball, clubs, or ribbon. For individual competitions, each gymnast performs four routines, each using a different apparatus. For team competitions, five gymnasts perform together, doing one routine using clubs and one routine where two gymnasts use hoops and the other three use ribbons. Group rhythmic gymnastics became a part of Olympic competition in the summer of 1996.

✦ This sport emphasizes grace and athleticism, and combines the flexibility and dynamics of gymnastics, the technical knowledge of ballet, and the self-expression and rhythm of modern dance.

✦ Rhythmic gymnastics requires a high skill level in controlling and manipulating various apparatus while performing a routine on the floor mat. Rhythmic gymnasts must concentrate on expressing their choreography, demonstrating mastery of the apparatus, and performing leaps, spins, and rolls.

🌿 Throughout the routine, the gymnast must exhibit control, coordination, and balance. Turns, leaps, dances, and tosses are the most common moves done with any apparatus. Rhythmic gymnastics does not allow acrobatic moves, but most back-walkovers and elbow cartwheels are allowed.

🌿 Rhythmic gymnastics differs from artistic gymnastics in the body types, the flexibility, and the expression of the gymnasts. Artistic gymnasts are generally shorter and more muscular than rhythmic gymnasts, who are usually tall and thin.

🌿 Artistic gymnasts often turn to rhythmic gymnastics, which entails a lower rate of injury.

TRAMPOLINE GYMNASTICS

🌿 This relatively new form of gymnastics recently debuted as a medal event in the 2000 Olympics.

🌿 The events in trampoline sports include individual trampoline, synchronized trampoline, double mini-trampoline, and tumbling.

🌿 Trampoline gymnastics has individual events for men and women, and it also has competitions for pairs called synchronized trampoline.

🌿 Your child will excel at trampolining if she has the power required for top-level jumping so that height, and therefore time, are available to execute double, triple, and even quadruple somersaults and twists.

🌿 Beginners learn 30 or more different skills before doing any upside-down somersault movements.

🌿 Tumbling should only occur under the supervision of a coach who has obtained a trampolining coaching qualification.

Safety and Injury Concerns

🌿 Gymnastics has one of the highest injury rates of any sport, and the risk of injury increases with the level of competition. Each year, doctors treat over 86,000 gymnastics-related injuries, and more than 25,500 children ages 5–14 are treated in hospital emergency rooms.

🌿 To reduce the risk of injury, spotting is essential. An experienced coach should spot your child during all practice sessions when she is trying a new move or a complex one she's trying to master.

🌿 Gymnasts can suffer from sprains and rips on their hands from the bars.

With young kids, most of the risks involving tumbling are things that happen outside a gymnastics center, such as flipping on the couch or out on backyard trampolines. Here we have rules, such as one person on the trampoline at a time, that help to prevent injuries. From the very beginning we're teaching them how to protect their neck.

—*Leore, gymnastics instructor, Tumble Kids USA*

Injuries are inherent to gymnastics due to the difficulty of the skills. A qualified program with a lot of experience and organization can definitely make a difference in the injury rate. Overuse injuries can be a problem during high training times of the year, and need to be detected early and monitored.

—*K. Jay Hogue, Orlando Metro Gymnastics women's coach and owner*

🦋 Eating disorders are common among young gymnasts, thanks to the intense competition. See pages 173–175 for tips on what to do if you suspect your child may have an eating disorder.

Cost Considerations

🦋 Your child may need grips, which cost between $20 and $30, and for rhythmic gymnastics, your child may need to purchase some of her own equipment, such as a ribbon, ball, rope, or hoop.

🦋 Potential hidden costs include gym fees, private coaching fees (if extra help is needed on a skill or event, generally between $25 and $50 an hour), tournament fees, and travel expenses to get to them.

ICE HOCKEY

Overview

Ice hockey is a fast-paced, competitive sport involving two teams of up to six players each on the ice. Using long sticks with curved ends, well-padded players try to control the puck and hit it into the opposing team's goal, past the goalie. Ice hockey traces its roots back 500 years to field hockey players in Great Britain and France, who took their summer sport onto frozen ponds and lakes in the winter. The earliest North American games were played in Canada, first by British soldiers stationed there in the 1870s, and then by students at Montreal's McGill University on an ice rink. Ice hockey has been an Olympic sport since 1908. About 260,000 children under age 18 now play hockey on teams affiliated with USA Hockey.

An ice hockey game starts with the referee dropping the puck into a center circle for a face-off. The opposing centers try to gain control of the puck or pass it to a teammate. Unless a player has been sent to the penalty box, each team has six players on the ice: a goalie, left and right defensemen, and three forwards: left wing, center, and right wing. Players rotate onto the ice to play in shifts every couple of minutes, and substitutions can take place on the fly. This has to be done carefully, as a team may end up being penalized for having too many players on the ice simultaneously. Because hockey's fast-paced, aerobic action has players going all out in short bursts, hockey teams carry as many as 20 players in order to substitute players in and out of a game. Skaters move between 15 m.p.h. and 20 m.p.h., while the puck moves at speeds from 30 m.p.h. to 80 m.p.h. A regular game consists of three

At age 4, my son watched the 1988 Winter Olympics with as much intensity as his parents. Inspired by the hockey competition, he announced that he wanted to ice-skate. His grandfather bought him his first pair of skates, and the next fall, when he entered kindergarten, my son brought home a flyer from school announcing sign-ups for the area youth hockey program. His father and I knew we had to let him give it a try. He turned out to be a great skater, and though his father and I might have already been overzealous about his abilities, we chose for him to remain with his age group. Thus began eight consecutive seasons of youth hockey, several of them on traveling teams that took us from our central Wisconsin home to rinks all over the state and even to Minnesota on occasion. While many friends would look at us with disbelief about the cost and time we devoted to our son's hockey hobby, we truly enjoyed it as a family. The car rides gave us an opportunity to talk and play games. The hotel stays included team potluck suppers and gathering by the pool with families who were equally devoted, not just to the sport but to their kids in general. The focus wasn't just on the children's performance, it was on the whole experience.

—Linda, mom of Ben, 18

20-minute periods and teams change ends of the rink for each period. If a tie occurs, a sudden-death overtime period is played.

General Benefits

- Teaches fast reaction times, given the speed and quickness of the game
- Improves hand- and foot-eye coordination, balance, and agility

Your child develops skating skills for life, and it's a game he can play for life. I see 80-year-old men out there on the ice playing and it's fabulous. Plus, the kids get good exercise and have a tremendous sense of accomplishment. For the girls on my team, hockey has become a key part of their identities. They have taken on hockey-related screen names on the Internet, wear their team jackets to school, and have a strong sense of camaraderie. Plus, since it's still an unusual sport for girls, it creates a special connection whenever they meet another girl who plays. Now that they're 12, they want to go skating with each other rather than go to the mall.

—*Andy, dad of Samantha, 13, and Kimberly, 10*

The first time my son went to ice hockey practice he was scared and fell down on the floor at my feet. He said he was not going again, and would not leave the house. So my husband finally said, "Let's just go watch." They got there a little early, went up in the stands, and sat down. "Okay," Brian said to my husband, "I'm going to do it." But when he got to the door to the ice, he refused to go on. My husband said, "If you try this, we could stop for ice cream." My son watched the people on the ice for another five minutes, then went out there and skated. Now he loves it, thinks it's great, and is thrilled.

—*Bridgitt, mom of Taylor, 10, Connor and Chloe, 8, and Brian, 6*

Ice hockey players need a high level of physical skills (skating combining balance with strength, agility, and hand-eye coordination) with the ability to anticipate and quickly react to play action. Hockey involves almost continuous action, with players substituting in while the game continues. Although there are defensive and offensive "systems," there are very few set plays, which means players are constantly tested mentally. Players need self-control to maintain the focus required in this fast-paced and physical game

—*Sam Sherman, varsity girls' head coach, Martha's Vineyard High School, teaching for 17 years*

ⓔ Provides aerobic exercise

ⓔ Improves cardiovascular fitness

ⓔ Strengthens and tones muscles, particularly the legs from skating and the upper body from stick handling and shooting

ⓔ Gives players a strong sense of teamwork

Kids Who Tend to Excel

ⓔ Children who are solid skaters, athletic, agile, coordinated, and have a good sense of balance tend to do well.

ⓔ At the youth level no specific body type is needed, though the three forward positions require smaller, quicker players and the defensemen are usually bigger, stronger players.

Girls in Hockey

🌿 Although hockey is still a predominantly male sport, more and more girls are getting involved, with the number of female hockey players in the United States rising by over 50% in recent years. Surprisingly, women's ice hockey dates back more than 100 years, but has just recently risen in popularity.

🌿 Many towns and clubs now sponsor all-girls' teams and leagues. Recreational programs for girls usually fall into the following age categories: 12 and under, 15 and under, and 19 and under.

Best Age to Start

ⓔ Many hockey programs accept children as young as 4 or 5 in "learn to skate" programs. Most hockey coaches feel it is best for children to start off on hockey skates if they plan to play ice hockey.

ⓔ The entry-level groups, known as Junior Mites, are for all children under age 7, with mostly first graders, as well as some kindergartners.

What to Look For When Getting Started

🌿 Most programs fall into one of two divisions of youth hockey: house leagues and the more elite travel leagues. The house league competes only locally, usually with one practice and a game on the weekends, while travel leagues usually involve one additional practice a week and away games against neighboring towns or

⊚~⊚~⊚

Girls have a huge edge in ice hockey today because, thanks partially to the Olympics, girls' ice hockey is one of the fastest growing sports at all levels, including college. Colleges are hard-pressed for female talent and with new programs cropping up each year, I feel that trend will continue for a while. Ice hockey recognizes that girls can play a physically demanding game at an intense level with success. In my opinion, it is the most physical girls' sport and perhaps that contributes to the enthusiasm we are seeing in girls signing up.

—*Sam Sherman, varsity girls' head coach, Martha's Vineyard High School, teaching for 17 years*

⊚

In girls' hockey, there's no checking, so it's not as intense, plus you don't have that whole macho thing going on. With limited contact for the girls, it becomes much more of a team sport, with a focus on passing, finesse, and shooting. Of course, there are always exceptions. Yesterday my daughter Sam bumped this girl off the puck and the girl turned around and slashed her in the shins with her stick. She responded by lashing out. But the risk of injury is small if your child has lots of padding on.

—*Andy, dad of Samantha, 13, and Kimberly, 10*

leagues. Each practice session typically runs for an hour on the ice, but practices are a dramatically greater time commitment for travel teams. Practices usually consist of drills and scrimmages.

🏒 The age classifications for youth hockey are as follows: 17 or under (Midget); 14 or under (Bantam); 12 or under (PeeWee); 10 or under (Squirt); 8 or under (Mite).

🏒 Look for a youth league that prohibits checking from behind and limits body checking, and ask about the number of coaches in relation to the number of players.

🏒 Hockey practices can be scheduled very early or very late in order to get ice time. Many hockey parents bemoan the crack-of-dawn practices and games, often starting as early as 5:30 a.m.

Safety and Injury Concerns

🏒 Ice hockey involves a significant risk of injury, given its speed, hard puck, sideboards, hard ice surface, and body contact. A high percentage of the ice hockey injuries occur when a player is hit from behind by an opposing player and strikes the boards of the rink.

🏒 Most injuries result from the use of body checking, a move in which a player bumps or slams with either his hip or shoulder into an opponent to block the opponent's progress or to throw him off-balance. Body checking can be used only against an opponent who controls the puck or was the last player controlling it. As a result of body checking, many players collide with goal posts or the boards.

🏒 Body checking doesn't start until age 12 at the earliest, and girls' leagues do not allow it.

Ice hockey is one of those sports where your child really does need to learn to skate early, but there's a big debate about whether to start on hockey or figure skates. I started my son on figure skates, which taught him better edging and backward skating when he switched over to hockey skates. At the end of the day, hockey is all about skating well. The kids can always learn stick handling later.

—*Jane, mom of Carolyn, 17, and Peter, 11*

Many girls start around age 6, some as young as age 5, but it's a myth that you can't pick this sport up later. I have five girls on the team I coach who just picked up ice hockey at ages 13–14. Some have never skated before, and they're all doing great.

—*Andy, dad of Samantha, 13, and Kimberly, 10*

Max started ice hockey late, going into the beginner PeeWee level in third grade, where he was two years older than the rest of the kids. But with hard work, by the end of that year he had caught up with his friends. He had to put up with a humiliating year with kindergartners, but he got the basic skills he needed and went on to play with his peers. That having been said, I don't know how much longer he can keep it up. The really serious kids go to power skating or hockey camps. I've been having an argument this summer with Max about going to two weeks of this kind of camp at the end of the summer. He's on the fence, but I think I'm going to send him, because he can't keep up. The kids who excel have Type-A personality, along with balance, coordination, speed on skates, a lot of aggression, and a strategic sense of being in the right place at the right time. Being big helps too. Max is not aggressive, but he's enjoyed the game and has been content not playing on an A team.

—*Sylvia, mom of Max, 13, and Kate and Zoe, 10*

Beginner leagues should have a "no checking" policy under which players are prohibited from using their bodies to push each other away from the puck.

🐟 Kids' hockey is strictly regulated, and referees are trained to immediately stop illegal moves, checking, or other aggressive behavior. Most children's leagues have a zero-tolerance policy for violence.

🐟 Protective equipment is one of the most important factors in minimizing the risk of injury in hockey. Make sure your child's equipment fits properly.

🍀 The main concern is the potential for catastrophic head or neck injuries, which are rare, thanks to headgear and strict officiating. There is still a high rate of concussions and face lacerations.

🍀 Most injuries are minor, involving muscle sprains and bruises of the leg, knee, and ankle, though fractures do occur. The improved protective equipment has helped lessen the frequency of these injuries.

Ice hockey definitely involves a specific breed of parents. They're not the Brie and white wine crowd that I associate with soccer. They're down to earth but totally into the sport. The bad rap for parents mainly stems from boys' hockey, where there's a tendency to skate fast and it gets intense quickly. Plus, your child has armor and a stick that is basically a weapon.

 —Andy, dad of Samantha, 13, and Kimberly, 10

Be prepared for early ice time. I will never forget our 5 a.m. away game, which was an hour drive, on the day of a Daylight Saving Time change! Plus, in ice hockey, you tend to see lots of dads trying to live vicariously through their sons, either because they didn't play in their youth or had played and played well themselves.

 —Jane, mom of Carolyn, 17, and Peter, 11

Learn all you can about a program before registering your child. Be sure to watch kids playing and ask a veteran mom or dad about their feelings toward the program.

 —Steve Malley, master USA Hockey coach, coaching high school and college teams for 15 years

Hockey, like many other sports, requires mental preparation and self-confidence that only comes through positive development built on a coach's reinforcement and successful experiences. Complex skills should be broken down into simple steps that can be accomplished through practice and that build confidence. Overloading beginners with advanced skills can make them feel inadequate and create a negative mind-set.

 —Sam Sherman, varsity girls' head coach, Martha's Vineyard High School, teaching for 17 years

Cost Considerations

🏒 Ice hockey is an expensive sport. Not only is ice time costly, but hockey players need a ton of equipment. A full set of equipment for a youth hockey player costs around $500, but it's easy to spend double that outfitting your child. Used hockey equipment is readily available through hockey equipment swaps and used sporting goods retailers.

🏒 Your child's most important piece of equipment is his skates. They need to be the correct size to give good support during skating. Beginners can usually get a good pair of skates for about $125, while advanced players generally spend between $200 and $450.

🏒 A helmet will cost between $40 and $100. Be sure your child keeps the chin strap fastened. The face mask comes in two versions: full shield or screen. The full shield offers a better field of vision but can fog up from moisture, while the screen face mask offers better ventilation but only adequate vision.

🏒 If your child is just beginning to play hockey, you don't need to be too particular when choosing a stick. As your child becomes more experienced, however, selecting the proper stick becomes important:

➤ Wooden sticks are less expensive but they are also heavier and break easily. Sticks with aluminum shafts are more durable, but more costly and

The most common injuries are the normal bumps and bruises from falling or getting hit with the puck. Properly fitted equipment prevents a vast majority of injuries. A good hockey shop will fit each piece of equipment, and not let a parent buy it big so the player will have it longer. It is very important to have a proper-fitting skate. I often see kids with their ankles bent, which is usually an indication of a skate that is too big, or a skate that doesn't offer enough ankle support.

—*Matthew Mincone, Martha's Vineyard High School boys' varsity coach for 4 years*

Hockey played under USA Hockey rules has become one of the safest sports for children under 15 since the requirement to wear helmets and face masks. Properly fitted equipment is very important. Referees and coaches attend training sessions that help them in controlling the game on the ice. Unfortunately, despite all efforts, injuries do take place and will take place. Few of the injuries have been severe or life-threatening.

—*Ron DeGregorio, vice president, USA Hockey, and youth hockey coach*

As an ice hockey parent, you worry a lot about injuries. In my son's league, they start checking this year, and it makes all the parents nervous about their kids getting clocked with a stick.

—*Jane, mom of Carolyn, 17, and Peter, 11*

Ice hockey is the most expensive sport you will ever find. The necessary and required equipment is pricey and sometimes hard to find. Besides equipment, league "tuition" is so expensive that the teams set up monthly payment plans! A nonmonetary cost is also time. If you are on an in-house league where there is no travel, playing times are usually very early in the morning—like 5 a.m.! If you are on a travel team, some games may be three to four hours away and you must plan accordingly.

—*Nancy, mom of a son age 13*

Ice hockey equipment is definitely an investment if your child wants to play the game. It will cost you $400–$700 to dress your kid from top to bottom, and you'll still end up having to resolutely tell your child, "No, you can't have the $500 skates or the cutting-edge gloves that cost $150."

—*Jane, mom of Carolyn, 17, and Peter, 11*

Kids outgrow their hockey equipment like crazy. We've learned that you can suit up your child with used stuff and be fine.

—*Sylvia, mom of Max, 13, and Kate and Zoe, 10*

can get bent. Graphite shafts are the most expensive and not as durable as aluminum.

- Most children starting out usually use a stick with a number 5 or 6 lie, which is the angle between the blade and the shaft of the stick. To check the lie, have your child stand normally on the ice with his stick out in front of him. If the toe of the stick's blade doesn't reach the ice, he needs a lower-numbered lie; if the heel is off the ice, he needs a higher-numbered lie. If your child skates low to the ice, choose a lower-numbered lie.
- The stick should come up to your child's chin when standing with his skates on.
- Sticks come in left and right models. In the left model, the blade bends inward slightly, while in the right model it bends outward. Most players place their dominant hand at the top of the stick, and thus pick the opposite

model stick (so a right-handed player will usually use a left stick).
- Sticks cost between $15 and $100 depending on type and size. Your child may use as many as 10 sticks over the course of a season.

⚜ Padded gloves cost between $35 and $140, and your child should be able to move his fingers easily within the glove. Shoulder-chest pads protect your child's upper body, and cost between $25 and $125. Padded hockey pants protect the lower spine, hips, and thighs, and cost between $50 and $160. Elbow pads cost between $15 and $60. You want to make sure that your child's elbow fits directly into the center of the elbow cup.

⚜ Shin pads cost between $15 and $85. They should fully cover your child's lower legs and the cup of the pads should fit directly over the kneecaps. A protective cup for boys and pelvic protector for girls help protect the groin area, and cost about $15 each.

⚜ USA Hockey recommends wearing a mouthpiece to protect the teeth and soft tissue of the mouth. Mouth guards cost about $15 for the "boil and bite" models, while custom mouth guards made by a dentist generally cost between $75 and $200.

⚜ If your child plays goalie, he will also need the following equipment:
- a different type of skate than the rest of the players, with low, flat, duller blades for better balance and padded sides to protect ankles from hard puck shots, which costs between $75 and $450;
- a mandatory face mask to protect his head, which must fit securely and typically costs about $110;
- goalie pads, which cost between $75 and $1,000, and include arm, elbow, and shoulder pads, and a chest protector;
- a goalie's catching glove ("trapper") which looks similar to a baseball mitt, and a flat, large, padded glove ("blocker") on the hand that holds the stick, which cost between $125 and $500 for the set.

⚜ As your child moves up, league fees typically run $400–$700 per season, with some travel teams charging more than $2,000. These cover not only the coaching staff but also ice time and referees.

INLINE/ROLLER HOCKEY

Overview

Inline, or roller, hockey developed when kids put on inline skates and started skating around deserted parking lots and tennis courts with hockey sticks and balls. The sport rapidly developed as a puck replaced the ball, new indoor tile-floor complexes with sideboards were built, and club leagues formed. Within the last three years, inline hockey has become one of the fastest-growing sports in the world and has actually grown bigger than ice hockey in the United States. A recent survey of the National Sporting Goods Association found over 2 million people playing inline hockey, compared to the 1.5 million who play ice hockey. The sport has been growing by quantum leaps internationally as well. As a result of its rising popularity, more facilities are being built to enable league and tournament play.

Inline hockey offers the skill building, fast pace, and fun of ice hockey. Since roller hockey minimizes physical contact, as opposed to its ice hockey counterpart, both boys and girls play it. Kids who like to skate naturally migrate to roller hockey.

The game is played using rules derived from ice hockey, with modifications made to allow for more offensive play and fewer line calls. Most ice hockey rules apply to roller hockey, with a few notable exceptions. Games consist of four 12-minute quarters, and each side has only four skaters and one goalie on the rink at one time. Roller hockey has one less player on each team in order to utilize the more open playing surface. There are no blue lines, just a center red line to divide offensive and defensive ends. On average, more goals are scored than in ice hockey.

General Benefits

◉ Easier to learn than ice hockey, while matching its fast-paced action

◉ Provides an intensive cardiovascular workout

◉ Develops strong leg muscles, coordination, and balance

◉ Improves conditioning, hand-eye coordination, and strength

◉ Teaches teamwork

Roller hockey is almost a completely different game than ice hockey. When played in its true form, roller hockey is a much faster and more competitive sport than ice hockey could ever hope to be. True inline hockey is played 4 on 4, not 5 on 5 like ice hockey. Also, there are no offsides or clearing in roller hockey. This allows for a much faster and wide-open game with completely different strategies than ice hockey.

—*Paul Mansfield, president, New Jersey Hyper Bandits, coaching for 5 years*

The top players in our sport generally skate well and have natural scoring ability.

—*Dan Brennan, manager of USA Hockey InLine and hockey coach for 12 years*

Kids who excel at roller hockey are dedicated to the game of hockey. They don't miss a practice or game and are eager to listen and learn. They work hard at learning new skills to become better players but also know how to have fun.

—*Phil Butta, Groton Parks youth roller hockey coordinator, teaching for 6 years*

Kids Who Tend to Excel

The kids who excel most at inline hockey are hardworking, determined, and willing to experiment with new skills.

Some kids have previous ice hockey experience, but many learn roller hockey without ever having played ice hockey before.

Best Age to Start

While children can begin inline skating at age 3, "learn to play" programs start for four- and five-year-olds, though many kids pick up the sport much later.

Between ages 8 and 10, most children move beyond basic skills into understanding strategy and how the game should be played. Because the skill level be-

The USA Hockey InLine Learn-to-Play Program provides a pressure-free environment for children to become comfortable on skates, with no leagues or tournaments.

—*Gary Del Vecchio, Jr., director of USA Hockey InLine*

I would honestly recommend going to check out the facility first off. The facility should be a place that you and your child will want to spend time at. After that, talk to the people in charge of the league, ask them any questions you may have; they should be willing and able to answer anything you may ask. Finally, ask around the rink or people you may know and see what they have to say about the program.

—*Eric Godzich, Cheektowaga Inline Hockey League coordinator, coaching for 7 years*

With any sport, pick a coach, and the league that shares your belief regarding sports. If it is all about winning, then I would stay away. Look for teaching in a fun, friendly environment, where winning isn't everything. I wrote a code of conduct for my parents in our house league—things have gotten that bad.

—*Ray Flood, Vineland Inline Hockey, coaching for 22 years*

comes fairly sophisticated during this period, it is more difficult for a newcomer to join a league.

What to Look For When Getting Started

❧ In lessons, children are first taught individual skills of skating, stick handling, puck control, passing, receiving, shooting, and scoring. Next, they learn position-based skills for playing forward, defense, and goal tender. After this, team skills become the central focus, including offensive attacks, fore-checking, and face-offs.

❧ Look for a league that promotes equal playing time for all players in the starting years regardless of skill level. Coaches should ideally have national certification, such as youth coaching certification from the National Youth Sports Association (NYSCA), and additional sports-specific training from organizations such as USA Hockey InLine.

❧ There are extensive opportunities for competition for youth inline hockey, with local, regional, and national tournaments, many of which are sanctioned by USA Hockey. Youth competition divisions start at 10 and under. There are 500 inline hockey leagues across the country. Kids can play in house league or select traveling leagues, with competition up to the junior world teams. The highest level of competition that an inline hockey player can achieve is playing on Team USA at the Pan American Games.

Safety and Injury Concerns

♣ Roller hockey is a relatively safe sport if players wear safety equipment, but kids do sometimes get hit by a puck or another player's stick.

♣ Unlike ice hockey, body checking is not allowed, further reducing the threat of serious injury.

♣ The most common injuries are minor cuts and scrapes to the arms and legs—areas not protected by pads and exposed when players fall. Players also receive bruises if struck in an unprotected area by a roller hockey ball or roller puck.

♣ Other typical injuries are bruises, particularly to the knee, shoulder, or wrist. Occasionally a child will have a torn ligament, other knee injuries, sprains, or fractures.

Cost Considerations

♣ Equipment for inline hockey can be fairly costly, easily amounting to about $300 or more for good equipment. Inline hockey skates cost between $100 and $200. Make sure not to buy them too large in the hopes your child can get an extra season out of them, as it can interfere with his skating ability and cause physical damage to his feet.

♣ A helmet with full-face shield or cage costs about $75. The helmet should fit your child's head snugly, but not tightly. A mouth guard that straps to the helmet is recommended.

When all required equipment is worn and fitted properly, inline hockey has very few injuries compared to ice hockey. This is because inline hockey is a non-contact sport. It is based more on speed and technique than just the pure violence of ice hockey.

—*Paul Mansfield, president, New Jersey Hyper Bandits, coaching for 5 years*

Players should always wear full gear during practices and games, and coaches need to supervise players to make sure this is enforced. Players oftentimes try to play without elbow pads, which can be disastrous if a player takes a bad fall.

—*Jake Mersberger, national hockey director and assistant executive director, USA Roller Sports*

♣ A hockey stick costs between $25 and $175. In terms of stick length, measure it when your child is in his skates. The butt-end of the stick should be between your child's chin and nose when it is standing on its blade tip. Hockey gloves cost around $60. Make sure that they fit well; if they're too big your child will have difficulty controlling the stick.

♣ Shin guards, knee and elbow pads cost around $45 total. In addition, your child will most likely need an athletic or pelvic protector, padded hockey shorts, light-

Roller hockey is much cheaper to play than ice hockey. However, that does not mean that roller hockey at the higher levels of play is not expensive. Equipment for inline hockey is comparable to ice hockey. However, the rink time and tournament fees are usually much cheaper.

—*Paul Mansfield, president, New Jersey Hyper Bandits, coaching for 5 years*

To play in our travel league, it costs roughly $125 per person. Away tournaments usually run $400 a weekend (usually 4–6 games). That does not cover travel cost, hotels, meals, and stuff like that.

—*Ray Flood, Vineland Inline Hockey, coaching for 22 years*

Some people want high-quality, high-priced skates, while others are not so concerned about this. The difference in skate quality, especially when speed skating, can be like driving a Volkswagen vs. a Porsche.

—*Jim Blair, inline speed coach, Roswell Roller Rink, for 10 years*

weight shoulder pads (optional) specially designed for roller hockey, and pants and jerseys.

❧ Maintenance costs include replacement sticks, as sticks easily break, stick tape, and a few sets of roller wheels and bearings.

❧ Most leagues require you to pay a league fee, usually around $100 to $150. Plus, all players participating in inline hockey will have to pay an inline hockey insurance fee in case of injury, which is usually about $20.

LACROSSE

Overview

Originally, lacrosse was a ceremonial religious rite for Native Americans. They used it to resolve disputes, heal the sick, and develop strong, virile men. It also served as a substitute for war, with as many as 1,000 players per side on a field as long as 15 miles. Called "baggataway" or "the little brother of war" by the Native Americans, the contest would last for days. In the early 1800s, the French pioneers in Canada began playing the game. It now holds the title of Canada's national summer sport.

Men's and women's lacrosse were played under virtually the same rules, with no protective equipment, until the 1930s. At that time, men's lacrosse began evolving dramatically to allow limited stick and body contact, necessitating protective equipment. Women's lacrosse continued to limit stick contact and rough checks and prohibit body contact, similar to the original Native American game.

Known as the fastest game on two feet, lacrosse is one of the most challenging team sports. Its rapid growth and increase in participants has been attributed to the fact that it is a combination of many different sports. The speed parallels that of hockey, the team defense is similar to basketball, and its physical intensity resembles football.

Today, lacrosse, commonly called "lax," is one of the fastest-growing sports in America, with over 125,000 kids playing lacrosse in the nation's youth and recreational programs. Lacrosse is primarily a youth sport, with about half of the U.S. players under age 15. Participation in lacrosse nationwide has been increasing by about 15% a year, with over 4,500 lacrosse programs now spanning the United States. Tournaments take place around the country, with divisions starting for 10-and-under teams.

For years, the game was played solely in Canada and the northeastern seaboard of the United States. However, the game is now going national and booming in places such as Texas, Florida, and California. For many years, lacrosse was an upper-class game, played principally in prep schools and Ivy League–type colleges. Now, most major colleges in the eastern United States have both men's and women's teams, and many schools and towns sponsor league teams. Lacrosse's fast pace and intense competition appeals to many children.

General Benefits

◉ Since lacrosse revolves around speed and running, it improves fitness, strength, cardiovascular development, and hand-eye coordination.

In boys' lacrosse, you find the same mentality as in ice hockey. Give a boy a stick and a helmet, and watch out! It's fascinating. Lacrosse is technically not a brute-force game, but actually a game of finesse when played professionally. Boys tend to play it very physically. Lacrosse is played on a huge field, there's lots of running, lots of players, and lots of mistakes and incorrect plays as the boys slowly learn the rules. You have to watch out for kids getting whacked.

   —Jane, mom of Carolyn, 17, and Peter, 11

Boys' lacrosse is much more physical than girls', resulting in more safety equipment. Boys use a stick, elbow pads, shoulder pads, gloves, and a helmet. Whereas the girls, allowing for zero contact, only use a stick. There is also a difference in sticks as well. Because boys are being knocked around more, their rules allow for a deeper pocket (the mesh at the end of the stick that holds the ball). Girls' rules require a flat pocket.

   —Bill McNamee, head coach at Irvine Youth Lacrosse and assistant high school coach for 8
      years

We girls like to call men's lacrosse "football with sticks!"

   —Cadi Marshall, girls' lacrosse coach for 6 years

- Players gain arm and leg strength from running and throwing.

- Lacrosse also builds balance and strategic thinking.

- All lacrosse players are involved in both the offense and defense in each game, so the team responsibilities are shared, promoting teamwork and cooperation.

Kids Who Tend to Excel

- Quickness, a willingness to work hard, and athletic ability distinguish the best lacrosse players.

- While there is no classic body type for lacrosse, the fast-paced game, involving sprints, abrupt starts and stops, precise passing, and dodging, requires speed, coordination, and agility.

◎ Lacrosse requires hand-eye coordination, as players must catch the ball in a netted stick while running, often at full speed.

Lacrosse is great exercise, requiring both endurance and bursts of speed, much like soccer. The lacrosse community is one of the most welcoming, diverse, and close-knit communities I have found anywhere, and that is part of what makes the sport so great. Take your child to watch some of the top collegiate teams play, as their skills are breathtaking and so much fun to watch.

> —Alexis Longinotti, president of Northern California Chapter of U.S. Lacrosse, former captain of Stanford University women's team, teaching for 2 years

At the more competitive level the qualities that set apart the best lacrosse players are speed and the ability to change speed quickly (acceleration), awareness of their position on the field relative to the ball, determination, and an unwillingness to give up. Yet speed is definitely not everything. Some of the best players of the game have not been fleet of foot, but rather had excellent stick and game skills. As with all team sports, lacrosse requires the ability to work together. More often than not, the player who comes up with the ball is the one who works the hardest and smartest for it, and the player who scores the most goals or has the most assists is the one who works best with her teammates, not who has the most accurate shot or pass.

> —Alexis Longinotti, president of Northern California Chapter of U.S. Lacrosse, former captain of Stanford University women's team, teaching for 2 years

Some kids start in early grade school with basic skills, while others wait until middle school years or even in high school. For this reason, "best" age is tough to say.

> —Jeff Harris, varsity lacrosse coach at Brunswick School, coaching for 21 years

There is no best age. Some of the best players in the world didn't start until they were in eighth grade. My personal feeling is fourth or fifth grade is early enough.

> —David Hallam, president of the Vermont Chapter U.S. Lacrosse, coaching boys' youth lacrosse for 10 years

Self-starters with quick reflexes and who make fast decisions, can run fast, have fast hands, and work on the basics on their own do best at lacrosse.

> —*Matt Holman, owner and head boys' varsity lacrosse coach, East Meets West Lacrosse Camp, teaching for 13 years*

Boys who do well in lacrosse are quick athletes, adept at hand-eye coordination for catching and throwing the ball, have the vision to "see" the field and understand team concepts, and are appropriately aggressive and ready for rough-and-tumble action. Unlike in some sports, size is not necessarily as important as speed, and a smaller athlete can be very successful if he or she is quick and has strong stick skills.

> —*Jeff Harris, varsity lacrosse coach at Brunswick School, coaching for 21 years*

Kids who excel are all-around athletes with speed, smarts, the ability to use both the left and right hand, mental toughness in stressful situations, and the endurance to keep up with all the running.

> —*Stephanie Pavlick, Holycross College head women's lacrosse coach for 3 years*

Best Age to Start

◉ While children can begin playing lacrosse as young as age 6, most coaches recommend that your child get involved in competitive lacrosse between the ages of 10 and 11. Most organized lacrosse teams begin around fifth or sixth grade.

◉ Depending on your child's athletic skills, lacrosse's learning curve can be very short.

What to Look For When Getting Started

❦ Look for an experienced coach who teaches the fundamentals of throwing, passing, catching, and scooping the ball, along with dodging and checking techniques.

Look for programs that encourage fun. Kids don't have fun while standing on the sidelines watching others play. Some parents pull their child out after they have seen a game or two because they didn't realize that lacrosse is a contact sport.

—*Bill McNamee, head coach at Irvine Youth Lacrosse and assistant high school coach for 8 years*

At the youth level, age 14 and below, we do not allow, "take down checks," i.e., lining someone up from more than five yards away and putting your shoulder into them for the express purpose of putting them on the ground. The height and weight differences at this age level are too great. This is not glorified football.

—*David Hallam, president of the Vermont Chapter U.S. Lacrosse, coaching boys' youth lacrosse for 10 years*

🪁 Catching and throwing with a lacrosse stick is difficult to learn and requires practice to get comfortable with the fundamentals. One of the more difficult tasks in lacrosse is keeping the ball secure in the shallow net while running with it between opponents who try to "check" or dislodge it by slapping at the ball carrier's stick. The player running with the ball tries to protect it by cradling or twisting the stick in a coordinated motion of the arms and wrists. This skill requires quick hands, which is one way a smaller player can compensate for her size.

🪁 Younger players often use modified equipment such as softer balls, play with fewer players, and have a shorter playing time.

🪁 At the youth level (middle school) no "checking" (using one's stick to hit an opponent's stick to knock the ball out) should be allowed. Checking is generally allowed at the high school level and above.

Safety and Injury Concerns

🪁 Bruises, strains, sprains, and ligament tears are the most common injuries in lacrosse, and broken bones are rare.

🪁 Running into any other player is prohibited in grade school lacrosse. In middle

If players have been coached inadequately, dangerous or rough checking may occur, leading to the possibility of being hit in the head or the face, but these incidents are usually avoided by diligent refereeing. Most high school coaches encourage their players to avoid checking or encourage them to only check if an opponent presents her stick and the check can occur safely.

—*Alexis Longinotti, president of Northern California Chapter of U.S. Lacrosse, former captain of Stanford University women's team, teaching for 2 years*

I have not seen many serious injuries in my years of coaching. In high school level play, there are some concussions, but research shows that lacrosse is a safer sport than soccer.

—*Jon Fox, middle school head lacrosse coach for 10 years*

In youth lacrosse, the common types of injuries are rolled ankles and shin splints. Under 8th grade the kids aren't big enough and are well protected with equipment so as not to get any serious injuries on a frequent basis.

—*Bill McNamee, head coach at Irvine Youth Lacrosse and assistant high school coach for 8 years*

school and older leagues, contact may only be made between the shoulders and the waist and from the front or side.

🦴 Referees maintain strict rules to prevent excessive force or checking from behind. Players must wear lots of pads above the waist including shoulder, arm, and rib pads, gloves, a mouth guard, and a helmet, which is designed to keep players from being hit by a hard-thrown ball or erratically swung stick.

Cost Considerations

🦴 Your child will need to purchases her own stick, which runs anywhere from $30 to $200. The typical stick (crosse) costs between $70 and $90, while the top-of-the-line titanium sticks cost between $150 and $170. Balls cost around $2 each.

🦴 All players must wear protective mouth guards ($2) and cleats ($15 to $20).

Unfortunately, lacrosse can be an expensive sport for a new player, as equipment can be pricey. Depending on where you live in the country and how much support the town or county gives to your league, sign-up costs can vary. When shopping for lacrosse equipment for a new player, go to a lacrosse retailer online or look for a catalogue and ask about a new-player package. Many stores will have a good deal on youth-size equipment in a package deal for a lower price.

—*Bill McNamee, head coach at Irvine Youth Lacrosse and assistant high school coach for 8 years*

✦ In girls' lacrosse no helmets or body padding is worn (except for the goalie), only mouth guards. Some girls wear gloves, which are optional, and cost about $25. Girls generally play in kilts, as in field hockey.

✦ Protective equipment for boys, which costs $200 on average, includes helmet and mask ($65–$100), gloves ($30–$70), rib and shoulder pads ($25–$55), arm pads ($20–$35), elbow pads ($25), and athletic supporter and cup ($10–$20).

✦ Additional goalie equipment includes throat protectors ($15), chest protectors ($65), and goalie stick ($80–$260).

✦ Helmets and face masks should be NOCSAE (National Operating Committee on Standards for Athletic Equipment) approved.

✦ League fees can run $100–$300 depending on the league and level in which your child participates.

MARTIAL ARTS

Overview

Modern martial arts evolved from various methods of unarmed combat that have developed over the centuries in Korea, China, and Japan. Each martial art is replete with complex histories and philosophies, mostly stemming from Zen Buddhism. Today there are over 40 million people in 140 countries who practice martial arts. Many advanced students consider martial arts to be a way of life and striving for perfection of character as opposed to just a sport. Many children who study the martial arts never enter competitions.

Most martial arts emphasize mastery of the body, integrity, self-defense, self-confidence, and concentration. They also focus on teaching how to harness ki (or ch'i or qi, "internal energy") through meditation and breathing exercises. The instructors usually teach nonviolence and how to avoid conflict, particularly in children's classes. However, some combat styles do teach aggressive fighting techniques, offer weapons training, and allow physical contact in sparring exercises. Thus, you need to look carefully into the type of martial art being taught before enrolling your child.

As a concerned parent, you may be wondering if by signing your child up for

My son started karate in first grade. He brought a flyer home from school for American tae kwon do and said, "I really want to do this!" All I knew about it was that it involved kicking. So I agreed to go check it out. It proved a wonderful fit. He took it three times a week, year-round until eighth grade, and achieved his third-degree black belt. I find it beneficial that he can now walk into any karate school as a paid instructor.

—Joy, mom of Chris, 15, and Victoria, 11

Karate focuses children and makes them think about their personal interactions outside of class in a very careful way. It does this in a way that is wonderfully magnetizing to children, especially boys, who are drawn to karate because they see it as controlled fighting. Yet the real beauty of it is that kids ultimately learn how to avoid conflict and control themselves. As kids advance to a high enough level, karate becomes a great athletic activity, plus it includes good stretching. For girls or boys less into fighting, karate is a huge self-confidence builder and it makes them self-aware as they pay more attention to their bodies.

—Karla, mom of Karl, 9, Max, 6, and Leo, 3

The general benefits of karate are acquired like building blocks. One benefit inevitably builds on another. The first block is confidence or when you hear the kids say, "I can do it." With confidence comes character. Kids learn who they are and how to be a good person. With character comes self-respect as well as a respect for others.

—Michael Graves, Olympic coaching staff, teaching karate for 24 years

From an adult's perspective, we see karate as an art form. From a kid's perspective, it takes time to realize that it's so much more. In my class the other day, I asked, "Who thinks that karate is just about punching and kicking?" A couple of hands went up. Then I explained how in karate, you learn to concentrate and really focus your mind on where you want to throw that punch. I then asked, "How many of you find it very difficult to stay seated and sit still at school and not shout out in class?" More hands went up. I said that the focus you learn in karate is the same focus you can bring to school and your classroom. The kids have come to realize that their acquired focus, discipline, and self-control are all links to their world outside our karate training.

—*Cheryl Nadeau, Choice Martial Arts Kenpo Karate sensei, teaching for 8 years*

Our first grader thinks tae kwon do is great, and we love it, as it has taught him discipline, self-confidence, to respect himself and others, and to listen. It also involves a lot of physical exercise and the chance to let off steam after school two times a week. Ben started with friends who have since dropped out, but he doesn't care, because he loves it so much. He gets very upset if he misses a class and loves getting tested for the belts. It's been great for him.

—*Andy, dad of Rachel, 10, Ben, 7, and Josh, 3*

My daughter started karate in second grade mainly because her brother was taking it. It was good discipline for her, and she stuck with it until she received her black belt. For my very petite daughter, it has given her a really wonderful sense of strength, and she can protect her body by being able to say, "Don't come near me. Don't hurt me. I am woman and don't mess with me. I'm strong and I'm good."

—*Joy, mom of Chris, 15, and Victoria, 11*

Judo teaches coordination, balance, strength, flexibility, fluidity of movement, and the development of specific skills that can be lifesaving.

—*Jim Hrbek, chairman of junior development and on national coaching staff for U.S. Judo, head coach and owner of Judo America, teaching for 26 years*

martial arts, you risk turning him into the schoolyard bully. It's a popular misconception that martial arts focus on attacking and injuring an assailant. In reality, most martial arts teach that the first line of defense is nonviolence and escape, and strongly discipline kids against aggression, bullying, or showing off. The training, self-discipline, and self-confidence that martial arts teach help prevent your child from either becoming a bully or becoming the victim of one.

General Benefits

◎ The essence of martial arts is based on discipline, respect, and perseverance, including learning respect for a teacher, classmates, and opponents.

◎ Martial arts help shy kids overcome timidity or withdrawal, and teach aggressive kids the self-discipline to control anger, hostility, and aggression.

◎ Breathing techniques teach focus and inner calm, and training sessions help children develop a longer attention span and greater concentration.

◎ Martial arts training improves physical conditioning, strength, body control, coordination, balance, and flexibility. Plus, training provides an aerobic workout.

◎ It gives kids street awareness and the ability to defend themselves in a dangerous situation.

◎ In martial arts, children go at their own pace and there is a constant reward system earning stripes on their belt and then earning new belt levels.

Best Age to Start

◎ While some children start training as young as age 3, most children start between ages 5 and 9. By that time your child has enough self-control and muscle mastery to punch, kick, and turn safely. However, martial arts is a discipline that can be picked up at any age.

In terms of the age to start martial arts training, it's very individualized and there is not set age to start. I've taught two-year-olds with excellent focus and twelve-year-olds who lack the concentration it takes.

—Cheryl Nadeau, Choice Martial
   Arts Kenpo Karate sensei, teaching
   for 8 years

◎

Kids who do best are very independent thinkers who thrive on individual challenges instead of team events. Even though there are certain rules to follow, kids who can think outside the box are the ones who do well.

—Joy, mom of Chris, 15, and
   Victoria, 11

Kids Who Tend to Excel

◉ All types of children can excel in karate, even those who are not especially athletic, because it does not require sheer muscle power or speed.

◉ Those children who can focus intensely do well, as well as those who have balance and flexibility.

◉ Girls thrive in karate as well as boys, and many achieve the ultimate goal of a black belt alongside boys.

Having a son with ADHD who's a little obsessed with violence and fairly aggressive himself, I had steered clear of karate. Two years ago, we tried karate and it's been the one activity that my son has stuck with. He's very proud of his accomplishments and belts, and hangs his certificates on the wall in his room. So while it seems counterintuitive to give an aggressive kid an aggressive sport, it has worked out really well for my son.

—*Anonymous*

My son has ADD and I found that the combination of exercise and discipline was incredible for him as a great energy outlet. Especially for those times when he got too wound up at home, I could take him to the studio to get rid of excess energy.

—*Joy, mom of Chris, 15, and Victoria, 11*

The best sport for our middle guy, who has Asperger's syndrome, was karate. It gave him an activity that did not involve competing with anyone else. It has built up his self-confidence, muscle control, and flexibility.

—*Cyn, mom of three kids ages, 12, 11, and 7*

The kids who get the most out of martial arts are the ones who have the greatest physical or mental challenges to overcome. They often develop much faster than the naturally gifted, relative to their own starting points.

—*Rick Foley, director and chief instructor in tae kwon do and hapkido, Elmwood Center, teaching for 26 years*

Karate for ADD/ADHD Kids and Other Special Needs

✦ Karate has become known as tending to help ADD/ADHD (attention-deficit disorder/attention-deficit hyperactivity disorder) kids calm down, as they learn focus and self-discipline.

✦ As a result, many martial arts instructors have extensive experience working with ADD/ADHD children and have developed programs that address their specific needs.

What to Look For When Getting Started

✦ Because martial arts encompass a tremendous number of disparate styles and approaches, from self-defense to deadly moves, you should become familiar with them all before choosing the best one for your child. It is possible to generalize which styles tend to focus on well-being, integrity, and self-defense, but much of the difference lies in the philosophy of each school.

✦ The most important things to find out about schools are their philosophies on fighting, and the message they give children about violence.

✦ Visit several schools before committing to one. Have your child take a class, or sit in on one yourself. If you can, make an appointment to watch part of both beginning and advanced classes. If the school offers a free introductory class, have your child take it. Your child should be grouped with others his same size and skill level for sparring. Questions to ask about classes:
  - What are the size and makeup of classes?
  - Are the classes organized by age or by belt and skill levels? Will there be any other students in the class at your child's skill level?
  - If classes have a mix of skill levels, what is the range of belt levels within each class?
  - When are classes offered and how long does each class last?
  - What is the student/teacher ratio? The teacher should be able to give adequate attention and some individualized instruction to each child.

✦ When looking at martial arts studios or classes, realize that choices differ dramatically and are often lumped under the general heading of karate. Each martial art has its own colorful history and approach to training, whether it stems from the traditional martial arts of Japan, China, and Korea, or in newer American variations. Take your child's temperament into consideration when choosing styles that range from evasive self-defense to offensive sparring training.

Selecting a Karate Master

✦ Find out who will teach your child's class. A larger school will have several senseis (instructors) whose personalities and teaching philosophies create tremendous differences in training. If you join a school because of a celebrated martial arts master, make sure your child will have access to him in some capacity. Many masters only work with students at higher levels, and will not even come in contact with beginning students.

✦ Find out details about teachers' backgrounds such as who they have trained with, whether they compete in national tournaments, if they affiliate with a larger school or organization, or if they enter their students into local, regional, or national competitions.

✦ All instructors should have black belts and have a minimum of three to five years of training. Look for the following:

Ask whether the karate instructor is going to talk about karate in terms of forms and competition or use examples from real life. A number of parents in my child's class were upset when our teacher mentioned scenarios involving kidnapping or fighting someone carrying a weapon. Also, look for an instructor who fosters a spiritual attitude about martial arts, connects with kids, and is both creative and energetic.

—*Karla, mom of Karl, 9, Max, 6, and Leo, 3*

Tae kwon do has been a terrific experience due to a wonderful instructor. He fills the class with many "life lessons," and he teaches the children self-confidence, discipline, poise, coordination, and respect.

—*Linda, mom of Alison, 11, Amanda, 5, Michael, 3, and Ginny, 1*

Patience is the most important quality of a good instructor because children don't listen through yelling. If the instructor is calm, the children will be calm. Also, martial arts instructors have a code of ethics, just like doctors, and parents should know about this.

—*Michael Graves, Olympic coaching staff, teaching karate for 24 years*

➤ Does he emphasize self-defense and self-control over violence and conflict?

➤ How does the teacher behave during a sparring session? What kinds of behavior does he encourage in his students? Is contact allowed? What types of safety precautions are in place?

➤ Does the instructor have to raise his voice to control the class?

➤ How does the instructor interact with the students? Is he respectful? Are the students respectful of him?

➤ Do the students bow as they enter and leave the dojo (training area), and show other signs of respect and self-discipline?

❧ Ask whether your child's teacher, another instructor, or the head of the school will give the belt test. If someone other than the teacher who has worked directly with your child gives the belt test, this may prove more stressful for your child.

Earning Ranks and Belt-Testing

❧ The most traditional Chinese, Japanese, and Korean systems offer eight to ten belt levels, from white, for beginners, to black belt. The more advanced belts have degrees of skill within them.

❧ Students earn new belts by demonstrating proficiency in a number of movements, forms, sparring, and defense techniques. Some schools

---

Kids tend to progress fast in the beginning, which is good motivation when they're just starting out, but then have to obtain the maturity to slog through the forms for the next several years. Also realize that your child's black belt is often different from that of an adult's black belt.

—Karla, mom of Karl, 9, Max, 6, and Leo, 3

In my children's school, they termed it "belt promotion" and stressed to everyone that you can't fail. They only invite you once they know you're ready. You still have to come and do it in front of this big group of people, as well as break your board (and it takes some kids five tries). It's kind of like a dance recital. It's a good experience and it taught my son, Chris, no matter how scared he was on the inside, he could do it.

—Joy, mom of Chris, 15, and Victoria, 11

guarantee a belt after a few months, though most require students to pass a test to rise from one rank to another.

🗡 An instructor who moves students through the ranks regardless of his skills does your child no favors and may be more interested in supplementing his income than teaching your child.

🗡 Some instructors give other awards to the children, such as patches that they can earn or trophies at the end of the session.

Popular Styles of Martial Arts
AIKIDO

🗡 This Japanese nonviolent martial art was developed in the early 20th century from jujitsu and means "way of harmony."

🗡 Aikido is considered a gentle martial art, using "soft," graceful, circular movements and letting the opponent defeat himself without causing either opponent serious injury. Aikido does this by emphasizing evasion and escape techniques using minimal effort on the part of the defender. Training focuses on learning to redirect an opponent's attack and to subdue an opponent without using force, but by applying pressure on vulnerable areas such as on the elbow, shoulder, or wrist.

🗡 Aikido is not practiced competitively, though it does include weapons training. Training in this style usually involves some spiritual component, as it is one of the more philosophical martial arts.

HAPKIDO

🗡 This Korean fighting style, meaning "the way of power and coordination," combines tae kwon do with jujitsu and emphasizes kicks, throws, and joint locks. It includes both "soft" moves, as found in aikido, and "hard" karate-like moves.

🗡 Hapkido's philosophy is nonaggressive, using moves that turn the attacker against himself. However, some of these moves are potentially lethal. Hapkido originally focused on pressure-point strikes, joint locks, and throws, but now also includes kicks and hand strikes.

🗡 Hapkido is not a competitive sport, and is known more as an art of self-defense.

JUDO

🗡 This traditional Japanese martial art, meaning "gentle (or compliant) way," was also developed from jujitsu in the early 20th century. Its popularity grew as its practitioners began to routinely defeat students of other martial arts. Eventually it became incorporated into the curriculum of Japanese schools. Judo places a strong emphasis on morality and character development.

✦ Like jujitsu, Judo uses an attacker's moves against him and includes throws, grappling, and other wrestling-style moves. Judo emphasizes the use of leverage instead of strength to throw your opponent off-balance and onto the ground. Once down, a variety of chokes or joint locks are used to force the opponent into submission.

✦ Developed and taught as a competitive sport, judo became part of the Olympic Games in 1964, with women's judo added in 1992.

JUJITSU

✦ This Japanese martial art, meaning "gentle practice," evolved from the samurai warrior art of weaponless fighting and looks similar to wrestling. It dates back to the 16th century, when kicks and strikes had little effect against the battlefield armor the warriors wore, so chokes and joint locks were used to attack unprotected areas.

✦ Jujitsu emphasizes evasive self-defense but includes moves designed to disable or kill an opponent if necessary. This competitive form of self-defense focuses on using an opponent's weight and strength against him. The most common moves are throws, locks, holds, trips, and hits.

✦ Jujitsu is a well-rounded style and involves sparring and weapons training.

KARATE

✦ This Japanese discipline, literally translated as "empty hand," is a weaponless form of martial arts characterized by quick, sharp movements. It originated on the Japanese island of Okinawa in the 1600s and developed as a means of self-defense because weapons were outlawed on the island. It is probably the most popular style of martial arts in the United States. Karate is competitive and part of the Summer Olympic Games.

✦ Karate is a powerful fighting style and involves a great deal of high-energy punching, strikes, kicking, and hard blocks. In training, students learn intense concentration to focus strength on impact. Karate stresses offensive as well as defensive moves, but traditional karate also aspires to the more lofty lessons of discipline, respect, and honor, making violence unnecessary. Forms (kata) and sparring play an important role in training.

✦ Karate uses a system of colored belts, starting at red or white for new students, and progressing through yellow, orange, purple, green, brown, and finally black belt. The higher belt colors often have three levels that must be achieved before progressing upward. There are ten levels of black belts.

KENDO

✦ Kendo is a Japanese form of sword fighting that means "way of the sword," and stems from samurai warriors.

✦ Practice involves extensive armor (padding, mask with metal bars, shoulder pads, chest and torso protection, gloves) along with a split-bamboo practice sword (ashinai), which is wielded with two hands.

KENPO/KEMPO KARATE

✦ Kenpo (Japanese) or kempo (Chinese) karate means "empty hand, way of the fist." Chinese, Japanese, and Hawaiian martial arts contributed to kenpo's techniques, which were first popularized in Hawaii.

✦ This style emphasizes self-defense and avoidance of violence. However, it is based on street-fighting tactics and includes forceful moves meant to disable or kill an opponent in a life-or-death situation.

✦ As the name suggests, kenpo involves a lot of hand techniques, both blocks and offensive strikes. Training involves learning numerous training forms (kata), along with rapid-fire hand techniques, kicks, and combinations.

KUNG FU

✦ Kung fu is a generic term describing any Chinese martial art (called "wu shu"), and means "well done." Innumerable forms of kung fu are taught, differing in how much power is brought to the techniques. The most popular forms of kung fu can be traced back to the Shaolin Monastery, where monks developed defense techniques against roving bands of robbers.

✦ This complex style is fast-paced and aerobic. It involves more dynamic moves than karate and includes throws, grappling holds, and weapons. It also uses smooth, continuous moves patterned after animals such as the tiger, crane, and praying mantis.

✦ Self-defense is also emphasized, but because of the extreme diversity within kung fu, look carefully into the instructor's teaching style and philosophy before enrolling your child.

NINJITSU

✦ This ancient training, meaning "the art of stealth," stems from the feudal days in Japan when ninjas carried out missions of espionage and assassination against warlords. Ninjas had a reputation for mercenary ruthlessness, but training in ninjitsu primarily stresses self-protection and avoidance of danger.

✦ A relative of judo, ninjitsu emphasizes utilizing a number of styles in order to be more unpredictable to an opponent.

✦ Although training does include empty-hand techniques and some unarmed combat, most techniques involve weapons such as the sword, dagger, dart, weighted chain, and throwing star.

SHOTOKAN KARATE

✦ Shotokan karate is a popular traditional form of Chinese martial arts, meaning "way of the empty hand," and is designed to be a lethal hand-to-hand combat art.

✦ Though the style does not involve the use of weapons, shotokan is quite aggressive, including lethal moves calculated to disable or kill an opponent. Much of the focus is placed on balance and one's center of gravity, with movements described as "hard" and linear. It also embraces a fighting theory of "one strike, one kill."

TAE KWON DO

✦ This Korean martial art, developed in the 1950s, is similar to Japanese karate and means "way of kicking and punching" or "way of the foot and fist."

✦ Tae kwon do is power-oriented, free-form fighting, though self-defense and avoiding conflict are stressed, since moves are meant to be nonlethal.

✦ Developed as a military art, tae kwon do uses kicks and punches to energize the body, along with breathing and meditation to provide focus.

✦ This form is known for its high, powerful kicks and impressive footwork. Hand techniques are used only as follow-up.

✦ Tae kwon do has been part of the Olympic Games since 2000.

TAI CHI

✦ Tai chi, also known as tai chi chuan, is a Chinese exercise and fighting style practiced mainly for its health and healing benefits. It means "great ultimate fist."

✦ Tai chi's slow, relaxed, graceful movements are stylized renditions of original arm and foot blows. With its focus on balance and stretching, it increases flexibility.

✦ As a method of self-defense, tai chi teaches using an attacker's moves against him in order to neutralize or evade the attack. Training emphasizes self-awareness.

WING-CHUN

✦ A variant of kung fu, wing-chun, meaning "eternal springtime," was named after the female student of the woman who developed this style. It's one of the most popular Chinese martial arts.

✦ Wing-chun involves explosive moves, using low kicks and fast hands, encompassing both defense and attack moves. This style teaches close-quarter fighting techniques, and emphasizes economy of motion.

✦ The low kicks and use of an opponent's attack to defeat him make wing-chun a less strenuous sport and one at which a small child can feel successful.

✦ The style itself varies significantly from one school to another and philosophically embraces change and innovation as part of its teaching style.

WU SHU

✦ Wu shu covers martial arts styles from mainland China, and means "martial skills." Wu shu is a competitive sport.

✦ This popular class of Chinese martial arts teaches graceful and flowing dance-like movements, along with flashy moves and acrobatics. These moves become part of coordinated sparring forms and fighting with spears or swords.

Changing Between Styles

✦ Most instructors recommend learning the basics of one type of martial art before learning another style.

✦ If you switch your child from one type of martial arts training to another, discuss this change with his new instructor. Ask the instructor how your child's belt level will translate into the new school's system. He may have to start as a white belt or retake a belt test.

Safety and Injury Concerns

✦ It's generally only in beginner classes that your child could get injured with sprained toes, fingers and other joints. Make sure the school provides extensive protective gear to protect your child's head, hands, and feet.

✦ Martial arts schools vary dramatically in the type of equipment and amenities they offer. Some are large and modern, while others operate out of a local gym or share space with a gymnastics or dance facility.

Ben doesn't use karate outside class. The one time he did was on his sister when she was making him crazy and bugging him. All of a sudden we heard the scream "Haiiii!" then a thud, then Rachel running out crying. I confronted him. He told me, "Rachel was bugging me. I told her to stop, and she wouldn't, so I hit her." From fighting stance, he demonstrated a front punch straight to the stomach. I said, "Ben I'm going to tell Master Bai. Would Master Bai let you do that?" Ben got very upset and said no. I asked why. He said you only use tae kwon do for defense and begged me not to tell and has since then never done that again. Even at school when a kid was bugging him and pushed him down in the playground, he said that it was not right to use karate back.

—*Andy, dad of Rachel, 10, Ben, 7, and Josh, 3*

There can be hidden belt or certification fees that go up in price as your child advances. Some schools start you out at $25 a belt then go up to $100 each belt, then have a black-belt test costing over $200, above and beyond your monthly fee. Also some schools rope you into a four- to six-month program.

—*Douglas Veronesi, kempo and jujitsu studio owner and instructor for 4 years*

Check out the facility where your child will take lessons. The equipment should be clean and the room should be well lit with mirrors along one wall. There should be enough space and equipment for all students, and weapons should be secured away from the children's reach when not being handled by instructors or their assistants.

❧ If sparring or training with weapons is part of the class, you need to ask:

～ What protective gear do children wear? What safety precautions does the teacher use when children handle the weapons?

～ When sparring, what kind of contact is allowed? Many schools have no-contact rule for sparring.

～ How closely is sparring supervised?

～ How old or experienced do children have to be before sparring or weaponry is introduced?

～ Are children paired by age, size, or experience when sparring?

～ What type of weapons do the older children handle? How many students handle weapons at one time?

Cost Considerations

❧ Some schools allow children to take a few classes before committing long-term. Ask whether trial lessons are available on a pay-as-you-go basis. Ask as well about the cost of private, one-on-one lessons if your child needs additional individual instruction.

❧ If you pay by the semester or season, find out if you can be reimbursed for missed and canceled classes or if your child quits halfway through the season.

❧ Find out which costs you must pay for separately, such as uniforms, belt-testing fees, badges or team uniforms. Karate uniforms generally cost between $40 and $120.

🌿 If the dojo will encourage your child to participate in tournaments, find out what fees will be involved. Tournament entry fees generally average between $15 and $30.

RODEO

Overview

Early cowboys used to do roping and riding tricks for entertainment when rounding up their cattle. This activity became so popular that ranches and communities began to hold competitions. While rodeo has been traditionally a male-dominated sport, cowgirls have become an integral part of the rodeo scene as well. Women have ridden, roped, and wrangled for years, but now cowboys and cowgirls are competing in the same events. Children are judged mainly on their ability to manage and control the movements and speed of cattle and horses. Most children do rodeo with their families. Rodeo has been named the official state sport by the Texas legislature. Today, rodeo attracts thousands of entrants and millions of spectators to major and local events across the United States and Canada.

Kids learn valuable life lessons through rodeo in teamwork, overcoming self-imposed obstacles and fear. They take pride in knowing they are in control of a big animal like a horse or can rope the horns of a steer or ride a mechanical bucking bull for eight seconds. All of these are confidence builders and lessons in experiencing something new.

—Jo-An Turman, cofounder of Winds Ranch Foundation and rodeo instructor

I have enjoyed being involved in rodeo because I enjoy the time I get to spend with my family. Rodeo can really be a family thing, Mom, Dad, and the kids; you can all participate together. Each time I took my daughter to a rodeo event we got quality time together.

—Patricia Schaffer, national director for Nebraska High School Rodeo Association for 7 years

All kids can excel in one or more areas of rodeo. Some become better ropers than others, so they are chosen to represent their groups for this event or they do horseshoes, roping stationary steer heads, riding the Mighty Bucky for 8 seconds, or the rodeo relay horse race, in which four kids pass a baton.

—Jo-An Turman, cofounder of Winds Ranch Foundation and rodeo instructor

Some kids start when they are old enough to get on a horse. Our state has a peewee class of 6 and under. Those that start young can start riding sheep. Still others don't start till they are in high school. I have found that it is really never too late.

—Patricia Schaffer, national director for Nebraska High School Rodeo Association for 7 years

General Benefits

◉ Strength, agility, precise timing, and quick thinking

◉ Teaches your child riding skills and to appreciate horses and other livestock

◉ Builds hand-eye coordination and memorization skills by weaving patterns with twirling ropes.

Kids Who Tend to Excel

◉ Children who excel at rodeo usually are athletic, outgoing, mentally tough, and able to concentrate under pressure.

◉ Rodeo is physically demanding and requires strength.

Best Age to Start

◉ The usual age to start rodeo lessons is between 10 and 13, but many children start as early as age 5.

◉ Rodeo associations have junior members between the ages of 5 and 18.

◉ Age groupings in junior rodeo events are often ages 6 and under, 11 and under, and 13 and under.

What to Look For When Getting Started

❧ The program should teach your child how to ride a horse in both directions around the arena at a walk, trot, and canter, how to halt the horse effortlessly, and also turn it without a problem. Programs also teach grooming and saddling, as well as show etiquette. Once your child masters riding, then training can begin in rodeo riding events.

❧ Almost all rodeo events have junior rodeo categories, grouped by both age and gender.

❧ For girls, barrel racing, pole-bending events, breakaway calf roping, and goat tying are popular. For boys, popular events include calf roping, calf wrestling, and bareback riding.

Typical Rodeo Events
BAREBACK RIDING

❧ If your child chooses to ride bareback, no saddle is placed on the horse. In order to earn the most points, your child's legs need to be in the proper position. He cannot touch the horse, and his spurring technique also earns him points. However, almost half of the points are earned by the horse's performance.

SADDLE BRONCO RIDING

❧ This classic rodeo event, similar to bull riding, has its roots in the Old West, with ranch hands gathering to compete over who had the best style while riding horses not yet broken in.

❧ In this competitive event, the rider must stay on the horse for eight seconds, and the rider's style factors heavily in the judging. Points are also awarded for the strength of the horse's bucking, the control throughout the ride, and the length of the spurring stroke.

❧ As in bareback riding, your child starts with his feet over the shoulders of the horse and cannot touch the horse. In addition, dropping the rein or slipping a foot out of the stirrup results in disqualification.

CALF ROPING

❧ Like bronco riding, calf roping originated in the Old West, where unhealthy calves were roped and tied down to be treated. Today, calf roping requires skills in riding, roping, timing, and coordination, as well as good horsemanship.

❧ After the calf is released, both horse and cowboy chase it. The rider then ropes it, dismounts, runs to the calf, and ties any three of its legs together using a "pigging string" he carries in his teeth. When the cowboy is finished, he raises his hands to signal to the judge, then gets back on his horse, letting the rope become slack. The calf must stay down for six seconds for the run to be valid. At that point the cowboy's time is scored.

TEAM ROPING

❧ This is the only team event in rodeo. The first rider, called the header, chases and ropes the steer around the horns or neck, while turning it to the left. The second rider, called the heeler, follows close behind and then ropes the steer's hind feet. If the heeler only ropes one hind leg, he receives a five-second penalty. If the heeler tosses his loop before the header has turned the steer to the left, it's called a "crossfire" and the ropers are disqualified. Their ropes are then tightened, and they position their horses facing each other on opposite sides of the steer. This entire event happens in seconds. When the slack is taken out of both ropes and the riders are facing each other, the clock is stopped.

MOUNTED BREAKAWAY ROPING

✦ The roper is on horseback with one end of his rope tied to the saddle horn by a piece of string. The calf is released and the cowboy will pursue it with the lasso swirling above his head. The loop must land completely over the calf's head. When the calf pulls away from the rider, the rope will grow taut and the string will break away from the saddle horn.

GOAT TYING

✦ Girls and boys race their horses up to a goat, dismount, catch the goat, and then tie up its legs. (The riders carry a short rope in their teeth.) The fastest person wins.

RIBBON ROPING

✦ The roper tosses a loop on a calf while the ribbon runner waits in the arena. When the roper dismounts and makes contact with the calf, the ribbon runner, or cowgirl, runs to the calf and snatches the ribbon tied to the calf's tail.

✦ The ribbon runner then races back to the finish line.

BARREL RACING

✦ Barrel racing is traditionally a female event, but it is becoming more coed. The rider must maneuver the horse through a "cloverleaf" pattern of three (sometimes four) barrels. There is a five-second penalty for knocking down a barrel. In addition, if the rider breaks the pattern, she is disqualified.

✦ Speed, agility, and riding ability are skills needed for this timed event.

POLE BENDING

✦ Also a traditional female event, pole bending uses six poles set in a straight line, twelve feet apart from each other, down the middle of the arena.

✦ In this timed event, the rider must run the horse in a straight line down the length of the poles, turn the horse around the first pole, and then maneuver through the poles in a zigzag pattern as fast as possible.

STEER WRESTLING AND STEER ROPING

✦ The art of steer roping was created on the ranges as a means of getting control of cattle in need of medical care by getting the animal safely to the ground and securely tied. Wrestling a steer requires brute strength along with leverage, and is not usually done by children. Steer roping is one of rodeo's oldest events, but held only in large arenas due to the large space required. A steer wrestler starts on horseback behind a barrier, and chases a steer that has been given a head start. After tossing a rope around the steer's horns, the steer roper brings the steer to the ground, and then must tie three of its legs together. As with calf roping, the steer must remain tied for six seconds.

Safety and Injury Concerns

🐾 Your child will need to wear a protective helmet, riding boots with a riding heel, and long pants.

🐾 Equipment should be in good condition, with no frayed or weak ropes and all riggings adjusted and tightened.

🐾 A protective vest is recommended to help absorb the shock of a blow from hitting the ground or being stepped on or horned by an animal. Some use spandex shorts to protect their buttocks and thighs while riding. Boys should consider using jock straps and protective cups.

🐾 Mouthpieces can be worn to protect your child's teeth.

🐾 Gloves are also recommended, especially for stock events.

Cost Considerations

🐾 The greatest cost involves your child having access to a place to ride and practice. For many, this means having a horse of their own. Purchasing a horse can be anywhere from $1,000 to $25,000. Other equipment you will also need is a pickup and trailers. Kids can lease horses, which can run around $700 a year, plus the cost of insurance.

🐾 Entry fees vary from state to state, with each event costing between $10 and $40.

🐾 Membership fees in local rodeo associations are around $130, which includes national and state dues and a required insurance policy.

🐾 Other rodeo equipment your child may need include a face mask, handle pad, mouthpiece, and rosin.

SAILING

Overview

While competitive sailing used to be virtually off-limits to anyone without a yacht club membership, it has now become widely accessible. The easiest way for your child to get started sailing is to attend a summer sailing camp, where she can learn the basics and decide if it's an activity she wants to pursue. Sailing is a sport that your child can enjoy throughout her adult years. An Olympic sport since 1900, sailing races involve either fleet or match racing. In fleet racing, all boats race against each other at the same time, while in match racing, two boats compete one-on-one.

General Benefits

◉ Sailing improves hand-eye coordination and balance, and develops upper-body and lower-body strength along with hand and finger strength.

◉ Trimming sails requires endurance and strength in the arms and chest. Because a sailor will most likely encounter heavy winds, she has to know how to maneuver herself when the boat wants to heel (lie up on its side in the water). The sailor has to keep the boat flat on the water to move quickly and in the right direction, also use her legs and abdominal muscles to flatten the boat out by hiking the body outside the boat. Hiking out and sheeting the sail in and out (using a line to adjust your sails) works the abdominal muscles, quads, and arm muscles.

◉ Sailing solo will keep your child active and agile. It also teaches quick reaction times.

◉ Racing gets kids interested in storm fronts, wind shifts, and aerodynamic design principles.

◉ Being able to navigate a craft and control wind is an exhilarating experience that increases a child's independence and self-esteem.

◉ Sailing helps children appreciate the awesome power of nature and learn about scientific principles, such as why a sailboat moves forward, how the rudder deflects water, and how the centerboard or keel works.

Kids Who Tend to Excel

◉ Kids must be water-savvy and not afraid to fall into the water. Having a good sense of balance and good hand-eye coordination is also helpful.

◉ Sailing requires thinking about multiple conditions simultaneously. Children

Sailing requires constant thinking and deciphering of information around you. Because of the many elements, you have to be confident in your skills and judgment as a sailor. I have seen three types of kids excel. First, there are the kids who want to race and compete. These kids are competitive, perfectionist types, with intelligence and the ability to stay calm and collected during stressful situations. The second type of child is the one who enjoys sailing for recreational purposes only. These kids typically have great person-to-person skills, confidence, and are typically very easygoing. The third type is the child who likes a little bit of both, and enjoys racing and recreational sailing on almost an even scale.

—*Matthew Barrowclough, youth sailing instructor for 2 years*

Active kids who love the water do well at sailing. It is a great sport for bright kids who are naturally analytical and inquisitive, because you have to figure out the wind, currents, and all the controls on a boat to make it move.

—*Stephanie Doyle, varsity women's sailing coach, University of South Florida, and youth coach for 10 years*

Kids who excel are athletic, strong, and coordinated. Different boats require different physical types for different positions, making sailing very versatile.

—*Amy Gross-Kehoe, director of sailing, Stanford University, and U.S. Sailing Association Developmental Coach of the Year 2000*

Kids who excel at sailing typically have good mental visualization skills. It takes a certain knowledge of the wind to become a very proficient sailor, which is best learned by spending time on the water.

—*James Foster, California State University Monterey Bay youth sailing instructor for 3 years*

who are able to react quickly to changes and enjoy taking risks do well. Kids who have a mind of their own, and like to use trial and error to figure out what makes them go fast, love to sail and do well at it. Sailing tends to attract people who are very mathematical and analytical.

Kids can start sailing about age 6, with an introduction to competition around age 8. Age 13 is when to decide how seriously the child should take competition, but this can happen later. Sailing is a lifetime sport. In the last Olympics, the McKee brothers won a silver medal in one of the most physically demanding classes of boats, and they were about 40.

—*Karl Knauss, head sailing coach,*
U.S. Coast Guard Academy,
teaching for 11 years

Best Age to Start

◉ The trend has been to start teaching sailing to kids between the ages of 7 and 10, but this depends on your child's maturity, swimming competence, ability to follow instruction, stability of boats used, and the instructor's patience. Many schools don't start teaching children to sail solo until their teenage years.

◉ Depending on how big or tall she is, an eight- or nine-year-old can take out a beginner boat with close supervision, staying near the shore. A child should weigh at least 50 pounds in order to hold the boat down when a breeze picks up.

What to Look For When Getting Started

🐟 A well-run sailing school will have a combination of an on- and off-the-water curriculum. The sequence doesn't matter entirely and is often decided by the weather, but many schools first explain basic sailing principles on land using chalkboard, visual demonstrations, and question-and-answer sessions. Then they let the kids go out on the water to practice what they have learned.

🐟 Instructors should be experienced sailors, ideally certified by the U.S. Sailing Association and trained in safety and handling water emergencies. A good ratio of students per instructor is about 7 to 1. The students should be divided by ability, not age.

🐟 In the beginning, your child will need a place to sail with little boat traffic and calm water, such as on a lake or pond. Yet there should be a steady breeze, as sailing in light air can be dull and frustrating.

🐟 Take a look at the type of boats the program uses. Make sure the program uses stable beginner sailboats, such as the Sunfish, Optimist, Hobie Cat, or Laser, which are easy to handle. These smaller boats, with usually just one sail, line, and daggerboard, keep controls close at hand and are easy to sail single-handedly. Check to see if the sailing program has a variety of boats or a fleet of identical boats. Go and observe the facility to see if the boats are up to date and well maintained.

🐟 An introductory sailing program should teach your child how to control the sails, steer, right a boat after capsizing, do proper rigging, sail trimming, and avoid getting hit on the head by the boom coming about.

🐟 Ask if the instructor will be in the boat with your child or on a dock or boat nearby. Your child will probably be paired up with another child so they can take turns sharing skipper and crew responsibilities.

Sailing is a highly intellectual sport. Good sailors need to be able to understand complex concepts such as aero- and hydrodynamics. They need to make tactical and strategic decisions in a fluid, constantly changing environment. Junior sailors need to be able to fully concentrate for the duration of a race. When sailors compete, they compete against multiple opponents. Additionally, sailors who use their own equipment need to learn how to take care of and maintain it, which is a great lesson in responsibility.

—*Karl Knauss, head sailing coach, U.S. Coast Guard Academy, teaching for 11 years*

When children first start sailing, they are usually very intimidated by the elements such as wind and water, as well as all the lines and mechanisms on a boat. When children see that they can brave the elements and make a boat move, they gain self-confidence in becoming successful at something that once looked very daunting.

—*Matthew Barrowclough, youth sailing instructor for 2 years*

Kids gain a sense of independence and appreciation for outdoor activities as well as respect for the ocean and nature. Physically, sailing is quite strenuous from the combination of sustained concentration, holding the boat down in heavier winds, and being out in the sun all day.

—*James Foster, California State University Monterey Bay youth sailing instructor for 3 years*

Our kids have taken sailing lessons each summer, as it's an important family activity that we do together. This summer we took two months off and sailed up the East Coast as a family. It's been great for my husband, as the thing he likes most is to be out in the ocean on his sailboat.

—*Sylvia, mom of Max, 13, and Kate and Zoe, 10*

Sailing is *very* frustrating at first. It goes against all ideas of common sense and is hard for children to understand. At first it is just long, maybe cold, wet, and frustrating. Plus, it seems like a dangerous sport for young children, which makes them have to be bold and conquer their fears all on their own. Once kids figure it out, they think it's awesome and want to stick with it.

> —Carrie Howe, Boston College Advanced 420 Race coach for 5 years

Typically, yacht clubs have greater resources and are more in sync with the needs of a junior sailor. This is not to say that there aren't any fine community sailing programs or children's day camp programs that include sailing. Just from my experience, children who receive coaching from a yacht club typically do better.

> —Matthew Barrowclough, youth sailing instructor for 2 years

Sailing can be done either as a team or an individual sport. As a team event, it allows students to specialize in specific skills, such as sail trim or helmsmanship, while as an individual sport, it requires children to be efficient at everything. The solo sailor needs to both understand sail trim and have a steady hand on the helm.

> —Marlene Sassaman, sailing instructor for 21 years

❧ The Small Boat Certification, based on having demonstrated certain nationally recognized basic sailing skills, is the first step in the U.S. Sailing certification system that your child can achieve as her sailing credentials develop.

❧ More advanced classes will teach racing and regatta fundamentals, navigation and maneuvering skills, rules of the road for safe boating, and spinnaker work.

❧ Once the fundamentals have been mastered, instructors often use races as a way to motivate children to build their sailing skills, and learn things such as hiking out and reading the wind in order to keep constant tension on the sail.

❧ Most instructors set up courses with buoys or other landmarks that force kids to practice certain skills, contain the sailors, and let the instructors better monitor their progress and safety. Instructors should use whistles or megaphones to get children's attention and alert them of storm warnings.

🐟 Sailing is both a team and an individual sport. The bigger the boat, the more of a team sport sailing becomes. Working on a small boat requires a lot more strength and athleticism, because there's much more to be done.

🐟 If your child joins a sailing team, expect practice at least three times a week for three to five hours, depending on the competitive level of the team.

Safety and Injury Concerns

🐟 There are risks anytime water is involved, but sailing risks are relatively few. Make sure your child wears a life jacket with enough buoyancy up high to keep her head above the water's surface.

🐟 Your child should be taught how to right a capsized boat as soon as she starts sailing.

🐟 Make sure the program or facility has enough working safety powerboats to rescue sailors in the event of bad weather or an emergency. Your child's sailing program should have a rescue boat to tow in sailboats if the wind completely dies down or to bring children in if bad weather unexpectedly hits. Rain is fine, but a sailboat's metal masts make them ideal lightning rods. Your child should not be sent out in unsafe weather conditions.

🐟 If the sailing instructors are out on the water, they should have a dependable way of communicating with a designated person onshore in case of emergency.

Cost Considerations

🐟 The cost of sailing can run very high, mainly because you have to find a boat to sail, and children whose families do not own sailboats need to join a sailing club. Start out in a program where boats are provided or leased by the season. If your child decides to continue on to competitive sailing, then most instructors recommend getting a used boat to start out with, which will typically cost around $2,000.

🐟 Public learn-to-sail programs are the cheapest and generally run less than $300 for a program. Yacht clubs are more expensive. Learn-to-sail programs generally provide boats and equipment for the children.

🐟 If the school does not provide personal flotation devices, you can buy one at a local marine store for $25–$40. Make sure it is comfortable, yet tight.

🐟 If a child decides to race, equipment is very expensive, unless the club or school provides it and kids can share. Gloves, sailing boots, spray suits, and dry suits all tend to be costly. Other costs include:

Parents who want their kids to just check out sailing can start fairly cheaply. The initial cost would be the price of the program and the purchase of a life jacket. If the sailor starts to take sailing seriously, parents are looking at buying boats and that can get expensive. I believe they can find a used Optimist dinghy (or Sabot in California) for about $2,000, but sailors over 14 are not allowed to race Optimists. Most junior boats cost around $5,000 new, but that does not include a trailer, dolly, and extra equipment such as compasses. Lines and sails need to be replaced regularly. One thing to realize about the boat cost is that most junior boats hold their value fairly well, so much of the up-front purchase can be recouped when the boat is sold. More specialized clothing will need to be purchased, and there may be some travel costs.

—*Karl Knauss, head sailing coach, U.S. Coast Guard Academy, teaching for 11 years*

As your child gets older and improves, he will typically want to get his own boat. At younger ages, the Optimist boat is primarily used, costing from less than $1,000 used to over $3,000 new. Fortunately, they have great resale value, and parents are able to recoup some of the costs by selling to upcoming junior sailing families. As children get over age 14, the boats they will use can cost from $2,000 to $6,000, depending on the boat and its quality.

—*Matthew Barrowclough, youth sailing instructor for 2 years*

- foul weather gear, which can cost up to $200
- a string or tie to secure glasses or sunglasses
- sunblock, a hat, a water bottle, and old sneakers that you don't mind getting wet
- maintenance and care of a boat, yacht club fee, or paying for a sailing program or boat rentals
- racing and sailing team fees

The costs of sailing sometimes catch parents off-guard. As with any sports activity, the further you go in the sport, the more you are expected to spend on better equipment and better instruction.

Sailing programs for new junior sailors typically have boats that the child is entitled to use.

Yacht club instruction can start from $300 a session (2–4 weeks) to over $800 a session. Yacht club memberships often cost around $250 a year, with prices going up significantly as your child gets older.

SKIING

Overview

Skiing has been around for centuries, and continues to grow in popularity, thanks in large part to the extensive media generated during the Winter Olympic Games. Skiing has its roots in Scandinavia and colonized America. Rock carvings found in caves in the Arctic rim show people on skis more than 5,000 years ago. Skis, originally called snowshoes, were used to travel over the deep snow in Norway and Sweden. All these early skis had a boot mounted to the ski at the toe, with the heel free to move up and down. This style of ski is now called a Nordic or cross-country ski. The first organized events in skiing—jumping and a type of cross-country race—started in the early 1800s using Nordic skis.

In the mid-1800s the invention of a heel strap by a Norwegian from the town of Telemark enabled the control necessary for downhill alpine skiing. In the 1850s,

It's interesting to note that there are ski areas located places where it snows very little, if any. There's even a ski area in Alabama! Snowmaking has become quite an art, and all that is needed is water and cold temperatures at night.

—*Steven Dean, alpine skiing instructor, Purgatory Resort, teaching for 11 years*

Ski racing is big in the Pacific Northwest, the Sierras, the Rockies, and in the mountains of the East Coast. Nevertheless, some very good ski racers have come from small hills in the central United States. One of the best in the world, Kristina Koznick, came from Buck Hill, Minnesota, which has about 200 feel of vertical elevation.

—*George Thomas, head coach, Colorado Mountain College Ski Team, and regional coordinator of U.S. Collegiate Ski Association, coaching for over 15 years*

Obviously, when people think of skiing in America, their first thoughts go northeast to New England or west to the Rocky Mountains. Actually, there are resorts as far south along the East Coast as North Carolina. In the upper Midwest, where most folk figure it's just flat as well as cold, there are a good number of places to strap your boards to your feet.

—*Jay Pagluica, Blandford Ski Resort owner and instructor for 20 years*

Scandinavians at California mining camps created straight-ahead downhill racing on 14-foot skis, reportedly reaching over 60 m.p.h. and attracting hundreds of spectators. Alpine skiing debuted at the 1936 Winter Olympics, at the same time as the invention and installation of ski lifts.

Today, there are over 40 million alpine skiers, with 11 million of those in the United States, with skiing popular both as recreation and a competitive sport. Almost every ski resort hosts junior racing teams and competitions. Best of all, skiing has become a popular pastime enjoyed by the entire family.

General Benefits

◉ Provides both aerobic and anaerobic conditioning

◉ Gives the whole body a workout, especially strengthening the legs

◉ Helps kids improve balance and hand-eye coordination

◉ Racing and training in inclement weather builds mental toughness and resilience

◉ Both cross-country and downhill skiing are great family sports. You can enjoy the beauty of the outdoors while getting exercise.

Skiing is truly a family winter sport. It can be an invigorating flight down the bumpy steep slopes or a leisurely scenic tour down every beginner trail on the mountain, but the family can do it together! You get out into the wilderness during a beautiful time of the year and often see mountains with white-capped peaks in the distance. Plus, skiing will turn your child into a lover of the winter season.

—Jay Pagluica, Blandford Ski Resort owner and instructor for 20 years

◉

Physically, ski racing is very demanding. A race itself is usually less than a minute, so it taxes the anaerobic system, and to be successful, athletes need to develop strength, power, agility, coordination, and balance. Many successful ski racers develop a strong aerobic base with cross-country running and track, then gradually turn their focus to developing strength and stamina in activities requiring less volume and more intensity, such as sprints, weight training, and sports such as mountain biking or soccer.

—George Thomas, head coach, Colorado Mountain College Ski Team, and regional coordinator of U.S. Collegiate Ski Association, coaching for over 15 years

Any child can excel at skiing. They just have to want to be there. What's great about skiing is that you don't have to be an athlete to be a great skier.

> —*Shannon McDermott, children's specialist, Ski & Snowboard Schools of Aspen, teaching for 23 years*

Skiing has such diverse aspects that kids who are perfectionists and driven toward accuracy and discipline may head toward racing. There are snowboard half-pipe and terrain parks for those who are more courageous and part of the 'Mountain Dew era,' and there is simple cruising and socializing for those who like the more social or easygoing parts of the sport.

> —*Megan Harvey, instructor trainer, Ski & Snowboard Schools of Aspen, and member of the PSIA National Alpine Team, teaching for 14 years*

In ski racing, success is often measured in hundredths of a second. To find the right combination of equipment, athletic ability, mental preparedness, technical skills, and coaching support to achieve those fine margins of time gained is elusive. For many kids, the sport becomes very frustrating and in the end futile.

> —*George Thomas, head coach, Colorado Mountain College Ski Team, and regional coordinator of U.S. Collegiate Ski Association, coaching for over 15 years*

Kids who excel in skiing develop a "go for it" attitude on the hill. They enjoy endless self-discovery by perfecting the ability to play on their skis or board.

> —*Charlie MacArthur, instructor and trainer, Ski and Snowboarding Schools of Aspen, and member of PSIA Alpine National Demonstration Team, teaching for 23 years*

Independent, fearless, kids whom like being outside do best. But it can take years to become an expert, so don't expect an overnight sensation. If children are having a good time skiing green or blue runs, don't pressure them to go down black runs.

> —*Steven Dean, alpine skiing instructor, Purgatory Resort, teaching for 11 years*

Kids Who Tend to Excel

◉ A skier requires balance, fine motor control in the knees and ankles to steer, and strong leg muscles.

◉ Ski jumping requires strength, technical control, and a certain degree of fearlessness.

◉ Cross-country skiing demands endurance and strength.

Best Age to Start

◉ Most children are not ready to try skiing until age 3 or 4. Resort ski schools generally place the minimum age between 3 and 5, and the children's ski school is a

Our kids started skiing at age 3, but that mostly consisted of getting them all dressed up, and then pulling them along by a pole on their skis. When they were around age 4, we enrolled them in ski school until they got proficient enough to come out on the slopes with my husband and me. We compromised about where we went skiing for many years, going to basically a bump of a mountain. We stayed at this very small ski area until our kids became good enough skiers to take them to a larger ski resort with the kind of skiing we most enjoyed.

   —*Sheri, mom of Allison, 11, and Eric, 9*

My husband and I are avid skiers, and it was important to us that our kids become passionate about skiing too. Even before age 3, we had them enrolled in ski school. We found that our kids were so much better at taking instruction from someone other than their parents.

   —*Lisa, mom of CJ, 10, and Maddie, 8*

Between ages 11 and 12, the kids with talent start to break out of the pack. By the time children move into the 13- to 14-year-old age group, future U.S. Ski Team members start to make their presence felt, even though a spot on the U.S. Ski Team is still five or more years away.

   —*George Thomas, head coach, Colorado Mountain College Ski Team, and regional coordinator of*
      U.S. Collegiate Ski Association, coaching for over 15 years

We started skiing as a family when our youngest kids were 4 years old, and we think it has been so worth the investment of time and expense. It took them three years until they were able to ski well on their own, and now we can all go out together and hit the slopes as a family.

—*Dean, dad of Evan, 10, and Olivia, Justin, and Shelby, 8*

combination of introduction to skiing, play in the snow, and childcare. Before that, many parents will take children out themselves on the beginner hill.

Your child needs sufficient motor skills and strength to control the direction of her skis, turn them into a wedge in order to make turns and control speed, and stay on balance. Make sure your child is physically strong enough to walk around in skis and boots, and can last at least one hour outside in the snow and cold. Being ready to ski also depends on your child's attention span, stamina, willingness to fall down in the snow, and the desire to just try it.

Ski racing can start as early as 8 years old, but most successful athletes begin their ski racing careers typically at the ages of 9 and 10.

Nordic, or cross-country, skiing, can start between the ages of 4 and 7, although most kids do not start until around age 10.

What to Look For When Getting Started

Look for a program with staff who specifically works with children and is affiliated with the Professional Ski Instructors of America (PSIA). Try to avoid a ski school that uses its children's program to train adult instructors.

A children's ski school should have a separate beginner's teaching area from the slopes, with a relatively flat or gently sloped terrain.

The teaching area should be filled with colorful props and teaching aids, ranging from cones to structures to ski around or through.

PRIVATE VS. GROUP LESSONS

Skiing professionals recommend investing in lessons for your child even if you are an experienced skier. For a beginner ski lesson, a half-day program is plenty. In

Skiing isn't for everyone, and some kids don't like the cold weather. A new pair of gloves, jacket, or boot heaters may solve the problem. Others don't like the peer pressure and can feel embarrassed that they can't keep up with the group. In this case, a child should be moved to another group where they feel more comfortable. A good instructor should be able to spot these problems and tell you.

—*Steven Dean, alpine skiing Instructor, Purgatory Resort, teaching for 11 years*

Investment in a conveyor belt–type lift (commonly called a flying or magic carpet) shows that a school has a commitment to teaching children. The teaching area and personnel should give you a secure feeling.

—*Mark Spieler, supervisor, Mammoth Mountain Sports School, teaching for 25 seasons*

It is always good if the kids' ski school has a well-groomed adequate-sized beginner area. There should be terrain features, flags, objects, and carpets set up for kids to use in a lesson.

—*John Armstrong, president of Professional Ski Instructors of America, teaching for 30 years*

Smaller resorts tend to have much more affordable program costs and make your child feel at home with small groups in a small facility. Once your child is comfortable with that, then take a trip to a large resort.

—*Eliza Kuntz, director, Montana's Red Lodge Mountain Resort Snowboard & Ski School, teaching for 13 years*

beginner lessons, your child will become comfortable with the equipment, work on a wedge turn and snowplow stop, and ride a chair lift. Most lessons start children off without ski poles. Children's instructors often use descriptions like "make your skis into a pizza" or "make your skis like French fries" to teach snowplowing and skiing parallel.

❦ Many kids prefer group lessons because they enjoy being with a sibling, friend, or peer group.

Check the group size. At weekends and holidays some schools need to make larger class groups in order to accommodate as many guests in lessons as possible. At those times a private lesson in the morning may be best, and then you can ski or ride with your child later in the day. Be sure to ask the instructor what the child was able to achieve, and what they are working on now. The instructors should be able to give you a couple of movements and concepts to work on with your child. (If they can't, it would be good to try another instructor.)

—*John Armstrong, president of Professional Ski Instructors of America, teaching skiing for 30 years*

Group lessons offer social interaction, but even more, they offer a chance for kids to see other kids their age trying new things. I find children try things more freely and willingly in a group lesson.

—*Megan Harvey, instructor trainer, Ski & Snowboard Schools of Aspen, and member of the PSIA National Alpine Team, teaching for 14 years*

I highly encourage private lessons. I personally find I can teach 100% more to kids when I am working one-on-one, and even small groups are hard. Some kids feel frustrated, alone, and overwhelmed in a group lesson, while others feel more challenged by trying to keep up with the group. Certification is a nice thing to look for in instructors. However, most instructors move up through ski school ranks to become certified later on. While it may be important for an instructor to have a goal of becoming certified at some point, only about 19% of kids' instructors will be certified, so this should not be a concern when looking for a program for children.

—*Kent Bry, director, Adventure Ski and Snowboard School, teaching for 30 years*

I always recommend a one-on-one lesson for all children ages 3–6 who are trying skiing for the first time. This private instruction is well worth the extra money, and you can choose which instructor will teach your child. Ski instructors today are trained not only in ski technique, but also in child psychology and physiology, as well as lift safety and first aid. They are professionals in group dynamics and understand the disparate learning styles of the different age groups.

—*Eliza Kuntz, director, Montana's Red Lodge Mountain Resort Snowboard & Ski School, teaching for 13 years*

The group lessons that I find most successful for the younger set (ages 3–6) have indoor facilities for breaks and lunch. They need low student/teacher ratios, with only three or four children to one instructor. They also need beginner areas separate from the main stream of traffic with lots of flat terrain for learning the basics, gentle slopes, and easy-access beginner lifts like handle tows. Very young children, exceptionally coordinated children, and shy children can benefit from private lessons, which allow for more attention and feedback.

—Alison Clayton, coordinator, PSIA Children's Program, and ski instructor at Vermont's Stratton Mountain, teaching for 23 years

---

✦ If your child has a difficult time in a large group environment, it may be worth investing in a couple of private lessons with a children's ski instructor. The private lessons will often accelerate the learning curve.

JOINING A SKI TEAM

✦ The U.S. Ski and Snowboard Association (USSA), the governing agency for ski racing in the United States, offers opportunities to compete from age 5 upward. Kids can start NASTAR, another form of mountain racing, which is inexpensive and an excellent means of testing the waters, at under 4 years of age.

✦ Most ski areas have their own ski and snowboard teams, and usually open their doors for kids around ages 8–10. These teams teach the very basics of racing competition. As your child's skills improve, she can move toward more competitive teams, both locally or at the bigger mountain resorts.

Most Popular Kinds of Skiing Competitions
ALPINE SKIING

✦ *Downhill.* Skiers go down a specific course with gates that must be skied around and jumps to go over without falling. The fastest time determines who wins. Downhill skiing features the longest course and the highest speeds in alpine skiing.

✦ *Slalom.* Shorter than the downhill course. Skiers have more short, quick turns around as many as 75 gates. Each skier makes runs down two different courses on the same slope. Both runs take place on the same day. The times are added together, and the skier with fastest total time wins.

✦ *Giant slalom.* A tougher and steeper course than slalom, with fewer gates and wider, smoother turns. The competition runs the same as the slalom.

✦ *Super giant slalom.* A mix of downhill and giant slalom that combines the speed of downhill with the precise turns of giant slalom. Each skier makes one run down the course, and the fastest time wins.

NORDIC SKIING

✦ Cross-country involves long, thin skis and hiking-type boots attached to the ski only by a front binding. It provides an intense aerobic workout. In the classic style, the skier uses a back-and-forth motion to move, while in skating style the skier pushes out to the side like an ice skater. You can cross-country ski just about anywhere there is snow, from parks to golf courses. There are lots of competitions for juniors, and the fastest time wins.

✦ In ski jumping, skiers take off from a ramp and are judged for distance, style, technique, and landing standing up. It is an event requiring both fearlessness and elegance.

✦ Nordic combined mixes ski jumping with cross-country skiing, and traces its roots back 5,000 years to Norway.

Ski racing programs can introduce fun events that are timed or scored when kids are around 8 years of age. Racing becomes a little more competitive at ages 10–12, and very competitive at age 14, and coaches can tell if the athletes have a true talent for it.

—John Armstrong, president of Professional Ski Instructors of America, teaching skiing for 30 years

In ski racing, there are no second chances, no teammates to pick up the slack, no rebounds, overtimes, or late innings. Step up to the gate and it's all on the line. Ages 8–12, the muscle memory years, are critical to lay a foundation and for a good racer to pick up the fundamental stance and mechanics that will be automatic at age 25.

—Shep Snow, director of the Independence Ski Racing Team and owner of The Snow School, coaching for 7 years

Ski racing is an individual sport, just one person against the clock, but with few exceptions, it is practiced in a team environment. Consequently, the sport breeds competitiveness and the will to win on the part of the individual, but this is molded within the context of a team working together.

—*George Thomas, head coach, Colorado Mountain College Ski Team, and regional coordinator of U.S. Collegiate Ski Association, coaching for over 15 years*

Keep in mind that ski racing is really not a "team sport," although your child may be a part of the team. A team's overall score may make them winners, but only one skier takes first place. So you can be "beaten" by your own teammates in a competition, and for some kids that can be hard to take.

—*Steven Dean, alpine skiing instructor, Purgatory Resort, teaching for 11 years*

Nordic skiing is a sport for all ages but in order to compete requires countless hours of practice. An athlete heading down that road would have to prepare for training every day for at least a decade and be an aerobic "mutant" in order to reach a competitive level. Needless to say, you have to be very strong mentally. You have to like spending time with yourself, having only a beating heart as your training partner. It is a sport where you have to be so disciplined that you will go out and exercise no matter if it is raining, hailing, or storming. Results only come as a consequence of total commitment and persistence.

—*Knut Nystad, University of Denver head cross-country skiing Nordic coach for 8 years*

FREESTYLE SKIING

🌀 Freestyle skiing developed in America in the 1960s, and was originally a mixture of alpine skiing and acrobatics. The International Ski Federation (FIS) recognized freestyle as a sport in 1979, and today it has become an Olympic sport.

🌀 Ballet is a routine of jumps, spins, and steps set to music.

🌀 Moguls involve stunts performed on a steep course with two jumps and many moguls between the jumps.

🌀 Aerials are acrobatic moves, stunts, and flips set to music.

Safety and Injury Concerns

🌀 Each year more than 40,000 skiing-related injuries to children under age 15 are treated in hospital emergency rooms. The most common skiing-related injuries are knee, ankle, wrist, and finger sprains and fractures, as well as head injuries.

🌀 Your child should wear a specially designed ski helmet to prevent or lessen head injuries from falls and collisions.

🌀 Goggles help protect eyes and enhance visibility, depending on the weather.

🌀 Bindings are designed to release during a fall and should be set based on your child's weight and ability. Have a ski shop check to ensure that your child's ski bindings are properly adjusted.

🌀 Teach your child to watch out for rocks and patches of ice, always stay on marked trails, and take easy trails at the end of the day when being tired leads to most injuries.

Helmets are a must. In addition, kids should be kept under control. Kids don't always realize the risks surrounding them. Be aware that altitude sickness can also be a problem.

　　—*Larry Wren, instructor, Breckenridge Ski Resort, teaching for 8 years*

🌀

Skiing is a gravity sport that requires balance while traveling at high speeds. Falls are inevitable, and with them come all the varied kinds and degrees of trauma injuries. Superior ski-binding design has virtually eliminated most broken legs, which are more apt to come from collisions with trees or obstacles. On the other hand, ruptured ligaments have become much more common, and while relatively painless, usually require surgery and a long rehabilitation process before returning to skiing.

　　—*George Thomas, head coach, Colorado Mountain College Ski Team, and regional coordinator of U.S. Collegiate Ski Association, coaching for over 15 years*

🍁 Frostbite can be an issue when the temperature drops low, and often it is much colder at the top of the mountain than at the base lifts. Dress your child warmly, in layers, and in clothing that allows her to move freely. Mittens keep fingers warmer than gloves, and waterproof ones are a necessity. Snow pants keep legs from getting wet and cold. A hat is essential, as most body heat gets lost through one's head.

🍁 Have your child use sunscreen, as it's easy to get sunburned from the sun reflecting off the snow.

Cost Considerations

🍁 Between lessons, lift tickets, clothing, transportation, food on the mountain, and equipment, skiing quickly adds up to an expensive sport.

🍁 Lift tickets often cost around $35 a day for your child, but can run upward of $55. Check to see if you can buy cheaper lift tickets off-site. If your family or child is really committed to skiing, look into buying a season pass. Look for "learn to ski" packages. Most start around $50 for a lift/lesson/rental ticket and should include a complete rental package, a group lesson, and a lift ticket for the day. Multi-day packages are often available for even greater savings.

🍁 Renting equipment often makes the most sense for your child, as she will likely outgrow her gear each year. When just starting out, rent from the ski resort so that you can exchange boots that your child finds uncomfortable and have bindings adjusted or fixed for free. Get there early to avoid crowds at the rental shop. Rentals run about $15–$25 a day.

🍁 You can even lease a package of skis, boots, and poles from a ski shop for an entire season, often for around $150–$200. The advantage of renting from a ski shop near your home is that the ski shop at resorts often gets crowded, and it can take a lot of time if you're just there for the day to get equipment fitted and rented.

🍁 A beginner's ski, boots, and pole package of new equipment starts at around $300.

🍁 Once your child becomes a skilled skier, boots alone can run between $100 and $600. Look for boots with front entry buckles, as they provide the best support and greatest mobility. With your child wearing one medium-weight pair of socks, there should still be enough room in the boot for her toes to wiggle.

🍁 Skis and bindings start around $250 and can exceed $1,000 for high-end equipment. Shorter skis are easier for your child to control. Look for skis that reach between your child's chin and nose. Parabolic skis with a narrow middle and wide tips and tails enable easier turns. Your child won't need ski poles until she uses the chair lift and has mastered turning. The right height for poles is determined by having your child stand gripping the poles upside down with the grips touching the floor. Have your child grasp the pole just below the basket and choose a height where elbows form a 90-degree angle and forearms are parallel to the floor.

The costs of ski racing can be very exorbitant as athletes develop. For younger kids, many regions stipulate that racers can only use one pair of skis for all events. As kids mature, they will need multiple pairs of skis for the different events, plus training skis. Serious junior racers attend summer race camps such as at Mount Hood in Oregon and Whistler in British Columbia. When you tally equipment, coaching, travel, race entry fees, food, and camps, you can anticipate a typical child age 13 to 14 needing a budget of around $2,000–$3,000 or more for a full season of racing and training. Older children can easily run up bills of more than $10,000. For the talented few, athletes who demonstrate outstanding skills and achievement, more and more of their costs for equipment, various races, and projects will be underwritten by their division or region as they approach criteria for making the U.S. Ski Team.

 —*George Thomas, head coach, Colorado Mountain College Ski Team, and regional coordinator of U.S. Collegiate Ski Association, coaching for over 15 years*

Racing team programs have tuition fees from $700 to $3,000, which includes coaching and lift pass. While equipment can be bought used at around $100, it can cost as much as $3,000 new. On top of that, your child will have race and traveling expenses. It adds up quickly.

 —*Kyle Crezee, director and head coach, Tahoe's Northstar Ski and Snowboard Team Race Team, teaching for 10 years*

Ski racing becomes very expensive at age 13. The competition changes and athletes must train three to four days a week to be competitive. Everyone has multiple sets of skis, and travel requirements increase in frequency and distance. Have your child ski on used gear until reaching the elite levels of competition. Perfectly good one-year-old race gear is available at ski swaps at up to 40% off the cost of new equipment.

 —*Shep Snow, director of the Independence Ski Racing Team and owner of The Snow School, coaching for 7 years*

✦ Cross-country costs less than downhill skiing, as you do not have to pay lift fees. You have to pay trial fees instead, with an annual pass usually costing between $50 and $150. Purchasing equipment costs $300–$400, and up to $1,500 for an advanced skier. Clothing can range from $100 to $500.

✦ If you want new equipment for your child, the best discounts are usually at the end of the ski season in March and April, when shops want to clear out merchandise. If you do buy skis for your child, make sure to get them waxed and the edges sharpened in a once-a-season tune-up. Look for a ski shop trying to unload some of "last year's gear."

✦ Used gear and equipment leases can be found at most ski shops, which your child can use for a season or two before growing out of it. Another option to save money is to buy used equipment at a local ski shop or ski swap.

✦ Also consider the cost of getting to the snow, such as gas, lift tickets, and hotel costs if going overnight.

SNOWBOARDING

Overview

Emerging as *the* winter sport, snowboarding has often been called "skateboarding on snow," as many snowboarders perform daredevil jumps and other tricks off half-pipes on downhill ski slopes. Snowboarding is a sport that combines elements of surfing, skateboarding, and skiing. It developed in the mid-1960s with a short, thin board with a rope attached at the nose without bindings. In the late 1970s, snowboarding became popular and snowboarders began to "invade" traditional ski resorts, often meeting opposition from skiers, who tried to exclude the snowboarders from the mountain.

The snowboarders who first hit the slopes were primarily rebellious teenagers, and a major culture clash erupted between skiers and snowboarders. Competitions began in the 1980s, when board-construction technology had evolved to the point that snowboarders had the necessary control over the board to carve turns and do tricks. By the 1990s, almost all ski resorts accepted snowboarding. Snowboarding made its Olympic debut in 1998 with alpine and freestyle competitions for both men and women. It returned to the 2002 Winter Olympics in Salt Lake City with two events, the half-pipe and parallel giant slalom.

Snowboarding is now one of the fastest-growing sports in America.

Approximately 30% of all lift tickets in North America are sold to snowboarders, and snowboarding continues to soar in popularity with children. In addition to the formation of the American Association of Snowboard Instructors (AASI), which certifies instructors, the Professional Ski Instructors Association has also created a snowboard instructor certification program that has led to newborn respect for the sport and an increasing number of adult converts. One of the great things about snowboarding is that it doesn't have to be competitive. Snowboarding is fairly easy to learn, and almost every ski resort now offers it.

Introducing your kids to snowboarding is a great luxury, as playing together on a ski hill is one of the best family activities I can think of and involves spending time in a truly magical place.

—*Greg Daniells, Whistler Snowboard Camp owner and instructor for 16 years*

Besides the fresh air and exercise, kids gain camaraderie with other snowboarders, balance, muscle control, as well as a sense of adventure, excitement, self-achievement, and fun.

—*Shaun Cattanach, AASI National Team member and examiner, resort project manager for Burton Snowboards, teaching for 13 years*

Snowboarding is a great activity that promotes individuality, athleticism, coordination, and social skills. Most important, it gets kids outside, away from television and video games, and engages them in a sport that lasts a lifetime.

—*Lane Clegg, supervisor, Snowbird Mountain School, and member of the National Snowboard Demonstration Team, teaching for 16 years*

There once was a quote from a famous snowboarder, Craig Kelly, who said, "I know a lot of people who used to ski, but I don't know anyone who used to snowboard."

—*Tom Collins, executive director of the U.S. Amateur Snowboard Association (USASA)*

General Benefits

- Improves strength, cardiovascular fitness, agility, balance, and athleticism
- Develops a positive attitude and persistence

Kids Who Tend to Excel

- Snowboarding requires muscle strength, stamina, and aerobic fitness.
- It relies on hip and knee movements to steer and complete turns, so leg muscles need to be strong.
- Balance is important.

Kids who excel at snowboarding tend to be active, physically fit people. Kids who like skateboarding, wake boarding, surfing, or mountain biking, usually *love* snowboarding.

—*John Tickner, training director, Mount Hood Meadows Ski and Snowboard School, and snowboard chairman for the Northwest Division of AASI, teaching for 15 years*

You don't need to be tall or fast or strong to snowboard. You just need basic balance and a desire to have fun. Snowboarding is hip, cool, and stimulates kids to get out and be active.

—*J. Randy Price, coach of the AASI national snowboard team, teaching snowboarding for 18 years*

Kids who do best are comfortable outdoors, love an adrenaline rush, are persistent, athletic, and have a positive attitude!

—*Greg Daniells, Whistler Snowboard Camp owner and*

Best Age to Start

- While your child may be able to start skiing as young as 3, snowboarding should be started several years later, because it requires more muscle strength and coordination. Unlike skiing, your child cannot simply slide straight on a snowboard, but instead must have strong enough muscles to turn the board. In addition, learning to snowboard demands a great deal of focus and attention from your child.

- Most programs begin offering snowboarding lessons for children as young as age 5, but most children lack the control and coordination needed until ages 7–10. The advantage of starting snowboarding when your child is young is that he doesn't have too far to fall, has little or no concept of fear, and has relatively few inhibitions.

I do not feel kids 7 or under should start off snowboarding, though many express an interest in it. Your child should learn to ski first. Ankle flexibility is vital in snowboarding, and kids under 7 can't do this as well. Also, the upper body develops before the lower body, so this throws kids off balance when snowboarding too early. By age 7 or 8, if kids want to snowboard, there is no reason why they need to ski first, although they will still have an easier time if they have first had some skiing experience.

—Kent Bry, director, Adventure Ski and Snowboard School, teaching for 30 years

The best age to start your child snowboarding is about 8 years old. Because of the way kids develop physically, younger kids have difficulty with some of the movements needed to move sideways. That's not to say that very young kids can't have fun. They will just need an adult helper to get around, get in and out of their bindings, and move across the flats.

—John Tickner, training director, Mount Hood Meadows Ski and Snowboard School, snowboard chairman for the Northwest Division of AASI, teaching for 15 years

What to Look For When Getting Started

🍀 Many ski resorts provide all-day or half-day lessons for all levels and abilities. Private lessons and specialty workshops are also available if your child wants individual attention or to specialize in one area of the sport.

🍀 The caliber of a snowboard school is a function of the quality of the staff. Ask if the staff is experienced working with children, and has been certified by either AASI or PSIA. Both organizations offer an ACE (Advanced Children's Educator) certification. Look for an instructor who works specifically with your child's age group.

🍀 Lessons should include basic skills such as edging, how to apply appropriate pressure to the board, and steering. If your child does not know how the edges of a snowboard work, he can take some pretty hard falls from catching the downhill edge and eventually become very frustrated. In the beginning, your child will need to determine his stance on the board. Most riders board with their left foot forward. However, some snowboarders go "goofy," leading with their right foot. The instructor can help your child find his best lead foot to gain maximum control and comfort. Lessons speed your child's progress and ensure his skills are solid.

Ask to see where the kids are taught. It should be an area that seems safe, relatively large, and open, not a narrow trail that simply was not being used. Remember, snowboarding is more about fun than proficiency. If at the end of the day your child still can't turn but had a fabulous time, then it was a great day. Everyone learns at their own pace. Learning to ride should not be looked at as a path to competition. Snowboarding is one of the few sports where the top riders are not racers, they're just out there having fun.

—*J. Randy Price, coach of the AASI national snowboard team, teaching snowboarding for 18 years*

Snowboarding can be overwhelming, and a good instructor makes all the difference in the world. Look for an instructor who's friendly, safety-oriented, professional, patient, and properly certified.

—*Greg Daniells, Whistler Snowboard Camp owner and instructor for 16 years*

Private lessons are a great way to begin the learning process. The one-on-one instruction helps your child progress quickly with the least frustration. However, private lessons are often expensive, and beyond the first few times a student goes out, a class lesson can be the most entertaining for kids. They get the camaraderie of riding with other students their own age and often develop friendships that last over time. I recommend a smaller class, something around six or fewer children for the best lesson. Once a child has reached a competent level of riding, he may desire additional coaching in specific areas like a half-pipe or gates in order to be a good candidate for competition.

—*Lane Clegg, supervisor, Snowbird Mountain School, and member of the National Snowboard Demonstration Team, teaching for 16 years*

The USASA is introducing a new division for training snowboard instructors and coaches, so look for instructors wearing a USASA Trainer pin. Once kids have mastered the basics of riding and show the ability to think several turns ahead of them, they will be able to come to any of over 350 local USASA events across the country, with kids starting as early as age 6.

—*Tom Collins, executive director of the U.S. Amateur Snowboard Association (USASA)*

🐟 Your child has to persevere through the intense initial stages of learning. Snowboarding is not as easy as it looks, and your child will need determination to succeed. Usually it will take a child one to three days to get the basics down.

Competitive Snowboarding

🐟 Most children who decide to compete move into competitive programs between 10 and 16 years old. Snowboarding has two basic disciplines: racing and freestyle.

🐟 Snowboard racing is similar to skiing, and racers compete in the slalom and giant slalom events. Giant slalom parallels its skiing counterpart. In parallel slalom and parallel giant slalom, two snowboarders race down parallel racecourses of identical design. The fastest total time over one run on each course advances to the next round, and eventually determines the winner. In "snowboard cross," each heat consists of 4–6 snowboarders racing pack-style down the same course, with the first two finishers advancing to the next round. The event is fast, with lots of action and contact.

🐟 Freestyle is divided into two disciplines: slope-style and half-pipe. In slope-style, the snowboarder rides down the slope, performing as many tricks as possible over natural and man-made obstacles such as rails, bumps, and other barriers. Half-pipe is an acrobatic, ballet-like event, conducted in a U-shaped tube, which is several hundred feet long, and bounded by two steep parallel walls of ice. Judges rate the snowboarder's performances, similar to skiing freestyle competitions.

Amateur snowboard competitions are broken down into age groups, so kids as young as 9 or 10 can compete with their peers. Don't push the competitive aspects, though. Snowboarding is all about freedom, fun, and self-expression, which can take a back seat when competition becomes the focus.

—*John Tickner, training director, Mount Hood Meadows Ski and Snowboard School, snowboard chairman for the Northwest Division of AASI, teaching for 15 years*

There are certain beginner or novice injuries, but if you stay within your abilities, most people will be fine. Knowing mountain safety etiquette is key.

—*Greg Daniells, Whistler Snowboard Camp owner and instructor for 16 years*

Safety and Injury Concerns

🐟 Snowboarding has a slightly higher risk of injury than skiing. While skiers tend to have more knee and leg injuries, snowboarders typically suffer from arm, wrist, and shoulder trauma.

✦ The risk of injury is higher for beginner snowboarders, who are more vulnerable to falling over. Risks can be reduced by having your child wear wrist guards and kneepads.

✦ Your child should always wear a helmet to prevent head injuries from falls or collisions. Using a helmet can prevent or reduce the severity of more than half of the head injuries to children younger than 15 years old.

✦ Goggles will also help protect your child's eyes from flying debris and enable him to see the terrain better.

Cost Considerations

✦ In terms of cost, snowboarding and skiing are on a par. Snowboarding is not a cheap sport after adding up the cost of the clothing, equipment, and lift tickets.

✦ Most resorts have beginner packages that include rental equipment, lessons, and lift tickets. These can range in price from $20 to $100 for anywhere from an hour to a full day of snowboard lessons.

✦ A lesson price can vary greatly, but expect to pay between $100 and $150 for a full-day lesson, which includes a lift ticket and equipment.

THE BOARD

✦ Snowboards are made of a wooden core wrapped in fiberglass and coated in a fiberglass or plastic cap with metal edges, and vary in size and shape. The performance of a snowboard is influenced by a combination of factors, including stiffness, length, weight, and shape.

✦ Your child's board length will depend on his weight, riding style, and the type of conditions he will ride in most often. In terms of height, your child's board should reach between his armpits and chin. The waist width of the board will depend on the size of his feet.

✦ Renting is a great option while your child is still deciding whether snowboarding will be a passing phase or a winter obsession. Some resorts will even offer bundle rental packages with a lift ticket and beginner lesson. You can rent equipment for your child by the day or week, which is highly recommended for novices. In addition, some ski shops will apply the price of rentals toward purchasing new equipment. Some ski shops offer the option of leasing equipment for an entire season, which is beneficial to children, who quickly outgrow gear.

✦ If your child wants to stick with it, avoid the temptation to buy everything slightly larger so he can grow into it, as this will make snowboarding much harder to learn correctly. When purchasing a snowboard for a child, consider the following:

➤ A shorter board is easier to handle. The longer the board, the faster your child will be able to go.

➤ Your child's toes and heels should reach the edges of the board, which makes it easier for him to turn the board on the snow.

➤ Your child's snowboard should be flexible to help make turning easier on snow.

➤ A racing board has a flat tail and rounded tip, as only forward momentum comes into play. Freestyle boards have both ends rounded to accommodate forward and backward riding used in half-pipes as well as around obstacles.

✦ Spending $500–$1,000 for a new snowboard is average.

✦ When you finally decide to purchase equipment for your child, you can go to a local ski shop or snowboard swap and buy used equipment to cut back on costs. However, stay away from garage sales and be careful at ski swaps, because you may wind up with gear that is outdated and inappropriate.

✦ There are four basic types of snowboards once your child gets more advanced:

➤ A free-ride board is easy to learn on and can be used anywhere on the mountain. If your child wants to ride many different types of terrain in various snow conditions and spends most of his time on the ground, then free-ride is the board of choice. Often called all-mountain boards, these versatile boards have directional shapes and a varying flex.

➤ If your child wants to go anywhere and do anything, then a freestyle board could be the best choice for him. A freestyle board allows a snowboarder to go forward or backward, in powder or hard-pack, and in the air or on the snow. The freestyle board has a directional shape with a longer tip that helps with flotation in choppy snow, along with a stiffer tail for more power. Freestyle races are judged based on a point system, similar to freestyle skiing competitions.

➤ For a child who loves "getting air," performing jumps, and mastering complicated spins and tricks, then a technical freestyle board may be right for him. This type of board has twin tips, which means that it has an identical blunt tip and tail shape for riding forward or backward.

➤ A free-carving, or alpine, board, tends to be the stiffest, narrowest type of board. The front of the board curves, while the tail lies flat. Although stable at high speeds, the free-carving board is not used for performing tricks or all-around riding. This board will allow the rider to go really fast and lay down inch-deep tracks on hard-pack or groomed snow.

BOOTS

✦ Riders wear boots specifically designed for snowboarding, and their feet are attached to the board with bindings that typically strap across each boot. Boots cost between $170 and $220.

❧ Your child will struggle with turns if the boots do not fit correctly. Boots should fit snugly enough that your child cannot slide his foot around or lift his heels, but not too tight that the boots compress his toes. Make sure your child walks around in the boots after trying them on in the store. If he walks stiffly, the boots are probably reaching too high up the calf. Kids should be able to walk in snowboard boots and be comfortable.

❧ Look for a simple boot for your child, such as one with a single lace or velcro. Small hands wrapped in mittens often have trouble with complicated laces out on the mountain. Your child should be able to put on his boots and strap them into their bindings by himself.

❧ Most children between the ages of 5 and 7 haven't developed enough coordination to use both edges of the snowboard and need a pair of hard boots to help protect the ankles and enable them to use the toe-side edge of their boards. Another advantage of hard boots is that children will be able to get in and out of his snowboard by themselves, which at this level really helps to promote independence.

❧ Unlike ski bindings, snowboard bindings do not release when your child falls. Always make sure that his boots are compatible with his board and bindings, and the style of riding he will be doing. Freestyle, free-ride, and technical freestyle snowboarding require soft boots. The support from soft boots comes from the rigid structure of the high-back or low-back bindings into which your child will strap his boots. Soft boots give a snowboarder greater flexibility. Free-carve and alpine snowboarders wear hard boots with a more rigid, plastic shell that lock into plate bindings. These hard boots keep a snowboarder steadier and increase control on high-speed turns.

Clothing should be loose-fitting (to allow for layering and unrestricted movement) and waterproof. Hats should be fleece or wool. Gloves should be waterproof and insulated. Socks should be a synthetic or wool blend. Good eye protection that fits is important all the time in the mountains. Boards should come up to about the chin and should be flexible enough so that the child can bend the board when standing on it.

—*Earl Saline, AASI Demonstration Team member, snowboard assistant manager for Winter Park Ski and Snowboard School, teaching for 12 years*

SOCCER

Overview

Soccer has emerged as the most popular and fastest-growing youth sport in America, with more than 40 million children now playing youth soccer annually in leagues and organized programs. Soccer is the second most popular American sport for boys, second only to baseball, and has become the number one sport for girls. By 1998, 41% of all U.S. players were female. In the past ten years, soccer participation has dramatically increased all the way to the high school level, with 76% more kids playing soccer than any other high school sport. There are also 204 countries in soccer's governing body, FIFA (Federation Internationale de Football Association)—more countries than in the United Nations.

One reason soccer has become such a popular sport is that it is easy to learn and does not require much in terms of equipment. Most children already know how to run and kick a ball, and the object of knocking the ball through a goal is simple to understand. Soccer is also truly a team sport, and only the goalie is subject to individual scrutiny, as she attempts to prevent the ball from entering the goal.

Youth soccer leagues have become so pervasive that the term "soccer mom" has become embedded in our vocabulary, conjuring up images of suburban moms shuttling kids to and from practices and games. Soccer is also an international phenomenon. Soccer's popularity has created intense competition starting in the elementary grades as children try out for traveling and competitive teams. So many kids want to play that fields, referees, and qualified coaches can be hard to find. Team selection and playing time are based on subjective decisions by coaches.

General Benefits

◉ Soccer is the ultimate starter sport, with various formats offered to children, including small-sided fields and smaller-sided teams.

◉ Soccer improves muscular strength, endurance, joint flexibility, cardiovascular fitness, coordination, agility, and balance.

◉ It also improves mental focus and strategic thinking.

◉ Soccer teaches teamwork and the ability to work with others while constantly moving. Because passing the ball is essential to a team's success, players must communicate well and be consistently aware of their team members' whereabouts on the field. Even though more accomplished players will likely handle the ball more

With only one ball to share among 22 possible players, kids gain a sense of teamwork. Since there are no timeouts, it gives the kid a sense of leadership throughout the game and ability to be proactive and creative within the rules of the game.

—*Nat Gonzalez, University of California, Riverside, men's head soccer coach for 13 years*

As a constantly moving contact game with limited substitutions, a flow and a rhythm develops that makes soccer a unique game. Of all the sports, soccer is one of the best for players because there is so little coaching done during the game. The players must implement the tactics they have learned through the years based on their own individual skills on the ball.

—*Jimmy Young, boys' youth soccer head coach and former varsity high school coach*

Soccer has four fundamental elements: technical (what you can do with the ball); tactical (your thinking and how you understand the game); fitness (endurance, coordination, agility, and speed); and mental/psychological (coachability and resilience). Good soccer players excel at all of these. With little kids, the ones who look sharp are those who are well-coordinated and fast, and people will say, "Wow, what a great player." These children may score more goals and look very dominant, but then in two to three years everyone's caught up with them in coordination and speed, and they find that they're either not extraordinary or have fallen behind. A famous approach used by a Holland team involves thinking of soccer in terms of "TIIPS"—technique, insight, intelligence, personality, and speed. Yet that same team scouts kids backward by "SPIIT": looking for those who are fast, confident, and charismatic, and figuring that they can give them the technique and skills needed. Great soccer players have to be pretty fast and have personality, and the rest comes with great coaching.

—*Dean Conway, state head coach and director of coaching for Mass. Youth Soccer Association*

Soccer is the ultimate team game. It's literally impossible for a single player to dominate the game, as there are usually 11 players on each side. One of the more interesting facets of soccer is that individual statistics aren't that meaningful. For example, the player who shoots a goal may have had the least actual contribution to the team's scoring. If you look at European sports pages, such as the London *Times*, the articles on soccer focus on the writer's view of how well individual players performed in the game and contributed to the team's overall effort rather than being filled with facts about goals scored.

—*Ron, nationally licensed youth soccer coach and dad of two, ages 10 and 8*

than others, every child is able to be involved in the action and contribute.

@ Many children learn determination from soccer, starting out frustrated when someone steals the ball from them, then learning to hustle to get it back. Eventually kids learn how to get right back up after having been knocked down without looking for a parent's shoulder to cry on.

@ An abundant number of programs exist to provide opportunities for many children, and are able to accommodate players with different athletic abilities and skills.

@ Soccer has also become a lifetime sport with people well into their sixties playing recreational soccer.

Kids Who Tend to Excel

@ Virtually all children can learn to play soccer, whatever their physical abilities may be, which accounts for the sport's wide appeal. Though having some height can be an advantage, smaller players can use skill, agility, and intelligence to outplay a stronger player. Muscle tone and muscle strength both matter, but the most critical attributes are speed and the ability to sprint.

The most successful soccer players are good athletes with lots of speed and foot quickness and a strong desire to learn and grasp the mental part of the game as well as the physical. They also must be able to make snap decisions and be somewhat of a risk taker.

—*Joseph D'Amato, Jr., middle school assistant principal, coaching soccer for 15 years*

Kids who excel have a desire to succeed, discipline in terms of physical conditioning, a willingness to work on individual soccer skills on their own time, and enjoy every minute they are playing.

—*John Starr, head girls' coach, Franklin Heights High School, coaching for 15 years*

@ Soccer does not require strength, height, or size, but rather speed, coordination, balance, eye-foot skills, cardiovascular fitness, and endurance.

@ Your child should also be appropriately aggressive for the level at which she is playing. She should be moving to a loose ball, kicking the ball hard, but never knocking down the other players.

@ The best players are generally regarded as the team leaders.

@ Coaches find radically shifting skill levels in soccer as children go through puberty, as some players slow down or are outplayed by their peers who have grown.

Best Age to Start

© Soccer is a great starting sport for younger children, as the rules are easy to grasp, and it doesn't take long to learn the basic skills. Unlike baseball or basketball where hand-eye coordination is so important, kids can start kicking a soccer ball around as soon as they can run. In addition, younger soccer leagues make it easier for your child to play the game, as there are only 3 or 4 players per team on the field for recreational play and 6 players for traveling teams. Eventually, your child will work her way up to play the official 11-sided soccer.

© Most children start playing organized soccer around first or second grade or ages 6–7, as that is when they begin to understand both the rules of the game and the techniques and strategies involved. At this age, children play on a smaller field, usually about a third or half the size of a full soccer field.

© Still, preschool soccer programs have now become the hot new league sport. But when deciding to sign your child up for a sport at such a young age, make sure she is ready for group play; you don't want to turn her off to the sport by signing her up too early.

© Before signing your child up for soccer, ask yourself whether she is physically ready to play. If your child hasn't developed the coordination to kick a ball, she may get so frustrated that she will want to hang up her cleats forever.

© Most soccer coaches believe that parents should wait until their kids are at least

Kids do fine starting at first grade, but should be in a noncompetitive learning-based program. It is too young to play real games and keep score or worry about much other than having fun. It is easy to turn kids off at this age. Some kids are not ready at first grade, and it is important for programs to accommodate newcomers who choose to join later.

—Ted Tye, president of Newton Girls' Soccer, coach for 13 years, and dad of an 18-year-old and 12-year-old twins

My daughter Sophie started soccer at age 3, and I think it was too young for her. It depends on the kid, but Sophie was shy and she cried the whole time. But it probably paid off because now she's a great soccer player at age 6 and loves being part of a team.

—Karen, mom of Max, 9, Sophie, 7, Celia, 5, and Jake, 2

5 or 6 years old before enrolling them in a league, since preschoolers and many kindergartners have difficulty learning soccer in a team setting and often become upset when a coach corrects them.

What to Look For When Getting Started

✿ Soccer, like hockey, is a very technical game with a variety of skills to master. Even though it looks easy to kick a ball down the field and shoot at a goal, the game can be difficult.

✿ Ask the following questions when evaluating a soccer program:
- How are children grouped: by age, by school, by grade, by neighborhood?
- How is the program structured in terms of practices, games, and travel?
- Are there registration fees, and do these include a uniform? Are there any other costs?
- Are the coaches paid or volunteer? Are experts brought in for special training sessions?
- Are tryouts involved? Of the kids who try out, how many get placed on a team?
- Are the better players concentrated on certain teams, or are team divisions made without taking skill into account?
- Will my child get relatively equal playing time with the other kids? Is this up to the coach's decision, or is there a playing policy (such as each child must play at least 50% of a game)?
- Will my child be exposed to every position? What happens if she doesn't want to play a particular position, such as goalie?
- What is expected of me as a volunteer, such as providing snacks or helping administer aspects of the team?
- If travel is involved, how far will this typically be?

✿ Team standings and playoffs should not happen until at least ages 9 or 10.

✿ From ages 6 to 8, you should expect your child to:
- learn the basics of soccer, such as dribbling, passing, and shooting;
- play games with a team of 3 or 5 players about 40 minutes in length on shortened fields with small goals;
- have fun, develop camaraderie, and remember more about the postgame snacks than the score;
- play with a size-3 ball.

✿ From ages 8 to 10, you should expect your child to:
- hone her ball-handling, passing, and shooting skills;
- focus on the more tactical aspects of the game;

- play games on a larger field with squads of either 6, 8, or 11 players, which include goalkeepers;
- participate in longer games;
- go to practices that focus for longer periods of time on skill-building drills;
- play with a size-4 ball.

From age 11 on up, you should expect your child to:
- play matches on a full-sized field with a regulation ball and goals;
- play on teams of 11 players, including a goalkeeper;
- practice two to three times a week for about 90 minutes, in addition to weekend games;
- play with a size-5 (full-sized) ball.

Ask if the coach has been certified. Beginning soccer coach licenses start with G and go up to A for the highest level in the United States. Part of each state's licensing process involves coaching tips and strategies, as well as learning from experts about how to best communicate soccer skills to children of various ages.

The soccer teams that our kids play on are part of the American Youth Soccer Organization, and their whole philosophy is for kids to have a fun time. They emphasize that it's not about winning, but about good sportsmanship. The coach and other kids have been incredibly supportive of our son, who isn't that strong a player, with the kids going out of their way to pass the ball to him during games.

—Karen, mom of Max, 9, Sophie, 7, Celia, 5, and Jake, 2

Our town has an incredibly competitive soccer program, and my daughter didn't make any of the travel teams in tryouts the first year as she thought she would. It turned out to be one of the best things to happen to her. Not having made the team, she asked to go to soccer camp that summer to get better. Through this happening, we learned that our daughter is a child motivated from within and has to really want something to be into it. So she set her goal, sought out how to achieve it, and made an elite soccer team the next year. She also found her position, playing defense or goalie. Soccer has been an absolutely fabulous experience for her, and she now plays on the second-best team in her division.

—Bridgitt, mom of Taylor, 10, Connor and Chloe, 8, and Brian, 6

Futsal

❧ Promoted as a game that improves touch and ball handling, Futsal has become a popular indoor winter soccer alternative. Futsal helps players develop quicker reflexes and extremely accurate passing.

❧ Top Brazilian players for years have attributed their world soccer success to Futsal. Futsal is an indoor soccer game played with five players on each team in an area the size of a basketball court. Players use a ball smaller, heavier, and with less bounce than a traditional size-5 soccer ball. Players have to use skill to move the ball, rather than being able to rely on the ball's bounce. Moreover, unlike traditional indoor soccer, there are no walls for the ball to rebound off back into play.

Safety and Injury Concerns

❧ The American Academy of Pediatrics (AAP) has estimated that 140,000 to 160,000 soccer-related injuries occur annually, with 22% being head injuries. The AAP recommends that participants in youth soccer should minimize heading the ball until more is known about the risks for brain injury. They further recommend wearing mouth guards, along with sports goggles to prevent injuries to your child's eyes.

❧ The most common injuries associated with soccer are bumps and bruises to the knee, thigh, shin, ankle, and foot. Shin guards protect your child from shinbone injuries, and are the only piece of protective equipment mandatory in most soccer leagues.

❧ Given the speed at which soccer is often played, serious collisions do occur, such as

Futsal is an excellent indoor activity that assists good soccer play. Indoor soccer (using walls) is useless, dangerous, causes injury, and teaches bad defensive technique.

—*Owen Boyd, youth soccer coach for*
 15 years

Common injuries with this sport at the young ages include being kicked, but that is where the shin guards come in (hopefully). Also, when kids are young their inability to control their kicks of the ball can sometimes cause head injuries if a child who is not paying attention gets hit by the flight of the ball. The best precaution a child can take is to always be aware, as soccer is always moving.

—*Nat Gonzalez, University of California*
 Riverside men's head soccer coach for
 13 years

Injuries are fairly rare for kids under age 12. After that age, the biggest concerns are ankle sprains, pulled muscles, and knee injuries. The best preventive medicine is to be properly conditioned and make sure injuries are properly evaluated and treated. If the game is being played in the heat, make sure breaks are frequent and kids get plenty of liquids.

—*John Starr, head girls coach, Franklin*
 Heights High School, coaching for
 15 years

when two players go to kick the ball and one ends up kicking the other. The impact can cause bruises as well as fractures, torn ligaments, and sprains.

Cost Considerations

✦ Soccer involves relatively little equipment, which makes it among the most inexpensive sports to play. In general, a pair of soccer cleats, shin guards, high socks that cover the shin guards, and a ball are all your child needs, and a pair of gloves if playing goalkeeper. Together these can all be purchased for under $100. Most teams ask that children bring their own soccer balls to practice, as many drills and activities require each child to have a ball. Younger children start off with a small, softer ball that they can more easily manipulate.

✦ The average cost for recreational teams is $50–$70 per season, but this cost increases for traveling teams. The fee generally covers uniforms and pays for referees at the games. Most soccer teams have a team uniform, which usually consists of a reversible shirt and may also include shorts and socks in the team colors. Sometimes you need to purchase the uniform separately.

✦ The big cost comes in league and club teams, with some clubs charging as high as $2,000 per player to cover yearly coaching, field, uniform, and referee costs.

SQUASH AND RACQUETBALL

Overview

While not traditionally found in schools, millions of children play the intensely aerobic games of squash and racquetball at clubs around the country. Over 5.6 million Americans play racquetball annually, and of these, there are 360,000 children ages 6–11 who play, and 906,000 children ages 12–17.

Joe Sobek invented racquetball in 1949 on a Connecticut handball court, combining the basics of handball and squash, and the sport caught on quickly. In the 1970s to 1980s, racquetball was one of the fastest-growing sports in America. World championships have been held biennially since 1981, and racquetball debuted as a Pan American Games sport in 1995. Younger players dominate the sport, with 59.4% of players falling between ages 12 and 34. According to the U.S. Olympic training center, an average racquetball game takes 20 minutes, during which a player will run a distance of approximately 3,650 feet—over two miles in one hour of play. Each year, the U.S. Racquetball Association (USRA) sanctions state, regional, and national championships for junior players ages 5–18, culminating in an annual international event, the Junior World Championships.

Squash is a less aggressive sport than racquetball. Played on a smaller court, squash uses a longer racket and a slower, softer ball that doesn't bounce as much as the one used in racquetball. Squash was invented in 1865 at Harrow School in England, evolving from a game called "rackets" played in an enclosed court. At the time, the soft rubber ball had holes in it, which caused the ball to collapse when hit hard, and thus the sport derives its name from this "squashy" ball. Squash is now played worldwide in over 120 countries. Because of squash's light racket and slow ball, children tend to excel.

Differences Between Squash and Racquetball

✦ Racquetball and squash are both racket sports played fundamentally the same way on indoor courts with similar dimensions. The racquetball court is longer, but a foot shorter in width. Squash balls are much smaller (about one quarter the size) and less lively than the racquetball, and squash rackets are narrow and longer. Also, in racquetball, a player gets two serves to put a ball in play, unlike squash, where a player only gets one.

✦ Squash has more restrictive rules about where in the court the squash ball may be played. A player may not hit the ball off the ceiling in squash, but this is permitted in racquetball. Squash also has a telltale, or "tin"—a narrow piece of metal that measures 17 inches off the base of the floor (all the way across) on the front wall that the ball needs to be played above, like a tennis net.

General Benefits

◉ Both sports involve a substantial cardiovascular workout, given intense short-distance running and sprinting to the ball, and build stamina.

◉ In addition to exhilarating ongoing action, these sports develop great balance, hand-eye coordination, footwork, agility, flexibility, coordination, speed, and quickness. They also build upper- and lower-body strength.

◉ Both games are mentally stimulating, requiring players to learn to develop and implement a strategy against each opponent, based on his strengths and weaknesses. They also teach focus, patience, discipline, endurance, and perseverance.

◉ Both racquetball and squash serve as excellent cross-training sports, helping children achieve success in other sports such as basketball, baseball, softball, and volleyball, all of which require quick reaction times, strong hand-eye coordination, and excellent lateral movement ability.

◉ Racquetball and squash are both great sports for kids who do not excel in tradi-

Racquetball is considered to be more of a power game with the object of the game being to end the rally quickly to score a point via a "kill shot" and an unforced error by your opponent. Squash is more of a control and finesse game with long rallies before a point is scored.

—*Mike Franks, racquetball instructor for 25 years, squash instructor for 12 years, and editor of wallbanger.net*

The bouncier ball in racquetball brings some guessing into the equation when trying to figure out where to go to return a shot, while in squash, it is a little easier to determine what your opponent's shot will be. In racquetball, the lack of an "out-of-play marking" at the bottom of the front wall (such as a net in tennis or a "tin" in squash) makes it too easy for a player to win the majority of the kill shots (played a few inches from the floor). Good players, thus, go for kill shots as early in a rally as possible, making those rallies very short in average. In squash, it is the opposite, as the better the level of play, the longer the rallies.

—*Tomas Fortson, head squash coach, Bowdoin College, teaching for 20 years*

From a player's perspective, squash and racquetball have about as much in common as Ping-Pong and badminton. Player movements are completely different. Squash tends to involve more of a "lunging" motion, and because rallies are longer, there is a greater emphasis on cardiovascular conditioning. Shot selection also tends to be more diverse in squash, incorporating more lobs, drops, and volleys. And the result of these differences naturally leads to different strategies between the two sports. From a spectator's point of view, the most immediate differences between the two sports are the length of the rallies—squash rallies generally last much longer and have been know to exceed 100 shots per point.

—*Stephen Gregg, USSRA director of junior development and squash coach*

The largest difference between the two is the ethos of each. Racquetballers have no compunction about hitting each other with the ball or even running into and over each other in the court, whereas squash players adhere to a strict ethic of always protecting their partner and opponent. A squash player is horrified to hit an opponent with the ball or racket or body, while a racquetballer looks to do it if there is an advantage to be gained.

—*Sean Sloane, head men's and women's squash coach, Haverford College, teaching for 32 years*

tional school team sports. They are games that can be played for a lifetime and can be played year-round indoors. Once they learn to play squash, most people get hooked for life.

Kids Who Tend to Excel

⊚ Strong hand-eye coordination, agility, speed, coordination, and being in good cardiovascular shape are all traits of children who do well in the game.

⊚ Both squash and racquetball have large intellectual components, and children who do best are good at strategic thinking, concentration, and the ability to anticipate and quickly react to an opponent's moves.

Best Age to Start

⊚ A child can start learning the fundamentals of squash or racquetball around ages 6–8, but most kids pick up the game at a later age due to the fact that facilities and junior programs are not readily available in some parts of the United States.

Kids love racquetball because the ball is almost always "in," unlike tennis. They can run and get it all the time. It makes them feel very successful, and they get pretty good, pretty quick. Racquetball burns about 600 calories an hour, as it is highly aerobic and uses all the major muscle groups. Time flies when you're playing, so you play forever and get in great shape. It also enhances your reaction times. I hear all the time about what great cross training racquetball is when these kids go play other sports.

—*Kelly Beane, head coach U.S. Junior Olympics racquetball team and racquetball pro for 17 years*

For children starting around age 8, squash is perhaps the simplest and most gratifying of the rocket sports. Children also build camaraderie and tend to have more intimate interaction with their coaches and peers due to the unique environment of the squash court.

—*Stephen Gregg, USSRA director of junior development and squash coach*

Squash is a fantastic source of physical exercise, better aerobically than almost any sport. In addition, since the ethics of the game demand cooperation and acceptance of an honor system, squash is a great teacher of character. Squash is also an excellent social game for meeting people.

—*Sean Sloane, head men's and women's squash coach, Haverford College, teaching for 32 years*

Both sports are highly social, and whether players develop into recreational or tournament players, friendships developed are typically longstanding and rewarding.

Players can typically use finesse and "smart shots" to overcome and defeat a stronger, power player who could be quite possibly a better overall athlete.

—*Mike Franks, racquetball instructor for 25 years, squash instructor for 12 years, and editor of wallbanger.net*

Squash is a great thinking game. Kids who excel think out the shots before they are played. Squash is also very physical, with no breaks in action. The ball is in play for 50% of the time, whereas in tennis, for example, the ball is in play for only 10% of the time.

—*Chris Spahr, squash instructor, University Club in Boston, coaching for 12 years*

What to Look For When Getting Started

🦋 Make sure that the instructors are committed to a junior squash or racket program and have experience teaching kids. Look for a club geared to youth activities that facilitates helping your child find other children to play.

🦋 Look for a racquetball instructor certified by the American Professional Racquetball Organization (AmPro), the U.S. Racquetball Association (USRA), or a squash instructor certified by the U.S. Squash Racquets Association (USSRA).

Safety and Injury Concerns

🦋 The main cause of injury is getting hit in the eye with a fast-moving ball. Your child should learn all the rules to ensure safe play, such as never striking the ball when your opponent is blocking the path of the ball to the front wall of the court. Protective eyewear eliminates this risk. You may want to encourage your child to wear a mouth guard to protect against injury to his teeth if struck by the ball.

🦋 Common injuries include strained knees, ankles, shoulders, and feet, as well as blisters on the hand from gripping the racket.

Cost Considerations

🦋 Rackets, nonmarking court shoes, and protective eyewear are mandatory.

I see kids 3 and 4 years old on the court just learning how to chase the ball around, and we have junior programs that start kids at age 6 for very brief lessons. Before the age of 8, there exist special multi-bounce rules to make learning the game easier.

> —*Patrick Bernardo, president of NY State Racquetball Association and owner of Racquetworld.com, teaching for 12 years*

Players in the elite levels of our National Junior Squash Program generally began playing between the ages of 8 and 14, though many of our top adults began squash in their college years or beyond.

> —*Stephen Gregg, USSRA director of junior development and squash coach*

We have divisions that begin at age 8 and under, but there isn't an optimum age to start; to excel, however, it helps to start earlier in life rather than later. It can take a while for children to learn the angles a ball travels and be able to play a "consistent" game where they are able to rally well. To help, we offer no-bounce and two-bounce junior divisions for beginners before they progress to the normal adult rule of one-bounce.

> —*Christopher Cole, U.S. Racquetball board of directors, U.S. Olympic Committee board of directors, and racquetball coach for 20 years*

Although squash is learned often as an individual sport, take every opportunity to get your young squashers on teams, because teams add a very healthy socialization component and fun.

> —*Sean Sloane, head men's and women's squash coach, Haverford College, teaching for 32 years*

Eye guards or goggles cost between $5 and $20, and many programs lend these to the kids.

🐟 A kid's squash or racquetball racket will cost between $30 and $50, though the

While being hit with a ball traveling at a high rate of speed is not dangerous, it does tend to "sting" and cause some significant discomfort.

—*Mike Franks, racquetball instructor for 25 years, squash instructor for 12 years, and editor of wallbanger.net*

price can be as high as $150. Make sure to choose a light racket with tight strings.

🍂 Balls cost about $2 each. Squash balls with blue dots on them typically have 30% extra bounce and are best for beginners, as rallies last longer and make for a more exciting game.

🍂 Squash and racquetball are almost exclusively played at private clubs, so your child will need to join a club with racquetball or squash courts. Club memberships typically run from $25 to $150 per month depending on the types of memberships offered and the quality of the club. Some clubs charge additionally for court time, with typical charges ranging from $10 to $20 an hour.

🍂 Lessons range from $15 to $60 an hour, depending on the qualifications and caliber of the instructor.

🍂 Additional costs for competitive juniors include a USSRA junior membership, which costs $30 a year, and tournament entry fees, which usually cost between $25 and $60 a competition.

SURFING

Overview

The sport of surfing involves riding across the face of an unbroken wave while standing on a specialized stiff board. Surfing takes place on waves ranging from one foot to over thirty feet high. Surfers claim that there's nothing comparable to the thrill of standing up on a surfboard and maneuvering it in a jumping, sliding rush across water.

Modern-day surfing originated in Hawaii in the 1770s but dates back centuries to Polynesians bodysurfing in the central Pacific. Improvements in board design and materials, as well as the development of the wet suit to keep surfers warm in cold water, helped speed the rise of surfing during the 1950s and 1960s. The current popularity of surfing has led to schools giving lessons just about anywhere there are breaking waves to ride.

There are three popular types of surfing. In body boarding, surfers lie on boards made out of lightweight foam about three feet in length and ride waves. In Malibu surfing, surfers lie on a long, stiff fiberglass board, using their arms to paddle and

The image of surfing has changed dramatically from a sport run by rebels and renegades to one where surfers are recognized as legitimate athletes. Surfing gives you a sense of a confidence. If you can surf big waves safely, then you feel you can do a great deal in other areas of personal challenge.

—*George Jones, Surf Guys School owner and teacher for 6 years*

Surfing works almost every muscle in your entire body and keeps you fit and energized. Each day is different and each wave is different, and you never get bored, as you can go to various beaches.

—*"Kahuna" Bob Edwards, surf school founder and instructor for 17 years*

Students are at one with Mother Nature and learn to respect her strength. Balancing on a wave that is part of nature can be a spiritual experience. It also builds upper-body strength, as you need to do push-ups going over waves and to get up and catch the wave. The surfer can do as many as 100 push-ups in a 3-hour session paddling out to the break.

—*Cowboy and Jenny Rosa, Waikiki surfing instructors for 40 and 15 years*

catch a wave. Once a wave is caught, the surfer stands on the board, tilting it to the side to ride along the face of the wave. In kneeboarding, surfers ride a specialized small board on their knees, in a compact and stable position, which enables steep drops, quick radical maneuvers, and tube riding.

General Benefits

- Strengthens the upper and lower body
- Builds stamina and endurance
- Provides an intense cardiovascular workout
- Teaches quick reflexes and decision making
- Fosters a sense of being close to nature and environmental awareness
- An activity that many families do together

Kids Who Tend to Excel

- Strong swimmers

- Kids who can tolerate cold water

- Those who are not afraid to fall

- Persistent children not discouraged by continually falling off the board

- Strong leg muscles are needed to shift weight forward and backward on the board, and move the board up and down on a wave.

- A strong upper body is needed to paddle the board.

Best Age to Start

- Most surfing schools start offering lessons to children between the ages of 8 and 9 for those who can swim very well, given the undertow and intensity of the ocean. Some kids start surfing as young as age 4, either riding on the board with a parent or having one person launch them and another catch the board.

What to Look For When Getting Started

🌪 Bodysurfing and belly-boarding are great pre-surfing activities, as they help teach your child wave judgment and strategy for catching waves, which many surfers consider to be the most difficult part of surfing to master. Every surf spot has its own unique wave pattern, which will vary based on any given day's tide, swell, and wind.

🌪 Every instructor should have lifeguard credentials, CPR certification, and training in first aid and ocean rescue. Make sure the instructor is familiar with the waters, tides, and reefs that your child will be learning in.

🌪 Ask about the instructor's personal surfing experience and surfing philosophy, and look for an energetic instructor with good communication skills.

🌪 With children ages 2–5 there should be one instructor to launch them and another to catch them. With children ages 6–10 there should be no more than three students to one instructor.

🌪 Kids 8 years and younger should not start out in water more than waist-deep, and children 12 years and younger should start out in water no higher than chest-deep.

Surfing is a fairly aggressive sport and tends to attract Type A personalities. Before starting, your child needs to be a very competent swimmer, as the ocean can be a brutal entity. We're out there challenging the ocean in surfing, and the ocean's vicious and takes no prisoners.

—George Jones, Surf Guys School owner and teacher for 6 years

Kids who do best starting out love the beach and have some knowledge of boogie boarding.

—"Kahuna" Bob Edwards, surf school founder and instructor for 17 years

Any age, any size, any sex can excel. We see a lot of kids who initially are not the most popular, extroverted, or physically fit. Surfing encourages physical development and interaction with others at events. You can progress at your own rate and enjoy being outdoors surrounded by nature in some of her most spectacular beauty.

—Paul West, president of the U.S. Surfing Federation and instructor for 25 years

The best surfer in the water is the one having the most fun. The only drawback to learning how to surf is being self-conscious.

—Steve Pinner, world-ranked professional surfer, coaching for 15 years

SURFING LESSONS: CATCHING THAT WAVE!

🦅 Most surfing lessons begin with instruction on dry land to teach kids the basic skills.

🦅 Your child should be taught how to carry a surfboard down to the beach, tie a leash that connects the board to his body, and learn how to paddle, catch a wave, stand up, and ride the wave. Foot placement is crucial, with the back foot planted near the tail of the board and the front foot somewhere near the board's middle. Your child will be taught how to be far enough forward so the board moves at its

Look at the background of the teacher. I've been surfing for 20 years and lifeguarding for 10 years. I just have a heart-and-soul passion for what I'm doing, and I love teaching my sport.

—*Rick Garrett, Safari Surf School owner and teacher for 5 years*

Safety should be paramount, with surfing etiquette and a solid dry-land program emphasized. Having maximum fun in a safe learning environment is what it's all about.

—*Michael and Milton Willis, founders of Willis Bros. Surfing and instructors for 10 years*

greatest speed, but lean far enough back so the nose of the board doesn't go underwater (otherwise known as pearling).

✦ Once your child is up and riding, surfing lessons focus on advanced techniques of paddling, direction control, paddling through a wave, and surfing an unbroken wave.

✦ Look for a surfing school that also teaches your child marine and ocean safety. Once past the beginning stages, your child should be able to look at the ocean before surfing to see how the waves are breaking, the size and direction of the swells, and if the surf is too big for his skills and ability level. Your child should also be taught about riptides, jellyfish, hypothermia, currents, and equipment care. It's critical to know where the rocks are, how the currents run, and if there's a strong undertow at each beach.

✦ Local and national competitions for kids are sponsored by everyone from amateur-sanctioned associations such as the National Scholastic Surfing Association (NSSA), to regional competitions such as those sponsored by the Eastern Surfing Association or Hawaii Amateur Surfing Association, to surf shops that hold their own contests. Judges give surfers marks based on their skills and the wave difficulty.

Safety and Injury Concerns

✦ Your child should never surf alone, or paddle out farther than he can swim back in without a board.

✦ A major safety concern in surfing is getting hit by someone else's board. Surfing lessons should teach your child how to dodge surfboards, tucking and diving on the opposite side when he sees a board coming at him, and ducking underwater before getting hit on the head.

✦ Learning surfing etiquette is extremely important. "Shoulder hopping," when someone takes off directly in front of you while you're riding a wave, is extremely dangerous and frowned upon.

We start every first surfing lesson on a balance trainer. Next, students learn how to paddle the surfboard, jump up on it, and learn to work with it. Gaining comfort in the ocean and on the board is a huge factor. You want an instructor who's very proficient in the art of surfing and has extensive ocean experience. Many teachers will teach you alongside your child, which makes it a fun family experience. I start everyone on long boards for stability and forgiveness, and you can just about guarantee beginners will be standing up quickly, often by their third wave, though sometimes it takes a week to learn. Word of mouth is your best guide for individual instructors.

—*George Jones, Surf Guys School owner and teacher for 6 years*

Watch the teacher in action and look for patience, as most kids are scared of the waves. We talk to kids from the time we teach them on the beach all the way to the line up, and keep saying that we will be with them the whole time. We tell them to relax and breathe, and when a wave comes, we say "Whee," like it is fun to bump up like on a horse or a roller coaster. Then it becomes fun. We encourage parents to swim out with us and catch their kids so they are in sight at all times.

—*Cowboy and Jenny Rosa, Waikiki surfing instructors for 40 and 15 years*

🐟 Jellyfish can sting painfully and your child should always watch out for them.

🐟 If there's a riptide of long shore current, or if the current in the water is moving very swiftly from north to south, or vice versa, your child has to be able to recognize it and be sure not to get caught up in it.

🐟 If bait fish are migrating in the fall, sharks may be present. Most people are bitten by small, juvenile sharks that have trouble sorting humans from feeding bait.

🐟 Aquatic footwear helps protect your child's feet from a rocky bottom. A personal flotation device helps guard against drowning. To protect against sunburn, your child should have on waterproof sunscreen. Rash guard cream can help prevent irritation on the chest and stomach area caused by the skin rubbing against the board.

Cost Considerations

❧ Look into renting a board before buying one. Surfboards are expensive, and a used board is generally your best bet when starting out. A new surfboard will cost between $300 and $600. You can generally find a quality used board for about $250. Beginners need a long board, between 8 and 10 feet long, as it's easiest to paddle and catch waves, giving a surfer more time to stand up. It provides a fairly stable platform when standing and is forgiving of small missteps. On it, your child can ride either small or big waves and make slow turns. Short little boards with ultra-

Kids getting hit on the head, especially by the fins on the bottom of a board, is a major concern. I always tell my beginners that the safest place to be is standing on the surfboard, because you know where it's at—under your feet. I never use a surf leash with beginners, as it can get wound around their feet, and I want the board away from them if they fall. I tell them to always come up from under the water with their palms up protecting their heads.

—*George Jones, Surf Guys School owner and teacher for 6 years*

Getting hit by your own board feels like getting hit by a baseball bat. We always tell students to protect their head at all times and to never dive off a board in shallow water, but rather to think like they are at the shallow part of the pool and do a belly flop.

—*Cowboy and Jenny Rosa, Waikiki surfing instructors for 40 and 15 years*

An adequate safety program covers natural hazards, like stingrays and jellyfish, and how to avoid them. Understanding ocean currents like riptides lets us use the ocean's energy and removes the danger.

—*Michael and Milton Willis, founders of Willis Bros. Surfing and instructors for 10 years*

The most common and debilitating injury in surfing is getting hit in the head with the board, which is why it is important to start kids off with a soft board. For children it is best to start out with larger and softer boards to avoid serious injury and ease them into it.

—*Steve Pinner, world-ranked professional surfer, coaching for 15 years*

light fiberglass shells are shaped for maneuverability, and are for advanced surfers only.

🏄 Unless the board comes with a traction pad, your child will need wax ($1 per bar) to rub on the board to create traction when paddling and standing on it.

🏄 Additional costs include repairs to the surfboard, for everything from a broken nose, snapped tail fins, to a board broken in half. Fins generally cost $45.

🏄 There are also the costs of a surf-rack, rash guard, and leash ($15 to $20).

🏄 A wet suit helps protect against the sun and against skin rash. In cold weather, it helps hold in body warmth. A wet suit will cost about $150.

Just like driving a car, you do not want a child to go out and try and learn to drive in a 12-cylinder sports car. A nice slow stable wagon works better initially. Most kids want to get a shortboard right away, when they could make 10 times the progress in the beginning riding a long board or a soft midrange. Longboards are typically nine feet and midranges are usually seven feet.

—*Paul West, president of the U.S. Surfing Federation and instructor for 25 Years*

Kids always want to get one of those sleek-looking, hard fiberglass surfboards, but they're hard to learn on, and if you get hit one time in the head, you get hurt and will just drop the sport. Get something thicker and wider for your child, so the board will be more stable, and something made out of foam for safety.

—*Rick Garrett, Safari Surf School owner and teacher for 5 years*

The board to begin on should be wide and thick as well as long enough to provide stability while still being challenging. Surfing is a step process. After mastering the first board, surfers move on quickly to more advanced equipment. Don't invest in a surfboard until you're sure your child will stick with it. When the time comes to purchase that board, seek professional advice from an experienced surfer.

—*Michael and Milton Willis, founders of Willis Bros. Surfing and instructors for 10 years*

✦ Expect to pay $35–$50 per hour for private lessons, though they can range as high as $100.

✦ Most competitions charge an entry fee of about $20 per event.

SWIMMING

Overview

Learning to swim and be safe in the water is critical for any child. Along with many other parents, you may consider swimming an essential skill for your child to master. Drowning is one of the leading causes of death among children 14 years and under; more than 1,000 kids drown each year. As a result, the American Academy of Pediatrics recommends swimming lessons for every child age 4 and up.

At some point in your child's life, she will be exposed to water situations and will need to know basic water safety to avoid drowning. Swimming or activities in pools, creeks, lakes, rivers, and oceans should not be a source of fear, but rather fun places to enjoy or spend a family vacation. Regardless of whether your child wants to swim competitively or recreationally, chances are you will want to enroll her in some type of swimming program.

Competitive swimming has become a year-round sport, with 40 new swim clubs joining USA Swimming, the national swim organization, in 2001. Swimming has been held at every Olympic Games since their inception.

I consider swimming to truly be a life skill. Swimming is something you have to learn when you're fairly young, as it's a much harder skill to learn when you're older. It's also a base for lots of other sports in the water, from sailing to waterskiing. You'll never feel like your child is very safe unless he knows how to swim. I see swimming lessons as critical and have told my boys that they can stop only once they get to a certain level of proficiency.

—*Deborah, mom of Philip, 10, Patrick, 8, and William, 3*

General Benefits

◉ Swimming improves strength, muscular conditioning, and endurance for all of the major muscle groups. It also increases flexibility in the upper body and shoulder area.

◉ It improves cardiovascular fitness and circulation, providing aerobic exercise that puts little stress on the body, and strengthening the respiratory system.

◉ Swimming competitively offers a lot of team camaraderie, cheering for each other at meets, and is one of the few sports that mixes kids of different ages together.

◉ Swimming allows overweight children to exercise with less risk of injury, since water reduces stress on joints.

◉ If your child has asthma, swimming has been found to be the least likely sport to trigger symptoms. Swimming can help your child increase her lung capacity as well as develop good breathing techniques. If you can, find a program capable of monitoring your child's lung function with a peak flow meter.

◉ Swimming is also a basic skill needed for other water sports, and for many social activities (such as pool parties and beach outings).

Kids Who Tend to Excel

◉ You don't need a particular body type to excel and, surprisingly, strength is not a factor in swimming. Rather, endurance and efficiency of strokes are more important.

◉ Having long arms and legs to help propel you through the water helps.

◉ Most kids who excel make a big commitment by swimming year-round, giving them a distinct advantage over those who just participate on a swim team and take lessons during the summer months. They also learn to master all the different swimming strokes.

Best Age to Start

◉ It's best to start your child early, before she has a chance to develop a fear of water. A good age to start formal swimming lessons on basic strokes is around 4 years old, and around 7 or 8 to start competing in swim meets, the youngest age bracket being 8 and under.

What to Look For When Getting Started

Kids who excel at competitive swimming have cardiorespiratory endurance, and master the mechanics of the strokes and the biomechanics of swimming. Flexibility in the shoulders, ankles, knees, and elbows plays a great role in doing the strokes.

—*Raegh swim coach and instructor for 54 years*

🌿 Some programs offer swimming lessons for infants with a parent. The goal is to get your child comfortable and acclimated to the water. Observe the class before signing your child up, and make sure it's taught in

> The key when starting your child in swimming lessons is that you want to think in terms of "drownproofing" your child. This involves becoming comfortable in water, learning to hold breath under water, and not panicking. Starting around age 3 or 4, kids can begin to be taught rotary breathing and kicking. We have kids as young as 4 on our swim team who swim about 12 yards in a meet.
>
> —*George Campbell, swimming program director for 20 years, middle school physical education director for 32 years, and dad of three grown kids*

such a way that your child feels like she's having fun while learning and being challenged to improve. Remember, though, that water-enrichment classes are not enough to really "drownproof" your child.

❧ The best introductory courses keep reliance on flotation devices to a minimum because children never really learn to swim; the device just holds children above the water and gives them a false sense of security.

❧ Ask if the instructor has certification as a water safety instructor from the Red Cross or YMCA or has taken a National Swim School Association course. Make sure there is one instructor for every five children and preferably another lifeguard on duty as well.

❧ Over time your child will learn four or five basic strokes, combinations of arm and leg movements that will move a swimmer through water. Teachers tend to teach the strokes in the following order: freestyle, backstroke, breaststroke, and then butterfly last. In addition, your child may learn the sidestroke. Ask about the order of stroke introduction when signing your child up for lessons, as it can make a big difference in terms of how your child picks up the basics.

❧ Group lessons work well for kids who are able to swim but aren't quite ready for a swim team. Enroll your child in a private lesson if you feel she needs individual attention for her stroke basics. Private lessons enable the instructor to focus attention and instruction individualized for each particular child's skills. The ideal time for a private lesson is a half-hour; after that, you tend to lose the child's interest, and she can tire out.

Swimming is an activity I consider critical for my kids to learn, as we spend summers by a lake, so lessons have been a high-priority investment. Of course, that having been said, it's been quite an odyssey, from having to drive 25 minutes to the nearest YMCA, to a town recreational Wee Swim class in which my kids complained bitterly about getting into the "freezing!" water. It took the peer pressure of an older friend and a bribe to finally get my daughter to put her head underwater. So you have to be prepared to tough it out when you're going to insist on a particular activity for your kids!

—Lisa, mom of Lars, 8, Elsa, 6, and Peter, 4

In my daughter's Mommy and Me class, we got in the water with the kids. We helped them float, blow bubbles, and swim with noodles. We stay in the shallow end, where it's only around 3.5 feet. My daughter swam halfway across the pool all by herself while I swam next to her after only after two weeks!

—Stephanie, mom of Eric, 5, and Tina, 3

Group lessons are a great way for your child to build friendships with the other kids in the group, but often too many kids can be distracting and your child can lose focus during the lesson and fool around. In a private lesson, your child can have the teacher's full attention.

—Ian Coffey, assistant swimming coach at Syracuse University, coaching for 8 years

What to Expect If Your Child Joins a Swim Team

❧ Becoming a competitive swimmer involves a huge time commitment, both in terms of practice and travel to swim meets. Many swim teams practice two to five days a week with four-hour meets on weekends. The key is to find a swim coach who makes practices fun, because swimming can become repetitive if it consists solely of swimming laps. Ask if the coach combines practicing in the water with conditioning and training on dry land to help build upper-body strength.

❧ Extensive training during swim practices aims to teach your child to increase her speed and how to pace herself. Swimming the first portion of long-distance races too fast can drain a swimmer's strength, while swimming too slowly can

Some kids are just naturally good with one stroke, while struggling with another, and start to specialize in a stroke as early as age 9.

—*Margy Halloran, swim team coach for 4 years and competitive collegiate swimmer*

During a swim meet, children cannot hear while they're in the water, but that doesn't stop parents from shouting instructions from the sidelines or yelling at their kids while walking back and forth the length of the pool as they swim. My daughter did competitive swimming up to age 12, when she declared that practices weren't fun anymore and her shoulder hurt from swimming five days a week, two hours a day. She clearly wanted to quit, and we just said, "That's okay." She got great conditioning from swimming and it's something she can do for fitness throughout her life.

—*Jane, mom of Carolyn, 17, and Peter, 11*

At a swim meet, you have many age groups, many events, and the races can last from a few seconds to twenty minutes. The meets are long and your child may not swim until hours after the meet has started and then swim for only forty seconds. As a parent, you have to be able to be patient.

—*Ian Coffey, assistant swimming coach at Syracuse University, coaching for 8 years*

make catching up impossible. When your child is just starting out, look for meets that allow her to swim short distances until she has the chance to build up endurance over time.

🐟 Short-distance races (50 and 100 meters) are an all-out full sprint.

🐟 The 200-meter events are considered the hardest to master, as they require pace as well as a controlled sprint.

🐟 The longer distances (400, 800, and 1500 meters) require constant awareness of muscle fatigue.

🐟 The individual medley, swum in 200- and 400-meter distances, features all four competitive strokes. A single swimmer swims one leg each in the order of butterfly, backstroke, breaststroke, and freestyle.

✦ In the medley relay, which is 400 meters, four different swimmers swim four strokes for each leg of the relay, swum in the order of backstroke, breaststroke, butterfly, and freestyle.

✦ In the freestyle relays, which are swum at distances of 400 and 800 meters, four swimmers each swim freestyle one quarter of the race.

✦ Many swimmers lose races due to poor starts, slow turns, and missed touches on a turn. At the start, once all swimmers are in the down positions, either a gun or an electronic tone signals the start of the race. If the starter believes a swimmer has dived early, the race will be recalled and that swimmer disqualified. In all events, the swimmer must touch the wall, either by somersaulting and touching only with the feet in freestyle or backstroke, or by touching the wall with a hand before executing the turn in breaststroke and butterfly.

Synchronized Swimming

✦ If your child likes to perform routines to music, she might enjoy synchronized swimming, which combines athleticism with creativity and music. This sport, formerly known as water ballet, is offered for women at the world championship and Olympic level, although recreational and early competitive levels are also available. The participants, coaches, and judges are almost exclusively female.

✦ In a synchronized swimming competition, swimmers' routines are judged for accuracy, control, execution, difficulty, synchronization, choreography, and poise. Competition consists of a set technical routine, with specific moves performed in a particular order, and a free routine, each performed to music and limited to a certain time. Routines are scored out of a possible 10, with the score reflecting both technical performance and artistry.

✦ The challenge of synchronized swimming is to maintain an illusion of effortlessness while making the strenuous moves, many of which are done upside down and underwater. Underwater speakers enable the swimmers to hear the music. A nose clip prevents water from coming up the nose.

✦ Synchronized swimming requires aerobic and anaerobic endurance, flexibility, grace, a high level of coordination, strength to hold the poses, and exceptional breath control. It requires a high level of commitment to a partner or team.

You have to be wary of overuse injuries in competitive swimming, as kids end up making the same shoulder motion again and again in their strokes. You also have to make sure that your child doesn't get mentally and physically fatigued, particularly if they are swimming day in and day out. I've seen plenty of kids who get burned out, don't want to swim anymore, and just walk away.

—*George Campbell, director of swimming for 20 years, middle school physical education director for 32 years, and dad of three grown kids*

Overtraining causes many injuries. Training should be gradually built up. Too many coaches do distance training with very young children, which is too much. Children 8 and under should pay a lot of attention to stroke techniques to avoid running into injuries later on.

—*Raegh, swim coach and instructor for 54 years*

Most competitive teams require a tuition, which covers coach's salary and registration with USA Swimming. There are additional inexpensive fees to participate in meets. On average I would say that you might spend a little over $1,000 total, though this varies per team.

—*Alyssa Bush, summer swim instructor for 5 years*

Safety and Injury Concerns

🐾 Swimming is the most injury-free of competitive sports. However, make sure coaches are trained in CPR, first aid, and water-safety instruction.

🐾 Some swimmers can develop shoulder, elbow, and knee injuries using improper techniques or from overuse.

🐾 Use goggles to prevent chlorine damage to the eyes, and if your child is susceptible to ear infections, have her wear earplugs.

Cost Considerations

🐾 All your child really needs is a swimsuit, goggles, perhaps a swim cap or earplugs, and a safe place to swim. For swim team, your child will have to get a team suit. For girls, swimsuits can be expensive, often costing around $40.

🐾 You may have to pay for access to a pool and for lessons. A competitive swimmer will train from 5 to 20 hours per week. Monthly dues are typically $50–$70. Private lessons range from $10 to $50 an hour.

TABLE TENNIS

Overview

Table tennis, essentially a professional sport similar to Ping-Pong, has 40 million competitive players worldwide and has been an Olympic sport since 1988. Millions also play table tennis recreationally and in major tournaments. In the early 1900s, the sport's official name was changed from Ping-Pong to table tennis. It is slowly becoming more popular in the United States, stretching beyond its reputation as a recreational game played in basements across America. There are over 230 table tennis clubs in the country, with many beginning to offer junior classes. In table tennis, two paddles, or "bats," are used to keep a ball moving from one player to the other until one of them fails to make a return. A typical game lasts about 30 minutes.

General Benefits

@ Table tennis is one of the best sports for developing hand-eye coordination.

@ It strengthens endurance, agility, finesse, and builds quick reflex reactions.

@ It is aerobic and offers a good cardiovascular workout.

@ Table tennis is accessible to all ages, genders and ability levels, even disabled players.

Kids Who Tend to Excel

@ great hand-eye coordination

@ quick reflexes

@ intense concentration and focus

@ the ability to think on their feet and strategize based on the skills and weaknesses of an opponent

@ creativity and a willingness to experiment with different shots and strategies

Best Age to Start

@ Table tennis can be picked up as soon as your child has the hand-eye coordination to make contact between the paddle and the ball, and the strength to hold up the paddle during a game.

Table tennis is a sport that teaches touch and finesse ahead of power, attributes that then can be transferred to other sports. It is also a sport that requires strategic thinking and tactics. Table tennis is one of the most gender-equal Olympic sports, and girls learn right alongside boys.

—*Ben Nisbet, director of American Youth Table Tennis Organization*

Table tennis has been called chess at warp speed. It's a very tactical game that teaches players to think on their feet. From table tennis, kids develop tactical thinking. Table tennis is often thought of as just a "game," but in reality, it can be a terrific workout. As kids become more proficient and the rallies grow longer, table tennis provides an excellent workout. Best of all, it's fun, so kids will enjoy it and keep at it, without even realizing the fitness benefits.

—*Larry Hodges, USA Table Tennis Club programs director and Maryland Table Tennis Center coach for 23 years*

Modern table tennis is about reading and producing spin and making the ball do what you want it to do. There is tremendous strategy and quick thinking involved. As you advance, you spend more time controlling outcomes rather than reacting. Kids who reach this level after about 6 to 8 months of practice get tremendous satisfaction out of creating a well-placed serve, forcing a predictable return, and following up with a precisely executed attack topspin winner. It requires patience, control and execution. As one advances, strategies overlay strategies and mental ability to sequence often wins out over physical talent.

—*Ben Nisbet, director of American Youth Table Tennis Organization*

Table tennis is one of the few sports where players of all ages can play on an equal playing field. Kids, parents, grandparents can all play. Size is relatively unimportant in table tennis. For example, the greatest woman player in history was Deng Yaping of China, who was 4'10" tall! Kids who excel at table tennis tend to be academic stars as well, as both involve tactical thinking and self-discipline. Top table tennis players are among the most disciplined and academically inclined of athletes.

—*Larry Hodges, USA Table Tennis Club programs director and Maryland Table Tennis Center coach for 23 years*

Most kids start off between ages 7 and 13, first learning Ping-Pong at home or at a local recreation center.

What to Look For When Getting Started

❦ Ask if the program has coaches who are USA Table Tennis certified.

❦ Every year, the primary junior tournaments are the Junior Olympics and Junior Nationals, with players from ages 7 to 21 competing in events in age categories starting with Under 10, in singles, doubles and teams, with equal events for boys and girls.

Safety and Injury Concerns

❦ Table tennis is relatively injury-free, except for wrist or shoulder sprains.

Cost Considerations

🐾 The primary cost is the paddle, with a decent beginning one costing around $30. Look for a wooden paddle with a smooth rubber surface. Rubber covering sheets for the paddle cost about $25 each and need to be replaced every 2 to 6 months, depending on how fast they get worn out. An orange or white ball is also required.

TENNIS

Overview

Tennis is the oldest of all racket sports. It emerged in its current form in 19th-century England on well-manicured croquet lawns, which were turned into courts for a racket game. While tennis was originally an Olympic sport in 1896, it went dormant from the Games for almost a century before being reintroduced in the early 1990s. With readily available indoor and outdoor facilities, tennis has evolved into a year-round sport. Tennis is also a lifetime sport; you can potentially play it well into your eighties. Tennis provides a great opportunity for your whole family to enjoy a sport together.

General Benefits

◉ Provides an aerobic workout that builds cardiovascular fitness

◉ Improves speed through sprints to chase down a ball

◉ Increases mobility, quick reactions, agility, flexibility, dynamic balance, and coordination

◉ Strengthens nearly every muscle group, particularly arms and legs

◉ Increases hand-eye coordination and footwork

◉ Develops fine motor control for touch shots like volleys, drop shots, and lobs

◉ Builds concentration, focus, and strategic thinking

Kids Who Tend to Excel

◉ Your child does not have to be naturally athletic or have a particular body type to excel in tennis.

◉ Players do need quick reflexes, outstanding hand-eye coordination, footwork, timing, speed, and quickness.

Tennis is a game for life. And you don't need nine other players to do it. You can even do it alone against a backboard, with a ball machine, or a bucket of balls. Learning tennis also serves as a steppingstone to adulthood because it teaches you to be a good sport.

—*Ron Perry, head teaching pro and USTA tennis professional, Brae Burn Country Club*

Tennis has a huge thinking element to it, forcing you to think several steps ahead, just like chess. Tennis also teaches you to be a problem solver, because you'll play against people with different styles and you have to figure out which of your strengths will work best against them.

—*Matt Helsel, head tennis coach, Elizabeth Town College, teaching for 9 years*

Tennis is a great sport that can be taught in a coed setting. The same techniques are taught to both boys and girls, who can even play against each other in the younger levels.

—*Martin Blackman, American University Tennis Team head coach for 4 years*

Focus, concentration, consistency, resilience, and determination also distinguish the best players.

Best Age to Start

Many programs and teaching pros start tennis lessons for kids between ages 5 and 7, though junior rackets and lessons are available for children as young as 3. This decision mainly depends on your child's interest and maturity, her ability to hold on to and swing a racket, and hand-eye coordination.

Of note, many kids are between ages 8 and 12 when they start formal lessons, though juniors who reach the tournament level usually start very early, sometimes before age 6.

What to Look For When Getting Started

Early tennis lessons will teach your child how to make contact between the racket and the ball, improve hand-eye coordination, footwork, and other tennis basics.

Find a tennis pro for beginners who is not a taskmaster, but is instead good with children, patient, with a sense of humor, and who has your child feeling enthusiastic about getting out on the court and hitting the ball.

Most children start out with group lessons because they cost less, run longer than a private lesson, and are generally more fun as they involve games and interactions with peers. Playing with a group turns learning tennis into a fun and a social activity. In group lessons, look for a ratio of four kids per instructor.

Tennis requires its participants to be highly self-disciplined and self-motivated. Successful players must have a great deal of emotional self-control and the ability to concentrate for two to three hours at a time; moreover, they must be able to think analytically under pressure. All successful players know that you win more matches with your mind than with your body. One of my favorite quotes along these lines comes from Wimbledon champion Boris Becker, who is one of the most physically gifted players to have ever played. When asked how much of the game is mental, he replied, "Only 90%." Children who do best are self-reliant, emotionally in control of themselves, and willing to persevere.

—Roger Mitten, head tennis professional, Mid-Town Tennis Club, and founder of
Tennis Opportunity Program for economically disadvantaged children, teaching for 15 years

Kids who excel in tennis tend to be "hyper" and have lots of extra energy or a strong desire to be outdoors exercising. Tennis also seems to attract kids who like attention and want to be rewarded for their hard work.

—Jeff Tarango, Tennis Wizard coach for 3 years and touring professional for 15 years

Most kids do not come to the sport with what some would call natural tennis skills. Also, tennis as a sport is very forgiving. We find kids with what would be called minor handicaps (like wearing glasses, overweight, slow, small, etc.) doing well at it.

—Hugh Waters, tennis teaching professional for 40 years

You don't have to be genetically gifted to be a successful tennis player. Tall players have an advantage on the serve and generally have a better reach, but shorter players can quickly change direction and find it easier to handle low balls. To be successful, kids must enjoy competition and dedicate themselves to constant and continued improvement. At the highest levels, world-class tennis players are very fit, have good foot speed, quickness, and agility. All champions adapt to different conditions and opponents, and learn to stay focused for an entire match.

—Kirk Anderson, USA Tennis national administrator, PTR and USPTA master professional,
teaching for 33 years

If some of the parents of my students had it their way, I might be waiting in the delivery room with a racket and ball. The reality is that children can be encouraged to learn the game at any age as long as the activities are appropriate. With children under the age of 4, I recommend that parents play with their child in a very open-ended environment—rolling balls, playing catch—anything that gives them a fun, positive association with the game. I have found that formal instruction can be worthwhile beginning at age 4. At this stage children are learning to follow direction from someone other than Mom or Dad and they have enough attention span to participate in group lessons and grasp some of the basic concepts of the game. I would add that each child is unique and there is not a chronological rule to follow. Parents would benefit from getting advice from a certified instructor.

> —*Timothy Smith, director of junior tennis at Longwood Cricket Club and codirector of New England Academy of Tennis, teaching for 18 years*

As a teaching professional, the biggest problem I have is when parents send me a three- or four-year-old child for an hour private lesson and it becomes more baby-sitting than tennis coaching. Once your child has the ability to strike the ball, serve, and play tennis, then private lessons make sense.

> —*Ron Perry, head teaching pro, Brae Burn Country Club, and USTA tennis professional*

❧ If your child seems to have a real passion for tennis, make sure she gets topnotch coaching so her future development is not hindered by a poor foundation in the basics. Both the U.S. Professional Tennis Association (USPTA) and the U.S. Professional Tennis Registry (USPTR) have certification for instructors, detailed in the Resources section. Ask the teacher about what level of players they typically coach, what certification they have, what teaching philosophy they adhere to, and whether they have a specialty.

❧ The U.S. Tennis Association (USTA) runs junior tournaments for kids ages 12–18. Whether or not your child is ready to enter these should be a joint decision by your child, her teaching professional, and you. A tennis match can involve two individual players (singles), two pairs of players (doubles), or a single player against a pair of players (Canadian doubles).

Juniors need to be nurtured through a long initial learning period, as it takes a good five years for a junior to acquire the tennis skills needed to excel. Qualities that help in very young children are a love of games, interest in a ball, good attention, and patient parents. Your child should come home from a tennis program inspired. If not, change programs. A great pro or a tennis program should hook your child—which is what you are looking for.

—*Hugh Waters, tennis teaching professional for 40 years*

Tennis is a highly technical sport, with a million different avenues for learning strokes and techniques, and kids can easily get frustrated trying to master it. Group lessons are more cost effective, but the best route for a beginner is to start with private lessons to get down the basic strokes. Then if your child needs help with specific issues, back to the pro. If your child gets serious about tennis, you want a coach who specializes, such as in serve and volley or doubles strategy. You also want a coach who is like-minded to your child, so for instance if your child is hyper-aggressive, you find a coach who teaches that style of play.

—*Matt Helsel, head tennis coach, Elizabeth Town College, teaching for 9 years*

I have found that a child should take a combination of group and private lessons when first starting out. Two clinics each week and one half-hour private lesson a week seems to be the perfect match for a child. This way the child will have fun with other kids his own age and learn to focus in his private lessons. Also, the coach will be able to see the child's weaknesses in the group lessons and then address those problems one on one.

—*Martin Blackman, American University Tennis Team head coach for 4 years*

Safety and Injury Concerns

🍂 Tennis can cause muscle sprains in the forearm and shoulder, shin splints, and tennis elbow. Common injuries are to the shoulder, wrist, elbow, and knee, as well as ankle sprains.

🍂 Balls should always be cleared off the court, as one of the most common causes of injury is tripping over an errant ball.

🐟 Your child should wear tennis shoes with good support to prevent ankle injuries or a torn Achilles tendon, which can result from quick starts, stops, and lateral moves.

Cost Considerations

🐟 Your child will need a racket of her own. Junior rackets are not too costly, and can often be borrowed from an instructor. A beginner's racket costs between $25 and $40, with racket costs for more serious players ranging from $120 to $200 on average.

🐟 The most expensive part of playing tennis, outside of joining a private tennis club, are lesson fees, with group lessons costing between $10 and $25 an hour. Private clubs charge more for their programs but offer a higher quality of instruction. A one-hour private lesson can cost anywhere from $30 to $80 an hour depending on the coach and his or her level of expertise.

🐟 Tennis can become expensive when your child enters the more advanced realm of weekly private lessons and tournaments. If your child starts traveling to competitions, there will be coaching fees, travel expenses, and tournament fees. Your child

We encourage the use of modified courts and equipment for young children. Lower nets, short racquets and large foam balls make the game much easier to learn, and rally skills can be developed much faster with equipment designed for young children. As soon as children can rally, they should be able to play a modified tennis game with other kids.

—*Kirk Anderson, USA Tennis national administrator, PTR and USPTA master professional, teaching for 33 years*

Being very patient and understanding is key when working with young kids, as well as the ability to make it fun. If kids aren't having fun, they won't come back, and young kids tend to have the most fun in group lessons. You want a pro who doesn't have long breaks talking or explaining something to the kids but rather one who hits while instructing, as kids prefer a hands-on experience. Also, make sure that the pro is USPTA or USPTR certified. You don't want someone teaching your child just because they have on a pair of white tennis shorts.

—*Ron Perry, head teaching pro, Brae Burn Country Club, and USTA tennis professional*

Young children will often start twirling or randomly swinging their racket at a moment's impulse, and other kids nearby can get hurt. Pros need to make sure that everyone's spaced far enough apart in a group lesson and that balls are not all over the court where a child can easily trip over them.

> —*Ron Perry, head teaching pro, Brae Burn Country Club, and USTA tennis professional*

In tennis, small-muscle groups in the ankle and wrist take a pounding. I always emphasize to my students to try to use large muscles to move the ball around, not their elbow or wrists.

> —*Matt Helsel, head tennis coach, Elizabeth Town College, teaching for 9 years*

Many kids watch the hard-hitting pros on TV and come out swinging too hard in their next lesson. A child should be taught that accuracy and form are the key to success, not pounding the ball out of control.

> —*Martin Blackman, American University Tennis Team head coach for 4 years*

Injuries occur more often with our advanced players, who train anywhere from 5 to 15 hours a week. Typical injuries show up in the shoulder and back and are often the result of overuse, improper technique, or lack of flexibility. When players begin to take the game more seriously, there is greater demand on the body. It is important for parents and players alike to take a holistic approach to the game and include an appropriate fitness program that will not only enhance their performance but also help to keep them injury free.

> —*Timothy Smith, director of junior tennis at Longwood Cricket Club and codirector of New England Academy of Tennis, teaching for 18 years*

will also need to have multiple rackets, in case one breaks in the middle of a match, and will wear out tennis sneakers about every two months.

TRACK AND FIELD/RUNNING

Overview

As your child races around the house from one room to the next, you might wonder if he will ever run out of energy. Perhaps all of your child's excess energy can be centered on a more productive activity than creating chaos in your home. Track and field is an excellent sport for any child who is quick, strong, and exhibits a bottomless amount of energy. This combination of running, throwing, and jumping will mold your child into an all-around athlete and give him the skills necessary to compete in other sporting activities as well. Cross-country running, track and field's counterpart, is also a perfect fit for those who have mental and physical stamina and prefer to run long distances.

With the sport tracing its roots back to ancient Greece, track and field is the number one participatory sport in junior high and high schools, according to USA Track & Field. In addition, millions of people run for health, fun, fitness, and competition, including three of the last four presidents of the United States. Running clubs have sprung up in almost every community in the country. Running programs exist for kids and sponsor events for families. Running is also the most accessible of aerobic sports. No matter where you live, an excellent area for running is almost always close by.

Running is a natural sport that requires very little equipment and very little funds to get your child involved. All he will need in the early stages are sturdy shoes and the appropriate clothing. In the beginning, it is also important that he determine his own pace and run only if it's fun and enjoyable. Each child has different endurance abilities and skill levels, so it is up to your child to know his limits.

General Benefits

◉ Both track and field and running build strength, endurance, and cardiovascular fitness.

◉ Since the "running boom" of the 1970s, much has been written concerning the psychological benefits of running, which include decreasing anxiety, reducing stress, relieving depression, enhancing physical self-esteem, and promoting a sense of well-being.

◉ Running allows for a flexible method of training in which your child can run at his own pace, with or without a partner, at whatever time suits him. Your child's body becomes the tool of the sport.

◉ Regular, moderate running can reduce the risk of osteoporosis and diabetes in your child.

Kids Who Tend to Excel

◉ For track and field, body type matters. Runners and jumpers are usually lean, whereas discus throwers and shot-putters are more muscular and stocky.

◉ Sprinters are usually more muscular and distance runners more slender. Mental toughness, speed, and endurance are key to succeeding in running activities.

◉ As individual sports, both track and field and running require self-discipline, commitment, and hard work.

Best Age to Start

◉ While there are programs for children as young as 8 to start jumping and field events, many kids do not start until ninth grade.

◉ Distance running should be postponed until adolescence. Even then, track programs for middle school–age children usually limit running distances to half to three-quarters of a mile at a time. At this stage in your child's development, his bones are still growing and the growth cartilage at the ends of the bones is softer than adult cartilage and thus more vulnerable to injury. Your child should not begin running races above 5 kilometers (3.1 miles) until he is at least 14 years of age. There are many shorter distance competitions available for your child to participate in, such as "fun runs" and team competitions.

◉ Most marathons are out of the question, as officials will not allow athletes under the age of 18 to enter due to possible skeletal injuries.

Track and field provides your energetic child with an outlet to do all the things not allowed in the house—running, jumping (on the furniture), and throwing things. If you have a child like this, then this a great option to keep your house in one piece and interest your child in activities that provide the basis for all other land-based sports. Kids should be encouraged to try all events from sprints, jumps, and throws, to some middle-distance events. Most young people should not enter distance running right away, as they first need to learn proper sprint form.

> —Scott Hal, head track and field/cross-country coach, University of Northern Colorado, chair for 24 years, USA Track & Field Men's Olympic Development Committee

◉

Risk takers and adventurous people do well in the pole vault, hurdles, and jumps. Kids who excel at sprinting and jumping have coordination and strength.

> —Stan Rosenthal, cross-country and track and field coach, University of South Carolina, coaching for 25 years

What to Look For When Getting Started

🍂 Since running is a natural action, your child will quickly develop his own form. He should be taught to relax his hands and face while running. A scrunched face and clenched fists indicate tension, which usually means the intensity is too high and he is struggling to continue rather than having fun.

🍂 In terms of distance, your child needs to learn how to gauge his own limitations and should run only as far as he is comfortable. He should be able to smile and carry on a conversation while running. Urge your child to slow down if necessary and keep his shoulders relaxed while steadily swinging his arms. There are many levels of competition, from local invitational track meets to school-sponsored events, up to regional, state, and national meets.

🍂 The ultimate goal of all track and field athletes can be summed up in three words: faster, higher, and farther. The track and field athlete competes to beat his best time, the opponent, and the record. On a team, your child will have the benefit of trying different events to see which ones he likes and performs at best.

Track: Running Events

🍂 Sprints, which also include hurdles and relay races, require the athlete to run at full speed. Sprinters blast off from a starting block and run full speed in races from 50 to 400 meters long. Hurdles are sprints where a runner must race at full speed while jumping over 10 obstacles along the way. A relay race consists of four team members, each runner covering a part of the course and passing a baton to the next runner.

🍂 Middle-distance races are between 800 and 5,000 meters long and require both speed and stamina.

🍂 Long-distance races are between 10,000 and 30,000 meters long, but are not typically done in school competitions.

Field: Throwing Events

🍂 The discus, hammer, and shot are thrown from within a circle, with the longest throw winning.

🍂 A discus athlete throws a solid, heavy disk using a spinning motion to build up power, and releases it with a sidearm motion.

🍂 A hammer is a heavy metal ball attached to a handle by a chain. A hammer thrower uses a good spin to power up a hammer throw, first spinning the hammer around his head and then spinning his body before releasing it.

✦ The shot put can be a difficult event for a child because the athlete needs to hop on one foot while throwing a large, heavy ball.

✦ Javelin athletes run and throw a long thin pole as far as they possibly can. The pole is usually made of metal, though it can be wooden, with a steel tip that must stick in the ground when thrown. Javelin athletes sprint down a runway to a foul line, at which point they throw the javelin. All the throwers have six tries to do their best, and the longest distance wins.

Field: Jumping Events

✦ In the high jump, the athlete has to jump up and over a bar raised to increasing heights.

✦ Long jumpers sprint down a runway, make a jumping leap from a takeoff point, and land in a sandpit. The jump is measured at the closest mark made in the sand.

✦ In pole vaulting, a pole carries the athlete up and over a high bar, with the athlete clearing the highest bar winning.

Safety and Injury Concerns

✦ The primary source of injuries in track and field and running are muscle strains and tears, torn ligaments, and shin splints.

✦ Before running, a five-minute warm-up followed by stretching exercises is essential. Although your child's body is more flexible than that of most adults, he should always begin a walk or run slowly in order to get the muscles warm and ready to run. He should also be shown how to stretch his calves, hip flexors, and hamstrings when cooling down at the end of each run.

✦ Whenever possible, your child should run on a clear, smooth, even, and reasonably soft surface. At first your child should avoid running on hills, which increases stress on the ankle and foot.

✦ Consult a physician to rule out any physical limitations that may prevent your child from participating in a running program, such as asthma.

✦ In recent years, a growing body of research has revealed that dedicated runners can become psychologically dependent and even addicted to running to the point where they experience anxiety and depression when forced to abstain from their running routine.

Stretching is very important. Being flexible helps prevent injury and makes a child a better runner, jumper, or thrower.

> —Stan Rosenthal, cross-country and track and field coach, University of South Carolina, coaching for 25 years

Over 800 kids have come through our program and there has been one broken ankle from landing wrong during running drills and two concussions: one from a seven-year-old girl falling on her head while jumping over a hurdle she was advised not to do and a seven-year-old boy was knocked on the head because he ran into someone swinging the shot in a sling during a warm-up. That is a great safety record when you consider we coach running, high jump, long jump, shot put, and javelin.

> —Ed Poirier, head coach of youth track and field team, Attleboro YMCA, coaching for 7 years

The triple jump is not recommended for young girls due to their physiological development. In regards to the throwing events, it's important to use lighter-weight implements if starting young.

> —Sergei Bykov, assistant track coach, Abilene Christian University, coaching for 4 years

✦ During hot weather, your child should run in the early morning or evening so he avoids heat exhaustion. Your child should drink 10–15 ounces of fluid 10–15 minutes prior to running and every 20–30 minutes along his route. Sunglasses and a hat should be worn to filter out UV rays and shade his eyes and face.

Cost Considerations

✦ One of the major benefits of running is that it can generally be done anywhere and anytime. However, if your child wants to become involved in regular competition or training, there will be some costs depending on your child's age and at what level he wants to compete.

✦ Track and field clubs usually have a registration fee to cover athletes under their insurance policy, and this fee goes toward coaching and equipment. Your child will also need to register with the appropriate state body if he wishes to compete in meets. Typical fees to compete at the local track meets are between $5 and $30.

🏃 When selecting a running shoe for your child, look for good shock absorption, which will provide stability and cushioning to the foot. Make sure that there is a thumbnail's width between the end of the longest toe and the end of the shoe. Look for a high-quality shoe that is made specifically for running or track and field events, with proper cushioning in the forefoot and heel as well as arch support. Depending on how often your child runs, replace his running shoes as soon as they show signs of breakdown, which usually occurs after three months of use. Running shoes typically cost $35–$50 for a pair. Spikes start at around $30.

🏃 Depending on the events your child takes part in, a tracksuit, warm-up shoes, and spikes or shoes appropriate for the specialized event will be needed. If your child wishes to specialize in field events such as the pole vault or hammer throw, additional equipment may be required.

VOLLEYBALL

Overview

While volleyball has traditionally been thought of as a fun pickup activity at a barbecue or while lounging on the beach, it is actually an up-and-coming, highly competitive sport both on the hard courts of gyms and on the sand courts of beaches. Volleyball was invented at a YMCA gymnasium in Holyoke, Massachusetts, in 1895. It was added to the Summer Olympic Games in 1964 and is now played by millions around the world. Volleyball ranks just behind soccer as one of the world's most popular sports.

Precise teamwork is one of the most important determinants of success in volleyball, as the explosive movements of six players in a relatively small space must all be highly coordinated, from spiking the ball to defensive moves. In volleyball, while individual performance is important, individual stars cannot make a team. Instead, top programs consistently win tournaments based on team unity. Your child will learn that consistency contributes more to her team's success than any single big play.

General Benefits

◉ Volleyball improves balance, hand-eye coordination, flexibility, agility, endurance, and overall body strength. It teaches tremendous concentration, focus, and discipline.

Volleyball keeps kids interested in moving, and gives them increased agility and quickness because it is an explosive, skill-driven sport. You can make an average athlete into a great volleyball player. Volleyball epitomizes what team sports are all about, because everyone needs to work together, such as having plays where one kid passes, one will set, and one will hit.

—*Kelly Boyd, volleyball coach at Southern Indiana University, coaching for 7 years*

Kids who excel in volleyball are aggressive, athletic, good communicators, and smart. They are able to analyze situations and react quickly, improving their reflexes.

—*Annette Kvamme, volleyball coach, Fort Hays University, teaching for 5 years*

As you rise in levels, volleyball offers a variety of positions, and we tend to find different mentalities for each position. Setters tend to be thinkers and leaders of the group, while hitters and defensive players tend to be more aggressive yet also thinkers.

—*Cassie Headrick, head women's volleyball coach, University of North Texas, teaching for 8 years*

It also teaches your child to rely on her instinctive reactions for split-second decision making and changes in direction. During long rallies, your child may have to run full speed to the back of the court, dig a spike, and then sprint forward to the net to assist a teammate in setting the ball, then jump as high as possible and spike the ball into the opposing team's court. The skills of vertical jumping and moving laterally can transfer to many other sports.

Volleyball is a wonderful sport to carry through adulthood, offering a fun, social way to stay in shape.

Kids Who Tend to Excel

Volleyball players are usually tall, quick, and able to jump high. Having a tall, lean body with a long arm reach helps, though short players who are quick can develop into effective defensive players.

Volleyball players need body strength to spike the ball and jump. They also need to move deftly in a small space, coordinating with other team members.

Volleyball requires perseverance and demands a high degree of energy to keep up with the intense competition. Kids with good motor skills and athleticism excel. Having a competitive edge also helps.

Best Age to Start

Most children start playing volleyball in seventh or eighth grade, although some programs now begin as young as age 5, having kids work with lighter balls or even balloons to start developing coordination and skills. Kids can get into competitive clubs starting at age 12 and under.

What to Look For When Getting Started

🦋 Look for a volleyball program specifically tailored to improve your child's skills and game performance. Your child might fare better starting with recreational volleyball, which has a softer ball, than highly competitive play.

🦋 Mini volleyball was specially designed for young children, with smaller courts, lower nets, and soft colored balls, which are easy to maneuver and manipulate. The simple rules focus on ball manipulation, with players rotating positions. Points are awarded for directing the ball onto the floor inside the opponent's court. This type of volleyball promotes coordination, agility, and the ability to move swiftly in order to handle changes in the ball's flight. Your child will develop a sense of touch, timing, and balance to direct the ball with precision and control and move in a dynamic and explosive way when jumping to attack or defend.

🦋 Find out whether the coaches in the program are paid professionals or volunteers, and how much experience each coach has. USA Volleyball Association certifies coaches through their Coaching Accreditation Program (CAP), with Level I for new coaches all the way through Level V for national coaches.

🦋 USA Volleyball also sponsors junior competitions that start locally, with teams qualifying regionally and then for a Junior Olympics. Age divisions start at 12 and under, and go for each year through 18 and under.

Your child's body has to develop a resistance to the ball, and playing with a lighter ball starts that process. Plus, it allows children to still learn skills correctly without having to use strength against a ball's weighted resistance. Lastly, the outdoor and indoor game fundamentally differ. Movement is more difficult outdoors and skills are also different, so I would recommend indoors when beginning.

—*Cassie Headrick, head women's volleyball coach, University of North Texas, teaching for 8 years*

Mini volleyball is the best way to start. The softer ball is kid-friendly, allowing small children to play without injury and be much more successful.

—*Sue Gozansky, head volleyball coach, University of California, Riverside, teaching for 32 years*

With the younger kids, I work on skill development, form, and how your body needs to look when you contact the ball. Once they have the skills down, I teach things like different ways to move your arms and how to spike the ball.

—*Kelly Boyd, volleyball coach at Southern Indiana University, coaching for 7 years*

Safety and Injury Concerns

✦ Volleyball's most common injuries are usually minor, such as facial cuts, bruises, or minor tendonitis, strains, or sprains. Bruising of the hands, wrists, or forearms can result from repeatedly hitting the ball. Most injuries occur because of incorrect technique.

✦ Some hard-court, indoor volleyball injuries include sprained or broken ankles, bruises due to hard landings on elbows or knees, and overuse shoulder injuries. Your child should wear kneepads to protect her when she falls or dives onto the court. Special pants, padded from the hip to the knee, can also offer protection from floor burns and bruises. Look for lightweight shoes that provide strong ankle and arch support and offer good shock absorption. Wrist supports can also be worn when competing.

✦ Beach volleyball often has the fewest injuries of all the types of volleyball. Pulled muscles, bruises and cuts, and sprained ankles will occasionally occur. Before playing outdoor volleyball, check the ground for sharp objects or divots that could cause ankle injuries.

Most injuries happen to the ankles and knees from all the jumping, and there can be many jammed fingers from blocking.

    —*Annette Kvamme, volleyball coach, Fort Hays University, teaching for 5 years*

To successfully play volleyball at the higher levels, your child must play with a volleyball club, and many clubs are quite expensive, often costing thousands of dollars each year.

    —*Sue Gozansky, head volleyball coach, University of California, Riverside, teaching for 32 years*

Volleyball has become very club driven. Volleyball moms travel with their kids to tournaments and have to spend extra money on motels and food, coaches and transportation. You can spend astronomical amounts at a competitive level. Parents sometimes look at it as an investment for college.

    —*Kelly Boyd, volleyball coach at Southern Indiana University, coaching for 7 years*

Cost Considerations

🐟 Volleyball equipment and participation is relatively inexpensive. All you need to participate are court space, a net, volleyball, athletic shoes, and kneepads for indoor play.

🐟 Competitive volleyball involves joining a club and paying dues, along with tournament fees.

WATERSKIING

Overview

Waterskiing was invented in the United States in 1922, when Minnesotan Ralph Samuelson built the first pair of skis and got pulled on them behind a motorboat. Waterskiing started as an exhibition sport and then officially developed into a competitive sport in 1939, when the first annual National Water Ski Championships were held. There are now over 11 million water-skiers in the United States.

Many children learn to water-ski at summer camp and then want to pursue it further. Water-ski clubs are a great way to get your child involved in waterskiing if you do not have a boat of your own. Many water-ski clubs around the country are geared toward racing, with experienced skiers, observers, drivers, and instructors on hand. For many, recreational waterskiing is a family activity, with each person participating at his or her own level.

Waterskiing competitions feature primarily three types of events. In slalom, the skier has to successfully navigate a course around six buoys. On each run, the boat increases its speed by two miles per hour until the maximum speed for each division is reached. After that, the towrope is then shortened by premeasured increments. The water-skier who clears the most buoys without a miss or a fall wins. In trick skiing, each skier performs two passes, which consist of a 20-second routine of maneuvers, each having a preassigned point value based on its difficulty. The skier with the highest number of points wins. Trick skiing, sometimes called "gymnastics on water," involves flips, spins, and tricks that the skier performs with the rope harness on his foot. Trick skiing requires strength, balance, and agility. In jumping, the water-skier who jumps the farthest distance wins. Maximum speeds for the boats are set for each division. The skier increases speed by going out to the wake on one side of the boat and then cutting hard into the jump ramp.

Thousands of tournaments take place throughout the world each year, ranging from local competitions for beginners, to national and world-level international tournaments for elite athletes. A water-ski race team consists of a boat driver, an ob-

Waterskiing is a sport where children progress at their own speed and feel really good about their individual skills. Children develop physical strength and overall body conditioning, which makes them good athletes overall.

—*Steve Lohr, senior judge, Level 3 AWSA coach and national competitor for 38 years*

I have seen kids start at all ages. My oldest daughter is 5 and will compete in slalom and tricks next summer. A friend of mine started when he was 60 and competes in the national championships now.

—*Roger Boskus, waterskiing instructor for 3 years*

server, and a skier. Waterskiing for elite athletes has become a full-time pursuit, with skiers meticulously working on techniques and cross-training out of the water. Because of the fierce competition in each event, most water-skiers specialize in only one or two events in order to excel.

General Benefits

- Builds upper- and lower-body strength
- Provides an aerobic workout
- Improves balance and coordination
- Allows children to embrace challenges and overcome fear

Kids Who Tend to Excel

- Those who have upper- and lower-body strength, balance, athleticism, and coordination
- Kids who have tenacity to hold on to the rope.
- Kids who are comfortable with speed

Best Age to Start

- Kids often start as young as age 6, depending on how well they are able to hang on to the towrope bar and balance when they come up out of the water onto their skis.

- Being unable to swim or ill at ease in the water is a large impediment. For this reason, swim lessons are often best before ski lessons.

What to Look For When Getting Started

❧ Ask if the instructors use a teaching aid for beginners to help keep their skis steady during takeoff. You also want to know whether an adult will be in the water with your child, helping her to get up out of the water and give her confidence in her first attempts, or whether they teach beginners from dry starts on land.

❧ The instructor should work with your child to teach her how to keep her knees bent, head up, weight leaning back, and arms straight, and also how to retain her balance. Once your child masters two skis and is able to cross the wake behind the boat, the coach should begin teaching her slalom. Most instructors first teach how to drop one ski, and then teach a deep-water start on a slalom ski.

🍃 There are many different types of regional, state, and national waterskiing competitions, with some geared just for beginner skiers, such as those sponsored by the National Ski League (NSL), a program of USA Water Ski. Local organizations also host grassroots tournaments. Regional and national competitions take place on weekends. The events are grouped by age, with boys' and girls' divisions as follows: Level 1 for ages 9 and under, Level 2 for ages 10–12, and Level 3 for ages 13–16.

Matching skiers of similar skill levels is not necessary, as each person skis individually. Your child can ski with a national champion or a new beginner and still have fun. It does help to have peers around in the program, though, as it makes the overall environment more fun and enjoyable.

—*Steve Lohr, Senior Judge, Level 3 AWSA coach and national competitor for 38 years*

Safety and Injury Concerns

🍃 Waterskiing is a relatively safe sport, as long as the boat driver uses care and keeps a lookout for other boats, swimmers, and debris. Your child should be taught signals that a person in the boat can understand, such as thumbs up for starting to accelerate, or the okay signal after falling, as she can't be heard over the boat's engine.

🍃 Occasionally a skier can get bruises from falling. Make sure your child's bindings fit properly to avoid injury, such as a sprained ankle from the ski not releasing from the foot during a fall.

Waterskiing competition is a very safe sport if done with professional coaches. A fall at slalom skiing at slower speeds is almost always injury-free. Ankle sprains and broken bones can happen in an extremely severe fall, which usually does not occur until the speeds get to 34 m.p.h.

—*Roger Boskus, waterskiing instructor for 3 years*

🍃 Your child should always wear an appropriate personal flotation life vest, should know how to swim, and not be afraid of the water.

Cost Considerations

🍃 Most water-skiers prefer to own their own skis, though some programs will supply skis. Expect to pay between $100 and $500 for a pair of new skis, and around $500 for a wakeboard with bindings.

Many worry about injury from falling forward onto your skis. However, since skis move the same speed and distance as you do, falling forward rarely causes injury. If your child gets more advanced and into competitive levels of waterskiing, the chance of injury does increase, such as in racing or jumping, where helmets are worn.

—*Lou Abel, waterskiing coach for 50 years*

🐟 Your child may need a pair of waterskiing gloves to prevent calluses from forming on her hands, which will cost around $15, and she will also need a life vest (personal flotation device), which will cost between $25 and $60.

🐟 When buying beginner water skis for your child, look for adjustable bindings, one ski that doubles as a slalom ski, detachable stabilizing bar or rope that holds the skis the proper distance apart, wide tips for stable starts, and shorter length for easy handling and quick learning.

🐟 Lessons cost anywhere from $25 to $100 depending on the experience and caliber of the teacher.

🐟 Other expenses include joining a water-ski club, lessons, competition entry fees, and the costs of renting or owning a boat, all of which vary dramatically by region. Often, waterskiing clubs have a club boat that members can use.

WINDSURFING

Overview

Windsurfing is a comparatively new sport, invented in 1968 by two Californians, a sailor and a surfer, who figured out a way to combine their respective sports into a new hybrid. By mounting a sail on a joint that can be tilted in any direction, a windsurfer can steer the board without a rudder, unlike sailing. Windsurfing became an Olympic sport in 1984.

Windsurfing combines the thrill of surfing and the waves with the strategy of sailing and the peacefulness of nature. Many kids learn windsurfing on warm-weather vacations and then want to continue at home. There are 1.2 million windsurfers in America and the sport is still growing fast.

Most windsurfing racing resembles yacht races. Participants go around a set course in a triangle configuration; the first one to complete the course is the winner. Other forms of competition are a slalom racecourse that runs only downwind where sailors must maneuver around buoys, and wave sailing, in which sailors are judged based on aerial skills, tricks, and board handling.

General Benefits

◎ Builds upper- and lower-body strength as well as endurance

◎ Improves balance and coordination

◎ Offers a great sense of peacefulness and stress relief, from being out on the water

◎ Teaches independence and self-reliance

Kids Who Tend to Excel

◎ Windsurfing relies on finesse and balance rather than strength.

◎ Kids who excel have to master the fundamentals of sailing and catching the wind.

◎ To master windsurfing takes perseverance, practice, and commitment.

Best Age to Start

◎ Most kids can get the concept around age 6 or 7, but there's no best age to start. Your child must be at the age when she can swim well and feel confident and comfortable alone in deep water. Many children pick up windsurfing in their teens and catch up with their peers who started younger.

What to Look For When Getting Started

🐾 Windsurfing is not an easy sport to learn. As a beginner, your child will be spending a lot of time

Kids gain an appreciation for the environment (nothing like seeing firsthand the drawbacks to water pollution!) and an experience of peace while flying across the water. They learn about the weather and the conditions that result in wind. Kids will also experiment with different things to go faster, jump higher, and plane longer, resulting in a real appreciation of cause and effect. Windsurfing is a solo sport but very social. Windsurfers love to hang out on the beach and talk about windsurfing.

—*Brian Collis, president of Southern Maryland Windsurfing Association, teaching for 4 years*

I have seen windsurfing give my son a more mature attitude, make him more safety conscious, learn to persevere, and inspire him to learn about the science of sailing.

—*Steve Elliott, windsurfing for 25 years*

Windsurfing is similar to ballet in that kids with no grace at all can do well enough to get the "bug," and as they excel, they become very graceful as they maneuver the board into and around the waves. Kids who excel are the ones that like a challenge. Most windsurfers will tell you that they've had horrible sessions, only to smile and show up to sail again the next time the wind blows. Kids who already love the water or already love boat sailing usually excel in windsurfing, because kids like to go fast. A windsurfer will go much faster than almost all sailboats.

—Brian Collis, president of Southern Maryland Windsurfing Association, teaching for 4 years

just learning to lift the sail out of the water, which takes a great deal of pulling and is exhausting.

🐟 Children with surfing and sailing experience will master windsurfing faster, but almost everyone takes close to 100 falls before getting the hang of it. Each fall entails pulling the sail out of the water, called "uphauling," to start again, which creates tired, sore muscles the next day. Make sure the sail is rigged tight and flat, as this will make pulling up the sail easier, with less water to drain off. Learners should keep knees bent to help protect the lower back when pulling up the sail.

🐟 As windsurfing is essentially sailing on a surfboard, your child will need to learn the basics of sailing, including understanding wind direction, points of sail, and how to tack, jibe, and change directions. Once your child masters these skills, along with a deep-water start, he will be ready for a shorter board. He will also learn how to utilize foot straps and a harness that enables body weight to counteract the pull of the sail, instead of just using arm muscles.

🐟 When looking at a windsurfing program, ask how they teach beginner surfers, whether they do beach or water starts, what kind of equipment they teach on, and if they provide life vests, water shoes, or wet suits. Look for a program that offers continuing intermediate and advanced lessons and for an instructor who has been certified by U.S. Windsurfing, indicating training in the latest techniques.

Proper equipment is important to a child's success, and children should start out with light-weight carbon masts and small sails that are easy to lug around.

—*Beth Powell Winkler, masters world champion, U.S. Sailing Team member, and windsurfing instructor for 20 years*

If you really want your kid to get into windsurfing, give it a shot yourself. If your child sees that you can do it or are learning alongside him, he'll be more likely to get into it. There are many windsurfing families, all having fun on the water. All over the country there are races, wave events, and freestyle competitions that kids are encouraged to compete in. Kids almost always do better in windsurfing than adults because they're lighter, and can plane in less wind. This allows them to blow past heavier adults, giving them the advantage on the water.

—*Brian Collis, president of Southern Maryland Windsurfing Association, teaching for 4 years*

Many people are taught windsurfing on old, heavy equipment because that gear can take the punishment of a learner. Unfortunately, the effort required to learn on this gear is excessive. In the last three years there have been significant improvements in the development of light and stable boards, sails, and associated gear that make learning the sport much easier for children and adults than it was as recently as five years ago.

—*Michael Alex, teaching windsurfing for 11 years*

Light-Wind Windsurfing

🦋 Kids should always learn light-wind techniques first. This is important both for safety and for learning advanced techniques and tricks.

🦋 Cruising is the most popular form of light-wind windsurfing. It is done in winds of 10 knots or under on boards that can easily support one's weight while not moving.

🦋 Freestyle, the second most popular form, involves doing a variety of tricks, turns, spins, and maneuvers with the board and sail.

High-Wind Windsurfing

✦ This advanced form of windsurfing, generally performed in high winds between 15 and 25 knots, involves smaller boards, which are more maneuverable at very high speeds. Controlling a board in high winds takes agility and quick reflexes.

✦ The three types of high-wind windsurfing are slalom (doing high-speed turns between runs), bump and jump (jumps, turns, and loops at high speed), and waves (windsurfing in an ocean or gulf on open swells).

Safety and Injury Concerns

✦ Windsurfing is a relatively safe sport. If your child falls into the water, she can just climb back on the board and start sailing again. That being said, your child should always wear a personal flotation device (PFD) and never sail out too far alone.

✦ A windsurfing wet suit will not only keep the chill off, but also offer protection from the sun and scrapes as your child climbs onto the board. Look for a wet suit with plenty of room in the forearms and shoulder area, and booties to protect your child's feet, as many learning areas have rocky bottoms. The wet suit also serves to protect your child's legs, knees, and feet from getting hurt if hit against the board's fittings during a fall.

✦ The two most common injuries in windsurfing are getting hit on the head from a falling rig (which can be prevented by raised hands protecting the head in a fall) and getting a foot trapped between the board and the rig. Both can be avoided by being taught in lessons how to keep your front foot on the stern side of the mast's base.

✦ Beginners should always windsurf with a breeze blowing toward shore, particularly if in the ocean, to ensure they are not pushed farther away from shore.

Cost Considerations

✦ Windsurfing equipment is composed of five primary pieces: board, sail, boom, mast, and mast base. Most instructional programs will either provide beginner's equipment or have it available to rent. To purchase a completely rigged board costs between $1,000 and $1,500. However, you can spend about half that if you buy used equipment. You'll also need a rack for your car.

✦ Some local shops will rent gear, costing between $40 and $60 per hour or $100 or so per day. Rates are different around the country, and may not include insurance against broken gear.

The difference between light-wind and high-wind surfing is the difference between driving a car for the first time in a parking lot versus 65 m.p.h. on Route 95.

—*Eddie Senechal, Cape Cod windsurfing instructor*

If the sailing site is safe for beginners in high-wind and your child already knows how to sail in light-wind, that is the quickest way to get them hooked. Light-wind is good for balance, strength, sail handling, and learning footwork. High-wind is good for upper-body strength, co-ordination, and balance. High-wind is exhilarating, addicting, and is the reason we sail. Once they experience sailing at speed and planing, they will be forever hooked.

—*Steve Elliott, windsurfing for 25 years*

Light-wind windsurfing is mostly a steppingstone to high-wind windsurfing, although much racing takes place in light-wind that requires much more concentration and discipline. Kids who struggle most with windsurfing get bored with light-wind but aren't aggressive enough to attempt high-wind.

—*Karen Marriott, national and Olympic trials competitor, teaching for 14 years*

Teaching a child to windsurf in over 15 knots of wind is like taking a new downhill skier to a double diamond and giving him a push downhill. Light-wind is laid-back and relaxing. Those conditions allow you to work on your board and sail-handling skills while having fun on the water. You'll usually see larger, longer, or wider boards with more volume on the water in these conditions, with larger sails. Sailing in 15–45 knots of wind is high-energy, heart-pumping excitement. You'll see smaller boards, smaller sails, bigger waves, or chop on the water, with sailors working on their jumping and planing skills. Both conditions are lots of fun with the right equipment.

—*Brian Collis, president of Southern Maryland Windsurfing Association, teaching for 4 years*

❧ Most beginners should start on a beginner's board with a centerboard and a fin, but need not have straps for the feet. Some beginner boards are wide, which makes them easier to handle. Ideally the starting-size sail should be a light, simple design. A lightweight carbon mast is best for both beginners and experts. Your child will need a boom that easily attaches to the mast with a clamp-on front end, and adjusts to fit the length of your child's sail.

❧ A wet suit typically costs between $100 and $200. A personal flotation device will cost around $50.

What's ideal for children is to sail with a club or at a location that rents gear suitable for children, as growing kids and their improving skills can require replacement of the equipment to something more suitable every year.

    —Michael Alex, teaching windsurfing for 11 years

Proper footwear is as important as life jackets.

    —Beth Powell Winkler, masters world champion, U.S. Sailing Team member, and windsurfing instructor for 20 years

Rent or borrow equipment to start. Once your child is comfortable with the basic skills, he'll have an idea of the type of sailing he wants to do—cruising, drag racing, bump and jump, freestyle, wave sailing—and can choose the gear that fits.

    —Brian Collis, president of Southern Maryland Windsurfing Association, teaching for 4 years

Having your own equipment is a motivating factor for a kid. My son likes to rig equipment around the house and practice sail tricks on the lawn.

    —Steve Elliott, windsurfing for 25 years

WRESTLING

Overview

Wrestling is an international sport, dating back over 5,000 years, and prevalent in virtually every country. At heart, it is a primitive, competitive sport, tracing historically from the Greeks and Romans to George Washington and Abraham Lincoln. Wrestling has been an Olympic sport since 1896. The professional wrestling seen on television, which is both violent and theatrical, bears little resemblance to the sport of wrestling. Sport wrestling prohibits strikes and penalizes or disqualifies competitors for violent or illegal moves.

Part of wrestling's popularity in the United States, with more than 270,000 high school participants, stems from multiple weight classes that allow kids of all sizes to compete. In all traditional styles, wrestlers compete in age and weight categories, so everyone has an equal chance. Moreover, since wrestling is an individual sport, participants must rely entirely on their own abilities to succeed.

Literally hundreds of wrestling styles can be found around the world, many countries having developed their own indigenous forms, such as sumo wrestling. The five styles of amateur wrestling practiced in the United States each have their own rules, techniques, and emphasis. The Olympics and other international competitions involve two styles of wrestling: freestyle and Greco-Roman. Freestyle and Greco-Roman both focus more on wrestling from the feet, the primary difference being that Greco-Roman is limited to upper-body holds. Folkstyle wrestling places greater emphasis on controlling and involves more mat wrestling.

General Benefits

⊙ Wrestling builds stamina, endurance, and determination. It also cultivates self-reliance as an individual sport, while still lending a sense of team camaraderie. Because of its intensity and the long hours spent practicing, wrestling can also foster deep friendships.

⊙ Wrestling is one of the few sports that works and significantly strengthens all the major muscle groups. It enhances overall physical strength, tenacity, balance, agility, flexibility, and coordination. It improves cardiovascular fitness.

Kids Who Tend to Excel

⊙ Mental toughness is key. Long-term success in wrestling has a lot to do with dedication, training, and competitive spirit.

> Wrestling gives kids a great sense of body control and leverage.
>
> —*Fred Miller, Oak Glen Junior Matmen head youth wrestling coach for 6 years*

> Physically, wrestling helps a child become much tougher. It causes tremendous muscular and cardiovascular development, while improving flexibility and balance. Overall, wrestlers learn how to utilize strength in different positions. The sport also incorporates a lot of different training aspects, including running, interval training, and strength training.
>
> —*Larry Shaw, head wrestling coach, Oak Glen High School, and 2002 National Wrestling Coaches Association State Coach of the Year, coaching for 24 years*

> Wrestling is without a doubt the most demanding contact sport. To compete at a high level, you need to be in top physical condition or you put yourself at risk for serious injury. As a coach, I make sure that our wrestlers are in great shape before taking the mat.
>
> —*Mark Delligatti, head wrestling coach, Fairmont Senior High School, coaching for 18 years*

Strength is important but so are stamina, speed, technique, strategy, intensity, power, and coordination.

Children who are strong for their weight and naturally aggressive and competitive tend to do best.

Kids do not have to be a certain size or shape to succeed, because they will compete against others of similar age and weight. Wrestlers are generally paired within a year of age and five pounds' weight.

Girls in Wrestling

Wrestling has traditionally been a male-only sport, but over the past ten years girls have also participated. At young ages, strength differences are minimal, but this changes dramatically with puberty, when boys tend to gain a significant advantage. So wrestling starts with boys and girls practicing and competing against each

Emotional control is essential because wrestling is such an emotional sport. Kids have to learn to use their emotions to give them a boost when they need it, but to keep them in check when things go against them. When two wrestlers are evenly paired, the match usually goes to the one with the most heart. Often, will and determination can overcome greater skill.

—*Fred Miller, Oak Glen Junior Matmen head youth wrestling coach for 6 years*

Wrestling is very tough, demanding sport both physically and mentally, and you have to be very self-disciplined. There is physical contact the entire time. It's you against someone else without much time for breaks like in other sports.

—*Jack Otera, middle school assistant wrestling coach for 3 years*

Kids who are competitive by nature do well. As kids move up through the ranks, ability and athleticism become more important, especially balance and body spatial awareness.

—*Larry Shaw, head wrestling coach, Oak Glen High School, and 2002 National Wrestling Coaches Association State Coach of the Year, coaching for 24 years*

other, but as kids get older, there is a women-only competition structure. It is likely that your daughter may still be the only girl on your local team and will have to be determined and tough to compete against boys.

U.S. and international freestyle competitions now include women's divisions. Women's freestyle wrestling has been added to the Olympic Games for 2004. Wrestling for women is very similar to freestyle wrestling, but neck holds are strictly forbidden.

Best Age to Start

Like most youth sports these days, starting younger seems to be the norm in kids' clubs where kids start as young as 4 or 5. Many kids do not start until middle school and still thrive.

In our youth program, we have several girls who do quite well. Opportunities for girls are opening up in all age groups, which is very exciting for wrestling. I feel that the more opportunities there are for girls, the more mainstream wrestling will become overall. On the scholastic and college level there are high school competitions and wrestling clubs and teams for girls in college. I think the more opportunities for girls, the better.

   —Larry Shaw, head wrestling coach, Oak Glen High School, and 2002 National Wrestling
      Coaches Association State Coach of the Year, coaching for 24 years

Currently at the high school level when girls wrestle it is against boys, but I am seeing more tournaments just for girls, not just at the beginner levels but all the way up to the college level. At the world level, where there are a ton of opportunities, I think it is great that it is becoming popular with girls.

   —Matt Diehl, Central College head wrestling coach for 14 years

We have girls wrestling at our high school, and they do very well. Younger girls do especially well, as they tend to develop faster than boys and this is reflected in their wrestling abilities.

   —Jack Otera, middle school assistant wrestling coach for 3 years

© Look for a club with a separate, less competitive regimen for your child under age 9, involving more fun, "tumbling" types of activities.

What to Look For When Getting Started

🐟 A good program should teach that every wrestling move has its countermove, whether to a throw or what seems to be an unbreakable hold. Every wrestler should be encouraged to develop his own favorite offensive moves, but must learn about them all so he can counter anything an opponent throws at him.

🐟 When just starting out, look for a program that offers opportunities for scrimmaging rookies against each other instead of one that stresses tournaments.

🐟 Wrestling tournaments can last for four to six hours, and wrestlers typically

Conventional wrestling wisdom would lead one to believe that to be a good wrestler one must begin wrestling at age 2, yet I have successful kids who start as late as age 15. It is important to note that nearly all wrestlers who make all-state and all-American start wrestling by age 6 or 8.

> —Daryl Hayes, high school head wrestling coach for 9 years

Kids are ready to wrestle as soon as they can pay attention to the coach. We've had some that did well at age 4, and others that weren't ready at age 8. Generally, I'd say around age 6 is a good age to start.

> —Fred Miller, Oak Glen head youth wrestling coach for 6 years

In my community, we start in kindergarten, but ideally, I think kids should start around 9 or 10 years old, when kids have the attention span needed.

> —Larry Shaw, head wrestling coach, Oak Glen High School, and 2002 National Wrestling Coaches Association State Coach of the Year, coaching for 24 years

Wrestling practice is rough and tumble, and kids have to learn how to train hard without hurting their practice partner. Wrestlers should have a chance to win before they run into a five-year veteran in the first round of an open tournament.

> —Fred Miller, Oak Glen Junior Matmen head youth wrestling coach for 6 years

compete in two to four matches. Tournament competition is organized by weight and age. Typical age brackets are 8 and under, 9–10, 11–12, and 13–14.

Most Popular Types of Wrestling
FOLKSTYLE

✦ Developed in the United States, this style is not used in international competition. Folkstyle wrestling emphasizes control, with points awarded for the length of time a wrestler controls his opponent. As a result, the wrestler in control works toward a pin, while the wrestler on the bottom tries to escape or reverse control. To pin an opponent, a wrestler must hold him on his back for two seconds. Hand locks are only allowed when pinning or taking down an opponent.

✦ Folkstyle rewards taking an opponent down and keeping him controlled on the mat. It differs primarily from freestyle wrestling by awarding points for defensive moves from the bottom position.

FREESTYLE

✦ Freestyle wrestling rewards attacks, throws, back exposure, and initiating action against an opponent. Freestyle wrestling concentrates on attacking an opponent's entire body, and wrestlers earn points by taking an opponent down to the mat and exposing his back. Wrestlers can use their legs and hold an opponent above or below his waist. In freestyle competition, the only thing the wrestler on the bottom tries to do is avoid being turned onto his stomach.

✦ Hard locks are allowed anytime and hand throws are encouraged. Extra points are earned by throwing an opponent off the mat with his feet going above his head. You can also grasp an opponent's legs to trip him. Wrestlers can pin an opponent by holding him on his back for one second. You can also win by scoring 10 points more than your opponent, which counts as a technical fall. Matches are generally one five-minute period, but two periods with a short break in between are often used for children under age 10.

GRECO-ROMAN

✦ Greco-Roman wrestling, stemming from the Greeks and Romans, who considered wrestling a great character-building activity, concentrates on taking an opponent down to the mat and exposing his back, but without using or attacking his legs. In the Greco-Roman style, a wrestler can never grasp an opponent below the belt line, trip him, or use the legs to perform an action. Wrestlers use only their arms and upper bodies to attack. Points for takedowns and exposures, scoring, and length of matches are nearly identical to freestyle.

Safety and Injury Concerns

✦ Youth wrestling is considered relatively safe, given the use of proper safety equipment that includes mouth guards, wrestling shoes, kneepads, headgear, and regulation mats.

✦ Most wrestling injuries are minor, consisting of sprains, strains, bruises, cuts, or nosebleeds. Other injuries include hurt shoulders, pulled muscles, foot, knee or ankle sprains, and hip or back pain. More serious common injuries include broken noses, dislocated fingers, and twisted ankles.

🐾 Wrestling officials look for any illegal positioning of the body and immediately penalize any unnecessary roughness. As a result, wrestling has a low percentage of serious, permanent or life-threatening injury, and fewer serious injuries than football, basketball, or ice hockey. Despite the fact that it is a contact sport, it does not involve speed, which makes it much safer.

🐾 Overuse injuries seldom occur because of the variety of wrestling moves.

Concerns About Weight Loss for Matches

🐾 One of the most important things when evaluating a wrestling program is how the coaches handle the issue of weight, particularly when it comes to making lower weight classes in competitions.

🐾 Wrestling has been associated with some boys going to extremes to achieve excessive weight loss right before a match in order to stay within a certain weight class.

🐾 While national governing bodies, such as USA Wrestling, now prohibit any form of rapid or unsafe weight loss, the issue continues to be one you need to watch out for. Weight control becomes more important at the high school level, but coaches should be aware of health and safety factors and prohibit their wrestlers from engaging in any unhealthy weight loss.

People mistakenly think wrestling is really violent, when if fact it's a very safe sport. The kids are on a padded surface, they are the same size and age, they are not running at each other, not throwing objects at each other, and there is an official right there with the kids. There can be some impact injuries, such as bruising, stress on the joints, and muscle sprains. There is also the occasional bloody nose or busted lip, but nothing to get too worried about. Incidents of more serious injury are relatively low.

—Larry Shaw, head wrestling coach, Oak Glen High School, and 2002 National Wrestling Coaches Association State Coach of the Year, coaching for 24 years

We've seen very few injuries over the years, aside from nosebleeds, the everyday head-butts, mat burns, a few broken wrists and knee injuries.

—Fred Miller, Oak Glen Junior Matmen head youth wrestling coach for 6 years

You have to be very careful to keep an eye out for eating disorders, which some kids develop in order to keep their weight down.

> —Jane, mom of Carolyn, 17, and Peter, 11

Weight is an issue in wrestling. Today we are a lot smarter about the correct ways to do it, and there are national regulations to follow. With our youth kids we do *not* ask them to lose weight. We want kids to train their bodies, get in shape and develop good cardiovascular conditioning, and grow up into weight classes. When issues of weight loss do come up with older children, we are very safe about it.

> —Larry Shaw, head wrestling coach, Oak Glen High School, and 2002 National Wrestling Coaches Association State Coach of the Year, coaching for 24 years

Weight cutting, which has been a black eye for wrestling over the years, is becoming less of an issue. To dehydrate yourself is crazy. Because we have weight classes and everyone wants the advantage, there is pressure on kids to go down a weight class. But I think people are becoming smarter about this, and not cutting as much weight.

> —Matt Diehl, head wrestling coach, Central College, for 14 years

Cost Considerations

🔱 Wrestling is not a very expensive sport. Programs cover large expenses such as practice facilities and mats, and individual athletes need very little equipment.

🔱 The standard wrestling uniform ("singlet") is made of stretchy material and designed to fit snugly so that it does not restrict the movement of a wrestler. Many teams provide this as part of their uniform, but if not, it typically costs between $20 and $35.

🔱 Headgear prevents outer ear injuries and bruises, and generally costs between $16 and $18.

🔱 Kneepads are optional, and cost between $12 and $30.

✦ Lightweight wrestling shoes, made of soft leather without heels, offer increased ankle support and fit tight to the foot to facilitate movement. They cost between $25 and $50.

✦ Tournament entrance fees generally run between $10 and $20.

✦ Travel expenses to events is one cost variable to consider. Wrestling in a youth league can be very expensive, mainly due to travel expenses that can run as high as $400 a week for hotels, food, and the cost of getting there.

9

Other Physical Activities

STRENGTH TRAINING

Overview

Strength training is endorsed by the American Academy of Pediatrics Committee on Sports Medicine, provided the program is properly designed and supervised, as a way to build muscle strength, improve a child's fitness level, or rehabilitate a sports-related injury such as tennis elbow. The American Orthopedic Society for Sports Medicine, the American College of Sports Medicine, the President's Council on Fitness and Sports, the U.S. Olympic Committee, and the Pediatric Orthopedic Society of North America all now endorse strength training as safe and beneficial for children.

Strength, or weight, training, which focuses on using resistance to build strength, completely differs from weightlifting and power lifting, which are competitive sports not recommended for children, as they focus on lifting as much weight as possible. Strength training should be only one aspect of your child's exercise routine, and he should feel comfortable with it and look forward to the next session.

There have been many misconceptions concerning children and strength training. The media sometimes portrays resistance training as involving competitive weightlifters straining to lift as much weight as they can. Yet children get introduced to strength training with little or no weight, focusing instead on body weight calisthenics, partner exercises, and lightly resisted exercises. Prepubescent children actually gain strength by improving the functional ability of the nervous system rather than by dramatically increasing the size of the muscle. Muscles don't really grow larger until puberty stage, when testosterone, estrogen, and progesterone increase.

—*Greg Gibbs, USAW Olympic Club coach, director of Power & Pride Strength & Conditioning, and personal trainer for 10 years*

A kid jumping off a bench at recess experiences far greater loads on his joints than he would trying to do a squat. With proper supervision a young athlete can be set onto a great path by weight training at a young age. In Europe, athletes are introduced to weights at 8 years old, and if administered properly, this can give them a huge advantage over their peers as they mature. The increased strength gives them the ability to advance into more complex exercises and technique work depending on their sport. Weights should be a common activity for a motivated child at ages 12–14, and free weights are far superior to machines, because they allow joints to move freely.

—*Jonathan Edwards, Triple Jump Gold Medal Olympian and youth strength and conditioning expert*

General Benefits

- Increases muscular strength, balanced strength around the joints, and endurance

- Improves sports performance, posture, and helps to prevent overuse injuries

- Decreases the likelihood and severity of sports injuries by increasing the strength of tendons and ligaments and density of bones

- Facilitates rehabilitation after a sports injury, as one of the fastest ways to heal many injuries is to strengthen muscles surrounding the injured area

Best Age to Start

◉ Once your child starts participating in organized sports such as T-ball, soccer, or gymnastics, and is around age 7 or 8, he's ready for very basic strength training.

What to Look For When Getting Started

🌿 Most strength training takes place in private gyms, and you need to find an instructor who has experience working with children the same age as yours. Your child should always be directly supervised by a trainer or coach when weight training. The National Strength and Conditioning Association (NSCA) offers the only nationally accredited certification programs in the fitness industry. It issues two types of certifications. A Certified Strength and Conditioning Specialist (CSCS) possesses the knowledge and skills to design and implement safe and effective strength and conditioning programs. A Certified Personal Trainer (CPT) is a professional who works one-on-one with clients.

🌿 A training program for your child should use high repetitions with low weight, no more than three days per week with at least one day off between weight-training sessions. The focus of each training session should be on proper form and technique. Your child should never do heavy weights with low repetition training. Putting on muscle mass should not be the goal of his strength-training program.

🌿 Kids between the ages of 5 and 12 can do bodyweight resistance exercises such as push-ups, sit-ups, squats, arm curls, calf raises, and pull-ups.

🌿 Only after your child has passed through puberty should he even consider concentrating on

As soon as children have signed up to play a sport, I believe that they should also sign up to prepare their bodies to handle the rigors of playing that sport. Even children as young as 5 should do some sort of resistance work to improve athletic performance and strengthen bones. By the time kids get to high school, they should be doing speed, agility, and quickness drills twice a week. Weight training should take place two to three times a week with light resistance weights for one to three sets of 6–15 reps, and stretching.

—*Mike Nitka, chairman of NSCA High School Coaches and director of strength and conditioning at Muskego High School, coaching for 30 years*

I train children as young as 13 years old. Whether or not I decide to work with a child has quite a bit to do not only with the child's level of maturity but also with the parent's rationale for hiring a personal trainer. Overweight children who are in need of friendly motivation are good candidates, as are child athletes. A personal trainer should be utilized in addition to sports and activities, not as a replacement.

—*Brian Day, FitnessByDay.com personal trainer for 5 years*

Prepubescent boys' and girls' programs should focus on agility, balance, and muscular endurance as opposed to absolute strength and power. As a child advances beyond puberty, a good trainer will tailor the program to include exercises that improve power for sports and activities specific to the child's interests, such as football, soccer, tennis, running, swimming, or martial arts.

—*Brian Day, FitnessByDay.com personal trainer for 5 years*

Here are my basic guidelines for resistance exercise progression in children. Age 7 or younger: Introduce a child to basic exercises with little or no weight, develop the concept of a training session, and keep volume low. Ages 8–10: Gradually increase the number of exercises focusing on technique; start gradual progressive loading of exercises. Ages 11–13: Continue progressive loading of each exercise and introduce more advanced exercises with little or no resistance. Ages 14–15: Progress to more advanced youth programs in resistance exercises, add sport-specific components, and increase volume. Proper progression, program monitoring, and supervision are essential to meet the changing needs of children.

—*Greg Gibbs, USAW Olympic Club coach, director of Power & Pride Strength & Conditioning, and personal trainer for 10 years*

adding muscle bulk. Starting in seventh grade, work on weight machines can be added, but no free weights until ninth grade. When introducing a child to strength-training exercises with free weights or on machines, no resistance weight should be used at first. When your child has mastered the proper form and technique, weight can be added gradually.

Safety and Injury Concerns

✦ Most competitive youth sports pose greater injury risks than resistance training. Age-appropriate exercises, correct techniques, and competent supervision are key.

✦ Your child should never be unsupervised when lifting weights, and stretching and warm-up should always be done before and after strength training.

✦ Permanent damage can result if your prepubescent child tries to lift weights too heavy for his bones and muscles, and his growth plates—the parts of long bones where mass gets added as he grows—could sustain acute or chronic injuries.

Cost Considerations

✦ While group lessons average around $15 a class, private training can run between $20 and $100 an hour. Your child may also need to get a junior health club or gym membership.

YOGA

Overview

Although the ancient science of yoga originated in the Far East, it has become immensely popular in the West during the past few decades. With the mainstreaming of yoga, there are now over 18 million yoga enthusiasts in America, and the growth of children's yoga classes in the past few years has been increasing exponentially. Just as adults are turning to yoga in record levels to reduce stress and stretch out muscles, more and more parents are enrolling their kids to reap the same benefits. Many parents turn their children on to yoga as a way to relax, and counter stress from the accumulation of homework, competitive activities, and packed schedules.

Yoga postures, accompanied by specific breathing techniques, are designed to stimulate specific areas of the body and the brain, resulting in the release of tension. The word *yoga* comes from the ancient Indian language Sanskrit and means to "yoke" or unite the mind, body, and spirit. The result for many is a powerful feeling of relaxation, inner strength, and the ability to quiet one's mind in order to be fully present in the moment. Children practice sitting still and engaging in the quiet art of controlling their bodies. These practices lead them to emerge calmly from their classes.

Yoga has become an antidote for overstimulated kids, as it gives them time for quiet introspection and teaches them to be calm and centered. Along with this decreased stress, certain postures also help to build strong muscles and increase flexibility.

Most Popular Styles

There are innumerable types of yoga taught throughout the United States and the world. Often it's a matter of finding a style that resonates with your child. The most common forms taught include:

Yoga provides a sanctuary away from our competitive society as well as a place where a kid can just be a kid without worrying if she is the best, the prettiest, the smartest, or the strongest. Removing the competition from the practice of yoga helps children to be more tolerant and less judgmental of others and, more important, less judgmental of themselves. Yoga provides a noncompetitive forum where every child is perfect. When children learn new poses, they gain a strong sense of accomplishment and pride without ever having to win or lose. In yoga, children are encouraged to practice deep breathing for stress control, meditation for focus and concentration, and respect and love for themselves, the earth and all its inhabitants. In my opinion the primary benefit really comes from the peace and equanimity that yoga fosters.

—*Shana Meyerson, founder of Mini Yogis, teaching for 3 years*

Yoga should not be confused with exercise or an extracurricular activity. Only yoga recharges our battery when we perform it; with everything else our energy is being expended. Yoga helps to balance emotional ups and downs, especially during pre-puberty, puberty, and adolescence. Yoga is all about "harmonizing head, heart, and hands" as said Swami Sivananda Saraswati of Rishikesh, India.

—*Ayesha Venkatrao-Holcombe, director of the Satyananda Yoga Center, Austin, teaching for 20 years*

❧ *Hatha yoga.* Focuses on poses that help unify the two energies of *ha* (the left) and *tha* (the right), and merge them into the center of the spine.

❧ *Iyangar yoga.* Focuses on moving one's body into alignment. Much attention is given to aligning the postures correctly, and props such as straps, blocks, and pillows are often used. Breathing into the postures is taught to help sustain and increase each posture's effect.

❧ *Kripalu yoga.* An introspective and meditative form of hatha yoga focusing on slow moving postures, breathing, opening body energy, and stress reduction.

❧ *Kundalini yoga.* Focuses on strong breathing and dynamic exercise.

❧ *Viniyoga.* This relaxing, restorative yoga focuses on flow and breathing techniques to enhance the therapeutic effects of each posture.

🔸 *Ashtanga, or power, yoga.* This high-energy, dynamic form of yoga requires strength to keep up with the rigorous, dynamic pace. Class involves a constant flow of nonstop, connected movements, along with the use of deep breathing and locks. These help intensify the effects of the postures by building internal heat in the body. Power yoga is not for children, because it is too intense and strenuous.

General Benefits

◉ Yoga provides increased flexibility, agility, coordination, balance, and strength.

◉ It helps kids learn to unwind, develop relaxation techniques, and emerge from class calmly.

◉ Breathing exercises teach your child how to breathe fully and deeply, cultivating a still mind along with improved concentration and focus. These exercises, along with the meditation used in many yoga classes, can also teach your child stress management, such as using deep yoga breathing to relax before a big game or test. Yoga can also help kids learn to be less impulsive.

◉ Yoga is a noncompetitive physical activity that allows your child to work at her own level, and teaches your child to connect to and ground herself in her body, become more self-aware, have more self-control, and formulate a calm, focused energy.

◉ Yoga teaches kids about body alignment, builds body awareness, and helps prevent injuries from occurring in sports.

Yoga teaches clear thinking, calmness, and focus. It imparts strengths, flexibility, and a stronger immune system.

—*Lisa Megidesh, director of Center for Yoga and Healing and instructor for 16 years*

Yoga not only works the muscles but massages the internal organs at the same time. So, while children utilize every muscle from their biceps to their baby toes, they are also taking care of their kidneys and stomachs, thyroids, pituitaries, and every organ in between. This allows for healthy regulatory, digestive, circulatory, and nervous systems.

—*Shana Meyerson, founder of Mini Yogis, teaching for 3 years*

Yoga helps children to develop strong, flexible and healthy bodies as well as increase their concentration, focus, and attention. Through yoga, kids explore their creativity and imagination while simultaneously opening up to a peaceful, relaxed state of body and mind. Anatomy and body awareness are inevitably discovered, and so is the fun!

—*Jodi Komitor, Next Generation Yoga, teacher for 5 years*

Children with hyperactive tendencies do benefit from the practice. It helps to calm their minds, calm their bodies, and get them to focus. Deep breathing, relaxation, meditation, and some of the more complex poses challenge a child's concentration and force her to live in the present moment with a calm, still mind (the literal meaning of *asana*—the name given to each yoga pose).

—*Shana Meyerson, founder of MiniYogis, teaching for 3 years*

For kids who are easily distracted, moving from one thing to the next, learning yoga can keep them more grounded.

—*Linda, yoga teacher, Rose Institute*

I have witnessed hyperactive children do yoga and become more focused and less impulsive. As well, I have seen low-energy children become stimulated, energized, and more aware.

—*Jodi Komitor, Next Generation Yoga, teacher for 5 years*

Hyperactive and Attention-Deficit Children

🐟 Yoga has been shown to benefit both hyperactive and attention-deficit children by helping to instill calmness, relaxation, and body awareness.

🐟 Yoga has been known to help with other medical conditions, such as asthma, insomnia, digestive problems, and learning disabilities.

Best Age to Start

◉ There are classes introducing yoga to kids of all ages, including even babies. Generally, preschoolers around ages 4 and 5 start doing some of the postures on their own.

When a child is capable of following simple directions and controlling her basic motor skills, she is ready for yoga. I encourage parents to join their children's classes if the kids are under age 5. It helps children to focus and feel secure. Children's yoga is a fairly new practice, grounded in a sound understanding of yoga and its precepts, and flourishing through creativity. There are different types of children's practices out there. Some are very serious—more like the adult classes, just scaled down for kids—and some are more playful. Personally, I recommend the playful classes, as they allow children to drop their defenses and apprehensions and really dive into the moment. There is no such thing as excelling in yoga class. The integrity of yoga is held in the effort, not the execution, and the only "talent" really required is an open mind.

—*Shana Meyerson, founder of Mini Yogis, teaching for 3 years*

Children as young as 3 can "play" yoga and have fun learning. But at about age 7 the child will start verbalizing the benefits to the teacher, saying things like, "I feel calmer," or "I used the breathing at school today." They love to tell you how they use yoga in their daily lives. A child's class moves more quickly than an adult class, and they like concrete examples and the use of props such as eye pillows, straps, or a yoga ball.

—*Lucy Wagner, director and founder of Central Mass. Yoga Institute, teaching for 10 years*

Children's yoga is *very* different from adult yoga. Kids are playful, spontaneous, and they like to make noises, sing songs, and create stories. It is important that the teacher and the environment be child-friendly and able to meet the kids' needs.

—*Jodi Komitor, Next Generation Yoga, teacher for 5 years*

What to Look For When Getting Started

🐾 Look for a class that is fun, less strict and less intense than adult classes, and one that introduces an element of playfulness. Children's classes usually run about 45 minutes. Many yoga studios offer Mommy and Me programs that you can do with your infant or toddler.

The only injury I've personally encountered was a splinter that a child got practicing on an outdoor patio. Yoga, when done mindfully, does not easily lend itself to injuries. Quite the opposite, it is meant to be a healing and gentle practice. Children are encouraged to listen to their bodies and respect their limits. They should be told to never do anything that hurts or feels wrong and never worry about what anyone else is doing. There are six billion people on this planet and six billion different ways to do each yoga pose, including not doing it at all. As such, children have to be made to feel comfortable "opting out" or modifying the poses to whatever works for them.

—*Shana Meyerson, founder of Mini Yogis, teaching for 3 years*

I have never had a student hurt him- or herself. I remind them not to work their bodies or necks in ways that hurt. There is a difference between a good stretching hurt and a painful hurt.

—*Jodi Komitor, Next Generation Yoga, teacher for 5 years*

Ask what kind of breathing exercises they teach. Certain kinds of deep pranayam breathing exercises are not appropriate for prepubescent children.

—*Lisa Megidesh, director of Center for Yoga and Healing and instructor for 16 years*

🐦 A typical class will include not only yoga postures and stretches but also relaxation, meditation, and quiet breathing time. Your child will learn how to get into and hold various poses that build both upper- and lower-body strength.

🐦 Yoga for children keeps the postures relatively simple and incorporates games and animal postures such as the downward-facing dog, the lion, the cat, and the cobra.

🐦 Children learn to become aware of their bodies as they move through different postures. Classes end with a form of guided meditation, which for kids often means imagining themselves somewhere else, like a wondrous beach, floating in the waves. Often classes begin and end with the Hindu salutation "Namaste," which means, literally, "I bow to you."

🐦 Look for a certified instructor who has previous experience teaching children and someone who is not only passionate about yoga but also about children.

Safety and Injury Concerns

🐦 Make sure that the instructor does not force your child to bend or contort her body in any way that feels uncomfortable. Also, look for an instructor who does not do exercises that require your child to balance on her neck or head.

🐦 The temperature in the yoga studio or practice area should be warm, to help keep the muscles flexible, resilient, and injury-free.

Cost Considerations

❦ Classes tend to run about $5–$15 each session and you can usually get package discounts.

❦ Yoga requires little equipment. Your child may have to bring a sticky mat, which costs about $20, or a towel to class, and she is usually asked to wear comfortable clothes. Most studios provide the mats for children's classes.

10

Sports Resources

GENERAL SPORTS RESOURCES

National Alliance for Youth Sports (NAYS)

2050 Vista Parkway
West Palm Beach, FL 33411
(800) 729-2057 or (800) 688-KIDS
nays@nays.org
www.nays.org

The NAYS runs a national education program that has trained 1.3 million volunteer youth sport coaches.

President's Council on Physical Fitness and Sports (PCPFS)

200 Independence Avenue, S.W.
Humphrey Building, Room 738-H
Washington, DC 20201.
(202) 690-9000
www.fitness.gov

The PCPFS works to promote, encourage, and motivate Americans of all ages to become physically active and participate in sports. Its Web site has extensive research, resources, and tips to get kids fit.

Institute for the Study of Youth Sports (YSI)

Michigan State University
213 IM Sports Circle
East Lansing, MI 48824
(517) 353-6689
ythsprts@msu.edu
http://ed-web3.educ.msu.edu/ysi/

The YSI researches the benefits and detriments of participation in youth sports, and the Web site has extensive educational materials for parents, coaches, officials, and administrators.

National Council of Youth Sports (NCYS)

7185 S.E. Seagate Lane
Stuart, FL 34997
(772) 781-1452
youthspts@aol.com
www.ncys.org

The NCYS represents over 90 youth sports organizations with over 52 million participants between them.

RESOURCES FOR GIRLS IN SPORTS

National Association for Girls and Women in Sport

1900 Associate Drive
Reston, VA 22091
(800) 213-7193 ext. 453
www.aahperd.org/nagws

This organization, which is part of the American Alliance for Health, Physical Education, Recreation and Dance, focuses on educating the public about Title IX issues and promoting opportunities for all girls and women in sport.

Tucker Center for Research on Girls & Women in Sport

University of Minnesota, 203 Cooke Hall
1900 University Ave. S.E.
Minneapolis, MN 55455
(612) 625-7327
info@tuckercenter.org
www.education.umn.edu/tuckercenter

An interdisciplinary research center that studies many related aspects of women and sports, and offers copies of the President's council report, "Physical Activity and Lives of Girls."

Women's Sports Foundation

Eisenhower Park
East Meadow, NY 11554
(800) 227-3988
wosport@aol.com
www.womenssportsfoundation.org

Founded in 1974 by Billie Jean King, the Women's Sports Foundation is dedicated to ensuring equal access to participation and leadership opportunities for all girls and women in sports and fitness. Great articles can be found on its Web site.

RESOURCES FOR SPORTS FOR SPECIAL NEEDS CHILDREN

Disability Sports Web Site

http://ed-web3.educ.msu.edu/kin866/

This fabulous site, created by the Department of Kinesiology at Michigan State University, has extensive information on disability sports, inclusion issues, sports offerings, and competitions for disabled athletes.

Special Olympics International (SOI)

1325 G St. N.W., Suite 500
Washington, DC 20005
(800) 443-6105 or (202) 628-3630
www.specialolympics.org

Special Olympics is an international organization dedicated to empowering individuals with mental retardation, cognitive delays, or significant learning issues to participate in sports. SOI offers children starting at age 8 year-round training and competition in 26 Olympic-type summer and winter sports. Today there are over one million participants in the Special Olympics from 150 countries.

Disabled Sports USA (DS/USA)

451 Hungerford Drive #100
Rockville, MD 20850
(301) 217-0960
dsusa@dsusa.org
www.dsusa.org

DS/USA offers nationwide sports rehabilitation programs to anyone with a permanent physical disability, with activities ranging from skiing to water sports to horseback riding.

National Disability Sports Alliance (NDSA)

25 West Independence Way
Kingston, RI 02881
(401) 792-7130
info@ndsaonline.org
www.ndsaonline.org/main.htm

The NDSA is the national governing body for competitive sports for individuals with cerebral palsy, traumatic brain injuries, and for survivors of stroke.

U.S. Association of Blind Athletes (USABA)

33 N. Institute St.
Colorado Springs, CO 80903
(719) 630-0422
info@usaba.org
www.usaba.org

The USABA promotes athletic competition for individuals who are visually impaired or blind. Sports include cycling, judo, swimming, wrestling, and skiing.

USA Deaf Sports Federation (USADSF)

102 N. Krohn Place
Sioux Falls, SD 57103-1800
(605) 367-5760
homeoffice@usadsf.org
www.usadsf.org

The USADSF is the American sports organization for deaf athletes, and sponsors competitions in a wide range of sports.

Wheelchair Sports, USA

3595 E. Fountain Blvd., Suite L-1
Colorado Springs, CO 80910
(719) 574-1150
wsusa@aol.com
www.wsusa.org

This organization hosts sports competitions for those with spinal cord injury, spina bifida, poliomyelitis, and other lower limb impairments.

American Association of AdaptedSports Programs (AAASP)

P.O. Box 538
Pine Lake, GA 30072
(404) 294-0070
aaasp@bellsouth.net
www.aaasp.org

The AAASP creates adapted competitive sports programs in local communities, working with schools, parks and recreation departments, YMCA/YWCAs, hospitals, parents, and other community groups.

ARCHERY

National Archery Association (NAA)

One Olympic Plaza
Colorado Springs, CO 80909
(719) 578-4576
info@USArchery.org
www.USArchery.org

The NAA is the official governing organization for archery in the United States. Its national Junior Olympic Archery Development (JOAD) is a youth archery program with five age-based divisions that enable kids to compete: pre-cadet (9 and under), cadet (12 and under), junior (15 and under), and intermediate (18 and under). The JOAD program is often offered through community-based organizations such as the Scouts, the Boys and Girls Clubs, the YMCA, and 4-H.

National Field Archery Association (NFAA)

31407 Outer I-10
Redlands, CA 92373
(800) 811-2331
www.nfaa-archery.org

The NFAA is dedicated to the conservation and preservation of the game and its natural habitat, and has more than 1,100 affiliated clubs, sponsors, and nationwide tournaments.

National Alliance for the Development of Archery

14260 W. Newberry Road, #334
Newberry, FL 32669
(352) 332-9984
nadaemail@aol.com
www.teacharchery.com

This organization trains and certifies archery instructors, and its Web site can help you find an archery program or instructor in your area.

BADMINTON

USA Badminton (USAB)

One Olympic Plaza
Colorado Springs, CO 80909
(719) 866-4808
usab@usabadminton.org
www.usabadminton.org

This organization is the recognized national governing body for the sport of badminton in the United States, oversees all U.S. badminton competitions, and prepares the best players in America for the Olympic Games. Its Web site includes program listings, a tournament calendar, where and how to play, spectator's guide, rules, news, and links. The organization has also just recently launched a coach-certification program. The organization sponsors regional tournaments, along with a world junior championship.

BASEBALL, SOFTBALL, AND T-BALL

T-Ball USA

2499 Main St.
Stratford, CT 06615
(203) 381-1449
teeballusa@aol.com
www.teeballusa.org

This national nonprofit youth sports organization is dedicated to the development of T-ball.

Little League Baseball

P.O. Box 3485
Williamsport, PA 17701
(717) 326-1921
www.littleleague.org

This organization was founded in 1938 and began admitting girls in 1974. Each Little League program is community-based, with more than 7,400 Little League programs in more than 100 countries.

USA Baseball

P.O. Box 1131
Durham, NC 27702
(919) 474-8721
info@usabaseball.com
www.usabaseball.com

USA Baseball is the national governing body for baseball, overseeing more than 20 million amateur players.

Softball Association (ASA)

2801 N.E. 50th St.
Oklahoma City, OK 73111
(405) 424-3855
info@softball.org
www.softball.org

The ASA is the national governing body of softball in the United States and fields annually over 80,000 youth softball teams comprising 1.3 million players and 300,000 coaches. The Web site enables you to find a regional association near you.

Amateur Athletic Union (AAU)

www.aausports.org

The AAU is a large, multi-sport amateur sports organization, with a baseball program for ages 8–18 for teams that like to travel and can already be playing in other leagues.

American Amateur Baseball Congress (AABC)

www.aabc.us

The AABC has organized leagues in 42 U.S. states, Puerto Rico, Canada, and Mexico for children from ages 7 to 18. The 8-and-under division alone has 1,134 teams. Play culminates in a World Series.

Babe Ruth Baseball and Softball

www.baberuthbaseball.org

With over 7,315 leagues worldwide, Babe Ruth offers baseball for players ages 13–18 and a new division for ages 5–12, with over 886,500 players. There is also a softball division, ages 5–18.

Continental Amateur Baseball Association (CABA)

www.cababaseball.com

Offers tournaments for ages 9–18 in 32 states.

Dixie Youth Baseball

www.dixie.org

With leagues in 11 Southern states, Dixie offers three divisions of baseball, ages 12 and under, 13–14, and 15–18, and also has a softball division. The league mandates that all players participate in every game. Although the league emphasizes local play, teams do compete in a World Series.

Dizzy Dean Baseball

www.dizzydeanbbinc.org

Dizzy Dean Baseball is a recreational youth baseball program for ages 5–19 located primarily in the South as well as the Midwest.

National Amateur Baseball Federation (NABF)

www.nabf.com

The NABF has organized leagues throughout the United States and Canada with divisions starting at age 10 and under and going through college. It hosts over 50 annual regional tournaments, 8 national championship tournaments, and a World Series.

Pony Baseball and Softball

www.pony.org

PONY, which stands for "protect our nation's youth," sponsors baseball and softball programs for players ages 5–18. To help young players transition to a regulation-size diamond, PONY incrementally increases the distance from home plate to the pitcher's mound and between the bases as players get older. It also allows leading off bases, metal cleats, and "big barrel" bats.

U.S. Amateur Baseball Association (USABA)

www.usaba.com

The USABA offers a baseball program for ages 11–19 in 50 states culminating in nine National World Series Tournaments.

BASKETBALL

USA Basketball

5465 Mark Dabling Blvd.
Colorado Springs, CO 80918-3842
(719) 590-4800
fanmail@usabasketball.com
www.usabasketball.com

USA Basketball is a nonprofit organization and is recognized as the national governing body for men's and women's basketball in the United States by the International Basketball Federation (FIBA) and the U.S. Olympic Committee (USOC).

Youth Basketball of America (YBOA)

10325 Orangewood Blvd.
Orlando, FL 32821
(407) 363-9262
yboahq@msn.com
www.yboa.org

YBOA promotes youth basketball worldwide, sanctions local, regional, and national tournaments, and hosts three major tournaments each July. It also offers league development, educational clinics, and scholarship programs.

Amateur Athletic Union (AAU)

P.O. Box 22409
Lake Buena Vista, FL 32830
(800) 228-4872
www.aauboysbasketball.org; www.aaugirls-basketball.org

The AAU boys' teams are organized by grade level, starting with third grade and under, and going through to the end of high school. The girls' organization sponsors travel teams that compete in local and regional tournaments, culminating in an annual national tournament at Disney World. Teams are grouped by age, with divisions for ages 10 and under through age 18 and under.

BOWLING

USA Bowling

5301 S. 76th St.
Greendale, WI 53129-0500
(800) 514-2695
info@usabowling.org
www.bowl.com/bowl/usa

USA Bowling is the sport's national governing body in America. USA Bowling certifies instructors, with its bronze-level coach competency, to coach beginning bowlers. The other level, silver, indicates coaches able to coach bowlers with intermediate to advanced skills.

Young American Bowling Alliance (YABA)

5301 S. 76th St.
Greendale, WI 53129-1192
(800) 514-Bowl (2695)
info@youthbowling.com
www.youthbowling.com

This organization coordinates junior bowling tournaments and has links to junior bowling associations around the United States. Youth league bowlers have to become members for $12 a year. The YABA has 400,000 members, over 18,000 programs, and presents over 1.3 million awards each year.

CHEERLEADING

American Association of Cheerleading Coaches and Advisors (AACCA)

6745 Lenox Center Court, Suite 318
Memphis, TN 38115
(800) 533-6583
jimlord@aacca.org
www.aacca.org

This nonprofit educational association serves over 50,000 cheerleading youth, junior high school, high school, and college coaches across the United States and works to ensure that student cheerleading is practiced safely. In addition to its safety manual, it runs cheerleading safety certification programs nationwide.

National Cheerleading Association (NCA)

(800) 622-2946
www.nationalspirit.com

For over 53 years, NCA has been providing camps, events, and championships for cheerleaders across the nation. It runs over 400 summer camps as well as regional and national cheerleading competitions. Its youth leagues start for ages 9 and under. The organization also certifies coaches.

CLIMBING

U.S. Competition Climbing Association (USCCA)

P.O. Box 502568
Indianapolis, IN 46250
info@usclimbing.org
www.usclimbing.org

The USCCA is the official sanctioning body for national competition climbing for adults and youth. Its Web site has both information about youth competition and links to USCCA-sanctioned gyms. This organization has over 10,000 kids participating in rock climbing.

American Mountain Guides Association (AMGA)

710 10th St., Suite 101
Golden, CO 80401
(303) 271-0984
info@amga.com
www.amga.com

This nonprofit organization certifies rock-climbing guides. Level I guides have been certified for easier routes, while Level II certification indicates a person able to guide the full spectrum of rock climbing in non-alpine environments. Its Web site enables you to find certified guides by location.

IndoorClimbing.com

www.indoorclimbing.com

This site has an easy directory helping you locate worldwide indoor climbing gyms, with detailed contact information.

CREW/ROWING

U.S. Rowing Association

201 S. Capitol Ave., Suite 400
Indianapolis, IN 46225-1068
(800) 314-4ROW
www.usrowing.org

U.S. Rowing is the national governing body for the sport of rowing in the United States. It selects, trains, and manages the teams that represent the U.S. in international competition.

CURLING

U.S. Curling Association (USCA)

1100 Center Point Drive, P.O. Box 866
Stevens Point, WI 54481
(888)-CURLERS
usacurl@charter.net
www.usacurl.org

The USCA, founded in 1958, nationally represents, governs, and promotes the sport of curling. It is a member of the U.S. Olympic Committee and the World Curling Federation, and has over 130 member clubs in 11 regions.

DIVING

U.S. Diving (USD)

201 S. Capitol Ave., Suite 430
Indianapolis, IN 46225

(317) 237-5252
usdiving@usdiving.org
www.usdiving.org

USD is the national governing body of diving. Programs for junior divers, ages 18 and under, are conducted through 42 local diving associations, encompassing more than 300 clubs nationwide. Anyone participating on a U.S. Diving team must register with USD for a $30 membership fee. Its Web site enables you to find a local diving club near where you live. USD also certifies instructors who have taken their U.S. Diving safety-training course, as well as CPR and first-aid training.

EQUESTRIAN SPORTS

USA Equestrian

4047 Iron Works Parkway
Lexington, KY 40511-8483
(859) 258-2472
information@equestrian.org
www.equestrian.org

USA Equestrian oversees all equestrian sports in America, from the grassroots to the Olympic Games. This Web site includes information about equestrian competition both nationally and internationally, as well as links to other equestrian sites.

American Riding Instructors Association (ARIS)

28801 Trenton Court
Bonita Springs, FL 34134
(239) 948-3232
aria@riding-instructor.com
www.riding-instructor.com

This site includes information about the ARIS riding instructor certification program and a directory of certified riding instructors.

U.S. Pony Club

4041 Iron Works Parkway
Lexington, KY 40511
(859) 254-7669
memberservices@ponyclub.org
www.ponyclub.org

Pony Club, one of the leading junior equestrian organizations in the world, has over 600 individual clubs in 48 states with more than 12,000 members. The term "pony" reflects the age of the members, not the size of the horse. Pony Club organizes competitions for children up to age 21. Dues are $70 annually. The Web site enables you to find a local club near you.

U.S. Dressage Federation

220 Lexington Green Circle, Suite 510
Lexington, KY 40503
(859) 971-2277
usdressage@usdf.org
www.usdf.org

This nonprofit organization represents the national dressage community, with 133 affiliated clubs and over 38,000 members. It organizes junior competitive events nationwide for children under age 21.

National Reining Horse Association (NRHA)

3000 N.W. 10th St.
Oklahoma City, OK 73107
cbarnett@nrha.com
www.nrha.com

The NRHA is the governing body of the sport of reining. It approves more than 240 youth 14–18 competitions and over 220 youth 13-and-under competitions.

U.S. Combined Training Association (USCTA)

525 Old Waterford Road
Leesburg, VA 20176
(703) 779-0440
info@eventingusa.com
www.eventingusa.com

The USCTA promotes and develops combined training, or eventing, which combines the disciplines of dressage, cross-country jumping, and show jumping. The association has over 12,000 members and holds over 260 competitions nationwide. Its young riders program for children up to age 21 culminates in a North American Young Riders Championship.

FENCING

U.S. Fencing Association (USFA)

One Olympic Plaza
Colorado Springs, CO 80909
(719) 578-4511
Fax: (719) 866 4270
www.usfencing.org

Founded in 1891, this organization is the national governing body for fencing. Its Web site provides links to fencing clubs nationwide as well as information about tournaments. Your child must be a member of the U.S. Fencing Association to compete in local or national tournaments, with fees running between $30 and $40. Tournaments sanctioned by the USFA include youth divisions for under age 10, under age 12, and under age 14. Membership in the USFA costs $40 per year, which includes regional newsletters, *American Fencing* magazine, registration required for most competitions, and personal injury insurance, as many health plans exclude sporting activities.

FIELD HOCKEY

U.S. Field Hockey Association (USFHA)

One Olympic Plaza
Colorado Springs, CO
(719) 866-4567
usfha@usfieldhockey.com
www.usfieldhockey.com

This association is the national governing body for U.S. field hockey. It has approximately 15,000 members and is dedicated to promoting field hockey by sponsoring a number of programs.

National Field Hockey Coaches Association (NFHCA)

11921 Meadow Ridge Terrace
Glen Allen, VA 23059
(804) 364-8700
jjgoodr@attglobal.net
www.eteamz.com/nfhca

The NFHCA is a nonprofit organization serving field hockey coaches from across the United States. Its Web site has listings of clinics and summer camps for players.

FIGURE SKATING

U.S. Figure Skating Association (USFSA)

20 First St.
Colorado Springs, CO 80906
(719) 635-5200
usfsa@usfsa.org
www.usfsa.org

The USFSA is the national governing body for the sport of figure skating in the United States and representative for the International Skating Union. It has 585 member clubs across the country, and more than 125,000 members. All regional, sectional, and national figure-skating competitions in the United States are sanctioned by the USFSA and conducted by member clubs. Its Web site enables you to find skating clubs near you.

Professional Skaters Association (PSA)

3006 Allegro Park S.W.
Rochester, MN 55902
(507) 281-5122
office@skatepsa.com
www.skatepsa.com

The PSA is the official coaches' education, certification, and training program of the USFSA. The PSA trains and rates coaches from the beginning level of register through certified, senior, and then master. Ratings are offered in areas of specialty, including figures, freestyle, pairs, dance, group, program director, synchronized team, choreography and style, and moves in the field. The Web site provides a list of PSA-rated coaches around the nation.

Ice Skating Institute (ISI)

17120 N. Dallas Parkway, Suite 140
Dallas, TX 75248-1187
(972) 735-8800
www.skateisi.com

The ISI was founded in 1959 as a nonprofit organization for owners, operators, and developers of ice-skating facilities. The institute provides all different levels of skating programs and hosts four recreational skating competitions annually, including world championships for synchronized skating and one for recreational skaters. It also certifies coaches with ratings of bronze, silver, and gold.

FOOTBALL

Pop Warner Little Scholars (PWLS)

586 Middletown Blvd., Suite C-100
Langhorne, PA 19047
(215) 752-2691
pwlsreg@aol.com
www.popwarner.com

PWLS is a nonprofit organization that provides 360,000 young people ranging in age from 5 to 16 with over 5,000 youth football and cheer and dance programs in 41 states and several countries around the world. PWLS, founded in 1929, requires its participants to maintain academic standards in order to participate.

Women's American Flag Football Federation (WAFFF)

8802 Bailey Road
Wyndmoor, PA 19038
wafffdirector@aol.com
www.wafff.com

The WAFFF is an organization dedicated to the promotion of amateur flag football for women and girls throughout the United States and Canada, and its Web site has listings of regional leagues.

GOLF

U.S. Golf Association (USGA)

P.O. Box 708
Far Hills, NJ 07931
(800) 223-0041
www.usga.org

The USGA has served as the national governing body of golf since its founding in 1894. More than 9,100 private and public golf courses, clubs, and facilities make up the USGA. The nonprofit organization writes and interprets the rules of golf, conducts national tournaments, and oversees the golf handicap system.

American Junior Golf Association (AJGA)

1980 Sports Club Drive
Braselton, GA 30517
(877) 373-2542
ajga@ajga.org
www.ajga.org

The AJGA is a nonprofit organization that provides junior golf tournament information and college scholarships for junior golfers. With a junior membership of more than 5,300 and a full-time staff of 42, more than 160 AJGA alumni play on the PGA and LPGA Tours and have earned more than 240 Tour victories.

LPGA Girls Golf Club

100 International Golf Drive
Daytona Beach, FL 32124-1092
(386) 274-6200
lpga-usga@fans.lpga.com
www.lpga.com

LPGA-USGA Girls Golf is a developmental junior golf program that encourages girls ages 7–17 to learn to play golf, organized by the LPGA in partnership with USGA. More than 2,400 girls participate in over 100 sites nationwide.

Professional Golf Association (PGA)

100 Avenue of the Champions
Palm Beach Gardens, FL 33418
(561) 624-8400
www.pga.com

The PGA runs the Golf Professional Training Program (GPTP), which certifies instructors. The Web site enables you to search for a PGA Professional in your area, as well as providing information about regional juniors tournaments. The PGA has launched www.Juniorlinks.com, a new Web site for youth, which offers a master database of junior golf programs in the United States.

U.S. Golf Teachers Federation (USGTF)

1295 S.E. Port St. Lucie Blvd.
Port Saint Lucie, FL 34952
(888) 346-3290
info@usgtf.com
www.usgtf.com

The USGTF trains and certifies golf teaching professionals and has over 13,000 members. The USGTF issues four levels of certification, from Level I for beginner instructors through Level IV, master teaching professionals. The Web site can help you find a USGTF-certified teaching pro in your area.

GYMNASTICS

USA Gymnastics Federation

Pan American Plaza, Suite 300
201 S. Capitol Avenue
Indianapolis, IN 46225
(800) 345-4719
rebound@usa-gymnastics.org
www.usa-gymnastics.org

This nonprofit organization is the national governing body for gymnastics in the United States. Its Web site has a directory of gymnastics clubs nationwide.

ICE HOCKEY

USA Hockey

1775 Bob Johnson Drive
Colorado Springs, CO 80906
(719) 576-8724
comments@usahockey.org
www.usahockey.com

USA Hockey is the national governing body of recreational hockey in the United States. Its Web site has links to local junior leagues across the country. Of its over 29,000 registered teams, more than 75% play in the age classifications of 17 or under. USA Hockey runs coaching clinics around the country, and certifies coaches from beginning to master level.

INLINE/ROLLER HOCKEY

USA Hockey InLine

775 Bob Johnson Drive
Colorado Springs, CO 80906-4090
(719) 576-8724
usahockeyinline@usahockey.org
www.usahockey.com/inline/main/home/

USA Hockey InLine is the official inline hockey program of USA Hockey, Inc., the national governing body for the sport of hockey in the United States. Since its inception in 1994, it has developed programs for players and coaches and sanctions tournaments nationwide and become the largest inline hockey organization in the world. The organization registers and trains coaches nationwide but does not have a certification process. Its Web site helps you find a local league from the more than 600 local and travel leagues nationwide.

USA Roller Sports (USARS)

4730 South St.
Lincoln, NE 68506
(402) 483-7551
hockey@usarollersports.org
www.usarollersports.com

USARS is the national governing body for all roller sports in the United States, including roller hockey. It oversees junior national teams, and has listings for leagues nationwide.

LACROSSE

U.S. Lacrosse
113 W. University Parkway
Baltimore, MD 21210
(410) 235-6882
info@lacrosse.org
www.lacrosse.org

U.S. Lacrosse was founded in 1998 as the national governing body of men's and women's lacrosse, merging a number of formerly independent national organizations, including the Lacrosse Foundation, the U.S. Women's Lacrosse Association, the National Junior Lacrosse Association, the U.S. Lacrosse Officials Association, the U.S. Lacrosse Coaches Association, and the U.S. Club Lacrosse Association.

KARATE

Aikido Association of America (AAA)
1016 W. Belmont Ave.
Chicago, IL 60657
(773) 525-3141
aikidoamer@aol.com
www.aaa-aikido.com

This association provides a list of aikido dojos in almost every U.S. state.

American Amateur Karate Federation (AAKF)
1930 Wilshire Blvd., Suite 1208
Los Angeles, CA 90057
(213) 483-8262
www.aakf.org

This nonprofit organization, with 1.5 million members nationwide, represents the International Traditional Karate Federation for America. The AAKE conducts regional and national junior traditional karate (as distinct from newly developed forms of karate) tournaments.

American Judo and Jujitsu Federation (AJJF)
780 N. McCarran Blvd., PMB #299
Sparks, NV 89431-5278
(800) 850-2553
co@ajjf.org
www.ajjf.org

This nonprofit federation represents jujitsu, judo, and other martial arts schools across the nation, with links to dojos from its Web site. It also tests and issues national black belt ranks, and runs regional and national tournaments.

American Taekwondo Association (ATA)
6210 Baseline Road
Little Rock, AR 72209
(501) 568-2821
atausa1@aristotle.net
www.ataonline.com

This association has a Karate for Kids program as well as a Tiny Tigers program for children ages 2–6, and enables you to find tae kwon do dojos from its Web site.

Shotokan Karate of America
c/o Maryknoll Japanese Catholic Center
222 S. Hewitt St., Room 7
Los Angeles, CA 90012
(213) 437-0988
hq@ska.org
www.ska.org/karate.shtml

The Web site has a lengthy directory of affiliated dojos in almost every state.

U.S. Judo

One Olympic Plaza, Suite 202
Colorado Springs, CO 80909
(719) 866-4730
secusji@aol.com
www.usjudo.org

This organization is the national governing body for the sport of judo in the United States, as well as a member of the International Judo Federation. It conducts regional and national competitions for juniors. U.S. Judo membership is $50 per year, and your child must be a member to compete.

U.S. Jujitsu Federation (USJJF)

3816 Bellingham Drive
Reno, NV 89511
www.usjujitsu.net

This nonprofit organization is the national governing body for jujitsu in the United States. The Jujitsu Federation hosts a number of jujitsu clubs, camps, and national jujitsu junior competitions as well as a number of seminars. The Web site enables you to find programs around America.

USA National Karate-do Federation (USA-NKF)

P.O. Box 77083
Seattle, WA 98177-7083
(206) 440-8386
karate@usankf.org
www.usankf.org

This organization is the official national governing body for the sport of karate in the United States. It has links to schools across America.

U.S. Taekwondo Union (USTU)

One Olympic Plaza, Suite 104C
Colorado Springs, CO 80909
(719) 866-4632
feecback@ustu.org
www.ustu.com

The USTU, founded in 1974, is the official organization for tae kwon do in America.

RODEO

National Little Britches Rodeo Association (NLBRA)

1045 W. Rio Grande
Colorado Springs, CO 80906
(800) 763-3694
info@nlbra.org
www.nlbra.org

The NLBRA is the oldest national junior rodeo association in the country, for children ages 8–18. It organizes rodeos and provides scholarships.

American Junior Rodeo Association (AJRA)

4501 Armstrong St.
San Angelo, TX 76903
(915) 658-8009
ajra@gte.net
home1.gte.net/ajra/ or www.ajra.org

This youth rodeo association hosts rodeo competitions for kids ages 8–18.

National High School Rodeo Association (NHSRA)

12001 Tejon St., Suite 128
Denver, CO 80234
(800) 466-4772
www.nhsra.com

The NHSRA has an annual membership of over 12,500 students from 39 states, five

Canadian provinces and Australia, and sanctions over 1,100 rodeos each year.

SAILING

U.S. Sailing Association

P.O. Box 1260
Portsmouth, RI 02871-0907
(800) USSAIL1
info@ussailing.org
www.ussailing.org

This is the national governing body for the sport of sailing. Its Web site has links to sailing programs and clubs around the United States. U.S. Sailing certifies coaches from Level 1, beginning coaches, to Level 3, advanced coaches, based on testing, teaching experience, and continuing education.

SKIING

U.S. Ski and Snowboard Association (USSA)

Box 100, 1500 Kearns Blvd.
Park City, UT 84060
(435) 649-9090
special2@ussa.org
www.ussa.org or www.usskiteam.com

The USSA is the national governing body for Olympic skiing and snowboarding, managing competition and athletic programs coast to coast. It is also the designated U.S. representative for skiing and snowboarding by the International Ski Federation. Its Web site has information on ski team programs throughout the country.

Professional Ski Instructors Association (PSIA)

133 S. Van Gordon St., Suite 101
Lakewood, CO 80228

(303) 987-9390
admin@psia.org
www.psia.org

This association of over 25,000 instructors certifies ski instructors nationwide, and its Web site can help you locate an instructor for your child.

SNOWBOARDING

American Association of Snowboard Instructors (AASI)

133 S. Van Gordon St., Suite 102
Lakewood, CO 80228
(303) 988-0545
aasi@aasi.org
www.aasi.org

The AASI is a nonprofit association dedicated to promoting the sport of snowboarding through instruction. The association develops certification standards for snowboard instructors and education materials to be used as the core components of most snowboard training. AASI is an education partner with, and program of, the Professional Ski Instructors of America.

Professional Ski Instructors of America (PSIA)

133 S. Van Gordon St., Suite 101
Lakewood, CO 80228
(303) 987-9390
admin@psia.org
www.psia.org

This association of over 25,000 instructors certifies ski instructors nationwide, and its Web site can help you locate an instructor for your child.

U.S. Amateur Snowboard Association (USASA)

P.O. Box 3927
Truckee, CA 96160
(800) 404-9213
www.usasa.org

The USASA is the first governing body exclusively for competitive amateur snowboarding and serves as the U.S. representative for the International Snowboard Federation.

U.S. Ski and Snowboard Association (USSA)

Box 100, 1500 Kearns Blvd.
Park City, UT 84060
(435) 649-9090
special2@ussa.org
www.ussa.org

The USSA is the national governing body for Olympic skiing and snowboarding, managing competition and athletic programs coast to coast. It is also the designated U.S. representative for skiing and snowboarding by the International Ski Federation.

SOCCER

U.S. Soccer Federation (USSF)

1801 S. Prairie Ave.
Chicago, IL 60616
(312) 808-1300
socfed@aol.com
www.us-soccer.com

The USSF is the national governing body of American soccer. It oversees the U.S. national teams (men's, women's, Olympic, and youth), as well as coaching and referee development.

National Soccer Coaches Association of America (NSCAA)

6700 Squibb Road, Suite 215
Mission, KS 66202
(800) 458-0678
www.nscaa.com

Founded in 1941, the NSCAA is the largest single-sport coaching organization in the United States, with more than 15,000 members. It provides coach educational clinics, academies, and seminars, as well as diploma courses in all fifty states.

American Youth Soccer Organization (AYSO)

5403 W. 138th St.
Hawthorne, CA 90250
(800) USA-AYSO
www.soccer.org

With its 625,000 registered players ages 4–18, 92,000 volunteer coaches, and 47,000 referees, AYSO's emphasis is on participation of all players and recreational play. It mandates a 50% of each game play policy. Community programs are organized into regions with volunteer coaches.

U.S. Youth Soccer Association (USYSA)

899 Presidential Drive, Suite 117
Richardson, TX 75081
(800) 4-SOCCER
nationaloffice@youthsoccer.org
www.youthsoccer.org

America's largest youth soccer organization, with more than 3 million children ages 5–19 playing in its affiliates, this nonprofit organization has member associations in every state. The USYSA sponsors both recreational and competitive leagues, along with regional and national championships. Teams are divided by age. The organization serves as the youth division of U.S. Amateur Soccer, which includes high-level play through the Olympic Development Program.

Soccer Association for Youth

4050 Executive Park Drive, Suite 100
Cincinnati, OH 45241
(800) 233-7291
www.saysoccer.org

This independent regional youth soccer organization is located mainly in the Midwest and serves more than 100,000 members and youth players ages 4–18.

U.S. Futsal Federation (USFF)

P.O. Box 40077
Berkeley, CA 94704-4077
(510) 836-8733
futsal@futsal.org
www.futsal.org

The USFF, under U.S. Soccer, is the national governing body for Futsal in the United States. Futsal is the only internationally approved form of indoor soccer.

SQUASH AND RACQUETBALL

U.S. Racquetball Association (USRA)

1685 W. Uintah
Colorado Springs, CO 80904-2906
(719) 635-5396
racquetball@usra.org
www.usra.org

The USRA is a nonprofit organization and is recognized as the national governing body of the sport by the U.S. Olympic Committee. The USRA sponsors the American Professional Racquetball Organization (AmPro), which issues certification for racquetball instructors and pros, offering clinics and testing throughout the United States. The USRA includes over 3,000 facilities with racquetball courts. It also serves as headquarters for the International Racquetball Federation (IRF), the international governing body for racquetball.

U.S. Squash Racquets Association (USSRA)

P.O. Box 1216
23 Cynwyd Road
Bala Cynwyd, PA 19004
(610) 667-4006
office@us-squash.org
www.us-squash.org/squash

The USSRA has 33 local districts, and its Web site can help you find the nearest school, club, or facility with squash courts. It also runs a certification program for coaches.

SURFING

U.S. Surfing Federation (USSF)

P.O. Box 1070
Virginia Beach, VA 23451
(888) 987-7873
www.ussurf.org

The USSF, founded in 1980, is the national governing body for competitive surfing within the United States. It coordinates competitions open to all levels of surfers nationwide

National Scholastic Surfing Association (NSSA)

P.O. Box 495
Huntington Beach, CA 92648
(714) 536-0445
jaragon@nssa.org
www.nssa.org

With over 2,000 active members, the NSSA is an amateur U.S. competitive surfing association divided into five geographic regions.

SWIMMING

USA Swimming

One Olympic Plaza
Colorado Springs, CO 80909
(719) 866-4578
www.usa-swimming.org

This official national governing body for the sport has links to affiliated swimming clubs and camps nationwide, as well as local, regional, and national competitions.

U.S. Synchronized Swimming

201 S. Capitol Ave., Suite 510
Indianapolis, IN 46225
info@usasynchro.org
www.usasynchro.org

This organization sponsors national and international competitions for synchronized swimming teams, and its Web site will help you find a club near you.

American Red Cross Swimming

431 18th St., N.W.
Washington, DC 20006
(202) 639-3520
www.redcross.org/services/hss/aquatics

The American Red Cross has been the leader in swimming and lifeguarding instruction since 1914 and set the standard for many courses taught. Its Web site has a local chapter locator.

American Swimming Coaches Association (ASCA)

2101 N. Andrews Ave., Suite 107
Fort Lauderdale, FL 33311
(800) 356-2722
asca@swimmingcoach.org
www.swimmingcoach.org

The ASCA is a professional organization for swim coaches in the United States. It certifies coaches on five different levels, with Level 5 being the highest and comprising the top 2%–5% of coaches in the nation.

TABLE TENNIS

USA Table Tennis (USATT)

One Olympic Plaza
Colorado Springs, CO 80909-5769
(719) 866-4583
usatt@usatt.org
www.usatt.org

USATT is the national governing body of table tennis and certifies coaches from youth instructor level to club, state, regional, and finally national level. Its Web site has a list of table tennis clubs and coaches in the U.S.

TENNIS

U.S. Tennis Association (USTA)

7310 Crandon Blvd.
Key Biscayne, FL 33149
(305) 365-8782
jrcomp@usta.com
www.usta.com

Found in 1881, the volunteer-based USTA can now be found in all 50 states and American territories, and is composed of 17 geographical sections that further divide into districts, each of which establishes its own tournament schedule and issues its own rankings. You can use its Web site to find local tennis programs.

U.S. Professional Tennis Association (USPTA)

3535 Briarpark Drive, Suite One
Houston, TX 77042
(713) 978-7782
(800) USPTA-4U
uspta@uspta.org
www.uspta.org

Founded in 1927, the USPTA is the oldest and largest association of tennis-teaching professionals, with more than 12,500 members worldwide. It certifies teaching professionals, and the certification exam is structured so that a professional's rating indicates job qualifications. For example, members who earn a Professional 1 rating, the highest level, have at least three years of teaching experience and the qualifications to work as a director of tennis or head tennis professional. For the Professional 2 rating, in addition to passing on-court and written exams, they must have some teaching experience, while the Professional 3 rating indicates having passed the exams without any teaching experience acquired yet.

U.S. Professional Tennis Registry (USPTR)

P.O. Box 4739
Hilton Head Island, SC 29938
(800) 421-6289
ptr@ptrtennis.org
www.usptr.org

With over 10,300 members in 122 countries, the USPTR educates and certifies tennis teachers and coaches. PTR certification ratings include PTR professional, instructor, and associate instructor based on performance on five areas of testing (written, skills, teaching, drills, and error detection). Teachers can supplement their current rating with 1A, 2A, 3A, and 4A levels of professional development through workshops, courses, conferences, degree programs, or other educational activities.

TRACK AND FIELD

USA Track & Field (USATF)

P.O. Box 120
Indianapolis, IN 46206-0120
(317) 261-0500
www.usatf.org

USATF is the national governing body for track and field, long-distance running, and race walking in the United States. It has over 100,000 members, and oversees 2,500 local clubs. It sanctions grassroots tournaments through regional, state, and national competitions—including an annual Junior Olympics—runs training programs, and issues certification for coaches. Its Web site has links to programs and coaches around the country.

VOLLEYBALL

USA Volleyball

715 S. Circle Drive
Colorado Springs, CO 80910
(888) 786-5539
postmaster@usav.org
www.usavolleyball.org

USA Volleyball is recognized by the U.S. Olympic Committee and the Fédération Internationalé de Volleyball as the national governing body for the sport of volleyball. It has junior memberships as well as regional affiliates. Its Web site gives you contact information for 39 regional offices as well as summer volleyball camps.

American Volleyball Coaches Association (AVCA)

1227 Lake Plaza Drive, Suite B
Colorado Springs, CO 80906
(719) 576-7777
www.avca.org

The AVCA has more than 3,100 members comprising national and international coaches, including high school, club, and youth coaches. The Web site has links to help you find club teams around the country.

WATERSKIING

USA Water Ski (USA-WS)

1251 Holy Cow Road
Polk City, FL 33868
(863) 324-4341
usawaterski@usawaterski.org
www.usawaterski.org

USA Water Ski is the national governing body for organized waterskiing in the United States, with a dual mission of promoting recreational waterskiing and organizing and governing competitive waterskiing. It has over 35,000 members in five regions across the country, with 70% of members involved in tournament competitions. It certifies waterskiing instructors, and sponsors learn-to-ski clinics and programs to develop junior water-skiers. It has approximately 800 affiliated local water-ski clubs, as well as specialty divisions, which include the American Water Ski Association, the American Barefoot Club, the American Kneeboard Association, and the National Show Ski Association.

International Amateur Water Ski, Wakeboard, and Kneeboard

P.O. Box 283
Black Diamond, WA 98010
(253) 887-1606
fun@intleague.com
www.intleague.com

This nonprofit organization, self-described as the "Little League of Waterskiing," offers water-ski, wakeboard, and kneeboard competitions in 30 states that group individuals by skill levels. Competitors receive points based on how they finish at an event, culminating in state finals at the end of each summer, and each division's state finalist continuing on to the U.S. Championships, held each October.

WINDSURFING

U.S. Windsurfing Association

326 E. Merritt Island Causeway, Suite 300
Merritt Island, FL 32952
(877) 386-8708
uswa@aol.com
www.uswindsurfing.org

U.S. Windsurfing is a member-based organization working to grow recreational and competitive windsurfing in the United States. It sponsors regional and national tournaments, and junior membership costs only $10. The Web site contains useful information about the basics of windsurfing, windsurfing clubs, instruction, equipment, events, research reports, and current news. This site also has useful links to windsurfing publications and great travel sites for windsurfing.

WRESTLING

USA Wrestling
6155 Lehman Drive
Colorado Springs, CO 80918
(719) 598-8181
usaw@concentric.net
www.usawrestling.org and
www.themat.com

USA Wrestling—the national governing body for amateur wrestling in the United States, with over 140,000 members, 11,000 coaches, and 2,400 chartered clubs—coordinates grassroots and elite wrestling programs across the country. Regional competitions are open to athletes who are age 9 or older, while for national championships wrestlers must be over age 14 to compete. USA Wrestling also runs a national coaches education program that certifies national coaches: copper, for beginning coaches, through bronze, silver, and gold for international-caliber coaches.

STRENGTH TRAINING

The National Strength and Conditioning Association (NSCA)
1955 N. Union Blvd.
Colorado Springs, CO 80909
(800) 815-6826
nsca@nsca-lift.org
www.nsca-lift.org

The NSCA, which serves as the national association for strength training and conditioning, offers two national accreditations: certified strength and conditioning specialist (CSCS) and NSCA certified personal trainer (NSCA-CPT). The Web site has a section to help you locate personal trainers in a specific geographic area.

YOGA

Because of the decentralized nature of yoga practices, and the numerous yoga disciplines, there is no one centralized resource or certification process for yoga. To find children's yoga classes in your area, check your local parents' paper and ask around for recommendations from other parents. The following site may be helpful:

National Yoga Alliance
120 S. Third Ave.
West Reading, PA 19611
(877) 964-2255
info@yogaalliance.org
www.yogaalliance.org

Yoga Alliance is a voluntary alliance of diverse yoga organizations and individual yoga teachers dedicated to establishing voluntary national standards for yoga teachers and providing support for yoga professionals in the United States. The Web site has a registry of yoga teachers who have met the voluntary standards.

PART III

ART AND PERFORMING ARTS

11

General Music Considerations

Approximately 62 million people in the United States play a musical instrument, and 97% of parents polled feel children benefit from a music education. Because music is often no longer included in the mainstream curriculum of schools, it is up to you to decide the best way to introduce your child to music. Deciding if or when to start private lessons, selecting an instrument to study, and choosing the right teacher are key decisions.

I view music as a sports alternative: You have sports parents, you have ballet parents, and then you have music parents. Most of these parents have musical backgrounds themselves. With our oldest son, we're dealing with a child whose passion for music is all-consuming. We're not pushing him to do it, but it's more like we're getting yanked along. Our son may have the wherewithal to make a big contribution to the discipline and it may be his career. Therefore, my wife and I take it seriously. With a gifted kid, it is incumbent on you to find the best programs, the best teachers you can, and take musical education as seriously as you would take regular school.

—Jim, dad of Ben, 10, Emma, 7, and Spencer, 4

I have Ben taking sax, even though he's great at the piano, because I feel he's a kid who's not going to be an athlete and music could end up being an important part of his life. Plus, piano is too solitary, because you can't play it in a social or school setting like orchestra or band. I know that I'm socially engineering his life to an extent, but it's in places where I think he'll find lots of happiness and be able to do stuff with other kids.

—Janine, mom of Ben, 10, and
Andrew, 7

For me music was a passion, and I have sung and performed semiprofessionally. While in college, I traveled with the glee club, which was a fun thing that led me to meet lots of new people. I have no grand aspirations for the kids when it comes to music. I simply want them to love and have fun with it. To me music is a joy, and I want it to be that for them too. I want Ben to be the one playing the guitar as everyone else sings along in college. Are either of my children music prodigies? No. Do they enjoy it and have fun with it and have something that they can say is theirs? Yes.

—Andy, dad of Rachel, 10, Ben, 7, and
Josh, 3

GENERAL BENEFITS

In addition to learning music for its own sake, musical study can influence your child throughout her life. As a result of music-listening and music-making experiences, your child develops musical intelligence, and a better sense of tempo and rhythm.

Music gives your child an outlet for self-expression, and the pride and sense of accomplishment of being a musician. Performing in concerts and competitions also boost your child's confidence and self-esteem.

Playing a musical instrument improves manual dexterity, fine muscle control, hand-eye coordination, poise, posture, memorization, listening skills, concentration, and self-discipline. Wind instruments build respiratory strength.

Music also has social benefits, as many bands, orchestras, and singing groups travel together.

Recent studies suggest that early childhood music education has a direct effect on the development of the brain's neural circuitry, which can improve spatial, temporal, and abstract reasoning skills, which apply to math, science, and chess.

A research team led by physicist Dr. Gordon Shaw of the University of California at Irvine made an enlightening discovery when they embarked on their two-year experiment with preschoolers. The children who were given piano or keyboard training performed 34% higher on tests measuring spatial-temporal ability than the other children included in the study.

Music primarily gives children another language in which to express themselves.

—*Paul Verona, international concert pianist and teacher for 25 years*

Both my son and daughter can sit down and play quite a few pieces from memory. My favorite memory is when we want into a hotel near Chicago to meet some cousins from out of town. While we were waiting, my two kids took turns sitting down at the piano in the lobby and playing different pieces from memory. What a boost to their self-confidence and sense of accomplishment when people, including some men working nearby, stopped what they were doing to listen.

—*Shannon, mom of an 11-year-old daughter and a 9-year-old son*

Playing a musical instrument exercises both the right and left side of the brain. The creative side is developed through musical expression, and the logical side through learning to read music, count note values, and learning other aspects of musical theory.

—*Tanah Haney, professional performer and private harp, piano, and recorder teacher for 12 years*

ENCOURAGING MUSICAL INTEREST IN YOUR CHILD

🎵 Rather than making it your ambition to produce a musical genius, help your child develop a lifelong enjoyment of music. Your child does not need innate talent, as music can be learned and developed. Like any skill worth learning, playing a musical instrument well takes effort and dedicated practice.

🎵 You can encourage your child's love of music and nurture her musical talents in the following ways:
- Surround your child with musical experiences.
- Listen to music together on the radio.
- Listen to a mix of classical and jazz music, as well as popular and

contemporary music, with your child to develop her musical ear for different rhythms, harmonies, and melodies.

- Provide your child with regular opportunities to hear, sing, or play music with and for family and friends in a relaxed setting.
- Attend concerts, community music events, and musical festivals.
- Help your child to understand the story or composer behind the music. Check out books from the library, and read about fascinating stories such as Mozart's early genius.
- Have your child join you in watching music and arts programs on television.
- Encourage your child to participate in general music classes and performing ensembles.
- When school offers band or string instrument instruction, help your child choose an instrument.
- Visit the classroom to gain a better understanding of what takes place in the music program.
- Volunteer to chaperone trips to music events and work to bring outstanding performers to your child's school.

If your child is shy or reluctant, don't force the issue. However, if your child isn't too nervous to play informal mini-concerts, encourage her, as she may be better prepared to deal with and conquer stage fright later on.

Kids Who Tend to Excel

Children who gravitate to music and excel at it usually have:

- an appreciation and love for music, and a genuine desire to play and learn
- a good ear for pitch and tone
- a long attention span, patience, and creativity
- initiative when it comes to practice
- an open mind about different styles of music

Best Age to Start

For children, starting at the right age is a key element in the success of their lessons. If a child starts lessons too soon, she may feel overwhelmed and frustrated, and want to quit—an unfortunate situation that might be prevented by waiting a few years.

Kids who excel are not necessarily those who are innately gifted, but rather those who are self-disciplined about practice, tenacious, and love music.

—*Betsy Binder, private flute teacher for 12 years*

The most successful students at a young age have "an ear" for tone and pitch, and they seem to instinctively find it on the instrument.

—*Gary Keller, saxophone professor, University of Miami School of Music, teaching for 20 years*

A student who excels in music usually has a supportive environment in which to practice, study, and rehearse. The student needs to demonstrate some musical ability: pitch recognition (singing along with the radio or choir), rhythmic sense (dancing or clapping to the beat), musical curiosity. The student need not be a potential prodigy to study. Self-discipline is a plus, but not needed to get started. Many times it is a wonderful byproduct of musical training.

—*John Mueller, assistant professor of trombone and euphonium, University of Memphis, and professional musician, teaching for 21 years*

Opinions differ widely on when to start traditional music instruction, and each section that follows on specific instruments offers age guidelines. By ages 5–8, many children are ready for one-on-one music lessons. Some instructors prefer to start their students around age 8. By this point, a student can read, begin note reading, and focus on a weekly half-hour lesson.

Realize that the younger your child is, the more you will have to help out with practice time. Postponing lessons for a year or two sometimes proves beneficial, as older children tend to progress faster and do very well starting later than the earliest recommended age.

For your preschooler who has a keen desire to begin music, a group preschool music class in a game-oriented setting will give her a foundation of basic principles that will prove helpful later with private lessons. At this age, private lessons generally do not work unless your child has had experience in a formal learning environment.

● Younger students often benefit from shorter lessons, perhaps 20 minutes twice a week for the first six months.

● Consider your child's social needs. You may want to consider group lessons if being with peers would be more interesting for your child and make her more enthusiastic about learning. Group lessons are often better for younger children because they feel a sense of belonging and believe they are achieving something together. The one disadvantage of this is the lack of individual attention.

● Group lessons for younger children (ages 3–8) can relieve the pressure, make it a social activity with peers, and are less expensive.

Suzuki Method

❧ Suzuki students start between ages 2 and 4 and learn to listen, absorb, and play music themselves by ear before they can even read music.

❧ Dr. Shinichi Suzuki, a Japanese music teacher, found children could learn music very young when using a teaching method that relies on a child's natural ability to learn language.

❧ Suzuki instruction starts without your child having to be able to read music, and relies on learning through imitation and teaching your child to play by ear.

❧ If your child learns the Suzuki method, she will start by playing numerous variations of familiar songs, starting with "Twinkle, Twinkle, Little Star." Each variation is designed to teach your child specific musical skills.

If you do Suzuki, music is seen as a normal part of living. Instead of the Russian tradition of learning to read music, then scales, and finally play musical pieces, Suzuki starts a student playing easy pieces from memory. Kids develop an ear and have the constant reinforcement of playing real music. It can be so much fun. Over the course of eight or nine levels, more and more complexity gets introduced. In most programs, parents are required to be in class so they can reinforce what the teacher has taught.

—Jim, dad of Ben, 10, Emma, 7, and Spencer, 4

CHOOSING A MUSICAL INSTRUMENT

Which instrument should your child play? If ever there was a time to encourage your child to experiment, this is it. Chances are your child will want to try out at least a couple of instruments before settling on one.

Expose your child to instrumental music as early as you can. With some early music instruction in a church or community choir or even at home, she may be able to pick up an instrument quite rapidly. All instruments fall into four categories: string, brass, woodwind, and percussion. Piano is considered a basic instrument (many music programs expect "piano proficiency"). It also provides a good basis for picking up a secondary and portable instrument. Many students make the easy switch to a different instrument within the same family, such as from clarinet to saxophone.

How to Choose

🎵 Learn with your child about the different families of instruments: strings, woodwinds, brass, and percussion. Try to find an instrument that meshes well with your child's personality.

🎵 Seek out local band or orchestra concerts with your child and, if possible, a friend who knows something about music. Take your child to an orchestra concert and talk afterward about what you saw and heard.

🎵 Listen to musical pieces that feature a range of instruments. Listen to a classical station on the radio and try to identify the instruments.

🎵 Set a budget for your musical instrument. Some instruments, such as the French horn, tuba, bassoon, and oboe, may be a bit on the pricey side, but school music departments usually have a small number of these instruments in their inventories.

🎵 Let your child try out a few instruments by borrowing from a friend or going to a music shop. She will also likely have the opportunity to try a few out in music class at her school, as music instructors often let students borrow equipment.

🎵 Your child's school band or orchestra director should know someone who can lend your child an instrument.

🎵 Keep your lifestyle in mind. If either space or mobility is an issue, go with the portability of a small instrument like clarinet or violin.

🎵 Strategically choose your child's instrument instead of falling back on conven-

Select an instrument that your child seems excited about playing, and that a professional has advised your child will have success on. For instance, kids with an underbite should never play brass instruments, as they will always have trouble getting a decent tone. Some instruments like the tuba and horn require a better than average ear, so only those who score higher on the ear training test should select those instruments. Still the best hint of success is if a child is truly excited.

> —*Scott Watson, professor of tuba and euphonium at University of Kansas and professional musician, teaching for 23 years*

I believe that children should be allowed to choose which instrument they would like to play. The most successful students have been the ones who bugged their parents for an instrument and lessons. Some people believe that certain physical characteristics indicate which instrument a child should play, but I disagree. Expose your child to a variety of instruments at a young age. Many orchestras offer concerts for kids that show off the instruments. A strong desire and good orthodontia can overcome bad physiology!

> —*Marlene Metz, private flute and recorder teacher for 8 years*

A child should listen to the sound a good player can achieve on all the different instruments through recordings and seeing a demonstration of the instruments, which are often given at the beginning of school years through band and orchestra programs. Then they should be allowed to play what they desire to play. Parents who "force" a child to do music usually do not have much luck. And children often have a strong opinion of the particular kind of instrument that they want to play. Trying to choose an instrument "for" a child is almost always a mistake.

> —*Julie DeRoche, clarinet faculty member, DePaul University School of Music, and Chicago Symphony substitute, teaching for 25 years*

ience. Whether the piano teacher lives right around the corner or the music teacher gives free violin lessons at school, if the instrument is not a good match for your child, she will be frustrated, and the experience will have been a waste of your child's time and your money.

Physical Suitability

✦ Talk to the school band or orchestra teacher about your child's interest, as well as her size, before making a decision.

✦ Consider physical restrictions when choosing an instrument. Some instruments, such as a cello or tuba, may be too cumbersome or heavy for a small child, and some instruments may require dexterity or extra breath support.

✦ Unless you plan on driving your child to and from school each time she needs to bring her instrument home, a tuba is probably not going to be a good choice. Stay away from an instrument with a case that's difficult to manage on a crowded school bus.

✦ Few instruments come small enough for little fingers and bodies, so your child may be limited in the scope of available instruments. The player needs to be able to see and reach all parts of the instrument.

✦ Because stringed instruments are built in proportionally smaller sizes, children as young as 3 can play them.

✦ Recorders and flutes are available in smaller sizes for younger students.

✦ Due to their size, weight, and length, wind and brass instruments are generally better suited to older children.

✦ Small children can usually handle a regular piano keyboard with an adjustable chair or footstool.

✦ Some teachers recommend trying to find an instrument in the same range as your child's singing voice.

Your Child's Preferences

✦ Spend some time talking to your child and get a sense of what sounds she likes. Which instruments appeal to her?

✦ Be sure to let her hear every instrument she has the option of choosing. You may decide to go to a local music shop to try out different types of instruments, or ask your child's teacher if she would be willing to do this during music class.

✦ Don't balk if your child tells you she wants to play a "less popular" instrument. Often this means more opportunities to play in a group setting.

It's good to go with the instrument your child expresses the most interest in, since few things can turn a child off music more than unwanted lessons in an instrument they don't like. The best thing you can do is to expose your child to many different kinds of music and different instruments, and see if any pique his interest. There are lots of ways to do this. Most symphonies hold matinee family concerts, where you can take your child to see all sorts of musical performances. There are also general music programs (Kindermusik or Music for Young Children), where they can have fun learning about rhythm, tune, and movement without having to worry about mastering a difficult technique. If there is a music program at your child's school, this can be a good place to start—whether it be singing, band, dance, or musical theater.

—Tanah Haney, professional performer and private harp, piano, and recorder teacher for 12 years

Keep in mind that your child may change his mind a few times. Of course, you also want to encourage stick-to-itiveness, and the development of good practice habits. Give each instrument a few months at least before giving up, unless your child really seems to be miserable. A child might hit rough spots, where he becomes discouraged or distracted, and it's good to encourage him through those times. However, if the child is obviously very unhappy, consider switching instruments or teachers.

—Tanah Haney, professional performer and private harp, piano, and recorder teacher for 12 years

It's Okay to Switch

🐦 It may help to think of your child's first instrument as the first of many. Many beginning musicians have much greater success with their second instrument than with their first. Remember that only a few professional musicians actually began on the instrument they now play.

🐦 This is another good reason to rent an instrument instead of buying one. Your child may play for three months and announce that she has decided that it's actually the violin, not the flute, that she desperately wants to play. For this reason, make a short-term commitment if you're renting an instrument. Also, many rental agreements will allow you to continue the agreement with a different instrument.

GROUP PLAY IN ORCHESTRAS AND BANDS

🐿 Most school districts start band in fourth or fifth grade.

🐿 In addition to school bands, some towns or counties offer youth orchestras or marching bands.

🐿 Orchestra and band teach teamwork, particularly in learning to play in time with everyone else and realizing that in group play no one person assumes center stage.

🐿 Band and orchestra will allow your child to participate in performing groups, especially if she doesn't like solitude.

🐿 Because of the sense of camaraderie, belonging to a musical group may motivate your child to practice harder and make it less likely that she will want to quit.

🐿 For older children, band instruments become an option. Perhaps your child has

There is absolutely no question that a child will be more interested and more successful if she is able to play in a group. It gives children a sense of belonging and a sense of accomplishment.

—*Karen, private teacher of flute, recorder, clarinet, and saxophone for 27 years*

Regardless of the type of instrument that a student plays, the social and intellectual experience of being a member of a performing ensemble is immeasurable. Children learn to work together to produce a performable great event, such as a concert, and make friends and have fun doing it.

—*Julie DeRoche, clarinet faculty member, DePaul University School of Music, and Chicago Symphony substitute, teaching for 25 years*

Group participation in orchestras creates a sense of belonging and camaraderie that can't be fulfilled just in the private studio.

—*Linda Bolander, private violin and viola teacher, teaching for 10 years*

A band or orchestra program needs to be very organized and disciplined. A large ensemble by definition is led by one person (the teacher/conductor) who should demonstrate that she is in charge and has a plan. Large and active parent support groups (i.e., band boosters) are necessary and a good indicator of the quality of the program. Check to see how often the group rehearses and performs. Observe a rehearsal or two and a performance if possible. See if the students are behaving, having fun, and focused. Beware of programs that overemphasize competition results (too narrowly focused) or have no direction (unfocused).

—*John Mueller, assistant professor of trombone and euphonium, University of Memphis, and professional musician, teaching for 21 years*

been to band or orchestra concerts and has a desire to be in one, or she saw a demonstration of band instruments in school and saw one that she might like to play.

🎜 Once your child has made a decision, find an instrument and determine if a private teacher is necessary.

RENTING VS. BUYING AN INSTRUMENT

General Cost Considerations

🎜 If finances are a consideration, take this into account from the beginning when offering your child instrument choices.

🎜 Think about whether you want to rent, buy, or rent the instrument with the option to buy it. Like a car, the value of a musical instrument depreciates as soon as it becomes yours. Make sure your child knows that this is a long-term commitment, not a month-long endeavor. Once you commit to the music shop, you commit to the instrument and to the financial responsibilities that accompany it. Even though some music shops will let you switch instruments, they will not let you end the commitment altogether. Make your child keep her end of the bargain and encourage her to practice.

✤ Renting may involve the least amount of commitment if you're unsure about the degree of your child's passion. Let your child try an instrument out for six months to a year before purchasing one.

✤ Finding the right music store or dealer to buy or rent an instrument from involves making a careful decision. It could save you hundreds of dollars and infinite aggravation, especially when dealing with repairs. Your music teacher can probably give you a couple of referrals to the best music stores in your area. The advantages of renting from a music store are:

➤ The instrument your child receives will be in good playing condition. If you decide to rent to own, be sure you start out with a new instrument that is not reconditioned, as you may end up purchasing it.

➤ Repairs and maintenance, which can sometimes be quite expensive, will usually be included in the rental fee. You also don't have to pay more than a quarter of the total rental fee for the commitment, so if your child wants to quit or switch instruments, it's not expensive to make the change.

➤ A school music distributor deals exclusively in band and orchestra instruments. This type of merchant usually has a knowledgeable staff of professional players and educators, along with a competent repair department. If you have questions about a dealer, ask your child's music teacher, since this is often how your school district obtains instruments.

Types of Rental Plans

✤ One option is to rent from your local music store on a month-to-month basis if you are not sure whether your child will take to the instrument.

✤ Consider renting used, name-brand instruments by the school year. You can often save half of what a monthly rental would cost by making one payment to rent by the school year.

✤ Read the fine print before signing an agreement. Many stores have "rent to purchase" plans where a portion of your monthly rental could be applied to the purchase price. Look for plans that offer prepayment discounts and 100% credit of the rental fee applied toward the purchase of an instrument. You usually can apply your

Your child's teacher should *always* be consulted when buying an instrument. The teacher will know the best type of instrument for your child, and help find the best place to purchase it. Besides that, if your child shows up for lessons with a type of the instrument the teacher doesn't like, it can become a real problem. Plus, if you are thinking of buying your child an instrument to begin on, first ask yourself the question: Would you buy your child a new car when she is just getting her learner's permit?

—*Thomas Bacon, international French horn soloist, teaching for 40 years*

lease fee to the retail price of a new instrument, often with substantial additional discounts. Check to see whether all of your payments apply to the purchase of the instrument, and what that purchase price will be.

🎵 Oftentimes your equity buildup can be applied to any instrument in the store, though some stores only apply the rent credit to the instrument being rented.

Insurance

🎵 Many dealers offer insurance to cover damage and theft of their rental instruments. Consult your insurance company about coverage for your musical instruments. While your homeowners policy may cover theft, it likely does not cover damage.

🎵 The replacement costs for rental instruments fall anywhere from $400 to well over $1,000. Without insurance, you could be responsible for all repairs or replacement if your child loses her instrument.

🎵 Musical instruments can break easily. When you take advantage of the dealer's insurance, you eliminate all the worrying you'd be doing about theft or damage. Accidents inevitably happen, no matter how diligent your child is about taking care of her instrument.

🎵 The cost of theft and damage insurance is reasonable, usually costing $2–$3 per month or $12–$20 on school year plans.

Rental vs. Purchase Cost

🎵 When deciding whether to rent or buy, your decision will most likely depend on the difference in monthly cost. If you can purchase a quality instrument at a price equal to or less than the monthly rental cost, then you will want to purchase it.

✦ Cost effectiveness may vary depending on the instrument and the quality of the instrument. If your child studies for some time, buying can definitely be a better value, as you can resell the instrument when she moves on to a different or more advanced one.

✦ Depending on the price, some instruments have a shorter "payback" time than others. For example, a $700 clarinet will pay for itself in less time than a $1,600 French horn.

✦ Keeping your child's best interest at heart, you'd do better to rent a good-quality instrument than buy one of poor quality. An instrument that plays badly will discourage your budding genius and could make her lose interest altogether.

HOW TO CHOOSE A MUSIC TEACHER

✦ Music goes beyond playing the notes on a page and involves being able to understand and interpret the emotions behind them. You want a teacher who can give your child an experience of joy in music.

✦ Private instruction is perhaps the best way to learn to play a musical instrument, but joining a band or ensemble in addition to private lessons will also enhance your child's learning. Depending on your child's age, private lessons may or may not be appropriate.

✦ You may find yourself overwhelmed by the prospect of picking a music teacher for your child, especially if you have no musical background yourself. Here, we offer some suggestions for deciding if your child is ready, selecting potential instructors, and interviewing them. Keep in mind that a renowned performer isn't necessarily the best choice if your child dreads her lessons. The most important part of selecting a private teacher is to find the right match. Your child's education and long-term success are often dependent on a good relationship with her teacher.

Where Do I Begin the Search for a Teacher?

✦ Ask for recommendations for good music instructors from friends, neighborhood parents, teachers, music teachers, piano tuners, music stores, and others in your community.

Friends are the best source for referrals when it comes to finding a good teacher. Luckily, we found our piano teacher from music lessons at summer camp, but we now have eight friends who use the same teacher based on our referrals. Now at recitals there's a cohort of kids who know each other, which has been nice for them and for the parents.

—*Amy, mom of Sacha, 11, and Libby, 8*

🍂 Your search may depend on your goals for your child. If your child is a beginner, make sure your emphasis is on the relationship between your child and the teacher to ensure that your child's experience will be a positive one. If your child is serious about pursuing an instrument, you will want to look for a conservatory-level teacher.

🍂 Contact the music department at a local college or university. You're likely to find some music professors who run private studios or who can at least recommend some good teachers in your area. Many retail piano stores offer inexpensive lessons in their showrooms, but evaluate these the same way you would choose a private teacher.

Interviewing a Prospective Teacher

🍂 Music lessons differ widely in content, technique, and educational objective. The most important part of selecting a private teacher is to find the right match for your child.

🍂 Visit a candidate and sit in on a lesson to see what the teacher and her method of teaching are like. You may also want to attend her students' recital.

🍂 Schedule an interview with the teacher and be sure to bring your child. You may have to pay for the teacher's time, but a meeting is essential in the decision-making process.

🍂 A successful student-teacher relationship is crucial to your child's musical success. How does her personality fit with that of your child?

🍂 Qualities to look for include patience, a positive attitude, and a creative approach to teaching music in a way that is clear and engaging.

🍂 Discuss with the instructor how she plans to build up your child's self-esteem and encourage her during lessons.

🍂 How much of a perfectionist is the teacher? Your child may find herself miserable if she feels as though she is unable to please her instructor.

🍂 What teaching materials and approach does the teacher use? Are you comfortable with her techniques?

✦ Does the instructor teach the students how to memorize? To improvise? To compose? To sight read?

✦ Does the teacher allow children to play contemporary music and/or play by ear? Students who want to play songs from the radio will become frustrated by a teacher who will never let them try. Yet it is important for students to learn classical music and technique as well.

✦ Ask for clear policies regarding fees, payment schedule, absences, vacations, illness, lateness, and telephone or other interruptions. Find out how best to be in touch with the teacher, whether it's via voicemail or e-mail. Many teachers will make up a lesson if you give enough notice, but expect to pay for last-minute cancellations.

✦ Listen for prejudices. Does she negatively discuss other teachers or students?

✦ Inquire about time commitment and practice requirements. How much practice time does the teacher expect each week?

✦ The best teachers schedule occasional recitals and concerts to give students performance experience. Other performance occasions could include contests, music festivals, master classes, chamber music, piano ensembles, and accompanying.

✦ Check out her studio. Is it a well-equipped and spacious environment conducive to learning?

✦ Ideally, she should encourage students to play in recitals but not insist to the point a stage-shy beginner will quit lessons. If appropriate, the teacher should also encourage her students to participate in festivals and competitions.

✦ Teachers often charge a recital fee to cover the cost of space rental, a piano accompanist, program printing, and the teacher's time in arranging and conducting the event.

✦ Even if a teacher with high credentials and consistent success record comes highly recommended, she still may not be right for your child.

✦ Find out if the teacher specializes in beginners or advanced students or if she teaches all ability levels. A very young beginner may be intimidated in a studio of older, advanced students. Conversely, an older child may feel uncomfortable around young students.

✦ A good teacher will be able to sense your child's moods and needs. She'll know when to include movement in the lesson, when to make a student sit still, and when to let your child take a break.

✦ She should weave music theory into her lessons.

🎵 Inquire whether she offers group lessons.

🎵 Look for an instructor who will provide formal or informal evaluations of your child's progress.

🎵 Ongoing points to consider when deciding how well the match is between the teacher and your child:

- ➤ You want a teacher who will inspire your child as she grows musically, and whose techniques suit your child's personality and learning style.
- ➤ Your child should have her interest sparked by the teacher and want to learn more.
- ➤ Does your child feel comfortable asking the teacher questions?
- ➤ What goals does the instructor expect your child to achieve by the end of the season or year? Do these goals mesh with your own?
- ➤ How does your child relate to the teacher?
- ➤ Does she have a warm rapport with your child, showing an interest in aspects of her life outside of music?

You need to find a teacher with a personality type compatible to your child's, so that a laid-back kid is not with a Type A teacher.

—Jim, dad of Ben, 10, Emma, 7, and Spencer, 4

What I love about Ben's teacher is that she makes it fun. She never berates or browbeats him. She understands that kids are busy and some weeks will be better than others. Some weeks my son is more focused and sometimes he has a tough week and doesn't have enough time to practice. She never makes him feel bad. The teacher holds a recital once a year in which all her students play. In addition, she sets up 25 different times throughout the year when various students go with her to play at nursing homes or community functions. These are very low key and serve as great practice playing in front of an audience. Best of all, playing the piano is a passion that Ben and I share together.

—Janine, mom of Ben, 10, and Andrew, 7

At first we had a terrible piano teacher. She was a child prodigy from Romania who expected my daughter Chloe to be one as well. My daughter and I went together and interviewed a different teacher. Chloe liked that the teacher asked her about her favorite singers. She also asked about expectations for practicing. Since then, I've learned to have my children cut the deal on what works. It's no longer my contract with the teacher.

—*Bridgitt, mom of Taylor, 10, Connor and Chloe, 8, and Brian, 6*

Our piano teacher comes twice a week to our house, which is great because the kids can do the lessons at home, even in their pajamas sometimes, in a relaxed setting.

—*Amy, mom of Sacha, 11, and Libby, 8*

Kids need opportunities to play in public at an early age, as they will not develop stage fright if they consider it normal to go and play in front of someone. At my son's music school, every Friday night is a recital. In order to play at a recital, a child first plays in front of a workshop, and once the child's playing has been approved (and improved) by the teacher and workshop instructor, then the child can play in a recital. That means that by the time they reach a recital performance, the kids play their pieces really well. They think that performing is a natural part of what's expected, and they get applauded for it by a group of enthusiastic parents.

—*Jim, dad of Ben, 10, Emma, 7, and Spencer, 4*

➤ Does the teacher appear to be actively engaged with your child or just going through the motions?

Education and Involvement

✦ Make sure your prospective teacher has enthusiasm and a love for what she's teaching. Is teaching a hobby or career for her? If she has a passion for the instrument, the odds are that your child will have that same passion.

✦ Find out about the teacher's educational background and training. Look for a music teacher who graduated from a well-known music school and who now per-

Teachers have to figure out what kind of music a child wants to play. I noticed that one child I worked with was only doing sonatas and classical, and she needed a change. So I chose something different, slower, and with more harmonies—something completely different that made her smile. It's important to realize that teaching piano needs to be more than just buying levels 1, 2, 3 and so on of piano books in the store: You need a repertoire so that a child can work on more rhythmical things and on what she loves. It has to be very individual. Moreover, piano teaching books just contain arrangements: The melody is not what the really great composers have written. Once my students complete a level, I bring them a "very special treat" as a reward for their progress. Most of the great composers did write music for children, and that's what I bring as a treat. I bring each a very beautiful piece of music that's slightly more difficult than they're used to, and which we work on for several weeks.

—*Violeta Stoyneva, private piano teacher for 4 years and freelance bassoonist*

After you've chosen someone, carefully evaluate your child's progress. Don't expect quick miracles, but you should hear some progress in the first few weeks. If you don't, ask the teacher why. Be sure and "listen between the lines" when hearing the explanation. Don't forget, the teacher doesn't want to lose a student, so listen carefully to the explanation for lack of progress. The bottom line is, if you're not happy, don't be reluctant to look for another teacher. That being said, a student needs consistency of instruction in order to improve, so don't bounce your child from teacher to teacher.

—*Jerry Peel, professor of french horn, University of Miami School of Music, teaching for 30 years*

Look for a teacher with experience, coupled with a cheerful demeanor and the ability to listen well. Children can have difficulty articulating their concerns sometimes and it is important that the teacher be sensitive to this. For beginners, a teacher does not necessarily need to be a virtuoso player, but he or she should have a real understanding of the instrument and the technique involved in playing it.

—*Paul Combs, professional musician and private saxophone instructor for 32 years*

Trust your instincts and ask lots of questions. Before committing to a teacher or program, have a conversation or interview with the person who will be teaching your child. Prepare questions ahead of time and listen with your intellect and heart. Ask for references and any brochures or literature that the teacher has prepared for parents. Look for someone committed to teaching children. You need to find someone whose approach will be a good fit with your own values around education and child rearing. Ask if you can have a trial lesson before making a commitment for a longer period. Have the teacher explain what method(s) she uses and why. Ask how long she has been teaching, but don't be afraid to take a chance on someone new to teaching, especially if she has just graduated from a reputable college or university music education program.

—*Celeste Ellis Whitting, owner, Celestial Resonance Violin Studio, teaching for 6 years*

haps works with a local orchestra or civic light-opera company. How long has she been teaching?

🐠 Furthermore, how experienced is the teacher in dealing specifically with kids? Does she have any formal early-childhood training?

🐠 You don't want a music teacher who focuses solely on popular, jazz, country-western, or rock and roll. Your child should start with classical training because it will enable her to eventually pick up other styles.

🐠 Ask your candidate if she performs somewhere, such as a church or club, and go listen. Her performance may not reflect her teaching abilities, but you'll know if you're dealing with a qualified musician.

🐠 Under whom did she study? Is she certified by a professional organization or examination system? How does the teacher continue her professional development? See the Resources section for national associations for each instrument and what certifications they issue.

Communicating with Your Child's Teacher

🐠 Clarify expectations with your child's music instructor about:
  - what supervisory role you should play;
  - if and how often you should sit in during practices;
  - how, and how often, you will get feedback from the teacher on your child's progress.

✦ When issues come up, approach your teacher in a nonconfrontational manner.

✦ Make an appointment to discuss matters at a mutually convenient time.

✦ State your concerns as specifically as you can, listen carefully to the teacher's response, and continue to ask follow-up questions as necessary.

GETTING YOUR CHILD TO PRACTICE

Your child has chosen an instrument and anticipates playing it day and night. You've found the best teacher around with a slot for your budding Mozart or Miles Davis. However, the biggest challenge is yet to come—getting your child to channel that energy into her daily practice. Your encouragement, persuasion, and guidance will most likely be needed at times to get your child to practice. *Repetition* comes from the French word for practice or rehearsal: Good practice by nature should involve lots of repetition. In the long run, hard work and effort are as important as talent for kids who excel in music.

✦ Most kids have a universal opinion about practice: They don't like to do it. Not only do you have to contend with daily practice, but you also have to help your child get through the boring parts of mastering the basics. Once she reaches a level of proficiency, she can start playing music that interests her most.

✦ You may be lucky and have a child who loves music and practices on her own initiative. However, you'll likely find yourself with a resistant student at some point along the line. There are bound to be dull, tedious moments for your child, but her persistence will be tied to her passion for her instrument.

✦ In the early stages, you should be in the room with the child during at-home practice periods to offer encouragement and praise ("That was really good! Would you play it again for me?").

✦ Schedule practice time for your child on the calendar just as you would soccer practice.

✦ Make sure that your child's practice sessions are as free as possible from distractions.

Practice is such a huge and hard issue. Practicing every day is critical and distinguishes those kids who excel. But I think kids hate practice if parents insist on it. Like the father who sits in a lounge chair next to the piano reading his newspaper and makes his son practice; that's what his son will remember—his father looking at him over his newspaper with one eyebrow raised. In the ideal case, the children will practice on their own. But some children say to me that they want to practice, but forget and the week flies by. For these kids, parents should be involved in organizing their time because every child needs help building practice into the day.

—*Violeta Stoyneva, private piano teacher for 4 years and freelance bassoonist*

Know in advance that your kids will complain about practicing. Be prepared for it and be armed with your response ahead of time. Both my kids were very excited to start playing, but both have complained "long and loud" at one time or another about how mean I am to make them practice. Then, after a while, they just accept it and move on—a bit like homework and going to school. I think because my husband and I decided this was a family value and we haven't wavered, it has helped us get through the challenging times. I am starting to see the light with my daughter now where she only occasionally shirks her practice time (but I still remind her!).

—*Shannon, mom of two, ages 11 and 9*

For my oldest son, music is his thing. He can't imagine a life without it. Goodness knows, though, we still fight over practice. My son likes to play the fun pieces and compose music, but finds practice boring. He has never threatened to quit piano, just to quit practicing. When he has to do scales, he wants to put the metronome at 130 beats/minute and make his fingers fly. I bring some work into the music room and I sit on one of the chairs while he plays. Having me around listening has helped. Of course, there are other times when I just say, "It's time for you to practice, young man. Or should I tell Mr. Byer you won't be coming this week?" To which my son says a resounding, "No!" Then he practices.

—*Jim, dad of Ben, 10, Emma, 7, and Spencer, 4*

I bought a battery-run kitchen timer because we were having too many fights over practice. I assigned each of my kids the amount of time they have to practice each day, based on their age. My eleven-year-old has to practice 22 minutes, my ten-year-old 20 minutes, and my eight-year-old 15 minutes. When they begin practice, the time starts, and the rule is that they have to stop the timer for any interruptions, such as going to the bathroom or taking phone calls. While my kids all complain about practice, they take pride in what they've accomplished and will sit down with friends after school happily playing away. They're also the first ones to enthusiastically volunteer to perform at the different musical events at their school. I've come to think of their moaning as just mouthing off, and it's sort of become background noise that I almost don't even hear anymore.

—Naomi, mom of Talia, 11, Arielle, 10, Aaron, 8, and Daniella, 5

We have a "good practice box." Whenever my daughter practices her violin without complaining or procrastinating, she gets to pick a "prize" from the box. Inside are all sorts of things: sugar-free gum, nail polish, money, 30-minute coupons to watch cartoons, and the like. It has made a total change in her entire attitude toward practicing, and she's even getting better on the violin.

—Mary, mom of Jonathan, 8, and David, 3

Creating the Ideal Practice Environment

✦ Help encourage practice by creating a quiet, well-lit setting. Hopefully, this will facilitate the concentration your child needs. In particular, make it a space free of siblings, TV, and other distractions.

✦ Determine whether your child likes to practice in her room, alone, or where you and the rest of the family can hear her. If your child craves privacy while she practices, make sure she has adequate space in her room. Set up a little nook with appropriate lighting and a music stand.

✦ If your child enjoys your listening to her while she practices, create a space for her in your living room or study so you can be present without the added distractions of a common living area (i.e., television, noisy siblings).

✦ If your child relies on you for motivation, play an active role in structuring practice sessions and rewarding effort.

✦ If your child is self-motivated, provide encouragement by praising her progress.

✦ Refer to practice time as "playing time." Your child will respond better to music if it does not seem like work. Making practice a game is much more appealing.

✦ Positive reinforcement helps most in your child's progress. Try awarding points for every part of a piece she masters. Encourage other family members to applaud your child's efforts.

✦ Don't hover over your child or give her constructive criticism—let your child's teacher correct problems. Also, don't make judgments about the musical quality of your child's practicing. Listen and show enthusiasm for her efforts and achievements. Learning an instrument requires lots of squeaks, scratches, and incorrect notes.

✦ Explain to your child that learning often happens in stages. Your child may be working on her music for what seems like a long time with no apparent improvement, and then will suddenly make a breakthrough. Reassure your child that sticking with it and practicing during these learning lulls will pay off.

Scheduling the Time

✦ Find a regularly scheduled time for practice during your child's preferred time of day. Pick a practice time that also coincides with your child's peak hours. Some children are at their best right after school, while some do best in the evening when they're relaxed, but not tired.

✦ Some children prefer to work continuously until a practice session is completed. Others prefer to take breaks. The goal is to have focused practice time. Figure out which works best for your child. If your child can concentrate better for ten minutes at a time, that's the best schedule for her.

Making Practice Fun

✦ Keep in mind that practice is not naturally a childlike activity. Children love to play instruments, not practice them. Acknowledge up front that practice and lessons will not always be fun or enjoyable for your child.

✦ Practice can be very tedious. Feel free to encourage your child to play silly games to make it more bearable. For instance, if she's decided to play one passage four times, have her play it once normally, then once standing on one leg, then once looking out the window, and once with her eyes shut. Encourage experimentation.

✦ Throw an informal "jam session" where children can get together for treats and games that involve playing the instrument they are studying.

Improving Technical Aspects and Measuring Progress

❧ When your child finds a place in a musical piece that always goes wrong, have her decide which notes are at the heart of the problem. Encourage your child to work on the difficult bits separately over and over before playing the whole piece through.

❧ A half-hour practice routine might go like this: Warm up for a few minutes, play a fun, familiar piece for a few minutes, work on a new or difficult piece for a few minutes longer than that, work on scales or arpeggios for another few minutes, and end with something fun.

❧ Point out to your child that while playing familiar songs may be more fun or comfortable, playing nothing else will not help her improve.

❧ However boring and pointless they may seem, scales are crucial to your child's learning. Nothing else gets a student's fingers into such good shape, and helps a student to practice patterns of notes that will occur over and over again in all sorts of musical pieces. Once she knows her scales, your child will be glad she spent all that time perfecting them.

❧ Both you and your child need to be patient with her playing. Everybody makes mistakes, and many of us make the same ones over and over. Remember that those mistakes are a large part of your child's growth experience.

❧ Have your child set realistic goals. Be wary if she says, "I'm going to play this whole piece with no mistakes at all," and encourage something more like, "I'll play the third line four times over, and then I'll stop even if there are still mistakes." It's a good idea to record the problem areas in a notebook so she can remember them for the next day's practice.

❧ Give your child a gold star on the days she's practiced her scales for you or learned a new segment of a piece. This way, not only is she reminded that she needs to practice, but she can also see how her work is paying off.

❧ Help your young musician set practice goals. Keeping a journal, not just a practice chart, helps track the peaks and valleys of learning a new piece or improving fundamental skills.

Guide to Specific Instruments

PIANO

Technically a stringed instrument, the piano makes an excellent first instrument, and many teachers of diverse instruments feel that piano study should be encouraged for any musician. Music teachers all agree that piano forms an excellent basic foundation for any further musical experiences your child pursues. Even if your child chooses to switch to another instrument later, the melody, rhythm, and sense of harmony she acquires with piano education will carry over.

ADVANTAGES

❧ Piano offers a great way to learn the basics, from rhythm and tempo to reading music.

❧ As an instrument, the piano provides your child with the instant gratification of a good-sounding note with the simple strike of a finger. Other instruments require careful finger position, breathing, or mouth control before pleasing sounds can be obtained.

Pianos are everywhere: in schools, churches, and the house next door. Once you have the skills to play it, you can enjoy playing it everywhere, and it gives you a wonderful base in music that you can use to play any other instrument.

—*Thomas Bacon, international French horn soloist, teaching for 40 years*

Piano is a strong instrument for learning music theory, as it's all visible on the keyboard. For example, half steps and whole steps are easily discernible on a keyboard while less so on other instruments.

—*Sandie Apuzzo, Kindermusik educator and violin instructor, teaching for 6 years*

The value of piano training cannot be overstated. Piano develops the right and left side of the brain, gives children a foundation in harmony and musical structure of all kinds, and develops coordination.

—*Stephanie Jutt, associate professor of flute, University of Wisconsin-Madison, teaching for 30 years*

The piano provides the best visual model for learning the Western music tradition. Accurate pitch and acceptable tone are immediately available, and all aspects of musical structure can be realized, including harmony, without a group to assist.

—*Jeanne Hurlburt, private music teacher and performer for 22 years*

🎵 A pianist hears the complete musical piece when she plays, while string and wind players generally hear only one part of it.

DOWNSIDES

🎵 Playing the piano can be a very solitary endeavor. It's only as an advanced player that your child may be able to play with an orchestra or jazz band.

The piano is a great instrument for children to start on because anyone can make a sound on the piano immediately. Children can work on the concepts of notes and rhythm without having to hold anything up. Also, it gives kids a great introduction to harmony and the theory of music, which are much better explained on an instrument capable of playing more than one note at a time.

> —*Jane Carl, acting assistant principal clarinet, Saint Louis Symphony Orchestra, and associate professor of clarinet, University of Missouri-Kansas City, teaching for 31 years*

It also involves reading two staves of music in two different clefs, which can be confusing.

BEST AGE TO START

Many children are ready to start traditional piano lessons between 5 and 6 years old. Children start Suzuki lessons as young as 3. For traditional lessons, most teachers prefer that your child:

- have some basic reading skills or knowledge of the letters A through G
- can concentrate during lessons and practice for 15 to 30 minutes at a time

For piano, physical size or strength, such as that needed to hold a large wind instrument, is not an issue.

Offer lots of encouragement and don't let your child give up too soon. If your child seems too young, take a break, and try restarting lessons after six months have passed.

COST CONSIDERATIONS

An electronic keyboard is generally smaller and less expensive, but many teachers prefer to start children on a normal acoustic piano. While some teachers will allow your child to start piano lessons with a keyboard, they usually insist on an acoustic piano within a year, if not sooner. If you start your child on an electronic keyboard, make sure the keys are the size of an acoustic piano and touch sensitive, as all beginning methods introduce forte (loud) or piano (soft) after a few lessons.

A vertical piano generally costs between $2,000 and $3,000, and works well if

First and foremost, the most important thing to look for is a piano with a full keyboard (88 keys), a good working action, good strings and hammers, a resonant soundboard (no cracks), and a sturdy pin block, pegs, and working pedals. I do not recommend an electric keyboard, even the weighted ones. The action is absolutely different, your child will not acquire the sense of deep tone or facility, and keyboards do not have pedals like a real piano. It makes no sense to invest in an instrument that you will have to eventually replace.

—*Paul Verona, international concert pianist and teacher for 25 years*

space in your house is limited. Note that the taller the piano, the longer the strings and the better the tone. Grand pianos can start at $3,400 and go up to $95,000. Many stores offer rent-to-own plans, where your rental payments apply to the purchase price should you decide to keep the piano.

✦ You might also consider a used piano, but before buying one, you should have a knowledgeable piano technician look it over.

✦ Other costs include the lessons themselves—which can range between $20 and $50 on average per lesson—sheet music, and music books.

MAINTENANCE

✦ Keeping your own piano in good working order usually involves twice-a-year tune-ups (usually spring and fall), costing between $75 and $175 depending on the work needed.

BRASS AND WOODWIND

✦ Brass instruments are made of brass or other metal and produce sound when a musician blows air inside by making a "raspberry" noise against the mouthpiece. Brass instruments include the bugle, cornet, French horn, trombone, trumpet, and tuba.

✦ Woodwind instruments produce sound when a musician blows air inside— either across an edge, such as with a flute; between a surface and a reed, as with the clarinet; or between two reeds, as with a bassoon. Woodwind instruments include bassoon, clarinet, flute, oboe, piccolo, and recorder.

🕉 Brass instruments, such as the trombone, trumpet, French horn, and tuba, as well as many of the woodwind instruments, such as the oboe, saxophone, and bassoon, may be too cumbersome or heavy for your child before the age of 9.

🕉 Prior to this age, your younger child will probably lack the strength or dexterity required to play instruments of this type. They also demand significant breath control and special mouthing techniques.

🕉 Still, there are a few notable exceptions in the woodwind family, such as the recorder and the flute, which your child will have an easier time playing at a younger age.

Bassoon

The bassoon, the largest instrument in the woodwind family, has an eight-foot-long wooden tube folded in on itself. To play it, you blow through a reed that vibrates to make the sound, with different notes produced by using a system of keys that cover and uncover holes. The rods and levers that operate the keys tend to be very long.

The bassoon is *not* a good instrument for children just starting out. It is too large and awkward, requires well-developed hands, and poses significant drawbacks in dealing with its delicate reeds. Bright nonconformists excel at the bassoon.

—*Robert Barris, professor of bassoon and co-chair Department of Music Performance Studies, Northwestern University, teaching for over 40 years*

Most kids start on something else and switch to bassoon in late middle school or high school. Many school systems don't own bassoons and not all instrument shops rent them. The big advantage is, most bands and orchestras are dying to have a bassoon, so there's not much competition and you can walk into an ensemble that never would have accepted you on flute or clarinet.

—*Melissa Mackey, freelance bassoonist teaching for 6 years*

ADVANTAGES

♣ The bassoon is an orchestral instrument and is also used in wind bands. There are not many bassoonists around, which will make your child highly sought after.

♣ By the time your child reaches fourth or fifth grade, learning the bassoon is comparable to playing any other woodwind instrument.

♣ The bassoon can be taken apart into several pieces and packed into a carrying case about three feet long, which makes it easy to carry.

DOWNSIDES

♣ The bassoon is rather large and heavy.

♣ An immense amount of lung capacity is key to playing the bassoon.

BEST AGE TO START

◉ Your child will need hands big enough to reach the keys and sufficient breath strength, which generally starts around the age of 12 or 13. Your child will also have to "bite" the reed fairly hard.

◉ Your child should play another instrument, such as clarinet, for at least a year or so, before attempting the bassoon.

COST CONSIDERATIONS

♣ A small bassoon has been especially created for beginners, and generally costs between $3,000 and $5,000. You need to remember that your child will eventually outgrow her first bassoon and you will need to replace it with a normal-sized version of the instrument.

♣ More advanced players often play the contra-bassoon in orchestras, which is so

Basic repairs can be handled by most wind repairmen. Bigger jobs need to be handled by a bassoon specialist, and they can be very hard to find. The bassoon is a double-reed instrument, so reeds will need to be purchased every few months, maybe more often at first while the student learns to care for them. More advanced students learn to make their own reeds.

—*Melissa Mackey, freelance bassoonist teaching for 6 years*

big and heavy that it is supported against the floor instead of slung from the player's neck.

✦ New bassoons cost $12,000–$35,000 and the school or orchestra always provides the instrument. Even many universities will supply the student with a bassoon.

✦ The reeds are inexpensive and usually last several months. Your child will need to have a couple of spares.

MAINTENANCE

◉ Bassoons often have expensive repairs because their wood gets easily damaged if knocked or dropped.

◉ Every few years, the soft pads fixed to each key that close the holes off have to be replaced.

Clarinet

With a clarinet, your child holds the instrument in front of herself, blowing into the mouthpiece. The mouthpiece is a reed, which vibrates to make a sound, similar to what happens when you blow a blade of grass between your thumbs. All ordinary clarinets are the same size. However, alto clarinets and E-flat clarinets, more appropriate for advanced players, are of different sizes.

ADVANTAGES

✦ The clarinet is particularly easy to start, and your child will be able to play tunes in a couple of weeks.

✦ The instrument comes apart and fits easily into a small case.

✦ The clarinet can be played in orchestras, concert bands, wind bands, jazz groups, and clarinet choirs. Band programs need lots of clarinets, so there are many opportunities to play in a group setting.

DOWNSIDES

✦ For smaller children, the clarinet is hard to hold. Also, your child will have to "bite" the mouthpiece quite hard.

✦ Since the clarinet is fairly popular, the competition for spots in orchestras and bands can be fierce.

If the student is big enough, the clarinet offers a medium amount of resistance to blowing—more than the flute, but less than the oboe. It is relatively easy to produce a tone in the low register, it has a mellifluous sound, the widest dynamic and pitch range, and is best for playing both classical and jazz.

> —*Michael Webster, associate professor of clarinet and ensembles at Rice University, artistic director of the Houston Youth Symphony, teaching for 39 years*

The clarinet is relatively easy to produce a sound on, and plays its entire range more easily and uniformly than any other wind instrument.

> —*Wilbur Moreland, professor of clarinet, University of Southern Mississippi, teaching for 38 years*

BEST AGE TO START

Most children start the clarinet between 9 and 11 years old, but it depends more on your child's size than his age. Because having arms strong enough to support this relatively big and heavy instrument is essential, many people start when they are older.

COST CONSIDERATIONS

Many beginners start on a used plastic model, which can be purchased for around $125, but can cost as much as $600.

A good student-model clarinet is around $400–$700, though professional models range anywhere from $1,500 to $5,000.

The reeds cost little, and can last several months. They cost around $25 for a box of ten, and beginners usually need four at a time.

MAINTENANCE

Clarinets are very sturdy and mechanically simple, but they don't fare well when dropped or knocked.

Always have your child swab out the instrument after playing, removing the reed and cleaning out the mouthpiece.

A child with small hands might have difficulty at first in covering the holes, which in the right hand are fairly large and spaced fairly far apart. Also, a poor mouthpiece on a great horn will also produce inferior results.

—*Wilbur Moreland, professor of clarinet, University of Southern Mississippi, teaching for 38 years*

Some children find a full-sized clarinet rather large for them to handle, but starting around age 10, when most kids start, smaller clarinets do not work well because they are in a different key, have a different tone color, and do not suit a band well.

—*Julie DeRoche, clarinet faculty member, DePaul University School of Music, and Chicago Symphony substitute, teaching for 25 years*

For children who are quite small in size, there are a few things to watch out for. When holding the clarinet properly, the weight of the instrument rests on the right thumb. For some kids, this can be quite uncomfortable. There are some things that can be done to minimize the discomfort. One is adding a thumb rest cushion, which will make where the thumb rest touches less sore. Another is use of a neck strap to remove most of the weight from the child's hands. Also, sometimes children with thin fingers have a more difficult time covering the last two open holes on the right hand. Your child will go through lots of reeds because they are fragile and wear out fairly quickly, but a good reed in good condition really enhances the ability to play and learn. As your child progresses, you will need to upgrade his mouthpiece and perhaps his instrument.

—*Jane Carl, acting assistant principal clarinet, Saint Louis Symphony Orchestra, and associate professor of clarinet, University of Missouri-Kansas City, teaching for 31 years*

Flute

After the piano, the flute is one of the most popular starting instruments, particularly for girls, who fall in love with its high pitch, melodious sound, and elegant look. Flutes can be modified for young children, and the compact size makes it easier for a child to play. The trickiest challenge is learning to create the proper mouth position. By blowing across an open hole, your child can easily play notes and produce sounds in a simple process similar to blowing over the top of a soda bottle.

ADVANTAGES

✦ The flute is highly portable, and a child who plays flute can be part of a marching band or a school or community orchestra if she is interested in engaging in a musical group activity.

✦ Playing the piccolo, the smallest and highest-pitched instrument in an orchestra, is much like playing a flute, and could become an option for your child later on.

DOWNSIDES

✦ Flute technique gets complex quickly. To help your child offset some frustration, ask the teacher to let you know when she's getting to a more difficult technique.

✦ Although it's easier for your child to produce a sound with a flute than with other woodwinds, she will still need to develop breathing skills.

BEST AGE TO START

◉ Because the flute is easier to start off with than other woodwinds, your child may be ready to start taking traditional private lessons as young as third grade, but flute lessons most typically start in fifth grade as part of a school's band program. Children who start on flute in the third grade often do not have long enough arms to reach all the notes, so they use a special curved flute to start.

◉ Many teachers believe children should have some basic reading skills and attention span before starting lessons.

COST CONSIDERATIONS

✦ A quality full-sized student-model flute lists for between $400 and $1,000, though dealers generally discount the manufacturer's recommended price and there is often room to negotiate.

The flute is a comparatively small instrument, so it's relatively easy to hold and carry around. Because it is a melody instrument, coordination is initially less demanding than piano or stringed instruments, which require hands to do separate tasks simultaneously, such as bowing with one hand and fingering notes with the other.

> —*Laura Vincent, flute and piccolo instructor, Rivers Music School, teaching for 20 years*

Most kids will tell you that the reason they decided to play the flute is that they thought it was pretty and they liked the sound. Parents tell me that they like the flute's portability, affordability, and the relative softness of its sound, as compared to the trumpet, for instance. For girls, peer pressure also becomes a factor. There are tons of little girls who choose the flute in fifth-grade band because their friends play it too.

> —*Marlene Metz, private flute and recorder teacher for 8 years*

The flute is excellent for learning proper breathing techniques and breath support. A flutist uses the same breathing techniques as a singer.

> —*Mark Thomas, founder and honorary life president, National Flute Association, teaching flute for 51 years*

Kids can learn flute at around age 6 in a Suzuki program using a curved head joint so the child can reach the flute's keys. Otherwise, have your child start at about 10 years old with a straight head joint.

> —*Stephanie Jutt, associate professor of flute, University of Wisconsin-Madison, teaching for 30 years*

🐟 A used flute can usually be found for between $100 and $350, but you will likely have to pay an additional $150 or so for a complete overhaul and check of the instrument.

❧ Because a younger child will need a modified flute, it's a good idea to rent one first, with rentals costing around $20–$25 per month.

MAINTENANCE

◉ A flute has to be cleaned inside after being played, and have an annual cleaning, oiling, and adjustment. Flutes should never be washed with soap or immersed in water.

◉ Flute repairs are generally costly, and have to be done by a specialist.

French Horn

The French horn consists of a very long, narrow tube of brass coiled around on itself. Blowing a "raspberry" with your lips into the cup-shaped mouthpiece makes the sound, which comes out of a flared bell. Your lips vibrate like the reed of a clarinet, and this vibration becomes musical sound as it passes through the bore of the horn.

ADVANTAGES

❧ The horn is used in both orchestras and wind bands, so plenty of opportunities abound for playing in a group.

❧ There are almost never enough horn players to go around, so you will find little difficulty getting into local youth orchestras. Horn players are also in demand for chamber music, as composers frequently write parts for them in woodwind and other ensembles.

❧ The horn is carried in one piece in a rigid case. Despite its strange shape, it is not difficult to carry.

DOWNSIDES

❧ The horn is not an easy instrument to start. Some students start on the trumpet and later change to the horn. Additionally, the open notes are much closer together. Therefore, it's more difficult to control movement between them.

BEST AGE TO START

◉ A child must be able to hold the horn in the proper position while blowing a steady stream of air.

The French horn (more commonly referred to as the "horn") is widely acknowledged to be the most difficult instrument in the brass family to learn and among the most difficult of all instruments to master. Some manufacturers have dealt with this problem by designing smaller horns similar to half- and three-quarter-size violins for younger students. Playing the horn is not an exact science. It requires a certain individualistic approach that borders on fearlessness. The pedagogy for learning the horn should be the same for all beginning players. Most horn students are trained in the "orchestral style," which includes the development of a characteristic sound using proper production techniques and the fundamental mastery of technical and lyrical playing.

Students' horns come in basically three types. Beginner students start on a single horn in F or in Bb (the latter of which is shorter in length and easier to produce clean notes without mistakes; however, some teachers are purists and believe that the only true horn sound comes from a Bb horn). Many years ago, manufacturers saw the need to combine the stronger qualities of each of those instruments into one single instrument. Thus was born the idea of the "double" horn, which combines these "two" horns with a shared lead pipe (that's where you put the mouthpiece) and a bell section and bell flare. The rest of the horn, or the guts of the instrument, is actually two instruments. Students as they advance often move on to a double horn.

—*Jerry Peel, professor of french horn, University of Miami School of Music, teaching for 30 years*

◉ Players need a lot of puff, so it's rare for children to start before they are 11 or 12 years old.

COST CONSIDERATIONS

🎺 Horns are expensive to buy, with the purchase price of new horns starting around $1,500. The price of used horns can vary widely depending on their condition, brand, and quality. Professional quality horns start in the $2,500 range and can go up to $8,000 or more.

🎺 French horns are all the same size, but beginners may be able to cut costs by using a single, rather than a double, horn at first.

MAINTENANCE

◉ Since it has few moving parts, there is little to go wrong with a horn. However, any brass instrument is easily dented and this can be expensive to repair, especially if there is damage to the lacquer that protects the brass surface.

◉ Overall, the horn does not require much maintenance, but it will need valve oil and slide grease every few weeks.

Oboe

The oboe, a member of the woodwind family, is played by blowing directly through a reed. The reed then vibrates to make a sound, with the notes being produced by covering and uncovering holes via a complicated group of keys operated by rods and levers.

ADVANTAGES

✦ The oboe is a key part of an orchestra, as well as some wind bands, which creates many opportunities for ensemble play.

✦ Usually, the oboe comes in two pieces, and packs fairly easily into a small case, which is not difficult to carry and offers excellent protection.

DOWNSIDES

✦ The oboe requires a lot of breath, and is fairly difficult to learn.

✦ In the beginning, your child will make a squawking noise before mastering the sound.

BEST AGE TO START

◉ Most children start learning the oboe between the ages of 10 and 14.

COST CONSIDERATIONS

✦ A beginner's used oboe may be purchased for $500, but the average new instrument costs between $1,000 and $2,000, with higher-quality instruments reaching as much as $5,500 new.

✦ Plastic oboes are advised for young students, as wood is prone to cracking, and are generally of higher quality than similarly priced wooden instruments.

The oboe is a poor choice for a first instrument. It is not appropriate for children under 10 years of age, and 10 is too late to begin studying music, so younger children should be learning piano, strings, or recorder prior to playing the oboe. Oboists tend to self-select, showing above-average academic ability, and a desire to distinguish themselves from the crowd.

—Jeanne Belfy, professor of music, Boise State University, teaching oboe for 28 years

MAINTENANCE

Oboes generally need little maintenance, but if dropped or knocked, the repairs are expensive. Plus, chipped plastic cannot be repaired at all.

Every couple of years, the soft pads fixed to each key that close the holes off must be replaced.

Commercial reeds are inexpensive, generally costing around $2 each, but as your child advances, good oboe reeds are often handmade and obtained from the teacher, costing about $10–$20 apiece, and lasting about a month each.

Recorder

ADVANTAGES

The recorder is smaller and lighter than a clarinet and has open holes down the front, making it more manageable for a young child.

A recorder's finger patterns are not complex and are quite logical. Each time a child lifts a finger from an opening, the sound gets higher. If she puts a finger down, the sound gets lower.

Because it's easier than other woodwinds, the recorder is a great instrument to start with. Your child can advance to another instrument as she gets older.

The recorder is taught in many elementary schools as part of music class.

DOWNSIDES

While recorders are played in some music classes, they are not played in orchestras or marching bands.

The recorder is a fantastic instrument for young children because the plastic ones are cheap (less than $10), virtually indestructible, and super easy to play. Parents can find out if their child has musical ability without making much of an investment. The kids learn to read music, play by ear, and develop good practice habits—skills useful on any instrument. Many of the fingerings on the recorder are the same on other woodwind instruments.

—*Marlene Metz, private flute and recorder teacher for 8 years*

BEST AGE TO START

◎ Since the recorder is so small and simple, a child as young as 4 years of age may be able to play it. Also, by this time, children have usually started reading, a skill that many teachers believe children should have before starting lessons.

◎ Wait until your child has some degree of attention span. She should be able to concentrate in class and practice for 10 to 30 minutes at a time.

COST CONSIDERATIONS

✦ Compared to other woodwind instruments, recorders are fairly inexpensive. You can purchase a plastic recorder for under $10 at music stores, though wooden recorders can cost up to $100.

MAINTENANCE

◎ In terms of care and storage, the recorder is a low-maintenance instrument.

If choosing between the saxophone and the flute, as many children do, it will be much easier for your child to produce sound on the saxophone.

—*Paul Combs, professional musician and private saxophone instructor for 32 years*

Saxophone

Saxophones come in several different sizes. The smallest is the soprano saxophone, which is straight. The next size up is the alto saxophone, which has a curved mouthpiece and bell and usually hangs from a sling around the neck. The even larger tenor saxophone is the same, and the baritone saxophone has its tube coiled to reduce its length. Most saxophonists start on the alto saxophone, some on the soprano. Though it's not a good idea to start on a tenor or baritone, your child can always switch later.

ADVANTAGES

🎷 It is easy to produce a sound and learn a few notes in a couple of lessons, which gives your child a instant sense of gratification as a beginner.

🎷 The saxophone is a versatile instrument that can be used to play many different types of music, integral in wind bands and jazz bands, as well as pop and country music.

🎷 Like the clarinet, the fundamentals of saxophone are fairly easy to learn, and by the time your child gets to fourth or fifth grade, there is little difference between learning the saxophone and learning other woodwind instruments.

🎷 Saxophones come apart in several pieces and pack into cases according to their size. A soprano or alto in particular is not difficult to carry.

DOWNSIDES

🎷 To play the saxophone, your child needs arms strong enough to support the instrument and hands big enough to reach the keys. There are no small instruments for beginners, although the soprano saxophone comes closest.

🎷 To play the sax, your child will have to "bite" the mouthpiece fairly hard, which is easier once she has her adult teeth.

The biggest disadvantage for young saxophone students is a cheap instrument. There are a lot of inexpensive but poorly made saxophones that make learning to play it unnecessarily challenging. Braces can make playing the saxophone more difficult but not impossible. School bands will try to limit the number of saxophones, as there are usually more students who want to play saxophone than needed.

—*Rhett Bender, chair of music, Southern Oregon University, and professional saxophonist*

The saxophone is one of the easiest instruments to play badly. Especially the larger saxophones (tenor and baritone) have rather large finger stretches and can be too heavy for young students.

—*John Sampen, distinguished professor of music, Bowling Green State University, playing saxophone for 40 years*

🔱 Many pieces of orchestral music do not have parts written for the saxophone.

BEST AGE TO START

◎ It is common for children to wait until ages 10–12 to start on the saxophone because of its large size and weight, and the lung capacity needed to sustain long musical phases. Some children start earlier on a curved soprano saxophone.

COST CONSIDERATIONS

🔱 A good alto saxophone can be purchased for about $750–$2,000. However, you can often find a quality used saxophone for as little as $400.

🔱 For a beginner, look for fairly soft and inexpensive reeds.

Normally children under fifth grade can't play the sax, as the instrument is too big, heavy, and hard for them to hold. The hand span is also a little too large.

> —*Russell Peterson, instructor of saxophone and jazz studies at Concordia College*

◎

The saxophone is a very delicate instrument. From start to finish, it has over 5,000 production and assembly procedures. Most student-level horns come in sturdy cases, but the student still must be careful when hauling it around.

> —*Miles Osland, professor of saxophone and director of Jazz Studies at University of Kentucky (Lexington), teaching for 26 years*

◎

Teach your child to regularly clean out the mouthpiece for sanitary purposes, plus it can just plain get gross. Also, you need to regularly buy reeds for the instrument. They don't last forever, and each student should have at least three or four "good" ones at all times. I tell the parents that if their child chose photography as their art, they would have to keep buying film. With saxophone, they have to keep buying reeds.

> —*Lisa Osland, professor of saxophone, University of Kentucky (Lexington), teaching for 23 years*

MAINTENANCE

◉ Saxophones are normally tough, and need little repair unless dropped.

◉ Like the clarinet, there is little maintenance. Annual checkups avoid more costly repairs and keep the saxophone in good working order, and small adjustments are periodically necessary. Every couple of years, the soft pads fixed to each key that close the holes off have to be replaced.

Trombone

The trombone, a large relative of the trumpet, has a narrow tube of brass folded in upon itself to conserve space. It is played by blowing a "raspberry" with your lips into the cup-shaped mouthpiece, as well as by moving the slide, which alternately lengthens and shortens the tubing.

ADVANTAGES

✦ The trombone is relatively easy to learn, and does not require a strong breath to sustain the notes. It is also easy to transport, as it comes apart into two main pieces, with a rigid carrying case for protection.

✦ There is usually a shortage of trombone players for ensemble play, which allows for many opportunities with orchestras, wind ensembles, jazz bands, small brass ensembles, and marching bands.

DOWNSIDES

✦ The biggest disadvantage to the trombone is that it can be awkward for smaller children to hold and play.

✦ When playing in an orchestra or wind band, the trombone's music is written in bass clef, yet when played in a brass band, its music is written in the treble clef, so your child will have to learn to play both.

BEST AGE TO START

◉ Many trombone players begin at 11 or 12 years of age, when their arms are long enough to push the slide out to its longest position, and sustain the breath required.

◉ Seventh position, with the slide completely extended, is a long way out for children with a small stature, who sometimes start on a trombone with an "F attachment," a thumb-operated valve that allows notes in longer positions to be played closer in on the slide.

An advantage to playing trombone, especially in school music programs, is that it is often overlooked by students, so trombonists are often in demand and this provides an opportunity for your child to stand out.

—*Jeff Albert, freelance musician, teaching trombone for 12 years*

The trombone is relatively easy to make a sound on the first day. Also, there is (usually) only one moving part, the slide, rather than three valves on a trumpet or horn or the millions of intimidating keys on a clarinet or saxophone. The size of the mouthpiece is great for children with braces, as it is larger and more forgiving than a trumpet mouthpiece, but not as overwhelming as that of a tuba.

The main disadvantage is that it is a large instrument, and can be cumbersome. There are no notches in the slide to show you where the positions are, so you really have to be able to hear the pitch, and see and feel the position you're going to, in order to play well in tune.

—*Brian French, principal trombone, Winston-Salem Symphony Orchestra*

COST CONSIDERATIONS

Trombones typically cost between $400 and $850 for a new student-model trombone.

MAINTENANCE

Little can go wrong with a trombone, as it has only one moving part, the slide. The slide needs to be handled carefully, as the trombone won't play if it becomes bent or damaged. It also needs to be lubricated once or twice a week.

The trombone itself can easily be dented, which can be expensive to repair, especially if the lacquer that protects the brass surface has to be redone.

Trumpet

Trumpets are essentially orchestral instruments, although they are frequently used in jazz bands as well. The cornet is very similar to the trumpet, but is mostly used in brass bands. The cornet has a softer, sweeter sound and is a little more agile, while the trumpet has a hard, bright sound orchestral composers love. You hold the trumpet in front of you with the mouthpiece to your lips and the bell directly forward. One hand operates the valves, while the other supports the instrument.

ADVANTAGES

🎵 The trumpet can be played in orchestras, wind bands, jazz bands, brass bands, and sometimes pop groups. The cornet is used in brass bands principally, but can also be seen in jazz and wind bands.

🎵 Trumpet is an easy instrument to start.

🎵 You'll find a plethora of trumpet teachers around.

🎵 The trumpet and cornet fit into convenient cases and are easy to transport. The modern ones are quite small and light.

DOWNSIDES

🎵 Trumpet is an extremely popular instrument, which makes finding ensemble opportunities difficult.

BEST AGE TO START

◉ Both trumpet and cornet are easy instruments to start, but they require a lot of breath and a lot of strength to hold up the instrument comfortably, so students usually don't begin before they are age 9 or 10. It helps to have experience on a prior instrument, such as the recorder.

◉ Some students start on the trumpet and transfer to the more difficult French horn later, which can be a smart move, since there are lots of trumpet players and not many horn players.

COST CONSIDERATIONS

🎵 Trumpets are relatively cheap, costing around $300 for a beginner model, while cornets are slightly more expensive.

MAINTENANCE

◉ The trumpet is easily dented, and this can be expensive to repair.

◉ It also needs to be kept clean inside after having been played.

◉ The lacquer finish wears off, although this does not influence the instrument's sound, and can be redone every few years. Silver plate lasts much longer but needs occasional polishing.

There is little maintenance required on a trumpet, but the tuning slides need to be greased from time to time, and the valves will need a little special valve oil.

There is something glorious about the trumpet, as it has a special place in our history, harking back to when it was played for kings and queens. The kids who excel have a "built in" love for music. Music is natural to them, and they don't make a big deal about practicing because it gives them great pleasure. You need great ears to play the trumpet, so that you can hear and recognize notes before you actually play them.

—*Marek Skwarczynski, professional musician and private trumpet teacher for 5 years*

Trumpet is a leadership instrument, as it is very prominent, and as a result kids learn a lot about self-confidence. When I was choosing an instrument, I heard a trumpet during the *Messiah* performance around Christmas, and I loved the sounds. Kids should choose an instrument that they have heard before and have a strong feeling for and attraction toward the sound.

—*Jeff Reynolds, professor, University of Toronto, and professional musician, teaching trumpet for 30 years*

The trumpet is shiny, loud, fun, and kids "right off the bat" are playing an adult instrument that makes them feel special. Besides, angels in heaven don't play flute!

—*Roddy Lewis, senior brass tutor for Gwent (UK), teaching for 16 years*

As the smallest brass instrument, the trumpet can be started younger than the others, between 9 and 11 years old. A cornet, being more coiled up (but the same pitch and fingering as the trumpet) and shorter, is easier for young students to hold. It is easy to switch from the trumpet or cornet to the horn or baritone [euphonium], and not difficult to switch to the trombone or tuba.

—*Stephen Chenette, emeritus professor of music, University of Toronto, and former orchestra principal trumpet, playing for 60 years*

Tuba and Euphonium

The largest of the brass instruments, the tuba has a conical bore consisting of a gradually widening tube of brass folded around itself to save space. Notes are produced by blowing a "raspberry" with your lips into the cup-shaped mouthpiece and operating three valves with one hand. The euphonium, or baritone as it is also called, is the brass family's lyrical tenor voice.

ADVANTAGES

🐟 The tuba is relatively easy to learn, and does not require strong breath control.

🐟 It comes in smaller three-quarter sizes for children just starting out.

🐟 The tuba is used in orchestras, wind bands, brass bands, and jazz bands, which creates many opportunities for ensemble play, especially as there usually aren't many tuba players around.

DOWNSIDES

🐟 The real difficulty is the sheer size and heaviness of a tuba, which does not come apart in pieces and is hard to both transport and hold.

🐟 Tubas come in different sizes, keys, and clefs. When played in an orchestra or wind band, the tuba's music is written in the bass clef, but in a brass band the music is written in treble clef. Your child will have to decide which clef to learn.

🐟 There are few occasions to play it with an orchestra, so it is mostly played with a band.

🐟 Your child will have to learn how to provide an internal pitch for her lips to buzz the correct note.

BEST AGE TO START

◉ Most children start playing the tuba or euphonium between fourth and sixth grade because of the instrument's size.

◉ Some children may start playing other tenor horns and then later switch over to the tuba.

COST CONSIDERATIONS

✦ A good new model Bbb tuba would be $1,750–$3,000. However, quality used model Bbb tubas can be found in the $500–$1,500 range. There are also some half-size student-model tubas. Tubas go up to $12,000 for a new professional model. For this reason, many schools and orchestras supply them to students. Euphoniums start at $2,000 and go up from there.

MAINTENANCE

◎ The tuba is not particularly prone to damage, and has few moving parts. Yet it can be easily dented, which can be expensive to repair if the lacquer that protects the brass surface has to be refinished.

◎ The tuning slides need to be greased every couple of months, and the valves oiled weekly. The instrument should undergo a yearly cleaning and adjustment by a repair expert.

The tuba family is quite a diverse lot! Tubas are part of the bugle family (like all brasses) and known as "keyed bugles." They are named for the lowest note one can play on them without any valves. Students start out on a Bbb ("contrabass B-flat") tuba, also known as a double B-flat tuba. In the U.S. most kids play what are called "Bbb" tubas—while most professionals play Cc and F tuba. Eb and F are bass tubas. The euphonium or baritone horn is the tenor tuba. Clear as mud!

—*Ryan Schultz, principal tubist, Seattle Pacific Northwest Ballet Orchestra*

The tuba provides the foundation of whatever ensemble in which it is played. The student must have inner confidence, as he or she is going to be relied on to have great rhythm, a good sense of the bass in the harmonic scheme, and (not to be smug about this) a sense of power!

—*Gary Buttery, tuba instructor, University of Rhode Island and Connecticut College, teaching for 30 years*

The tuba, being very free blowing, is far easier to get an initial tone out of when compared to some of the high brass instruments such as trumpet and horn. It is also a full body experience: The resonance of the tuba can be felt by a student down to his toes! The social aspects of playing in a band and orchestra are why playing the tuba and euphonium is often a lifelong hobby for thousands of dedicated amateurs throughout the country. Both instruments have one of the lowest rates of kids who quit the instrument.

—*Scott Watson, professor of tuba and euphonium, University of Kansas, and professional musician, teaching for 23 years*

Depending on the age of the student, seriousness, and usage, you will either be looking at a Bbb or Cc tuba. Most all school directors are knowledgeable about Bbb tubas, though the Cc has become a very good option, as the fingerings are the same as the written notes of the trumpet. The Cc also has a less tubby sound, and is great in smaller combos, jazz, and folk settings! No matter if it is a Bbb or Cc tuba, purchase a four-valve instrument. You will regret the purchase of a three-valve after a year or two, even if the student quits. Resale on a four-valve is twice what a three-valve is and you usually make a buck or two as well. Always have a professional player give the okay on the instrument you are looking to buy. Intonation problems, stuffiness, and leaky and ill-operating valves can turn your student off to the instrument and tuba in general.

—*Gary Buttery, tuba instructor, University of Rhode Island and Connecticut College, teaching for 30 years*

STRINGED INSTRUMENTS

The sounds of stringed instruments come from strings being plucked, as with a harp or guitar or with a bow drawn across the strings, as with a cello or a violin. Stringed instruments include the violin, viola, cello, double bass, harp, and dulcimer.

ADVANTAGES

✦ Stringed instruments are great for smaller hands, since they come in smaller sizes. As a result, a child of 6 or 7 might start on a violin, viola, or cello that is a quarter or half the size of a regular one. The smaller instrument's size makes it easy to carry to and from home, school, and lessons.

✦ Stringed instruments are sometimes called social instruments, since your child may play in school or community orchestras with other children her own age, which offers her many opportunities for social interaction. Starting lessons at an early age can prepare your child to join a group in a few years.

DOWNSIDES

✦ Your child will need some extra time and patience when learning a stringed instrument. Unlike a piano, where a note is hit and the player has instant results, someone playing a stringed instrument has to learn to position her fingers and draw the bow correctly before she can create a pleasant sound.

✦ Though stringed instruments may be frustrating at times, encourage your child to stick with it. Reassure her that practice and perseverance will help her achieve beautiful music.

BEST AGE TO START

◉ Most children start traditional lessons when they're between the ages of 6 and 8, though children as young as 3 can start with Suzuki lessons.

◉ Some excellent players don't start until they are 9 or older, while others even as old as 13 or 14 catch up with those who have been playing longer. Progress will be slow, though, no matter what age your child starts.

◉ Most teachers warn parents and students that it takes twice as long to notice improvements on the violin as it does on most woodwind or brass instruments, as a result of the complexity and subtlety of the technique required to play stringed instruments. For quite some time the sound of your child playing her violin will not sound great, so be patient.

COST CONSIDERATIONS

✦ Before purchasing a stringed instrument, take into consideration that your child won't move to a full-sized instrument until about seventh grade. A rent-to-own program will make much more sense for your young child. Otherwise, you may end up buying two or three different-sized instruments.

✦ Look for rental programs at music stores, which allow you to transfer all the rental money paid on the smaller instruments toward the purchase of a full-sized instrument. Rental programs for stringed instruments can start at around $25 a month.

Stringed instruments in general are good for children because they teach very complex coordination and motor skills, advanced analytical ability, and mental discipline. Many children are drawn to the soothing sounds of stringed instruments. Viola has an especially mellow sound and often plays harmony roles in music, allowing older and more advanced students to benefit from the feeling of being in the middle of the music rather than being on the top (violin) or bottom (cello/bass).

—*Jenny Shallenberger, private viola and violin instructor for 20 years*

One of the advantages of any stringed instrument (and piano) is that you can get a sound out of it right away. With wind instruments it requires some coordination in facial muscles and breath control before this can happen.

—*Linda Bolander, private violin and viola teacher, teaching for 10 years*

✦ There is no standard cost for lessons. If you live in a metropolitan area, you might pay as much as $25 to $40 and up per session. In smaller towns, you might start at $12–$15 per session and increase from there.

✦ Instrument accessories include rosin for the bow, shoulder rest, cloth to wipe strings, cleaner and polish for the instrument and can add up to around $150–$200 per year. A carrying case with enough space for accessories runs between $100 and $200. Other supplies include a music stand and a tuning fork.

MAINTENANCE

◉ Because stringed instruments are technologically simple and have changed so little over the years, many things can go wrong with them. But, for the same reasons, repairs are also fairly cheap, though you will need to bring the instrument to a professional repairer.

◉ Some common problems:
  - ⌒ Strings break often.
  - ⌒ The bridge may snap. Also very cheap to replace, but you'll probably need a repairer to do it for you.
  - ⌒ The fingerboard (the black strip of wood under the strings) may come off.

With stringed instruments, new is not necessarily better. Old instruments have been played more and often are better made with a more delicious tone.

—*Molly Bidwel, private viola, violin, and piano teacher for 40 years*

Wooden instruments need special care. No leaving in the car—*ever!* In the winter, care must be taken to keep the instrument from getting too dried out. An extra set of strings is often important, as they can break easily, and the bow hair should not be touched by sweaty hands.

—*Molly Bidwel, private viola, violin, and piano teacher for 40 years*

〜 The tail-gut (which holds the tailpiece to the bottom of the instrument) may break.
〜 The stick of the bow may snap.
〜 The horsehair of the bow will gradually wear out, so the bow will eventually need re-hairing or replacing—they cost almost the same.

◉ The most serious damage can occur to the wood of the violin such as knocks or cracks that may just spontaneously appear all by themselves. Do not try to repair these yourself, as modern adhesives can seriously damage the instrument's sound and value.

◉ Approximately once a year, your child's bow will need to be re-haired ($35–$100) and the instrument will need a new set of strings ($25–$100).

Cello

Many people consider the violoncello, or cello for short, to be the most beautiful of all instruments. Essentially it is a large violin, although the body is much thicker. Cellists read their music from the bass clef (like the left hand of the piano) although more advanced players have to be able to read the tenor or C clef as well. The cello is played resting on the floor, between a musician's legs.

ADVANTAGES

🗡 The cello is not a particularly difficult instrument to start. Like the violin or viola, the technique is complex, but, the cello's larger size and more natural playing position, sitting with the instrument held between the legs, makes it a little easier.

🗡 Orchestras can accommodate as many as 16 to 18 cellists.

DOWNSIDES

🗡 The fingerboard has no marks to indicate exactly where the fingers should be placed, and it takes a while for the hand to become accustomed to the best position.

🗡 The cello can be a rather difficult instrument to carry for a young child and can be a challenge to transport to school if your child relies on the bus.

BEST AGE TO START

◉ Most children start in fifth grade, or sometime during middle school, but often cello is an instrument picked up in later years as well.

COST CONSIDERATIONS

✦ A new cello costs around $1,900. The cello balances on a metal spike that extends from the bottom, and to avoid possible damage to the floor, invest in a "mushroom"—a round plastic or rubber gadget that grips the floor and holds the spike securely.

MAINTENANCE

◉ Unfortunately, the large size of the cello renders it vulnerable to accidental damage.

◉ The strings are also expensive, but don't usually need replacement more than once a year. Often they don't break at all, but need replacing because the steel outer casing has become worn and sharp edges have appeared. Otherwise, see the maintenance section above for stringed instruments.

Double Bass

The double bass is a sort of giant violin, although it has sloping shoulders instead of the very round shoulders of the violin or cello. It has four thick steel strings and a short, heavy bow. Players stand behind the bass and one hand stops the strings against the fingerboard. Double bass music is written in the bass clef.

ADVANTAGES

✦ The double bass is not very difficult to start with. Double basses come in different sizes, with a mini-bass available for children, followed by a half-size, which can be handled well by most children starting around age 12. A height-adjustable bar stool can help your child reach the top of the instrument. Many players stay with a three-quarter-size bass, as the full-sized one can be unwieldy.

✦ It's a very versatile instrument essential to orchestras and jazz bands, played in many different kinds of ensembles such as folk or pop groups, and there is always a dearth of players.

The biggest disadvantage to playing the bass is its size. You will need a big car and a lot of patience!

— *Mark Bergman, principal double bassist and education director of the New Haven Symphony Orchestra, player for 22 years*

DOWNSIDES

🎵 The fingering system is different from that of any other stringed instrument, with the strings tuned in fourths instead of fifths as on the cello, violin, and viola, and the thick strings are more difficult to "stop."

🎵 It's difficult to transport, as it is quite large and awkward to carry.

BEST AGE TO START

◉ Most children start around age 11 or 12, but there is a tradition of older players transferring from other stringed instruments.

COST CONSIDERATIONS

🎵 A new student-quality double bass starts around $500, with very small and full-sized instruments costing on average $1,000–$1,500.

MAINTENANCE

◉ The double bass is very resilient and damage rarely occurs. Sometimes the neck comes loose from the instrument's body, but the repair is inexpensive. The chrome steel strings are expensive but almost never break.

◉ With proper care, it will need minimal maintenance. The bow needs to be re-haired once a year, and strings replaced every couple of years.

Guitar

With six strings stretched along the fingerboard and across the curved body, the guitar is a relatively simple instrument. You play by plucking or strumming with one hand and stopping the strings against the fingerboard with your other hand.

Your child will need to choose among several types of guitars. When making this

Children enjoy the guitar because it is part of almost any kind of music they hear. The guitar is compact and can easily be taken along, such as to camp. It teaches children responsibility, because owning a guitar involves care and maintenance. Guitars are also great for the development of fine motor skills and attention to detail, because it is harder to produce a nice sound on a guitar than on a lot of other instruments.

—*Chris Zahnleiter, professional musician and private guitar instructor for 8 years*

Our son kept begging for guitar lessons because he saw his sister taking piano lessons, and watched me sit down with her each night as I helped her read the music. We tried to dissuade him, but after weeks of his pleading, we went to a guitar instructor whom we knew personally. Ben went in and after talking with him, the instructor said we should try it. Ben's been doing it for four months now and loves it. I don't push him to practice. I'll just ask him if he wants to practice and when he's into it, I'll sit down with him and he sees it as a fun time together with Dad, just the two of us. He's even beginning to learn to read music. He looks at it like a game.

—*Andy, dad of Rachel, 10, Ben, 7, and Josh, 3*

choice, expect to be influenced by the specialty of the guitar teacher you hire to give your child lessons.

🔸 Folk guitar relies on basic chords, is easy to learn, and is the best style for accompanying oneself or others in singing.

🔸 Classical guitar is quiet and beautiful to listen to, but not well suited to group play. It is very difficult to learn, as the finger picking can get very intricate, and your child's progress is likely to be slow.

🔸 The Spanish guitar is more noisy and energetic.

🔸 The electric guitar is mainly used to play pop or rock music.

ADVANTAGES

🔸 The guitar is a good instrument for children because it is easy to get quick results. In a few weeks your child will be able to play an easy song.

🎸 Guitars are used in many different musical styles, and are great for accompanying singers in casual settings.

🎸 The guitar is also easy to transport.

DOWNSIDES

🎸 Your child will have limited opportunities to play in an orchestra or band, but can instead look for folk groups to join.

BEST AGE TO START

◉ A few children start the guitar around age 6, but many children pick up the guitar much later, even into their teens.

COST CONSIDERATIONS

🎸 You can start your child on a three-quarter-size guitar, which costs about $90. With a smaller guitar, your child can more easily hold the guitar the right way and put the right amount of pressure on the strings.

🎸 New acoustic guitars cost between $200 and $400. A child-size electric guitar costs about $100, and an amplifier starts at around $50.

Many of the kids that I teach have inherited a guitar from either their parents or older siblings. However, it is important that a kid have an appropriate-size guitar of decent quality, as this is the single most important thing that will guarantee success.

—*Randy Browning, professional musician and private guitar instructor for 4 years*

Generally speaking, it does not matter whether a student starts with a acoustic or electric guitar, but most children and teenagers tend to prefer electric because it enables them to play the styles of music they like more. I've even found that most students who start out on acoustic eventually switch to electric.

—*Chris Zahnleiter, professional musician and private guitar instructor for 8 years*

MAINTENANCE

@ You can anticipate spending around $9 every couple of months on new strings. The thin wood on an acoustic guitar can become easily damaged if dropped.

Harp

ADVANTAGES

🎵 When learning the harp, your child simultaneously learns two clefs (bass and treble).

🎵 The harp sounds beautiful even during the very first lesson, and you will never tire of listening to your child practice.

🎵 There are few harpists around, which means many opportunities to perform with orchestras, performing groups, and religious services.

DOWNSIDES

🎵 Harps tend to be inordinately expensive, and while they vary greatly in size, most are large, bulky, and difficult to transport. The harp itself tends to be "tippy," so it needs to be located where it won't be bumped into and knocked over.

🎵 While it's easy to make a sound on the harp, it's difficult to become proficient. It is also a very solitary instrument and involves spending a considerable amount of time practicing alone.

🎵 It can sometimes be hard to find an experienced harp teacher for beginning students, as harp is seldom offered in school lessons.

BEST AGE TO START

@ Most children start learning to play the harp in fourth or fifth grade, although some teachers will start children as young as 5. Many harp teachers recommend that students start first on piano.

COST CONSIDERATIONS

🎵 Small harps tend to work better for kids, as they can lift and carry them themselves, and they are also far less expensive.

🎵 Harps vary greatly in size and style, and the cost of a new one can range from $300 up to $100,000. The more expensive pedal harps often have to be budgeted

Most children are enchanted by the harp. They seem to find it almost magical. They love to simply run their fingers up and down the strings. There are also lots of neat "sound effects" you can get on the harp, without even knowing how to play. Posture is really important when playing the harp, and the harp is truly a "full body" experience, even though from an outsider's perspective it may seem that only the hands are involved.

—*Tanah Haney, professional performer and private harp, piano, and recorder teacher for 12 years*

The harp is an excellent instrument for a young child. It is of course glamorous and attracts much attention. For this reason it is wonderful for a shy child or one who needs to build self-confidence.

—*Marjorie Chauvel, lecturer in music at Stanford University, teaching harp for 63 years*

The students who do best at the harp tend to be imaginative and independent, and possess strong aptitude in several music skill categories, such as melodic memory, reading, rhythm, and hand-eye coordination.

—*Stephanie Osborne, harp instructor, California State University Los Angeles, teaching for 11 years*

the way you would a small car, while a "lap harp" (small folk harp under 25 strings) is much more affordable. A new small nonpedal harp costs about $700. A new lever harp runs from $2,000 to $5,000. A pedal harp costs between $8,000 and $45,000. Harps tend to retain their value, and can be traded in for models with more strings, or exchanged when moving from a lever to a pedal harp.

✦ Renting is definitely the best option when your child is starting out on the harp. A typical rental fee for a small harp is between $60 and $100 a month, though it can sometimes be difficult to locate rental instruments.

✦ Other expenses can include an adjustable chair or bench ($100), music stand ($25), metronome, and even a dolly to move the harp ($265).

Playing the harp, a child is immediately "unique," as she is playing an instrument that everyone admires and thinks sounds lovely.

>—*Carrol Mclaughlin, professor of harp, University of Arizona, teaching for 25 years.*

A harp is a wonderfully "forgiving" instrument because once you get it tuned, when you play a "wrong" note it still sounds wonderful, as opposed to some early violinists or instruments where one has to "find" the note on the string.

>—*Jane Wilcox Hively, private lever harp and voice teacher for 25 years*

As the harp sounds beautiful from the beginning, children are not frustrated by squawks and scratchy sounds as with many string, brass, and wind instruments.

>—*Elizabeth Richter, professor of harp, Ball State University, teaching for 22 years*

As much as I love the harp, I think there are several disadvantages for children starting out. The instrument is very expensive, and sometimes it's hard to find the right-size instrument to fit the child (and still have a good instrument). It is also very difficult to learn and to play well. The harp requires a tremendous amount of coordination and quick reflexes, as well as a quick mind. I prefer that my beginning harp students have some musical background before beginning harp, preferably piano. The harp is so difficult that it is better if they can concentrate on learning to play it rather than learning how to read music.

>—*Jan Jennings, professional harpist and teaching for 37 years*

If a child is going to play a harp, it will require a real commitment on the part of the parent. Until the child is old enough and has had enough experience, the parent will have to tune the instrument every day, which takes about 30 minutes for a beginner and moves down to a few minutes for a pro. In general, harps can be a royal pain for parents. But for children, they are a very special opportunity.

>—*Stephanie Curcio, former harp teacher at Phillips Exeter Academy and private teacher for 40 years*

The beginning harpist has to learn to coordinate 8 fingers, 36 strings, and 2 clefs. Of my five eighth-grade students right now, the three who started before middle school can play incredibly and are working on difficult music. The other two started in sixth grade and can barely keep up with the orchestra.

—*Serena O'Meara, professional harpist and recording artist, teaching for 25 years*

I will teach kids as young as 7 years old using the Suzuki method. I find it improves their memories, since it relies on playing by rote and ear.

—*Kathleen Attanasi, principal harpist for Walt Disney World for 25 years, teaching for 27 years*

The harp needs dusting, frequent tuning, may need string replacement, and the lever harp may need some technical adjustments to the levers and tuning pins. The pedal harp is a much more high-maintenance instrument, which needs regulation every one to two years. Both types of instruments need a regulated amount of humidity, and should not be near heaters.

—*Susan Knapp Thomas, harp teacher for 20 years*

MAINTENANCE

The strings need to be constantly tuned, which is something your child will learn how to do, but might need your help with initially. An electric tuner costs $40.

Occasionally, broken or worn strings have to be replaced, and you should keep extra strings on hand. Lever harp strings cost $4–$8, while pedal strings are $2–$35.

For the pedal harps, yearly maintenance is required to regulate its mechanical system and cables, costing around $250.

Viola

The viola is simply a larger version of the violin, with a proportionally shorter neck and fatter body, which are not noticeable to the untrained eye. The strings are tuned like the violin's, but are five notes lower and also a little thicker.

ADVANTAGES

⚜ Although the viola is not a useful instrument in wind bands or jazz bands, no orchestra can find enough violists. Some violinists switch over to viola, since there are never enough viola players.

DOWNSIDES

⚜ One disadvantage of your child playing the viola is that viola uses its own clef, called the "viola clef" or the "alto clef." Therefore, violinists and violists don't read the same line of music. However, it doesn't take too long to get used to the difference.

BEST AGE TO START

◎ Suzuki programs start with children as young as 3 or 4, but most kids start later on in fourth or fifth grade.

COST CONSIDERATIONS

⚜ Although the viola does come in small sizes like the violin, the most common thing for young viola beginners is to get a small-sized violin and have someone re-string it with viola strings. This works perfectly well and is much cheaper than buying a purpose-built small-sized viola.

⚜ A new beginner viola costs between $400 and $750, with more advanced models costing between $3,000 and $4,000.

Viola is a big instrument. There are small versions, but with a few, very expensive exceptions, they sound really quite horrible, especially on the lowest (C) string. So it is generally wiser to start on the violin and change over to the viola after a couple of years when the child's hand grows a bit. Further, I don't recommend that a child play viola unless it appears that he will be a relatively tall adult or has long arms and fingers.

—*Molly Bidwel, private viola, violin, and piano teacher for 40 years*

Unlike violin or cello, viola is also an ideal choice for many, since it comes in several different sizes based on a player's arm length.

—*Jenny Shallenberger, private viola and violin instructor for 20 years*

Violists don't get "the tune" part in most musical pieces. I always teach that violists are the ones who make a "pretty" violin tune exquisite through great harmonization. I remind my students that many composers were violists, as it helps them to understand what role the viola plays in the harmonic structure of the ensemble.

Stringed instruments are tremendously difficult because of the myriad of simultaneous actions required just to produce a note. It's not like the piano, where anyone can sit down and make a noise. (Not to belittle great pianists who have mastered that instrument!) I don't start violists until fourth grade unless a child is exceptionally disciplined and able to concentrate for 20–25 minutes at a time.

—*Sarah Borchelt, professional violist, teaching for 20 years*

It is best for your child to start by age 11, before hands become tense and less flexible.

—*Molly Bidwel, private viola, violin, and piano teacher for 40 years*

For a musical career in performance, musical training should start as early as possible, definitely by 8 years of age. Often the best results come from students who have switched to viola after a good start on violin, or other unrelated instruments such as piano.

—*Brant Bayless, violist, Utah Symphony, and private viola teacher for 4 years*

> When buying a viola, look for a size compatible to your child, not too big, healthy appearance (no cracks), good set-up (pegs that work and/or tuners, proper bridge), an instrument that speaks easily, and a good bow.
>
> —*Marilyn Baker, private violin and viola teacher, formerly adjunct faculty at Pepperdine University, teaching for 25 years*

Violin

The violin, the foundation of all orchestral string sections, has changed very little over the last 300 years. It consists of a thin wood box and an elegant neck and scroll with tuning pegs at one end. Four steel strings are stretched across the body. The instrument is held under the chin with one hand, and the other hand is used to pass the bow across the strings to make sound. The bow is a stick with horsehair stretched across it. A player rubs the horsehair with rosin (from pine trees) to make it sticky.

ADVANTAGES

☙ The violin has a particular advantage for very young players since it comes in small and graduated sizes.

☙ Violinists are always wanted in orchestras, though depending on the area, this can also make competition more intense for those positions.

DOWNSIDES

☙ The violin is a complex instrument, and progress may be very slow at first.

BEST AGE TO START

☉ Most children start between the ages of 5 and 8, depending on their level of maturity and attention span, but this also depends on the method they choose to learn.

COST CONSIDERATIONS

☙ As your child grows, he will move through different sizes of violin. Many children start with a half-size or three-quarter-size violin. When your child is still growing, don't commit to a purchase quite yet.

🐦 A quality student violin can start at $400, but they typically cost between $800 and $1,000. A higher-level instrument for serious middle and high school students costs between $2,000 and $6,000.

The violin is one of the most challenging instruments to learn, as it requires children to really listen to what they are playing and develop a feeling of where to place their fingers in order to find the right notes. With most other instruments there are specific keys you press. Violin takes a great level of discipline and patience.

Don't look at expensive instruments in the beginning. Until a child is in a full-size violin, the quality isn't very good and it would be a waste to spend a lot of money on something your child will just grow out of. There are places available that will rent the smaller instruments until your child gets to a full-size.

—*Suzanne Mortimer, private violin instructor for 7 years*

Violin benefits brain development because it uses so many senses (listening, reading, tactile touch) requiring acute precision and coordination, which is why violin teaching is so popular at the elementary level. Even though many other musical instruments also develop the brain, the violin has the added burden of creating your own tones using your ear at a minuscule level of coordination. Add to this the task of having to read notes off a page, coordinate left hand and right hand, listen and correct incorrect intonation, and integrate all this to a rhythm. This does not even include creativity in music coming from the right brain.

Typically any age below 10 is the best time to start, because after that, the finger muscles don't respond as well.

—*Kavan Rambukwelle, private violin and piano teacher for 15 years*

Playing the violin is essentially the same pursuit it was in the 17th century. It draws on and fosters development of enduring human qualities: patience, perseverance, endurance, self-knowledge, and discipline. Learning to play the violin can cultivate spatial reasoning, problem solving, aural skills, music literacy, fine motor development, and body awareness. So even if your violin student doesn't aim for Carnegie Hall, the benefits are lifelong and carry over into other pursuits.

—*Celeste Ellis Whiting, owner, Celestial Resonance Violin Studio, teaching for 6 years*

Because the violin has no frets, it is hard to get and stay on pitch. Often teachers will put tape on the instrument to indicate finger placement, but I consider this a crutch that can create a lazy ear. Pitch is so important on the violin that ear training should begin immediately instead of making a visual aid. An inborn good ear helps, but I believe this can be taught to a large extent if the passion is there.

For a beginner, I recommend renting an instrument at a reputable local music store. Remember that the child will likely go through several sizes, and provision for changing should be in the contract. When you are choosing a higher-performance instrument, a shop that specializes in violins is the best place to look. Make sure someone trained in sizing violins is on hand to measure the child. This is important—a violin that is too large can do harm to hands. Err on the side of caution and go smaller when in doubt. Make sure this person considers the finger length of the child, not just the arm length. I have seen disasters because this was ignored.

—Linda Bolander, private violin and viola teacher, teaching for 10 years

As methods, studies, and exercises vary from student to student, so does a specific starting age. Most eminent violinists started around the age of 4; yet there are others who started a little later in life. It depends on your child's ability to observe and absorb language and physical movement from the teacher.

—Stanley Kushner, private violin instructor for 25 years

DRUMS AND PERCUSSION INSTRUMENTS

Most percussion instruments make sounds when hit, such as a drum or a xylophone, while others make sounds when shaken, such as maracas. Percussion instruments include chimes, bells, cymbals, drums, timpani, and triangle.

Drum practice is similar to martial arts. It simultaneously develops timing, focus, control, coordination, dexterity, understanding patterns, and creativity. Drumming releases tension and aggression, enables self-expression, and is the most physical of the instruments.

ADVANTAGES

❦ Drums can be played in everything from orchestra sections to rock bands, offering your child tremendous versatility in terms of what type of music to play.

DISADVANTAGES

❦ Your child needs to learn proper drumming technique to ensure he doesn't hurt himself physically by developing wrist tension or carpal tunnel syndrome.

❦ Another issue is the loudness of the drums, both in terms of potentially damaging your child's eardrums, as well as impinging on your family's or neighbors' noise tolerance level.

BEST AGE TO START

◉ In general, kids can start around 8 years old.

COST CONSIDERATIONS

❦ Your child could start with a $30 drum pad. New drum sets generally cost between $300 and $800, and ones costing higher than this are likely more professional than a child needs to start. Drumsticks cost around $8 a pair.

MAINTENANCE

◉ Drum sets need very little maintenance. The cymbals and the chrome/metal of the hardware and snare drum can be polished with special cleaners.

◉ The drumheads occasionally need to be replaced if they get dented or worn, and usually range in price from $7 to $25, depending on the inch size. They take only about 10 minutes to replace.

◉ The drumsticks should be checked every once in a while and replaced if they get frayed or show cracks.

Drums are the most natural musical instrument in that they capture the basic rhythm we have in our heartbeat and all around us in our environment.

—Brad Dutz, professional drummer and teacher for 10 years

Drums are fun, and you can get something happening pretty quickly. It doesn't take too long before you can play your favorite songs or at least keep a beat.

I find more and more girls coming in for lessons, which is wonderful. The old thinking that drums are a guy thing and too physical for girls is completely wrong.

—Ken Serio, private drums instructor for 15 years

Playing the drums serves as a truly effective outlet in which to positively channel both physical and mental energy. Hand technique develops speed, power, endurance, and hand control.

For concerns about the volume of drums, some of the development and practice can be achieved on a low-volume drum pad. There are also several types of muffling systems available for the drum set. Moreover, the use of earplugs is widely accepted by the professionals in the drumming community.

—Dan Britt, private drums instructor for 5 years

Voice Lessons and Group Singing

OVERVIEW

General Benefits

◉ Teaches concentration, expression, posture, breathing, and self-improvement techniques.

◉ Performance instills confidence and self-esteem.

◉ Often learns songs in other languages, primarily French, Italian, and German.

Best Age to Start

◉ Be careful not to let your overeager child damage her vocal cords.

◉ Many voice teachers say that a girl should be at least 14 years old or past puberty before starting voice lessons and a boy should wait until after his voice changes.

Aside from the sheer enjoyment they get from singing, children develop awareness of their body, how to relax tense muscles, and gain confidence that translates into other areas of their life by performing in front of an audience.

—*Chrys Page, director, Sing Your Life Studio, teaching voice for 30 years*

Voice lessons for children under 14 are best held in small groups and should center on ear training, rhythm, and developing a child's awareness and use of breath and ease in singing. Individual lessons in intense vocal technique or difficult songs are counterproductive. Training children to belt out songs and be "Annie" can be extremely damaging to the voice.

—*Karen Peeler, professor, Ohio State University School of Music, teaching for 30 years*

Studying voice aids in developing mental and musical discipline, strengthening memory, developing aesthetic sensibility ("good taste," if you will) and realizing that worthwhile goals may take a long time to achieve. Exposure to more complex musical patterns has been demonstrated to aid in neural development in the brain as well.

—*Ben King, professor of voice, Houghton College School of Music, teaching for 30 years*

Until these hormonal changes occur, the larynx and vocal cords grow at different rates, and voice lessons might pressure and damage these muscles.

However, since these hormonal changes now occur much earlier than in previous generations, some children are ready for private vocal lessons as early as age 10. Some teachers say that this is way too young—even if hormonal changes take place earlier, your child's voice does not actually mature until about age 16.

In addition, many other factors contribute to when your child should begin lessons. Her rate of physical and emotional growth as well as her interests and talents are all indicators. Your child's teacher must be familiar with the physiology and psychology of young singers.

Try to remember that males and females differ in vocal development as much as they differ in physical and emotional development. Your son and daughter may not be ready for voice lessons at the same points in their adolescence.

The best age for a child to begin lessons is 15 years of age. By then, the voice has usually changed, and the student is mentally able to understand the concepts of correct posture, breathing, resonance, support, and vowel formation. Also, a 15-year-old is mature enough to stay on task in a 30-minute lesson and enjoy the work—younger children are easily bored with the vocal exercises involved with the classic technique. Be very wary of teachers who are willing right away to teach your child under 12. They probably just need the money.

—Rebecca Flaherty, WeJoySing music teacher and private voice instructor for 3 years

I usually don't take children under the age of 16 as voice students unless they are already highly motivated, have other musical background, and/or are involved in musical activities. Many children aren't mature enough vocally or psychologically. But there are some who do very well because of early maturity.

—Henrietta Carter, chair, Golden West College Performing Arts, teaching voice for 39 years

Since I do not work with the vocal cords themselves, we can start a student as young as 4 years old. We start with ear training and develop their muscle memory. Then we work on breathing, which can be very therapeutic for hyperactivity, and a lot safer than Ritalin.

—Chrys Page, Sing Your Life Studio Director, teaching voice for 30 years

In my opinion, the best time for training the voice is after puberty. Much can be done with a child musically before that time, and some training of the breathing instrument can begin. But until puberty (and for some time after) the vocal mechanism is changing so much it's a little like learning to play a violin that is constantly changing size and shape.

—Nancy Walker, associate professor of voice, University of North Carolina at Greensboro, teaching for 28 years

That having been said, voice instructors vary dramatically in the ages they will take on children as students.

Kids Who Tend to Excel

Kids who excel:

- love music and singing

- are open to trying and experimenting with new sounds (many of the exercises in a voice lesson can sound very silly)

- lack inhibition and can overcome any performance anxiety in singing for others

- have a good ear (i.e., are able to match pitch)

WHAT TO EXPECT IN VOICE LESSONS

❧ Voice lessons involve learning proper breathing techniques, along with developing the vocal cords and increasing lung capacity. A teacher will focus on your child's voice expression and resonance, along with proper breathing, posture, relaxation, and stage presence.

❧ Healthy singing does not leave your child hoarse or cause her to strain her neck, clench her jaw, or breathe in gasps. Your child should learn to breathe from her diaphragm, not from her chest. Her shoulders should stay down when she inhales, rather than "shrugging up." This type of breathing allows for healthier and greater airflow, and keeps the neck and chest muscles relaxed.

❧ For several centuries, voice teachers have debated the use of "chest resonance" (chest vibrations felt while singing low notes) versus "head resonance" (mouth or head vibrations experienced while singing higher notes). Singers must systematically blend the two. Your child will naturally use one of these resonances based on her personality, chest and head size, and both the music and language to which she's been most exposed. Avoid a teacher who insists that your child use only one of the resonances, as both are needed in healthy singing.

❧ Each voice teacher will usually emphasize a particular style of singing, from classical to musical theater, jazz, light opera, and pop.

Why Your Child Doesn't Sound Perfect Yet

❧ Just like acquiring any other skill, your child will likely feel frustrated at times. A good teacher can recognize frustration and discuss it openly with both you and your child.

Kids who excel most are self-motivated and have an idea about what they want in terms of their vocal development. I like when students come to me with goals like, "I want to get a role in the school musical" or "I want to sing better in the church choir." Those students have the drive to succeed. Studying voice is a big responsibility—the student is really in control of his or her development. The teacher serves as a set of well-trained ears to help the student learn what sounds are healthy and natural, and what sounds are manufactured, and then assigns exercises and songs to help the student with specific issues.

—*Rebecca Flaherty, WeJoySing music teacher and private voice instructor for 3 years*

The development of musicianship before beginning voice training in private lessons is a decided advantage for the singing student. I encourage motivated singers of all ages to learn to play an instrument such as piano to facilitate their learning of songs, and for studying music fundamentals and music theory. I also encourage them to attend live performances of outstanding performing artists and to participate in or observe group activities such as choirs and workshops.

—*Henrietta Carter, chair, Golden West College Performing Arts, teaching voice for 39 years*

Kids need perseverance, aural acuity, good memory, and an emotional empathy.

—*Ben King, professor of voice, Houghton College School of Music, teaching for 30 years*

Kids who excel are those with an unquenchable passion for singing. That passion drives them through the challenges and frustrations that come with mastering the most complex musical piece there is!

—*Nancy Costlow, private voice teacher for 7 years*

I teach the classic Italian bel canto technique. *Bel canto* means "beautiful singing" in Italian. It is the technique that has been passed down for hundreds of years and used by most opera and classical singers. I use this technique because it serves to help students find their natural sound and strengthen it, rather than other techniques in which singers try to make their voice have a certain sound. Bel canto is the healthiest way to sing, because in order to do it well, you must be very relaxed.

—*Rebecca Flaherty, WeJoySing music teacher and private voice instructor for 3 years*

I teach in the classical tradition, based on the vocal principles developed in Italy in the 17th and 18th centuries, because I'm convinced that its breathing techniques, vowel production, and resonance offer the most secure foundation on which to build a personal singing style.

—*Ben King, professor of voice, Houghton College School of Music, teaching for 30 years*

I teach classical vocal production. Classical vocal production has been time tested, and has been passed down through the ages for a reason: It's clear, healthy, and natural vocal production. If you learn correctly, you can sing your entire life with no laryngeal problems. Styles that are "in" are not necessarily the best styles (i.e., high heels). I equate much of pop singing (I hate to even call it singing) with high heels. Wear them/sing it long enough and you will develop calluses and vocal nodules, and a variety of other problems. Much of pop singing is merely controlled yelling, which is why so many pop stars have hoarse, husky-sounding voices when interviewed.

—*Renée de Wolf, voice adjunct college faculty and private voice teacher for 12 years*

🍂 Remember that professional music recordings are often the result of a sound engineer and producer electronically manipulating perfection, and that your child cannot produce the same quality or sustained volume as an adult professional singer.

🍂 Many of your child's favorite popular or classical singers have studied singing and continue to do so throughout their careers. Most credible teachers of pop and musical theater insist students first master the fundamentals of healthy singing before branching off into the different vocal styles and techniques required for those crafts. This does not happen in a few lessons or months, but develops as the child matures, practices, and has the guidance of a good teacher.

Helping with Practice

🎵 Your main role as a parent is to make sure that your child practices, and to provide encouragement and your ears when your child asks for them.

🎵 When just beginning, your child might practice only 15 minutes, 4 days a week. The longer your child studies voice, the longer practice time will become.

🎵 Whether or not you are a singer or have performing experience, resist the urge to correct or comment unless your child asks for help, and even then, start by asking, "What would your teacher say about this?"

🎵 Suggest that your child tape a few of her lessons. This way she can hear herself sing and recap her lessons for you, and you can hear what's going on. Also, your child can refer to the tape during practice time if she needs to remember something about her technique or the music she is learning.

🎵 If she does not already do so, ask your child's teacher to jot down practice hints in a student notebook.

I like to give all of my students the opportunity to learn from their peers as well as from me. For instance, I had an eight-year-old once who didn't want to sing anything but R&B, but she had a voice that wasn't really suited for these types of songs. I put together a revue of Broadway show tunes and included her in the production with other older students. She ended up loving this music and couldn't wait to get to the karaoke store and buy up all the show tunes she could find. And when the audience gave her standing ovations for her efforts, she decided to try out for *The Music Man* production at the local community theater and got to play a major role. And no one even dreamed that there was this *voice* inside this little girl. Well, no one except me.

—*Chrys Page, director, Sing Your Life Studio, teaching voice for 30 years*

🎵 Your child may be sensitive to practicing when the family is around, so afford her some privacy if this is the case.

🎵 Remind your child that she needs to practice her singing just as she would any other instrument.

Helping Your Child Take Care of Her Voice

🎵 Warn your child to avoid abusing her voice. She shouldn't do anything that results in hoarseness or throat pain, such as yelling, screaming, and singing at an excessive volume. In very noisy environments, conversation should be kept to a minimum.

🍀 When she has a cold or laryngitis, she should not try to talk or sing.

🍀 Monitor your home environment for smoke and dust.

🍀 Avoid drying medications such as antihistamines and anesthetic throat sprays.

🍀 Have your child use a humidifier in her bedroom during the winter.

🍀 Drinking plenty of water is crucial for her vocal health.

🍀 Don't let your child rehearse or perform without warming up first.

CHORUS AND CHOIR

🍀 A terrific way for children to gain general musical experience is to join a children's chorus, whether sponsored by a church or synagogue, school, community, or national organization.

🍀 Group performance does not require the same commitment as a private instrument. Chorus exposes a child to a wide range of music, encompassing many styles and cultures. In the process, your child will learn about reading and singing music in a non-classroom, social setting.

🍀 Even if your child doesn't have an amazing voice, chorus gives her an opportunity to sing, as well as learn to read, perform, and enjoy music.

🍀 A good voice teacher will not take on individual students until their voices have changed, between ages 11 and 14. Choruses give children a forum for singing without damaging their young voices. For children younger than 11, joining a children's choir or a preschool singing program enables them to learn how to use their voices properly, in a fun, relaxed way.

🍀 Individual music lessons can be isolating, but a chorus is an ideal way to put those musical skills to work in a social setting.

🍀 Participating in a chorus also teaches children how to listen to each other, improving their musical, ensemble, and communication skills.

🍀 If you're lucky, your child's chorus may travel to interesting places around the country or the world.

🍀 The National Endowment for the Arts found that 1 in 10 American adults sing in a chorus each week. Many of these adults began their singing careers in a childhood chorus.

🍀 Singing in a chorus teaches your child about making positive contributions to

Choir for kids is great because you sing individually but experience a group dynamic. Also, the cooperation that kids learn is incredible.

> —*Diana, mom of a high school–age daughter*

A vocally well-trained choral director can provide what amount to group lessons in their choral warm-ups.

> —*Ellie Edwards, president, Boston Chapter of the National Association of Teachers of Singing and private voice teacher for 30 years*

For chorus or choir, take a look at the performance schedule. If groups perform too often, they will be underrehearsed; if they perform too infrequently, the singers will become bored with the repertoire.

> —*Patty Thom, director of music, Walnut Hill School for the Arts, and instructor of voice, Boston Conservatory, teaching for 16 years*

the community, from performances in nursing homes, to community events, to recordings.

🎵 The centuries-old tradition of a boys' choir continues today, with much attention garnered by well-known groups such as the Vienna Boys Choir and the Boys Choir of Harlem. These choirs tend to be highly selective, with boys participating only until puberty, at which time their voice changes and they can no longer reach the soprano notes. Local music schools, churches, and religious organizations often offer a boys' choir program. These large, well-known programs recruit nationally.

What to Look For in a Voice Teacher

🎵 A voice teacher helps students develop the physical, mental, and emotional aspects of singing, referred to as technique, and guides your child in musical style. The teacher should not try to make everyone sound the same. Rather, she should focus on your child's individual voice.

✦ Both voice teachers and coaches need to be excellent musicians, although a good voice teacher does not necessarily play the piano. Frequently, a voice teacher will hire an accompanist to play her lessons.

✦ A young singer may do damage to her voice by using incorrect techniques or by moving along at too fast a rate. A well-qualified teacher will prevent this from happening. Look for a teacher who is a member of the National Association of Teachers of Singing.

Cost Considerations

✦ If your child studies with an accomplished singer who holds an advanced degree, that teacher will likely charge from $20 to $50 for a half-hour, depending on where you live and the level of the teacher. There will also be periodic costs for purchasing music, usually costing between $40 and $60 a year.

✦ Ask if your child will be expected to pay an accompanist or contribute to a facility rental for performances.

For little kids, find a teacher who will just let your child sing, learning phrasing, musical issues, diction, without trying to "build up" your child's voice. Avoid belting, just as lifting heavy weights should be avoided, as it will ruin the vocal mechanism in an undeveloped child.

—Kari Windingstad White, regional governor, National Association of Teachers of Singing, voice teacher at UCLA (retired), and private voice teacher for 18 years

A good voice teacher will have already completed at least an undergraduate degree in voice performance or voice pedagogy, will still be taking voice lessons herself, and will be performing on a regular basis. It's very important that the student is able to develop a good rapport with the teacher—a lot of trust is involved in this relationship! Also, make sure the teacher has a good attitude about teaching—oftentimes singers who can't get jobs turn to teaching just because it's an easy way to make money, not because they really want to do the work and help students craft their voices. Make sure this teacher loves to teach.

—Rebecca Flaherty, WeJoySing music teacher and private voice instructor for 3 years

The correct teacher should have taught other children in the age range of your child. He or she should have at least a B.A. in music, several years of experience or a qualified mentor to turn to when questions come up. Belonging to a professional organization such as the National Association of Teachers of Singing shows that the teacher is interested in improving his/her skills. But the number one, most important trait of a good teacher is chemistry between the teacher, the child, and the parent.

—*Nancy Costlow, private voice teacher for 7 years*

Sit in on some lessons to listen to students who have been with that particular teacher for a while. If they sound as though they're straining, singing as loud as they can, or are hoarse—run, don't walk, away. If the teacher refuses to let a parent sit in on lessons beforehand, I would consider that a warning signal as well.

—*Renée de Wolf, voice adjunct college faculty and private voice teacher for 12 years*

If you live near a school that offers degrees in singing, call and see if they have a "community school of music" where graduate students teach who have access to advice and opinions of other teachers at the university.

—*Rebecca Flaherty, WeJoySing music teacher and private voice instructor for 3 years*

Theater and the Performing Arts

OVERVIEW

Whether your child insists on donning high heels and makeup or mimicking a grumpy schoolteacher, her imagination develops early. Children express themselves freely and creatively, combining gestures, movements, and voice intonations to create fictional characters. Your child's dramatic play may be the beginning of a theatrical interest.

By dreaming themselves into a different time and space, children can escape the pressures of everyday life. There are many ways to be onstage. Evaluate whether your child would prefer to be in small class performances for parents or a full-drama production for the public. Since the arts have taken a back seat in school curriculums, more children have been enrolling in drama classes and children's theater organizations.

General Benefits

◉ Theater develops the imagination, allows for self-exploration and freedom of expression, and provides a healthy release of stress.

As humans, we have multiple intelligences, and theater exercises them all. It gets children moving and using their imagination. Acting develops kinesthetic skills, visual and spatial understanding, verbal linguistic skills, musical rhythm and the ability to communicate an idea. Designing sets and working on costumes also promote mathematical and logical reasoning.

    —*Susan Chenet, Louisiana high school drama teacher in gifted program for 10 years*

Children gain more understanding of their bodies, voices, and imaginations when they create theater. They learn to feel comfortable in their bodies and how to best use their voice to communicate what they need to say. Children learn how to listen, to collaborate, and find new solutions to problems while expressing what's on their minds and in their hearts in nontraditional ways.

    —*Sharon DeMark, director of education, The Minneapolis Children's Theatre Company*

Theater allows kids who are not part of a team sport to experience the feeling of teamwork. We teach the idea that everyone is like a puzzle piece. If you are not all there, in the right place, then the picture is incomplete, no matter who is missing. Theater is an art of compromise. Kids learn to appreciate someone else's talent for what that person adds to their own. A lot of kids learn how to let go of boundaries and just play. Theater also teaches more complex expression: facially, physically, and vocally.

    —*Brian Milauskas, creative director of Kidstock Children's Theater, teaching for 17 years*

Children learn how to focus on others and allow themselves to be focused on. Acting is all about listening and reacting. Focused listening does not come naturally to everyone.

    —*Nina Schuessler, artistic director, Harwich Junior Theater, teaching for 25 years*

© Imitation and re-enactment, by allowing children to experience different emotions and situations, promote empathy and understanding of others. Acting teaches emotional discipline and develops grace under pressure.

© Drama promotes innovation, spontaneity, risk-taking, and fearlessness. Being onstage helps children overcome shyness and conquer performance anxiety. It helps children with low attention spans learn to focus and channel their energy. It also develops language, communication, and memory skills.

Best Age to Start

© Your child may begin theater and performing as early as age 6 or as late as her teen years. One way to judge whether or not your child is ready to participate in theater or drama classes is to observe how she plays at home. Children of all ages love to perform, enjoying mimicking what they see and playing make-believe. If your kindergarten child likes to create crazy stories, act out roles, or imagine fantasylands, then she might enjoy exhibiting that behavior onstage.

I have taught one kindergarten child who was so incredibly motivated that even though she couldn't read, she memorized seven pages of lines overnight. I made a tape for her of her lines, and she just kept listening to it until she had them all down pat. It is quite impressive what motivated kids, even at a young age, can accomplish in drama.

—*Michelle Vyadro, Chestnut Hill Camp drama instructor for 3 years*

Laid-back drama games with very little emphasis on performance or technique are appropriate for first and second grade. Third grade is a good time to take a slightly more structured class, which may lead to playwriting, performance, and musical theater.

—*Sean Hartley, program director, Lucy Moses School, teaching for 14 years*

Creative drama is for all ages. Preschoolers enjoy it just as much as teens.

—*Brian Milauskas, creative director, Kidstock Children's Theater, teaching for 17 years*

© Children don't usually begin formal script reading and participating in formal performance dramas until ages 10–12.

Kids Who Tend to Excel

© Outgoing, enthusiastic, creative, and energetic kids often don't mind taking risks or feel inhibited by what others will think of them.

© Shy children, who may need more coaxing initially, often gain the most from the experience. Many find acting to be a new, freer form of expression, and introspective kids often love thinking about and getting into a character.

© Hyper kids can often channel that extra energy into improvisation. However, in staged drama productions, fidgeting, wandering off every few minutes, and not listening become a real problem.

© Being able to concentrate is critical.

Kids who have a sense of self-confidence and can translate their ideas to a kinesthetic form thrive in theater. Children may have great stories in their heads, or ideas of how a story can come to life, but they need to then be able to physically transform those ideas to be successful in theater.

—*Sharon DeMark, director of education, The Minneapolis Children's Theatre Company*

©

Some kids with great acting abilities and beautiful voices simply fall apart when it comes to audience performances. It helps if your child can take risks and project onstage, which can be quite scary.

—*Michelle Vyadro, Chestnut Hill Camp drama instructor for 3 years*

©

Nonjudgmental kids or those who are open to new ideas and willing to try *anything* will love acting. I usually tell people that the kids who do well are the kids who color outside the lines.

—*Lisa Evans, artistic director, Concord Youth Theater, teaching for 20 years*

Imaginative children who love to pretend usually have an easy time of it. Theater can be great for a child who needs more attention. Improvisation helps rigid children become a little looser. Often "class clown" types, who may act out in school, get a chance to be rewarded instead of punished for their jokes and hijinks. Musical drama, especially choral singing, can be very good for bonding "loners," who might have trouble making friends with the rest of the group. Angry children or children with emotional problems may find creative dramatics a useful or therapeutic release mechanism.

—*Sean Hartley, program director, Lucy Moses School, teaching for 14 years*

My son, who has Asperger's syndrome, a mild form of autism, enjoys theater, where he designs and runs all the lighting. He's even gotten into some acting himself, doing great with a part in musical theater recently. For him, theater offers the chance to be social, and to hone his social skills. It's almost a sneaky form of therapy for him.

—*Debbie, mom of Zachary, 12, and Lily, 10*

What to Look For When Getting Started

❧ Early theater classes should be geared toward having fun. Your child will learn the basics of performance and begin to get comfortable expressing herself in front of a group. Emphasis is placed on cooperation and observation. To ensure more individualized instruction, look for 12 students and under per class.

❧ In class, your child may work on dramatic skills such as projecting, learning to communicate feelings, pantomime, and individual character work. These skills are often taught through movement, story improvisation, vocal exercises, and character development.

❧ In classes for younger children, drama teachers often use theater games and group storytelling, in which the teacher may narrate a story that the children can act out.

❧ In intermediate classes, your child may be assigned a monologue and begin to do scene-work with scripts.

❧ Advanced acting classes enter into the realm of audition practice. Students practice comedic or dramatic monologues and scenes and learn techniques of reading a piece in an audition that they have not seen before.

❧ If you have the time, observe a theater program or acting class before enrolling your child. Here are some questions to consider:
- ∿ What do the classes offer?
- ∿ Are the students under a lot of pressure to perform or is it a more relaxed environment?
- ∿ Are there creative aspects or is the goal to produce a formal play?
- ∿ What upcoming shows will they be producing?

❧ Take your child to see a production by the program. Consider these questions when evaluating the quality of the play: Did the actors exhibit a high level of skill and were the characters believable? Were the costuming, sets, and lights creative?

Very young kids create their own characters—something like monsters, magicians, or make-believe characters—and just learn to be comfortable acting out. What does a monster with a deep voice sound like? We get them comfortable acting with their bodies physically, emotionally, and verbally. For the older kids, we play improv games like on the show *Whose Line Is It Anyway?* We talk about character development, exposition, text, and subtext to teach the technical aspects of theater.

—Lisa Evans, artistic director of Concord Youth Theater, teaching for 20 years

In a typical children's class the kids will fly, run, jump, freeze, grow, and soar and laugh a lot! Beginning classes should place an emphasis on story (beginning, climax, ending) and whole-class involvement where every child gets a chance to shine. One of the great parts of children's theater is engaging one's imagination, learning to collaborate, and sharing the spotlight versus having to be the STAR.

—Jill Bloede, artistic associate, Charlotte Theater for Children, teaching for 12 years

For some of our kids, we make them yell at the top of their lungs for a week in order to get them to project their voices. Then the audience is able to hear them when they get up onstage and naturally become more muted.

—Michelle Vyadro, Chestnut Hill Camp drama instructor for 3 years

Lots of little kids want to be in the spotlight. When they're young and in a production, they're cute no matter what they do. But as they get older, they're no longer cute and start to feel the pressure of having to perform well to please an audience. It can be a really jarring experience, and you want to find a program that helps your child train for and smoothly make that transition.

—*Leora Falk, Improv Drama instructor for 4 years*

You can give generalized information to a child about how to act, but you cannot tell him exactly how to do it. There is a danger in the director saying exactly what she wants. It needs to be collaborative. Also, age-appropriate material is important. A child has to be able to emotionally connect to it. We ask each of the children to write a biography of the character they play, even if it is well defined in the book or script.

—*Lisa Evans, artistic director of Concord Youth Theater, teaching for 20 years*

🧩 Your child may initially be shy and not particularly thrilled about getting up in front of a room full of people. Allow your child to explore theater in an environment where there is less pressure.

🧩 Find out the director's style and personality. Some directors focus only on the lead, while every other kid fades into the background.

Clarify Performance Time Commitment

🧩 Depending on whether your child is taking acting classes or participating in the production of a full-scale play, the amount of time commitment will vary greatly.

🧩 If your child has a part in a play, she may have to rehearse lines at home nightly.

🧩 Ask the director:
  ～ What times are rehearsals?
  ～ How long do they last?
  ～ What do the kids do while they're not onstage?
  ～ Does the schedule accelerate toward production?

The real hidden cost of having your child participate in children's theater is all the time consumed by rehearsals, outside regular class time, for ten weeks leading up to a play. It's an enormous commitment.

—*Alexa, mom of Adam, 10, and Sophie, 6*

In my experience, the classes generally meet once a week. There is often some homework from week to week, such as memorizing lines, and writing or creating a character. But usually, an hour or so preparation time per week is sufficient, except right before performances. Larger parts and longer plays obviously require more preparation.

—*Sean Hartley, program director, Lucy Moses School, teaching for 14 years*

AUDITIONING

✦ When auditioning for a musical role, urge your child to stay away from pop songs. Your child may be tempted to imitate the artist's style, a method that may encourage bad technique. Instead, look for children's show tunes, offering a wide selection from which to choose an appropriate song.

✦ Encouragement before an audition is very important, but telling your child she excels in areas she doesn't may be detrimental in the long run. If her acting is strong but her singing is weak, encourage her to concentrate more on theater than on voice. If your child is not cast in the part she wants, telling her she should have gotten the part will only worsen her auditioning blues.

✦ Some acting schools offer classes just on auditioning. Students learn how to project a positive attitude and to do cold readings and monologues.

TYPES OF PERFORMING ARTS

Creative Drama and Improvisation (Improv)

🜚 "Process rather than product" is the mantra for creative drama. Unlike traditional script-based drama, creative drama can include dramatic play, story enactment, theater games, music, and dance.

🜚 The improvisational aspect of creative drama teaches children to react without deliberation, express first impulses, and not worry about failure. Students are taught to accept whatever circumstances they are presented with and then to move the moment forward.

🜚 Improvisation is more laid-back than traditional drama. Teaching takes place through acting games, and it involves far more imagination than being in a full-fledged production with memorized lines.

🜚 Students and teachers use improvisation and inventive play to communicate emotion and ideas. Learning to act without inhibition is extremely difficult, especially in a culture where children are taught just the opposite.

🜚 Improvisation provides children with creative freedom, a necessary building block for all performing arts. In its essence, creative drama is reflective and based on the other participants. A shy, reluctant child is encouraged but never forced to participate. There are no "wrong" lines or actions.

Rachel didn't get the lead in the play after auditioning last year and was very upset. She felt that she sings better than the girl who got the part. So I asked her about the audition and what happened, and she said she got very nervous, even though we had practiced singing before. She admitted she sang with her head down and buried in her paper. This was the very first time she really wanted something and did not get it. But she took the smaller part she had and still had fun with the play. Of course she already told me that she wants the lead this year! And I think that she'll have more confidence this time around. But she also realizes that if she doesn't get the lead, it's not the end of the world.

—*Andy, dad of Rachel, 9, Ben, 6, and Josh, 2*

There are no starring roles in improv. In theater productions, every child wants to be the star. When a director announces role assignments, egos can get bruised. At home, every child is the shining star, but when it comes to a production, there may be more talented kids, or simply someone who better suits the physical characteristics of the lead role. Children often smolder if they get a small part, while their friend gets the lead. Many kids think they want to be in a play, but have no real idea of what they're getting into. Plus, there are stressful auditions to contend with. In improv, everyone takes part in roles of equal significance.

—*Leora Falk, improv drama instructor for 4 years*

Kids are just waiting to be asked to act, especially in a noncompetitive, nurturing environment. Most children really respond to creative drama, as it's like focused play. As they get older, children learn how to establish an aesthetic. A teacher should bring technique in slowly so it is something that children develop for themselves.

—*Nina Schuessler, artistic director, Harwich Junior Theater, teaching for 25 years*

Theater Arts

✦ Theater arts is the more traditional theater arrangement in which actors perform a play on a stage.

✦ Besides enjoying the exhilaration of being in front of an audience of many people, children may also enjoy working behind the scenes. Set design, costume design, stage-managing, stage crew, set building, lighting, and publicity can all be fun and rewarding activities.

✦ The play performed could be a drama, a musical, a documentary, or movement theater.

Musical Theater

✦ If your child loves to dance, act, *and* sing, musical theater will be an entertaining way to combine these talents. Choreography, vocal range, musical interpretation, phrasing, breath control, projection, diction, and intonation are often included in musical theater curriculum. Solo, duet, and group singing may also be rehearsed.

My son has always been my little drama king, making any incident into a big deal. In first grade, he decided that he wanted to audition for elementary school plays, and he landed roles in those. When the time came to choose a high school, he went to a drama magnet that offers lessons at the school with actors and actresses. He also takes acting lessons with a group one night a week for three hours. During the summers, he studies and performs with civic and Shakespearean theater companies that run summer camps.

—Joy, mom of Chris, 15, and Victoria, 11

Since she was small, my daughter has been innately friendly and outgoing, very dramatic, and has thrived on performing before an audience. Not only does she love to sing and have a good voice, but the music teacher in her school pulled me aside when she was in kindergarten to tell me that my daughter has talent. So instead of regular voice lessons, I found a local children's theater group that she could join. My daughter was offered a lead part in *The Sound of Music* this year, but after much discussion we decided to turn it down. She's only 6, and I didn't think she (or I) could sustain the 9 hours of rehearsal time each week, on top of everything else she does. She agreed that it was too much, and I thought that she handled making the decision very well. She took a minor role instead, and *loved* performing onstage. The audience burst into spontaneous applause in the middle of a song during her one solo performance that made her grandparents and me very proud. The three-hour performance didn't end until 10:30 p.m. (hours past her normal bedtime), and I still couldn't get her to bed after the adrenaline high of performing in front of an audience.

—Alexa, mom of Adam, 10, and Sophie, 6

❧ If a musical theater class is in a larger studio, dance experience may be required prior to enrollment.

Cost Considerations

❧ Besides the cost of classes, ask about costs for your child's costume, props, or set design.

❧ While you may not expect to pay admission to see your child in a performance, this is often the case.

Dance

OVERVIEW

You may find yourself marveling when your two-year-old joyfully dances away to music. At this stage, you join the ranks of parents searching for classes for their budding "stars." When is the best time for your child to begin dance, and what should you look for in a dance school?

Dance can be treated as an art form, sport, or something in between. As an art form, it is disciplined and expressive with an emphasis on individual and class achievement. As a sport, it is disciplined and rule-bound with an emphasis on pleasing judges and teachers and acquiring trophies and medals. Most dance forms emphasize artistry and performance rather than competition. However, a few forms of dance are competitive, such as Irish step dancing and the latest form of ballroom dancing, called DanceSport, that has just been officially recognized by the Olympic Committee.

Although recitals are often stressful and labor intensive, they can be a very rewarding way for your child to showcase her talent and newly acquired skills. Usually, recitals take place at the end of the first year of classes and offer a great opportunity for family and friends to gather to witness nine months of hard work. Recitals can help to ease stage fright and teach showmanship. Stage performances can also help motivate a child and give her the incentive to practice hard. Furthermore, watching the set crew, light positioning, and backdrop changes is exciting and will make your child feel she is part of a larger whole.

One day my daughter turned to me to announce, "I think I'm going to be a pop star and actress, so I need to do dance or gymnastics in addition to the music I'm doing." I said, "Okay," as I realized that my kid is telling me at a young age that she's really focused. I quickly got her enrolled in a five-hour-a-week dance program at a recommended dance studio. The studio requires all the kids to take ballet and jazz before anything else, and after that my daughter threw in tap, hip-hop, and modern dance. The extended practices culminate in a huge extravaganza performance in the auditorium of a local college. My daughter is not the strongest dancer there, but she loves it, is extremely focused, and never says she's too tired or doesn't want to go.

—*Leslie, mom of Alexandra, 10, and Jack, 9*

General Benefits

- Allows children to hold themselves with grace and balance

- Teaches how to isolate different parts of the body

- Increases endurance and muscle tone, working both sides of the body equally

- Builds stamina

- Improves posture, alignment, flexibility, agility, sense of timing, coordination, peripheral vision, spatial sense, and memorization skills

- Teaches how music, rhythm, and movement work together, and develops rhythmic ability

- Provides exposure to new and different types of music and performance

- Cultivates a personal style and the ability to express emotion through movement

- Offers an alternative to competitive sports as a physical activity

- Develops focus, dedication, and discipline

- Helps shy children learn to become relaxed and confident in front of a group

Rachel doesn't know a single girl in her dance class, and she's been doing it for seven years! And she doesn't care because she loves it so much. Since she doesn't know anyone in class, she's just herself and not self-conscious. She really enjoys it. It's a type of self-expression, it's fun, and a time to let loose. Dance has given her self-confidence. Plus, I love that it's physical activity, given that in school she only has gym two times a week for 45 minutes.

—*Ellen, mom of Rachel, 9, Ben, 6, and Josh, 2*

Dance teaches kids to trust their bodies. They gain a qualitative understanding of their physical extension and inflection, like learning how to move the top of their body separate from the bottom of their body. We have a natural spiral in our body where every position has a natural opposition. For example, if you move your left leg forward, your right shoulder goes back. General alignment is a huge benefit. Some kids are totally out of alignment. Rolled-in knees, fallen arches, turned-in feet. Dance helps get bones in place when they are pliable. A teacher who cares about alignment will notice these things. If a child is not comfortable in her body, she won't be comfortable in her mind.

—*Kara Keating, founder and director, Movement Art, teaching for 20 years*

Best Age to Start

◉ If you think your child might be interested in pursuing dance, encourage her to start moving and shaking at a young age. Dance around the house and ask your child questions like "Besides standing, how many ways can you balance yourself?" and "How many different ways can you move your head, arms, and legs?" Get your child to clap, rock, or hop to music on the radio. Bop to familiar songs, nursery rhymes, or rhythmic noises around the house.

◉ By the time a child is 3 to 6 years old, she uses physical expression to communicate. Children are warehouses for enormous amounts of energy, and dance helps channel this energy in positive ways. A good pre-dance program or a movement class supports creativity, curiosity, and natural movements, and is usually offered locally through parks and recreation departments or local dance studios. Even the most basic of movements like walking, running, jumping, skipping, bending, stretching, twisting, and swinging can all be combined to form dance steps. These activities will help your child become more aware of her body and internal rhythm.

After these initial explorations, your child can move on to more specific, technique-focused dancing.

◉ An early start helps develop the flexibility and strength in a dancer's muscles and bones. Best ages to start specific types of dance:

➤ *Creative movement or pre-ballet classes.* For children between the ages of 2 and 6, these playful classes are a helpful precursor to ballet, and children often learn the principles, music, and stories of classical ballet. With a little imagination, hula hoops, balls, and batons turn into fun ways of experiencing sound and action. If your child is more disciplined or "classically inclined," suggest ballet.

➤ *Ballet.* For a child with good coordination, strength, and balance, a good age to start is 6 to 8 years, while pre-ballet classes will start as young as age 3.

➤ *Modern dance.* Some instructors advise beginning modern dance before other dance types. Others suggest taking ballet first as a foundation. Either dance will strengthen and prepare your child for the other and encourage her to think about her body in relationship to dance. If your child is especially excited about dance, consider enrolling her in ballet and modern dance simultaneously.

➤ *Jazz.* Children typically start at age 6 and up, although pre-jazz and pre-ballet classes can start as early as 3 years old.

➤ *Tap.* Classes usually start around age 6, when children can remember move sequences.

Creative movement classes can be taught as young as age 3 or 4, but technique classes should not be taken until a child is 6.

—*Jefferson James, executive director, Contemporary Dance Theater, teaching for 30 years*

◉

My daughter is in a KinderCombo dance class, a mix of tap and jazz, and loves getting dressed up in tights and tutus. She got interested after watching her older cousins in recitals. At first my daughter didn't want me to leave her alone in the dance studio. She kept running outside in the hallway to find me. Now, in her new dance class, they have a big window the parents sit behind and watch the class. It is just enough to keep her inside.

—*Stephanie, mom of Eric, 5, and Tina, 3*

Dance education is wonderful, fun, and beneficial even if your child does not want to become a professional. For those interested in dance recreationally, attending classes twice a week is adequate. Students who want to train in a professionally focused program will take classes three days per week during their early years. By the time they are 14, they should be taking classes 5–6 days each week.

—*Rachel Moore, director of dance education, Boston Ballet, and former professional ballerina, teaching for 20 years*

The more classes per week, the better the child gets. We try not to burn the kids out, so most of the time they take one class per week until ages 7–8; then they gradually add a class. Ballet is stressed until 8, and then they can take a jazz or tap class. I don't start them working at the barre until age 6—or until they learn not to hang on it!

—*Carol Richmond, Dance Kids of Monterey County, teaching ballet for 27 years*

My daughter started ballet at age 3, because an older girl next door would come over to play and show us her latest moves. She's stuck with it, and is now going into her fourth year of lessons. I had always felt myself to be ungraceful, and I wanted my daughter to learn the grace that ballet teaches. When she started, it was just a lot of hopping around to great music and standing on dots on the floor for performances. Over the years, it's escalated to the point where there's more work than play.

—*Alexa, mom of Adam, 10, and Sophie, 6*

➤ *Irish step dancing.* Children can start as early as 4 or as late as their mid-teens.
➤ *Salsa.* Some schools offer classes for children as young as 3 and 4.
➤ *Ballroom dancing.* While classes will start for children as young as age 7 or 8, most children do not start until middle school or junior high.

◉ Things to keep in mind when looking at classes:
➤ Children ages 3–5 can focus for 35–45 minutes at most, and should not be in a class with more than 15 students.
➤ Children ages 6–8 can practice for one hour a week, but more than 20 other students in the class can make it too hard to concentrate.

- Children 8 years and older can concentrate for longer periods of time and are more interested in skill building.
- Children 9 years and older can practice for more than an hour a week and can handle a class with a large number of students.

Kids Who Tend to Excel

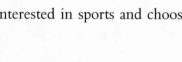

Kids who do best:

- have physical strength and grace

- need to have focus, discipline, and perseverance

- love to dance, and keep working on moves until they've "got it"

- are sometimes quieter children, who are not interested in sports and choose dance instead

Talent without determination is useless, while great determination with even the smallest bit of talent can lead to great success. Allow your child the time to master skills and gradually develop the dedication necessary to become good. Becoming good happens over the course of four to five years, not just in one or two years.

—Bob Thomas, dance director, Dean College, teaching for 26 years

For children to excel, they need a love of movement, self-discipline, and a certain amount of natural gifts such as arched feet and a ballet body. Hard work can compensate for a lack of natural talent, but the child who has everything obviously has an advantage. Ballet takes years to master, and in this age of instant gratification, some children are not willing to do the time. Also, as they reach the teen years, other activities seem more important. In order to become a dancer, you must have a passion for dance.

—Willa Damien, director, Dance Loft Studio, teaching ballet for 27 years

Success at ballet comes with a mixture of desire and talent and a lot of concentration. I have several students who aren't as talented but do far better because of their focus and ability to take corrections to the next class. Certain physiques more naturally adjust to ballet. Students who aren't as flexible need to work harder. It is hard to teach really rambunctious children, as they may be good at leaps and jumps but ballet is too restricting for them. They get bored and antsy.

—*Susan Endrizzi, Jose Mateo's Ballet Theater, teaching for 5 years*

The more disciplined child will gravitate toward ballet. If a child is really talented, a ballet academy or specialized ballet school will most likely be recommended.

—*Gene Murray, owner of Gene Murray School of Dance, teaching for 40 years*

Really physical kids pick up the steps in a snap, and kids who have more of an internal rhythm are better at making up their own stuff.

—*Eve Agush, The Dance Complex, teaching tap and jazz for 15 years*

A child needs to have a fairly good athletic ability, along with a particular interest in mathematics, since there is a fair amount of counting involved in Irish step dancing. Kids need to hold themselves confidently and have excellent posture.

—*Niall O'Leary, former world champion and Irish step instructor for 10 years*

Boys in Dance

In the United States, girls dominate the dancing scene, while boys are less likely to participate. If your son is on the fence about whether or not to try dance, suggest a class specifically geared toward sports development. Stretches, leaps, and jumps are fantastic ways to develop strength and dexterity.

It may be tough to get your son over the initial "Ewww, dance is for girls" mentality, but try not to let that prevent him from trying a highly rewarding and exciting activity.

My son asked to do ballet, and we're glad to give him some physical exercise. He comes out with a beet-red face, so he's working hard in there. He just does it for fun. His best friend is in class, which inspired him to do it. There are 2 boys and 21 girls in his age group. I told him that in a couple of years, he's going to like that a lot.

—*Jim, dad of Ben, 10, Emma, 7, and Spencer 4*

Boys don't usually last in ballet classes. There is something about the word *ballet*. They usually get pressured from friends and drop out. Tap, jazz and especially hip-hop are more popular. Nevertheless, boys can come to ballet as late as their teens and still become great dancers.

—*Kara Keating, founder and director, Movement Arts, teaching for 20 years*

What to Look For When Getting Started

✦ Checking the yellow pages and asking around town are two quick and easy ways to start investigating dance lessons. Also, try visiting a dance studio to talk with other parents. Ask them what they like about their child's teacher as well as what they do not like. Ask the staff at a dancewear store. They may be dancers and have the inside scoop.

✦ Check to see if your city or town has a local dance council that may be able to make recommendations. The best schools offer something for both serious students who need training and students who just want to have fun. If your child is on a more serious track, check the credits of the teacher's former students. Look for teachers whose students are on scholarships in colleges and universities or are working professionally.

✦ The learning environment should not intimidate your child, but instead make her feel at ease.

✦ When looking at a dance program, observe the following:
- ➤ Is the floor resilient and well maintained? A suspended wood floor is best, to avoid physical stress, but certain treatments over cement and tile are acceptable if the dancers are not doing lots of jumps and landings.
- ➤ Is the floor space big enough to accommodate the number of students in your child's class?

~ Is the equipment first rate? Are there quality ballet barres and mirrors?

~ Is there proper lighting and up-to-date musical equipment?

🍂 Questions to consider when signing your child up for dance class or program:

~ Does the teacher concentrate not only on movement exploration, but also on individual development and creativity?

~ Does the class have a warm-up and cool-down before and after exercises?

~ Is the class appropriately challenging or too stressful for your child's level?

~ How much class time is devoted to recital preparation?

~ How many children are in the class? How much individual attention and correction do students get? Beginners need a great deal of both.

~ Is the atmosphere warm and pleasant?

~ Does the teacher instruct the class in the use of the head and arms, not just the legs and feet?

~ Usually, private lessons are only necessary for advanced students who want to get ahead in competitions or prepare for an audition. If, however, your child would like more time to practice, approach his teacher and ask if there is room in his schedule to provide private lessons.

~ Year-end shows often pack a big punch, so make sure you are comfortable with the details before proceeding. Ask how much rehearsal time will be involved and whether the costume fee is included in the total cost or

Look for a studio that is not high-pressure, but instead encourages fun and bolsters self-esteem. There is already a lot of pressure in the world, and I believe kids should not have to face more of it in a dance class.

—*Maria Scalzi, Scalzi School of Dance, performer and teacher for 49 years*

Any program that offers classes in jazz, tap, modern, and ballet probably does not have a really strong ballet training. A school associated with a company or a private ballet school would have a stronger program. A ballet class should have no more than 15 students per class. Ask questions such as: Do they accept all students? Do they give everyone attention or just the more talented students? Do they teach everyone the same regardless of whether or not they want to be a professional?

—*Susan Endrizzi, Jose Mateo's Ballet Theater, teaching for 5 years*

Most classes begin with a warm-up, something ritualistic. You can see the growth pattern as children begin to memorize the ritual. Kids love rituals and repetition, like hearing the same music again and again. If the kids are young, I like to do a "follow me around the room" exercise. For the older kids, we face the mirror or cross the floor to teach a new step. I always like to do some kind of improvisation. We'll go around in a semicircle and they'll each have to dance on their own, something spontaneous or something we learned in class. They know they are not going to be corrected and they enjoy that.

—Eve Agush, The Dance Complex, teaching tap and jazz for 15 years

additional. Some studios may ask you to sew your child's recital costumes, or pay extra and find your own seamstress. If you are busy, this can be an unexpected inconvenience.

What to Look For in a Dance Teacher

✦ A strong teacher will have had training at a major school, company, or professional dance-training program and may even have performed with a professional company. However, being a professional dancer is not mandatory. Good training and a focus on quality and detail are much more important than extensive performing experience. Almost anyone can open a studio.

✦ Be wary of a teacher who is an "expert" in ballet, jazz, modern, and tap. Good studios offer a variety of dance classes and employ several teachers to specialize in their area of expertise.

✦ Questions to think about when considering a teacher:

- Does the teacher hold the attention of the class or are the students running around and chattering? Is she self-assured and authoritative?
- Does the teacher take apart or "break down" new or complicated movements? Does she explain what she wants in a language your child can understand? Does she correct steps or just demonstrate and let the students fumble along?
- Does the teacher encourage the children to be individually expressive? Is she teaching dance as an art form?
- How does the teacher look when she moves? Is she enjoyable to watch? Would your child want to imitate this person?

I love my daughter's teacher! She makes ballet light and sweet, is loved by all the girls, and brings a great sense of fun to class. This fall we had a substitute teacher, covering for a teacher on maternity leave, who was incredibly serious, and it diminished my daughter's enjoyment.

—*Alexa, mom of Adam, 10, and Sophie, 6*

See how your child reacts to the teacher and vice versa. Watch the class. Someone with wonderful credentials may not be able to teach. There should be a happy medium of knowledge and commitment to the art.

—*Mario Battista, professional ballroom dancer and owner of Battista Dance Studio, teaching for 13 years*

The basic personality of the teacher is crucial. She should enjoy working with children. The best dancer is not always the best teacher. In my opinion, 90% of parents find the personality of the studio owner and the teacher to be most important.

—*Maria, dance teacher and studio owner for 31 years*

A teacher should instill a good work ethic within her students, but students should not work hard because the teacher is mean.

—*Susan Endrizzi, Jose Mateo's Ballet Theater, teaching for 5 years*

Credentials are very important, as there is no licensing system for dance teachers. Look at a teacher's background, training, and professional experience rather than convenience of time and location.

—*Gene Murray, owner of Gene Murray School of Dance, teaching for 40 years*

BALLET

European peasants were the first to perform the classical art form that is today known as ballet. During the Renaissance, ballet made its way into the more elite sections of society, and was used as an accompaniment to classical music, poetry, and song in the royal courts of France and Italy. When professional ballet dancers began to appear in the 17th century, their skirts became shorter and the stages higher so as to accentuate the fancy footwork. Originally, ballet dancers were men, while women had to earn their right to dance publicly. Today, ballet is often seen as the best foundation for all other types of dance.

General Benefits

◉ Provides children with an otherwise rare exposure to classical music and other classical art forms.

◉ Enhances the development of posture and general muscle control.

◉ Builds strong abdominal muscles, flexibility, and stamina.

◉ Teaches children how to show respect for an instructor and an art.

◉ Requires enormous concentration and internal effort.

◉ Provides lessons in tenacity and determination.

What to Expect in Class

✦ Ballet is an art form built on hundreds of years of tradition. A good ballet class commands respect for the instructor and the art. This means not slouching at the barre, not speaking out of turn, and beginning and ending an exercise with poise and full attention. Bowing or curtsying to your teacher after class is also a sign of gratitude and respect. These small touches can add clarity and precision to your child's skills as a ballet dancer.

✦ Your child's first ballet class will most likely include an introduction to the basics: the barre, jumps, and traveling steps. She will work at the barre with two hands and learn simple combinations of dance steps on the floor.

✦ If she is older, she will probably do barre work with one hand and learn how to move her legs in multiple directions. She will practice standing with her feet flat and then on demi-pointe. She will be instructed to move her legs both quickly and slowly at various degrees of height depending on her physical maturity. Ideally, the

I actually feel as if ballet has become an enormous part of my daughter's personality. It's given her self-confidence and grace, along with a lot of fun. My hope is that she will continue to enjoy it and stick it out through high school.

—Alexa, mom of Adam, 11, and Sophie, 7

working leg should extend 90 degrees without excess stress and her posture should be naturally controlled.

❦ More advanced classes will do these same exercises and finish with pointe work for the girls and jump practice for the boys. Advanced classes separate movements slowly, focusing on technique and performance. As children are able to remember more counts and combinations, training will progress to complicated movements and more careful footwork. By learning how to correctly use their bodies early on, children avoid injuring themselves later.

❦ When her feet, ankles, and back are strong enough, your child will move to pointe. Boys will be preparing for more challenging turns, beating steps, and partner dancing. At these high levels, class may meet from two to five days a week.

❦ Even though your child may complain about tights and leotards, the traditional ballet uniform is an integral part of dance training. The tights and tank leotards for girls and the spandex shorts and tight T-shirts for boys allow maximum freedom for movement. Form-fitting clothing helps teachers to better see students' bodies, correct mistakes, and more accurately place children by ability.

❦ Ballet slippers are around $20, leotards and tights cost about $40, and pointe shoes can run between $50 and $60.

When to Start Pointe Work

❦ First worn in the early 1800s, pointe shoes are made by hand using satin, heavy cardboard, light nails, cord, canvas, and special stiffening glue. They have a thin leather sole and a box that surrounds the ballerina's toes. At the end of the toe is a flat, hard tip about the size of a silver dollar.

❦ Pointe work is the essence of classical ballet. In the ballet world, *en pointe*—dancing on your toes while wearing special satin slippers—is an important and

Dance exercises are designed in a specific order to warm and condition your body so you are always ready for the next exercise.

—Susan Endrizzi, Jose Mateo's Ballet Theater, teaching for 5 years

My daughter started ballet at age 3, when class consisted mostly of dancing around dressed in ballet regalia, often with tutus and tiaras in tow, and looking at themselves in the mirror. Now she goes to the Boston Ballet school, where there's a strict dress code and rules about how they behave and hold themselves. Classes have become very structured, and they can no longer giggle, talk, play, and engage in theatrics. There's much focus on recitals, which involves extra practices and costumes. Maddie now holds herself straighter, and there's a confidence that comes out in her posture.

—Lisa, mom of CJ, 9, and Maddie, 7

prestigious rite of passage. It may appear that ballerinas waltz effortlessly across the stage, but pointe work actually demands an incredible amount of physical strength.

🦢 Your child should not begin dancing en pointe until she has developed enough muscular strength in her lower legs, feet, and back; strong body coordination; and proper skeletal alignment.

🦢 Usually, this is not before age 10 or 11. If she dances en pointe too soon, she could damage ligaments and tendons and harm the development of her ankles and feet.

🦢 Pointe shoes cost around $60 a pair and students go through around one pair a month. Lamb's wool, paper towels, or toilet paper can help cushion your child's toes within the shoe.

Getting Serious and Auditioning

🦢 Your child may approach ballet as an exciting activity, a passionate hobby, or career-oriented endeavor. Usually, serious dance training begins anywhere between ages 9 and 12 for girls and about 14 years old for boys. If your child pursues ballet in hopes of dancing professionally, she must audition for a full-time ballet school where both ballet and academic classes are offered. In this case, your child will most

To minimize problems, we err on the side of waiting until 12 to start pointe. Ankles can get turned, backs sometimes hurt, and hamstrings can be pulled. We bring in sports medicine experts to talk to our kids. My daughter, however, was not ready for pointe until 14. Family war ensued, but she just wasn't ready!

—*Carol Richmond, Dance Kids of Monterey County, teaching ballet for 27 years*

A lot of kids end up quitting when it comes time to dancing en pointe, around age 11 or 12, because they can't go en pointe easily.

—*Susan Endrizzi, Jose Mateo's Ballet Theater, teaching for 5 years*

As one progresses in ballet training, the demands on a student's time greatly increase. Students are forced to make choices about how they are going to spend their after-school hours. Some decide that they would prefer not to spend 5–6 days a week dancing.

—*Rachel Moore, director of dance education, Boston Ballet, and former professional ballerina, teaching for 20 years*

likely live at the school, combining academics with dance, music, drama, and choreography classes.

🐟 Auditions are normally required for class advancement and entrance into a ballet academy. Examiners will ask your child to dance so they can judge physique, sensitivity to music, and physical control. The examiners will accept dancers who have the potential to develop into high-level dancers. Audition applicants also have a physical examination to check their joints, foot shape, and the angle of their legs to see if they can do pointe work.

OTHER POPULAR TYPES OF DANCE

In addition to the types of dance detailed below, there are innumerable types of folk dancing your child can learn, from flamenco to belly dancing.

Ballroom Dancing

🌢 Recently, ballroom dancing has emerged as a popular competitive dance, even though it has long been an exciting social activity. Standard ballroom dancing includes dances like the waltz, tango, foxtrot, quickstep, and hustle. Latin dancing is another category of ballroom that includes the cha-cha, samba, lambada, rumba and paso doble.

🌢 Ballroom dancing offers an immensely diverse selection of dances, some originating in the nightclubs of Paris and others in the heat of the Dominican Republic. The U.S. Amateur Ballroom Dance Association reports that the younger generation is most attracted to the Latin and swing varieties.

🌢 While people frequently ballroom dance "just for fun," DanceSport, or competitive ballroom dancing, is gaining momentum. In fact, DanceSport just became an official Olympic sport. Children can enter competitions at young ages, with preteen sections for those who are under age 9.

🌢 In class, your child should wear clothes that have plenty of room for free movement. Most instructors prefer that girls wear a one-piece dress as opposed to a skirt and top, which may creep up and bare the stomach. In addition, girls should wear dance trunks to avoid embarrassment when performing dips, turns, and spins. Boys should wear comfortable pants and shirts.

🌢 Girls can wear dance shoes with a medium heel that have an instep or ankle

Parents bring children into my studio who are shy and awkward. Boys don't even know how to ask a girl to dance, and some boys put their hands in their sleeves so they don't have to touch the girl! Ballroom teaches kids social graces and how to interact with other children.

—*Mario Battista, professional ballroom dancer and owner of Battista Dance Studio, teaching for 13 years*

strap for security and a sole that won't stick to the studio floor. Boys' shoes should be more formal with ties for security and a sole that is appropriate for the floor. Often competitions require dresses for the girls and more formal attire for the boys, so ask the instructor about anticipated costs.

✦ Each instructor will have her own dress and shoe requirements, so it is important to inquire about her preferences when signing up for the class.

Hip-Hop

✦ Hip-hop is a non-partner dance that accentuates athletic body movements. We now see hip-hop on rap and R&B music videos, but the energetic dance started centuries ago in the Caribbean when rhythmic speech and dance were used to tell stories. Eventually, this form of expression became rap and break dancing, a movement that offered young urbanites an inexpensive form of self-expression. The break dancing of the '80s and '90s is based on the "break beat," or the part of a dance song where all sounds but the drums fade away.

✦ Hip-hop emerged out of break dancing and combines dance moves from all over the world in loud, bass-driven music. People use martial arts, reggae, gymnastics, capuera (Brazilian fight dancing), and even disco steps to create new hip-hop styles.

✦ Hip-hop today places more value on the ability of a group to move together in synchronicity rather than individual aerobic performance. While professional dancers make the fast moves look easy, they take considerable time and practice to master.

✦ B-boying, or break dancing, is a form of hip-hop rooted in the Bronx, in New York City. "Up rock," or dancing standing up, spinning, and freezing, or holding unusual gymnastic moves on the floor, are all tests of strength and stamina.

Irish Step Dancing

✦ Some call this unusual, graceful style of dance "ice of the body and fire of the feet" because of the rigid upper-body position and the fast-moving feet. Irish step is the only form of ethnic dance that relies solely on natural balance without the help of outstretched arms. In class, students learn to master the "sevens and threes," which is a side step followed by a 1, 2, 3 step. Hands held stiffly at one's side is one of Irish step dancing's most distinctive characteristics.

✦ Derived from folk dances in the Celtic tradition of the late 18th century, Irish step is now in great demand, and students of Irish step often perform for the public.

In the past six or seven years there has been a surge of media exposure for Irish step dancing. It is an art form that originated in people's kitchens, and now it is on Broadway. A lot of non-Irish people pursue Irish dance. There has also been a general increase in boys taking Irish dance.

—*Niall O'Leary, former world champion and Irish step instructor for 10 years*

The performances of Riverdance introduced Irish dancing to the public at large in the 1990s.

🍀 Beginners will do their "sevens and threes" while learning to hold hands and other arm positions. The teacher will place your child in a hand-holding figure of two, three, four, six, or eight.

🍀 In your child's second or third year of Irish step, she may become part of a four- or eight-person team to do traditional dances. As she increases her skill, your child will need a "hard shoe" fitted with fiberglass heels and tips. These shoes let your child make rhythmic sounds using toe, heel, and ball-of-the-foot combinations.

🍀 The Irish Dancing Commission certifies dance instructors so that their students can be in a *feis* (pronounced "fesh"), or dance competition. Applicants for the certificate must pass a grueling exam that tests their knowledge, ability to perform, and skill at handling students. Candidates earn certificates through three different tests: written, practical, and oral. Only if they pass all requirements will they receive the TCRG (The Coimisiún le Rincí Gaelacha) certificate. If your child wants to compete in Irish dance, her teacher must have a TCRG.

🍀 A *feis* can be found somewhere in the United States every month of the year, although the spring and summer months are the busiest. Dancers can compete solo, in pairs, or as part of a group. Students, as young as preschoolers, compete in one of five levels in the appropriate age bracket from beginners to former prizewinners. Judging is subjective, based on timing, steps, execution and method, and style.

🍀 A costume may be required for a competition or performance. Each school's costume policy will be different. If a profit is made performing for a function or private party, ask if the proceeds will be used to offset travel fees or costume costs, which can run between $50 and $400. Costumes are gabardine and a light wool blend. The Celtic embroidery accounts for about a third of the cost of the costumes. As they grow older, children may need a solo costume, which can run anywhere between $500 and $2,000, since they may be made of raw silk. Kids can choose whatever outrageous color they want. Some have jewels and studs and get very intricate.

🍀 Boys used to wear jackets and plain kilts, but starting in 1994, they began to wear black pants with a plain-colored shirt, a vest, a satiny shirt, and sometimes a tie.

✦ There are two types of Irish dance shoe, soft and hard. Your child will need to learn the basic steps on the soft shoe before moving to the hard shoe. The soft shoe has a suede, cushioned sole and runs between $35 and $70. The hard shoe runs between $70 and $110.

Jazz

✦ Since the 1920s, many creative dance forms have sprung from the explosive rhythms of jazz dance. Examples of jazz dance range from social dances like the charleston to big-band swing to the tap dancing of Fred Astaire.

✦ Jazz dance finds its roots in Africa. African folk culture influenced early 20th-century stage shows in both Europe and America. The infectious toe-tapping moves that accompanied ragtime and other honky-tonk music eventually became jazz dance. It wasn't long before this syncopated, loose style was popularized in ballrooms and dance halls. Today on Broadway, choreographers use jazz to create unrestricted dance moves filled with attitude and energy. Break-dancing, hip-hop, and modern dance are also all influenced by jazz dance.

> Jazz dance helps build self-esteem and body awareness. You use your whole body. It's a wonderful workout that certainly increases muscle tone.
>
> —Gene Murray, owner of Gene Murray School of Dance, teaching for 40 years

✦ Good jazz demands individual expression and improvisation. It can be identified by bursts of energy radiating from the hips, the isolation of body parts, large dramatic movements, and unbroken momentum. Jazz draws its inspiration from a wide variety of dances and social trends, fusing them in clean, efficient movements. Each dancer, choreographer, and director gives jazz a unique and personal interpretation. Jazz technique is more free, less emotional, and less academic than ballet.

✦ The average pair of jazz shoes costs between $20 and $30.

Modern

✦ By the late 19th century in Europe, ballet had reached a standstill. Many felt it had become a frilly showcase for pretty girls rather than a challenging mode of artistic expression. Modern dance was the result of a rebellion against ballet's rigid rules and refusal to change with the times.

✦ The new century was filled with uncertainties and excitement. The influx of TV and other media, as well as innovations in transportation, exposed people to different ideas and foreign cultures. Dancers wanted a way to express their diverse emotions. Modern-dance teachers like Martha Graham and Alvin Ailey rejected the traditional ballerina image, and instead used emotional impulse and cultural elements to create a more lyrical and poetic way of moving.

✦ Modern dance is less rigid than other types of dance, and will teach your child how to bend her body into spirals, contract herself in different positions, and tilt or extend her body in unusual, impressionistic ways. Modern dancers usually dance barefoot.

Salsa/Latin Dance

✦ When people hear salsa music, they usually find it harder to sit still than to get up and move to the beat. This hypnotic rhythm, the most popular type of which is called "mambo," finds its roots in both Europe and Africa. When Africans were transported as slaves to Haiti and Cuba, they brought their musical heritage with them. Mambo, like the conga and bongo, was originally a Bantu name for a musical instrument used in a ritual to mean "conversation with the gods." In the 18th century, this fiery African beat gradually blended with the European settlers' country-dances, or *contradanzas,* as they were known in Spain.

✦ The new mesh of Caribbean syncopation soon transformed into the strong beats and romantic lyrics of salsa. Children especially enjoy the freedom of being able to dance on or across any beat.

Tap

✦ Whereas jazz and ballet provide visual complexity, tap focuses more on intricate rhythms and musical phrasing. In other words, a tap shoe's metal sole turns into a percussion instrument.

✦ When black slaves were first brought to America, slaveholders prohibited the use of drums or any other African instrument out of fear that slaves would communicate over long distances and start a revolt. The slaves resorted to using their feet to keep their indigenous beats alive.

✦ This African dancing fused with Irish and British clog and step dancing to create what is now known as tap. Between 1850 and 1870, early forms of tap could be seen in American minstrel shows. White performers painted their faces black and imitated the dancing of black slaves. It wasn't until after the Civil War that dancers relaxed their posture, arms, and shoulders and added playful gestures.

✦ In the 1930s and early 1940s celebrity dancers like Fred Astaire helped spread a wave of tap dancing across the United States. Jazz rhythms like swing, big band, bebop, funk, and Latin all became popular tap accompaniments.

All children enjoy tap dancing. Tap is an anaerobic workout, and using your feet is a physical challenge. It is a skill-building activity and kids love to learn skills. Tap can teach simple mathematics and the ability to understand the shape of music. Kids also learn to work as a unit. When kids get a step, they feel so successful!

—Eve Agush, The Dance Complex, teaching tap and jazz for 15 years

One interesting tap variation is soft-shoe, in which a performer's shoes don't have metal taps. Some people say this leisurely dance looks and sounds like dancing on sand.

Today, tap has returned to the stage in modern Broadway hits. When talented tap dancers take the stage, an electrifying spirit of fun fills the air.

Tap shoes cost between $30 and $40. Having a metal sole on your shoe will make practicing tap more satisfying, although some beginner classes start with a snug, low-heeled, leather-soled shoe. If your teacher wants a non-leather sole, look for flat tap oxfords with screws, not nails.

Safety Concerns and Injuries

Injuries can occur in dance, but usually from misalignments, and muscle strains are common.

Even with the best training, accidents can happen, and overuse can injure fragile joints like the knee or ankle.

With a daughter in ballet, I am concerned about any emphasis on body image. It's something I'm extremely vigilant about, and deliberately picked a ballet studio with girls of all shapes and sizes. I didn't want a place that emphasized the traditional ballerina figure, which my daughter won't likely have.

—Alexa, mom of Adam, 10, and Sophie, 6

🌪 When your child goes en pointe in ballet, she may develop hammertoes (curled toes), ingrown toenails, and corns. Use padding to relieve pressure. If problems persist, contact your doctor to see if the corns need to be removed.

🌪 Similar to other physical activities where body size and slimness is an issue, body image can be a concern in dance, particularly for girls. See pages 174–175 for more information on signs of eating disorders.

We haven't hit the body issue yet, but sometimes Rachel will comment, "I don't want to get too fat," and I'll say, "You're perfect, so stop that."

—*Ellen, mom of Rachel, 9, Ben, 6, and Josh, 2*

Hopefully, students with body-image issues have a means of talking to the teacher or another student who is more comfortable with herself. If your child is sensitive about her body, look for a studio that does not take weight or height measurements and that may offer outside information on nutrition.

—*Jefferson James, executive director, Contemporary Dance Theater, teaching for 30 years*

At the Center for Dance Education at Boston Ballet, we have a trained psychologist work with our students on body-image issues. Students have seminars to learn about and discuss many issues associated with wellness. Students should always be encouraged to discuss their concerns with parents and teachers.

—*Rachel Moore, director of dance education, Boston Ballet, and former professional ballerina, teaching for 20 years*

Art

OVERVIEW

Art offers one of the greatest means of creative expression for your child, enabling her to experiment with and come up with manifestations of her own design. Kids love making original things, taking great pride in them and feeling a sense of accomplishment from the work they have done. In our fast-paced society, art can be surprisingly relaxing.

General Benefits

⊚ Teaches concentration, problem solving, critical thinking skills, and self-discipline.

⊚ Increased hand-eye coordination and fine motor skills.

⊚ Heightened focus and concentration.

⊚ Teaches creative thinking and an understanding of spatial relationships.

⊚ Teaches color sense, observation skills, and the ability to transform a conceptual idea into reality.

⊚ Expressing emotions through art gives your child an outlet for releasing built-up anxiety or tension.

Kids Who Tend to Excel

⊚ Art not only requires creativity and an open mind but also discipline, patience, the ability to sit quietly for long stretches, and concentration.

When we can explore our creativity through art, we become fuller human beings.

—*Aileen Gildea-Pyne, Artbeat Art instructor, teaching for 20 years*

Art teaches students that they can construct their own world. To create art using a visual reference, students have the opportunity to *analyze* an object or a scene, *evaluate* how they would like to represent that object or scene, and *synthesize* everything by bringing the elements together in a new way. Kids also learn the ability to focus, observe, fail without feeling defeated, problem solve, use high-level thinking skills, and develop spatial perception. The production of art can be a meditative process. Art teaches a child to focus and to use kinesthetic, visual, and auditory modalities.

—*Barbara Verchot, Orlando Museum of Art teacher for 16 years*

Art class brings together a lot of different types of kids who would not otherwise know or talk to each other. The drama queens get to talk with the sports fanatics while working on their projects. Kids are able to work independently on their project but also gossip and have fun at the same time.

—*Emily Grossman, Chestnut Hill Summer Camp art teacher for 8 years*

One of the greatest benefits of art is that it allows children to define in what ways they learn best. Some are more tactile, while others are visual or just great listeners. Another benefit is the sense of empowerment that children feel when they succeed. They realize, "Hey, I can do this," and feel really good about it. There is a huge gamut of children who excel in art. I've seen extroverts really have their personalities brought out in art, and I've seen introverts really come out of themselves because they don't have to speak. They can be in their own worlds and still enjoy art.

—*Pam Shanley, instructor, Arlington Center for the Arts, teaching for 18 years*

Art teaches problem solving. To create a work of art, students must grasp the assignment and see many solutions to it. From those solutions they must select the one that they can physically accomplish, and that pleases them aesthetically. They must plan, perform steps in a certain order, and deal with mistakes. Many kids have a hard time with mistakes. For most artists, taking the risk to make mistakes is where true innovation and success come from.

—*Marla Shoemaker, senior curator of education, Philadelphia Museum of Art, and art instructor for 30 years*

The main thing that kids get out of classes is a means of expressing whatever is on their minds. If they've got fantasy characters running around in their heads; stories about themselves that they want to share, or anything at all that they want to get out of their systems, art is a great outlet.

—*Andrew Farago, manager, The Cartoon Art Museum, teaching for 2 years*

Many of the kids who excel at art are often those who are just "gifted." They have it in their genes. They "see" differently than the rest of us, observe well, and make themselves open to information and suggestions. They have imagination and are intensely expressive. They are interested not only in duplicating and reinterpreting what they see, but imagining what they can't see.

—*Joan Rich, art teacher, Bethesda-Chevy Chase High School, and professional artist*

Students who excel in art understand art*work* takes *work*. Just as learning baseball requires repeated practice time swinging the bat to try to make contact with the ball, art takes repeated attempts at a particular skill. To learn, one must move out of the comfort zone into unknown territory, and be willing to fail. Innate ability may give an edge in the beginning stages, but desire, drive, and a vision to grow are the most important elements for greatness in this field.

—*Barbara Verchot, Orlando Museum of Art teacher for 16 years*

I have seen all types of children come in here, and it never ceases to amaze me who can be a wonderful artist. While some people have more innate artistic talent, it seems to me to be more of a steppingstone than anything else.

—*Gwyneth Welch, founder, Monart School of the Arts, teaching for 20 years*

Kids who do best have the ability to focus, think in new ways with curiosity, and come to solutions that evolve.

—*George Di Bouno, art specialist at Holdrum Middle School, teaching for 39 years*

To make the ordinary into something extraordinary, artists have to take risks! Too many children and adults assume that artists are born, not made. While some children do have innate abilities to "see" and to record what they see and feel, many more artists become successful after many hours, days, and years of practice, practice, practice. It takes hard work to be a successful visual artist.

—*Donna Banning, visual arts instructor, El Modena High School, member National Art Education Association (NAEA) board of directors, and practicing artist, teaching for 33 years*

It helps if your child has innate talent, but with patience, skill in art can definitely be developed.

In art, children who do well learn to be able to think "outside the box," learning to express themselves and solve artistic problems in innovative and original ways. They must also master materials and tools to achieve a level of craftsmanship that will enable them to be expressive with the skills honed.

Best Age to Start

While kids can get immersed in art at an early age, most children do not start formalized classes until age 6. However, art can be picked up at any age.

Parents who feel that their children are artistic prodigies often push them into organized lessons much too early. Early teens is time enough for serious lessons in art.

—*Donna Banning, visual arts instructor, El Modena High School, member NAEA board of directors, and practicing artist, teaching for 33 years*

Preschool is not too early, if the program you select is particularly geared for that age group. One huge caveat: Rarely is it a good idea to ask that your child be placed with a group older than his real age, because he seems to have special skills beyond those of his age-related peers. Art classes are a social activity as well as an art instruction time, and our experience is that students moved into a more advanced class do not enjoy the experience, and we often move them back. Also, just because your preschooler can draw well doesn't mean he can mix colors, or wrap with paper, or sculpt with clay.

—*Marla Shoemaker, senior curator of education, Philadelphia Museum of Art, and art instructor for 30 years*

What to Look For When Getting Started

🖌 The teacher should encourage your child to create her own unique art, rather than setting up a prescribed project with explicit instructions for the end result. Ask to see the projects that kids have done in previous classes. When looking into a serious art class, ask to see some of the portfolios of the teacher's students.

🖌 In order to ensure the type of individual focus that art demands, classes should ideally have no more than eight children per teacher. Make sure that the teacher is organized and able to pay attention to all of the students equally.

🖌 The teacher should be an experienced artist who has taught kids before. Make sure that she is not controlling, and she is willing to get dirty right along with the kids.

🖌 Kids don't want to be told what to do. Instead, an art teacher should offer ideas and make suggestions but ultimately leave it to them to discover their own artwork and abilities.

There are teachers who have children "copy" from a photo or other specific image, but I prefer an open-ended class. I took classes where a still life was set up in a room, you came in, started drawing or painting, and the teachers commented on your specific project as they walked around. In contrast, I think classes where a child is free to explore with a medium work best, as there's less copying and more creativity.

—Joan Rich, art teacher, Bethesda-Chevy Chase High School, and professional artist

The teacher should encourage kids to envision what they are going to create before they start the process of creating art. This not only improves their artwork, but it also improves and broadens their imaginations.

—Emily Grossman, Chestnut Hill Summer Camp art teacher for 8 years

A good instructor will place a dual emphasis on learning the art process with keeping an eye towards presenting the "product," such as an exhibit. A program should instill in students an understanding and appreciation of the important role art plays in life.

—Theodora Merry, executive director, Neighborhood School of the Arts, teaching for 9 years

A teacher should have a wide variety of skills to expose students to the widest possible variety of areas and mediums. Students who excel in one medium might be challenged in another. Avoid teachers who set up art projects with preplanned results, which are deadening. Instead, a child should have the opportunity to come up with creative personal expressions of a visual idea. Product without thought is not art, it's just "stuff."

—George Di Bouno, art specialist at Holdrum Middle School, teaching for 39 years

POPULAR TYPES OF ART CLASS

Animation/Cartooning

🌵 These classes teach inking, human proportion, perspective, use of color and tone, and basic drawing technique.

🌵 Your child will learn about key frames, line of action, captions, and lettering while creating comic book pages. Ask about the subject matter: Will your child be drawing superheroes or something autobiographical?

Calligraphy

🌵 Calligraphy, the art of highly stylized writing, teaches your child discipline, patience, and persistence. Some classes teach calligraphy in Chinese characters, as well as those of other foreign languages. Calligraphy can also be relaxing.

Ceramics, Pottery, and Wheel Working

🌵 Ceramics teaches making creations with clay—from sculpture to pinching, building with slabs or coils, and wheel throwing. Pottery is creating hand-built ware. A good teacher will explain where the clay is found, how it is manufactured, how it is fired, the appropriate temperatures to fire at, and how glazes, stains, and underglazes are made, applied, and fired.

Children tend to begin drawing a cartoon at the eyes or hands. A good instructor will notice this, get them to look at the overall picture, and start with simple circles for the stomach or head. I have also observed that kids who are insecure about their abilities tend to draw really small figures and kids who are secure draw big figures. Well, I try to get the insecure kids to draw big figures and break out of their insecurities.

—*Paul Rufe, drawing and cartooning instructor*

The best part of the pottery class my daughter took this fall was that she came home after the last class with holiday presents made for each family member!

—*Alexa, mom of Adam, 11, and Sophie, 7*

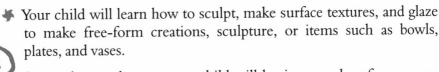

🌵 Your child will learn how to sculpt, make surface textures, and glaze to make free-form creations, sculpture, or items such as bowls, plates, and vases.

🌵 As classes advance, your child will begin to explore form, mass, scale, color, and texture, and will work with various types of clay medium.

Pottery and wheel working teach skill in manipulating a three-dimensional formless material into a three-dimensional result.

—*George Di Bouno, art specialist at Holdrum Middle School, teaching for 39 years*

In a pottery and wheel-working class, make sure that everyone gets adequate time on the pottery wheel. Twenty students and one wheel will not give students enough time to begin to develop confidence.

—*Marla Shoemaker, senior curator of education, Philadelphia Museum of Art, and art instructor for 30 years*

✹ Starting around age 8, your child may move on to wheel work, which involves centering the clay, opening up the piece, pulling up the walls, trimming the base, and glazing.

✹ Ask if kiln charges are included in your child's class cost.

Painting and Drawing

✹ In painting classes, your child will study techniques for watercolor, acrylic, and tempera paints. Classes work from your child's own imagination, photos from magazines, still lifes, or famous paintings. As she advances, your child will learn brush techniques, color theory, and composition. Beginner classes start with tempera paint and then move on to watercolor, each of these water-based paints having unique characteristics that take time to learn and master.

✹ In drawing classes, your child will work with pencils, charcoal, and ink.

✹ When choosing classes, keep in mind that there are widely divergent types of painting. Ask about what techniques or style the teacher emphasizes.

✹ Ask if materials will be supplied, as watercolor papers are expensive, and there is no substitute for a decent grade of paper, as well as quality flat, round, and linear brushes.

Painting and drawing offer your child the chance to observe, record, and manipulate the real. I teach my students to think of drawing as marks on paper, while painting is modeling on a two-dimensional surface.

—*George Di Bouno, art specialist at Holdrum Middle School, teaching for 39 years*

For painting and drawing, look for a studio where one can make a mess, as well as one that has high-quality brushes, paper, and drawing implements. A teacher needs to have a creative approach to introducing rendering in two dimensions, which is very hard for students.

—*Marla Shoemaker, senior curator of education, Philadelphia Museum of Art, and art instructor for 30 years*

Look for a teacher who emphasizes that there is no "right" or "wrong" way to draw, and respects each child's artwork as a unique creation. Find a program that really teaches students how to draw and how to use specific techniques. So often art schools will teach nothing, believing that this will "stifle the child's creativity." I always counter that the creative abilities of Michelangelo, da Vinci, Rembrandt, and Picasso were not stifled by learning how to draw and use media.

—*Gwyneth Welch, founder, Monart School of the Art, teaching for 20 years*

A drawing and painting course should be well grounded in the basics of the elements of art and the principles of design. Students should be provided with opportunities to "see" the world around them and produce works of art using a variety of materials. Students should draw the figure, the landscape, the still life, and use their imaginations to create works of art that build knowledge of composition, mood, and space and eventually express personal opinions and ideas.

—*Donna Banning, visual arts instructor, El Modena High School, member NAEA board of directors, and practicing artist, teaching for 33 years*

Photography involves aesthetics and chemistry. It offers the chance to capture some visual moment or mood and share it with others, along with the chance to manipulate light and shadow.

—George Di Bouno, art specialist at Holdrum Middle School, teaching for 39 years

Photography

✦ Classes teach fundamentals of using a camera, including how to frame, center, and focus a picture. Advanced classes teach film exposure and darkroom printing. Ask about whether your child will be taking black-and-white photos, color, or both.

✦ The instructor should also teach the elements of art and the principles of design, and how they are merged in photography.

✦ Equipment costs can be high depending on the level of the class, the type of equipment and film required, and whether the program provides the cameras.

Sculpture

✦ Sculpture offers your child the chance to explore the concepts of form and space.

✦ Sculpture brings unique challenges, as working in three dimensions is very difficult. It takes a special skill and understanding of form and materials to create interesting three-dimensional forms.

Kids learn to think three-dimensionally when they work on a sculpture. In sculpture, you manipulate real materials in real space and create a new object. Kids also learn how to manipulate wood, clay, plaster, and other materials.

—Harold Olejarz, professional sculptor and teacher for 14 years

Carving stone requires an inordinate amount of patience. Paper and cardboard sculpture is another challenge. Found materials can provide the student with an opportunity to recycle materials and use them in new ways and make them reflect on the commercialism, the throw-away generation, and the excess of our society. Wonderful statements about society in general and specifically can be made!

—Donna Banning, visual arts instructor, El Modena High School, member NAEA board of directors, and practicing artist, teaching for 33 years

In a sculpture class, look for one that introduces a variety of materials and techniques, from carving, assembling, and modeling to working with both soft and hard media.

—*Marla Shoemaker, senior curator of education, Philadelphia Museum of Art, and art instructor for 30 years*

Sewing, Quilting, and Needlework

Classes teach hand stitches, embroidery, quilting, patchwork, appliqué, button sewing, crochet, knitting, or machine sewing. Your child will work on anything from making a pillow to creating clothing. In the process of learning to sew, your child will work on measuring, spatial relationships, problem solving, and critical thinking skills.

Woodworking

Woodworking classes teach building and lathe (wood turning) work. Your child will create wooden items such as boxes, spinning tops, bookcases, and similar projects.

Students have to follow strict rules of equipment use, learn how the machines

Danny is one of these boys who absolutely love working with tools. Since age 3, he's had his own real hammer, and over the past couple of years we've added a real saw and pickaxe, which he uses at home. When we recently did a home renovation, the workers couldn't believe what he could do at age 4. So we have just signed him up to start a woodworking class.

—*Dee, mom of Carey, 8, and Danny, 5*

In woodworking, a beautiful, well-executed piece can speak to one the way a painting or a piece of music does.

—*George Di Bouno, art specialist at Holdrum Middle School, teaching for 39 years*

The tactile qualities of pushing a needle through the fabric, the hand-eye coordination and the exercise of small motor skills all benefit a child who is as young as 4 years old. The science of dyeing fabric is always a fun way to teach math skills as well as chemistry. Children can start sewing around age 4 or 5 with supervision and depending on their attention span.

—*Marjorie McWilliams, quilting teacher for 15 years*

are used, and learn craftsmanship. The program almost always provides safety goggles and woodworking tools.

Safety and Injury Concerns

🌢 Make sure the program uses age-appropriate art supplies. Students should always be instructed on the proper use of tools being used to create a project.

🌢 Make sure your child's art teacher uses nontoxic materials until students are mature enough to handle materials that are potentially harmful, such as turpentine or lead-based glazes for clay. Some fixative sprays and paint solvents are very toxic and potentially carcinogenic, but most are labeled as such.

🌢 Hot melt glue cans may cause burns if not used properly.

🌢 Be especially careful in sculpture and woodworking classes, where cutting tools are used.

Cost Considerations

🌢 Ask if there is a separate supply fee apart from tuition, or what supplies your child will be expected to purchase on her own. Tuition fees and supply costs vary dramatically based on the medium. Some classes charge as little as $20 for supplies, while more advanced classes can cost $100–$200 to cover materials.

🌢 Also ask if your child will have to pay for any special processes or contribute to exhibition costs.

Art and Performing Arts Resources

MUSIC

The National Association for Music Education (MENC)
1806 Robert Fulton Drive
Reston, VA 20191
(800) 336-3768
www.menc.org

Founded in 1907, MENC aims to advance music education, and has over 90,000 members representing all levels of teaching from pre-kindergarten to postdoctoral levels. The organization addresses all aspects of music education from band, chorus, orchestra, general music, to teacher education and research.

Music Teachers National Association (MTNA)
441 Vine St., Suite 505
Cincinnati, OH 45202
(888) 512-5278
mtnanet@mtna.org
www.mtna.org

The MTNA is a nonprofit organization of 24,000 independent and collegiate music teachers committed to advancing the value of music study and music making to society and to supporting the professionalism of music teachers. The Web site has a directory of nationally certified private teachers, who have fulfilled requirements that include a videotaped review of student performances, teaching demonstration, review of their policies and curriculum, and specific educational requirements.

American Harp Society

www.harpsociety.org

Organization for harpists.

American String Teachers Association with National School Orchestra Association (ASTA with NSOA)

www.astaweb.com

This association represents more than 11,000 string and orchestra teachers and players.

American Viola Society (AVS)

www.americanviolasociety.org

The AVS is an association for violists.

Guitar Foundation of America

www.guitarfoundation.org

America's leading guitar organization.

National Flute Association

www.nfaonline.org

An international organization for flutists with over 6,000 members. A student membership costs $30.

North American Saxophone Alliance

www.saxalliance.org

The North American Saxophone Alliance is a professional music organization for the saxophone.

International Clarinet Association

www.clarinet.org

The international organization for clarinetists.

International Double Reed Society

norma4IDRS@erols.com

The professional society for double reed instruments, the oboe and the bassoon family, with over 4,000 members.

International Horn Society

www.hornsociety.org

The national organization for horn players.

International Saxophone

www.saxophone.org

An extensive online information resource for saxophonists.

International Society of Bassists (ISB)

www.isbworldoffice.com

The ISB is an organization for the double bass.

International Trumpet Guild

www.trumpetguild.org

Organization for trumpet players around the world, with over 7,000 members.

International Trombone Association

www.ita-web.org

The national organization for trombonists.

Internet Cello Society

www.cello.org

Organization for cellists.

Percussive Arts Society (PAS)

www.pas.org

The PAS is a music service organization promoting percussion education, research, performance, and appreciation throughout the world.

The Piano Guild

www.pianoguild.com

This is the largest nonprofit organization of piano teachers and students.

T.U.B.A.

www.tubaonline.org

The International Tuba-Euphonium Association (ITEA) is an international organization to promote the euphonium and tuba.

Violin Society of America (VSA)

www.vsa.to

The VSA covers the violin, viola, cello, and bass.

National Association of Teachers of Singing (NATS)

4745 Sutton Park Court, Suite #201
Jacksonville, FL 32224
(904) 992-9101
info@nats.org
www.nats.org

The NATS is a nonprofit organization dedicated to encouraging the highest standards of singing, teaching, and promoting vocal education and research. With over 5,000 members, it is the largest association of teachers of singing in the world. NATS chapters and regions host annual "Student Adjudications" where singers perform and receive written feedback about their performance. The organization has a searchable database of teachers.

THEATER

American Alliance for Theatre and Education

c/o Dept. of Theatre, Arizona State University, Box 872002
Tempe, AZ 85287-2002
(602) 965-6064
aateinfo@asuvm.inre.asu.edu

This organization serves as a network for theater artists and K–12 educators who work with young people.

National Endowment for the Arts: Theater and Children

1100 Pennsylvania Ave. N.W.
Washington, DC 20506
arts.endow.gov

An independent agency of the federal government, NEA's Arts in Education Program focuses on arts programs in schools nationwide. You can select Theater and Musical Theater under "Art Forms" and find a "Resource Center" that provides more regional contact information.

DANCE

Dance has very few overarching national organizations, and the most comprehensive set of links to regional and local organizations can be found at two privately maintained sites:

ⓔ scarecrow.caps.ou.edu/~hneeman/dance_hotlist.html

ⓔ www.dancer.com/dance-links/

Dance/USA

1156 15th St. N.W., Suite 820
Washington, DC 20005
(202) 833-1717
danceusa@danceusa.org
www.danceusa.org

Dance/USA supports dance by addressing the needs and interests of the professional dance community. Its Web site has extensive resource links.

International Tap Association

P.O. Box 356
Boulder, CO 80306
(303) 443-7989
intertap@concentric.net
www.tapdance.org/tap/

The Web site enables you to find local tap programs, and includes information about traditional tap, clogging, and Irish step dancing.

U.S. Amateur Ballroom Dancers Association (USABDA)

P.O. Box 128
New Freedom, PA 17349
(800) 447-9047
www.usabda.org

This nationwide nonprofit organization, also known as USA DanceSport, serves as the official national governing body for amateur ballroom dancing and DanceSport, the competitive version of ballroom dancing.

National Endowment for the Arts

arts.endow.gov

An independent agency of the federal government, the Endowment nationally recognizes and supports projects of artistic excellence and aims to preserve and enhance diversity in our culture. Under the Resources heading is a long list of smaller dance organizations.

National Dance Association (NDA)

1900 Association Drive
Reston, VA 20191-1599
(703) 476-3436
nda@aahperd.org
www.aahperd.org/nda/

The NDA, founded in 1932, aims to increase knowledge, improve skills, and encourage sound professional practices in dance education.

ART

National Art Education Association (NAEA)

1916 Association Drive
Reston, VA 20191-1590
(703) 860-8000
Fax: (703) 860-2960
www.naea-reston.org

This nonprofit, educational organization has over 22,000 art educator members who come from every level of instruction: early childhood to college and university. Founded in 1947, NAEA's participants include all 50 states, most Canadian provinces, and 25 foreign countries.

PART IV

INTELLECTUAL AND COMMUNITY ACTIVITIES

18

Intellectual Activities

CHESS

Overview

Chess, the oldest skill game in the world, traces back centuries to China, India, and Persia. It quickly spread to Europe when the Moors, who learned chess from the Persians, invaded Spain and brought the game with them. Europeans gave chess pieces their current names. Their symbolism is fascinating, and a story you can tell your child. The pawns in abundance represent serfs, the laborers considered property of the landowners. The castle piece (rook) is the home, just as in medieval times. The knights represent the professional soldiers, and the bishops the church, a powerful force in medieval times. The queen, the only woman and the most powerful piece of the game, reflects her role as an adviser to the king. In medieval times, the surrender of the king would mean the loss of the kingdom to invading armies, and so the game of chess is lost by not protecting the king.

Chess has earned a reputation as the intellectual game for nonathletes, helping children excel academically, especially in math. The U.S. Chess Federation now has over 31,000 members ages 14 and under, up from only 3,000 junior members a decade ago.

> Chess is one of the few games I know of that appeals to all ages, genders, ethnic groups, and professions. It is a game that can never be completely mastered and, therefore, provides unlimited potential for study and improvement.
>
> —Susan Breeding, tournament director, U.S. Chess Federation, teaching for 14 years

General Benefits

◉ Chess teaches logic based on strategic planning of actions and reactions. It also helps your child anticipate the consequences of his actions and think creatively.

◉ It improves concentration, focus, self-discipline, calculation, and critical thinking skills.

◉ Chess enhances memory skills, as a player must remember prior moves and strategies to plan an attack and also because there are so many moves one can make in the first 10 moves of the game.

◉ As players must be keenly aware of position and an opponent's responses, reactions, and strategies, chess develops awareness and analysis and teaches pattern recognition.

◉ When played competitively, chess helps children make quick decisions under a great amount of pressure.

Kids Who Tend to Excel

◉ Typically, children who excel at chess have the ability to concentrate extremely well, and many are either music- or math-oriented.

◉ Children tend to be equally split between introverts and extroverts.

Best Age to Start

◉ While a child can be taught the rudiments of chess as young as age 5, most children join a chess club or start lessons around age 7, which is when most kids develop the ability to focus and concentrate on the game.

◉ The younger a child starts, the more difficult it will be for him to understand the complexities of the rules and strategies.

Chess teaches critical thinking skills, problem solving, patience, considering the consequences of one's actions, making the best choice from several good possibilities, and good sportsmanship. It teaches you to stay focused on one activity for an extended period of time. Socially, chess is an especially wonderful activity for children, channeling their time and energy in a very positive direction, and giving them the tools that allows them to interact with adults.

—*Susan Breeding, tournament director, U.S. Chess Federation, teaching for 14 years*

Chess is a cross-cultural, intergenerational activity played in every country of the world. Chess aids in the development of "visualization" and foresight, problem solving, critical thinking, and self-analysis. The mental skills required, and developed, by chess are transferable to other academic, intellectual, and social situations. For example, the time-management skills developed in using a chess clock have been shown to aid students who previously performed poorly on timed tests.

—*Omar Pancoast III, chess director, C&O Family Chess Center, teaching for 30 years*

The best thing kids can get out of chess is having an instructor who serves as a mentor to encourage them and teach them about life. There are many ways to relate chess to our journey in life. Patience, sportsmanship, problem-solving skills, and self-discipline are just a few.

—*Kevin Batangan, instructor, Success Chess School, and private tutor for 3 years*

Chess teaches kids logical thinking and concentration skills, from how to evaluate positions, select alternative courses of actions, analyze the consequences of a given set of actions, calculate their opponents' choices and responses, and live with the results of their decisions.

—*Peter Lee, chess club coordinator and coach for 5 years*

The typical qualities of children who most excel in chess are: a competitive spirit, an inquisitive mind, patience, a willingness to lose often in order to get better, and supportive parents or other influential adults.

—*Susan Breeding, tournament director for U.S. Chess Federation, teaching for 14 years*

They have a fighting spirit that brings out the best of their skills. They work hard at chess by reading books or taking lessons and they have a true love of the game.

—*Kevin Batangan, instructor, Success Chess School, and private tutor for 3 years*

Contrary to what many people believe, you don't have to be "smart" to play chess. In fact, I tell people that chess "makes you smarter!"

—*Omar Pancoast III, chess director, C&O Family Chess Center, teaching for 30 years*

What to Look For When Getting Started

✦ Chess can be engaged in on many levels from casual, social play through organized scholastic and club play, to local, state, national, and international competition.

✦ Find an instructor with the patience to teach children, especially younger ones. There's a common tendency among chess teachers to teach over the heads of students, resulting in both your child and teacher becoming frustrated by the lack of progress. If you are considering a private tutor for your child, look for an instructor willing to adapt to your child's needs and skill level.

✦ Seek out recommendations from parents of children who have been taking lessons from a specific teacher for at least a year, and interview the instructor to see if his personality complements that of your child. Many chess club programs offer free help for beginners from older players.

✦ In a group lesson, look for a ratio of at least 1 adult for every 8 students.

✦ Instruction time should balance teaching basic strategies and tactics with playing time. Ask whether instruction takes place in the form of short lessons or individual help. In some programs the children simply come and play for an hour or so while the instructor only works with a few of the kids.

🦃 It is highly recommended that children always play touch-move and touch-capture, as this rule applies to all tournaments. If you touch a piece with your hands, you have to move that piece as long as it has a legal move. This rule enables your child to understand true cause-and-effect thinking, which leads him to be a skillful and mature player. The difficult part of touch-move is if the piece touched has no good moves, then the player is stuck, has to move it, and will most likely lose the piece.

🦃 At chess clubs, children usually begin by playing others their own age or skill level, but your child can meet many different kinds of players with a wide array of styles. Because of the variety of players, your child will meet stronger opponents who will help him improve. Also, your child will have the chance to make friends who share his interest in chess.

🦃 The decision to enter tournaments depends on your child's emotional maturity. The first time your child plays, he will likely be up against more experienced players. Try to find an instructor who is actively involved with chess tournaments.

🦃 Most tournaments are timed, except for beginners, to ensure that each round starts on time and games do not extend too long. A chess clock, composed of two connected clocks, has two push buttons on top of each. When one is pressed, the other button is pushed up and causes that clock to begin ticking. The added time pressure makes the game more challenging, because if your clock runs out, you lose. Common time controls are either 30, 60, or 90 minutes, during which specified time each player must complete his moves or lose based on running out of time. Games with time controls between 10 and 29 minutes inclusive fall into the separate category of "Quick Chess" for ranking purposes.

Cost Considerations

🦃 Depending on an instructor's credentials, private chess lessons range from $15 to $50 per hour.

🦃 Depending on your child's age and if he wants to play tournament chess, membership in the U.S. Chess Federation has an annual fee of $13–$40 a year.

🦃 In addition to membership fees, tournament fees range from $10 to $50 per tournament. National fees are more expensive than local fees.

Many higher-rated teachers get extremely frustrated when the child does not always see what the teacher sees as second nature. Too many coaches focus on winning, when the focus should be on learning, improving, and becoming more competent at chess. As long as the child can go over his game, and understand where he went wrong, he's learned and hopefully will not repeat the same mistake twice.

—*Peter Lee, chess club coordinator and coach for 5 years*

With beginners and intermediates it is more important to have a teacher who is experienced with children and has the patience of a saint rather than to have a chess "master." Also of note, many girls who have been active, strong chess players during elementary school lose interest shortly after the onset of puberty. No one is sure of the reasons, but in spite of massive outreach within the chess community, chess after elementary school remains a male-dominated activity at all levels. Some of my top students have been girls, but without exception their level of involvement has dropped off sharply between the ages of 11 and 14. It's very frustrating!

—*Omar Pancoast III, chess director, C&O Family Chess Center, teaching for 30 years*

❧ If your child wants to play competitive chess, he will need a chess clock. While chess equipment is typically cheap, the chess clock ranges from about $25 to $120.

❧ Traveling expenses for away tournaments can become quite costly due to the hotel and meal expenses.

FOREIGN LANGUAGE STUDY

Overview

Between birth and age 8, your child's brain is uniquely hard-wired to absorb languages and to learn to pronounce words with a native accent. Children learn languages very differently from adults, with studies finding that children even store a second language in a different area of the brain. While children engage in fun activities in a foreign language, such as singing, storytelling, or cooking projects, they naturally take in and start to use the new language comfortably and effortlessly.

You may wonder whether learning a second language before your child has yet to fully master English will detract from his learning ability. To the contrary, learning the roots and structure of a second language typically enhances your child's English. As long as children hear these languages methodically and regularly, they can learn more than one simultaneously.

As children approach puberty, neural connections develop, and the nature of language learning and storage changes, becoming less flexible. Between the ages of 8 and 12, studies have shown that children lose the ability to hear and reproduce new sounds, resulting in a foreign-sounding accent in the second language.

General Benefits

◉ The benefits of learning a second language are linguistic, cognitive, social, and cultural, including: heightened creativity, enhanced problem-solving and spatial relations skills, improved listening skills, and ability to learn a third or fourth language more easily.

◉ Many children who learn a second language perform better on cognitive and verbal tests as well as on standardized tests such as the SAT. Research also suggests that learning a second language improves your child's analytical and math skills.

◉ Languages enable your child to understand other cultures, appreciate people from other countries, and potentially have a competitive advantage in the workforce.

◉ Studies now show that a child taught a second language after age 10 is unlikely to ever speak it like a native. Experts attribute this phenomenon to physiological changes that occur in the brain as a child enters puberty.

◉ Because kids are less self-conscious than adults, they rarely fear saying something funny or getting a concept wrong. This lack of embarrassment or inhibition aids them in pronouncing foreign words correctly and becoming fluent sooner than adults.

Kids Who Tend to Excel

A language student who excels:

◉ imitates easily

◉ displays verbal astuteness

Many English words share Latin roots with Spanish, French, and other Romance-language synonyms. Learning the meaning of foreign words develops a student's capacity to analyze the meaning of native English words. Consistently studying another language builds a student's inventory of root word similarities.

—*François Thibaut, founder of The Language Workshop for Children, teaching for 30 years*

Kids develop an understanding of other people and other people's ways of looking at the world. They experience a sense of accomplishment and pride upon successfully communicating with others who share the new language, and gain an enhanced perspective on their own language and culture.

—*Tove Dahl, language professor, University of Tromsø, teaching for 24 years*

- has strong skills in his first language
- has a good memory
- welcomes new challenges.

Best Age to Start

The earlier children start learning a second language, the better, even as early as one year old. Many teachers and linguists recommend starting the language learning process as soon as possible, even before children become verbal in their first

The interests and talents of those kids who excel can vary wildly. As long as kids can see that the language brings them closer to the kinds of things they like to do or know and sufficient resources for learning the language are available, any language can be mastered by virtually anyone. The bottom line is that those who are curious perhaps do best.

—*Tove Dahl, language professor, University of Tromsø, teaching for 24 years*

Surprisingly, there is not a lot of research that identifies the kids who excel in language classes. Basically, it comes down to good teachers and hard work by students, combined with parental support, motivation, and good learning strategies.

—*Craig Packard, ERIC Clearinghouse, Center for Applied Linguistics*

When children are not self-conscious, they aren't afraid of getting a new word wrong or saying it funny. Their lack of inhibition helps them verbalize foreign words and become fluent sooner.

—*François Thibaut, founder, The Language Workshop for Children, teaching for 30 years*

language. Even though children are not speaking at that point, they are actively absorbing and processing language.

By 6 months, children in English-speaking households already have developed different auditory maps, shown by electrical measurements that identify which neurons respond to different sounds, from those in Swedish-speaking homes. This is why learning a second language after, rather than with, the first is so difficult. The auditory map of the first language restricts the learning of a second language.

After the age of 10, children are unlikely to speak a newly learned language like a native. Still, it is absolutely feasible to learn a new language, and learn it well, as an adolescent or even an adult. For students in middle or high school, foreign language learning often becomes a part of their regular academic curriculum. It often helps to augment your child's classroom learning if he participates in a language club—where the language is used conversationally, led by a native speaker—or in a home-stay program during the summer, immersed in a country where the language is spoken.

What to Look For When Getting Started

Visual aids, workbooks, and songs are important to facilitate learning a different language.

Ask if the teachers are native speakers, as children absorb the accent they hear. If you're enrolling in a program, does the director speak that language such that he's capable of judging a teacher's accent and choice of vocabulary?

The earlier, the better is the usual wisdom. A child raised from the start with more than one language in the home or community can develop native-like skills in several languages; although if one predominates in frequency of usage, that will likely become the child's dominant language.

—*Nancy Stenson, associate professor, Minneapolis Institute of Linguistics*

Basically, there is no single "best age." One can learn a second language at any age, although some language-learning goals are more appropriate to certain ages than others. As a general rule, children who begin foreign or second language study before adolescence are more likely to achieve native-like pronunciation in a second language than those who begin such study during or after adolescence—that's perhaps the major difference. There is also evidence that learning a foreign language at a young age does make a significant contribution to academic achievement in general, mastery of communication skills, and cognitive development.

—*Craig Packard, ERIC Clearinghouse, Center for Applied Linguistics*

Between 10 and 20 months, toddlers start what linguists term their "one-word stage." Before that, they simply listen and store what they hear. This is the prime of what psycholinguists and neurolinguists term their "critical period" the time of their greatest neurological capacity to absorb and store language. During this stage, and until the brain begins losing plasticity at 12 or 13, children possess their greatest potential to absorb and retain languages. Don't let your child's prime time to learn a new language slip away. Words and phrases we learn *before* puberty will always be pronounced differently than words and phrases learned afterward. Why? Because language learned after puberty is stored in a completely different place in the left hemisphere's Broca's area. That is why my accent will always be "charming."

—*François Thibaut, founder of The Language Workshop for Children, teaching for 30 years*

🐟 Be wary of programs classified as using a "proven method." Make sure the program has a method, and that students are not just singing and playing in another language.

🐟 In terms of your involvement outside of formal lessons, you do not have to speak the language your child is learning in order to help him be successful. Find ways to expose your child to the new language and encourage him to use the language outside of class. Check out language books from the library, buy children's music in the language, and watch videos in the language.

🦋 While children over 8 years old can be effectively privately tutored, they often thrive with stimulation and company of other children. Consider arranging group language lessons with friends at someone's home, where a group of five kids can learn the language together.

Language Immersion Programs

🦋 Immersion means that from the moment that children walk into the room, all activities are conducted entirely in the foreign language. Young children are

For your child to sound like a native speaker, a native speaker must teach him. Pay attention to the accent your child is acquiring. Children absorb the accent they hear. We judge a speaker's education by the accent he uses. Ask whether your teacher is a native speaker. Also, children learn best through play, absorbing more in a relaxed, emotionally supportive, happy environment. The play must also be part of a structured, progressive curriculum, delivered with a consistent technique, so that your child will remember next year what he's learned.

—*François Thibaut, founder of The Language Workshop for Children, teaching for 30 years*

Most parents don't have any idea about what is being taught in a language class and just put all their faith in the school. And sometimes the curriculum is inane—numbers, colors, simply copying the names of cities in South America, you name it. Are kids engaged in meaningful communication in their precious few minutes a week? Would the language the kids learn help them talk to people on the streets if they were to visit a town in Mexico or in the South of France? That's the kind of question parents don't usually ask and could. Also, avoid teachers with an excessive focus on grammar, as it drives most kids crazy. Kids can waste countless hours in programs where some foreign language is taught by drills. In such mindless tasks, kids put their minds in neutral. Their brain's learning centers are not truly engaged, and they just go through the motions of learning language.

—*Andrew Cohen, professor of applied linguistics, University of Minnesota, and director of National Language Resource Center*

I want my children to speak many languages, and languages are so hard. Their father is German, and I grew up speaking Chinese. So I make our oldest study both, a little every week. I've found that the only thing that makes this successful is to get really involved myself. So now we play German computer games, watch German videos, and take family trips to Germany. We've hired baby-sitters who speak German. The best has been peers who don't speak any English at all, but these kids are hard to come by! My oldest is now learning some, despite his reluctance. My middle son has an aptitude for languages and likes it.

—*Karla, mom of Karl, 9, Max 6, and Leo, 3*

Look for a teacher who has experience with children, a high level of fluency in the language, an understanding of the principles of language acquisition, and uses activities that are fun and age-appropriate. Maximum exposure time to language will maximize expertise, but frustration and boredom are issues, as with any academic subject. Little chance to use the language outside the classroom can damage your child's interest level as well.

—*Nancy Stenson, associate professor, Minneapolis Institute of Linguistics*

The key is to find a program that creates a fun, positive, nonstressful, and nurturing environment for kids to learn. Look for teachers with a unique combination of native speaking ability, passion for teaching, and tremendous energy.

—*Karen Gould, education director of Language Stars language immersion program for 1,500 children*

uniquely suited to absorb a second language as naturally as their first. They learn more effectively without translation or English equivalents.

🐟 Mostly English-speaking parents, who want to foster bilingualism, place their toddlers in these programs. Spanish, French, Chinese, and Japanese lessons are being offered at selected child-care centers and preschools.

🐟 A child's emotional, social, and intellectual growth are further developed by participating in various activities, such as storytelling, music, drawing, arts and crafts, blocks, counting, and reading, in a different language. In addition, engaging in routine activities, such as snacktime and cleanup, in a different language also fosters their skills.

🦋 Children learn best through relaxing and enjoyable play. However, if the play does not include a structured curriculum, taught with consistent technique, your child may have fun but will not have learned much.

Cost Considerations

🦋 Costs vary so dramatically, depending on the length of the language program and the materials included in the fee, that it is hard to give average costs.

🦋 Find out if your child will have to purchase any materials such as learning tapes or CDs or if they are included.

In our programs, teachers use dynamic presentation, colorful visuals, and sheltered language to accelerate a child's comprehension and active verbal skills. Our philosophy is to combine 100% immersion in the foreign language with 100% fun. Fun means we take our curriculum and linguistic goals and implement them through games, songs, drama, stories, movement, cooking projects, arts and crafts, and more.

—*Karen Gould, education director, Language Stars language immersion program for 1,500 children*

When kids land in an environment where it is natural and cool to speak the target language, some kids already speak it relatively well, and the staff models fun activities possible with the target language, beginners quickly aspire to be among the cool by becoming target language masters too. With that kind of linguistic and motivational scaffolding, amazing things are possible! One of the wonders of immersion programs is that learners are just as much teachers for each other as the hired teachers are. By speaking with each other, testing what kids have learned with friends in their daily interactions, their friends' responses give kids a good idea of how they are doing. Also, when friends use expressions that others don't yet know, the others are easily motivated to learn and adopt them into their repertoire too.

—*Tove Dahl, language professor, University of Tromsø, teaching for 24 years*

> Even the best immersion programs don't necessarily do the trick for all kids, as learning a language is so individual. Some flourish in such environments, but others shut down and do most of their cognitive processing in English. They are "languaging" in English, not in the target language, but the teacher can't see that.
>
> —*Andrew Cohen, professor of applied linguistics, University of Minnesota, and director of National Language Resource Center*

ODYSSEY OF THE MIND

Overview

Odyssey of the Mind emerged in the early 1980s in an industrial design class taught by Dr. Sam Micklus at Rowan University in New Jersey. He challenged his students to create such inventions as vehicles without wheels, mechanical pie throwers, and flotation devices that would carry them safely across a lake. The designs were judged not just by their success, but by the ingenuity and intellectual risk-taking that went into creating an innovative solution. The students had fun, word spread, and this international nonprofit organization now teaches creative problem-solving skills to millions of students from kindergarten through college. The organization is totally volunteer-run, except for an association manager, who sets up tournaments.

General Benefits

◉ Brainstorming, teamwork, creativity, and intellectual risk-taking are the foundations of the program.

◉ Children can relax and not worry about being belittled, because they are taught to make decisions as a group. The team is encouraged to ask, "How would that be helpful?" or "Could you explain that a little further?" to each proposed idea rather than criticizing it.

◉ Children learn to "think outside the box," take risks, and work as team members. They learn how to approach problems creatively and come up with innovative and imaginative solutions to open-ended problems.

◉ They also learn to appreciate the talents and ideas of others and learn to combine and integrate ideas to find the best solutions.

The years I spent coaching my daughter's Odyssey of the Mind teams were the most exciting and rewarding experience I have had with children. There is something absolutely thrilling in watching children learning to express themselves, thinking creatively, and developing the courage and confidence to tackle the most difficult of problems. I can't think of another activity that has enriched my life more. My daughter Amanda participated in Odyssey of the Mind from second grade through twelfth grade. Her teams went to World Finals three times. Now a senior at Kent State University, Amanda has returned to volunteer as a judge at regional and state tournaments and has also served as an official at the World Finals. So many times, she has told me how much her Odyssey experiences have helped her, both in her course work and design projects, and in coping with the daily challenges of living on her own.

—*Linda Winegar, director, Pennsylvania Odyssey of the Mind Association*

Kids Who Tend to Excel

ⓔ Odyssey of the Mind appeals to a wide range of kids, especially those who enjoy hands-on activities.

ⓔ Many Odyssey of the Mind programs in schools begin in the gifted and talented programs, since those children are very self-motivated and always looking for interesting and challenging things to do.

ⓔ Because Odyssey of the Mind eliminates fear of criticism, even shy children have an opportunity to open up and express themselves.

Any child can be successful in Odyssey of the Mind if he is willing to persevere and work together with a team. Shy children learn to express their ideas. Children who have talents outside the usual school curriculum find a place where their talents are appreciated and recognized. Winning is not everything or even the most important goal. Children learn to combine ideas and brainstorm in order to come up with their best ideas.

—*Beth Manley, North Carolina Board, Odyssey of the Mind*

> Because the problems often require delving into particular subject areas, kids develop re-search skills and expand their base of knowledge. The skills they learn are truly life skills, the kind of skills that help you when you hit the proverbial "brick wall." Rather than letting that brick wall stop them, they will figure out how to go around it, over it, under it, through it or tear it down!
>
> —Linda Winegar, director, Pennsylvania Odyssey of the Mind Association

Best Age to Start

Odyssey of the Mind enables children to participate in the following age divisions:

- Division I: under 12

- Division II: under 15

- Division III: under 19

- There are also noncompetitive "primary" problems for students ages 8 and under.

The Competitions

Odyssey of the Mind is an international creative problem-solving program for children K–12. Every year, Odyssey presents five competitive problems for the teams of five to seven kids to solve, ranging from natural and technical to artistic and performance. At the end of the season, teams participate in a competition presenting their solutions, as well as solving within 8 minutes a spontaneous problem given to them at the competition. They also practice and later compete on spontaneous problems they have not seen before and that they must solve as a team in 8 minutes.

Students usually start working on their solutions in October and finish in March in time for regional and state tournaments. Teams present their solutions at regional and state competitions, and some advance to the world competition. The World Finals is held on a different college campus each year, with teams from all over the world participating in a three-day event.

Each team has a volunteer coach working with them. Coaches act as facilitators, teaching kids how to come up with ideas by brainstorming, not coming up with solutions for them. They also schedule practice and work sessions, help the kids find materials for their creations, and teach basic skills such as how to use tools. The most important job of the coach is to encourage creativity and divergent thinking, helping children to open their minds to new ideas. Coaches can help by asking the team open-ended questions to help facilitate their group problem solving.

🦶 Community groups or schools can enter one team per problem per division into a competition.

🦶 Teams usually meet once or twice a week, or sometimes more depending on the coach and team's preferences. The months leading up to a competition can involve intensive preparation, consuming hours after school and often on weekends.

Odyssey of the Mind Challenges

🦶 The challenges, except for structure, change every year and fall into six general categories:

- ~ *Mechanical/vehicle.* Teams design, build, and operate task-performing vehicles.
- ~ *Classics.* Ranging from literature to art, these problems involve anything from writing an extra chapter for a classical work of fiction to bringing a painting to life.
- ~ *Performance.* Teams present a performance around a specific theme and incorporate required elements, with past themes including animal themes, expressing human emotions, and folktales.
- ~ *Structure.* This challenge always involves teams designing and building

The children make all of the props, come up with *all* of the ideas to make every single thing, whether they write a script, build a structure, design a vehicle, or a create piece of artwork. A coach's job is to supervise, to keep everyone safe, and to assist by asking questions using the Socratic method. The questions allow the students to expand their thinking and solve the problems themselves. For example, if the students are testing the strength of a structure they made out of balsa wood and glue to hold weight, a coach might ask, "Where did the structure break first? Why do you suppose it broke there first? What can you do to make the structure stronger in that area?" So a coach who wants to have all the answers would not be a good fit for an Odyssey team.

—*Beth Manley, North Carolina Board, Odyssey of the Mind*

structures using only balsa wood and glue, which can hold as much weight as possible.

~ *Technical performance.* Teams make innovative inventions that incorporate artistic elements, such as creating a new type of instrument that plays an original piece they composed.

~ *The "spontaneous" problem.* This is usually messy, hectic, and hands-on (e.g., building a bridge using straws, toothpicks, and shaving cream) and emphasizes creativity, teamwork, and speed.

✦ NASA is a sponsor of Odyssey of the Mind and helped to develop one of the problems, both last year and this year.

Costs and Registration

✦ A member school or a community group pays a fee of $135 to enter teams to compete. A membership covers a team in each problem in each division (divided by age: under 12, under 15, or under 18) so a membership can cover many teams. Most memberships begin with interested parents asking questions.

✦ Usually, the hardest part is finding adults willing to coach the team. Once you find coaches, team members can either be assigned to a team or the team can form on its own.

✦ In order to register your child's school, go to www.odysseyofthemind.com and either download a registration form or register directly online.

19

Troops and Groups

Innumerable community-based activities aim to teach children values and life skills, enable them to make new friends, and teach them about cooperation. The largest of organizations offering such programs nationwide are the Girl Scouts, Boy Scouts, Camp Fire USA, and 4-H clubs. All these organizations rely heavily on parent volunteers, and the caliber of local programs often reflects the passion of the children and the commitment of their parents. Not only are parents called upon to serve as leaders in each of these organizations, but many projects' success depends on parents and children working together on them at home.

It's important for parents to realize that they need to be an integral part of the group's success. Society has changed, and volunteers, such as group leaders, are not as prolific. Parents may be needed to serve as leaders themselves. They may be needed to act as assistant leaders, helpers, drivers, and general volunteers.

—Pam Marino, leader, board of directors of Camp Fire USA and involved in the Greater Bay Area Council for 21 years

Participation is key for parents, and I can't stress that enough. Even if not leading a group, parents should plan on continuing to participate by attending field trips, helping with the candy or cookie sales, going camping, helping with a special activity, or just being there as an extra pair of hands.

—*Bonnie Demorotski, executive director of Camp Fire USA for 5 years*

GIRL SCOUTS

✤ An informal educational organization dedicated solely to girls ages 5–17, the Girl Scouts comprise the largest girls-only group in the world, with over 2.8 million girls, and nearly 1 million adult members and volunteers. More than 40 million American women were Girl Scouts during their childhood.

✤ All activities have four primary program goals: developing self-potential, relating to others, developing values, and contributing to society. The activities through which girls earn badges are aimed at building self-confidence, responsibility, integrity, creativity, decision-making skills, teamwork, and leadership abilities.

✤ There are 316 councils throughout America, which administer local troops.

✤ Girls are grouped by age:
  ➤ Daisy Girl Scouts: kindergarten through first grade.
  ➤ Brownie Girl Scouts: grades 1–3.
  ➤ Junior Girl Scouts: grades 4–6.
  ➤ Cadette Girl Scouts: grades 7–9.
  ➤ Senior Girl Scouts: grades 10–12.

✤ Through its membership in the World Association of Girl Guides and Girl Scouts, Girl Scouts of the USA is part of a worldwide organization of 8.5 million girls and adults in 140 countries.

✤ Each member pays a yearly membership fee of $10 and the badges cost around $1 each, but both fees often get covered by cookie sales proceeds. Uniforms are not required. Each troop raises its own funds for activities it wishes to do. Because these activities are financed in large part by the Girl Scout cookie sale, a tradition for over 60 years, local groups also receive a percentage of the profits.

✤ The Girl Scout Web site has a Council Finder to help you locate a troop near you.

We consider Girl Scouts to be a value-based organization, focused on building girls as better individuals for the future. We see ourselves as reinforcing the values of family, educational and faith-based institutions, and the local community. And since we're totally focused on girls, we can meet the uniqueness of their needs. In Girl Scouting, girls have the opportunity to develop their own skills in a noncompetitive environment that emphasizes teamwork. The other powerful thing is that they feel part of something that links them to 3 million girls all over the country. Girls who are age 14 and older can apply to become part of national and international events. As well, many Girl Scout councils find ways to link for multiple council events. We have the stereotype of cookies, camping, and crafts, but none of these activities are required and in fact many troops focus on completely different areas.

—*Sharon Hussey, senior vice president for program, membership, and research, Girl Scouts of the USA*

Girl Scouts is great. Rachel started Brownies in first grade. Before that was Daisies, which she didn't do, but it was fine to join later. The kids do a lot of community service, like going to a local nursing home to sing songs. They have fun outings, such as a sleepover at a science museum, going to a place to make beaded crafts, going to a chocolate-making place, and a mother-daughter weekend campout trip. They also do a lot of crafts and holiday projects in addition to earning badges. They meet two times a month at their elementary school. There are four mom leaders who have stayed with the troop for several years, and there's a wonderful camaraderie among the girls.

—*Ellen, mom of Rachel, 9, Ben, 6, and Josh, 2*

Before signing girls up to be in the Girl Scouts, parents should know that it is a volunteer-based program. The program for their daughter will only thrive if the parents are willing to get involved in the leadership of the troop. The most important and unique benefit of Girl Scouts is that it is a girl-directed program and all girls excel. Girls are involved in the decision-making, planning, and leadership of the activities. Those who are willing to step out of their comfort zone to try new things are provided the opportunity, and those who are more hesitant are supported in their choices while being gently coaxed to challenge themselves.

—*Heather Montgomery, outdoor manager, Girl Scouts of North Alabama*

The girls, particularly as they get older, make more and more of the decisions about what the group will do. For example, if a group likes to travel, they will probably spend a lot of their time planning and taking trips to amusement parks or museums or historical sights in another state. A group that's interested in community action might volunteer at a soup kitchen or a nursing home or tutor at a public library. Some girls just want to hang out and discuss the issues that are on their minds at the moment. Most troops get involved in a number of different kinds of activities, and the local Girl Scout council trains every volunteer who works with children.

—*Harriet Mosatche, senior director of research and program, Girl Scouts of the USA and Girl Scout leader for 10 years*

Girl Scouting is an organization designed to help girls develop to their full potential by teaching them good morals, self-esteem and how they can be an asset to society and their community through service. Parental support is necessary for success. The most important benefit of participating is the many things girls learn by interaction—with each other, with their leaders, and with the community.

—*Felicia Ann Brobson, Girl Scouts service unit manager and troop leader*

The average troop size is 12 girls, and the frequency with which troops meet is based on the preferences of the girls guided by their volunteer leaders.

A brand-new program called STUDIO 2B has been introduced for girls ages 11–17 with the focus on a "by girls, for girls" approach. This program includes activities and discussions that coincide with what preteen and teen girls want, such as offerings in sports, self-defense, high adventure, and stress management.

BOY SCOUTS

The purpose of the Boy Scouts of America—incorporated on February 8, 1910, and chartered by Congress in 1916—is to provide an educational program for boys and young men to build character, become trained in the responsibilities of participating citizenship, and develop personal fitness.

✦ There are over 2 million Cub Scouts and over 1 million Boy Scouts, in more than 55,000 packs. Volunteer adult leaders serve in more than 300 local councils, 28 regional areas, and national boards in volunteer executive boards and committees.

✦ The 10 stated goals of Scouting are character development, spiritual growth, good citizenship, sportsmanship and fitness, family understanding, respectful relationships, personal achievement, friendly service, and fun and adventure.

Cub Scouting

✦ This program for boys in grades 2–5 centers on activities emphasizing character development, citizenship, and personal fitness. Tiger Cubs (first graders), Wolf Cub Scouts (second graders), Bear Cub Scouts (third graders), and Webelos Scouts (fourth and fifth graders, with Webelos standing for "WE'll BE LOyal Scouts") meet weekly.

✦ Most children start Cub Scouts in first and second grade, and they are encour-

I feel we are a premier organization in terms of teaching values and character development in a safe environment. We've been around for 92 years now with a very strong proven track record.

—Al Westberg, national director of Cub Scouting, Boy Scouts of America

I was a Boy Scout for many years, and Cub Scouts has been great for my son. He has den meetings with all the boys in his small group once a week in the evening, and a pack meeting once a month, which is for all the boys in grades two through five. My son is very motivated to earn the badges, which involve acquiring diverse life skills such as planning a meal in your house, setting the table, and helping to serve and cleanup. Other activities include designing a little pine derby car and having races, woodworking, baking cookies, learning about things connected with U.S. citizenship, and going on outings such as a recent one to a huge model railroad. The boys also get to meet a bunch of new kids.

—Ken, dad of Carey, 7, and Danny, 5

aged to join a neighborhood-based pack, which is often affiliated with elementary schools, community organizations, or religious institutions.

🍂 Members join a Cub Scout pack and are assigned to a den. A typical den will have 8–10 boys, and the number of dens in a pack varies regionally. Many of the activities happen right in the den and pack, although some parents and sons work on projects at home and bring them in to the cubmaster for approval.

🍂 Once a month, all dens gather together for a pack meeting.

🍂 A child registers for a yearlong program, and pays a national $7 registration fee. Additional fees depend on the projects the pack undertakes.

🍂 Currently, there are over 980,000 Cub Scouts in over 54,000 packs.

Boy Scouting

🍂 85% of all Boy Scouts were first Cub Scouts.

🍂 This program for boys in sixth grade through the end of high school involves a vigorous outdoor program and development of peer group leadership under the guidance of an adult Scoutmaster.

🍂 Boys earn merit badges after mastering each Scout skill, and with over 120 merit badges available, Scouts must earn 21 to qualify for Eagle Scout. Of this group, 12 badges are required, including First Aid, Citizenship in the Community, Citizenship in the Nation, Citizenship in the World, Communications, Environmental Science, Personal Fitness, Personal Management, Camping, and Family Life. In addition, a Scout has a choice between Emergency Preparedness or Lifesaving and a choice among Cycling, Hiking, or Swimming. Boy Scouts also engage in community service projects.

🍂 The time commitment parallels that of Cub Scouts, with frequent meetings as well as extended weekend or longer outings as a group.

🍂 A jamboree involves hundreds or thousands of Scouts camping together in the spirit of friendship.

Venturing

🍂 This program, the first coed offering from the Boy Scouts, is open to boys and girls ages 14–20. It focuses on challenging high-adventure activities, sports, and hobbies that teach leadership skills and provide opportunities to teach others.

CAMP FIRE USA

✦ Camp Fire USA, organized into 120 local councils across the nation, has over 650,000 kids participating, 46% male and 54% female. Camp Fire is unique because it offers coed programming in club activities. Camp Fire offers a great opportunity for families with both a son and daughter to get together as a unit and enjoy the club program.

✦ With a stated mission to "build caring, confident youth and future leaders," programs focus on leadership, self-reliance, after-school groups, camping and environmental education, and childcare.

✦ Camp Fire USA's programs are designed and implemented to reduce gender-role, racial, and cultural stereotypes and to foster positive intercultural relationships.

✦ Camp Fire groups are organized by age:
  ∿ Starflight: kindergarten through second grade
  ∿ Adventure: grades 3–5
  ∿ Discovery: grades 6–8
  ∿ Horizon: grades 9–12

✦ Originally founded in 1910 as Camp Fire Girls, the organization's name was subsequently changed to reflect the inclusion of boys, starting in 1975. Camp Fire USA is all-inclusive, welcoming children regardless of race, religion, socioeconomic status, or disability.

✦ "Give service" is Camp Fire's watchword. One program, Character Counts, teaches children their six pillars of character: trustworthiness, respect, responsibility, fairness, caring, and citizenship.

✦ Recognition is an important part of all Camp Fire USA programs. For their participation, growth, and achievements, many youths receive distinctive items such as beads, emblems, pins, and certificates. All are designed to convey special messages through symbolism, color, design, and shape, and each recognition item relates to a particular program level, according to grade or activity.

✦ Camp Fire costs vary from councils throughout the states. Program fees are $15 for youth, $10 for adults, and $35 for a family. Members purchase vests ($15 each) or T-shirts ($8–$15 each) depending on what the club decides. An annual candy sale helps pay for activities in which the groups engage.

From personal experiences, I can say that I would *never* have had the opportunities I had or accomplished what I did if it were not for being involved in Camp Fire. My club was very involved in camping. We went on 23 individual camp trips. I have slept in a cave with bats, been at numerous state parks and campsites, have slept on a submarine docked by Navy Pier in Chicago, camped in treehouses and even a historical castle. Our weather was cold, extremely hot, damp, rainy and even snowy. So, we have a lifetime of memories, all of which I hold dear! My daughter, now 27, grew up in Camp Fire, and I can see how she has been affected the same way. At my daughter's wedding 3 years ago, three of her bridesmaids were her Camp Fire friends!

—*Linnea Pioro, program administrator, Camp Fire Chicago Council, involved in Camp Fire for 21 years*

Outdoor skills, camping, nature, and the environment are at the center of what we do at Camp Fire USA. The kids excel because they have another adult beside their parent who cares about them and shows an interest in them. That is the secret for the success of all children. The children get to learn from adult role models, work with a small group of children whom they bond with, and they get to be a part of the process in selecting what activities they will work on.

—*Bonnie Demorotski, executive director of Camp Fire USA for 5 years*

Camp Fire is a terrific opportunity for busy families. Since we are coed, brothers and sisters, moms and dads can be involved together. It's a great way for families to have fun, learning experiences together, as well as with other families. Because the program is flexible, any activity can be emphasized depending on the interests of the children. Most clubs do a wide variety of activities, such as arts and crafts, field trips, camping, and service projects in the community.

—*Pam Marino, leader, board of directors of Camp Fire USA and involved in the Greater Bay Area Council for 21 years*

4-H

✦ Universally recognized by its four-leaf-clover emblem, 4-H is one of the largest youth organizations in the United States, with more than 6.8 million youth participants ages 5–19, and over 495,000 adult volunteers and 116,000 teen leaders. More than 45 million people are 4-H alumni.

✦ The program is administered cooperatively between the U.S. Department of Agriculture, land-grant universities, and county governments. When children enroll in 4-H, they usually sign up for a club at the local county extension office.

✦ The program aims to give the nation's young people knowledge, skills, and attitudes that will enable them to become productive and contributing members of society.

✦ The 4-H pledge captures the program's philosophy: "I pledge: my Head to clearer thinking, my Heart to greater loyalty, my Hands to larger service, and my Health to better living, for my club, my community, my country and my world."

✦ Young people participating in 4-H come from the following areas:
  ∿ 10% live on farms
  ∿ 32% live in towns under 10,000 and open country
  ∿ 23% live in towns and cities of 10,000 to 50,000
  ∿ 9% lived in suburbs of cities of over 50,000
  ∿ 26% lived in urban areas of cities of over 50,000

✦ Of the youth members, 52% are girls and 48% are boys, and 30% come from minority racial-ethnic groups.

✦ Founded in 1902, 4-H programs began as a way to give young people access to better agricultural education. The overall objective has remained the development of young people as individuals and as responsible and productive citizens.

✦ Members can participate in more than 110 program areas, including community service, communications, arts, consumer and family sciences, environmental education, earth sciences, healthy lifestyle education, leadership, plants and animals, and science and technology. Many 4-H activities remain career-driven, though activities range from building model rockets to organizing canned food drives for the needy, raising guinea pigs, or delivering speeches to local government officials. Summer camping programs, school enrichment programs, and fairs are also typically offered.

✦ 4-H publishes manuals for each project choice, which cost between $2 and $4 each.

✦ Activities involving animals, cooking, sewing, and natural resources are popular.

✦ When visiting a 4-H club meeting, look at what types of activities the club does and whether these interest your child. For example, if your child becomes really interested in gardening and learning about plants, then he would probably not be happy in a livestock club where everyone is raising cattle and pigs. Most county extension offices have a long list of clubs available in the local community.

✦ There are no membership fees for 4-H. How much fund-raising occurs really varies from club to club. If the club has decided to raise $40,000 to build a house for a needy family, then they are probably doing a lot of fund raisers. If the club only needs $300 for project books for the year, then they are probably only going to do a couple.

✦ 4-H has spread internationally through the International 4-H Youth Exchange (IFYE) program, where 4-H alumni live with host families in other countries and do agricultural work, volunteer at an adult training center, or work with a local youth development program similar to 4-H.

At 4-H, we are not only cows and plows! You don't have to own an animal or live on a farm to be in 4-H—it's for every kind of young person. 4-H provides safe learning environments for children covering a huge range of topics, from animals, rockets, computers, community service, food and nutrition, to money management. Learning by doing is a critical component of all 4-H programs. All 4-H clubs also perform some type of service to the community, whether that is cleaning up a park, visiting a nursing home and putting on a talent show for the residents, raising guide-dog puppies for the blind, or helping at a soup kitchen. Families often work together on a 4-H club project, so the young person is engaged with parents and siblings. Many families talk about how 4-H adds warmth and depth to their family life, helping them discover things that they can do together.

—*Ami Neiberger-Miller, state 4-H program specialist, University of Florida, working with 4-H for six years*

Costs vary greatly with the projects. While the horse project costs are large (initial purchase, equipment, feed, housing, etc.), the costs are minimal for forestry or entomology. If kids decide to exhibit what they learned at the local fair, additional costs could be perhaps $10 for poster materials or a display box for $25 to 65.

—*Natalie Carroll, associate professor, Purdue University, involved with 4-H troops for 25 years as a youth, parent, and professional*

20

Resources for Intellectual and Community Activities

CHESS

U.S. Chess Federation (USCF)
JTP Program
3054 U.S. Route 9W
New Windsor, NY 12553
(845) 562-8350
inquiries@uschess.org
www.uschess.org

The USCF is the governing organization for chess in the United States with over 90,000 members and nearly 2,000 USCF-affiliated chess clubs. More than 100,000 chess players participate in USCF-sanctioned tournaments every year, including national championship events. Its rating system ranks the performance of chess players in these tournaments. The junior section of the USCF aims to expand and promote the role of chess in the youth of

American society. The USCF publishes a bimonthly chess newsletter just for kids, *School Mate,* with articles to teach your child techniques to become a better player.

FOREIGN LANGUAGES

American Council on the Teaching of Foreign Languages (ACTFL)

6 Executive Plaza
Yonkers, NY 10701-6801
(914) 963-8830
headquarters@actfl.org
www.actfl.org

The American Council on the Teaching of Foreign Languages, consisting of more than 7,000 foreign-language educators, is a national organization dedicated to the improvement and expansion of teaching languages at all levels of instruction.

National Network for Early Language Learning (NNELL)

www.educ.iastate.edu/nnell

The NNELL is an organization consisting of foreign-language teachers united in the cause to teach children at least one language in addition to their own.

American Association of Teachers of French (AATF)

www.frenchteachers.org

The AATF, founded in 1927, is the largest national association of French teachers in the world, with nearly 10,000 members.

American Association of Teachers of German (AATG)

www.aatg.org

With over 6,500 members, the AATG is for teachers of German at all levels of instruction and all those interested in the teaching of German.

American Association of Teachers of Italian (AATI)

www.italianstudies.org/aati/

The AATI promotes the study of Italian language, literature, and culture in schools, colleges, and universities in North America. It has approximately 1500 members worldwide.

American Association of Teachers of Spanish and Portuguese (AATSP)

www.aatsp.org

This nonprofit organization has links to teachers nationwide.

National Council of Japanese Language Teachers (NCJLT)

www.colorado.edu/ealld/atj/ncjlt/

The NCJLT is an organization dedicated to the promotion and development of Japanese-language teaching at the elementary and secondary level across the United States.

ODYSSEY OF THE MIND

Odyssey of the Mind Program

1325 Rte. 130 South, Suite F
Gloucester City, NJ 08030
(856) 456-7776
info@odysseyofthemind.com
www.odysseyofthemind.com

In addition to general information about the program, the Web site has a list of state directors and contact information for each director.

TROOPS AND GROUPS

Girl Scouts of the USA (GSUSA)
420 Fifth Ave.
New York, NY 10018
(800) 478-7248 or (212) 852-8000
www.girlscouts.org

Boy Scouts of America
National Headquarters
1325 W. Walnut Hill Lane/P.O. Box 152079
Irving, TX 75015-2079
(972) 580-2000
www.scouting.org

Camp Fire USA
4601 Madison Ave.
Kansas City, MO 64112-1278
(816) 756 1950
info@campfireusa.org
www.campfire.org

National 4-H Council
7100 Connecticut Ave.
Chevy Chase, MD 20815
info@fourhcouncil.edu
www.fourhcouncil.edu

Information about 4-H can also be found at these two Web sites:
www.4-h.org
www.national4-hheadquarters.gov

PART V
CONCLUSION

21

Final Thoughts

"If you had fun, you won!"
—*Sign above a gym door at a public elementary school*

I see childhood becoming shorter and it saddens me.
—*Lisa, mom of Connor, 10, Garrison, 6, and Mitchell, 1*

Sometimes being the parent means simply saying no.
—*Dana, mom of three children, ages 9, 7, and 5*

REMEMBERING WHAT ULTIMATELY COUNTS

We worry about our children's lifelong success, and feel gripped by the anxiety that choices made at ages 3–10 may affect their long-term prospects for a happy, fulfilled, successful life. We feel that the stakes are high, and that it's our mandate to invest time, energy, and emotion to ensuring that our kids will "be all that they can be" and "just do it." The end goal has become more about "packaging" a child for college admission officers than helping her develop and mature.

As a culture, we wrestle with opposing notions of what it means for a child to succeed. Is it by being internally satisfied, feeling good about oneself, approaching life joyously, and deeply connecting to others? Or is it measured by external measures of success, such as what school your child attends, what jobs she goes on to have, how much money she makes, or what neighborhood she lives in?

The focus has changed from having fun, exploring new things, gaining new skills, to glory, mastery, and triumph. Our societal values have shifted from character to achievement, from virtues to status, from best efforts to a checklist of goals obtained. It's very hard to resist the hectic pace and whirlwind of activities that have become part of the fabric of our children's everyday world. Much of this activity mania stems from wanting to give children every competitive edge in a world that has elevated success and fame above all else.

Yet, what beliefs do you want your child to take into adulthood with her? What kind of message does your child take away from all of this? What is it that you want her to value, to embody? How do you define a successful child? Instead of having our children feel we are confident in their growing up to be successful and loved, our anxiety and uncertainty fuels similar feelings in them, making them nervous about their own future as well.

Ultimately, you want to raise your child to find hobbies, activities, or sports that she loves, feels passionate about, and will carry into adulthood. You also want her to learn how to make responsible decisions, have an outlet for her energy and her stress, have close friends and be well liked by her peers. You want to be proud of your child's personal qualities of boldness, spirit, independence, self-respect, and confidence.

All these activities are driven by our own sense of anxiety over our children's ultimate success, yet the true way to judge success should be your child's overall attitude about himself. When a child feels good about himself, confident, loved, secure, and connected with friends—that should be the answer. When I see my son enjoying his activities with good friends, I feel great about where he's at in his life.

—*Janine, mom of Ben, 10, and Andrew, 7*

I do not expect my kids to be like anyone else or be the star on a team. I appreciate them for whatever they can accomplish. In sports, I want them to play fair, play well, and love what they're doing. I just worry about them being happy.

—*Dean, dad of Evan, 10, and Olivia, Justin, and Shelby, 8*

Take a moment to close your eyes and visualize your child all grown up 20 years from now. What kind of person do you hope that she becomes? How do you want her to look back on her childhood? What do you think she'll tell you about her experiences with sports and activities? What qualities will you value most in her?

Here are some surprising but wonderful insights on the topic from my daughter, Kyle. Returning to my desk after taking a break from writing this book, I saw the following note taped to the computer screen: "Activities are one of the most important things in a child's life. It's one of the things that makes them outgoing, smart, confident about their day, and never feeling bored. If your child doesn't like sports, try dance, chess classes, art or clay classes, or gymnastics." How true, I thought, realizing that even my ten-year-old has a passionate opinion about sports and activities, thankfully positive ones so far. It served as a reminder of how important it is to touch base with your child about her perceptions of sports and activities in her life.

HOW WILL THIS ALL PLAY OUT? THE EXPERIMENTAL GENERATION

It's unclear how this activity frenzy will play out as our children mature into adulthood. Will our children be accomplished Masters of the Universe, adept at all things under the sun, or will they be burned out, easily bored, and dependent on external validators to assure them of their self-worth? At the end of the day, you do not want to turn your child into an activity junkie.

It remains a conjecture whether or not children who spend vast amounts of time in structured activities really grow up to be better-adjusted, content adults. An emerging phenomenon of "adultolescence" has appeared with the first generation of activity-saturated kids who had no time to develop independence. To the dismay of college officials, many eighteen-year-olds have been struggling to adjust to the freedom of college life because suddenly they have blocks of unstructured time, without schedules set or modulated by parents, and don't know how to manage their time. Not surprisingly, they continue to rely on parental direction and protection well into their twenties. These kids return home to live with parents in record numbers, with 60% of college students now planning to live at home right after graduation, and 21% planning to stay at home for more than a year.

There is no evidence yet that all this frenzy is going to produce a happy, thriving set of adults. If anything, activity-drenched and exhausted kids arriving at colleges have sparked alarm among college deans, as indicated by a recent letter from Harvard College. Three top Harvard officials published an article in *The New York Times* urging kids to slow down, uncover their true passions, and not to just enter

We really have no idea until our kids are adults what "worked" and what "working" even means.

—*Amy, mom of Sacha, 9, and Libby, 7*

I want my kids to have hobbies when they're older. When I was growing up, I loved being involved in sports, music, and other extracurricular activities, and hope my kids will see it as a fun part of life. For so many kids, between after-school programs and numerous activities, there's too little downtime at home. Unfortunately, we won't know until our kids are grown up what the real impact will be.

—*Karen, mom of Max, 8, Sophie, 6, Celia, 4, and Jake, 1*

the résumé-padding madness. They expressed deep concern that sports, music, dance, and other recreational activities have become training for college admissions, scholarships, and the brass ring of fame and wealth, as seen with top athletes, entertainers, and CEOs.

WHAT'S TO BE DONE?

It's doubtful that you can single-handedly change our entire culture. It will likely take a group effort to turn the cultural tide, but until that happens, listen when your inner voice tells you it's too much, either for your child or for you. Just because "everyone else is doing it" does not mean that it will benefit your child in the long run or ensure her a rich and full life as a happy, mature adult. You need to make a conscious decision to be more thoughtful and less driven about your child's choices and perfection. The key is moderation, as well as taking your child's unique temperament and interests into account.

When in September, January, and June backpacks come home stuffed with flyers and announcements giving you the chance to enroll your child in just about every extracurricular activity under the sun, make your resolve for each new season not to allow your child or yourself to get overextended. Run a sanity check before allowing your child to take on any new commitments and learn not to say yes to everything your child wants to pursue. Instead, teach your child to pick the activities most meaningful to her, and that enable your family a respite from constantly being on the go.

Next time your child asks you if she can "please . . . please . . . please" take yet one more activity:

❧ Choose carefully. Seek out sports and activities that allow your child's talent and passions to flourish.

❧ Go for extracurricular activities in moderation. Do not say "Sure!" to any new activity until you have carefully evaluated its costs, including logistical, financial, emotional, and time involved.

❧ Have the courage to set limits and say no when needed. Don't take it as an inevitable fact of modern life that your child's life is going to be over the top, crammed with activities.

❧ Pick activities that work with your whole family's schedule. In letting your child choose her activities, set certain parameters on how much you're willing to have those activities override other competing schedules of your household.

❧ Don't be afraid to do something different than the kids next door. Matching your child to an activity she's well suited to and passionate about is the key.

❧ Preserve family time for yourself and your child. Find out when practices will be scheduled and make a decision about how many nights a week you're willing to have family dinners eroded by a quick bite on the run. Dashing with kids in the car from one activity to the next doesn't count as family time spent together.

❧ Recognize and embrace those critical times when less is more, as downtime needs to be part of both your and your child's life. Don't let yourself get caught in the compulsion to account for every minute of your child's time productively until you end up with an activity-saturated child. Constant busyness erodes your child's attention span and creates an insatiable need for organized activities. Your child

When I read the paper, I feel humbled by how lucky our lives are. Thinking about the horror stories of families in Afghanistan selling children into slavery in order to feed their other kids quickly puts things into perspective. Whenever I feel myself getting stressed out about which activities my kids should be doing, I tell myself, "Forget it! Get a grip!"

—*Sarah, mom of Taylor, 7, and Cameron, 5*

needs breaks in the action and time to hang out. It's your job to ensure unstructured moments in your child's week. Time to rest, engage in unhurried conversations with you to talk about stuff, play board games, read for pleasure, and immerse herself in her own creative endeavors.

✦ Engage your friends in a dialogue about this issue of activity mania, as there needs to be a group dynamic that lessens the intensity.

SELECTED BIBLIOGRAPHY

Amoroso, Mary. "Back Off and They Will Bloom," *The Pressured Parent* (April 16, 2000).

Andersonn, Christopher, with Barbara Andersonn. *Will You Still Love Me If I Don't Win?* Dallas, TX: Taylor Publishing Company, 2000.

Bailey, Pat. "Too Many Activities Can Stress Children," *Investor's Business Daily* (August 29, 2000): 1.

Barasch, Douglas. "Nurturing Talent," *Family Life Magazine* (October 2001).

Bellisimo, Y., Sacks, C. H., and Mergendoller, J. R. "Changes Over Time in Kindergarten Holding Out: Parent and School Contexts," *Early Childhood Research Quarterly* (October 1995): 205.

Belluck, Pam. "Parents Try to Reclaim Their Children's Time," *The New York Times* (June 13, 2000).

Ben-Tovim, Atarah, and Douglas Boyd. *The Right Instrument for Your Child: A Practical Guide for Parents and Teachers.* New York: William Morrow, 1985.

Bigelow, Bob, with Tom Moroney and Linda Hall. *Just Let the Kids Play: How to Stop Other Adults from Ruining Your Child's Fun and Success in Youth Sports.* Florida: Health Communications, 2001.

Brazelton, T. Berry. "Helping Children Learn from Sports," *The Washington Times* (March 4, 2001).

Brody, Jane. "Fitness Gap Is America's Recipe for Fat Youth," *The New York Times* (September 19, 2000).

Brogan, Jan. "Playing Too Hard: Organized Sports Create a Generation of Kids with Grown-Up Stress Injuries," *Providence Journal-Bulletin* (March 30, 1998).

Brooks, Andree Aelion. *Children of Fast-Track Parents: Raising Self-Sufficient and Confident Children in an Achievement-Oriented World.* New York: Penguin Books, 1989.

Caballero, Paula. "Running Out of Time: Scheduling Too Many Activities for Children Can Result in Unnecessary Stress," *The Fort Worth Star-Telegram* (December 24, 2000): 1.

Carlson, Peter. "A Treatise Against the Tyranny of Tots," *The Washington Post* (May 26, 1998): C1.

Century, Douglas. "The Boys of Summer Get Younger All the Time," *The New York Times* (March 11, 2001).

Cheever, Susan. *As Good as I Could Be (A Memoir of Raising Wonderful Children in Difficult Times).* New York: Simon & Schuster, 2001.

Cohen, Katherine. *The Truth About Getting In.* New York: Hyperion, 2002.

Coles, Joanna. "Hyper-Parenting Has Become the Most Competitive Sport in New York. Are We Pushing Our Children Too Hard?" *The Times of London* (April 13, 2000).

Coltin, Lillian. "Enriching Children's Out-of-School Time," *ERIC Clearinghouse on Elementary and Early Childhood Education* (May 1999).

Cordes, Helen. "Overscheduled Youngsters May Miss the Real Enrichment of Childhood: Spontaneous, Creative Play," *The Washington Times* (October 29, 2000).

———. "Schedule Overload Can Lead to Burnout for Kids," *Minneapolis Star Tribune* (October, 2, 2000): D1.

Coutts, Cherylann. "How Busy Should Your Kid Be?," *Parenting Magazine* (October 1998).

Creager, Ellen. "I Quit! What to Do When Your Child Athlete Decides to Hang Up the Cleats," *Seattle Times* (September 4, 1999): D1.

Critchell, Samantha. "Doing Nothing Might Be the Best Thing for Your Child," *The Associated Press* (July 17, 2001).

De Houwer, Annick. "Two or More Languages in Early Childhood," *ERIC Digest Clearinghouse on Languages and Linguistics* (October 1999).

Doherty, William J. *Take Back Your Kids: Confident Parenting in Turbulent Times.* Notre Dame, IN: Sorin Books, 2000.

Edelhart, Courtenay. "Bringing Up Baby: Parents Look for Ways to Give Their Little Ones a Developmental Edge at a Younger Age," *The Indy Star* (April 01, 2002).

Ehrensaft, Diane. *Spoiling Childhood: How Well-Meaning Parents Are Giving Children Too Much—But Not What They Need.* New York: Guilford Publications, 1997.

Elkind, David. *The Hurried Child: Growing Up Too Fast Too Soon.* Cambridge, MA: Perseus Books, 2001.

Ellers, Fran. "Kids Can Overcome Hyper-Parenting and Find Their Own Interests in Life," *The Courier-Journal* (March 9, 2000).

Engh, Fred. *Why Johnny Hates Sports.* New York: Avery Penguin Putnam, 1999.

Evans, Sandra. "Play's the Thing; Children's Days Are Often Booked Solid. So When Do They Learn to Goof Around?," *The Washington Post* (June 24, 1997): Z10.

Ferguson, Andrew. "Inside the Crazy Culture of Kids Sports," *Time* (July 1999): 52.

Fine, Carla. *Strong, Smart and Bold: Empowering Girls for Life.* New York: HarperCollins Cliff Street Books, 2001.

Fishman, Charles. "Smorgasbord Generation," *American Demographics* (May 1, 1999).

Fletcher, June. "Kids Call For a Time Out," *The Wall Street Journal* (August 25, 2000).

Fortin, Cassandra. "Best Gift Parents Can Give a Child Is Time," *Chicago Tribune* (July 2, 2000).

Freely, Maureen. "The Birth of the Hyper-Parent," *The London Evening Standard* (June 9, 2000).

Galletta, Jan. "Parents Take Back Children," *Chattanooga Times* (October 11, 2000): E1.

Gardner, Marilyn. "Parents Face Pressure to Push Their Children into Many Activities and to Be Involved As Well," *The Christian Science Monitor* (January 23, 2002).

Gilbert, Susan. "For Some Children, It's an After-School Pressure Cooker," *The New York Times* (August 3, 1999).

———. "Sports Your Child Shouldn't Play," *Redbook* (April 1, 1996).

Goff, Karen Goldberg. "Banishing Boredom," *The Washington Times* (August 5, 2001).

Goodman, Gary. *101 Things Parents Should Know Before Volunteering to Coach Their Kids' Sports Teams.* New York: Contemporary Books, McGraw-Hill, 2000.

Goodnow, Cecelia. "Life in Fast Lane Leaves Kids Stressed for Success," *Seattle Post-Intelligencer* (July 31, 2001).

Graber, Janna. "One Requirement for Summer: Time to Goof Off," *Chicago Tribune* (June 20, 1999): F1.

Greenberg, Susan, and Karen Springen. "The Overscheduled Baby: Too Much Structure Can Stress Parents and Children," *Newsweek* (October 2000).

Grimes, Le Datta. "Extracurriculars: Extra Fun or Extra Burden? Some Kids Thrive, Others Don't on Hectic After-School Schedules," *Lexington Herald-Leader* (November 16, 2000).

Grolnick, Wendy. *The Psychology of Parental Control: How Well-Meant Parenting Backfires.* Mahwah, NJ: Lawrence Erlbaum Associates, 2002.

Gutherie, Elisabeth and Kathy Matthews. *The Trouble with Perfect: How Parents Can Avoid the Overachievement Rap and Still Raise Successful Children.* New York: Broadway Books, 2002.

Harris, Marlys. "Trophy Kids: A New All-or-Nothing Philosophy Is Forcing Your Children to Compete," *Money* (March 1997).

Hartley-Brewer Elizabeth. *Raising Confident Girls.* Cambridge, MA: Fisher Books, 2001.

Healy, Melissa. "All Work, Less Play Is the Burden of Kids Today," *Los Angeles Times* (November 9, 1998).

Hofferth, Sandra, "Changes in American Children's Time, 1981–1997," University of Michigan's Institute for Social Research, Center Survey (January 1999).

Hunker, Paula Gray. "Learn to Plan: Coordinating Activities Can Make School Year Less Hectic," *The Washington Times* (August 25, 1998): E1.

Kelly, Katy. "Today's Kids: Overscheduled and Overtired," *U.S. News & World Report* (October 16, 2000).

Kindlon, Dan. *Too Much of a Good Thing: Raising Children of Character in an Indulgent Age.* California: Miramax Books, 2001.

Kirn, Walter with Wendy Cole. "Whatever Happened to Play? Kids Are Spending Less Time Frolicking Freely, Though Fun Is One of the Best Things for Them," *Time* (April 30, 2001).

Kochakian, Mary Jo. "When Parents Push Too Hard," *The Hartford Courant* (January 31, 2000).

Kuchenbecker, Shari Young. *Raising Winners: A Parent's Guide to Helping Kids Succeed on and off the Playing Field.* New York: Times Books, 2000.

Kutner, Lawrence. "Too Much of a Good Thing Is Too Much for Kids," *Star Tribune* (November 12, 1992): 12E.

Lach, J. "Cultivating the Mind," *Newsweek Special Issue: Your Child—From Birth to Three* (Spring 1997): 38.

Lombardi, Kate Stone. "After-School Routines Leave Little Time for Traditional Play," *The New York Times* (May 16, 1993): 1.

Machover, Wilma, and Marienne Uszler. *Sound Choices: Guiding Your Child's Musical Experiences.* New York: Oxford University Press, 1996.

Mahany, Barbara. "While Some Cry 'Enough!' Other Parents and Kids Thrive on a Packed Schedule," *Chicago Tribune* (April 25, 1999).

Marcos, Kathleen. "Why, How, and When Should My Child Learn a Second Language?" *ERIC Clearinghouse on Languages and Linguistics, Parent Brochure* (Washington, DC, 1997).

McCarthy, Laura Flynn. "Raising a Stress-Free Child," *Family Life Magazine* (October 2001).

Meltz, Barbara. "Don't Drive Your Kid Crazy with Too Many Activities," *The Boston Globe* (September 13, 2001).

Met, Myriam. *Critical Issues in Early Second Language Learning: Building for Our Children's Future.* Reading, MA: Scott Foresman-Addison Wesley, 1998.

Micheli, Lyle. *The Sports Medicine Bible for Young Athletes: What Every Parent and Coach Needs to Know About Improving Children's Health Fitness Programs Preventing Acute and Overuse Injuries and Rehabilitation.* Naperville, IL: Sourcebooks, 2001.

Mitchell, Alanna. "When Parenting Becomes Too Intense: This Generation of Mothers and Fathers Finds It Difficult Not to Program Their Children's Lives, but There Has to Be a Limit," *The Globe and Mail* (May 26, 2000).

Moss, Meredith. "Making Family a Priority: Parents, Kids Rediscover Fun of Unity," *Dayton Daily News* (September 7, 2000): 1A.

Murphy, Shane. *The Cheers and the Tears: A Healthy Alternative to the Dark Side of Youth Sports Today.* San Francisco: Jossey-Bass John Wiley & Sons, 1999.

Napier, Dawn. "Helping Kids Escape from the Activity Treadmill," *The Toronto Star* (July 10, 1996): A19.

Nettleton, Pamela Hill. "Put Me In, Coach: When Your Kid Is on the Bench," *Sports Parents Magazine* (September 1998).

O'Crowley, Peggy. "Stress-Proofing Your Child; Yoga and Other Relaxation Techniques Help Keep a Minor's Anxieties from Becoming Major," *The Record* (May 26, 1996): L01.

Postman, Neil. *The Disappearance of Childhood.* New York: Vintage Books, 1994.

Quigley, Linda. "Keeping Pace: YWCA Classes Help You Live Better, Learn More," *The Tennessean* (September 7, 1996): 1D.

Quindlen, Anna. "Doing Nothing Is Something: The Overscheduled Children of 21st-Century America, Deprived of the Gift of Boredom," *Newsweek* (May 13, 2002).

Raymond, Joan. "Kids Just Wanna Have Fun," *American Demographics* (February 2000).

Richter, Marice. "Are Kids Overloaded?: Crammed Calendars Are Cool with Many Youngsters, but Some Could Use More Days Devoted to Plain Ol' Fun," *The Dallas Morning News* (June 8, 1999): 5C.

Rimm, Sylvia. *Keys to Parenting the Gifted Child.* New York: Barron's, 2001.

Robinson, Thomas. "Reducing Children's Television Viewing to Prevent Obesity," *Journal of the American Medical Association* (1999): 282(16).

Rosenfeld, Alvin, and Nicole Wise. *The Over-Scheduled Child: Avoiding the Hyper-Parenting Trap.* New York: St. Martin's, 2000.

Rotella, Robert, and Linda Bunker. *Parenting Your Super Star: How to Help Your Child Balance Achievement and Happiness.* Chicago: Triumph Books, 1998.

Sachs, Brad. *The Good Enough Child: How to Have an Imperfect Family and be Perfectly Satisfied.* New York: HarperCollins, 2001.

Sagon, Candy. "Dinner Time: Working Parents, Busy Kids, Hectic Lives: But Everything Stops for the Family Meal," *The Washington Post* (March 3, 1999): FO1.

Schembari, James. "Practice Makes Perfect (and Poorer Parents)," *The New York Times* (January 27, 2002).

Scoggins, Chip. "Kids Feel Pressure to Focus on One Sport," *Minneapolis Star Tribune* (August 8, 2001).

Shore, Kenneth. *Keeping Kids Safe.* New York: Prentice Hall Press, 2001

Silby, Caroline, and Smith, Shelley. *Games Girls Play: Understanding and Guiding Young Female Athletes.* New York: St. Martin's Press, 2000.

Simons, Janet. "Busy, Busy, Busy Kids Need More Family Life," *Scripps Howard News Service* (March 28, 2001).

Singer, Beth Wolfensberger. "Raising a Perfect Child," *The Boston Globe* (March 26, 2000).

Sitz, Rick. "Sportsmanship: Encouraging Our Kids to be Good Sports," *Winnetka Alliance for Early Childhood Newsletter* (September 1998): 3.

Slatalla, Michelle. "Overscheduled? Here Are Some Ways to Get Your Family Off the Treadmill—and Still Keep the Kids' Piano Lessons," *Time* (July 16, 2000).

Soltes, Fiona. "Off in All Directions," *The Tennessean* (September 7, 1997): 1F.

Stovsky, Renee. "Being a 'Hyper-Parent' Is a Recipe for Burned-Out Dads," *St. Louis Post-Dispatch* (March 5, 2000): 1G.

———. "Time Out!," *St. Louis Post-Dispatch* (August 14, 1997): 1G.

Sundberg, Jim, and Janet Sundberg. *How to Win at Sports Parenting: Maximizing the Sports Experience for You and Your Child.* Colorado Springs, CO: Waterbrook Press, 2000.

Taylor, Jim. *Positive Pushing: How to Raise a Successful and Happy Child.* New York: Hyperion, 2002.

Trestrail, Joanne. "Overscheduled, Overwhelmed: A Calendar That's Too Full Can Drain Kids' Energy," *Chicago Tribune* (September 2, 2001).

Tyre, Peg. "Bringing Up Adolescents: Millions of Americans in Their 20s and 30s Are Still Supported by Their Parents and the Me-Generation Is Raising the Mini-Me Generation," *Newsweek* (March 25, 2002): 34.

Vallo, Mary. "Is It All Too Much?" *The Bergen County Record* (November 20, 1997).

Vobejda, Barbara. "More School, Structure Found in '90s Child's Life," *The Washington Post* (November 9, 1998): A2.

Votano, Paul. *The Trouble with Youth Sports.* Philadelphia: Xlibris Corporation, 2000.

Wapshott, Nicholas. "The Quest for Quality Time," *The Times of London* (March 29, 2002.)

Welk, Gregory. *Promoting Physical Activity in Children: Parental Influences.* Washington, DC: ERIC Clearinghouse on Teaching and Teacher Education, 1999.

White, Nancy. "Fast Times for Families: Sports, Lessons, Clubs . . . Kids' Schedules Are So Full, Some Parents Are Saying: 'Enough!'" *The Star* (October 7, 2000).

Whitely, Joan. "Stress Check," *Las Vegas Review-Journal* (March 4, 2001): 25A.

Williams-Allred, Amy. "Extracurricular Overload When Kids Do Too Much: Parents Often Are the Reason," *The Charleston Gazette* (October 22, 1995).

Wilson, Susan. *Sports Her Way: Motivating Girls to Start and Stay with Sports.* New York: Fireside, 2000.

Wise, Nicole. "Parents Shouldn't Be On Call All the Time," *Newsweek* (August 7, 2000): 136.

Wolcott, Jennifer. "Helping Kids Slow Down," *The Christian Science Monitor* (October 25, 2000).

Wolff, Rick. *Good Sports: The Concerned Parent's Guide to Competitive Youth Sports.* New York: Dell Publishing, 1998.

Zimmerman, Jean, and Gil Reavill. *Raising Our Athletic Daughters: How Sports Can Build Self-Esteem and Save Girls' Lives.* New York: Doubleday, 1999.

Zipp, Yvonne. "Penciling In Time to Play," *The Christian Science Monitor* (November 13, 1998): 1.

INDEX

ABOUT THE AUTHOR

Stacy M. DeBroff is a nationally acclaimed parenting expert and author of *Mom Central: The Ultimate Family Organizer* and *The Mom Book: 4,278 of Mom Central's Tips for Moms, from Moms* (2002, Simon & Schuster). She is the founder and president of Mom Central, Inc., a company dedicated to providing busy moms with smart household and parenting solutions.

Stacy has made numerous television appearances, from NBC's *Today Show* to *Oxygen Live* with Gayle King. She has also been a guest on more than 1,200 national radio programs such as *Daybreak USA, Date Line Washington,* and *Working Mom on the Run.* Articles about Stacy have appeared in the *Chicago Tribune,* the *AP Wire, USA Today, Boston Globe,* and *Chicago Tribune,* as well as numerous magazines, including *Parenting, Child, American Baby, Babytalk,* and *Publisher's Weekly.* Stacy has also spoken to hundreds of parenting groups and conferences, and e-mails her monthly Mom Central, Inc. newsletter to over 10,000 moms around the globe.

Stacy is also the co-founder of Mom Quest, a consulting service that provides unique marketing expertise in reaching women and moms, guiding entrepreneurs, and launching new authors. She works directly with these individuals to create their ideas into powerful book proposals, services, and products designed to reach and assist moms nationwide.

Working at Harvard Law School from 1990 to 1999, Stacy helped launch a generation of law students into public interest work by founding and heading an office staffed by seasoned public interest attorneys, which served as a model for other law schools across the nation. Stacy's publications at Harvard include *The Public Interest Job Search Guide,* published yearly by Harvard Law School, and *The Great Firm Escape,* a book co-authored with fellow lawyers from Harvard Law School's Office of Public Interest Advising, which she founded in 1990.

The American Lawyer recognized Stacy for her entrepreneurial contribution to law with an in-depth profile in their issue on the "Top Forty Lawyers Under Forty." *Massachusetts Lawyers Weekly* also chose her as one of the "Top Ten Lawyers of The Year" in 1998. Stacy garnered extensive coverage for her work at Harvard from the media, from *National Public Radio* to the *National Law Journal* and *The Wall Street Journal.*

Stacy holds a B.A. in Psychology and Comparative Literature from Brown University, *magna cum laude* and Phi Beta Kappa; and a J.D. from Georgetown University, *magna cum laude.* She lives in Chestnut Hill with her husband and two children, ages 10 and 9.

For more information on Stacy M. DeBroff and insider parenting tips, please visit:

www.momcentral.com